D1560856

PRINCIPLES OF SOCIOLOGY

PRINCIPLES OF SOCIOLOGY

William J. Goode

Columbia University

McGRAW-HILL BOOK COMPANY

*New York   St. Louis   San Francisco   Auckland   Bogotá   Düsseldorf
Johannesburg   London   Madrid   Mexico   Montreal   New Delhi
Panama   Paris   São Paulo   Singapore   Sydney   Tokyo   Toronto*

This book was set in Palatino by Black Dot, Inc.
The editors were Lyle Linder, Jean Smith,
and James R. Belser;
the designer was Joan E. O'Connor;
the cover photograph was taken by
Bill Longcore;
the production supervisor was Angela Kardovich.
R. R. Donnelley & Sons Company was printer
and binder.

PRINCIPLES OF SOCIOLOGY

1234567890DODO783210987

Library of Congress Cataloging in Publication Data

Goode, William Josiah.
      Principles of sociology.

      Includes bibliographies and index.
      1. Sociology. I. Title.
HM51.G636   301   76-55315
ISBN 0-07-023758-1

CONTENTS

PREFACE

Sociological inquiry is exciting. It explores and analyzes the important issues of both our personal lives and the larger world: war and the bomb, race and caste discrimination, the feminist movement, political power, how we are molded in childhood, the pollution of our environment, and how the massive forces of social change affect our future.

Sociology helps us to understand why we act as we do. Sociology also offers us a particular intellectual skill: the ability to probe beyond the hurts and joys of everyday life to the social forces that often move us without our perceiving that they do so. Thus, it aids us in seeing how we might change those social arrangements which now shape our behavior.

This introduction to sociology speaks primarily to students who will not go on to become sociologists themselves. It aims at presenting the very best thinking of contemporary sociology as simply as possible. Sociological thinking has changed greatly over the past generation, and at a more rapid rate over the past decade. This book seeks to explore and present these changes. Thus, it is an introduction to the newest and best in contemporary sociology, not just a summary of the past.

This book speaks to several different audiences. Some students want only to be entertained; sociology is admirably suited to that need. It abounds in fascinating details—of juvenile delinquency and organized crime, of sexual behavior and divorce, of youth rebellion and the feminist movement, and of the seeking and awarding of prestige in every sphere of life from baseball to nuclear physics.

Other students will want more intellectual substance; they will seek some explanatory principles to illuminate their understanding of those gaudy details. To those students sociology offers a fruitful way of analyzing both large and small events, from a date to a revolution. It continually shows us how those specific events or processes can be viewed as examples of larger regularities, principles, or recurring social patterns. It thus provides us with the intellectual tools for examining still other social behaviors and thereby opens the door to a richer view of the world around us.

Finally, I hope that among my readers there will also be a few students who will decide sociology may become their vocation. They have not been neglected, for the underlying theoretical framework and orientation of this book represents, I think, a step toward the sociology that has been emerging throughout the past decade of fierce debate in the field.

That conflict came to public notice with the student revolts of the late 1960s. Before they had become widespread, I wrote that sociological thinking was entering a phase in which a new theoretical orientation would be discerned.* This perspective does not reject the hard-won knowledge of the past, but its approach is both fresh and more faithful to our direct experience.

The new sociological perspective emphasizes the social roles that emerge in interaction more than social statuses that are fixed. Thus, it focuses more on dynamics than on statics. It is less likely to "explain" events by describing the traits of individuals (for example, "radical-conservative") and is more likely to analyze events by seeing them as processes, as social transactions between two or more sets of actors. The newer work also focuses far more on the tensions, strains, and conflicts within the social structure. It understands that whatever stability the world exhibits is achieved because many people make an effort to keep it so, against resistance from others.

The newer orientation notes, as sociology always has, that people's norms and values do guide them somewhat in their daily lives. However, it notes as well that this guidance is only partial. Norms do not "explain" social behavior—they are sometimes contradictory; we change them when we are in different situations; they may change over time; we violate them; and we are often guided by our own self-interest, which may run counter to what we and others consider "right."

Current sociology is also returning to an intellectual position that was dominant in the field before World War I: The best of contemporary analysis is once more becoming comparative as well as historical. That is, when we offer a sociological principle, we self-consciously ask ourselves, "Does this apply as well to other societies? Does it apply to societies of the past? Will it apply to a world that is rapidly changing?"

Sometimes, indeed often, we cannot as yet be sure of the answers. However, the questions should be part of our thinking. They keep us from supposing that our personal experience, at this particular time in history, is all of social reality. And they sometimes make us think of more valid interpretations or principles.

Further, in accordance with my earlier prediction, modern sociology has been devoting more attention to the importance of force and force-threat (sometimes called "power") in social relations, and to a better interweaving of socioeconomic forces in its analyses. Often this takes the specific form of "exchange theory," a theoretical framework that views much of social interaction as exchanges of various kinds of social behaviors, such as gifts or services, insults and deference. I believe that development will continue.

*On these points see my "General Introduction" to *Dynamics of Modern Society*, New York: Atherton, 1966, pp. ix–xv.

A final emphasis in modern sociology may be illustrated from deviance theory, although it applies to much other social interaction as well. Long ago, sociologists stopped viewing the "deviant" as a special kind of depraved person who rejected the proper norms of society. However, a modern view goes far beyond that bit of wisdom. If we refer to the deviant at all, we must see him or her as part of a larger interactional *process*, which includes what he or she does, how others respond, what the deviant does as a consequence—and the larger social system that produces or generates that continuing process.

This emphasis on the contingent and tension-laden aspects of social life does not deny the obvious, and sometimes dismaying, stability of traditional social patterns. Indeed, it is the tensions and conflicts that often contribute to that stability, and thus we cannot ignore either when we analyze social action. Consequently, we must examine the stability even when we are focusing on conflicts and tensions. Similarly, even when we temporarily focus on stability, we must ask whether the forces that create it are fleeting, and will soon give way to new social patterns. At every point, we must be aware of possible social changes, too.

This book aims, then, at serving the needs of students who will be content with interesting descriptions of social behavior as well as those who seek more basic intellectual skills. In addition, I hope it has achieved a more difficult goal: to lay the foundations for serious, advanced study in the field. I do know, from long experience in teaching basic sociology to thousands of students, that sociological analysis can be more than a challenging professional task. I hope that for each of you it can also become a continuing source of personal discovery, and of direct pleasure.

Perhaps more than any research monograph, a basic textbook is an expression of the author as teacher, and thus is influenced by all the great (and some of the lesser) teachers he or she has had. Although I still wonder at the mystery of good teaching, I was privileged as a student and as a professor in experiencing much of it.

I began my academic life as a philosophy student at the University of Texas. Most of the future sociologists who went through that school in the 1930s—the list includes such people as Kingsley Davis, Logan Wilson, C. Wright Mills, Marion J. Levy, Ivan Belknap, and me—were at least for a while students of a great teacher, the economist Clarence E. Ayres. Ayres had also been Talcott Parsons' teacher earlier at Amherst, and still earlier had been Thorstein Veblen's assistant at the University of Chicago. To note further the interlinkages of students and teachers, I (like many sociologists of my generation) was influenced greatly by Talcott Parsons, for two of *his* abler students, Kingsley Davis and Wilbert E. Moore, were in turn my teachers. All the dedicated teachers and students in this complex network had very different styles, but I think we shared two important teaching goals: to encourage independence and creativity, and to insist on intellectual rigor.

As a junior professor at Wayne State, I had the fortunate experience of teaching at a time and in a city where, with no planning at all, one made friends with many talented people. I have an affectionate collective name for these chance members of my life, but I shall not disclose it here. They include the legal philosopher Tom Cowan, Peter Blau, Melvin Tumin, Nicholas Babchuk, Zena Blau, Eugene Litwak, C. West Churchman, Russell Ackoff, Arthur Danto, the great social interpreter of Russian literature Vera Sandemirsky Dunham, Irving Fowler, Irving Rosow, Arnold S. Feldman, H. Warren Dunham, and Alfred McClung Lee.

In 1950 I moved to Columbia University, a school that has not earned a large reputation as a relaxed, affectionate *Gemeinschaft*. However, my own department has generally offered some compensating advantages: Colleagues actually read each other's publications, they encourage each other's creativity, and they generate many new ideas. I believe they have improved my skills as a social analyst during my long association with them. And they have been generous to me in their gifts of warmth and friendship.

Our interactions have been various in content, as might be expected in a department from which almost no senior professor has taken his doctorate and which includes many who have not even taken it in sociology. For example, Robert M. McIver (an outstanding amateur mycologist) was my mushroom teacher. Peter McHugh, Alan Blum, and Stanley Raffel were dedicated ethnomethodologists, and our arguments centered on fundamental issues of epistemology. Immanuel Wallerstein tried to make me more interested in the modern politics of Africa than its classical anthropology. Sigmund Diamond, Allan Silver, and Robert K. Merton taught me renewed respect for the problems of using historical data for sociological analysis. Paul F. Lazarsfeld demonstrated repeatedly his talent for transforming a vague theoretical hunch into a concrete, feasible project. Both he and Benjamin Zablocki (with some help from others outside the department, such as Peter H. Rossi, James S. Coleman, and Frederick Mosteller) have continued to nurture my very small talent in research methods, outweighed sadly by my keen interest in the topic. Always an eager student of Chinese and Japanese culture, I have been fortunate in having Herbert Passin as a guide in these esoteric matters. The range is indeed wide, and I am pleased to use this occasion to thank all my colleagues here, listed and unlisted.

Some of my stimulating colleagues are in other departments or other schools, and most do not even know they have been my teachers. These are again too many to list, but some merit special mention: Johan Gat-

lung, John K. Galbraith, Barrington Moore, Staffan Linder, Gary Becker, Harry Eckstein, Lawrence Stone, Peter Laslett, Conrad Arensberg, George C. Homans, Elaine Walster, Charles Tilley, Stanley Schachter, Ralf Dahrendorf, Alvin W. Gouldner, Paul A. Samuelson, George P. Murdock, C. Ray Carpenter, Nikko Tinbergen, and Konrad Lorenz.

Most of my students have been unwilling to suspend disbelief while working with me, and have instead attacked me enthusiastically. If the professor can survive that treatment, she or he is likely to learn from it, at a minimum, considerable humility. Among the Columbia University students who have thus aided me to some greater intellectual clarity (even if they did not believe I achieved it) are: Walter Goldfrank, Terence K. Hopkins, Stanley Raffel, Cynthia Fuchs Epstein, Joel Telles, Mary E. Curran, Carol A. Finkelstein, Robert H. Somers, Helen M. McClure, Albert J. Szymanski, Nicholas Tavuchis, Nechama Tec, Mary J. Huntington, Larry Mitchell, Frank Furstenberg, Angela Aidala, Lenore J. Weitzman—and many, many others.

Most of this book was written and rewritten during a sabbatical year in Berkeley, the only year I ever spent away from my home campus. On the West Coast I learned from both old and new friends: William A. Kornhauser, Arlene Skolnick, David Matza, Jerome Skolnick, Seymour M. Lipset, Phillip Selznick, Alex Inkeles, Morris Zelditch, Gertrude Selznick, Neil Smelser, Leo Lowenthal, Arthur Stinchcombe, Guy E. Swanson, Richard Ofshe, Judith Davis, Harold L. Wilensky, Kingsley Davis, and (again) many others.

Three of my research assistants were especially helpful in digging up useful data and steering me away from errors: Jo Ann Costello and Mark Baldassare of the University of California (Berkeley) and Mark Johnson of Columbia University. Lenore J. Weitzman gave me thoughtful criticisms of this manuscript as it went through several drafts, and often warm encouragement as well, when the writing was difficult. Erich Goode generously let me read some of his still unpublished thinking about deviance, and so helped me in clarifying my thoughts on this process. Charles H. Page read some early draft chapters and gave valuable advice—as he did for earlier articles of mine, when he was editor of the *American Sociological Review*. As she has often done in the past, Charlotte Fisher lifted my spirits more than once by locating a clear line of exposition within what must have seemed a most untidy, over-corrected set of pages.

If as a student I was blessed by exciting teachers, so was I as a professor. Clearly, my debts are so many that I could never hope to list them all. I am even more fortunate than that statement suggests, for as Ithink of that galaxy of colleagues who have given me some enlightenment, I fell it is necessary to precede almost every name with "My friend"—Melvin Tumin, Peter H. Rossi, Erving Goffman, Alice Rossi, Robert

K. Merton, Paul F. Lazarsfeld, Arnold S. Feldman, Walter Goldfrank, Cynthia Fuchs Epstein, Allan Silver, Herbert Passin, Sigmund Diamond, Eugene Litwak, James S. Coleman, Amitai Etzioni, William A. Kornhauser, Harold Garfinkel, Everett C. Hughes, Ralf Dahrendorf, Larry Mitchell, Kingsley Davis, Wilbert E. Moore, Peter McHugh, C. Wright Mills, Gresham Sykes, Harriet Zuckerman, Jonathan Cole, Orville G. Brim, Harvey Farberman, and Raymond Mack.

Within the limits of my own capacities and the historical development of the field itself, I have tried to do what has been common in economics and somewhat less common in sociology: to present the best thinking in the field, as simply as possible. If I have succeeded at all in achieving that ideal, I shall feel my labor has been well rewarded. The task has been both frustrating and exciting. With the completion of the book, much of the frustration has gone away, but I hope that the reader will continue to share with me some of that excitement.

William J. Goode
Hog Creek, Long Island

PART ONE

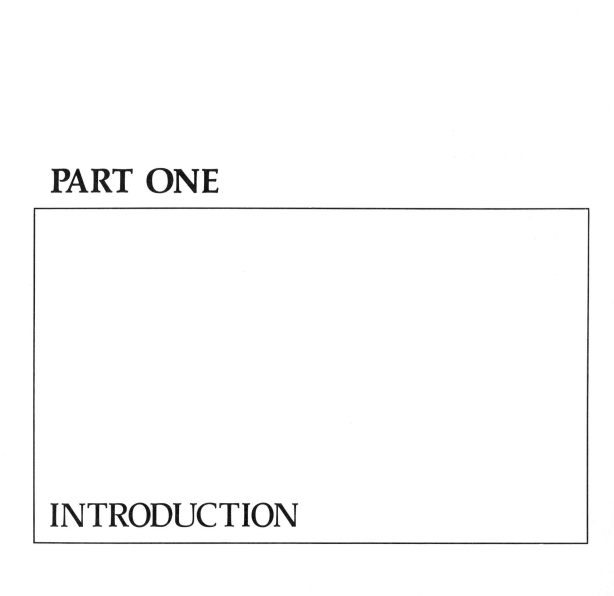

INTRODUCTION

CHAPTER ONE

THE SOCIOLOGICAL PERSPECTIVE

THE SOCIOLOGICAL VISION

To explore society is ultimately a way of knowing ourselves better, for we make up that society. It is a rewarding task, but not an easy one. It is often hard to put aside what we are sure we already know and to look at the curious customs and rules of "our tribe" in the same "objective" way we would study the rules and customs of the forest Pygmies.

However, to develop our sociological vision we must do just that: We must be willing to look at our own society with cool detachment, careful observation, and scientific analysis. We must examine the groups we live in—our family, our neighbors, our classmates, our nation—as if we had just set foot in a new and strange land.[1] We must

see how all these people affect our lives, and how we affect their lives as well, often without meaning to do so.

As we master this new way of looking at ourselves we shall begin an exciting adventure, for we shall understand more clearly our own social world. We shall begin to discover many new things in the social behavior we observe every day and now take for granted.

DEFINING SOCIOLOGY

But what is sociology? What do sociologists really do? How is their work different from

---

[1]The use of metaphors as a way of introducing sociological thinking to the reader may be found in some worthwhile essays on sociology. See especially C. Wright Mills, *The Sociological Imagination*, New York: Oxford, 1959; Peter L. Berger, *Invitation to Sociology: A Humanistic Perspective*, New York: Doubleday, 1963; and Pitirim A. Sorokin, *Fads and Foibles in Modern Sociology and Related Sciences*, Chicago: Regnery, 1956.

that of political scientists, psychologists, or economists? In this section we will examine the sociological vision and try to answer each of these questions.[2]

What Is Sociology?

Sociologists have offered many different definitions of their task. Here are a few:

1 Sociology is "the scientific study of human social life."
2 Sociology "specializes in the study of human societies."
3 Sociology is "the study of group behavior and social interaction, rather than the study of the individual as such."
4 Sociology is "the systematic study of human relations."

Closer to what sociologists have actually done in this definition: Sociology generally studies (1) group memberships, (2) group values and norms, and (3) group pressures (or rewards), as they affect people's behavior and preferences. An example of each type of study might be helpful.

Let us consider the effect of *membership* in *religious* groups. Sociological studies have repeatedly shown that a higher percentage of Catholics than of Protestants will vote Democratic in each election. (It is not that a majority of Protestants will vote Republican, but simply that a higher *percentage* of Protestants than of Catholics will vote Republican.)

As to the effect of *group values and*

[2]Another way of introducing the field is to explore the problem of defining it. One thoughtful essay that uses this theme is Alex Inkeles, *What Is Sociology? An Introduction to the Discipline and Profession*, Englewood Cliffs, N.J.: Prentice-Hall, 1964. Reports on current trends in the field appear from time to time under the auspices of the National Academy of Sciences; see Neil J. Smelser and James A. Davis, eds., *Sociology*, Englewood Cliffs, N.J.: Prentice-Hall, 1969. For other analyses of the sociological enterprise see Robert K. Merton, *Social Theory and Social Structure*, enlarged ed., New York: Free Press, 1968, pp. 1–38; and William J. Goode, *Explorations in Social Theory*, New York: Oxford, 1973, pp. 3–32.

norms, we might compare Catholic and Protestant values and norms about divorce. By *values* we mean the *standards* that group members share. These standards are used to judge whether something is good or bad, beautiful or ugly, right or wrong, moral or immoral. Even though the values of Catholics and Protestants are closer to one another than in the past, Catholics are still more likely than Protestants to believe that divorce is wrong.

Values are typically supported by specific *norms*, that is, more detailed directions for proper behavior. Norms are the more specific rules or definitions of how we are supposed to act in a given situation. They are based on group values and are backed by group pressures. Thus, the Catholic belief that divorce is wrong is likely to be supported by specific norms that frown on the kinds of behavior that might lead to divorce. For example, if a Catholic couple has serious marital problems, their norms state that husband and wife should make a real effort to work out their problems, or to adjust to the situation. Their friends are likely to advise them to see a priest but not a divorce lawyer. This is especially likely to happen if the couple live in a Catholic neighborhood or if they attend church regularly.

As to *group pressures* (or rewards), we have just noted the possibility that friends in a Catholic neighborhood might advise a couple to talk to their priest, but many other examples could be found in the newspapers. For example, it is probable that Catholic candidates for political office are more likely than Protestant candidates to feel group pressures to take a stand against abortion. Executives of oil companies are under some pressure from stockholders and fellow managers to favor low taxes on oil. They are also given praise if their efforts are successful. On most United States college campuses students try to persuade each other to become enthusiastic about their football team.

Sociologists have generally studied the effect of *groups* on people's behavior and preferences, but they have a wide range of other topics: Some have examined the religion of primitive tribes; others have studied changes in the art market over several generations. Sociologists have also tried to find out how best to sell a wide range of products, from crunchy breakfast cereals to the Edsel motorcar. Many have studied political processes. A few have used historical records to study family behavior in the past. Still others have written thoughtful essays that might be called social philosophy or commentary. The subject matter of these inquiries is also claimed by other social sciences, and the variety is wide. Thus, it is not likely that we shall be able to create a neat definition of sociology by listing all the things sociologists study.

However, we cannot define other social sciences that way, either. All of them roam widely in choice of topic as well as theoretical perspective. Nevertheless, each of the social sciences is able to distinguish its separate tasks even when they all look at the same event. Psychologists are more likely to focus on the personality of individuals. Economists are more likely than other social scientists to focus on monetary costs and benefits; political scientists will focus on governmental agencies and processes; and sociologists are more likely to focus on the impact of group norms, values, and pressures.

For example, when social scientists from each of these disciplines investigate criminal behavior they are likely to use the perspective typical of their fields. The psychologist would be more likely than the others to study the personalities of criminals and to isolate which factors in their early lives might have led them to engage in violence, stealing, or robbery. The economist might try to calculate whether particular kinds of crime "pay" well, by figuring out how much a criminal can earn, what are the chances of getting caught, how much a trial lawyer costs, or the loss of spending years in prison. The political scientist might focus on the criminal justice system and examine the effect of alternative laws, police programs, and criminal penalties on the rates of different kinds of crimes.

In contrast, the sociologist would be more likely to study these topics: the work teams of criminals and how they learn their trade; how the norms and values of various groups (drug users, buyers of stolen goods) support criminal activities; or the life history of one or more criminals. The sociologist would analyze the group experiences that change a juvenile delinquent into a criminal. Several studies have viewed the prison itself as a kind of community or organized group, and have analyzed its norms and social pressures (or rewards) as they affect both guards and prisoners. Although none of these fields analyzes crime fully, each gives us a better understanding of it.

For any human activity, we can focus on the sociological aspect, while ignoring other kinds of factors. Even when sociological factors play a *minor* role, we can still examine the effect of those factors. For example, modern farming is a highly technical enterprise. If we think of it in terms of economic production or technology, sociological factors would appear to be of modest importance. However, we could decide to study only those aspects of farming which are tied to group behavior. One of these would be the process by which farmers come to adopt a new agricultural technique, such as hybrid seeds or the mechanical cotton picker.

Whatever the practical advantages of the new methods, social factors will determine which farmers accept them first. These social factors include the farmer's rank, friendship network, and social norms. Farmers with higher social rank are more likely to try new methods because they enjoy more respect and they can take more social (and financial) risks. Once they have adopted a new technique, additional farmers are likely to follow their lead. Friendship patterns among farmers will also affect *who* adopts the new technique and how quickly the new method spreads. If the farmers are linked in a close social network, the new technique is likely to spread more rapidly. Those who are well integrated into a friendship network are likely to adopt it before those who are more isolated. Finally, if there are conflicts among farmers, one subgroup of farmers may refuse to try the new method because it was introduced by another group. (For example, some local farmers have been reluctant to try excellent agricultural methods that were introduced by new "hippie" farmers.) In short, the acceptance of a new agricultural method is not determined only by agricultural engineering factors, but also by sociological factors.

In all these instances we would be examining certain *sociological* aspects of a human activity (farming) that appears to be *mostly* determined by technological or economic variables. On the other hand, we could examine human activities that seem far more determined by sociological variables or causes. For example, both religion and family behavior seem more essentially sociological than economic or political. Ethnic or racial groups use many economic and political techniques for attacking others and protecting themselves. Nevertheless, the underlying processes are strongly affected by sociological factors.

Whether we choose to study human activities that are not primarily sociological (farming, factory work) or instead choose situations that seem more fully determined by the sociological (religion), we are actually carrying out the same task in both instances: *We are studying or focusing on one special set of processes.* We are searching for a distinct set of sociological factors to explain the regularities of that social behavior. We are not trying to explain the entire pattern of human behavior.

How Sciences Are Set Apart from One Another

How, then, does any science separate its problem area from that of any other disci-

Figure 1-1 Sociological studies focus on individual aspects of processes, such as the sex or race of voters or candidates in an election. (Charles Gatewood.)

pline? To answer this question, we must first note that *each science studies only a part of the world we see.* No science can explain all aspects of any concrete phenomenon, whether it is a volcanic explosion, the unfolding of a flower, or a tennis victory. To understand the idea that each science focuses on only a narrow part of anything we see, we must first keep in mind that the sciences do not try to explain a specific *event* anyway, but a *class* of events: The classical physicist, in observing one particular pendulum, was trying to understand how *any* pendulum moves, of whatever length, size, or shape. And nineteenth-century biologists tried to understand what the liver contributed to digestion in any human body, not in just one particular body.

Second, scientists do not study all aspects or traits of even that class of events or things; *scientists study only a selected set of causes, factors, or variables.* They ignore many factors and focus on only the factors they believe to be important. Thus, economics studies supply and demand in the market, but has mostly ignored market transactions in native tribes. Even within modern markets it does not study all aspects and factors of market transactions. The field does not concern itself much with the legal systems that give market advantages to a ruling class, and it does not engage in many studies that focus on why people like one kind of commodity more than another. Economics does not often study how people acquire the standards or values by which they judge what a given commodity is worth. Each science attempts to analyze only a narrow slice of an infinitely complex reality.

Indeed, one might assert that the foundations of a science or of a new subfield within it are firmly established only when that new discipline discovers just what its small but important set of variables and factors really is, and which ones should be ignored—even though they do affect concrete reality in some degree. A formula that

describes the motion of a pendulum ignores its shape, the roughness of its surface, and the surrounding air pressure.

Similarly, in sociology we can predict that in a country with relatively easy divorce the rate of marital breakup of all kinds will be generally higher toward the *lower* social strata. In making that prediction we ignore the possible effect of psychological or biological variables, although certainly they may affect those rates to some degree. In psychology, too, most hypotheses or findings ignore the possible effect of sociological variables such as social class, religion, and ethnic background. In its effort to locate a set of sociological factors and to focus on the sociological dimensions or aspects of human activities, our field follows the lead of other sciences.

Moreover, as the grand enterprise of science has taken shape over the past three hundred years, each new field has typically emerged by locating its *own* set of problems, processes, and explanatory principles, *not* by utilizing the variables and findings of the more developed sciences. Chemistry was *not* first developed on the foundations of physics, biology on those of chemistry, or sociology on those of biology, economics, or psychology. It is only in the later and more mature stages of a science that researchers begin to see how the formulations of physics might be used in, say, chemistry, or those of biology in some branches of psychology.

Typically, each new science has separated from the others because it located what seemed to be new aspects of events, phenomena, or activities that were not explained by the traditional variables, and thus called for a new approach.[3] Sociologists have used sociological variables to explain

---

[3]On this point see Jonathan R. Cole and Harriet Zuckerman, "The Emergence of a Scientific Specialty: The Self-exemplifying Case of the Sociology of Science," in Lewis K. Coser, ed., *The Idea of Social Structure: Papers in Honor of Robert K. Merton*, New York: Harcourt Brace Jovanovich, 1975, pp. 139–174.

sociological phenomena, just as psychologists have used variables from their own field, simply because other variables seemed too weak. They explained too little of what we wanted to understand.

Although this view of the relations among different sciences emphasizes that each field makes it own contribution, and can illuminate some problems better than another field might, it also points to a correlative fact, which we stated before and now repeat: *Any concrete event or thing can be studied with the special ideas or from the distinct view of any given science.*

Thus, if we simply observe the movements of human beings through the day's activities, we can decide to focus on those movements only as responses to gravitational and other forces, or as energy transformations, just as a *physicist might. Instead, we might look at those movements as complex chemical* processes. On the other hand, we might ignore both and instead note that those movements are producing transistor radios or are guiding a truck along a highway—in short, they are producing commodities and services for an *economic* market. As sociologists, we might examine some of those movements as expressing deference and respect to superiors or showing affection, as when people bow before a monarch or embrace a friend. We need not even view those movements as a scientist might, but instead we might look only at how people produce art or music or a dance. That is, we could look only at movements that can be described in artistic or aesthetic terms. None of these approaches will capture the entire social reality. All can help us to understand in some degree.

The Sociological Perspective

Sociological research has proved fruitful, yielding many findings that help us to understand social life. Its effort to locate a distinct set of factors and processes for study is much like the historic efforts of more mature sciences. Nevertheless, that does not prove that sociology now possesses a special view distinct from that of the other social sciences. We have not yet answered the question of whether sociology can create its own laws and body of theory.

It can be argued that the field has simply passed through a historical stage of separating itself sharply from other social sciences and that its next step will move the other way. That is, it will look for laws of human behavior by searching for *any* explanatory factors that seem useful, whether they are sociological, economic, psychological, or even biological. It will no longer need to be "pure."

We cannot use the history of modern science to answer this question, for the major fields did not follow the same phases or take on the same intellectual structure. When any new field was begun in the past, it was not possible at that time to know whether such a field would ever develop. Centuries ago, philosophers were generally agreed that no science of human relations could be created, because (1) we cannot know the inner life of other people, (2) "free will" makes social or psychological laws impossible, and (3) human relations do not exhibit the same regularities that physical objects do.

However, those arguments against or for the possibility of a new field have had relatively little effect upon its development. Instead, whether a scientific field eventually develops independently, with its own laws, is determined far more by whether its founders have been fortunate or wise enough to perceive a set of relationships, processes, or variables that in fact *are* closely related and do have causal relations with one another.

Often they were not successful. The carefully labeled variables and processes of medieval astrology did not develop into a field of science and thus did not form the basis of astronomy. "Fevers" were once thought to be a special and major class of diseases, but they have turned out to be of minor empirical importance in medicine. Similarly, the subfield of physical anthropology once attempted, over many decades, to work out a scientific basis for classifying all human races and to link those biological factors with different cultural, social, and psychological behavior. The effort was a failure, for those variables did not in fact have much effect upon one another.

In fact, these are only a few examples of the dozens of new subfields that have been proposed over the past two centuries. Most of them achieved no independent status, mainly because the variables and processes they "saw" did not hang together in reality. Their leaders were not successful in generating a range of valid laws about the real world. By contrast, *sociology has increasingly been able to develop findings that do have validity and do show strong relations with one another.* We can therefore continue to be optimistic for its future.[4]

On the other hand, that view suggests that we should not be too "pure" in our view of sociology. That is, since we cannot yet be sure that we *have* located the key sociological factors or variables, we should not confine our attention only to them. We should not yet be rigid about stating that this or that factor is "not really sociological." As social scientists, we seek an understanding of social behavior. Precision and power in our hypotheses and explanations are a much more important aim than whether they are "purely sociological" as defined in the past. Indeed, we shall go on to suggest, as a step toward that openness, that we might include in our sociological view at least some attention to rational or self-seeking behavior as it affects social life, *outside* the economic market.

Openness may also be wise because other subfields of social science continue to use sociological insights and data. As a consequence, some of their studies will help us understand social behavior better, and we should not ignore them. This has been especially true in social psychology, which has increasingly used factors that we would normally think of as sociological rather than psychological. Some of these, for example, focus on the conditions under which people help one another or resist authority. Others focus on social patterns in negotiations or on the social processes by which members decide who deserve more rewards for their contribution to a group task.[5]

Nevertheless, although the intellectual boundaries among the social sciences may become less sharp in the future, we can safely predict on *sociological* grounds that the divisions will not fully disappear. People are trained as graduate students in their own discipline, and come to take pride in it. They make close social ties with colleagues within it. They develop a vested interest in its success as compared with that of other fields. Consequently, they are likely to protect it from attack. Correspondingly, scholars who have been trained in the sociological tradition will continue to view their own perspective, however difficult it may be to define verbally, as a helpful guide to understanding the dynamics of social life. They will continue to feel that a sociological view will explain some behavior better than other fields can.

It should be emphasized, however, that the intellectual boundaries of any scientific field have become clear only after decades or generations of research, and not primarily through arguments about what it should study. That clarity has never been achieved simply because someone offered a neat, de-

[4]For a less optimistic interpretation and survey see Alvin N. Gouldner, *The Coming Crisis of Western Sociology*, New York: Avon, 1970.

[5]See the analysis of these processes in George C. Homans, *Social Behavior: Its Elementary Forms* (1961), rev. ed., New York: Harcourt Brace Jovanovich, 1974, pp. 51–68.

fensible definition of the main task or view, which people in the field then accepted as the one true way. That definition, where it emerges, comes mainly from research work, not from philosophical debates. The research work, in turn, *defines* because it reveals order and cause, regularities and dynamics, in some set of events or processes. It opens up new areas for discovery and new relationships that can be tested. *The field is, then, defined ultimately by its work, its results, its body of research.*

THE SOCIOLOGICAL EMPHASIS ON GROUPS

Group Values, Norms, and Social Pressures (or Rewards)

As we noted before, amid the rich complexity of social behavior, the sociological vision has concentrated especially on the *impact of group memberships, group values and norms, and group pressures on people's behavior and preferences.* By *values* we refer to the standards that group members share, by which they judge whether an action or even an object is beautiful, good, right, or lawful, or whether instead it is ugly, immoral, or unethical. By *norms* we typically refer to a specific set of rules or definitions of proper behavior. These express the group's values and are backed by group pressures. Thus, it still remains true that people in the United States believe in the *value* of monogamy in marriage, (that is, one husband for one wife, and both should be faithful), however, they may violate that value in practice. Correspondingly, to bolster that value there are many *norms*, or guides for behavior. Thus, for example, in spite of the many announcements about the new sexual freedom of our time, most groups support norms that disapprove of married women and men dating others, going off separately with people of the opposite sex for weekends, or hanging around bars alone in the evening. If we

violate the norms, we are likely to face some social consequences or pressures, such as loss of esteem.

In focusing on the impact of group values and norms on the action of other groups or individuals, sociology also studies *which people or groups affirm or believe in one set of norms and values as against another.* In other words, how differently does one group act because members believe in a different set of norms and values? Sociology must therefore also focus on *how people are socialized*—that is, how children (and adults, too) are trained to *believe* in such norms and values.

Since people do believe in norms and values, they typically try to impose them on other members of their own group and to some degree upon members of other groups as well. As a consequence, we must study the *various social pressures (or rewards) that move people toward conformity with those norms or values* or indeed away from conformity. Sociology has given special emphasis to how being a group member or having a particular social position (for example, being a leader) shapes one's beliefs, values, norms, and behaviors and how pressures from *others* (in part because of their values and norms) affect *our* behavior.

Let us consider simple but classic examples. Hundreds of studies over many generations have described various differences in behavior within a given population—for example, the number of children in a family, their eating patterns and style of living, church attendance, voting, even occupational mobility—and have "explained" them by showing that they could be ascribed to differences between, say, rural and urban backgrounds. The underlying idea was that people from those different backgrounds would hold different values and norms and thus would behave differently. When the urban-rural differences were sharper in the United States, we could expect that people from rural backgrounds would have more traditional beliefs about marriage, divorce, and having a large family. They were somewhat less likely than people from urban backgrounds to have the attitudes and skills needed for success in the job world of the city. Similar analyses used the categories of immigrant–native born, black-white, or social class background to explain a wide range of differences in social behavior.

So primitive an analysis does not seem very powerful now, although many great social scientists used it over the centuries. However, the general perspective can become sharper and more fruitful. For example, we can sharpen that insight somewhat by finding out which are our *reference groups*.[6] That is, by whose standards do we evaluate our behavior? The idea of *reference* groups reminds us that sometimes we may not be members of the group by which we judge our own behavior. As sociologists, then, we must often ask, To which group does an individual "refer" his or her behavior or the behavior of others? For example, most people do use groups of which they *are* members as their reference groups, but people who are socially moving upward often look beyond their group to another, whose social standing is *higher*, as a proper source of values and norms. That is, they do not weigh their behavior by whether members of their *own* group approve of it, but by whether members of the higher group might approve.

By linking individual behavior to *group membership, group norms, and group pressures*, we understand much social action that cannot be explained by easy reference to "self-interest" or "rationality," meaning getting the most money profit in a market. And by keeping group values, norms, and pressures in mind, we can use a more fruitful, modern notion of self-interest or rationality that includes the individual's "rational" seeking of goals that are collective, or group-oriented. For example, we can show that people often give up the economic rationality of the biggest money profit in favor of getting respect or prestige from other group members. They may make that choice *rationally* and seek prestige in a thoughtful way. Since they are attempting to live by group standards and may even sacrifice themselves for the group, we can no longer use the term "self-interest" as it might be used in economic analysis.

Some additional illustrations of how the special sociological emphasis on group norms, values, and pressures (or rewards) can be useful in the analysis of behavior should be noted here. In succeeding chapters we shall consider many more.

Whether people are likely to judge the chances of promotion or upward mobility as satisfactory is determined more by how well they are doing in relation to *other* members of their group than by the "objective" chances of rising.

Because people in social groups or organizations usually want to support their groups as well as their rank in those groups, members will usually follow rules that keep out able people of the "wrong" sex or ethnic, religious, racial, or class backgrounds, even though such rules will result in lower technical efficiency.

General patriotic propaganda has far less effect on the fighting behavior of soldiers than does their membership in small, informal groups. Soldiers are more concerned with "not letting their buddies down" than they are with either job promotion or the great ideological issues of the war at the national level. Moreover, it is possible to break down individual morale in war prisoner camps by undermining the structure of small groups and the social ties among people.

[6]See Robert K. Merton and Alice S. Rossi, "Contributions to the Theory of Reference Group Behavior," in Merton, op. cit., Chap. 10.

In work situations where it is to the advantage of the individual to produce as much as possible in order to earn more, people typically form groups that keep the rate of production down to a level that does not put too great a burden on any member.

The traditional perspective that studied the effect of believing in group values and norms on people's behavior but paid less attention to the *group's pressure* on the individual has sometimes led sociologists into several errors. One is that the analyst may forget that *we cannot predict behavior adequately from simply knowing people's values and norms.* After all, a moment's thought will remind us that we often violate norms that we actually believe in; or we conform to norms that we inwardly reject. For example, almost all students believe that it is wrong to cheat on an examination, but almost all students have succumbed to that temptation at some time. Most males believe that they should not allow themselves to be pushed around by a bully, and there are strong norms in support of that rule, but certainly most males have at times not lived by that brave rule.

Overemphasis on the impact of group values has led to another type of error, *the assumption that all members of a group or population segment accept certain values and norms when in fact only some of them do.* There is usually a substantial amount of *dissensus* in a group, organization, social stratum, or society with reference to many supposedly important values. Every survey of public opinion shows that many people disagree with some of the supposed values and norms about working hard for success: for example, private property, most religious beliefs and observances (even among active members of a church), or whether everyone should have an equal vote.

Overemphasis on the impact of group val-

ues has sometimes led, in addition, to forgetting that *all individuals hold many divergent or contrary values and norms.* As a consequence, some investigators have been led into assuming that only one set of value commitments is relevant, when several actually play a role in each person's decisions and action. Beyond that, everyone is under *many* sets of group pressures. No one is simply a member of *one* group.

Although sociology, like other growing fields, has committed some errors of emphasis, its focus on the cultural differences among subgroups has led to important contributions to our understanding of social life, and its findings have justified its claim to standing among the social sciences. For example, as recently as the early 1920s, the pseudoscientific notion of "instinct" was widely used as an explanation of social behavior. That is, many believed that people married, protected the group, or sold goods because of some specific, built-in, biological trait. This came to be rejected as sociological inquiry showed that the so-called instincts were simply a product of being reared and trained in groups; they were not part of any built-in physiological mechanism.

Similarly, until fairly recently social analysts and philosophers had repeated the belief that the *biological* factors of race, which seemed to be an obvious differentiation among the peoples of the earth, were a significant cause of *national* differences. In opposition, sociological research has shown that if human beings can be divided into races at all, this division cannot be the cause of differences in national psychological or social patterns. Differences are rather to be ascribed to the various ways in which people grow up in different groups and cultures.

Sociological studies of role behavior have also shown that *personality* differences are not very useful in explaining behavior whose roots lie in the individual's *position* or rank within a group or an organization. We can better use group norms and socioeconomic pressures to understand the behavior of managers in their relations with employees, rather than looking for personality differences or psychodynamisms.

Numerous sociological findings have cast doubt on the economic assumption of maximizing profit as the major principle in social life. People will often forgo the economic advantages of a promotion because it will interfere with their family life, and thus members of their family oppose the move. Universities can continue to attract a high level of research talent, although their salaries are *lower* than in either business or government, because they offer both more freedom in research and higher prestige. As Thorstein Veblen pointed out many years ago in *The Theory of the Leisure Class*, people will undergo discomfort and awkwardness in many aspects of their life in order to be in fashion (see Figure 1-2); and they will waste much of their income in order to display to others how successful they are. That is, people are often *rational* in seeking various advantages, but *often the advantages or rewards are group respect or affection*, not mere money.

Perhaps one of the most persuasive proofs of the importance of the sociological view is that its findings and perspectives have been borrowed or utilized by other fields, such as history, political science, anthropology, and economics. That is, the particular view of sociology is fruitful enough to help explain some of the events and processes with which other social sciences are concerned.[7]

When Is a Set of People to Be Called a "Group"?

In view of our many kinds of relations with different people, can we apply the term

[7]For an analysis of these relationships see Neil J. Smelser, "Sociology and the Other Social Sciences," in Paul F. Lazarsfeld et al., eds., *The Uses of Sociology,* New York: Basic Books, 1967, pp. 3–44.

Figure 1-2 People are willing to undergo discomfort in the name of fashion. (Charles Gatewood.)

"group" to them? That is, is it true that much social action takes place *in* groups, or that *individual* behavior is shaped by *group* relations? If the term simply applies to any social behavior at all, then it seems too loose to be helpful.

Social interactions, by definition, take place between people. Otherwise they are not social. However, many do not seem to be real groups. The people we know may be linked in various ways, it is true, but they do not form a *unit*. At one point we may talk alone with a friend, then later with several acquaintances together, and still later we may join a loose gathering of people who are watching someone trying to start a car. However, we are not likely to think of any of those sets of people as a group, and certainly all of them together do not form a group. True enough, in daily life we may also interact with people who are part of an *organization*, such as students, professors, or deans of a *university*; a clerk in a *drugstore* or public utility; or our coworkers in a *corporation*. However, to use the term "group" for all these relationships seems at first to violate its meaning. More importantly, can we speak of "the group" as offering rewards or threatening losses to "members" if they are not members and there is no group—or, instead, if everyone belongs to hundreds of "groups"?

Let us begin with a stricter definition and see what is the central meaning of "group."

In the narrower sense, a *group* would be only those social actors or units which (1) clearly distinguish between members and nonmembers, (2) possess a set of norms and values different from those of others, (3) control their members by definite rewards and losses, (4) are fairly cohesive (they stick together), (5) contain members who know one another, (6) come together or meet once in a while, (7) create in members a feeling of being united with one another *because* they are members, and (8) play a large role in their members' lives. If we use so restrictive a definition, much social behavior must take place *outside* groups, and sociology would deal with only a small part of human relations.

However, in ordinary language the word "group" has a wide array of meanings, and sociology has used many of them. Thus, we may use the term to refer to a friendship dyad (two people) or a trio of friends. We may also use the term for a large formal organization such as the American Medical Association. However, both of these two examples would still be groups even under the strict definition above.

Beyond that, we may occasionally use the term to refer to what is no more than a *statistical category*, or *segment* of the population, when we want to speak of such a *slice* of the population as the poor, the disadvantaged, or people in the child-bearing years, but we feel the term "category" is heavy and awkward. We are still less likely to use the term "group" for categories if the people in them do *not* think of themselves as alike, do *not* recognize one another as sharing anything in common, and are *not* recognized by others as set apart: for example, all people who first married at ages twenty through twenty-four, those who have flown across the ocean, or everyone who is waiting in a bus station.

From that extreme we can move to "groups" which are at least recognized *by others* as sharing some common experiences, and which sometimes see themselves as alike, such as women, blacks, or Texans. They need not meet together and do not control each other's behavior much. On the other hand, they may at times speak of themselves as a "we," simply because they recognize that people like themselves are treated the same way by others. Membership in many of these categories or groups is relatively long-lasting, but it need not be. Thus, people may be temporarily blinded or crippled and may come to feel some kinship with others who share that handicap, while "normals" treat them as different, as set apart in various ways.

Sociologists also refer to many forms of groups in which there is a real social interaction, even if it is not intense or long-lasting. A family is a group, but so is a university class that lasts but a semester or a quarter. Youngsters may form a group for an afternoon of touch football. During that period they do set themselves apart from others, do obey certain rules, and do play a large if temporary role in each other's life. Some sociologists would include in this large category even an audience, a church congregation, or the passengers on an airplane, to the extent that they do share a common social experience, follow the same rules for that period, and engage in some social interaction. People walking down the street would not be a group, but if an accident caused them to come together as an audience and then to interact together, they could be called a group.

None of these "groups" in the previous paragraph is marked, however, by any *organizational* system. There are no written rules, no system of election to office, no set of formal offices with specific duties, no regulations about communications; in short, they are not *associations*. In a modern society these (often called *voluntary associations*) often have great social and political influence (the American Bar Association, the American Medical Association, or the United Mine Workers). They have membership lists and often dues as well. Usually, *unlike* a family or a friendship group, they have definite *purposes* (the armed services, a university, the United Nations). On the other hand, some of their members almost never see one another (the association is too big for that), and in all important associations it never happens that *everyone* meets together (members of a consumers' union, stockholders of the Xerox Corporation, members of the United Auto Workers). They do share interests in common, however, and many rules, which they have the right to change.

Sociology has failed to work out a generally accepted set of labels for all these various types of groups or groupings. In some contexts we can use the term "audience" without any confusion, whether or not we want to call that a group. We can also refer to a temporary gathering of people as an "aggregate" if we wish, and again the word is clear enough in context. These and other terms are sometimes used, but there is no *systematic*, organized set of terms to cover *all* forms of groups. Consequently, from time to time a reader may feel that the term has been stretched out of ordinary meaning.

Nevertheless, the situation is not really so messy as it seems, in part because the term is used very concretely with no special jargon that might confuse. We simply use the term very loosely as a way of bringing up the topic of social interaction, and almost never will a sociologist try to explain something by saying "Because it is a group."

Most important, however, is the fact that this analysis suggests *three important principles that bear on our earlier question about how groups can affect social behavior* if so little of our daily life seems to take place within "real" groups. First, the long list of traits that distinguish a group in the most restrictive core meaning of the term is really made of *variables*, that is, factors or elements that can be high or low in amount. A group can be more *or* less cohesive, can

possess more *or* less sharp boundaries that set it apart, or can control its members more *or* less. Actual groups vary a great deal in all these aspects. Consequently, the bewildering variety of concrete groups we observe *is* the social reality; they take many forms because they do vary in all these ways.

Second, even those groups, groupings, categories, collectivities, or associations which seem to be far removed from a group in the stricter sense nevertheless do have more of those traits than a quick glance might show. Indeed, this discussion should sharpen our attention to the many forms of group life in situations where we are not accustomed to seeing them. For example, let us consider a group of people on the street, gathered around a person who has fainted. It may not seem to be very "groupy." However, if we look more closely, we shall see that there *are rules*, one of the characteristics of a group. If a member treats the fallen person roughly, or pushes another bystander, or screams hysterically, she or he will be scolded by others. They are likely to talk about the event with one another and to think of it as an experience they shared together.

In short, the social analyst must become aware of the variety of ways (even weak ways) that group life appears, because it may affect human behavior even when the group itself does not fit a narrow definition.

Third, *groups affect human behavior even when the interaction does not take place within a group.* We noted, for example, the existence of social collectivities or categories which never meet all together and which do not claim to be a social unit, such as blacks, women, or the aged. People in these categories often share many social characteristics, or are more likely than people in other categories to share certain traits, in part because *they are viewed by others as being different* and are treated differently.

Consequently, interaction between two individuals may be shaped by the fact that each sees the other as a "group member" even when they are only members of a "category." For example, women and men, boys and girls, in our society typically approach each other and react to the other as *group* members *first*, and only later as individuals. Blacks and whites are likely to view each other as members of a group and to respond to each other as part of a group. The police *are* a group in the stricter sense, and the public is not, but police officers perceive "civilians" as a group.

In short, people in many social categories that we might be unwilling to call groups may nevertheless have common experiences that have shaped their lives, so that at least some of their behavior is similar; and *others* perceive *them* as different, as members of a group, and treat them differently. Thus, much social interaction between individuals is shaped by those memberships, even when the participants do not think of themselves as forming a unit.

Thus, although the field of sociology is changing, it continues to study the norms and values of groups, associations, or whole societies. Rather than rejecting the idea of groups and group norms, sociology has continued to discover more of its richness and variety, while *also* giving increasing recognition to the role of rational calculation and exchanges in social life. In a later chapter we shall analyze in much greater detail the many different kinds of groups that affect our lives.[8]

SOCIOLOGY VIEWED AS A SCIENCE

In this introduction we have noted that sociology aspires to be a *science*. Basically, a

[8]For a classic discussion of groups see Kurt H. Wolff, ed., *The Sociology of Georg Simmel*, New York: Free Press, 1950, pp. 26–39, 87–104ff.; and also Simmel's *Conflict and the Web of Group Affiliations*, trans. by Kurt Wolff and Reinhard Bendix, New York: Free Press, 1955, pp. 125–195.

science is a *method*, a way of obtaining objective, precise, and systematic knowledge about reality. Physicists obtain knowledge about *physical* reality. Sociologists, similarly, try to obtain objective, precise, and systematic knowledge about *social* reality, or social relations. Thus, sociologists try to obtain scientific knowledge about how people are affected by their various group relationships.

However, is it even possible to obtain valid knowledge about social action? Can there be a scientific field called "sociology"? Philosophers have argued about these questions for two thousand years. There are three main traditional arguments against the idea of sociology becoming a science. First, some philosophers have argued that we cannot get adequate descriptions of social reality if we have to rely on our senses (for example, our eyes and ears) because these are notoriously untrustworthy. Second, the information we get from other persons is unreliable. People can refuse information; they can hide. They can give twisted or false reports. How can sociology be a science when it must use that kind of information? Third, philosophers have argued that the human spirit is "free" and unpredictable; human beings are not as *regular* in their behavior as animals are. Thus, we cannot find any "social laws" in human behavior.

In answer to the first argument, *all* sciences would have to be cast out if we decide that our senses cannot be trusted. Sociology must do what other sciences do: develop better measuring instruments (films, the use of different observers, cross-checking with different people at different times, and so forth) to cut down the chances of errors from poor observation.

In answer to the second objection, we must admit that research in human behavior requires different techniques than do studies of rock strata or molecules. But in any growing science these are normal problems of technology; solutions do not depend on philosophical debate. Over the past fifty years much work in sociology has been devoted to research *methods*, that is, to discovering new ways of getting better information about social behavior.

Various forms of social experiments have been carried out, such as comparing what people *claim* to believe with what we see them actually *doing*. In interviews different forms of the same question are used in order to find out whether people give the *same* answer if the wording of the question is different. People can, indeed, distort their answers, but those very attempts to hide the truth also give us more facts about social behavior. We can also observe without asking at all. For example, in experiences on fatness we can count the sandwiches left in the refrigerator after the person has left the laboratory, without asking the subject at all about how he or she responds to temptation, or how much he or she eats. In short, a wide array of useful techniques has been worked out for getting valid and reliable knowledge about human behavior.

The answer to the third traditional argu-

QUESTIONNAIRE RESPONSE   7

		COLUMN	CODE
18	Generally speaking, does your mother think of herself as a Republican, Democrat, Independent, or what? 1 Republican 2 Democrat 3 Independent 4 Other (please specify)_____	45	_____
19	Is your mother presently employed? 1 Full time 2 Part time 3 Unemployed 4 Disabled 5 Retired 6 Deceased	46	_____
20	What kind of work does (did) your mother normally do? That is, what is (was) her job called? Occupation_____	47–51	_____
21	In which of these groups does (did) your mother's total income, from all sources, fall last year (or the last year she worked)—before taxes? 1 Under $1,000 2 $1,000 to $2,999 3 $3,000 to $3,999 4 $4,000 to $4,999 5 $5,000 to $5,999 6 $6,000 to $6,999 7 $7,000 to $7,999 8 $8,000 to $9,999 9 $10,000 to $14,999 10 $15,000 to $19,999 11 $20,000 to $29,999 12 $30,000 or over 98 Don't know	52–52	_____
22	How many brothers and sisters did you have? (Count those born alive, but no longer living, as well as those alive now. Also include stepbrothers, stepsisters, and children adopted by your parents.) _____	54–55	_____
23	How many brothers and sisters are still alive?	56–57	_____
24	During the last semester or quarter, how much time did you spend watching television during an average day? _____hours	58–59	_____
25	How many credit hours of course work did you complete during the last semester or quarter? 1 None 2 1–3 3 4–6 4 7–9	60–61	_____

Figure 1-3 One page of a sample research questionnaire. (Lin, Burt, and Vaughn, 1976.)

ment (that people are "free" and their behavior is unpredictable) is simply that it is being done. We cannot predict how *individuals* will act, but we can make some simple predictions about what *classes* or types of individuals are more (or less) likely to do. Indeed, the reader does this all the time. Every one of us possesses a vast amount of facts about how other people are likely to act under certain circumstances: our boss when we are careless about our work; strangers in an elevator when we talk to ourselves out loud; or other drivers if we do not stop for a red light. Whether or not people are "free" in some deeper sense, we can observe and analyze the patterns and regularities in their social behavior, and that is the task of the sociologist.

But modern sociologists increasingly ignore the ancient arguments that claim such a science is not possible. In ignoring these arguments they follow the history of the physical sciences. In all developed fields, once a substantial amount of verifiable fact has been created, researchers become concerned only with how to discover further regularities in nature. They ignore the question of whether it was possible to do what they were in fact already doing.

Similarly, although all researchers in sociology have studied this problem, at least as graduate students, once they begin to carry out research they spend little energy in analyzing whether objective facts *can* be reached, for they see they are doing just that. They see no fundamental barriers against obtaining scientific descriptions and analyses of social patterns.

All these facts prove that the foundations of sociology as a science are relatively secure, and that the field is building up a body of scientific knowledge that is worthy of serious attention.[9]

Sociology as a Generalizing Science

From its recognition as a new academic specialty at the turn of the century, sociology has had several aspirations that are somewhat different from those of its sister disciplines. First, more than other social sciences (except economics) the field has sought to become a *generalizing science*; that is, its leaders have repeatedly proclaimed that it should develop general "laws" that explain social behavior, not merely describe concrete social interaction. An anthropologist might be content to report the kinship system, the religious rituals, or the war customs of the Blackfeet Indians. A political scientist might survey the inner workings of the contemporary New York City government. However, the sociologist is more likely to use such details to demonstrate or discover a more abstract proposition or hypothesis, such as:

> The less the material benefits and respect given to a social class, the lower the percentage of that class who will feel much commitment or allegiance to the rulership or the social system as a whole.

This is not to say that sociological research ignores concrete descriptions. On the contrary, it begins with such details, as does all science. They are the necessary foundation of any general theorizing.

Further, many sociologists enjoy the discovery and analysis of specific social customs as interesting in their own right: for example, the occupational world of the pimp or the police officer, the social and time budgets of the alcoholic, the friendship patterns of lower-class blacks, changes in dress fashions, or how people with stigmatized traits such as being blind or crippled man-

[9]For further discussion of these issues see Marion J. Levy, Jr., "Scientific Analysis Is a Subset of Comparative Analysis," in John C. McKinney and Edward A. Tiryakian, eds., *Theoretical Sociology: Perspectives and Developments*, New York: Appleton-Century-Crofts,

1970, pp. 99–110. See also Paul Filmer et al., eds., *New Directions in Sociological Theory*, Cambridge, Mass.: M.I.T., 1973. On measurement see Eugene J. Webb et al., *Unobtrusive Measures: Nonreactive Research in the Social Sciences*, Chicago: Rand McNally, 1966.

age the problems of social interaction with "normals."

Though it is safe to say that most sociologists read these accounts of social customs with more pleasure and interest than is experienced when they read the grand theories of general sociology, the latter are viewed as closer to the aspirations and goals of the discipline.

Let us consider what is meant by a general, or abstract, hypothesis. It is not just a simple *summary* of descriptive data. For example, such a summary might assert that in all human societies people in informal social behavior (play, friendly talk) use a variety of techniques to support each other's self-respect and social standing (such as being mannerly or showing an interest in the other). Other such summaries might be these: Over the past half-century the divorce rate in all Western countries permitting divorce has risen; or the percentage of the world population living in cities has risen steadily for more than a century.

These last two are concrete descriptions, relating what occurred at a particular time and place. They would not be correct if we applied them to Europe in the fifth century. The first was also a description, but it does not specify either time or place; it asserts, "Sometimes people engage in these activities." It is thus similar to other lists of what people do, such as: Friends do favors for one another; parents nurture their children (but some do not, and all punish them as well); business executives support criminal activities. Such statements are in fact a warning that we should be alert to such behavior and should look at it; but they do not yet tell us what are the causes of the behavior or what are the social conditions that create more or less of it.

By contrast, a scientific hypothesis, proposition, or law states a relationship between two or more abstract variables (or factors), sometimes also giving the conditions where we can expect to observe that relationship. That is, a *scientific hypothesis predicts* the relationship between two or more factors or social patterns. If it is a fruitful hypothesis in sociology, it will apply to many concrete organizations, social interactions, or societies and will help explain many recurring social patterns. None of these relationships in sociology is as powerful or precise as those in the more mature sciences, and possibly the search for them is doomed to failure, but we should at least understand this aspiration. A simple example is this:

The larger the resources of prestige and wealth of family elders, compared to younger family members, the greater the amount of control family elders exert over who marries whom.

Let us consider several aspects of this hypothesis. First, being far less precise than the formulas in the physical sciences, this one does not specify a numerical or mathematical relationship between the two variables (resources and control). It does not tell us how close the relationship is or how *much* of that "control" is explained by the possession of resources. However, mathematical precision is not a necessary trait of an abstract or general "law," even though it may be an elegant ideal that many sociologists seek. That hypothesis does, nevertheless, *predict*; it tells us the conditions under which we can expect to observe a certain pattern of behavior.

Second, *the hypothesis applies to groups or classes of families; it is a statistical or probabilistic statement.* We cannot expect that *every* set of family elders with large resources will exert *high* control over younger members, or that every set with small resources will exert *low* control. Since many other variables will affect the amount of control achieved, the hypothesis will *not* predict how every case will behave. The hypothesis does not describe the effect of all possible variables, but rather the general effect of these few variables alone.

This is another way of stating that most

scientific laws or hypotheses contain a hidden or unstated clause, that is, "other things being equal" or "if other things do not get in the way." Since almost everything in the world can affect almost anything else, scientific descriptions would be hopelessly complex if they had to list every possible causal factor.

Instead, scientific statements about natural or social processes do not attempt to include everything. Consequently, in the hypothesis above in order to "make other things equal" we would compare families in the *same* place and time. Thus, we should compare poor families in nineteenth-century Japan with upper-class families in *that* society, and not with upper-class families in the twentieth-century United States.

Finally, it should be seen that this crude proposition can be used to help explain many other related social patterns or regularities. That is, a "general" proposition, if correct, contains factors or causes that can be observed to affect a wide variety of concrete processes and events. Here are a few that are related to our proposition, that is, when family elders control more resources, they also control courtship behavior more:

Even in an officially free system of choosing a husband or a wife upper-class families attempt to control their children's marriage decisions by controlling their social networks—for example, private schools, dances, and balls; vacations in areas that only the well-to-do can visit; debuts; restricted neighborhoods—more than lower-class families do.

The percentage of births out of wedlock will be higher toward the lower social strata (because they have fewer resources for controlling the courtship behavior of their children).

If a society begins to industrialize, so that young adults can earn money independently of their families, they will insist on more voice in the choice of their own marriage partners.

In a frontier situation, such as the nineteenth-century United States or Australia, where young people must make their own way independently of the families they left behind them, they will pay less attention to the wishes of their family elders.

Since in most societies young men have a greater opportunity than do young women to make their own way socially and economically, women are controlled more in their choice of mates than are men.

In hunting and gathering societies (where an adult's rank is very little dependent on her or his parents' standing) family elders are less likely to choose spouses for their marriageable children than are elders in agricultural societies (where rank is likely to be dependent on one's parents' ownership of land).

Doubtless the reader can think of still other social patterns or even personal experiences that are linked to the earlier proposition. We have created this example precisely to show that even at this modest level of theorizing, *the aim of sociology is to locate relationships between abstract or general variables or factors, not merely to describe what occurred at a particular time and place.* In this case concrete descriptions would simply have related how marriage partners are decided upon in a particular society or community, without stating the general factors that affect those decisions.

Sociology as a "Pure" Science

Another traditional aim of sociology, which it shares with most other university disciplines, is to become a "pure," not an applied, science: *The goal of sociology is main-*

ly to describe and analyze social reality, not primarily to solve social problems. In view of the great difficulty of solving even *one* such problem—for example, poverty, racial and sexual discrimination, violations of civil rights, the manipulation by corporations of government, white-collar crime—that humble stance seems fully justified.

However, sociologists surely took that position, not because of a wise humility, but because the more advanced sciences became most helpful in solving *practical* problems when they discovered the *general* laws or relationships that underlay those problems. Thus, diseases could be more easily cured once their underlying causes were discovered. The *general* or "pure" principles of astronomy helped to solve the *practical* difficulties of ocean navigation. Those of chemistry were essential in solving numerous industrial problems. Consequently, if sociology is to be helpful in lifting human beings from want, affliction, and oppression, the first step should be to discover the basic processes at work.

Some critics have made the charge (which is difficult either to prove or to disprove) that expediency or cool calculation was another cause of setting "pure" science as the ideal of sociology. Clearly, any aspiring social science might have been met with some skepticism at the turn of the century. However, one that tried to offer easy solutions for ancient social problems would also have met hostility (not to mention the withdrawal of funds). If it was intellectually correct for sociologists to admit that they had no sound first principles as yet, it was also politically wise to put on the safe and honorific mantle of "pure science."

Other critics have charged that it is both callous and cowardly to avoid problem solving when human misery is increasing. Many sociologists defend themselves by arguing that it is not possible to do research that will only *help* human beings. If the knowledge is valid, it can be used for good

or evil. Good research on social problems will yield important facts, and they can be used in many ways—not all of them good.

Against that defense, critics point out that the world's rulers have the resources with which to use any scientific findings to their own advantage, while the poor have not. Consequently, it is urged, sociologists should not wait until fundamental "laws" are discovered; instead, they should drop the pretense of pure science and help build a new and better society.

Are such charges justified? Political attitudes cannot decide the question. It is more fundamentally a question of fact. If sociologists could indeed reduce human misery by any substantial amount, but do not, surely they ought to change. If (as seems more likely) they simply do not know how to accomplish that feat, perhaps they are wise to be humble. That is, they should first learn how social processes work, before posing as expert problem solvers. There is no evidence at present that they are more skilled than anyone else at giving advice about solving major social problems.

Sociologists as informed citizens have taken sides in numerous public controversies, and their political sympathies have been more in favor of the underdog than those of most people. In any event, far from neglecting social problems, they expend much of their research energy on them. Most research funds at the present time are allocated to problem solving, not to pure research.

What are some of the challenging problems they are trying to solve? Here are a few: how to stave off the threat of overpopulation, reduce race and sex discrimination, improve the delivery of health care, educate handicapped children, alleviate the difficulties that old people face, work out better solutions for poverty than welfare seems to be, rehabilitate alcoholics and drug addicts. Nevertheless, sociologists whose research aims at uncovering general principles continue to enjoy more esteem than do those who attempt to solve the practical social problems of our generation.

At a more fundamental level, however, we should note that this controversy between pure science and problem solving revolves about a false issue. Long before *pure* science began to make solid contributions to ordinary problems, *practical* builders and engineers had built up an impressive body of useful knowledge. Great cathedrals were erected, suspension bridges were hung above deep gorges, and aqueducts carried water over hundreds of miles, long before science understood the general laws on which those achievements were based. *Both* pure science and practical engineering have contributed to our knowledge. In fact, if "pure" research is excellent, it can also become useful. If "practical," or applied, research is well done, it is likely to help us understand scientific principles better.

In social science an illustration of this point might be the "pure" research on the supposedly *biological* effects of race or sex on *social* behavior. This research has increasingly shown these biological effects to be small. However, that general conclusion also suggests practical changes. If the biological effects are small, then the worldwide discriminatory laws and customs that erect sexual or racial barriers against equal opportunity are inefficient and impractical. Far more people can achieve than have been *permitted* to do so.

Similarly, *pure* research on how to change people's attitudes has led to *practical* suggestions for the reduction of interracial tensions. From practical research on how to increase productivity or how to introduce changes in work habits, social psychologists and sociologists have derived *general* or "pure" principles of group behavior. For example, people are more willing to work for the group, or to change their behavior, if they take part in the decisions to do so, and if they are allowed to help work out the new

plans. In somewhat broader terms, people become more committed to their group and its plans (whether or not they were originally in favor of either) if their ideas are given attention and respect.

Consequently, "pure" and "applied" sociology are not opposed to one another. Rather, they contribute to one another. As any scientific field progresses, each will at times correct or extend the findings of the other. If theory is not practical, it is unlikely to be correct. If practice is not based on some general or theoretical truths, it is unlikely to be useful.[10]

Sociology as a Mathematical, Empirical, and Quantitative Science

As social sciences develop, they become more empirical, quantitative, and even mathematical. Sociology is no exception.[11] It has become more mathematical than any other social science except economics. It is more empirical (based on observations of the real world) than economics itself. Economic analyses are more likely to be based on mathematical reasoning than on observation. Sociology is more quantitative than political science, anthropology, or history. More of its data are stated in numbers. Since these characteristics are thought to be "scientific," one might suppose they represent progress and should be applauded. In fact, they may bring both problems and gains. Let us briefly examine them.

By definition, any science must be *empirical*; that is, it relies on systematic observa-

[10]Robert K. Merton, "On Theoretical Sociology," op. cit., chaps. 4 and 5, pp. 139–171.

[11]For an abstract but lucid discussion of tools now used in social science to explore relationships among variables, see Otis Dudley Duncan, *Introduction to Structural Equation Models*, New York: Academic, 1975; H. M. Blalock, Jr., ed., *Causal Models in the Social Sciences*, Chicago: Aldine, 1971; and Donald T. Campbell and Julian C. Stanley, *Experimental and Quasi-experimental Designs for Research* (1963), Chicago: Rand McNally, 1966.

tion of the real world. It seems obvious that we should gather data, and the more the better. It is especially tempting to gather more opinion data from surveys, since the research technology is available and research funds can be more easily obtained for such studies.

However, simply to gather more data while forgetting what the data are for is to confuse a method with the goal we seek. If our goal is to understand social reality better, our next best step may at times be (1) a careful reanalysis of existing information, (2) a new hypothesis, or even (3) a new theoretical approach. In social research, as in much of life, to ask "What is it good for?" may be embarrassing, but it may also lead to a wiser decision. Gathering still more observations or opinion data that are not guided by a penetrating question may be wasteful.

If observations are precisely made, it is likely that they will be stated in *quantitative* form, in tables of quantities or percentages. Especially in social research, the student must learn to count. One result of counting is that many commonsense beliefs that we have acquired from others begin to seem weak. They are simply wrong or at best half-correct. Is it true that "staying with the marriage is good for the children"? That "good researchers are poor teachers"? That "dictatorships are more effective than democracies at maintaining price controls"? Or "to him that hath shall be given" even more? These traditional beliefs can be tested, and the better answer is certainly not "Yes," but a numerical answer in percentages.

Modern statistics also permit us to dissect a situation that is too complex for ordinary observation. Then we can, for example, find out numerically how *much* a certain factor (such as education, IQ, class background, or race) contributes to a given result (such as occupational levels or lifetime income). Quantification also permits us to give a

more precise meaning to our judgments of, say, "much change" or "little change." We may disagree among ourselves about whether the change is much or little, but we can at least agree that the change amounts to about 25 percent.

However, we must not be tempted to suppose that using numbers will automatically make our research scientific, or its conclusions precise. It is all too easy to forget that numbers are *symbols*. They stand for certain observations or reports. If those are poorly made, or do not fit reality, no amount of later computations, tables of percentages, or sophisticated scaling techniques will substitute for the missing social reality. The modern computer is especially seductive, for once it has received the appropriate numbers, it can spew out thousands of tables in a few seconds. However precise they appear, they can be no better than the original archives, survey questionnaires, or field observations on which they are based. Numbers alone cannot make good science.

Moreover, as the experienced researcher knows, it is especially easy to quantify the trivial. Giving numbers to irrelevant factors will not help us to explain social action. Almost anything can be counted, but it may not help us to understand social behavior.

Perhaps just as importantly, in our zeal to appear scientific through the use of numbers we may be tempted to forget our distinguished tradition of *field research*. All sociologists have learned much from excellent field studies that were never put into quantitative form, for example, Elliot Liebow's *Tally's Corner*, or Erving Goffman's *The Presentation of Self in Everyday Life*.

Most people with a bent for science admire the intellectual elegance of *mathematics* even when they hardly have an inkling of how to solve that bugaboo of high school algebra, the quadratic equation. Sociologists do not typically become proficient in mathematics, though most sociological research is at least presented in a statistical form. However, for decades a small band of analysts has hoped to harness the power of mathematical tools in order to make discoveries in sociology. Thereby, they follow the early physicists who used mathematics to explain the laws of planetary motion.

Mathematics can be of great help to sociology as a science. Even the attempt to put relationships in mathematical form forces researchers to state relationships or ideas more exactly. In addition, it forces sociologists to see what they have left out. Thus, they can put into their equations all the factors that might be important. The mathematical style permits no eloquence that might distract readers from perceiving omissions in the proof. Gaps in logic are made painfully obvious. Most important, if the right variables have been located, and their relationships precisely stated, it may be possible to transform them in mathematical ways that will reveal as-yet-undiscovered social patterns.

Whether that promise will be fulfilled cannot be ascertained as yet. In their earlier phases most sciences did not follow physics in their reliance on mathematics as a tool for discovery. On the other hand, one social science did so: economics. Perhaps its example is instructive, for it is at once the most advanced of the social sciences and the one that has been most unwilling (until recently) to study the messy irregularities of real behavior.

In the analysis of social interaction it is difficult—or, as some critics would allege, impossible—to locate a few powerful variables that form some kind of a closed system. As a consequence, mathematics may not serve as a kind of all-purpose key to discovery. Indeed, at present the many achievements in mathematical sociology seem to be of most importance in (1) restating more precisely some relationships revealed first by traditional research, and (2) developing an entire new mathematical subfield that may become important in the fu-

ture. Mathematical discoveries in the past, too, were sometimes applied in other sciences only decades or generations after they were worked out in mathematics itself.[12]

THE COMPLEXITY OF SOCIAL BEHAVIOR

Individual Values and Group Values

Although mathematics may tempt some to simplify their assumptions, observations, and theories to fit its needs, *most sociological research accepts the great complexity of social behavior as its basic subject matter.* It must do so because it attempts to analyze reality as it is perceived through the eyes of a social actor, or participant. This mode of analysis is implicit in our earlier comments on the extent to which judgments, preferences, and actions are partly determined by the *position of the individual in a group or organization.* We cannot be content, however, with only the limited vision of one person, or even many. As sociologists we must ascertain how people feel and judge, prefer and evaluate, and how they alter their behavior in response to others. We must also *ascertain an order and regularity, a set of causes and effects, that the social actors themselves may not perceive.* Thus, we must begin with very concrete observations about what individuals believe they are doing, but we must then go on to construct more complex models or hypotheses about why they act in that way. We cannot be satisfied with their own explanations for their own behavior, or even with their own reports about their own behavior.

---

[12]The logic of scientific research that we have traced out over the last few topics above is currently the subject of much debate in the philosophy of science. One such discussion with a bearing on sociological research and with a thorough bibliography of the core literature is Imre Lakatos and Alan Musgrave, eds., *Criticism and the Growth of Knowledge* (1970), New York: Cambridge, 1974.

For example, we can ascertain that many people in our society who claim to be relatively free of class, race, or religious prejudice will in fact engage in some casual dating with persons from different social backgrounds. However, if we chart their progress from casual dating to steady dating and then to more serious relationships or even marriage, we shall note that with each step a smaller percentage of people will choose companions who do *not* share their social backgrounds. In fact, an overwhelming percentage of marriages ultimately take place between people of very similar origins (see Figure 1-4).

Such an example should not lead to the rule "Things are not what they seem; indeed, the opposite," for *both* aspects constitute the reality. Pueblo Indian dancers who believe they are making rain may not in fact make rain, but they are nevertheless engaging in social behavior that deserves attention in its own right. If we look only for contradictions between what people profess and what they do, we shall miss important factors in social reality. For example, until recently medical schools maintained a quota system that permitted only a certain percentage of Jewish, Catholic, and women students to enter each year. Blacks were excluded almost entirely from white medical schools. Almost without exception, boards of admission *claimed* that their nearly exclusive basis for admission was the candidate's promise of future excellence as a physician.

If we stopped at that apparent contradiction, we would miss a fascinating set of social processes by which young people

Figure 1-4 Most marriages take place between people from similar social backgrounds. (Left: Charles Gatewood; right, Black Star.)

were made into physicians. Among other things, we would miss the "sponsorship" process, by which a favored few candidates were given increasingly rich opportunities for learning and were supervised by their physician-sponsors. We would also miss one of the results, the development of medical skills above the ordinary in people (mostly male WASPS) whose endowment was not superior to many who were rejected at the onset. We might see how those favored few continued to control the departments in major medical schools, but might miss the fact that those leaders did (as they claimed) set high standards for both medicine and medical ethics.

In short, in our search for an understanding of social life, we must learn what the actor perceives and believes, for that is his or her reality. However, it is only part of reality, and we seek order and regularity even where the actor does not see its form or its causes. To grapple with so complex a set of processes is a difficult, exciting task.

But if the sociological imagination must take on the difficult task of including both the actor's view and the larger social structure, that broader task also yields some advantages. It brings to our attention the likelihood that *a social organization or a society may appear to be doing one thing, but some individuals and subgroups within it may see things very differently,* for their perspective will be different. Just as the society is not simply the sum of its parts, so do subgroups and individuals experience a different reality than does the society as a whole. For example, Emile Durkheim's classic study of suicide (1895) showed that some organizations (such as military forces or the police) successfully teach their members to be willing to sacrifice their lives for the larger group. Such people will also exhibit a high suicide rate (that is, members give up their lives for *personal* reasons). A century ago Marx pointed out that manufacturers had to avoid loss and seek profit if they were not to become bankrupt. Under that pressure they

contributed to the success of the broad socioeconomic structure called capitalism. Besides that large, unintended consequence, manufacturers also caused misery for their workers, since those same competitive pressures forced them to pay low wages.

Another advantage of the sociological view is that we avoid many false issues in contemporary debates. One of these is whether societies or social systems are characterized by harmony or by conflict, or whether sociology has focused unduly on harmony. Such an issue could arise only if we confine our view to the *larger* social structure and ask whether it is "harmonious." However, if we consistently ask about the larger system as well as how its *individual* members perceive and act, it is obvious that all social groups or societies contain *both* harmony and conflict.

People in some positions will see and experience more of one than of the other. The sociologist must analyze both. We can expect to find aspiring young executives who know they are in a fierce struggle for the same position, while their boss views that competition as a benign, harmonious working out of ordinary selection procedures. Organizations are in conflict with one another, with or without violence. Some must be in both conflict and harmony with one another, as, for example, a strong union and a corporation. One can even assert that warring nations must engage in both conflict and harmony: If a war or a battle is to occur, they must agree upon a wide range of rules and social definitions (who may be killed, and how; relations with neutral nations; or when a war has ended.)[13]

Social Reality: Behavior or Values?

Another false issue is the remnant of an ancient philosophical debate as to whether there is, after all, any genuine reality "out

[13]See in this connection Lewis Coser, *The Functions of Social Conflict*, New York: Free Press, 1964.

there," or only the shifting perceptions, experiences, and definitions of individuals. This question has been raised in some films that present several different versions of social reality as told by two or more characters in the story. It also appears in extreme formulations of "labeling theory," in which it is suggested that people who are called deviant were once like everyone else but unfortunately came to be labeled as deviant and thus were pressured into further deviance. And it is the theme of the classic story about the blind men who each examined only one part of an elephant and described his part as a whole.[14]

At the deepest level that philosophical problem cannot be solved. We shall never know whether there is a reality "out there" different from the reality we believe we grasp. However, the sociological view at least permits us to look at both the *individual* perception and action, and how they interact with the *larger* social structure. When contradictions are found between the two, that *is* the reality. We can measure how the individual view is shaped by a person's position in groups and societies, and how the larger social patterns are made up of individual actions and perceptions. Both are part of social reality, and the sociologist must analyze *both*.

Perhaps most important is that this view corrects an overemphasis in the sociology of the past generation, which might be called the "primacy of values," that is, treating values and norms as the main social reality. That emphasis was partly justified. If we define values as the *general standards* by which we judge the beauty, excellence, or rightness of our goals, and define norms as the *specific group definitions* of how we are

supposed to behave, then it is clear that all social action *begins* with values and norms. Unless we valued one goal more than another, we would feel no impulse to act at all. If the actor did not feel that some norms are better than others, she or he would not be able to choose a course of action. That is, all ways of acting would seem equally right, wise, or aesthetically appropriate.

It is partly for this reason that the sociology of the recent past emphasized values and norms. Also, by emphasizing values and norms the sociologists of the period after World War I were able to lay claim to a distinct problem area and thus could argue they were developing a new intellectual discipline.

Moreover, if we claim to be studying social groups, we are likely to emphasize values and norms, ideologies and preferences, attitudes and beliefs, for groups *themselves* often see each other as different in these respects. For example, if we were to give a conversational thumbnail sketch of an ethnic group (Armenians, Irish), an urban group (Parisians, Berliners), or a regional group (Vermonters, Appalachian mountaineers), we would very likely begin with their evaluations. Finally, to describe someone's values and norms is to report on that person's own view, how he or she looks at social reality.

However, no serious social analyst can believe that values and what people prefer will tell us how people will actually behave. From them we learn what the social actor would prefer, but we know that social reality will not typically cooperate with the actor's wishes. Other people may threaten us if we follow our preferred course of action, or they will reward us for following another. We may genuinely feel committed to the value of hard work, but living by that standard is costly. We may believe that we should *not* conform to others' notions about appropriate dress and manners, but conform just the same. In short, the external social reality, the larger social structure as well as

---

[14]For a brief historical, analytical review of the debate as it pertains to the sociological study of deviance, see Stephen Cole, "The Growth of Scientific Knowledge: Theories of Deviance as a Case Study," in Coser, ed., *The Idea of Social Structure*, pp. 175–220; as well as Erich Goode, *The Sociology of Deviant Behavior*, Englewood Cliffs, N.J.: Prentice-Hall (forthcoming).

people in our immediate social space, may well create a big difference between our values and norms and what we actually do.

Moreover, as we noted earlier, a closer look at even our evaluations will disclose that they themselves are complex and contradictory, both within each individual and within any social group or society. The reader of this book is likely to admire *both* austerity and hedonism; hard work *and* play; success *and* the rejection of popularity; or unabashed self-seeking as well as dedication to helping others. People who hold different social positions within an organization or a society are likely to disagree on many values and norms. Individuals sometimes learn to their surprise that when they change jobs they may well change their norms. Thus, a more careful look at people's values and norms will show they cannot serve alone as an adequate guide for our own action or for predicting other people's actions.

The Assumption of Value Integration

Sociological inquiry must, then, find out the values and norms of the individual or the group, for we need to know what they prefer. However, knowing how complex values themselves are will keep us from making a theoretical error that was common in the sociology of the past generation: the assumption of *value integration*, that is, taking it for granted that the needs and values of the individual and the group are integrated and harmonious. It seems clear that they cannot all be in conflict, or else no one could or would cooperate, and there would be no society or group at all. However, we cannot assume that integration. We must ascertain how *much* exists. We must be alert to the large amount of conflict and disharmony that may prevail.

That older view essentially assumed the existence of "the" group or society, which was the source of individual values and norms. According to that view people were socialized to believe in group values, and thus wanted or sought what the group needed. The group depended on individual contributions, while the individual was dependent on the group. In that view the values of both had to be integrated with one another, or else the group or society would break down.

A wiser view, by contrast, does not assume any such harmony, for clearly values and norms are in some conflict. Some people contribute to their group without believing in its values, because thereby they gain some rewards (money, respect). Some people feel what they get from one or another group is too little. Everyone is a member of *many* groups and of many social relationships that are not full-fledged groups. People feel in harmony with some of their groups, but not with others.

It is impossible to hold values and norms that are integrated with all groups, for groups vary greatly. Everyone must constantly decide how to allocate her or his energy and resources to various social relationships and groups. Thus, we cannot assume any such integration of values and norms between individual and group. Instead, we must view that harmony as problematic, as contingent, as varying from high to low or nonexistent. In short, we must ascertain under what conditions any such integration will be found.

Thus, prior socialization, or belief in a set of values and norms, does not guarantee conformity. Such beliefs are not an adequate guide to action because they are often too complex and contradictory. We are all members of many groups and social relationships that pull us in many directions. How, then, are we moved to act so that the various tasks of the society get done just the same? Or, more simply, amidst all this possible conflict, how do people get each other to act in ways that contribute to each other's needs, wants, values, and norms?

The commonsense answer is the correct one: Groups and individuals in groups command a *range of resources* with which to persuade others to live by their values or norms, that is, to contribute to the group, to cooperate, or even to sacrifice themselves in battle. One social science, economics, focuses on this set of persuasive processes as they shape the flow of one major resource, wealth, or money: how people, corporations, or nations acquire it and spend it; how companies or organizations fail when they cannot offer enough money to elicit the cooperation and contributions of members or potential members; or how prices offered or demanded become a social message about how much something is valued.

It is clear that not all our resources, or all the messages others give us concerning how much our cooperation is worth, can be expressed in dollars. Economic theories about market supply and demand do not explain enough. As we shall show in the chapter on *prestige processes*, another major social resource that can be earned or expended is the respect or esteem that groups or individuals give to one another. Indeed, it can be argued that much of sociology analyzes the processes by which more or less prestige or esteem is given to people who live by the values and norms of their groups (or do not). Two other such major resources are friendship, or being liked, and the ability to command force or the threat of force, often called "political power."

Although a division of most social resources into four great categories of prestige, wealth, power, and friendship offers some convenience, that particular set is not important for our immediate analysis. What is important is that in every social system, as in all continuing social relations among individuals, knowing people's values and norms is necessary but not sufficient to predict action. We must in addition find out how human beings see the chances of losing or gaining various resources if they comply with others' norms, customs, values, or preferences. In turn, people try to get others to act in desirable ways by letting them know how much they will be rewarded when they do. Even in the realm of economics, working for money is affected by many other complex social processes. Sociology must analyze a much wider range of actions and resources, and thus its problems of theory and data gathering are still more challenging.[15]

Group Rules and the Question of Rationality

The comments above raise this important theoretical question:

Is it correct or fruitful to think of people as calculating rationally how much it is worth to help others or to conform to group rules? That is, if people are moved by the possibility of losing or gaining social resources, do they actually plot or calculate those gains or losses? Most of us do not think of ourselves as coolly plotting our best advantage. The economic assumption that people maximize profit seems far from reality. How could that notion be useful in analyzing most social processes (mothering, friendship) where getting the most for oneself seems even less applicable than in economic processes?

Let us consider whether people rationally calculate the possible gains from their behavior. Philosophers have called human beings "the rational animal," while deploring

[15]See Peter M. Blau, "Mediating Values in Complex Structures," in *Exchange and Power in Social Life*, New York: Wiley, 1964, pp. 253–282; Alvin W. Gouldner, "Reciprocity and Autonomy in Function Theory," in N. J. Demerath III and Richard A. Peterson, eds., *Systems, Change, and Conflict*, New York: Free Press, 1967, pp. 141–170; and Rose Laub Coser, "The Complexity of Roles as a Seedbed of Individual Autonomy," in Coser, ed., *The Idea of Social Structure*, pp. 237–264.

the obvious fact that much of our behavior seems irrational. Sociologists have added a further complexity to the question of rationality by pointing out that much action is *neither* of the two, but is *nonrational*. That is, human beings create a body of symbols, religious beliefs about an invisible spiritual world, music, art, ethics, aesthetic rules, or ideals that do not deny reality or run counter to human goals (as irrationality does) but form a realm of their own.

A rational calculation can be tested by whether we are using good ways of reaching our goal, as measured by the best evidence we have. Thus, we can test whether we have worked out a sensible plan or technology for draining a swamp, or even for interviewing French business executives. We would label behavior "irrational" if we follow a plan that our best evidence shows will either work *against* our goals or be irrelevant to them. By that definition someone is behaving irrationally if he insists his car should start even without gasoline. It is irrational to claim it will not start unless he sings to it first. It is not rational to believe studying for an examination is unnecessary, because we will be sitting in a "lucky seat," Number 007.

However, much social behavior does not fall into *either* the rational or the irrational category. It is rational to assert that two oranges plus two oranges equals four oranges. It is *ir*rational to claim that two oranges plus two oranges equals, say, five oranges. By contrast to both categories, it is *non*rational to announce that a large pile of ripe oranges is beautiful or to place a pile of oranges in a bowl because they are beautiful. No amount of empirical or observational evidence can prove that nonrational beliefs or actions (value judgments) are "incorrect" or "correct." Our group norms and values, our moral or aesthetic principles—all our value judgments—are neither rational nor irrational, but are nonrational.

Thus, it is nonrational to believe one

should be respectful to parents and to show them respect; to admire impressionist paintings; to carry out religious rituals; to act virtuously because one believes it is right to do so; or to help the poor because that is a moral obligation. All these are value judgments, and facts cannot demonstrate the "truth" of any of these.

By contrast, we *can* show that in some social networks or circles it would be rational to follow these beliefs and practices if we want to gain the esteem or liking of others. They will disapprove of us if we violate those "rules." It would, correspondingly, be irrational to expect most police officers to respond with a friendly grin if we show disrespect to them or kick them.

Though these distinctions help us in our observations of daily life, we have come only a few steps closer to answering our original question. Let us rephrase it in this fashion: Clearly, what we do *is* shaped in part by what others are likely to do, but do we rationally calculate what others will do to us? Do we attempt to gain the maximum we can from any social interaction? Or, put more crudely, to what extent does people's behavior approximate the economic view, the view that each person gives as little as she or he must, and gets as much as she or he can?

In the chapter on prestige processes we shall consider this question further. We shall analyze how social actors (individuals, groups, or organizations) control each other's behavior to some extent by giving or withholding esteem for their qualities or achievements. Here we ask the reader to draw upon his or her own observations. If we ask how rationally we ourselves act and how others act, the most obvious answer must be a limp, unsatisfying "It depends."

Our social action seems to be a bewildering mixture of nonrational and rational decisions and behavior, with now and then a bit of irrationality. At one point we give help to a friend because we truly feel that is our

FOCUS

AN OBSERVER'S COMMENTS ON SOME
LIMITATIONS OF PARTICIPANT OBSERVATION

My immediate object in doing field work at St. Elizabeths was to try to learn about the social world of the hospital inmate, as this world is subjectively experienced by him. I started out in the role of an assistant to the athletic director, when pressed avowing to be a student of recreation and community life, and I passed the day with patients, avoiding sociable contact with the staff and the carrying of a key. I did not sleep in the wards, and the top hospital management knew what my aims were.

It was then and still is my belief that any group of persons—prisoners, primitives, pilots, or patients—develop a life of their own that becomes meaningful, reasonable, and normal once you get close to it, and that a good way to learn about any of these worlds is to submit oneself in the company of the members to the daily round of petty contingencies to which they are subject.

The limits, of both my method and my application of it, are obvious: I did not allow myself to be committed even nominally, and had I done so my range of movements and roles, and hence my data, would have been restricted even more than they were. Desiring to obtain ethnographic detail regarding selected aspects of patient social life, I did not employ usual kinds of measurements and controls. I assumed that the role and time required to gather statistical evidence for a few statements would preclude my gathering data on the tissue and fabric of patient life. My method has other limits, too. The world view of a group functions to sustain its members and expectedly provides them with a self-justifying definition of their own situation and a prejudiced view of nonmembers, in this case, doctors, nurses, attendants, and relatives. To describe the patient's situation faithfully is necessarily to present a partisan view. (For this last bias I partly excuse myself by arguing that the imbalance is at least on the right side of the scale, since almost all professional literature on mental patients is written from the point of view of the psychiatrist, and he, socially speaking, is on the other side.) Further, I want to warn that my view is probably too much that of a middle-class male; perhaps I suffered vicariously about conditions that lower-class patients handled with little pain. Finally, unlike some patients, I came to the hospital with no great respect for the discipline of psychiatry nor for agencies content with its current practice.

SOURCE: Erving Goffman, *Asylums*, Chicago: Aldine, 1961, pp. ix-x.

duty (nonrational). At another, we calculate that if we do her a favor now, she will pay it back later when we shall need it more (rational). We may purchase a Mozart recording because we think it is beautiful (nonrational) but also display it so that our visitors will see what good taste we have (rational). We may unthinkingly praise someone for a good tennis shot, but we also calculatingly praise our partner in order to encourage him to play better. We may selflessly spend time teaching a child to swim because we believe we should do so (nonrational) but may nevertheless be aware, out of the corner of our eye, that our parents are beaming with pride at our goodness.

It is at least clear that we may conform to group rules, or to others' values and norms, because we believe in them and wish to conform (real commitment); or because we want to keep our job or others' esteem or affection (calculation); or because of *both* commitment and calculation. We are less likely to *violate* the rules *without* some calculation, but we may violate them while believing in their rightness. We are likely to calculate *more* when we perceive that our own goals are being frustrated, for example, when we feel we deserve approval for being virtuous but no one has noticed. In later chapters we shall note other situations where people are more or less calculating or rational in their conformity. Nevertheless, we are far from a full understanding of these complexities. They make the task of sociological analysis more difficult, but also more fascinating.

We cannot state precisely when people are rational in their social behavior. However, we can at least see that people do not typically seek to maximize their possible gains in social interaction. Few people are like the textbook "economic man," demanding as much as the market will bear and giving as little as the market will permit. However, people do prefer more rather than less. Or, more cautiously, they prefer to obtain respect, money, affection, or pleasures and comforts somewhat *closer* to their view of what is more satisfying, not less. To obtain them, they will conform to others' pressures if the cost is not too great. If conformity is easier, because they already believe in those norms, what they demand for that conformity will be less. On the other hand, everyone is at times in situations where doing what others want is so difficult— because it violates his or her norms or the task is hard—that no payment is high enough. In even the most ruthless of dictatorships, some people will resist at any cost. In the most benign of anarchies, some people will drop out because they do not get as much affection or respect as they believe they deserve.

Thus, if people do not seek to maximize their gains and minimize their contributions in the most calculating manner, they are not irrational. They do not deny social reality. They do calculate costs and gains to some extent. As social analysts we must try to find out when and in what situations they do so. They may not be seeking gains in wealth or greatness, but the affection of friends or living by the standards they believe are right. People do want more respect rather than less, but we must also ascertain whether it is the respect of their friends or of their bosses. Moreover, we cannot suppose that people are *not* trying to get the most, simply because they do not seem to aim high. They may actually be calculating that the chances of getting there are *small*, and that their total gain will be just as much if they do *not* invest in those vain attempts.

It violates our observations of human action to assume that people are always social computers. They do not always figure out just how much they can exact from others in exchange for the least contribution. It is clear just the same that people *are* aware of how much they are receiving in various social rewards (pats on the back, party invitations, job offers, welcoming smiles, diplomas, raises in salary) for their achievements, contributions, obedience to the rules, or conformity with group ideals. Being aware, people do alter their behavior, sometimes to reduce losses and sometimes to increase rewards. Moreover, if we observe others carefully, we can see that people alter their behavior, even when they do not give much thought to those potential losses or gains. Much of their adjustment is spontaneous or unthinking. Social analysts who are alert to this wide range of generally rational behavior are more likely to increase our understanding of human action than those who limit their vision to only "rational people" or only those who blindly obey their values and norms.

SUMMARY

The exploration of social relations helps us to know ourselves better. It also offers many practical benefits. It is, however, most rewarding to those who feel that knowledge and science are worthwhile in themselves.

Happily, the advantages of making that exploration do not depend on whether everyone can agree on a precise definition of the field, and in fact sociologists do not agree among themselves. But that is true of other sciences as well. We have nevertheless presented some formal definitions of sociology and have then gone on to examine what sociologists actually do.

In sociology as in the other social sciences, practitioners study a wide variety of topics, by a wide variety of methods, and few sociologists reject any of those inquiries as "not really sociological." However, one special emphasis is common in sociology more than in the other social sciences: the attempt to explain social behavior by the *values, norms, and social pressures (or rewards) of the various groups* with which people are affiliated in some way.

We have used many examples to show

that this apparently simple emphasis or orientation does in fact help us to understand social behavior, and indeed uncovers many social patterns we might otherwise have missed. It is not, we stress, the sole emphasis in sociology, and later chapters will draw upon many other examples of sociological analysis.

Whatever the viewpoint that makes sociology so fruitful, it shares with other sciences an important limitation: It considers only certain aspects of the great complexity to be found in life itself. It does not attempt to explain everything, and only explains some classes or *types* of things. All sciences try, similarly, to uncover or discover *general* relationships among classes of factors. When they are successful, these general relationships help us to understand many concrete events, but science does not attempt to explain every detail of such events.

From a broad, philosophic point of view, many analysts have argued that sociology, and all other social sciences, cannot become real sciences because human observation is faulty, biases necessarily distort the research, people can hide what they feel or do, and human behavior is not like rocks or chemicals. We have considered this problem and have noted that *methodological* research gives us some practical ways of getting at social facts just the same. In addition, as any science actually begins to do important research its practitioners concern themselves much less with the grand issue of whether they can do what they are already doing.

Although values and norms do shape people's behavior somewhat, we have pointed out in detail why knowledge of these data is not enough for the prediction of social behavior: People believe in many different and contrary values; people may conform and not believe, or ignore the rule but believe in it; people belong to different groups with divergent values and norms; persons who change their groups or social positions may actually alter their beliefs. In short, knowledge of norms and values is but a first step toward understanding why people act as they do.

We also considered the place of rationality in social behavior. Can we reject the notion that people blindly follow their group's values and norms; and can we suppose instead that individuals are coolly seeking their own self-interest for maximum profit? Certainly, as we later point out in our chapters on political processes and class systems, people do seek political power, economic advantage, and indeed all other resources or advantages the society may offer.

To be alert to *whose* interests or goals are being served helps us to understand human action better and also corrects an overemphasis in sociology on what we have called the "primacy of values." That is, we assert now that knowing people's values alone will not give us enough understanding. But expecting them to be coolly rational for their own ends is wrong, too. If we study rational or self-seeking behavior, we can see that people do not always try to get the biggest money profit, either.

In much of social behavior people are seeking a very different set of goals than money, such as political influence, the respect of others, or affection and friendliness. Even when people seek such goals or resources in a calculating way, they are being influenced by group members, for members will not pay them such rewards if they do not conform with members' wishes or norms. We shall study these mutual social pressures, or *social exchanges*, still further in later chapters.

We pointed out that sociology as a field seems to have the aim of being "theoretical" (seeking general relationships) rather than merely collecting facts. It also aspires to be a "pure" rather than an applied science, even though there is no contradiction between these two aims. It has become more empirical, quantitative, and even mathematical. It accepts the contingency, complexity, and contradictoriness of real social life, even when that makes both description and analysis more difficult. Sociologists continue to agree, despite much debate, that there is a distinction between value judgments and empirical descriptions. Nevertheless, some also assert that it is a social *scientist's* responsibility (not merely a citizen's obligation) to give political support to those who suffer disadvantages in this society.

We have, finally, introduced an issue to be treated in more detail in the later chapter on various kinds of groups: Since we rarely actually "see" a whole group, and often do not think of ourselves as belonging to a group, how can sociologists assert that so much of human behavior is shaped by group norms and processes?

Part of the answer is that even when some of the people we see are not *strictly* to be called groups, they may nevertheless have *some* of the traits of a group, and thus they have some social effect just the same. In addition, careful observation will disclose that some of our casual interaction does have group qualities, or is shaped by group rules, even when we were not previously aware of it. Moreover, individuals or classes of people may be *seen by others* as group members, even when they do not form a real group (for example, blacks and whites in the United States), and our behavior is changed as a consequence.

All these considerations are only a first step toward understanding more about the dynamics of social life, and thus our place within it. We shall take many more such steps in the chapters that follow, and shall consider as well some of the problems that continue to challenge the sociological imagination.

READINGS

Peter L. Berger, *Invitation to Sociology: A Humanistic Perspective*, New York: Doubleday, 1963.

H. M. Blalock, Jr., ed., *Causal Models in the Social Sciences*, Chicago: Aldine, 1971.

Peter M. Blau, *Exchange and Power in Social Life*, ᐛNew York: Wiley, 1964.

Donald T. Campbell and Julian C. Stanley, *Experimental and Quasi-experimental Designs for Research* (1963), Chicago: Rand McNally, 1966.

Lewis K. Coser, ed., *The Idea of Social Structure: Papers in Honor of Robert K. Merton*, New York: Harcourt Brace Jovanovich, 1975.

N. J. Dermerath III and Richard A. Peterson, eds., *Systems, Change, and Conflict*, New York: Free Press, 1967.

Otis Dudley Duncan, *Introduction to Structural Equation Models*, New York: Academic, 1975.

Paul Filmer et al., eds., *New Directions in Sociological Theory*, Cambridge, Mass.: M.I.T., 1973.

Erving Goffman, *The Presentation of Self in Everyday Life*, Garden City, N.Y.: Doubleday, Anchor, 1959.

Erich Goode, *The Sociology of Deviant Behavior*, Englewood Cliffs, N.J.: Prentice-Hall (forthcoming).

William J. Goode, *Explorations in Social Theory*, New York: Oxford, 1973.

Alvin W. Gouldner, *The Coming Crisis of Western Sociology*, New York: Avon, 1970.

George C. Homans, *Social Behavior: Its Elementary Forms* (1961), rev. ed., New York: Harcourt Brace Jovanovich, 1974, pp. 51–68.

Alex Inkeles, *What Is Sociology? An Introduction to the Discipline and Profession*, Englewood Cliffs, N.J.: Prentice-Hall, 1964.

Imre Lakatos and Alan Musgrave, eds., *Criticism and the Growth of Knowledge* (1970), New York: Cambridge, 1974.

Paul F. Lazarsfeld et al., eds., *The Uses of Sociology*, New York: Basic Books, 1967.

Elliot Liebow, *Tally's Corner: A Study of Negro Streetcorner Men*, Boston: Little, Brown, 1967.

John C. McKinney and Edward A. Tiryakian, eds., *Theoretical Sociology: Perspectives and Developments*, New York: Appleton-Century-Crofts, 1970.

Robert K. Merton, *Social Theory and Social Structure* (1949), enlarged ed., New York: Free Press, 1968.

C. Wright Mills, *The Sociological Imagination*, New York: Oxford, 1959.

Georg Simmel, *Conflict and the Web of Group Affiliations*, trans. by Kurt Wolff and Reinhard Bendix, New York: Free Press, 1955.

Neil J. Smelser and James A. Davis, eds., *Sociology*, Englewood Cliffs, N.J.: Prentice-Hall, 1969.

Pitirim A. Sorokin, *Fads and Foibles in Modern Sociology and Related Sciences*, Chicago: Regnery, 1956.

Eugene J. Webb *et al., Unobstrusive Measures: Nonreactive Research in the Social Sciences*, Chicago: Rand McNally, 1966.

Kurt H. Wolff, ed., *The Sociology of Georg Simmel*, New York: Free Press, 1950.

CHAPTER TWO

CULTURE AND SYMBOL SYSTEMS

The human line of evolution is different from that of all other animals. Instead of adapting biological equipment (claws, teeth, fur, running ability) to the *physical* environment, the human species adapted mainly its brain to the increasingly *social* and *cultural* environment created by its fellow beings. Specifically, human beings developed social and cultural solutions, rather than biological ones, to their problems.

As a result of its unique evolution, the human animal still looks like its cousins, but its behavior is built on entirely different bases: It takes longer to become adult than any other animal; it communicates through language; it builds a wide array of tools; it passes knowledge on to the next generation; it creates mathematical, artistic, and religious systems; and it can organize as a group to do what no single member could do alone.

What is culture, which can form such a different base for the social life of this peculiar animal?

WHAT IS CULTURE?

Philosophers have argued for centuries about what culture "really" is. Many people would prefer to use the term only for "high culture," such as the great works of the masters or the expert knowledge and critical appreciation of "fine" art—opera, painting, sculpture, literature, dance, and so on. Others have applied the term mainly to the major great civilizations, such as T'ang China, Periclean Athens, or Augustan Rome, thus excluding thousands of nations and preliterate tribes.

By contrast, anthropologists and sociologists often apply the term to all the things humankind has done, made, or thought about—from unicorns to lobsters, from atomic nuclei to Picasso's collages, from quadratic equations to jungles. In the famous definition of a nineteenth-century English anthropologist, E. B. Tylor, culture includes "knowledge, belief, art, morals, law, customs, and all other capabilities and habits acquired by man as a member of society." It includes our dreams and attitudes, diamonds and street dust, cowboy films and pizza, Supreme Courts and pollution. It includes our food likes and dislikes, our modes of dressing and undressing, our various economic systems, and the many styles of walking or dancing that different societies learn.

Sociologists also use the term *culture* in a stricter sense to refer to the *system of meanings in any society*: its norms and values, its language and literature, its beliefs and ideologies, its art and religion, its science and the games it plays. That is, "culture" applies not to the physical movements of people engaged in religious rituals, but to the *meanings* of those ceremonies. Breaking bread at a meal can be merely an easier way to eat it, but it may also embody the cultural meaning of friendship, or part of the Christian ritual commemorating the Last Supper. Certain words can contain the legally binding formula of marriage, which imposes a wide range of obligations on husband and wife. In short, one set of words can symbolize a whole system of meanings.

Other animals engage in many of the same *social* acts as we do. They cuddle their young, play, join to attack or defend, keep each other company, or fight for dominance. But they do not create systems of symbols[1] for each of those behaviors, such as beliefs about parenthood, large groups of games to pass on to the next generation, ideologies about enemies or about one's own group, or political philosophies about leadership or kinship. Almost every human act is invested with meanings and symbolisms beyond the act itself. In human societies, for example, eating is almost never a simple biological act. By some cultural standards pig meat is taboo, while by others, beef is. Forks are proper here, chopsticks there. In most cultures eating together symbolizes some degree of equality, and people make judgments about each other's "table manners." In fact, almost everything we do or say is heavily weighted with cultural meaning. However, because culture is symbolic and abstract, let us consider whether it is a mere set of ideas, or *only* a set of abstractions.

Is Culture Only an Abstraction?

The foregoing discussion of what culture is makes it clear that although systems of symbols are abstract, they are not *only* abstract. They have an impact on the real world. However, let us consider this question further.

If we think of culture as a system of meanings in a society, we can see that parts of a culture may live on after the society dies (the philosophy, art, and literature of Greece form an example). Indeed, much of United States culture comes from many different societies of the past. This suggests that cultures have a real existence of their own.

Not only may parts of a culture live beyond the time period of the originating society; the culture may extend beyond the geographic limits of a single nation. European nations west of the Ural Mountains, for example, have shared similar marriage sys-

---

[1]As we note in the chapter on socialization, in George Herbert Mead's formulation a symbol or word calls out the same response in the speaker as it does in the hearer. Or, we can agree to use any gesture, mark, or sound to *stand for* something else; for example, a hand placed over the heart means "Love," and a traffic sign means "Stop!" But, as we discuss later, though animals can learn how to interpret what other animals do, that is, to predict what they will do next, they do not *agree among themselves* to use certain actions or gestures to mean or stand for something else. They do not make symbols.

tems for many centuries. Correspondingly, groups with very *different* cultures may co-exist within *one* nation.

This possibility exists because nation, society, and culture are different things. First, a nation, in ordinary language, is a population within a defined territory, subject to one independent government that claims the right to rule within that territory. Usually, of course, nations will be mainly composed of a single society, because the nation sets boundaries between itself and others and causes its inhabitants to interact more with one another than with other people outside that boundary. As a consequence, people within it are, or become, a *society*. For most purposes, then, we can say the Japanese nation includes the same people as does the Japanese society.

However, a nation is defined in political terms, and thus may not be quite the same as a society. The latter is a group or a population whose members speak the same language, interact socially with one another for the most part, feel a common destiny, and share a set of beliefs and values. Large nations and empires often include more than one subsociety because of past conquests (for example, gypsies, Indians). These subsocieties or groups must accept the *political* rule of the nation but may affirm allegiance to their own social system as well as to their own culture.

The power of the nation cannot always dominate these subsocieties or subcultures. The Manchus did not impose their culture on their Chinese subjects, although they ruled over them for almost three centuries. Instead, they became Chinese in culture. The Dutch did not undermine Javanese culture and substitute their own, and much of Javanese society remained intact. By contrast, Latin Americans are now European in culture, as a result of the Iberian sociopolitical domination of that region from the sixteenth century onward.

It seems reasonable to conclude, then,

that culture does have a real meaning and an existence in its own right. Although it seems "abstract," it not only shapes people's daily behavior; it also resists domination by conquest, and may extend over time and space, beyond the limits of either a particular nation or a single society. Thus, we can sometimes trace the path of some cultural pattern (such as a fad or a fashion) over time and space and can study the conditions that affect its movement or its variations. Nevertheless, cultures *are* carried by a particular kind of animal. Let us, then, consider the relations between culture and biology.

Biology and Culture

It is likely that the most relentless analysis of human anatomy and physiology would disclose none of the facts given above about culture. Biologically, human beings can be classified in many ways, such as by blood groups, eye color, or type of hair. But these so-called racial traits yield no information about their owner's cultural patterns. The most distant apelike ancestors and relatives of our species can be classified anatomically, but that information does not tell us whether they built their social life on a cultural base.

Human beings have a large brain, but even that biological evidence does not permit us to guess that this animal has a culture. After all, the porpoise and the elephant have large brains, too, but do not use them to create a culture.[2] It is not the size

[2]Here I deliberately use as examples two types of animals that have high intelligence and that some people would like to protect from human beings, perhaps by a United Nations Bill of Rights. However, our compassion and admiration for both elephants and cetaceans (whales, porpoises) does not alter the fact that they have not created a culture that they pass on to the next generation through socialization. The porpoise's large brain may be primarily devoted to echolocation; it is certainly not devoted to the creation of religious, mathematical, literary, or art systems.

of the human brain that makes it unique, but what it does: It creates vast inner realms of abstract reality and processes great quantities of information about the meaning of what other human beings do.

Human biology and culture are intricately dependent on one another, but neither fully determines the other. The human animal cannot survive without culture; nor can culture exist without its biological carriers. As an example of this interdependence, culture specifies our obligation to care for our children and to teach them all we know about coping with the social and natural environment. One of those duties is to socialize or teach the child to become a parent at the appropriate time and to pass on to his or her children the culture of the society.

Figure 2-1 Primates—including human beings—must experience affection and social interaction as children in order to become socially and psychologically normal adults. (United Press International Photo.)

Thereby the continuity of both the human species and the culture is assured from one generation to another.

We now know that monkeys and apes do not become normal adults if they have not engaged in cuddling and play with members of their social group (see Figure 2-1). They are not even capable of adequate sexual behavior if they have been socially isolated as infants. This is true of human beings, too. Socially isolated infants (a few cases have occurred) not only fail to learn a language; they do not even become intellectually or psychologically normal.

However, this similarity between human beings and other higher animals glosses over the profound differences that a culture-based society creates in the processes of becoming adult. To become human, it is not enough to be given love, play, or protection. In addition, children must learn the culture of their society: They must learn a wide array of social roles, norms, and values if they are to interact successfully with others. None of this is necessary for other animals to become adequate adults in their group.

Not only must children learn this content in the narrow sense of knowing what others do or require. They also must come to feel that these ways of acting or thinking are morally or ethically right, aesthetically satisfying, or worthy of respect. The process by which human beings come to learn and to feel committed to the social roles, norms, and values of their society is called *socialization.* It includes both formal teaching in schools and the intimate, or personal, interaction of children with other human beings.

Of course, human beings could not learn in this fashion without a special biological heritage.[3] It is special in two important

---

[3]For a richly documented, controversial summary of how much human behavior is shared with other animals, see Edward O. Wilson, *Sociobiology: The New Synthesis*, Cambridge, Mass.: Harvard, Belknap, 1975.

ways. First, human beings appear to have no instincts, or built-in biological mechanisms that are *specific* solutions to environmental problems.[4] They cannot build homes, hunt or find food, or begin a family without learning the content of their culture. Second, a compensation for the lack of instincts is the large human capacity both for creating new solutions and for learning old ones. The human species need not rely on *biologically* inherited techniques because it inherits adequate ones *socially*.

However, human biology is deeply affected by culture, and vice versa. Foods eaten with delight in one culture (fried maguey worms, squid, roast pork) may actually arouse physiological revulsion in another. Our culture requires us to control our "natural" biological impulses (sexual arousal, urination, belching). In many societies, the culture requires people to undergo considerable pain or discomfort (scarification, tattooing, fasting) at certain times.

Correspondingly, cultural patterns are "biologized"; they arouse real physiological or psychological responses. Violation of a cultural taboo (such as desecrating the flag) will cause onlookers to become angry, with all the physiological reactions that accompany that feeling. Or an authority figure such as a father or a chieftain can arouse the physiological reactions of fear in a child or a subject. And stress from attempting to meet contradictory or difficult cultural rules may lead to hypertension. These complex and intimate links between culture and biology transform norms, values, and beliefs from "mere abstractions" into *internalized* preferences and directives that guide our daily lives.

On the other hand, the many variations in cultural patterns should not make us think that beliefs, norms, and values can change or vary without limit. Social and natural environments as well as our own biology do set some constraints on variation and make some cultural patterns less likely than others. For example, in no intimate group is there a general permission to lie and steal from one another. House preferences are of many kinds, but nowhere is the cultural ideal a set of narrow, winding tunnels that require people to crawl most of the time. In no culture are people taught to prefer poisonous foods. Although some religious sects (for example, the Shakers) have made celibacy a norm, in no society as a whole has that been a requirement. Nor can a culture require its female members to produce triplets at each childbirth. Much of culture is made up of beliefs and directives about the real world—both natural and social—and about our bodies; their close interactions require that they be adjusted to one another. Both the real world and our bodies set some limits on what cultures are likely to demand of human beings.

Symbols

We can note a further sense in which culture is not an abstraction: The meanings of culture are *shared*. They are symbols. Here, too, we see a difference between the abilities of animals and those of human beings. Unlike other animals, human beings can *agree* among themselves that a red light is to be a symbol for "stop!" or that a set of arbitrary marks on paper means a lion. A deer will run if it sees another deer running, but—as far as we know—the first animal to run is not *telling* others to run, and they have not agreed to use this signal when they observe danger ahead. The difference,

---

[4]Of course, the human animal does have *drives*, that is, appetites or needs (such as hunger and thirst) that must be satisfied if the animal or species is to survive. Drives do not, however, contain their own solution: A hunger drive does not tell the animal how to get food. The animal also has *reflexes*, such as the blink of the eye when something comes too close to the eye, or the knee jerk. The human animal contains, it appears, nothing comparable to the instinctual ability of a bird to build an appropriate nest or to navigate thousands of miles at the right season.

then, is that human beings *know that others know.* Thus, they can create symbols for almost any act or idea they wish to express, from secret messages in code to religious worship.

Two further characteristics of this symbolizing process need to be noted. First, because language, symbols, and ideas can be manipulated in the human mind, vast systems of symbols can also be created, from elaborate rules of etiquette to musical or mathematical systems. In short, culture can be *elaborated* to a high degree.

Second, because symbols do stand for, or substitute for, some kind of "reality—a flag as a symbol of one's country, an equation for a chemical process—people *respond* to them as a reality in themselves. As a result, they can feel genuine anger or moral indignation when someone violates a religious or a moral rule or desecrates a symbol (a flag, a cross) that they revere. In simple terms, norms, values, ideologies, or systems of art or religion can become "as real as a rock." They cause people to sacrifice themselves and others for what might be viewed as "mere abstractions" if we did not see how powerful they are.

Language

The most fruitful cultural invention in human history is language. It is the base on which all culture has been erected. Although all mammals learn to respond to the sounds that their fellows make, they do not use language. They learn to distinguish threatening noises and movements, or courtship calls, as they might learn what a train whistle or a lion's roar means for their safety. Even clever chimpanzees do not create a set of symbols that all agree will "stand for" certain objects, acts, or events. Thus, one chimpanzee cannot report to another what happened yesterday.[5]

---

[5]In research over the past decade, chimpanzees *have* learned to use symbols, such as deaf-mute or Indian

The advantages of language   The use of language transforms the quality of human social life in the following ways:

1   It extends the range of information that people receive and think about. Other animals can learn only what they themselves actually observe and experience. They cannot pass on this information to others. Human beings can share their information with their fellows and can correct it by comparing different reports.

2   Human beings can create a time and space dimension in their knowledge. They can tell others about what happened "long ago, when the volcano erupted," or "far across the sea." (This is more than mere memory; it is the ability to inform others and thus to extend the amount of shared knowledge.) Moreover, the human time dimension includes the future: People can inform others about what they hope or plan to do tomorrow or next year.

All these advantages of language yield another, which has even greater effects on the quality of human life: Human beings can accumulate knowledge. People can acquire information from many other human beings, in different places and times, and build an ever-increasing storehouse of useful data. With writing, a next step in information retrieval, the process of accumulation becomes almost limitless. When the knowledge grows beyond the capacity of most individuals but there is no writing to preserve it, specialists may arise to preserve and pass on this part of the culture: for example, Polynesian navigation techniques, Maori genealogies, or Homeric epic poetry. With modern electronic means, of course, this storage capacity increases even more. Hundreds of volumes can be put on a computer disk,

---

sign language, or shapes presented by a computer, and to hold actual conversations with human beings. However, none has ever created a language that all can share, and chimpanzee society is not based on language at all.

and their information can be retrieved with high precision. Indeed, specialists in the retrieval processes themselves are trained to handle the problems created by the piling up of knowledge.

Accumulation of knowledge permits human generations to build on the past. We become the heirs of a culture to which any one person contributes only a small part. We need not each discover or create anew what others have already learned. Not every one has to be clever. What a few clever people discover can be learned by other members of the society, while talented people who come afterward can begin with *that* new level of knowledge.

The uses of language The advantages of language listed above make language, most importantly, a *social tool*. All mammals are social, and coordinate their activities to some extent. But language permits a much larger number of human beings to work together, doing far more differentiated tasks, as part of much larger enterprises. In addition, through language human beings learn how others think and feel. We share our inner lives with other members of the group. Just as individual experience and thinking cause human beings to be more different from one another than other animals are, social sharing brings them together.

So far, our analysis has focused primarily on the ways language "stands for" the real world or expresses the experiences that people have, whether in the present, past, or future. That is, people respond to words as to real things: For example, the word "apple" causes that image to appear in the mind's eye, together with the crunchiness and sweetness of the fruit. Sequences of words in a novel may cause us to cry.

But the symbolic quality of language also creates an entirely different kind of thinking than that which we have been examining so far. Words also can be used to express abstract relationships, such as valence,

Figure 2-2 Scientific accomplishments such as a space launch would not be possible if we did not have language and its product: the accumulation of knowledge. (NASA.)

solidarity, or loyalty. They can be extended still further, to refer to the displeasure of the spirits or the gods, the harmony of the spheres, or the singing of angels—which no one has ever directly experienced.

In short, human beings can respond to words as though they were *real things in themselves,* even when they symbolize no empirically observable thing at all. Thus, our history is replete with conflicts about the meaning of certain religious words or about words that were later judged to have had no empirical content: whether the world was really (or only metaphorically) created in six days; "phlogiston" in seventeenth-century chemistry; or "spontaneous generation" in eighteenth-century biology. Language is an excellent tool, but it can become an instrument of self-deception.

Even when language extends far beyond the world of the senses, it still expresses the culture that created it. Consequently, analysts of language assert that any natural language is adequate for symbolizing whatever ideas, events, religious doctrines, or objects are found in the culture of a society. When new cultural patterns arise, people change their language to satisfy these new demands.

Because of this seeming fitness between the language and the culture of a given society, some social scientists entertain the hypothesis (associated with the name of Benjamin L. Whorf) that the structure of language itself affects the way people see, think, or react. Thus, some languages place little emphasis on *when* (past, present, future) an act

happens; Chinese was thought to be so concrete that the society was hindered in developing the abstract ideas of science; the Eskimo used many words for various types of snow, thus alerting members of that society to these important differences. That is, the form of the language is said to shape people's observations and thinking.

It is difficult to know how one would test this intriguing notion, though some negative facts seem evident. For example, the Chinese people, whatever their "handicap," did develop abstract philosophical and scientific ideas hundreds of years ago, and more recently they adapted their language (as did the Israelis with Hebrew) to the needs of modern science. When Eskimos stop hunting on the northern ice, they become less alert to the myriad forms of snow, however rich their vocabulary is—just as Southerners in this country lost their store of words for different racial mixtures when race itself lost some of its high salience.

On the other hand, this hypothesis contains the small truth that *translation* may be difficult because the other language may not

Figure 2-3 Anger at a taxi driver is clearly conveyed by this man's body language. (Charles Gatewood.)

contain adequate words to express what is in the original. The complex ideas of Catholic doctrine could not easily be stated in Eskimo at first, and a novel about stockbrokering could not easily be translated into the Arabic of Mohammed's time. Nevertheless, this is because those cultures did not contain such ideas or experiences, and thus their natural language had no vocabulary ready for them.

Culture contains more language behavior than mere words, however. At different class levels people speak different forms of the same language. For example, black street language is different from the English spoken in upper-class private schools. Bedouin (desert) Arabs speak a more "classical" Arabic than urban Arabs do.

We have also become aware of a more subtle language behavior, called body language. Not only do we learn our society's gestures of anger, contempt, or welcome, but we also learn more refined, usually spontaneous, and often unconscious, ways by which people express emotions.[6] Often, we "get the message" even when another person does not try to send it, for example, when a person uses affectionate words but turns his or her body away. In modern society people who are thought to be especially acute in understanding others are probably skilled at interpreting the meaning of body language.

WHAT CULTURE DOES

By now it should be clear that it is erroneous to think of human beings as some kind of animal that has added a thin veneer of culture to hide its savage ways. Humankind has been *transformed* by culture, for it shapes our very biological impulses. People from different cultures act differently, whatever their common biological heritage.

A Design for Living

At the most fundamental level, the importance of culture is obvious in that the basic techniques for survival are part of it—how to distinguish poisonous from edible mushrooms or fish, how to build a fire, or how to operate a computer in space. Even the simplest culture contains a large amount of this necessary knowledge.

More generally, however, every culture is a "design for living"—in sexual and familial behavior, appreciation of art, types of games played, forms of dancing or walking, or dedication to work. We accept much of our culture without even being conscious that we have done so. And we learn how different our culture is from others only when we observe or interact with people in another country, or with people in our own country whose culture is different (Appalachian mountain folk, the Pennsylvania Dutch, Boston Brahmins). Then we can see how many of their patterns are different, from the way food is cooked and eaten to how people greet one another.

A guide or design for living creates *orderliness* in human activities by offering a ready-made plan for coping with most situations. For some problems the culture simply gives a set of solutions based on experience and knowledge, for example, how to build an arch. However, for many types of decisions there can be no "best" solution and no empirical proof that one way is wiser than another: Forms of art, morality and ethics, religion, and familial norms and values are examples. However, people are socialized to believe in their society's cultural patterns and thus do not have to "decide" every time they face such situations. On a social level, this is comparable to many personal habits or preferences, such as eating patterns, which shoelace to tie first, the di-

[6]For a summary of these ideas see Albert E. Scheflen and Alice Scheflen, *Body Language and Social Order*, Englewood Cliffs, N.J.: Prentice-Hall, 1972.

vision of labor between wife and husband, or the routines of daily living. That is, we follow our habits, rather than deciding each time what to do. Thus, we simplify our thinking. On both the societal and the individual level, our choices are made easier by cultural patterns that we learn from infancy on.

Although cultural patterns do simplify our thinking, they also impose some costs. We all are limited in our perception and understanding because we can "see" only certain kinds of choices or possibilities. If science asserts that the world is flat, people do not argue much about the best route for sailing around the globe. If magical and religious beliefs interpret disease as caused by individual violations of various taboos, people spend little time in developing a germ theory of illness. In science and religion, as in morals and art, our traditional ways of thinking and evaluating limit the range of new ideas we are likely to take seriously.

Values, Norms, and Roles

The orderliness that cultural patterns impose, for good or ill, extends to social as well as individual matters. One important consequence is that people are more willing to work together for common goals, to share with one another, or to defend their group. Since people in the group want or value a similar way of life, they feel some identity with one another. Following a similar design for living, they are more willing to interact with one another or to like one another.

Though cultural patterns create some orderliness—as contrasted with what would happen if there were no such patterns—inevitably they create conflicts as well. Some people simply do not accept the values of their group; others actively oppose them or set up countercultural ideals; and different groups within the same society believe in different religions, aesthetic principles, moral and ethical rules, or political ideologies. When such cultural differences are extreme, one group may mount a revolution to impose its beliefs on others. Precisely because people feel committed to their own cultural patterns, they are willing to punish, fight, expel, or jail others who violate or ignore them. A large part of social conflict—between classes, individuals, groups, organizations, castes, or political parties—arises from cultural differences, in norms, values, or any kind of evaluations or beliefs.

Throughout this chapter we have used the concepts of values, norms, and rules without examining them carefully. Since they occupy such a central position in sociological thinking (as noted in Chapter 1), let us now consider them in more detail.

Values The term *values* refers to the broad evaluations that people share with members of the group about what is good, moral, ethical, beautiful, or excellent. Thus, we speak of the value of democracy, monogamy, telling the truth, or helping others. Such values are not adequate guides for action and are not so viewed, except in rhetoric and rituals. For example, democracy has been a deeply held value in the United States, but at times millions of people have opposed giving the vote to various groups—to women, blacks, Puerto Ricans, or members of certain religious sects. Such people did not deny the *general* value of democracy. Rather, their interpretation of who should have political influence excluded specific groups as unprepared or unworthy.

Norms A general value is further defined by various *norms*, or more detailed evaluations or rules about how to act or feel under specific conditions. For example, norms that support the general value of democracy specify that officeholders should step down from office if they lose an election; that people should not bribe others to vote in a certain way; and that the winner should not put the loser in jail after the election. Similarly, the "romantic love complex" in the United States contains many norms regarding the rights or obligations of people who date, appropriate behavior for getting a date, the intimacy or privacy that is permitted to those who claim to be in love, or even how to behave when one of the two persons falls out of love.

Roles   We use the term *role* to refer to a social position, and thus to the rights, obligations, and behavior by which we distinguish one position from another, for example, the role of stranger, tourist, friend, sister, or pharmacist. If we wish to be more precise, we speak of a *role relationship*, since the norms, obligations, or behavior of any *one* social position refer to relationships with one or more persons in other, *complementary* positions. We do not ordinarily describe *all* these important social positions.[7] Consider, for example, how many would be required for the single position of "daughter" (niece, sister, cousin, etc.). More usually, we focus on one or a few of such relationships.

The interaction of values, norms, and roles
When we observe how people actually behave in their various role relationships, we can see why some sociologists propose that we abandon any concern with values and norms.[8] That is, people seem to ignore or violate the norms frequently. They are inadequate for predicting how people will act. Here are some reasons why our "knowing the norms" people hold is not enough for predicting what they will do:

1   Many people *in* any social position or role do not feel strongly committed to the norms of that position.
2   People *not* in that position disagree, too, as to the rights and obligations of that position.
3   When people change their social positions, they may change their commitment to and definitions of various norms or role prescriptions.
4   In every social position, people seem to believe in contradictory norms or values (love *and* duty, quality *and* quantity).
5   Everyone occupies *many* social positions (parent, boss, neighbor, citizen) and may face pressures in many different directions.
6   We may violate a norm while believing in it or conform to it while *not* believing in it.[9]

Why, then, should sociology lay such stress on the related notions of values, norms, and role prescriptions? Perhaps the primary reason is that if we examine our own behavior we perceive that we almost never make important decisions without reference to one or more norms. First, we would not even make plans or carry them out if we did not consider them worthwhile according to our norms and values. Second, in considering how to do something, we weigh our actions by many norms: aesthetic elegance, ethical justification, or even instrumental adequacy. Third, when we consider any plan, we guess how *others* will evaluate what we do—whether they will re-

[7]For the whole set of role relationships that are linked to one such position or status, Robert K. Merton suggests the term "role set." See *Social Theory and Social Structure* (1949), enlarged ed., New York: Free Press, 1968, pp. 422–438.

[8]See, for example, Don Bushell and Robert Burgess, eds., *Behavioral Sociology: The Experimental Analysis of Social Process*, New York: Columbia, 1969; Irwin Deutscher, *What We Say, What We do: Sentiments and Acts*, Glenview, Ill.: Scott, Foresman, 1973; and Jack P. Gibbs, "Issues in Defining Deviant Behavior," in Robert A. Scott and Jack D. Douglas, eds., *Theoretical Perspectives on Deviance*, New York: Basic Books, 1972, pp. 39–68, especially pp. 56ff.

[9]These points are more elaborately made in William J. Goode, "Norm Commitment and Conformity to Role-Status Obligations," *American Journal of Sociology*, 66 (1960), pp. 247ff.

spect us for having fulfilled our role obligations or reprove us for having ignored them.

Evidently, then, we believe that others believe in norms and that they may cause us to regret having violated them. If we know that others may judge our acts harshly, we will try to excuse or explain our behavior and make it seem worthy of esteem. In short, knowing people's values and norms is not enough if we want to know how they will act in a given role relationship; but merely describing their acts is not enough if we want to understand it.

Ideal norms and "working norms"   If a norm exists—if people really believe in it and press others to conform to it—then it has some effect on what people or groups do, even though violations may be frequent. However, to take account of the gap between ideal norms (how things ought to be) and reality, it is sometimes useful to refer to the "working norms" of a group or set of people in interaction. A *working norm* is the level of performance that others will tolerate without much objection.

A group of workers, for instance, will come to agree on what is a fair day's labor—not so much work as to be a heavy burden, but not so little as to arouse their supervisor's wrath. The supervisor and the workers will agree, after some silent or overt negotiating, that though the ideal norm is for workers to be conscientious, hard-working, and productive, such a norm may be difficult to achieve. Similarly, parents set various norms for their children's behavior, and the children may even agree to the norms. But if the norms are too high a standard for everyday performance, they come to agree that an ideal performance calls for some praise, while behavior below some acceptable, or working, level will elicit scolding.

People in interaction constantly adjust their normative expectations to the reality. They constantly renegotiate what each has a right to expect, or what each person can or will do. If they cannot agree on what is a tolerable, or working, norm, their relationship may break apart.

Myths, Rituals, and Religion

The importance of culture is nowhere so strikingly evident as in the creation of a realm inhabited by legendary heroes, gods, and spirits, and in the elaborations of rituals to commemorate, honor, or praise them. This is apparently so far removed from the development of practical knowledge to cope with the daily crises of the natural and social environment that it calls for some analysis.

Throughout history many important sociological theorists have been concerned with the place of religion in society precisely because this part of the culture cannot be easily explained by reference to self-interest or to rationality. Indeed, Emile Durkheim, a major French sociologist in the early part of this century, suggested this fact as proof that religion must be very important in the social process. He noted that analysts, viewing the spread of science and rationality in the nineteenth century, supposed that old superstitions such as religion would die out. However, he observed there had been no real decline in religious belief. More people were educated, and science had developed, but people still clung to their ancient faith. This tenacity of religion was another observation that underscored its importance in human societies.[10]

Even in modern society more than a half-century after Durkheim's analyses—

---

[10]Durkheim's most elaborate treatment of religion is to be found in *The Elementary Forms of the Religious Life* (1912), trans. by Joseph W. Swain, New York: Free Press, 1947. Earlier he pointed out the intricate relationships between religion and suicide in *Suicide* (1897), trans. by John A. Spaulding and George Simpson, New York: Free Press, 1941, Book II; see also Max Weber, *The Protestant Ethic and the Rise of Capi-*

when religion is under widespread attack, when the Catholic Church has experienced many challenges to its traditional beliefs, when many commentators believe that both religious faiths and morals are in a state of decline—more than 95 percent of the American population claim to be affiliated with some religion. Moreover, even people who are not believers feel that it is socially inacceptable to proclaim in public their opposition to religion. In communist countries, of course, the official position of the government is set against any church, for Marxist doctrine is explicitly atheistic. Nonetheless, observers note that in such countries communism itself comes to take on a nearly religious quality, and the great heroes of the past are treated almost like saints.[11] Moreover, in such countries, visitors continue to report the firmness with which many people continue to hold to some parts of their religious beliefs.

The sacred and the secular As a step toward understanding religion, sociologists have drawn our attention to an aspect of all societies, the distinction between what is *sacred* and what is *secular*. Some things (words, acts, or places) are defined as set apart and are viewed with awe and considered holy or worthy of high respect; others are regarded as workaday and are approached without any special emotion, or are evaluated with reference to their useful-

ness. This distinction is a continuum, a matter of degree. For example, the flag or the national anthem may be viewed as somewhat more "sacred" than an automobile, but they are not as sacred as an altar, the Torah, or a ceremony in which a person becomes a minister. In most societies magic is somewhat less "sacred" than religion, but more so than most other activities.

As social scientists, sociologists have no techniques for ascertaining the "truth" of religion, since its realm is by definition beyond the limits of empirical observation. Sociologists can only observe what people do or say in their roles as worshippers. Clearly, being so limited, they can report that *no* observable qualities set the sacred apart from the secular—*other than how believers view things* (see Figure 2-4). That is, a piece of bone from a saint looks exactly like one from any other person.

Another generalization is that all religions contain a body of beliefs or doctrines specifying the exact nature of the gods or spirits worshipped, the origin of human beings, how they should behave toward the gods, and a complex set of meanings that is to be found in religious ceremonies or rituals. That is, religions contain both a set of cultural meanings and a set of social obligations. The latter specify the kinds of activities people are supposed to engage in when they are worshipping the gods or commemorating distant events in the society's history that are viewed as somehow sacred. There is, in short, a "church" or *social organization*, a set of social practices, surrounding the process of worship, and not alone a set of symbols or beliefs.

The content of religions The content of religious beliefs illuminates the place of culture in human life and offers vivid testimony to human imagination. Analysts of religion have devoted many volumes to collections of stories, myths, doctrines, and the activities of the tens of thousands of spirits and gods

---

talism, trans. by Talcott Parsons, London: G. Allen, 1930, for another analysis of the key importance of religion. In addition, see Max Weber, *The Religion of China*, trans. by Hans H. Gerth, New York: Free Press, 1951; and *Ancient Judaism*, trans. by Hans H. Gerth and Don Martindale, New York: Free Press, 1952. See as well William J. Goode, *Religion among the Primitives*, New York: Free Press, 1951, especially chaps. 1–4.

[11]On this point see J. Milton Yinger, *Religion, Society, and the Individual*, New York: Macmillan, 1957, pp. 14, 66, 149, 234; as well as Paul Tillich, *The Shaking of the Foundations*, New York: Scribner, 1948; and Reinhold Niebuhr, *Christianity and Power Politics*, New York: Scribner, 1940.

Figure 2-4   Sociologists find out how believers view things: One country's sacred cow may be another's hamburger. (Paul Conklin, Monkmeyer.)

that are thought to inhabit the supernatural realm. These myths about the past and beliefs about gods or spirits may be as complex in a tiny society with a simple technology as in one with a fully developed technology. However, some common themes seem to emerge in almost all of them.

First, all people must die, and all people experience troubles that seem to be meaningless or cruel. Religious beliefs attempt to explain the tragedies of life and death in a way that gives them cosmic meaning. Interpreted by religious beliefs, life does not seem to be a set of unconnected, arbitrary events. Some doctrines assert that this life is but a preparation for the next one, where we shall all be evaluated on the basis of our virtue in this one; others assert that we shall be born again, perhaps many times, and if we continue to improve we may eventually escape the Wheel of Life altogether. Others assert that some gods and spirits are whimsical. Whatever those beliefs, they inform human beings that their acts and experiences on this earth have a significance that is deeper than their mere appearance. They explain, at least in part, why some

people temporarily enjoy undeserved success or suffer undeserved tragedy.

Religious beliefs also typically reaffirm the existing social structure by setting out which kinds of acts are to be viewed as moral, virtuous, or pleasing to the gods and which kinds of behavior are to be disapproved. Not all, however, assert that people should obey worldly authorities and submit to their domination, for some religions teach believers that only religious virtue counts, and that no one should bow to any authority other than the spiritual.

Even religions that do not stress the individual soul nevertheless affirm the personal identity of human beings, for they give all individuals some responsibility for their fate and assert that what they do has consequences for a spiritual world, not only for the secular world. Thus, religious beliefs serve in part to give some identity or selfhood to the individual. In addition, by laying out ceremonies and rituals to be carried out, they reenact mythical events of the past and suggest some actions to be taken when crises or tragedies occur. In most societies, for example, religious ceremonies are associated with the tragedy of death, and often with major status changes, such as baptism, adolescence or adulthood, and marriage.

The close relationship between the social structure and the cultural content of religion can especially be seen in some of the traits ascribed to spirits or gods in most religions. These supernatural entities are not always thought to have human bodies, but their values, attitudes, perceptions, and thoughts are "anthroposocial"; that is, they have "personalities" like those members of the society. Here are a few of those similarities:

1 The deities take notice of human action.
2 The spirits or gods act broadly to further human welfare, as members of the society define it.
3 The deities desire human attention; they are pleased by honor paid to them and displeased by neglect.
4 The spirits or gods usually punish human beings for not acting in accordance with the rules of the society.
5 The deities are not invariably "good," for some of them may also have "moods," while others are whimsical or destructive at times.
6 Human beings attempt to communicate with the gods and make promises to them, and they expect to obtain some approval and rewards in return.

One may say, in short, that in all religions there is some kind of dialogue between supernatural entities of all kinds and human beings. This is even true in religions that are theologically defined as nontheistic (where there are no gods at all), such as in Buddhism, Confucianism, and Taoism. However, ordinary people are never content with religious doctrines that make ethical, moral, or philosophical ideas the center of worship and that omit all references to gods and spirits. Typically, at local and regional levels, various legendary figures, spirits, distant ancestors, or historical personages come to be viewed as sacred. In a similar fashion, when Christianity is introduced in a country that has many local spirits or gods, it is rare that this monotheistic belief is able to eradicate totally the respect that people pay to their former spirits or gods.

Religious conviction and reality Although our analysis has pointed to some factors that make religion of continuing importance in even a supposedly enlightened age, we should consider further why it is that people do not typically test their religious beliefs against observation. After all, at least some religious doctrines state what will happen in this world under certain conditions: Some have ceremonies for rainmaking; others see disease as a consequence of sin, or death as punishment for violating some religious taboo, or good crops as a result of appropriate blessings. Why do people hold such beliefs in the face of contrary observations?

Actually, experience rarely gives us a clear-cut experimental test. Almost everyone gets sick at times, but in a society where disease is thought to be a result of the gods' displeasure at sin, the victim can always remember some immoral or sinful behavior in the past. If rain does not come after rainmaking ceremonies, perhaps they were carried out improperly, or perhaps the participants did not feel the appropriately reverential emotions. With respect to what happens in the supernatural world as a result of what we do in this one, there can be no test at all.

In short, religious beliefs are typically constructed so as to make it impossible for people to demonstrate the truth or falsity of the beliefs they hold. Instead, the true believer usually finds in daily experience some confirmation of religious faith.

Religion and Social Cohesion

Sociologists have frequently noted that religion contributes to *social solidarity*, or *cohesion*, that is, the extent to which people feel unified and identified with one another. By sharing rituals and ceremonies in which they honor their gods and spirits, people are affirmed in their beliefs and feel more closely bound to one another. However, that can be so only in a society with one religion or only *within one* religious group that is contained within a larger society.

By contrast, the effect of several religious communities—each cohesive, each affirming its own moral and spiritual excellence and convinced of the support of its own deities—is often divisive. The history of religion is a bloody one in which people have killed and tortured one another because of their beliefs. When India was partitioned into two nations, one Hindu and the other Moslem, millions of people were left on either side of the border, and hundreds of thousands of people were killed in the ensuing outbreak of religious hostilities. The United States has attempted to support religious toleration from its beginnings; but anti-Semitism has been common, anti-Catholic riots have occurred many times, and small religious communities or sects that challenge either the political authorities or other religions are constantly arising. Indeed, precisely to the extent that people *do* believe in their own religions, they are likely to be in potential conflict with people who assert a different faith.[12] The "religious pluralism" of the United States, which permits an almost limitless variety of religious practices and beliefs, can exist only because most people do not feel the passionate devotion to their faith that past generations did. In addition, there is a set of United States norms that state that we should all behave tolerantly toward all religions.

Cultural Relativism

Sociology as a scientific discipline is partly founded on the conviction that science can-

[12]For some contributions of religion to social conflict, see Norman Birnbaum and Gertrude Lenzer, eds., *Sociology and Religion*, Englewood Cliffs, N.J.: Prentice-Hall, 1969, Part III.

not prove or disprove most of the beliefs that are a part of culture: religious doctrines, aesthetic principles, moral preachments, or political ideologies. That is, it is no more possible to demonstrate scientifically that Vivaldi's music is beautiful than it is to prove that bananas are delicious. Not only do research reports on the social life of primitive groups, peasant villages, or different classes or religious communities in modern society suggest that there are many possible designs for living, but those reports cannot give scientific evidence to show that these different ways of life are superior or inferior. They do state that when these different cultures are viewed through the eyes of their members or believers, all seem to have some worth.

Consequently, sociologists and anthropologists typically uphold what is known as *cultural relativism*, that is, the principle that we should not evaluate another culture by one absolute standard, but *relativistically*. We should weigh a culture only by reference to its own perspectives, standards, and beliefs. Set against this notion is *ethnocentrism*, the belief that one's *own* community, group, tribe, or nation is most worthy and excellent and that others should be viewed with some disapproval—the greater their difference from us, the greater the appropriate disapproval.

Like intense religious belief, ethnocentrism creates a more cohesive community. People who really believe that their own ways are finer or nobler than those of any other group are more likely to be socially solidary, to be willing to defend themselves against attack, and even to share and cooperate with one another. If such a group lives totally isolated, that cohesiveness does not create special problems. However, ethnocentrism within a larger society often creates conflict, and at a minimum leads to various forms of discrimination.

In contemporary Western society liberally educated persons are expected to adopt a culturally relativistic attitude. They are ex-

FOCUS

RESEARCH NOTE: DRAWING SAMPLES
FROM THE ELITE AND THE UPPER CLASS*

The following aims of the publishers of *Who's Who*, are indicative of the nature of this elite index.

The present edition contains down-to-date "Who's Who" biographies of 31,752 outstanding contemporary men and women.

The names in *Who's Who in America* are selected not as the best but as an attempt to choose the best known men and women in the country in all lines of *reputable achievements*—names much in the public eye, not locally, but nationally.

The standards of admission divide the eligibles into two classes: 1) those who are selected on account of special prominence in creditable lines of effort, making them the subject of extensive interest, inquiry, or discussion in this country; and 2) those who are arbitrarily included on account of official position—civil, military, naval, religious, or educational.[1]

No index is perfect, nor any sociological classification as homogeneous as might be desired. We are aware of the inadequacies of *Who's Who* as an index of an American elite. In the first place, it is too heavily weighted with educators and churchmen relative to the organizing elites of business, government, and labor. Secondly, in the distribution of power in any large community, especially urban America, one must always remain aware of the social power exercised by those persons, such as the political "boss," who are not strictly of the respectable world. *Who's Who* gives no clue to the extent of this power in America. Finally, we are well aware of the fact that certain persons are included in *Who's Who* more because of their prestige or prominence than because of any real achievement in a functional sense.

On the other hand, whatever its inadequacies, *Who's Who* is a universally recognized index of an American elite and as such, contains accurate information about a class of persons which the social scientist would be unable to secure on his own; people in this category, as a rule, do not have either the time or the inclination to supply such data solely for the purposes of sociological analysis. Finally, and of utmost importance, *Who's Who* is a useful elite index because it is felt that one must be able to make comparisons between social structure[s] if one is to go beyond mere anecdotal description to generalization from a systematic analysis of empirical evidence; this index may be used to compare

---

*From E. Digby Batzell, "Who's Who in America' and 'The Social Register,'" in Reinhard Bendix and Seymour M. Lipset, eds., *Class, Status, and Power*, 2d ed., New York: Free Press, 1966, pp. 271–272.

[1] *Who's Who in America* (Chicago: The A. N. Marquis Company, 1940), pp. 1–2.

various types of communities as well as the same community at two different periods.

One of the important differences between *Who's Who* and the *Social Register*, and very indicative of the difference between an upper class and an elite, is the way in which new members are added from time to time. On the one hand, new families are added to the *Social Register* as a result of their making a formal application to the Social Register Association in New York. In other words, a family having personal and more or less intimate social relations (in business, church, school, club, or neighborhood activities) with the various members of certain families who are members of the upper class and listed in the *Social Register* reaches a point where inclusion within the Register seems expedient; someone listed in the *Social Register*, presumably a friend of the "new" family, obtains an application blank which in turn is filled out by the new family (usually by the wife) and returned to the Social Register Association in New York along with several endorsements by present upper class members as to the social acceptability of the new family; after payment of a nominal fee, the next issue of the Social Register, including all pertinent information on the new family, will arrive the following November. The new family might be listed in the Philadelphia *Social Register*, for example, somewhat as follows:[2]

Van Glick, Mr. & Mrs. J. Furness III (Mary D. Bradford)

R,RC,ME,Y'15

Juniors

Miss Mary Bradford—at Vassar
Mr. John F. IV—at Yale

Phone 123

Miss Sarah—at Foxcroft
Mr. Bradford—at St. Paul's

"Boxwood"
Bryn Mawr, Pa.

In contrast to the *Social Register*, persons are listed in *Who's Who*, not on the basis of personal friendships or recommendations by present members, but rather on the objective basis of personal achievement or prominence; one does not apply for membership in this index nor is there even a nominal charge for being included; "not a single sketch in this book has been paid for—and none can be paid for."[3]

[2] Insight into the structure and values of the upper class in America may be obtained by a perusal of the family listings in any contemporary volume of the *Social Register*. The ideal typical Mr. Van Glick, for example, belongs to three clubs in Philadelphia, the *Rittenhouse* and *Racquet* clubs in the city, and the *Merion Cricket* club along the Main Line; he is a graduate of Yale University in the class of 1915; he is educating his children at very acceptable educational institutions, and lives in a very fashionable neighborhood along the Main Line. The familistic values of this upper class are indicated by the frequent retention of family given names (J. Furness, Mary Bradford, or Bradford, the son) and the use of "III" and "IV" as symbols of family continuity. The maiden name of the wife is always given and serves a useful genealogical function. The patriarchal nature of this family is shown by the fact that the college attended, if any, by the wife is never listed. In other words, family, club membership, education, and neighborhood all perform the status-ascribing function within this upper class.

[3] *Who's Who in America*, p. 2.

pected to understand that other people have different beliefs and practices and that one's own are not necessarily superior. Indeed, the idea of cultural relativism *is* liberating to some extent, for it teaches students to become more objective with respect to their society. Sometimes this is a painful process, but it is enlightening as well. One of the distressing experiences that travelers undergo in other countries is to learn how curious or odd their own behavior seems to *others*; but thereby individuals learn to be objective and analytical about the customs and practices in their native country.

An important result of coming to view other cultures relativistically is that our view of "human nature" may change. Ethnocentric persons are likely to view the customs and practices of their own community as "natural," as the only way to do things. However, a wider view that embraces many cultures informs us that if social life and beliefs can be so varied, then they cannot be so deeply rooted in human biology; that they must have been created by human beings; and therefore that they can be changed. For example, the German and Japanese cultures gave high evaluations to military activities for many generations, as did the Italian for one generation, but these patterns could be altered and apparently have been. To many people, "it is only human nature" that men should be dominant and women submissive, but a goodly number of cultures now show evidence of some changes in those beliefs.

We may not wish to applaud all cultural changes. But an awareness that cultures are created and maintained by human beings at least makes us aware that the differences among societies are not likely to be caused by inborn or biological factors that cannot be altered.

Although within sociology no sharp challenge to the general notion of cultural relativism has arisen, many sociologists challenge the notion that we should not evaluate some customs, practices, social structures, or beliefs. They have not gone back to the nineteenth-century faith that science can somehow "prove" the rightness of some social pattern or ideology.[13] On the other hand, many contemporary sociologists would assert not only that they have the right, indeed the obligation, to evaluate cultural and social patterns, but that they should also make known what their *own* values are.

If one separates evaluations from objective measurement, one can still weigh the extent to which the United States socioeconomic structure falls short of the standard of equality. One can analyze the values of the United States population to ascertain whether it would support various proposals for equality. Then one can consider *objectively* whether a new governmental program would have the effect of equalizing income, wealth, respect, or civic rights in any substantial way. But such value analyses are not to be viewed as "culturally relativistic," for they deny that all cultural patterns are equally worthy. Such analyses assert that we should make our values known and that we can evaluate a social pattern by that standard. We do not have to agree that we should not judge. Instead, it is asserted that some humane values deserve our support, and that *if* we believe in them, we can objectively weigh some customs, beliefs, and social patterns by whether they are adequate ways of achieving those values.

ACCULTURATION AND CULTURAL DESTRUCTION

Almost never does any society live in complete isolation from all others. With each passing decade archaeologists acquire more

[13]For an extended analysis of this fundamental point, see William J. Goode, "The Place of Values in Social Analysis," in *Explorations in Social Theory*, New York: Oxford, 1973, chap. 2.

evidence that human beings have always been restless wanderers, invaders, traders, and explorers. Thousands of years ago amber from the North Sea found its way to the Adriatic seacoast through successive links of exchange, trade, or plunder. Perhaps as early as thirty thousand years ago, people began to flow from Asia into what is now Alaska and to fan out over the North American and eventually the South American continents.

In these wanderings and encounters, people learned from one another not merely new techniques for hunting or weaving but also religious ideas, art forms, dances, games of chance, and political systems. Every culture we know is partly made up of cultural items that were once borrowed from another. The process by which people acquire cultural items from others is called *acculturation*. (Some anthropologists call this process *enculturation*.)

Some General Principles

In the acculturation process the characteristics of both the culture and the two or more societies play a part. That is, some types of *cultural* items or patterns flow more easily from one group to another; and some kinds of *social* interaction cause more or less acculturation to take place. For example, the Plains Indians not only acquired the horse from the Spanish but developed an elaborate horse and buffalo cultural system or complex, becoming some of the best horsemen in the world. However, they probably had no *social* interaction at all with the sixteenth-century Spanish invaders. Very likely, they either captured stray horses or stole them.

The most general principle observed in the acculturation process is that a society borrows *techniques* most easily, and it is quickest to borrow techniques that are more efficient for a task it already engages in. Very likely, no primitive society ever rejected the steel ax or the rifle. All societies have to chop things at times, and almost all engage in some hunting if they can. By contrast, a Scots dry-fly fisherman would not have met with much success in trying to persuade the Northwest Coast Indians to give up their salmon nets and spears, which yielded far more fish than his sporting equipment could.

A society is also more likely to borrow a cultural item if it is not necessary to absorb a complex body of skills and knowledge along with it. Thus, some highly productive strains of corn and rice that were developed by the United States especially to help some underdeveloped nations were rejected because growing them required special care, heavy fertilizing, spraying, and machinery.

New cultural items impose costs, which some people may be unwilling or unable to pay. It is not usually difficult to persuade groups or individuals that it is more helpful to use modern medicine; they do have a keen interest in staying alive. However, boiling water to kill germs is a nuisance, and costly. Going through a long course of medical treatment may require repeated difficult trips, continuing over several weeks. Almost all birth control programs have failed, because the goal itself seems only moderately desirable (though more desirable to women) and because all such techniques cost money and require discipline.

Purely technical items flow more easily than religious or philosophical systems do, and kinship systems are least likely to be borrowed. In world history it is rare that any highly developed civilization has easily accepted either of these from another society, unless that civilization was first nearly destroyed. One of the few contrary examples is the extensive borrowing by Japan from China in the seventh and eighth centuries, and from the Western nations in the late nineteenth and early twentieth centuries. More commonly, the religious and philosophical systems of great nations are intricately embedded in many social institutions in which much of the population has a stake, such as temples and their priests, schools and their teachers and pupils, or stratification systems. All these people wish to preserve their institutions at least in part, and the wisdom or truth of alien religious systems is not self-evident.

In apparent contrast to that principle, however, is one broad pattern that is easily observable: Whatever their philosophical attitudes toward the relative merits of hunting or rural life versus urban culture, people generally have gravitated toward urban cultural patterns when the choice was open. Nomadic invaders have rarely been able to conquer and destroy cities and then move on (Tamerlane's warriors were one exception). Typically, they have remained to enjoy the fruits of conquest—and culturally have become city people, to be invaded in turn by a later wave of hardy nomads.[14]

Ancient cities were walled, but not to keep their inhabitants from rushing out to learn rural cultural patterns. By and large, cultural items, including the latest techniques in agriculture have mainly flowed in one direction, from urban to rural.

The Dynamics of Acculturation

A closer look at the trends of acculturation tells us more about its dynamics. Through much of history cities have grown slowly. They grow fast in periods of economic expansion, military conquest, and quickened social change. That is, people flock to the cities and become acculturated there when the costs of leaving their rural or hunting cultures are lower than the expected rewards in the city. This was, for example, the judg-

Figure 2-5 The double-deck bus was brought to Africa by the British; the tribe member who moves to the city uses this imported means of transportation. (Marc and Evelyne Bernheim, Woodfin Camp & Asso.)

ment of millions of European immigrants to United States cities in the latter part of the nineteenth century. However, that opportunity may not exist for generations on end; peasants with scanty incomes will not abandon the little they have for still less in the city. Rural people and hunters do not lightly choose a confusing, complex, and frustrating urban culture unless the likely payoff is fairly substantial.

It must be kept in mind that much acculturation has been *forced* on conquered tribes or societies by imperialist rulers—for example, Rome, the Mohammedans, the Chinese, Great Britain, and the Iberian conquerors of Latin America. Although this situation seems to be very different from the

[14]This process was perhaps first analyzed in detail by the Moslem sociologist Ibn Khaldun (1332–1406), in his *Muqadima*. (*The Muqaddimah: An Introduction to History*, trans. by Franz Rosenthal, ed. and abridged by N.J. Dawood, Princeton, N.J.: Princeton, Bollingen, 1969, is a convenient and authoritative edition.)

urban acculturation that occurs when rural or hunting populations move to cities, much of the dynamics is similar.

First, conquerors usually (though not always) have a superior technology, and those who are conquered must learn some of it in order to survive. Ruling groups, in turn, cannot easily exploit their subjects unless they teach them at least enough to operate at the lower levels of skill. This pattern is also observed among migrants to cities. Thus, one first step in deriving some benefit from a conquest is to force a conquered group to become at least partly acculturated. Even that first step, it should be noted, requires that some members of the subject population learn enough of the language of the dominant group to be able to understand commands.

Second, rulers do not usually want to assimilate their subjects *fully*; they do not let them acquire all the dominant culture. They wish to keep the best opportunities for themselves and to continue to draw a boundary between themselves and those whom they rule. Typically, they feel superior to their subjects, who, they are convinced, are not able to become adequately trained or educated. Thus, rulers typically bar them from many higher-level positions and thereby lower the motivation of conquered groups to acquire the new culture.

Third, the process of cultural learning is most facilitated when there is little force applied, when people are given the rewards of greater prestige and social acceptance as they master the new patterns, and when teacher and learner interact frequently and closely in many different kinds of social situations, rather than encountering one another only in a rigidly segregated, master-servant type of interaction.

Those ideal conditions perhaps have never occurred in a conquest situation, although the Romans, Mohammedans, and British came closer to it in their colonies than did the Japanese, Dutch, or Germans. The Por-

tuguese and Spanish conquerors of Latin America were successful in undermining the native Indian cultures and—except for remote and isolated tribal segments here and there—in imposing their Iberian cultures on those people. By violence, disease, overwork, and forced migrations, they undermined the native *social structures* that might have preserved the traditional cultures. This is similar to what happened to slaves in the New World. The Iberian conquerors also eventually removed all the native rulers from their positions and successfully destroyed most of the native political structures, which might have created some resistance to the Iberian pressures against their culture.

The Latin American populations did not, even under those extreme conditions, simply embrace the Iberian culture, for typically the rulers tried to keep them in their lowly rank by not giving them rewards for accepting the new culture, or by punishing them for being so presumptuous as to exhibit a mastery of some part of it. This applies even to Catholicism, in which the natives were not allowed to participate fully. As the result, it is only in the twentieth century that the process of acculturation in Latin America is slowly being completed.[15]

As is clear from the foregoing analysis, the acculturation process may be as trivial as acquiring a new way of playing an old game or as momentous as becoming an industrialized nation. It may proceed quickly or slowly, and may involve many people or few. Moreover, the process by which an individual or a family becomes acculturated may proceed at a different rate than that for a group. That can be best illustrated by the acculturation experiences of immigrants to the United States. Many children of those immigrants became fully assimilated within their own lifetime. However, even after gen-

[15]For a more detailed analysis of this case, see William J. Goode, "Illegitimacy, Anomie, and Cultural Penetration," in *Explorations in Social Theory*, chap. 10.

erations of this process, islands or pockets of ethnic groups persist in all large cities. The Creole French still maintain part of their culture in Louisiana, as do Italians in San Francisco and Greeks in New York City—although millions of descendants of immigrants have become fully American in culture. In addition, "ethnic politics" continues to play a large role in all important elections.[16]

Most of the descendants of nineteenth-century immigrants have become fully assimilated, but some (together with newly arrived immigrants) keep part of the European culture intact, even in the relatively absorbent United States culture. By contrast, where (as in most parts of the world until fairly recently) social conditions *impeded* the rate of acculturation, some ethnic groups have persisted for centuries without being absorbed by the dominant national culture. Partly as a result, many "nationalist" movements have grown within France, Spain, Great Britain, and other countries in recent years.

CULTURAL VARIATION, SUBCULTURES, AND COUNTERCULTURES

Although we take for granted that the cultures of other nations are different from ours, we can also observe that within any nation there are innumerable variations in language, religious beliefs, values, and norms among ethnic groups, class levels, or regions. Usually, these differences are not large. Thus, we observe such differences if we move from, say, Boston or San Francisco to a small Southern town, but most people experience no great difficulty in adjusting to

such changes.[17] That is, there are many *variations* in cultural patterns within any large cultural system, and these may be maintained for generations.

At any given time these, too, are changing and becoming more alike or different. Few variations continue for long in the direction of becoming large differences, because the people in such groups interact socially with others or exchange ideas and goods with others, and so the differences are absorbed or reshaped by the dominant cultural patterns.

However, some groups—such as Appalachian mountain folk, some religious communities, or rural ethnic groups—are more isolated than others. Other groups, such as communes or religious sects, are less isolated but make conscious efforts to hold on to their cultural differences. Still other groups live under such different social conditions that their cultural patterns vary considerably from those of the larger society—for example, lower-class blacks or rural poor Southern whites. When these differences seem *substantial*, we may refer to that cultural variation as a subculture.

The term *subculture* thus suggests that the group culture is a variation of the dominant culture but that the differences are affirmed or supported by the group, whose members believe their subcultural differences are desirable. Thus, many ethnic groups in the United States consciously attempt to maintain their subcultures, as do many Scots and Welsh in England. In all these cases *most* of the subculture is that of the larger society, but the group affirms its dif-

[16]For analyses of the processes involved, see the comments by Herbert J. Gans, "Foreword," in N. Sandberg, *Ethnic Identity and Assimilation*, New York: Praeger, 1974; the two volumes by Daniel P. Moynihan and Nathan Glazer, *Beyond the Melting Pot*, Cambridge: M.I.T., 1963; and Glazer and Daniel P. Moynihan, eds., *Ethnicity: Theory and Experience*, Cambridge: Harvard, 1975.

[17]Readers who protest that the differences *are* large raise the problem of measurement: How large must a difference be, to be called "large"? Note that though, to some people, Boston culture seems very different from Los Angeles patterns, neither is as different from the other as both are different from the culture of London, Paris, or Berlin. The two United States cities share most cultural patterns, while as observers we typically focus on the relatively small differences—which can still be enough difference to cause some people to migrate.

ferences as both important and worthwhile.

Some groups also affirm a *counterculture.* That is, they do not merely fail to live by many of the cultural patterns of the dominant society (as all of us do, at times); they actively reject them and *also* affirm a set of principles that may even be contrary to those of the larger culture. Most criminal behavior is *not* countercultural; it is simply a failure to obey the law or norms. By contrast, most of the thousands of communes that have been founded in the United States since the 1840s have proclaimed an allegiance to different beliefs and values.[18]

No common set of principles can be discerned in all these social experiments, for different ones rebelled against somewhat different parts of United States culture. The most usual principle, of course, is some type of communal sharing, as against the principle of individualistic self-seeking of capitalism. Some are religious, others not; some affirm the virtue of hard work, while others proclaim one should work only when inclined to do so. Some are ascetic, while others support a wide sexual freedom. The rate of failure has always been high, but many have been successful for long periods of time.[19]

Not all groups that develop a countercul-

[18]For an early account of some of these communes, see Charles Nordhoff, *The Communistic Societies of the United States* (1875), New York: Schocken Books, 1965.

[19]For a keen analysis of factors making for success or failure, see Rosabeth M. Kanter, *Commitment and Community; Communes and Utopias in Sociological Perspective*, Cambridge, Mass: Harvard, 1972. See also Kanter's *Communes: Creating and Managing the Collective Life*, New York: Harper & Row, 1973. An excellent account of both problems and solutions in a successful commune is to be found in Benjamin D. Zablocki, *The Joyful Community*, Baltimore: Penguin, 1972.

Figure 2-6 Members of this commune create countercultural patterns as they form their "mini-society." (Alan Winston, Editorial Photocolor Archives.)

ture seek to establish a commune. Some form only a social network within the city. However, a group that merely disagrees politically with the party in power is not usually a counterculture, and we should not use the term for any and all kinds of rebellious attitudes. To form a counterculture requires more than a dislike for the American addiction to television or automobiles. After all, *most* people disagree with some parts of their culture.

To form a counterculture, it is necessary that people actually create some type of group or network, affirm a set of cultural patterns that run counter to those of the dominant society, and *also* attempt to maintain that cultural variation by some approximation of a "mini-society." Thus, there should be some provision for both rewarding and punishing members and for socializing new members (including children). Most countercultural groups do not go that far in their efforts, but it is clear that no subculture or counterculture can maintain itself without the support of an active social group. Countercultures should not be viewed as merely a rejection of the culture; they are often the vanguard of the future, because they oppose some social behavior that others eventually agree is wrong, and they suggest alternatives that may come to be accepted.

Our historical epoch is, as we point out in the chapters on prestige as a control system and on political processes, an especially rebellious one. This is not the result of "permissive child rearing" in the United States, for student rebellions occurred in all the industrial nations where some political freedom exists. Moreover, dozens of political regimes have been toppled since World War II, and many formerly peaceful ethnic groups within nations have asserted their right to independence. Numerous countercultural groups have been formed that challenge the dominant social philosophy in many countries.

Although the immediate present seems quieter, we do not believe there is any strong swing to conservatism. The political and cultural forces that have been opposing the ruling system will very likely continue to grow. It is possible that at some point in the future some of the contemporary proposals of countercultural groups will become more acceptable to the majority—such as a lesser emphasis on a high Gross National Product as the measure of the quality of national life; greater political influence in the hands of local communities, women, blacks, and other disadvantaged groups; more equality among class and ethnic groups; or even a growing refusal to wage war for nationalist purposes.

CONCLUSION

Research over the past two decades has revealed that all higher animals have a rich social life, learn from their environment, and even make a few tools. But none except human beings builds its social life on a cultural base. Relying on cultural adaptations to the natural and social realms, human beings mature more slowly than other animals and develop an array of tools and techniques to substitute for their lack of long teeth or claws, powerful muscles, or defensive shells.

Sociologists and anthropologists have gradually accepted a basic definition of culture as including almost all the social acts, all the things that are viewed as part of the society—indeed, almost anything that human beings think about. Sociologists also define culture in a more restricted sense to refer to the systems of meanings in any society, to the content of the communications human beings exchange with one another. In this more restricted sense, culture sometimes appears to be an abstraction, having no base in reality and simply existing as a set of ideas in people's heads.

Clearly, human beings are able to create complex realms of meaning, even about things and events that no one has ever seen. This symbolizing process becomes the content of a process of communication. People *share* the meanings they create and *decide* what a certain symbol will "mean." Typically, there *is* a reality to which symbols refer, and that reality can be tested. In fact, the human capacity to view symbols as realities in themselves is unique and makes culture possible.

For human beings, the most fundamental connection between biology and culture is that we can no longer survive without our culture. The human infant is helpless for a long time after birth. Human culture teaches parents to care for their children, to train them to become adequate adults, to educate or socialize the children to become parents when they grow up, and thus to pass on their culture to the next generation. Thereby the continuity of both the biological species and human culture is assured.

The essence of socialization, or acquiring the cultural and social patterns of the society, is not merely to learn what other people believe, but to come to prefer it. Thus, cultural patterns are in fact "biologized," or imbued with emotion; and biological impulses are curbed and shaped by culture.

Because of these close links, it is not correct to suppose that beliefs, norms, and values can change or vary without limit. (Indeed, they impose limits on one another as well; e.g., the value of "progress" makes other choices less likely.) Our biological potential can tolerate much, but cultural patterns must not become so extreme that the species will die out. The cultural content of a society typically dictates that human beings engage in a wide variety of acts necessary for the biological survival of the human animal and thus for the survival of the culture.

The most fruitful invention in human history is language, which permits us to correct our knowledge by sharing our observations; to facilitate the accumulation of knowledge, thus extending our ability to coordinate activities and accomplish large tasks; and to share feelings and wishes, thus binding us closely.

Culture is a design for living that specifies appropriate behavior in a wide variety of social spheres. But it also limits our perspectives and observations by encouraging us to accept the solutions of our culture, rather than looking for other possibilities. Because people may come to believe passionately in their values and norms, and because people in different social positions accept different versions of the culture, they may engage in violent conflict with those who disagree.

Both values and norms form part of the social roles we play. Role relationships are guided in part by values and norms, but they are inadequate for predicting. When we examine our own behavior, we perceive that we engage in few important acts without reference to the norms we hold, and we believe that others will weigh or evaluate our acts by reference to their norms and values.

An important part of every culture is the realm of the *sacred*. It is difficult to think of this supernatural sphere of religion as abstract, for the events and figures in it are seen as concrete and powerful in their direct impact on human lives. Yet the realities of the supernatural cannot be tested by direct observation.

Religions are not merely a set of beliefs about the supernatural. Always, they contain rituals and ceremonies that symbolize the events described in religious traditions. Engaging in such ceremonies, people are likely to feel reaffirmed in their devotion to the religious beliefs themselves, and to be affirmed in their identity as members of their own society. Their beliefs typically give them some consolation for the crises and tragedies they experience and also imbue such events with a larger cosmic meaning.

As with cultural beliefs generally, the

practice of a particular religion creates a greater social solidarity among believers. On the other hand, the very intensity of such convictions causes people to feel that their own ways are right and also creates conflict.

Cultural relativism as an ideological position yields a deeper understanding of our own culture, as well as a faith that the many differences among human beings are likely to derive from cultural patterns rather than from built-in biological impulses that cannot be controlled. Many contemporary social scientists feel that stance abdicates our moral responsibility to be concerned about the welfare of others. They argue that it is not enough merely to describe and explain; we must also take some steps to wipe out injustices when we find them.

Social and cultural change are not new phenomena. We noted that a major part of past cultural change has come about through *acculturation*. We analyzed both the kinds of cultural items that flow most easily from one society to another and the social conditions that may facilitate that flow.

Almost everything we do, think, or feel is shaped by the culture we have acquired from infancy on; and even a casual visit to another society reveals how different our own culture is from that of others. We can also observe many subcultural and countercultural patterns in our own society. However, cultural forms do not fully determine what we do. Social behavior is also shaped by physical, biological, economic, or political factors—indeed, sociological analysis is difficult precisely because our concrete acts are affected to some extent by almost any factor we can think of. Pinning down how much each one contributes to those acts is a challenging task. That task is facilitated somewhat when we know how their culture shapes people's *perceptions* of the world, their *evaluations* of what goals are worth seeking, their *choices* of means, and the standards by which they evaluate others' social behavior.

READINGS

Frederich G. Bailey, *Politics and Social Change: Orissa in 1959,* Berkeley: University of California Press, 1963.

Robert Bellah, *Tokugawa Religion: The Values of Pre-industrial Japan,* New York: Free Press, 1957.

Peter L. Berger, *Invitation to Sociology: A Humanistic Perspective,* New York: Doubleday, 1963.

Norman Birnbaum and Gertrude Lenzer, eds., *Sociology and Religion,* Englewood Cliffs, N.J.: Prentice-Hall, 1969.

Don Bushell and Robert Burgess, eds., *Behavioral Sociology: The Experimental Analysis of Social Process,* New York: Columbia, 1969.

Irwin Deutscher, *What We Say, What We Do: Sentiments & Acts,* Glenview, Ill.: Scott, Foresman, 1973.

Emile Durkheim, *The Division of Labor in Society* (1893), trans. by George Simpson, New York: Free Press, 1964.

————, *The Elementary Forms of the Religious Life* (1912), trans. by Joseph W. Swain, New York: Free Press, 1947.

Herbert J. Gans, *The Levittowners: Ways of Life and Politics in a New Suburban Community,* New York: Pantheon, 1967.

Clifford Geertz, *The Interpretation of Cultures: Selected Essays,* New York: Basic Books, 1973.

Nathan Glazer and Daniel P. Moynihan, ed., *Ethnicity: Theory and Experience,* Cambridge: Harvard, 1975.

William J. Goode, *Religion among the Primitives,* New York: Free Press, 1951.

————, "Norm Commitment and Conformity to Role-Status Obligations," *American Journal of Sociology,* 66 (1960), pp. 246–258.

————, *Explorations in Social Theory,* New York: Oxford, 1973, chap. 2: "The Place of Values in Social Analysis."

Alex Inkeles, *What Is Sociology? An Introduction*

to the Discipline and Profession, Englewood Cliffs, N.J.: Prentice-Hall, 1964.

Rosabeth M. Kanter, *Commitment and Community: Communes and Utopias in Sociological Perspective,* Cambridge, Mass.: Harvard, 1972.

————, *Communes: Creating and Managing the Collective Life,* New York: Harper & Row, 1973.

Karl Mannheim, *Essays on the Sociology of Culture* (1956), London: Routledge, 1967.

Robert K. Merton, *Social Theory and Social Structure* (1949), enlarged ed., New York: Free Press, 1968.

C. Wright Mills, *The Sociological Imagination,* New York: Oxford, 1959.

Ashley Montague, ed., *Culture: Man's Adaptive Dimension,* New York: Oxford, 1968.

Charles Nordhoff, *The Communistic Societies of the United States* (1875), New York: Schocken Books, 1965.

Albert E. Scheflen and Alice Scheflen, *Body Language and Social Order,* Englewood Cliffs, N.J.: Prentice-Hall, 1972.

Louis Schneider, *The Sociological Way of Looking at the World,* New York: McGraw-Hill, 1975.

Pitirim A. Sorokin, *Social and Cultural Dynamics* (1937), New York: Bedminster, 1962.

Paul Tillich, *The Shaking of the Foundations,* New York: Scribner, 1948.

Max Weber, *The Protestant Ethic and the Spirit of Capitalism,* trans. by Talcott Parsons, London: G. Allen, 1930.

Edward O. Wilson, *Sociobiology: The New Synthesis,* Cambridge, Mass.: Harvard, Belknap, 1975.

Milton J. Yinger, *Religion, Society, and the Individual,* New York: Macmillan, 1957.

Benjamin D. Zablocki, *The Joyful Community,* Baltimore: Penguin, 1971.

PART TWO

PERSONAL
AND SOCIAL DYNAMICS

CHAPTER THREE

SOCIALIZATION

Since human beings are mortal, they must be replaced constantly by younger people in order for the activities of the society to continue. Thus, the society is steadily engaged in training younger generations to handle its tasks. The term *socialization* refers to all the processes by which anyone—from infancy to old age—acquires her or his social skills, roles, norms and values, and personality patterns.

Although sociology does at times consider all that broad range of processes, its primary focus is on a narrower set of processes, the acquisition of values, norms, or attitudes (often called the *internalization* of values). The significance of the broader view is obvious: It includes almost everything that makes us human beings. However, we must also see why sociologists give more attention to the processes by which people actu-

ally come to believe in the values and norms of their group or of the larger society.

To begin with, what a society needs to have done (production and distribution of food, protection from enemies, political order) must be done by human beings. Thus, people must be induced to do those things. It is easier to induce others to do something if they already believe it is desirable, worthy, beautiful, or preferable in some way. If we build into children a set of real preferences for certain ways of acting, they are more likely to do those things even if the likely payoffs, from one day to the next, are not high. Thus, Christian teaching tries to get children to *love* virtue, not merely to practice it to avoid damnation. Similarly, the best science teachers steer their talented students toward the excitement of discovery, not mainly toward the job advantages of frontier research. And in economic, or market, terms, if consumers actually *prefer* Leatherhide Cold Cream, they will pay more (in time or money) to get it.

In all societies and all subgroups, then, people spend some of their energy in trying to get other people—especially the young— to make the group's values and norms part of their inner needs, part of their personality. As we note in Chapter 4, the results are startling in some areas of behavior. With great pleasure the Eskimos ate foods (such as slightly fermented contents of walrus stomachs and whale fat) that disgusted Europeans. Millions of Westerners, and especially women, have been persuaded that almost anything to do with sex is "dirty," while other societies (for example, the Polynesian) considered it a delightful recreation. People learn to hate some ethnic groups or religions and to prefer others. Although most of us think of "doing our duty" as grim and burdensome, we are also likely to get some smug pleasure from having done it.

In short, if people are actually *committed* to the customs, values, norms, or attitudes of their group or society, they can be led more easily, or at less cost, to live by those standards than if they have to be persuaded to conform only because of the likely pay-offs (negative or positive). However, merely knowing that someone accepts a norm or value *inwardly* is not adequate information for prediction. As noted in our discussion of roles and values (Chapter 2) and in our analyses of both prestige (Chapter 4) and politics (Chapter 13), we may believe we should not hurt another person but do it just the same; we may also obey a rule but not *believe* in it. Nevertheless, all societies have followed the strategy of trying to get their members to *believe in*, to accept *inwardly*, the values, norms, and customs of the group, and they have started this process at birth.

THE TWO MAJOR ASPECTS OF SOCIALIZATION

Socialization includes "the knowledge and skills of the cultural patterns and of social relations" in the society or subgroup, but its foundations lie deeper still. Parents do try to transmit both knowledge and skills, but that *cognitive* emphasis is not enough. Beyond that is an *emotional* base. Very likely this begins with the efforts of parents to teach children to *want* to learn, to be socialized, to "grow up," to learn skills. That is, even the learning of cognitive materials begins with an emotional base or impulse that persuades children that it is desirable to learn.

More generally, we are all taught to *feel appropriately* about aspects of society— music and literature, games and work, other people and groups, religion, family life, and even ourselves. The importance of this emotional content in our lives can be observed in talk among friends. Much of their interaction consists of sharing each other's feelings and value judgments, rather than simply exchanging descriptions or analyses. Thus, friends exclaim or complain about the weather, the latest film or TV show, a poor lecture, or a boring date; but careful listening will prove that little of this talk describes the *facts* about those events. Mainly we talk about our own emotional or evaluative reactions to an event, rather than analyzing that happening.

Thus, socialization aims at making us *competent* to do many things and at teaching us to know about many things; but it also aims at getting us to *feel* appropriately about people, behavior, and a wide range of values. The social importance of these inner commitments merits further analysis.

Because other people are concerned about both our actions and our inner attitudes, they may judge us as having failed either at carrying out the overt *actions* they expect or at feeling the *emotions* they consider proper. Thus, a person may fail either to attend a kinsman's funeral or to show the proper emotional response at the kinsman's death.[1] Let us see how people respond to those presumed attitudes or feelings in children or adults.

First, attitudes or inner norm commitment is viewed as socially important because people are less likely to attend to duties if they do not care much about the duties, or if they do not feel committed to them. On the other hand, people do not inquire closely into others' *norm* commitments if others carry out the appropriate *acts*. Most parents, for example, will not question a child closely about his or her feelings about studying if the child does in fact study diligently. And people who regularly attend church are rarely grilled about their inner piety. Expressions of sympathy are accepted as genuine sorrow.[2] Thus, we will not always know whether someone is *really* accepting another person's acts as "real" or "sincere." But if we do at times accept the deed as indicating inner commitment and thus incorrectly perceive the intensity of someone's real emotions, we do try to judge accurately. Few people can hide their feelings all the time, and most people have some ability to guess how others feel.

---

[1] Ethnomethodologists have claimed that sociologists cannot simply assume that motives, wishes, aims, or norms are definite events or things within the individual that sociologists can study as one might study a rock. Instead, other people who are in interaction with the individual "construct" these things. See, for example, "Motives," in Peter McHugh, Stanley Raffel, Daniel O. Foss, and Alan Blum, *On the Beginning of Social Inquiry*, London: Routledge, 1974. People *do* construct others' motives and then respond to what they think others feel.

[2] But sociologists need not be taken in by people's acts. Our task is to unravel discrepancies where they exist. Erving Goffman suggests that in some interactions we all save one another's face by making a mutual nonaggression pact not to inquire too closely into people's motives or outward masks. See *The Presentation of Self in Everyday Life*, Garden City, N.Y.: Doubleday, Anchor, 1959.

Because parents generally believe that children will "do right" if they have the right attitudes, religious convictions, or moral beliefs, parents and other moral authorities are much more disapproving if they think a child rejects or does not care about "doing right." People are more likely to label an individual as "criminal" or deviant in some way if that person openly asserts a counternorm or a rebellious attitude (see Chapter 5). Society is much less tolerant of the heretic than of the sinner. The sinner can at least repent or offer excuses. (The child who says "I'm sorry" will usually be punished less severely than one who proclaims, "I did it, and I'm glad.") Thus, adults watch and correct children in both their actions and their feelings, while children learn either to conform to both types of demands or to make a good show of doing so. As a consequence, the processes of social learning can be very complex at times. In general, however, people do not separate these two aspects of learning: That is, children learn both the right actions and the right emotions when they acquire any social role behavior (how to behave when Grandmother visits), for they learn it as a whole unit.

All these aspects of social learning emphasize its central importance: It is not merely something children must do in order to survive; it is needed for *society* to survive. Thus, there should be relationships between what children are to learn and the larger social structure. Let us consider that aspect of socialization.

SOCIAL STRUCTURE AND THE CONTENT OF SOCIALIZATION

Since society aims at transforming helpless infants into socially competent and responsible adults (as defined by *that* society), members of society are likely to emphasize behaviors that they consider important. That is, what is important in the social structure is emphasized by socialization.[3] Thus, the son of a Japanese warrior family was once taught the *Bushido* code, which detailed high obligations of honor and courage.

Some social skills and norms are more problematic or difficult to learn than others. Certain ones are necessary if the individual is to be part of the society at all: learning to eat, drink, walk, talk, control one's toilet behavior, return home from a visit, or dress oneself (if clothing is worn). With few exceptions, children acquire such skills sooner or later as part of growing up. Learning to do them is generally rewarding, and they offer new experiences to children. With each step forward, other people show their pleasure as well. Physical or neurological maturation makes the tasks easier with each passing month, and children become thereby complete members of their families and social groups.

Another large area of socialization is somewhat more problematic, since it contains many complex skills or bits of knowledge that adults must master to cope with their physical or social environments. These include such accomplishments as killing a buffalo or a bird with a bow and arrow, memorizing a long ritual chant or a religious ceremony, driving a truck, or even learning a complex game such as baseball. However, for the most part these are productive activities that bring rewards of both esteem and material goods. Many are also self-rewarding; the ability to perform them permits one to be accepted as a full member of the society. Indeed, some groups have created special rituals, betokening "adulthood," to signal that children have finally reached a particular level of skill. Some tasks are repetitive (both agriculture and bureaucracy contain many such jobs) but also yield the reward of some control over the environment.

A third segment of socialization is more difficult to teach or learn, for it is made up of all the social roles that are the major elements in any social structure, and it focuses on the *obligations* people owe to one another. A role is any behavior pattern that we are to carry out within a social position: the behavior of children toward their parents; the interaction of siblings; the complex relations between a chieftain and his priest. Roles are often specific to a social situation; for example, a professor interacts differently with students during an examination than at a party.

What makes socialization of roles a different task is that a major element in all relations is what each person owes to (1) another individual, (2) a group, or (3) supernatural forces or gods. That is, the standards by which others evaluate our social or role behavior are ethical, moral, legal, or religious.

If we do not pay enough respect to our parent or to a police officer, if we steal from someone, if we are noisy when the priest is chanting, others are likely to be morally indignant. The very young may be excused for ignorance or immaturity. But if we violate such rules because we do not even accept them or do not have appropriate feelings, others are even more disapproving.

Socialization for this third set of roles is somewhat more difficult because (1) many of the rules seem arbitrary and without obvious justification other than "This is the custom"; or (2) what one is enjoined or forbidden to do is a burden or a self-denial. Thus, most religious prescriptions or taboos are said to be in accord with the wishes of supernatural entities or gods; but if one does not believe that, no other proof seems possible. Rituals should be carried out exact-

---

[3]Alex Inkeles states that "the requisites of any social system become the imperatives for any system of child socialization"; see "Society, Social Structure, and Child Socialization," in John A. Clausen et al., *Socialization and Society*, Boston: Little, Brown, 1968, pp. 78ff.

ly as prescribed, but why they are so prescribed seems obscure. However, it is relatively easy to convince most *children* that it is unwise to offend the gods by violating a ceremonial taboo. Moreover, precisely because one way of doing it does not seem worse than another, neither children nor adults usually are tempted to violate a ritual. At most, people are neglectful or careless.

By contrast, the demands of interpersonal rules—what each person owes to the other in a role interaction—are harder to teach to children. It is *common* that what is a right for one person is an obligation for another, and therefore what one individual wants will be obtained at the expense of another. Thus, there is much resistance to many of these rules on the part of children and later on by adults as well. Children do not easily absorb the rules of fairness or equality, for that may mean giving up a toy to another child. Almost every interpersonal rule we try to teach children contains this fatal flaw, which makes a child somewhat less than enthusiastic about it and continually introduces an element of potential conflict in almost any role interaction.

Thus, most role prescriptions are under some strain, because one or the other person in an interaction must yield, or obey, or give some service, and we are not constant in our allegiance to these rules when they apply to *us*. Children can, of course, parrot such norms at early ages; all that requires is memory. However, as we shall note later on, analysts of socialization believe that an understanding of such social or moral rules comes much later, perhaps just before puberty.

Thus, precisely because these social patterns contain the rights to services, esteem, money, or obedience that individuals or groups owe one another—because any action by one person may well infringe on the rights of another—*individuals' self-interests* are at stake in them. The keen observation of children does not fail to note this important fact. Very likely much of parental pressure—threats, cajoling, persuasion, bribes, beatings, payments—is aimed at this wide range of social interaction, because children can get some benefit by ignoring or violating the rule.

Whether arbitrary or morally justified, however, socialization for these roles requires individuals *not* to take as much as possible from others but to respect others' rights even if thereby one loses some advantage or pleasure. This is most easily observable if we watch children squabbling on a playground, or watch a teacher or group leader try to restore order when children are in conflict. In both cases the issue is who violated which rule about who owed what to whom, and typically the violation brought some advantage to the offender. This type of interaction is also carried out, with a bit more subtlety, among adults. Nations go to war about such issues.

The importance of socialization for *this* aspect of role behavior may be emphasized by the general *lack* of social rules that require children to enjoy themselves, to have fun, to do what pleases them. The theories embedded in social structures recognize that children can in general be counted on to do those things without being required to do so. Consequently, the socialization processes need not give much attention to them.

By contrast, rules that ask adults to sacrifice themselves in battle, or to give to a chief or to a government what they have earned, or to work hard for a group or a corporation, or to obey leaders, or to be unselfish in family relations cannot rest mainly on any obvious advantage to the person who follows them. Consequently, they must be built into the motivational system of children, so that they do not question too deeply just why those rules are right and just. Goodness and virtue are not easily achieved, in children or adults. Parents spend much of their energies trying to persuade children that though such goals

Figure 3-1 The motivation to share is desirable but difficult to instill. (James H. Karales, Peter Arnold.)

might be costly, they are desirable in themselves. Needless to say, some of us never become committed to some of these norms. Or we may be committed in childhood but later lose some of that commitment. We all falter and weaken in our commitment when tempted.

BIOLOGY AND SOCIALIZATION

Our knowledge about the social life of other animals and the general biological bases of action has grown in the past two decades (see Chapter 2). As a consequence, there has been a revival of attempts to explain human behavior through biological factors.[4]

[4]See, for example, the work of Edward O. Wilson, *Sociobiology: The New Synthesis*, Cambridge, Mass.:

Research has shown that more of the behavior of lower animals depends on learning and social experience than was believed a generation ago. On the other hand, it also asserts that more of human behavior is determined by biology than sociologists have been willing to concede. This debate will not be settled soon, but let us examine its issues.

The heart of the new debate is the ancient problem of nature versus nurture, or heredity versus environment; that is, are we human because of biological factors or because of socialization? All wise persons have known that *both* are important, and no one can show how *much* each contributes, but perhaps these elements in the modern discussion are somewhat new:

1 Studies of higher apes in their natural homes show that their life is based more on social learning, and their patterns of social interaction (cooperation, play, mothers' care of infants, adult males' protection of the group, deference, and leadership) seem more like ours, than was understood before. Since we assume their social life is determined by biology rather than culture, and the social patterns are similar, perhaps more of our own behavior is innate, or biologically inherited, than seemed possible twenty years ago.

2 Major strides in language study have shown that the inner structure of language behavior seems very similar among very different languages. It is suggested that neurological structures in the brain cause these similarities. That is, the way the mind works is determined by this underlying structure, which is revealed in language.

Harvard, 1975; as well as Nikolaas Tinbergen, *The Study of Instinct*, New York: Oxford, 1969; Konrad Lorenz, *On Aggression*, trans. by Marjorie K. Wilson, New York: Harcourt Brace Jovanovich, 1966; and such popular books as Lionel Tiger, *Men in Groups*, New York: Random House, 1970; and Desmond Morris, *The Naked Ape*, New York: Dell, 1969.

3   The study of language also suggests (but again does not prove) that the linguistic skill of even a four-year-old child is too complex to have been learned by simply adding one word after another and acquiring a basic grammar for putting the words together. Speech cannot be reduced to so simple a process, for grammars and dictionaries do not describe the subtlety and flexibility of making sentences. Even computers are not capable of translating from foreign languages or making up adequate sentences. In addition, children make such quick leaps in skill that we cannot see how ordinary punishments and rewards could have taught them to discriminate so easily between proper speech and nonsense.

Therefore it seems reasonable to guess that the human animal is "wired" or "programmed" neurologically for speech and that this underlying biological endowment determines our capacity for language.

4   Human infants also seem to be wired or programmed for maximizing social interaction, thus suggesting an innate "need" to be social. They burrow, or "root," into a person's arms, suckle, adjust their bodies to increase contact, and grasp adults. Again, this suggests that infants do not have to be rewarded to make them want social interaction. They are biologically "preset" to be social.[5]

5   Biochemical studies of physical growth, glandular secretions, the way messages are sent through the nervous system, and the effects of chemicals (for example, LSD) on both the mind and social behavior suggest that biological factors shape some part of mental and emotional stability, personality, and sex-role be-

havior. Once more, this suggests that much of what we had supposed was caused by social experiences may instead be caused by biological processes.

These "new" arguments are not proved; they are only one more step in the continuing debate about which aspects of human behavior are shaped more or less by society and culture. They teach us to be more alert to possible biological influences.[6] As we note several times in this volume, the *methodological* barriers to a full understanding remain the same now as in the past: From birth on, infants are shaped by social factors and are also maturing continually, so that by the time we can test any theory about the origins of human behavior we can no longer be sure how much comes from our biological endowment, from maturation, or from social experiences.

Nevertheless, we can at least clarify our thinking by listing a few basic principles about biology and socialization:

1   Human beings have no instincts, as far as we know. That is, there are no inborn mechanisms for solving complex problems, triggered by a need presented in the environment (for example, in birds, building a nest or migrating with the seasons). There are drives, such as hunger or thirst (needs for which the body does not give a solution); and there are reflexes (automatic responses to special stimuli, such as the eye blink when an object comes too close, or the jerk of the knee when it is hit on the lower side).

2   Physical *maturation* or growth processes continue from infancy onward, and thus the human animal can do some things

[5]See, for example, Mary D. S. Ainsworth, S. M. Bell, and Donelda J. Stayton, "Infant-Mother Attachment and Social Development: Socialization as a Product of Reciprocal Responsiveness to Stimuli," in Martin P. M. Richards, *The Integration of a Child into a Social World*, New York: Cambridge, 1974, p. 100.

[6]For additional discussion of these relations, see N. G. Blurton Jones, "Ethology and Early Socialization," in Richards, op. cit., pp. 263–293; and Francis H. Palmer, "Inferences to the Socialization of the Child from Animal Studies: A View from the Bridge," in David A. Goslin, ed., *Handbook of Socialization Theory and Research*, Chicago: Rand McNally, 1969, pp. 25–55.

later on that it could not do when younger. Even if social influences were to stay the same, the human animal itself would not. Children can therefore learn some things (such as toilet training or walking) more easily at one time than they could earlier. Maturation also creates new problems for socialization (for example, sex changes at puberty).

3 There are biological limits to what can be taught or tolerated. For example, it is not possible, by the most effective teaching techniques, to transform a human infant into a chimpanzee adult, or vice versa.

4 Though society and biology keep each other within some limits, the two sets of demands are not necessarily in harmony. Each places strains on the other.

5 Socialization can be complex or relatively simple, depending on how complex the social and cultural patterns are. However complex these are, _any_ biologically normal child can acquire the social roles and the culture that _any_ society imposes.

6 Most, if not all, cross-cultural differences (the differences among different societies) are caused by social, not biological, differences. (This is another way of stating the previous proposition.)

7 On the other hand, different social environments may develop some biological potentials more than other societies do. For example, Plains Indians could "see" farther than white people could, but not because their eyes were really keener; rather, they could perceive and interpret more accurately a tiny speck on the horizon (just as a keen birdwatcher can see a flashing wing and identify it as a crested flycatcher). That is, biologically determined ability can be enhanced or intensified by training.

8 Very great biological and psychological differences exist among _individuals_, and biopsychological differences are far more useful for explaining individual variation than are differences among different groups or societies. Some people are born mongoloid idiots, and some exhibit abilities at the level of genius. Some, even with coaching, remain awkward and clumsy, and others can become great dancers.

The differences among individuals are much too great to be accounted for by socialization. Had Mozart been born a poor black on an Alabama farm, he would not have written his _Coronation Mass_, for he needed some training to do that; on the other hand, almost no musically talented person with equally fine teaching could match Mozart's creativity.

9 Folk wisdom and parental observation also suggest that clear personality differences begin to appear before any great effect could have been produced by social molding (for example, "She was stubborn just like that when she was six months old!" or "He was sunny from the very beginning"). Efforts to identify and measure such personality traits have not been very successful.

10 In general, our knowledge about the effects of _deprived_ or _distorted_ socialization is much more secure and definite than about the effects of ordinary social experiences. An infant deprived of ordinary interaction with caring adults, or subjected to high or contradictory stress (such as being hurt or hated, or being asked to love but being rejected at the same time), will not usually grow up to be normal, even if its original physical and psychological inheritance was average.

These principles are important, but they are crude. Their main assertion is that we cannot make _precise_ predictions about how adults will act, given a normal biological inheritance, while the biological endowment does make *possible* (without determining) whatever the adults do later on. It is difficult to show there are *any* important social patterns that are determined by specific biological mechanisms. Our biological heritage requires that social patterns satisfy biological needs, of course. For example, if they did not produce food, we would die; and if they did not provide care for infants, the society would end. However, which *kinds* of social patterns are worked out for those biological requirements varies greatly, and thus they are not determined by biological mechanisms shared by all normal human beings.

The biological structure also makes some kinds of social solutions easier and thus more likely. Human evolution almost certainly makes us more attentive to social stimuli and more dependent on social learning than other animals are, so that social life itself is ensured.

All these interactions help us to understand the close interplay between biological and sociocultural factors, and they suggest not that the biological is determining, but that biological factors help to make social life *necessary* (for the human animal could not live otherwise) as well as *possible* (for social life is built on biological foundations). They also remind us that the particular biology we inherit makes some types of social arrangements more likely than others. On the other hand, the *exact* weight of biological factors in particular *areas* of social life doubtless varies.

HOW EASILY MOLDED IS THE CHILD?

Up to this point we have followed the usage of most other analysts in referring to the society's effect on the child. By and large, psychologists and sociologists think of the child as a passive object to be shaped by the massive forces of family and group. Moreover, a common assumption, drawn from a wide range of social behavior, is that the child is plastic and can be molded in almost any way. In the United States it is a general belief, too, that people are "not born but made," that the influences of family, group, or church will determine much of their fate (the opposite belief is also held—that people *can* overcome those handicaps of the social environment).

Such beliefs are reinforced by a general acceptance of *behaviorism*, the psychological doctrine or theory that animals and human beings acquire habits and attitudes when they are rewarded or punished appropriately. The noted behaviorist John B. Watson claimed in the 1920s that the correct reinforcement pattern could make an infant into almost any kind of adult one might choose. The contemporary behaviorist B. F. Skinner has not made so extreme a claim, but the main thrust of his popular argument is precisely that people can be shaped in almost any direction by following the correct system of *operant conditioning* (that is, getting the individual to do what is aimed at, and reinforcing that behavior by the correct rewards). Thereby we can get a pigeon to guide a rocket by teaching it to peck (through a glass porthole) in the direction of a target, or make a human being become law-abiding. It is easier to prove this for pigeons than for human beings.

It is important, if we are to understand the processes of socialization, to see that the child is *not* infinitely plastic, willing or able to adjust to anything; more fundamentally, the processes must be seen as *interactional*. Both parents and children contribute to those processes; and the outcome would be different if different parents reared the same children, or the same parents were to rear different children. The processes are the resultant of how *both* will conflict with or support one another.

We can see this if we consider the case of parents who report the child is *not* plastic. Parents typically claim that their children began to show personality differences almost at birth. Some are "sweet," and others seem shy or thoughtful. Some appear to resist or show anger easily, and some are slow to develop. However, even a modest amount of careful observation discloses that parents do not treat their children the same. Girls are handled differently from boys. Parents are more anxious with their firstborn children, and talk with them more. Thus, even when they think it is the child who is different, they are contributing to that result.

Second, it is also usual that parents do not perceive *all* their behavior with their children. They typically give more than one message or "reinforcer" to their children. For example, they may *believe* they are punishing their daughter for crying without reason or for being noisy, when they are really teaching her that the only way to get their attention is to create a disturbance. They may think they are teaching a boy not to hit his sister, when they are really telling him that girls and boys are different by nature and are reinforcing the usual social stereotypes about male and female sex roles. Parents may inform the child he or she should not be selfish; but they may exhibit selfishness themselves and may thus prove its advantages to their children. More technically, we may phrase that interactional aspect of socialization by pointing out these relationships:

1. Even if some acts of the parents might mold the child, the parents may never learn *which* acts or reinforcers would be the most effective rewards for *that particular child*.
2. Even if the parents did know, they might be unwilling to pay that high a price. Some parents feel they should not "bribe" the child with presents or "seduce" the child with love. They may believe the child should be good anyway and punishment is morally correct (even if it is ineffective).
3. Even if parents did know, and *were* will-

ing, they might be unable to be consistent, to be patient, to give a great deal of love, or to devote so much time to the child. That is, they *cannot change themselves* to fit the needs of the child.

Obviously, all three of these relationships underline the fact that the *interaction* of parents and children—and not merely the traits of the parents or of the children separately—shapes the socialization process.

In addition, many specific behaviors of children affect how much warmth and care they get.[7] This may be seen in a study of the *sensitivity* or the ability of the mother to know what the child needs and to take care of that need quickly. The more sensitive mothers accepted their children more fully, cooperated more with them, and made themselves more accessible or available to them. Their children obeyed them more, were more secure and independent, and later on accepted their norms and values more completely.[8]

However, the more striking finding is that the infants who *communicated more effectively*, whose cries or movement could be more easily "read" or understood (even by outsiders), made up somewhat for the lesser sensitivity of some mothers.[9] That is, even the less sensitive mothers were more likely to respond adequately to their needs. Again, it is clear that parents and infants in *interaction* determine what happens in the socialization process.

---

[7]Martin P. M. Richards, "First Steps in Becoming Social," in Richards, op. cit., p. 91.

[8]Although the trait of "obedience" may seem less attractive than "daring" or "exploring," note that children begin to be able to obey, to attach themselves to adults, and to move about on their own at about the same time, that is, the second half of their first year. Clearly, if they moved about and would *not* obey even when danger threatened, their lives might be somewhat shorter (Ainsworth, Bell, and Stayton, op. cit., p. 124). Children who are secure in their attachments will, in any event, explore *more*.

[9]Ibid., pp. 111–113.

LEARNING PROCESSES

Since socialization is social *learning*, we should review some of the processes by which human beings learn anything. Much of our basic knowledge about learning comes from experiments on animals (mainly white rats), and to apply it to human beings may require some correction or qualification. Let us first consider the most basic or elementary process of learning, then note why it does not quite fit all situations of human learning. After that we can examine some other learning processes.

Operant Learning Theory

Behaviorist theory, or *operant learning theory*, essentially states that animals (including human ones) learn when they are rewarded (by an "operant conditioner," or reinforcer) for taking the right steps toward a solution. A white rat can be taught to press a bar, then wait ten seconds for one of two lights to go on, then do one of two different tasks, depending on which light appears—the operant conditioner or reward being a food pellet. The experimenter can thereby build complex chains of acts by rewarding the rat for each part of the chain (usually beginning with the last step and working backward). So, we are told, the baby acquires complex social patterns, for at each step toward such a set of acts (speaking, eating at the table, going to the toilet) the infant is rewarded with smiles, hugs, food, and praise.

Although doubtless this basic process determines much of human learning, the inadequacies of the behavioral approach seem clearer now than in the past, even as applied to other animals. The theory of operant conditioning has mainly been tested on animals that were being taught to do something they did not care about, in a situation (laboratory cages and human apparatus) wholly different from what was normal for

their species. If they "solved" the problem set by the experimenter, such as learning how to run through a maze or pressing a bar to get water, it had to be through trial and error, or accident, since that situation did not present the kinds of information the animal would get in its natural setting.

Problem solving and learning in wild animals are much more complex and less distant from human learning processes than most laboratory experiments suggest. The kinds of thinking that are revealed in natural settings seem profoundly different from those exhibited in laboratory settings. Consequently we may have to broaden our view of learning processes for both human and other types of animals. Here, let us list some findings that require a broader view of learning:

1 Animals are neurologically better organized for solving their own problems than for solving problems human beings give them. Different kinds of animals seem to have different kinds of minds, while laboratory experiments do not ordinarily reveal those qualitative differences.
2 Animals appear to solve new problems by thinking about them creatively. They do not work out solutions only by accident.[10]
3 Animals engage in playful problem solving and also explore new ways of doing things, or even new environments, whether or not they have to do so.
4 At least higher animals learn by watching others and following their solutions.
5 The higher the animal, the more complex is the learning process: More social-emotional factors affect what is learned and projected; and whether the animal *wants* to learn becomes more important. The relations of the animal (hu-

[10]For some examples see M. Brewster Smith, "Competence and Socialization," in Clausen et al., op. cit., pp. 290–293.

man or other) with its teacher become more important.

6 As the animal matures, it may show leaps in understanding that do not seem to be easily ascribed to the adding up of many individual experiences or to reinforcement by rewards and punishment.

For all these reasons it seems likely that human socialization or social learning is not entirely explained by theories based mainly on experiments with white rats in a laboratory. Even conceding the *general* importance of operant conditioning, we must not confine our thinking to its principles. We must extend our understanding to other learning processes, without rejecting the basic importance of operant conditioning.

Modeling

Another learning process, of special importance in human experience, is imitation, or *modeling*.[11] Research on modeling suggests that children imitate the behavior of others when they have been given some kind of reward or reinforcement, as well as when they see a reward or reinforcement given to the model. Children are more likely to model after others if they know that the model is especially competent or esteemed. Modeling is much more likely to occur if a child *identifies* with the model, that is, wishes to become like the other person or to please that other person. As might be expected, children in general will imitate warm and rewarding models more than distant and cold ones.

On the other hand, the *stage* of development of the child will affect modeling. At very early ages imitation is less frequent, and it becomes more frequent as the child approaches school age; but by the third grade and higher school levels children are rather selective about whom they model after and what kinds of behaviors are affected.

At the stages of infancy and early childhood, what *looks* like imitation may turn out to be the *parent imitating the child* (for example, laughing or making sounds like words). Whether earlier or later, it is very difficult to ascertain whether imitation, or modeling, is accompanied by *internal* changes of attitudes or values, or whether the child is merely acquiring modes of external behavior like those of a model.

Since most of this research has been done by psychologists, the process of learning by imitation has been interpreted as basically *operant* learning; that is, the child learns by imitation because he or she is rewarded for it in some way. On the other hand, larger segments of behavior may be learned at some step through modeling, rather than being acquired through the addition of small bits of behavior to each other over a longer period of time. Moreover, in real life some of the rewards themselves come, not from social approval or affection, but from the pleasure the child gets in mastering a new skill or exploring a social role, such as imitating an adult's behavior.

Problem Solving

Naturalistic observation of both young children and animals reveals another learning process, which may be called *problem solving*. That is, at some phase in infants' development they begin to show some ability to grasp the parts of a problem and figure out a solution, without being told how to do it, and without first learning all the parts individually. This may be as trivial as putting a stick into a hole or as subtle as tricking a parent into taking the child from the playpen. Problems and solutions both become more complex as the child matures. They

[11]See "The Role of Imitation in Childhood Socialization," by Willard W. Hartup and Bryan Coates, in Ronald A. Hoppe et al., eds., *Early Experiences and the Processes of Socialization*, New York: Academic, 1970, pp. 109–142; as well as Justin Aronfreed, "The Concept of Internalization," in Goslin, ed., op. cit., pp. 280ff.

apply to social as well as physical situations. Some children are clever at figuring things out for themselves, and others are less so; and some are better at social than physical problems.

Underlining the importance of both imitation and problem solving as learning processes suggests the more general view that infants do appear to begin thinking about their outside world at some point and to distinguish (as many analysts have noted) between themselves and other objects and people. It is characteristic of human beings that whenever they are awake (and much of the time when they sleep) their mind is actively processing fantasies, information from the senses, memories, language inputs, and stimuli from inside their bodies. They solve problems in their head whether or not they carry out the solution.

That is, the human mind is not merely responding constantly or being conditioned by other people's actions. The mind is endlessly active on its own, attempting to understand what others do and say, working out plans for action, or attending to the minute problems of adjustment in social interaction. In short, some part of the total social behavior the child acquires is not directly determined by conditioning, but is the result of the thinking and problem solving he or she does. Thereby, far more learning takes place than is caused by operant conditioning directly.

Direct Teaching

Whether we should consider *direct teaching* as a separate learning process is not clear. It takes place in and outside the classroom, and its importance is that concentrated masses of information about the social and physical world are absorbed faster than they could be acquired by direct experience. Very likely most of that is to be understood through operant conditioning, since children are rewarded for their quick mastery of that

material, and they are also rewarded for accepting the role of pupil. In any event, even in primitive societies without schools, adults and peers spend some time in instructing the young in both the skills of agriculture or hunting and the more esoteric knowledge of religious ceremonies.

Maturation

Still another learning process may be, like formal instruction, *not* very distinct in its dynamics but nevertheless difficult to harmonize with the basic theory of operant conditioning: These are developmental processes, or *maturation*. Studies of learning in animals reveal that at certain *phases* of development the animal's learning may be far too rapid to be explained as the simple addition of skills reinforced by rewards.[12] In ducks and geese, for example, newly hatched birds are quickly "imprinted"—that is, they form a deep attachment to their mother, who is the first large social object they experience in the wild. However, if no mother goose or duck is there, they may equally well form an attachment to an inappropriate social object, such as a human being. If the human being steps on their toes (thus a *punishment* rather than a reward), they may form an even deeper attachment. However, this process can occur only for a very short time after birth, that is, only at a particular *phase* of development. Later on, the imprinting will not occur, and the punishment will arouse fear and withdrawal.

Similarly, it was once thought that dogs could be taught to hunt only after they were fairly mature, beginning at more than one year of age. Now it is known that a more critical phase occurs at about six months, and field training is more effective at that age. Infants cannot, even with great effort, be taught to speak at three to six months,

[12]For a review of some research in this area, see Eckhard H. Hess, "The Ethological Approach to Socialization," in Hoppe et al., eds., op. cit., pp. 19–36.

but their great leaps in verbal understanding in the second year of life seem too swift to be explained by a careful schedule of "reinforcers" such as praise or food. Still later, children of six to eight years can repeat the rules of a game, but usually have not yet understood that the rules are created and agreed upon by the group. They have not yet grasped the fact that rules can vary, depending on what the group itself decides. That understanding seems to require a further phase in maturation.

All these instances suggest that how and what we learn is shaped fundamentally by our phase of development, or maturation. Since theories about socialization or social learning have often taken the form of phases or *stages* of development, it is to these we now turn.

STAGES OF GROWTH

The developmental stages of human beings are so obvious that it might be supposed we now have a clear theory of socialization or childhood development, or, at a minimum, a precise *description* of each stage of social maturation. It is self-evident that the human being starts as an infant, then crawls, toddles, and speaks. After becoming old enough to play with other children, the child is likely to move in same-sex groups at school and, later on, to enter the stage of puberty, or sexual awakening. At that time intense relations with children of the opposite sex become more common. Toward the end of the adolescent period the individual begins to take on adult roles one after the other. We could go on to list the various stages of human life to old age and death, but this is enough to show how obvious the notion is and how it fits what we observe daily.

Nevertheless, careful researchers have not been able to agree on what these stages are or how we can distinguish each from all the others. Some infants skip the crawling stage. Speech can come before or after toddling. In many parts of the world no one bothers much about toilet training, but bowel control occurs just the same—to be sure, long after a middle-class United States child would have been coerced into conformity. The closer we examine developmental stages or compare them in different societies, the more difficult it is to agree on what stage comes after another, how to distinguish each one, and whether each person must go through every one of them, in the prescribed order.[13] For these reasons the phases of maturation that one researcher reports do not correspond with those of another, while all assert that social learning is very different at different stages of growth.

Social Psychological Theory

George Herbert Mead is not often viewed as a theorist of developmental stages, but his social psychological theory of the relations among the mind, the self, and the society does contain hypotheses about socialization as a developmental process.[14] For Mead, the growth of mental activity is fundamentally a *social* process. This activity occurs as a result of speech with others and internal dia-

[13]One of the more famous *descriptive* studies of child development, with special reference to the ages at which each kind of behavior emerges (rather than how socialization proceeds), is the Gesell study. See, for example, Arnold Gesell and Francis L. Ilg, *Infant and Child in the Culture of Today*, New York: Harper, 1943; *The Child from Five to Ten*, New York: Harper, 1946; and Arnold Gesell, Frances L. Ilg, and Louise B. Ames, *Youth: The Years from Ten to Sixteen*, New York: Harper, 1956; for criticism of this work, see the retrospective review by Lois Meet Stolz, "Youth: The Gesell Institute and Its Latest Study," in Edward Zigler and Irvin L. Child, eds., *Socialization and Personality Development*, Reading, Mass.: Addison-Wesley, 1973, pp. 211–223. The Bayley Infant Scales, developed by Nancy Bayley and her associates, are based on more recent measurements; they show the levels of development to be expected at a given age.

[14]His classic work is *Mind, Self, and Society* (1934), New York: Morris, 1961.

logues with oneself and others. When children acquire language, they acquire both the meaning of words and the emotional contents of words, and both are social. They learn to think about the things others are concerned with and also use that knowledge to think about themselves and others.

The first stage in this development is the "conversation of gestures," a social process that is even found among animals.[15] Infants can engage in a conversation of gestures with an adult and can learn to understand what the adult's gestures mean, even though infants are not conscious of what they are doing. Infants can also make noises, and can respond to their own noises, and thus engage in an *internal* conversation of gestures with themselves. Each of the infant's acts stimulates further response, even though no other person is there.

At a later stage the child is able to "play," to take the role of another temporarily or to play a part in a small interaction. This may be as simple as the toddler's engaging in playful threatening noises with an adult who has *initiated* threatening noises or gestures, both then dropping that role as they move into laughter and affection. Such playful episodes give the child further understanding of the differences in roles, and over time the child learns a great number of such partial roles. The child may also engage in playing *both* roles of an interaction while alone. Thus it may play the role of "mother" as well as child, speaking some of the mother's words and responding to them as itself, while both roles are simply played for the moment.

The stage of real games comes later, for games require that children know many rules and keep them in mind simultaneously. Even a simple game of hide and seek requires that each child understand what every other child is supposed to do during that period. During this later stage the child

[15]Ibid., pp. 59ff.

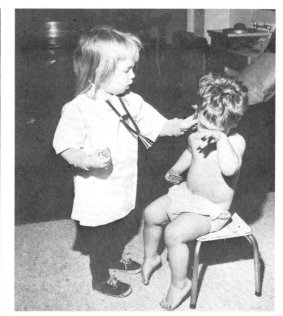

Figure 3-2 Early play situations help children to understand various social roles. (Ray Shaw, Photo Trends.)

still takes the roles of others, but now takes a number of them simultaneously.

Essential to this development is not only learning how people respond to one another, or the judgments people make about each other, but also seeing *oneself* as others see one. As Charles Horton Cooley suggested with his concept of "the looking-glass self," we learn who and what we are by observing how others respond to us. We acquire that self, as Mead says, by taking the role of others who are responding to us. Thus, even the sense of self is acquired through social interaction.

Taking the role of the other becomes a general ability of the child and the adult. This is first done, as already noted, in play. At an early stage the child takes on the attitudes of *significant others,* who will usually be members of the family. These are the persons who are most significant in shaping the child's attitudes, and they are the source of his or her standards of evaluation and emotional response. As the child acquires a larger set of roles from interaction with still more people, she or he will respond with what Mead called a *Generalized Other*, a distillation of the knowledge and moral rules that apply to her or his social life. This corresponds to the community that the child sees as her or his own. It is more generalized than the significant other, for it is not merely the specific roles or attitudes of a particular person that the child acquires, but the general attitudes and beliefs of the larger society.

During this stage the child knows his or her own self in relation to others, and also their relations to each other. That is, he or she takes the role or point of view of the larger community. Much of that self is simply the rules and customs of the group (what Mead called the "Me"), but some part of it (which he called the "I") is creative, unique, impulsive, and thus not quite predictable.

Freudian Theory

Still earlier than Mead, Freud had proposed a set of stages by which the instinct-driven infant is finally shaped into a conscience-harried adult. He saw this development as primarily determined by the individual's relationship to her or his *sexual* phases. Born polymorphous perverse—that is, able to respond sexually to any kind of caress and directed only by the pleasure principle—the infant moves into the *oral* stage, in which its sexuality is mainly expressed in suckling, its main attachment is to its mother, and thereby the infant makes its first distinction between itself and another person.

The next phase is the *anal*, in which the child's sexuality is expressed in the pleasures and difficulties of excretion, toilet training, dirt, or holding back and letting go its feces. The next stage, from about two or three years to about six, is called *phallic*, and this is when the "Oedipus complex"

arises. In this phase of development the Freudian interpretation focuses more on the boy than on the girl, though a similar process (the "Electra complex") is asserted to occur in the girl's life as well. The boy develops a sexual attachment to the mother, expressed in the wish to marry her and to kill the father. However, both love and fear combine to repress that incestuous wish. The boy feels his father will castrate him. By repressing both fear and the incestuous wish, the boy can express love for his father, identify with him, and want to grow up like him.

At about age six the child enters, according to Freud, a *latency* phase, in which little interest in sexuality is shown, the child now identifies with the parent of the *same* sex, and children of different sex avoid one another. Children come to identify, then, with the "appropriate"-sexed parent, and thus acquire a *superego*: They now begin to accept the moral attitudes of their parents.

When the child enters the *genital* phase of puberty, the sexual impulses are reawakened, relations with peers of the opposite sex are created, and the superego conflicts sharply with the animal impulses that play so large a role in the life of the growing adolescent. That conflict between internal moral demands and fears about sex, on the one hand, and the increasing sexuality of the teenager, on the other, creates much of the emotional stress associated with adolescence in Western society.

The Freudian view of growth stages has not fared well. It suggests that different modes of suckling, weaning, and toilet training might have important effects on the adult personality, but careful study denies those assertions. It views human beings as basically animals, held in check by repressions of reality, instead of being thoroughly social. It also asserts the nonsexuality of the latency phase, when observation in both the United States and other societies would show a continuing increase in apparent sexuality during that period. Perhaps most researchers would not agree, either, with the specific years in which Freud claimed each stage would occur.

On the other hand, in conformity with Freud, a goodly number of studies suggest that the period of about six years (say, five to seven) is one that continues to show up as a turning point in the child's development: In learning experiments the mental, or cognitive, behavior of children is more like that of adults after that age, many other behavior changes occur at that point, and the adult IQ can best be predicted then.[16]

Piagetian Theory

The Swiss child psychologist Jean Piaget also views the period from five to seven as an important stage of development. Focusing less on the interaction between parents and children and more on children's play, he views children's acquisition of moral rules as part of their general mental, or cognitive, development.[17] He asserts that there are *qualitative* changes in the thinking of the child, and that at each stage the child's grasp of the moral rules will be different.

The earliest stages, up to two years, can be broken down into several substages, but essentially this is a sensorimotor phase, in which infants learn about space, time, and

their relationship to objects. Infants, as in Mead's thought, have no "self" at first, and only gradually see objects as independent things, without regard to what they are doing to them. Thereby, children can imagine or think about an object even though it is not in sight.

Much of Piaget's early theory of moral development was derived from observing the marble playing of children two to fourteen years of age from the poorer sections of two Swiss cities. However, his observations and ideas include far more types of games and social behavior. Because of the ages of the children involved in this activity, his second stage (two to five years, approximately) is one in which language becomes more important. Children are able to reason with symbols, and not only by manipulating objects as in the first sensorimotor stage.

This second major stage Piaget calls *egocentric*. In this phase the child observes examples of organized games, or is told about them by adults, and begins to imitate these examples of rule-directed activity. However, the child continues to play mainly alone, without going to the trouble of finding playmates for the game, or plays with others but does not try to win. That is, the child is concerned mainly with himself or herself in relation to the game, but does not try to put together the different ways of playing.[18] In this second stage the child engages in regularities or rituals of behavior (that is, repeating some way of playing) but does not yet follow *rules*, because he or she does not feel that the rules impose any real social *obligation* or have any moral force.

The next stage occurs at about seven to eight years (Piaget believes the specific ages are statistically likely but not absolutely fixed), when the child seems to want to understand the rules, to cooperate with other players, and to win. Children know

[16]S. H. White, "Evidence for a Hierarchical Arrangement of Learning Processes," in L. P. Lipsitt and C. C. Spiker, eds., *Advances in Child Development and Behavior*, New York: Academic, 1965, vol. 2, pp. 184–220.

[17]Jean Piaget, *The Moral Judgment of the Child* (1932), trans. by M. Gabain, New York: Free Press, 1965; see also his book *On the Development of Memory and Identity*, Worchester, Mass.: Clark University Press, 1968. See also John Flavell, *The Developmental Psychology of Jean Piaget*, Princeton, N.J.: Van Nostrand, 1963; and Lawrence Kohlberg, "Stage and Sequence: The Cognitive-Developmental Approach to Socialization," in Goslin, ed., op. cit., pp. 347–480. Kohlberg's work begins from Piaget's research but also contains many criticisms of it. See also Susan Harter, "Piaget's Theory of Intellectual Development: The Changing World of the Child," in Zigler and Child, eds., op. cit., pp. 224–245.

[18]For a description of these stages, see Piaget, *The Moral Judgment of the Child*, pp. 32–65.

the rules, but not in detail; and they differ among themselves in their reports of what the rules are. They do not look only to adults or older children for information about the rules, but now two or more children as equals may agree on this or that rule between themselves.

It is not, however, until after the age of ten (on the average) that children come to view the rules of the game, or of a social group, as the outcome of independent action taken by their own group. That is, they now see that they can make and unmake sets of social, moral, or game rules by common consent. Rules are not simply imposed by others or decided on arbitrarily between two friends. At this stage children begin to enjoy rule making for its own sake.

Jean Piaget has continued to broaden and refine his theories over many decades, and thus not all of his thought can be easily summarized. However, an important theme remains central in his thinking: that the moral and social development of the child is determined to a considerable extent by changes in the quality and structure of the child's thinking. That is, the intellectual and cognitive development of the child is an important source of moral growth.

Criticisms of Developmental Theories

The many attempts to chart stages of the child's socialization process and thus its stages of maturation have been subjected to many criticisms.[19] First, the samples of infants or children being studied are usually small (both Piaget and Cooley drew many conclusions from observing their own children) and are commonly middle-class. Thus, we cannot be sure these findings apply to most children. Second, when certain stages are predicted to occur at a specific age, say, eighteen to twenty-four months, many children do not fit the chart but seem normal just the same. Third, the indices or criteria for deciding a child is in, say, Phase 3 are often unclear, so that other observers cannot be sure whether that phase has indeed been reached. This is especially a problem for activities involving the inner meaning of a moral rule.

Finally, must the child go through *all* the stages, and in that order? Are there subgroups or whole societies that remain at one phase without developing what these analysts call "moral maturity"? Or are the more mature phases simply to be classified as value judgments, as a set of personal preferences that the analyst wants everyone to accept?

On the other hand, developmental studies do point to at least two important conclusions: (1) How the individual accepts the values, attitudes, or customs of the society is in part shaped by the structure of ideas or *thinking* he or she does. (2) The growing child does not merely add item after item as he or she becomes adult; instead, real changes in the quality or structure of thinking and feeling take place. The adult can solve not only larger quantities of problems, but very different problems, both moral and intellectual, than the infant or young child can. The process of socialization is shaped by these qualitative changes, as the infant moves through early childhood to adolescence. The changes do not occur without social interaction, but they also affect in turn how that social interaction is experienced inwardly. Finally, even when we cannot clearly distinguish each stage from the next in accordance with the blueprint offered by one or the other analyst of socialization, it is clear that each analyst does

---

[19]See, for example, Hartup and Coates, in Hoppe et al., eds., op. cit., pp. 109–139; Smith, in Clausen et al., op. cit., pp. 293–304; Kohlberg's various comments on Piaget; Eleanor E. Maccoby, "The Development of Moral Values and Behavior in Childhood," in Clausen et al., op. cit., pp. 231–240; W. H. Sewell, "Infant Training and the Personality of the Child," *American Journal of Sociology*, 58 (1952), pp. 150–159; and John A. Clausen, "Socialization Theory and Research," in Clausen et al., op. cit., pp. 20–64.

make us aware of some of the inner dynamics of social interaction, by which the child gradually internalizes the various rules and patterns of the society.

SOCIAL DEPRIVATION

The importance of social interaction for normal human development is proved most convincingly by observations of children who have been *socially deprived*. Some children have been reared in social isolation or in residential institutions (orphanages, schools for the retarded or psychotic). Some have been reared by brutal or neglecting parents; others have been treated with great hostility or coldness.

A much-cited study of a generation ago documented a finding that numerous observers had reported for centuries: Infants and children deprived of adequate socioemotional care die off at a rapid rate.[20] In the institution under inquiry, none of the children was older than three. Infants spent most of their day without human interaction, for there were only a few nurses, and all the children suffered from lack of normal attention and cuddling. Two years later, one-third of the children had died, and those who remained in the institution were retarded.

Eighteenth-century data on foundling homes and hospitals that received abandoned children suggest an even higher mortality, though some of this must be attributed to ignorance about diet and disease.[21] In addition, those who directed orphanages or institutions for the retarded often profited

by giving inadequate physical care. Nevertheless, it seems likely that the death rate of infants and children in institutions has typically been much higher than that of children who lived with their families but in great poverty. Indeed, the same conclusion has been drawn from studies of *adults* in modern prison camps: Where inmates give each other socioemotional support the mortality is much lower than where they do not.

The human animal does not, then, respond well even *physically* to social deprivation. *Socially*, the differences are equally striking. The human being does not grow up to be normal either emotionally or intellectually if he or she has not been engaged in continual social interaction with *caring* others. (This is also true of apes.)[22]

From time to time, children have been discovered who were kept in isolation for years, or who lived away from human contact.[23] These children could not speak, showed great difficulty in handling human objects or understanding their uses, and seemed unable to respond with trust and affection to adults who tried to give them substitute parental care. Depending on the severity of the earlier deprivation, some were able eventually to move toward normal social behavior, after undergoing an enriched program of social experience.

Far more frequent are the cases of child abuse, that is, cases of parents punishing children with burns, broken bones, and

[20]René Spitz, "Hospitalism," *The Psychoanalytic Study of the Child*, 1 (1945), pp. 53–72; and "Hospitalism: A Follow-up Report," ibid., 2 (1946), pp. 113–117.

[21]W. L. Langer, "Checks on Population Growth: 1750–1850," *Scientific American*, 226 (February 1972), pp. 92–99. For an earlier period, see Richard C. Trexler, "Infanticide in Florence: New Sources and First Results," *History of Childhood Quarterly*, 1 (1973), pp. 98 ff.

[22]H. F. Harlow, "The Heterosexual Affectional System in Monkeys," *American Psychologist*, 17 (1962), pp. 1–9; "The Maternal Affectional System," in A. M. Schrier, H. F. Harlow, and F. Stollnitz, eds., *Behavior of Nonhuman Primates*, New York: Academic, 1965, vol. II, pp. 299–309.

[23]As far as we know, there are no true "wolf children," but some children have lived outside human contact, on the edges of human settlements. In addition, the cases of Anna, Isabelle, and others are instances of children reared in more or less complete isolation, and with little contact even with their own mothers. For a discussion of these cases, see Kingsley Davis, *Human Society*, New York: Macmillan, 1949, pp. 204ff.

even killing.[24] Usually child-abusing parents impose standards of performance that are too high for the child (for example, demanding that a two-year-old keep her or his room neat) and then respond to that failure as the child's denial of love and respect for the parent. Those parents were, in turn, typically deprived of love and attention when *they* were children.

Still more common than battered children are those who are cared for physically but deprived of warmth and affection. Ability to bear a child has almost no connection with ability to give love or understanding to the child. Many parents are insensitive to the emotional needs of their children; that is, they simply do not "read" or interpret the child's wishes.[25] Others may feel warmth for the child, but have little capacity for letting the child know this.

The destructive effects of social deprivation have been emphasized in J. A. Bowlby's inquiry into the attachments between mothers and children.[26] The critical period, he argues, occurs between six months and three years. Children who are reared during that period in orphanages, or by insensitive or uncaring mothers, are more likely to be dependent, anxious, and fearful. They are mentally, physically, and socially retarded. Some are damaged for life.[27]

More recent studies suggest that residential institutions and other organizations for collective child care need not damage the child, but research continues to emphasize the damage done by socioemotional deprivation.[28] *Some* institutions do furnish a reasonably adequate social experience for children: attention, frequent interaction, more information, fewer negative comments, more explanations, play, warmth, and security. Indeed, some children from very deprived homes may actually do better in speech after they have been in a more adequate institutional environment. When such institutions create that type of atmosphere, the absence of the child's own mother causes little or no harm.[29]

Adequate tests of these relationships are difficult, because the most disadvantaged children at one stage of life are less likely to enter institutions that will offer them a rich socioemotional experience to make up for the earlier handicaps. Children who *continue* to stay in such institutions may not develop well, but that failure may also be caused by their *initial* lack of adequate social development, which in turn lowers their chances for placement in an affectionate foster home, and thus causes them to stay in those institutions. In any event, later studies do emphasize the possibility that institutional care can be adequate, while they underline the damaging effects of socioemotional deprivation on the development of the child.

[24]For data on battered children, see D. G. Gill, *Violence against Children*, Cambridge, Mass.: Harvard, 1970; R. E. Helfer and C. H. Kempe, eds., *The Battered Child*, Chicago: University of Chicago Press, 1968; and William J. Goode, "Force and Violence in the Family," in Suzanne K. Steinmetz and Murray A. Straus, eds., *Violence in the Family*, New York: Dodd, Mead, 1974, pp. 25–43.

[25]See again in this connection the insightful work of Ainsworth, Bell, and Stayton, op. cit., pp. 99–135.

[26]J. A. Bowlby, *Attachment and Loss*, New York: Basic Books, 1969.

[27]For generally confirming data, see Jack Tizard, *Community Services for the Mentally Handicapped*, London: Oxford, 1964.

[28]See, for example, the further specifications of which factors in institutional care can be improved, in Jack and Barbara Tizard, "The Institution as an Environment for Development," in Richards, op. cit., pp. 137–152. See as well Edward Zigler and Irvin L. Child, "Specialization," in Gardner Lindzey and Elliot Aronson, eds., *The Handbook of Social Psychology*, 2d ed., vol. III, *The Individual in a Social Context*, Reading, Mass.: Addison-Wesley, 1969, pp. 533–542.

[29]On the general consequences of adequate collective care, see the brief summary by F. Ivan Nye and Felix M. Berardo, *The Family*, New York: Macmillan, 1973, pp. 394–401.

WHAT MAKES SOCIALIZATION EFFECTIVE?

In the nineteenth century, children became responsible adults—at least as good as human beings generally are—when they were punished severely; but in most primitive societies they were indulged a good deal and punished rarely, with exactly the same result. That is, as far as we know, *all* societies have been fairly successful in rearing the younger generation to take on normal adult obligations and to uphold the norms of the group or society. The differences in socialization techniques from one society to the next may have produced very different kinds of people, but we do not know what those differences were. Great nations and small societies have done very stupid and cruel things, but we cannot explain them by pointing to failures in socialization.

On the other hand, within a given society or group, some families are more effective than others in getting their children to be committed to their values, norms, and customs. When we observe people (parents, teachers, other children) trying to socialize others, it seems clear that some of their efforts are likely to create hostility and rejection in the child, rather than kindliness and acceptance. Some children become adults who believe in the ideals of their group or attempt to create an even better life for people around them, while others grow up to be indifferent. What are some of the social factors that determine whether socialization is more or less effective?[30]

Methodological Problems

Before considering the variables of effective socialization, let us take note of some major methodological problems in this area. Since we cannot create neat experiments with

[30]For summaries of findings from research on socialization, see the relevant headings in William J. Goode, Elizabeth Hopkins, and Helen M. McClure, *Social Systems and Family Patterns*, Indianapolis: Bobbs-Merrill, 1971, Eleanor E. Maccoby, "The Development of Moral Values and Behavior in Childhood," in Clausen et al., op. cit., pp. 227–269, especially pp. 247–248; and Justin Aronfreed, "The Concept of Internalization," in Goslin, ed., op. cit., pp. 263–323.

Figure 3-3 Three young boys in New Guinea are being taught an important skill, part of their socialization. (Courtesy of the American Museum of Natural History.)

human beings as we might with white rats, the data for any conclusions on these processes are *typically* insufficient. Wise people who have done research in these areas disagree on many important points. It is difficult to pick out which of the thousands of possible causes of adult behavior might have had the effects that we see in the lives of human beings, and many of them may not have come from differences in socialization. To make proper comparisons, we would need at least the following data:

1   We need to have adequate measures of whether people actually *do* believe in the values, norms, customs, or attitudes that they profess. Mere behavioral or verbal conformity does not prove that they are committed to those evaluations.

2   We must show that both parents and children share these value positions.

3   We must prove that the similarities between parents and children were not caused simply by the ordinary social pressures of rewards and punishments from *other* people in their class, neighborhood, or school. That is, we have to show that the *parental* patterns of socialization themselves had this effect.

4   It is necessary to ascertain what in fact *were* the socialization techniques used by the parents. It is not enough to have the parents' reports on their own behavior. We need real observations of their interaction with their own children.

5   We need to ascertain, in addition, whether the children *correctly* perceived what their parents' beliefs or values were. Obviously, if they saw them as very different from the parents' true beliefs, then the consequences of socialization might have been very different.[31]

[31]As Frank Furstenberg has shown in his extensive survey, "Transmission of Attitudes in the Family," (Ph.D. dissertation, Columbia University, 1967), Chap. 1, only a handful of researches on socialization have managed to obtain even most of these categories of information.

Because of these methodological problems, we cannot be certain that we have as yet discovered which factors are likely to cause a higher commitment to the values, norms, customs, and beliefs of the family, group, or society. We must, then, confront such findings with our own observations and consider further how they may be tested more adequately.

Factors in Effective Socialization

Here are some of the factors that have been reported to be especially important in effective socialization:

Warmth, nurturance, and affection from parents or other persons (teachers, peers) who are trying to socialize the child

Identification of the child with the parent or socializer

Authority of the parent

Consistency

Giving freedom to the child

Explanations and reasons

Punishment

Although we have been focusing more on the actions of parents, still other people will become significant others, or reference groups, as the child moves into play groups, the school, organized groups, the church, and jobs. Many people will eventually have some socializing effect on any individual, and we shall discuss those effects in a subsequent section. However, the factors listed above are likely to be of great importance later on, just as they are in the earlier family situation. Indeed, they are important in the processes of social control as well as those of socialization itself.

Since the possible impact of these factors is fairly clear, only a brief discussion of them is necessary.

Warmth, nurturance, and affection The extent to which parents are warm, nurturant, and affectionate toward the child is linked with several consequences. First, if the parents are loving, the child is also likely to love the parents, and thus to care about their wishes or feelings. Warm parents are more likely than others to be attentive to the needs of the child and thus to offer many rewards that will reinforce what they consider good behavior. The warm parent can more effectively arouse guilt or concern in the child by the withdrawal of love, while the hostile parent cannot use that potent weapon as easily. The child who perceives coldness or hostility has much less to lose by disobedience.

On the other hand, for effective socialization only a modest amount of nurturance or love is necessary. Phrased negatively, non-nurturant, cold, or hostile parents will not be very effective socializing agents, but there is no evidence that very intensive loving is more effective than ordinary warmth.

The effect of a warm relationship between parent and child is especially apparent when the father or mother uses the withdrawal of love as a mode of socializing the child. The effect is different from that of ordinary punishment, for punishment itself closes the sequence of acts and in effect wipes out the importance of the violation for the immediate present. Withdrawal of love is different, for then the child must *change* his or her behavior *before* being reinstated in the prior love interaction. Withdrawing love continues, then, until the child is good again. It has a more lasting effect, as a consequence.

Identification with socializers A warm, nurturant, affectionate relationship is also more likely to motivate the child to *identify* with the parent. Thus, what hurts the parent also hurts the child inwardly. When the child identifies with the parents, his or her pleasure in good behavior becomes pleasure in itself; the child thus takes pleasure in his

or her own goodness. Through the process of identification, the child takes on the duties of the parents; those role patterns become part of the child's personality. They are not merely what others press the child to do; by doing them the child feels fulfilled, for that demonstrates that the child *is* like his or her own adult models.

Authority New nations and new political regimes (as we note in Chapter 13) must face the problem of achieving authority, and so must parents and other socializing agents. Indeed, social commentators frequently complain that modern parents and teachers have lost their authority. This means that young people do not accept their *right to command*. Often, that state of affairs is contrasted with the commentators' childhood, when (they claim) children *did* obey their parents, teachers, and other authority figures.

Children are more likely to obey if their parents have authority, for in general people with influence and power are obeyed more. However, here we are focusing on the effect of authority on the child's *commitment* to the values of the group or society. Authority seems to have both an effect of its own and an especially strong effect when combined with warmth or affection. That is, the combination of love *and* power has a very great impact on the child's belief in or commitment to the values and norms of the group.

This factor can have little effect in the first year or so of the infant's life, since the question of the *right* to command simply does not arise. Parents can and do control the child physically. The problem of obedience becomes more important as the child's ability to move about improves and the parents begin to make more demands on the child (toilet training, keeping out of danger, not breaking things).

As in social interaction generally, authority must not be confused with willingness to use force. Indeed, the use of naked force by parents or other socializing agents is likely to increase simple obedience out of fear, but *decrease* the child's moral commitment to the rules.[32] In short, parents who justify their demands on the basis of strength merely cause the child to calculate how to avoid getting caught and hurt, rather than to accept the rules themselves.

In childhood, the most important element in parental authority is the ability of parents to convince the child that they stand for the moral community itself—what George Herbert Mead called the "Generalized Other"— so that the rules they lay down are not whimsical or selfish but part of the moral order of the universe. Punishment is not, then, an expression of personal anger or hostility. Rather, the parent is simply carrying out the rules of ethics, morality, religion, or justice. This is most effective when parents themselves obey those rules. It is also more effective when the parent would prefer *not* to punish but the rules themselves require it.[33] Thus, the child's disobedience and even the punishment are both viewed as hurting the parents; that is, the parents are *required* to do so, but do not want to do it.

Consistency The effect of authority is greater if the discipline by parents and other socializing agents is *consistent*, that is, if

punishments and rewards are usually forthcoming in accordance with the rules of the family or group. However, learning theory is somewhat complex on this point. First, it is impossible for parents to be completely consistent, because they simply cannot know all the things the child does throughout the day. Second, consistency can mean several different things: whether different socializing *agents* actually conflict with one another (father versus mother, parent versus teacher); whether *reinforcement* is contradictory (praise this time, punishment the next); whether reinforcement simply does not *always* occur (praise this time, no praise the next). These different ways of reinforcing will have different effects on the child's inner commitment.

Third, at least one form of inconsistency, being rewarded much of the time but *not* all the time (called an *intermittent reinforcement schedule* in psychology), is especially effective in creating a deeply held belief or attitude, which later experience will not easily erase. Readers will note this pattern (being rewarded or punished sometimes, but often not) is very common in childhood. Among its consequences is a continuing expectation of hope that if one is good, *this* time one will be rewarded; or an inner anxiety because when the child is tempted to violate a rule—precisely *because* the reinforcement *was* intermittent—the child can never feel sure of getting away with the violation.[34]

Freedom Giving freedom to the child increases the child's inner commitment, al-

---

[32]The types of families that Diana Baumrind calls Harmonious, for example, do not appear to use force, or even to assert authority; they seem to *have authority*, without ever needing to exercise control. On this point, see Diana Baumrind, *Early Socialization and the Discipline Controversy*, Berkeley: University of California, January 1974, p. 56 (prepared as a General Learning Press module); see also "Child Care Practices Anteceding Three Patterns of Preschool Behavior," *Genetic Psychology Monographs*, pp. 75 (1967), pp. 43–88.

[33]In the Indian tribe called the Zuñi, in the southwestern United States, parents take this process one step further, for rather than threaten the child themselves or assert their own authority, they constantly make clear that whatever punishment the child will experience will come from the spirits or the ruler of the cosmos.

[34]For the reader who is convinced that an absolutely consistent schedule of reinforcement is more effective for teaching a social pattern that is very difficult to erase later, consider our response to a mechanical device. If it works every time (or even every fifth time) but then at some point fails to work on schedule, we assume that the system itself has broken down, and we are likely to waste little time in continuing to press the lever that is supposed to start it. On the other hand, if the device works only now and then, we are likely to be optimistic that "this next time" it will start. This

though common sense might suggest the opposite conclusion (that is, that if the child is allowed to choose, it will violate the rule). However, readers can find some observations in support of our general assertion: For example, we are much more likely to *believe* in a rule if we have chosen it ourselves than if it has been imposed on us. This is, in fact, a powerful human pattern that underlies the continuing attractiveness and the social effectiveness of democracy once it has been established, for people do not easily give up a system in which they make their own rules. Much experimentation confirms the general rule that members of a group who make a decision together are more likely to believe in it and to follow it with action than are people who have a decision imposed on them.

Related to freedom is an important finding in learning research called the theory of *cognitive dissonance*.[35] It states essentially that if a person can be induced or persuaded to do something he or she did not really want to do, afterward the person becomes more committed to that choice (that is, the person has some freedom not to do something but decides to do it anyway). By contrast, strong threats and punishments, or even high rewards, will induce obedience, but they are not likely to change the child's attitudes. The child simply learns what actions will pay off better, without altering his or her opinion of what would be more desirable.

To be persuaded or induced to conform, without really wanting to do so, is a common childhood experience. As a conse-

quence, the child comes to see itself as the kind of person who does that sort of thing freely.

Thus, the pattern of (1) strong punishments or high rewards that leave little alternative is less effective than (2) being gently induced to conform without really wanting to do so. A third alternative (3), a truly *permissive* pattern in which the child is allowed his or her own way almost entirely, does not create much inner commitment to the rules. Then the child does not learn what others believe is desirable and sees no reason to care (since neither rewards nor punishments are linked with his or her behavior). Moreover, completely permissive parents are likely to persuade the child that they simply do not care what the child does and are neglectful of the child's interests.

Explanations and reasons Readers will already have noted that the foregoing factors or variables are reinforced by *communication*, by the explanations and reasons that parents or teachers may give the child. Both adults and children are more likely to accept rules as their own if others explain *why* the rules should be followed.

This result is partly caused by the elementary fact that giving reasons requires more social interaction, more social contact, and more caring between the person being socialized and the person doing the socializing. It thus persuades the individual that she or he is part of the rule-making process. Second, it links the *specific* rule with the larger system of moral rules and the community as a whole. Third, it helps the child to take the role of the other, for explanations show how this rule affects other people. It also gives esteem and respect to the child, for thereby she or he is treated not as a helpless person being commanded but as a person whose opinions are being considered. Giving explanations makes it easier, in

---

expectation system applies to many other areas of life, such as gambling and fishing. The infant does experience a consistent reward system at first, and later the child is rewarded only now and then.

[35]Leon Festinger, *A Theory of Cognitive Dissonance*, Evanston, Ill.: Row, Peterson, 1957. It is called *dissonant* because the individual feels an inconsistency or dissonance between his or her self-image and what he or she is actually doing.

short, for the child to understand that it is good to obey rules.

Punishment Punishment has many complex—and even contrary—effects on the socialization of children, and indeed its effects on even white rats are puzzling, too.[36] As we note in Chapter 5, punishment has very strong, lasting, crude, and negative effects. It does not teach the person to explore or to create, but much socialization consists in *prohibitions* anyway (not to play with matches, not to break things, not to hit one's brother).

Punishment is less *precise* than rewards, for it does not inform the child what is *right*. One can learn in a hundred instances that one is wrong, without ever learning what is right. Again, however, much socialization does not *aim* at precise prohibitions or avoidances. Groups and societies do not want the individual to calculate just how closely he or she can come to a violation or wrongdoing. Instead, any approach to a forbidden way should arouse fear, anxiety, and rejection.

Punishment is more effective when it is only a temporary phase that interrupts warmth or love. Indeed, if the parent-child relationship is affectionate, even nonreward may be experienced as punishment. Scolding from someone who is usually hurtful is more of the same old thing, and we do not suppose we could improve matters by much if we were to be virtuous. By contrast, a scolding from one who usually gives us love and cuddling is more painful, and we then are moved to reestablish that relationship by being better.

The *timing*, or *phasing*, of punishment, then, is important. Punishment has a greater impact if given at the moment of

misbehavior or just before, and it loses impact if it is delayed. If given later, the effect is to remind the child of the costs, rather than to persuade her or him that the misbehavior is simply *wrong* in itself. Punishment also has a greater effect if it is accompanied by explanations and reasons, for it is experienced as the outcome of the moral rules themselves.

Somewhat more intense punishment is more likely to increase the child's commitment; but if the punishment is *very* intense, it arouses much resentment and a rejection of the lesson being taught. Parents often face the problem of how to grade the intensity of the punishment they give to their children; and it is not common that parents are extraordinarily wise in these matters.

The loss of affection or respect is a nearly inescapable element in all punishment: It is very difficult for anyone to punish another without expressing anger, disesteem, or moral indignation. Thus, whatever *other* punishments are used, these emotional forces are also part of it.

All societies use some techniques for punishment, though many have used physical punishment only rarely. For example, even in the traditionally severe Japanese society, parents almost never whipped their children. On the other hand, (1) the mother was always close by, to see what the child was doing and to control him or her; and (2) parents and family used shaming techniques effectively. All societies impose many sexual and religious taboos, which are usually based on the punishments of social criticism, physical hurt, ridicule and shame, or the possible anger of the gods and spirits.

The social traits of responsibility, honesty, and sharing are rewarded in all societies. Responsibility and honesty are also reinforced by punishment for failure, since in both cases what is underlined is a *prohibition*. That is, the prohibition is against neglect or breakage and against lying. On the other hand, punishment is not

---

[36]For some of these effects, see Ross D. Parke, "The Role of Punishment in the Socialization Process," in Hoppe et al., eds., op. cit., pp. 81–108. See also the thoughtful review by R. L. Solomon, "Punishment," *American Psychologist*, 19 (1964), pp. 239–254.

used very successfully to persuade children that they should *achieve* at a high level or be creative.[37] Thus, we cannot simply say that the "virtues" are best reinforced by rewards, for most people rate honesty and responsibility as very worthwhile. The foundations of every social group and larger society are based upon a widespread set of prohibitions and avoidances: for example, not to hurt others, not to steal, not to break other people's possessions, not to kill, not to set fire to an enemy's house. Life would hardly be bearable if we did not build into the younger generation a deeply laid pattern of rejecting these antisocial behaviors.

We do not, in fact, know that the most *efficient* way of implanting these attitudes or values in children is through punishment, though in fact societies use it widely at the earlier stages of life for just those purposes. We cannot suppose that human societies have hit upon the most effective system of socialization. It may well be that people use punishment very widely simply because it seems to cost the *punisher* much less in time and energy than giving rewards, being patient, and staying close by to be sure the appropriate acts and behaviors are carried out.

NONFAMILY SOCIALIZING AGENTS

The principles and factors of socialization emphasized above do not lose their importance when we move from the family to the outside world, but the structure of the child's reality does. First, the sheer number of possible authorities increases to include older playmates, teachers, religious leaders, scoutmasters, music and athletic coaches, bosses and friends on the job, and important figures in the field of one's work.

[37]For a hypothesis about which early experiences affect the need to achieve, see B. C. Rosen, "Family Structure and Achievement Motivation," *American Sociological Review*, 26 (1961), pp. 574–585.

Figure 3-4 Many nonfamily socializing agents affect the role of *kibbutz* residents. (Willem van de Poll, Monkmeyer.)

Second, necessarily some of those authorities will try to get the child to be committed to values and norms that are in conflict with those of the family. Thus, to some extent the family socialization will be undermined at later stages of the child's growth.

Third, in some areas of activity the school, church, and family may instead reinforce one another, at least in the earlier years. This was especially true in small villages or societies of the past.

Fourth, as the child matures, the goals of the group or organization shift somewhat, from attempts to change the attitudes or norms of the individual to simply shaping his or her behavior by convincing the person that it is wiser or more rational to be virtuous or to live by the rules. In primary groups, members want each other to *believe*—to be committed to the same values. How others feel or believe is almost always important. Nevertheless, behavioral conformity may be enough in many situations.

Two consequences of the conflict among

socializing agents should be noted. One is that maturing children are less inclined to agree that any single agent has much *real* authority. Adolescents are quick to tell their parents that a respected teacher disagrees with the values of the family or that a political leader opposes what the parents wish. Thus, older children are less willing to agree that their parents have the *right to command*. It should also be emphasized, however, that this has been true of United States children for at least 150 years; they have generally felt freer to oppose their parents than European children feel.

Second, this conflict also generates a public competition among social institutions and agencies; each strives to capture the allegiance of the younger generation. That is, older children and adolescents are also shaping the behavior of adults. The sheer size of the teenage cohort makes it an impressive economic and political market (see Chapters 12 and 13). Many of the fads in this economic market (popular music, clothing, books and magazines) are determined by the political and social attitudes of the younger generation. The very survival of some institutions (for example, the church) is dependent on competing successfully for social authority. And since the voting age has been lowered, political candidates who aim at elections a few years away may wish to shape their policies so as to attract young people now and thus obtain their support later on. In short, social institutions, agencies, and individuals continue to try to socialize older children, and thus they must compete among themselves for the normative or value commitments of younger people. Thereby members of the younger generation gain more influence over their own development.

It is partly for these reasons that in most primitive societies the older generation did not worry much about whether their infants would be "successfully socialized." A Polynesian or Zulu child could not even imagine a "counter-Polynesian" or "counter-Zulu" way of life, while in the modern United States there are countless prophets who offer "counter-cultural" ideals and modes of living to the young. At present, the child in any industrial society as well as in any formerly "primitive" society can choose new authorities and can obtain some rewards for following their philosophies, as against that of the dominant group, class, or society. The child in most primitive societies of the past could not escape to a different group, could not encounter new prophets or preachers outside the group (occasionally one appeared within the group), and would not usually get payoffs for any deviations.

It has been widely noted that a high percentage of the students who were politically active in the late 1960s and early 1970s were not from the disadvantaged lower classes but from educated, liberal, middle-class families. Moreover, student rebellions were much more widespread at elite universities and colleges in the industrialized countries. Much analysis has been devoted to this relationship, but at least one central fact seems clear: The activist students were not genuinely *rebelling* against their parents' political or moral philosophy. They were rather attempting to manifest those philosophies through action. The battle was much less a fundamental disagreement about values or basic aims; it was more a countercharge by young people that their parents, and the whole society, had failed to live up to those values.[38]

Sociologically, a somewhat more interesting subgroup is found among contemporary children in various disadvantaged social strata of the United States. For example, black children of school age are much more likely now to express dissent from established val-

---

[38]With reference to the socialization dynamics within such families, see Baumrind, op. cit., p. 59, based on research done by J. H. Block, N. Haan, and M. B. Smith, "Socialization Correlates of Student Activism," *Journal of Social Issues*, 25, no. 4 (1969), pp. 143–177.

ues, as are some white ethnics, Indian children, Chicanos, and Appalachian children. What is most striking is that they are, unlike young people of college age from middle-class families, much less able to protect themselves from school authorities who find their negative attitudes objectionable. They are aware of the social turmoil of the past decade, and they often understand some of the major issues in this conflict. Black children, especially, are likely to know far more about race issues and specific black political leaders than do many white adults.

These children confront their own parents with a difficult dilemma. The parents worry about whether to encourage their children to continue rebelling against official doctrines, and thus to increase the chances that they will encounter hostility or punishment in school and outside, or to persuade them to conform, thus denying the reality and justice that are so clear in their minds. It seems likely that the present disadvantaged children will take a much more active role in attempting to redress what they view as the injustice of the larger society.

Thus, in contrast to most past societies, in which parents did not often worry that they were failing, many modern parents believe that they have lost authority and that they may be harming their children by inadequate or damaging modes of child rearing. It is doubtless for this reason that millions of books are sold annually on the general topic "How to Grow Children Successfully."

COLLECTIVE CHILD REARING

In our earlier discussion on socioemotional deprivation, we asserted that the harmful effects of institutional living do not always occur, because the developmental needs of children *can* be met adequately by collective child rearing if it is properly done. Public day-care centers have existed for half a century in France; collective living and child rearing have been practiced for still longer in the Israeli *kibbutzim*; and a complex system of day-care nurseries and schools has continued for decades in the U.S.S.R. The Israeli *kibbutzim* and the Soviet collective nurseries and schools especially have attempted to mold infants into loyal adult members of a communal society. A view of child rearing in the U.S.S.R. should help us to understand socialization better, since its aims in certain areas of activity are so different from those of the United States.[39]

As in the United States, the responsibility of rearing the younger generation wisely is thought to be an important task of both family and school in Russia. Children must be taught to be competent and loyal citizens. Public speeches refer to these tasks. Books on child rearing are sold in huge editions. However, some small and large differences in child-rearing patterns can be observed.

First, Soviet parents have more *physical* contact with their children. Mothers generally breast-feed their children, and both parents and older children are more likely than in the United States to hug little children. Second, relations with children are highly emotional, both in love and in criticism. Third, parents are more restricting. They are more concerned that their children will get into trouble or danger and do not allow as much freedom to do so. They are also more concerned about *other* children, and correct them far more than United States adults would consider proper.

Fourth, Russian parents expect and get more obedience from their children. Both in school and outside, children are expected to

[39]A thoughtful account of socialization in the *kibbutz* is that of Melford Spiro, *Children of the Kibbutz*, New York: Schocken Books, 1965. An extensive comparison of child rearing and the school system in the United States and the U.S.S.R. is that of Urie Bronfenbrenner, *Two Worlds of Childhood: U.S. and U.S.S.R.*, New York: Russell Sage, 1970. See also Jack and Barbara Tizard, "The Institution as an Environment for Development," in Richards, op. cit., pp. 137–152.

be disciplined. This philosophy is expressed by one Soviet source as follows:

Obedience in young children provides the basis for developing that most precious of qualities: self-discipline. Obedience in adolescents and older school children—this is the effective expression of their love, trust, and respect for parents and other adult family members. . . . We shall be asked: what about developing independence in children? We shall answer: if a child does not obey and does not consider others, then his independence invariably takes ugly forms. Ordinarily this gives rise to anarchistic behavior, which can in no way be reconciled with the laws of living.[40]

Soviet schools attempt to carry out these ideals and largely succeed.

In Russia some 10 percent of children under two years of age are in public nurseries, and about 3 to 6 percent of preschoolers, while 5 percent of school-age children are in boarding schools or prolonged daycare schools. Within these schools physical punishment is rare, reasoning and explanations are widely used, and praise is a frequent reward—not so much for doing one's task well as for trying harder or doing more than expected. Common punishments include both scolding (that is, dispraise) and loss of love.

Reinforcement schedules are based on behaviorist psychology, which is generally accepted in Soviet Russia. By eighteen months toilet training is completed, and toddlers are learning to dress themselves. Children are taught to be self-reliant in the sense of taking care of themselves. They are also given intellectual and aesthetic stimulation. Far from the traditional gloomy picture of "public institutions," these schools attempt to create an environment of affection as well as encouragement for growth.

[40]Bronfenbrenner, op. cit., pp. 10–11.

In any group of children some are mischievous at times. When that happens in Russia, the child is not likely to be punished. Instead, the teacher directs the attention of the class to one or two others who are doing *good* things.[41] In behaviorist terms, this means that bad behavior is not rewarded with attention (and should die out), while good behavior is praised and thus will be reinforced.

From the beginning, much stress is placed on *collective* doing and owning. This is linked with the general Soviet ideals of morality, service to the group, love of country, and sharing with others. Where possible, *competition* is collective. That is, children join together to outdo others in some service, such as cleaning up a playground. Thus, children identify with the group and put less stress on their *individual* success. Consequently, they also see achievement as requiring the help of others.

As children mature, they may "adopt" younger ones in the school, reading to them and serving them as escorts or teachers. They are given grades for this activity. Still more collectivistic, and reinforcing the influence of the group, is the practice of group criticism and evaluation. This practice has a built-in motivation, since often the group is punished as a unit when a member of it does something wrong—a system used in the United States armed forces as well. Those who misbehave, who are negligent or careless, may thereby threaten the group. As a consequence, the class may spend time in analyzing an individual's behavior and deciding what system to follow in both punishing the individual and improving the behavior. Aside from that attention to specific individuals, the class may at times engage in

[41]This is one of the reinforcement techniques that has been widely studied by Robert L. Hamblin and others in a variety of social settings, often with children who are especially disruptive, or who are apparently unable to learn. See Robert L. Hamblin et al., *The Humanization Processes: A Social, Behavioral Analysis of Children's Problems*, New York: Wiley, Interscience, 1971.

FOCUS

THE SCHOOL GROUP AS A SOCIALIZING AGENT*

Rewards are more common than punishments in Soviet schools, but classmates often make decisions about both. Here we observe how some classmates responded to boys who had done some unsupervised swimming (their parents had already promised to punish them).—W. J. G.

But punishment by the parents was only an ancillary penalty. The main disciplinary action, I learned, would take place at four that afternoon when the *soviet druzhina*, or executive council, of the school Pioneer organization would deliberate over Ivanov's case.

Let us attend the meeting. We find ourselves in the council room, an impressive chamber lined with banners and trophies. Around the large table, covered with a deep-red cloth, sit the elected members of the Council. . . . There are thirteen of them, nine girls and four boys, representing all classes from the fifth grade upward.

Ironically, Ivanov, as commander in the fifth grade class, is a member of the group. After completing the routine totaling of class points for the weekly standings in interclass competition in behavioral excellence, the Council turns to its special business. Ivanov is asked to stand and tell the group what he has done. The answer is barely audible, "I went swimming."

As his answers are written down by the secretary, a girl asks: "You and who else?"

He names seven others.

Second girl: "Fine thing, you the commander leading your men."

A boy: "Do you realize that last year a child drowned in that very pond?"

The questions and accusations continue, mostly from the girls. The major effort is two-sided: first, to impress Ivanov with the fact that, in violating the rule, he had jeopardized the lives of his classmates as well as his own; second, that his act constituted a betrayal of the faith invested in him as a Pioneer commander. Ivanov is now speechless. He trembles slightly and is struggling to hold back the tears. The direction of questions shifts: "Who suggested the idea of going swimming in the first place?" Silence. "Was it you?" Ivanov shakes his head. "Then who was it?" No answer.

One of the older girls speaks up. She is a ninth-grader and already a *Komsomolka*, or member of the Young Communist League. "All right, Ivanov, if you won't tell us, how would you like it if your whole class doesn't get to go on our five-day camporee next week?"

Another girl: "You will all just stay here and work."

*From Urie Bronfenbrenner, *Two Worlds of Childhood: U.S. and U.S.S.R.*, New York: Russell Sage, 1970, pp. 66–68.

Still another: "Think how the rest of your classmates will feel about you then."

Third girl: "Why punish the rest of the class? They didn't have anything to do with it."

Someone suggests punishing just the boys. Now the male council members, who have said very little, raise an objection. The full collective is responsible for the conduct of its members, they say. Besides, they argue, punishing only the boys would set up a division between the sexes, and that is against Communist principles!

Other measures are proffered. Someone suggests that the boys be restricted from swimming for the rest of the summer. Others feel that they should be disqualified from participation in summer camp. There is a proposal that they be given special chores to do during the vacation, such as watering trees. During this discussion, the adult leader of the Pioneers, who had come in some time after the session had started and had been listening attentively on the sidelines, asks for the floor. He suggests that it makes no sense to impose a punishment for the rest of the summer, since the offense itself will be forgotten and only the punishment remembered. As for finding the instigator, the rest of the offenders should be required to speak for themselves. "Let's call in the rest of them."

Seven boys file in. The previous procedure is repeated. Each one is asked if he participated in the swimming and each admits it. Then each is asked if he initiated the enterprise. All either deny it or refuse to answer. Again the Council members explain the seriousness of the offense and discuss possible punishments. Again there is talk of forbidding the boys to attend the five-day camporee, the school's major spring outing. Mention is also made of special work assignments. And one new idea is introduced. A girl member proposes that until further notice the boys be deprived of the privilege of wearing their Pioneer kerchiefs. The boys are having a hard time facing their accusers. Some bow their heads; others give in at the knees.

Again it is the adult leader who eases the pressure. Although his voice is stern, the effect of his remarks is to set aside one of the severe suggestions: "This is certainly a serious matter. I would recommend that all eight of the offenders be placed on strict probation for the coming week, and if any one of them deviates so much as a jot or a tittle from the code of proper conduct, he will be deprived of the privilege of attending the camporee."

The Council accepts the suggestion but in its final decision adds two further penalties. All the boys look up as sentence is passed in solemn instruction by Nadya, the Council President: "Ivanov, first of all, it is your responsibility to see to it that beginning on Monday, neither you nor any of your men are to wear your Pioneer kerchiefs." The President continues, "Second, during the coming week, while you are on probation, each of you is to carry out an extra work assignment by watering all the newly planted trees on the school grounds every day. Finally, before you go home this evening, all of you can scrub down and wax the floor in the school assembly."

When I left the school at 6:15, the last part of the sentence was being carried out, as the boys worked their way across the wide floor of the auditorium.

analyzing its *own* shortcomings and deciding on a course of action to remedy them.

As a consequence of these socialization patterns, deviation by an individual or a small group is seen as an emotional betrayal: They have shown a lack of concern or affection for their own comrades. Their friends, then, respond by withdrawing their respect and warmth. Such a system yields much security, social support, and satisfaction for the individual as long as he or she stays within the group and conforms to its rules. It also reduces considerably the amount of deviation from those rules. Within that system it is taken for granted that if an individual sees another doing something that is "antisocial"—for example, violating the rules, going off for an unsupervised swim, or failing to follow a schedule—he or she ought to report it. The child learns, in effect, that there is no satisfying way of life outside the group or against group rules.

Leaders are likely to be girls, and deviants are likely to be boys, but almost all children of both sexes gain esteem from others and achieve self-esteem by conforming to group rules. In Russia peers punish those who deviate; in the United States peers are more likely to support deviates, or at least to look away and refuse to inform teachers or other adults of the violation.[42]

Such a system of socialization creates a firm motivational foundation for a society that does not permit its citizens to travel freely outside the country, that punishes even trivial deviations like painting modern abstract pictures or writing satires on the leaders, or that does not permit even its own newspapers to publish "bad news" such as mine cave-ins or plane crashes. It is a society that has never understood the toughness and resilience of democratic practices, and perceives only the disorder and conflict that are so widespread where citizens are allowed to express their disagreement with their leaders or the government. Clearly, the average Soviet citizen is trained to be fearful that any individual deviation might undermine the system itself.

Though we may disapprove of that system, it does illuminate some of the processes of socialization. And we can see that it might give much security to most people in it. Although it seems to control its children more than is necessary to obtain political or social control, it does attempt to teach them it is more worthy to contribute to the common good than to calculate how to exploit others for one's own ends. We can understand some of its advantages without approving the system as a whole.

CLASS DIFFERENCES IN SOCIALIZATION PRACTICES[43]

For well over a generation, students of socialization have remarked on a wide range

[42]Jessie Pitts reports that French children will usually ally with school authorities by not cooperating with or supporting a deviant child. See "The Family and Peer Groups," in N. W. Bell and E. F. Vogel, *A Modern Introduction to the Family*, New York: Free Press, 1968, pp. 278ff. However, this is not because the school captures the allegiance of the French child.

[43]This section relies heavily on the work of Viktor Gecas, "The Influence of Social Class on Socialization," in W. R. Burr et al., eds., *Theories about the Family* (forthcoming).

of differences in the parent-child relationships of people in different social classes.[44]
Generally, this literature has asserted that
there were profound differences in the ways
middle-class and working-class parents
reared their children, and that these ways
affected the adult personality patterns and
social behavior of those who came from
such backgrounds. Among the findings or
assertions are that lower-class parents used
physical punishment more, were much more
restrictive in their control over children with
special regard to obedience, did not encourage them to use their own judgment, did
not train them to defer gratification in order
to achieve an important but later goal, and
were much more concerned with their authority than with teaching the child to become an independent adult.[45]

Let us now consider the differences that
have emerged with some consistency from
the data.[46]

One of the commonest claims in the literature on social class and socialization is that
lower-class parents use physical punishment
more in controlling their children. This observation also fits the middle-class stereotype of people in the lower classes as being
somewhat more violent. Present data bear
this finding out, but to only a very limited
extent. The relationship between class and
the use of physical punishment is weak and
highly variable. In most studies the difference is not statistically significant. Moreover, recent studies suggest a smaller difference than in studies of the past.[47] In simple
language, the difference may exist, but it is
a very small difference.

Melvin Kohn has suggested that it is less
important to know whether parents use
physical punishment than to know the conditions they feel *justify* the use of physical
punishment.[48] His data suggest that lower-
class parents are not likely to distinguish
carefully between a child's losing his or her
temper and becoming extremely wild in
play, for in both situations the child is likely
to do something that has bad consequences.
By contrast, the middle-class parent is concerned with the child's *intention* more than
with whether the behavior has actual destructive consequences.

This hypothesis was tested later by comparing the reaction of parents to the situation of intentional disobedience versus accidental breakage. Middle-class parents are
much more likely to use physical punishment for intentional disobedience than for
accidental breakage, since the latter situa-

[44]A recent summary of some of the *consequences* of
supposed class differences in socialization practices is
found in Margaret J. Lundberg, *The Incomplete Adult*,
Westport, Conn.: Greenwood Press, 1974. For an important summary of apparent class differences, and
some evidence that class differences in socialization
practices were diminishing over time, see Urie
Bronfenbrenner, "Socialization and Social Class
through Time and Space," in E. E. Maccoby, T. M.
Newcomb, and E. Hartley, eds., *Readings in Social
Psychology*, New York: Holt, 1958, pp. 400–425; and
"The Changing American Child—A Speculative Analy-
sis," *Journal of Social Issues*, 17 (1961), pp. 6–18. The
work of William H. Sewell is especially important for
an understanding of the impact of factors predicted by
psychoanalytic theory (for example, age of toilet train-
ing, weaning) on later personality patterns. See "Infant
Training and the Personality of the Child," *American
Journal of Sociology*, 58 (1952), pp. 150–159; and
"Some Recent Developments in Socialization
Theory and Research," *Annals of the American
Academy of Political and Social Science*, 349
(1963), pp. 163–173.

[45]For some parallel differences, based on the distinctions between parents who have a job in a bureaucracy
and parents whose work requires them to make independent managerial decisions, see D. R. Miller and
G. E. Swanson, *The Changing American Parent*, New
York: Wiley, 1958.

[46]The reader should keep in mind that the quality of
several hundreds of studies, published over some four

decades, varies greatly. Some of these studies are largely collections of anecdotes, while others are longitudi-
nal attempts to obtain reliable and valid observations.
In any event, the problems of research techniques are
great, since most findings have been based on parent
reports, not actual observation of natural behavior in
the home.

[47]Gecas suggests that class accounts for about 4 percent
of the variance in the parental use of physical punishment.

[48]Melvin L. Kohn, *Class and Conformity: A Study in
Values*, Homewood, Ill.: Dorsey, 1969.

tion was not intended. By contrast, lower-class parents distinguish much less between these two situations.[49] Studies of class differences in socialization practices have also suggested that middle-class parents are more likely to use reasoning or psychological techniques (such as shaming). Here the studies have been somewhat more consistent than with reference to physical punishment, though again the differences are not large.

In harmony with the general belief that working-class parents were more likely to use physical punishment and were less likely to be concerned with motive are the reported class differences in the *ideas* of what constitutes a "good child" or a "good mother." Various authors have suggested that the working-class parent prefers a child who is obedient and neat and does not get into any trouble, either with the parent or with outside authorities. The ideal child should not talk back.

By contrast, the middle- or upper-class parent is more likely to prefer a child who will understand the rules, and even disobey them if, in the child's moral judgment, the rules themselves are wrong. Correspondingly, the middle-class parent is thought to be less concerned with whether the child is neat or clean.

These differences are related to the life problems of people in these classes. Note, for example, that people who are poorer may have a somewhat greater problem in keeping their children neat and clean, and these middle-class values are thought to be worthy of emulation. These general differences have been summarized by the finding that middle-class parents are somewhat more willing to accept a generally equalitarian relationship between parents and children, while working-class parents are more in favor of an autocratic relationship between parent and child.

[49]See Viktor Gecas and F. Ivan Nye, "Sex and Class Differences in Parent-Child Interaction: A Test of Kohn's Hypothesis," *Journal of Marriage and the Family*, 36 (1974), pp. 742–749.

Parallel to the differences summarized above is the finding that middle-class parents are somewhat more likely to show emotional support and affection, or to be more attentive, helping, or willing to engage in play with the child, than are working-class parents. The findings are not uniform, and the differences are not large, but they are relatively consistent. Bronfenbrenner has asserted that in working-class families fathers are likely to be somewhat more affectionate and easygoing with their daughters, and mothers with their sons, whereas the sex differences are much smaller in middle-class parents.[50]

From the foregoing differences we would expect that middle-class parents are more likely to emphasize independence and achievement in their children than are working-class parents. This finding is generally confirmed in most of the studies that have focused on this issue.[51]

Over the past half-century thousands of commentators and presumed child experts have offered advice to American parents on how to rear their children. Over time, parents have become much more concerned about how they rear their children, and some evidence suggests that class differences have gradually decreased as the advice from experts becomes more widely known.

[50]See Urie Bronfenbrenner, "Toward a Theoretical Model for the Analysis of Parent-Child Relationships in a Social Context," in J. C. Glidewell, ed., *Parental Attitudes and Child Behavior*, Springfield, Ill.: Charles C Thomas, 1961, pp. 90–109.

[51]With reference especially to achievement motivation, see B. C. Rosen, "Family Structure and Achievement Motivation," *American Sociological Review*, 26 (1961), pp. 574–585. This finding is related, in turn, to the general difference in communication patterns between parents and children in different classes. It is not merely that middle-class parents talk to their children more, but that their communications are less likely to be simple commands or threats, and are more likely to contain reasons, explanations, and requests for obedience. That is, the nature of the communication itself suggests to the child that he or she is being encouraged to think independently and to make a judgment in the specific situation. Or, phrased somewhat differently, the middle-class parent emphasizes somewhat more the ideal of self-regulation.

On the other hand, as we have just noted, some persistent differences continue to emerge in the research literature, and these suggest that class differences in child rearing partly arise from the differences in life problems that parents face in different class positions, and from deep-seated differences in the values they hold.[52] It is evident that the differences we have noted are also likely to be associated with education, because formal education emphasizes both values and socialization practices that are more common in the middle class. Thus, the more education parents have, the closer are their socialization practices to those of the middle class. We can also suppose that as the level of education rises in the United States, some of these class differences will diminish.

On the other hand, as sociologists we can predict that as long as the life situations in different social strata are different, and thus parents must help their children to adjust to the different problems faced at those class levels, there will be persisting class differences in the socialization practices of parents, in this or any other country.

ADULT SOCIALIZATION

Although children do resist the forces of socialization, they are more easily molded than adults, and the most important part of socialization occurs before adulthood. Nevertheless, socialization is a continuous process, and the individual is not "completed" until death.

In Chapter 4 we note that everyone is constantly being evaluated for his or her qualities and performances and is being urged to live by the norms of the group.

[52]This difference has been stated by a number of analysts, but see especially Melvin L. Kohn, op. cit., p. 8. Kohn adduces data from several studies to show that in fact the values held by middle-class and lower-class parents do differ consistently, and that they are not to be explained by race, religion, national background, or community size.

New situations arise for which previous social learning has not adequately prepared us, and we must adjust with whatever personal resources we command. In addition, others continue to try to shape our behavior and norms or to improve our character in ways they would prefer. In short, people try to socialize us from birth to the end of our life.

For many of the situations that develop in adulthood we are partly prepared by *anticipatory socialization*. That is, we are socialized for a social role before we have any opportunity of trying it out. For example, consider George Herbert Mead's observation that the child plays various adult roles, such as "daddy," "truck driver," or "nurse." Even the toddler has already learned some of the behavior required in that role, and knows how to carry out part of it.

Direct teaching occurs, too, at every stage of life. The child is told that he or she will grow up some day and become a parent or work at a job, and is also told about some of the responsibilities to be assumed in the future. Children are told what is proper adult behavior when a friend or kinsman dies. By watching and imitating, by engaging in playacting a role, or by being explicitly taught, people experience some anticipatory socialization long before they actually have the opportunity to assume the full responsibilities of a social position.

Less is known about adult socialization than about childhood socialization because it has been studied less. It also presents some subtle difficulties of observation. For example, how much change in norms, attitudes, and values actually occurs in adulthood? We can assume that adults are trying to change the *inner* commitments of children, but in adulthood people may be simply trying to change others' behavior. Do the efforts at changing others' *behavior* also change their *attitudes* just the same?

Certainly people's *behavior* changes as they learn the rules of a new job, a club, or a community, but little of this requires any basic changes in their values or norms.

Some attitude changes occur with age; for example, people become somewhat more conservative politically and socially. But does this occur because of socialization? From personal experience we know that we can adjust to a new social position without altering either our personality or our norms. Consequently, we cannot suppose that behavioral changes in other people prove that they have become committed to different values or norms.

However, most sociologists define the general processes of socialization as including *all* the ways by which we learn new roles. Thus, we need not separate carefully value or normative changes from behavioral ones. We can focus on any processes by which adults are pressed to learn new roles.

This broad view of adult socialization is also justified by an important social regularity: Nearly all the more effective techniques for social control are also used when the aim is to get others to become committed to new values and norms. Moreover, in much adult socialization those who are trying to teach others how to act in new social roles do not ordinarily distinguish between these two aims: They seek to change both inner values and outward behavior. Where the two aims are distinguished at all (such as in training for the priesthood), and a greater emphasis is put on inner changes, the social arrangements for social learning are somewhat different (for example, more social isolation, fewer resources permitted to the trainee, more training time devoted to beliefs).

If we examine our own experience, we can see that we undergo both processes as adults. To make a trivial case, if we join a social group or a stamp-collecting club, we have to learn the technical rules of when people meet and where, how people dress, who are the leaders—in short, all the "microsocial patterns" to which we must adjust. However, very soon we are likely actually to *feel* annoyed or indignant when a fellow member violates a rule or ignores the inter-

ests of the group in favor of his or her own. That is, we do more than merely learn the rules as a kind of social map; we also accept the rules inwardly—they become part of our selves.

It is also obvious that in adulthood as in childhood people do care about others' commitment to values and norms, because it is widely assumed that if others are committed to the "right" values they are more likely to act in approved ways. They can be trusted more; that is, people assume others will do the "right thing" even if no one is watching. If people are committed, we suppose they will obey the rules even if their profits or payoffs are not high. On the other hand, as we have emphasized, no social system or group relies *only* on normative or value commitment. There are always social control mechanisms for observation and for handing out rewards or punishments for acceptable or inacceptable behavior.

The most important generalization about adult socialization is that the broad principles of learning we analyzed earlier apply here as well. People are quicker to acquire the new roles if the socializing agents are warm and welcoming and if they have more rather than less authority. They also learn more quickly if the socializing agents offer reasons, explanations, and corrective information; if they themselves live by the rules; and if most fellow members also follow the rules. If rewards and punishments are handed out in accord with the rules, that is a further support for socialization. Adults may be less easily shaped than children, but the processes of social learning are not basically different.

Differences between Adult and Childhood Socialization

In an industrial society adult socialization is different from childhood learning in two important ways, which have many further consequences. First, most of it is *specific* to a particular role, and thus the people who try

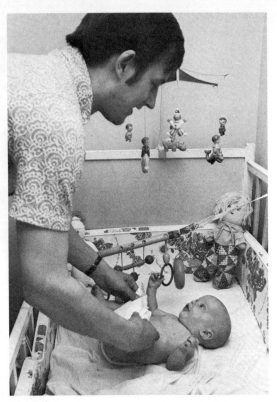

Figure 3-5 A common experience of adult socialization is that of the young adult learning the new role of parent. (Erika, Peter Arnold.)

to socialize the individual for one role may have only a mild interest in what that person does in another. Fellow employees tell the newcomer what the rules on the job are, but they usually have only a gossipy interest in telling him or her how to act as a parent. Phrased differently, the family, school, and church try to shape the child as a whole person, but this is much less so for the adult.

The second basic difference is that the adult has far more resources with which to resist the socialization pressures of others. Except for the role of parent, adults can change their social links with specific others. Unlike children, adults have some economic resources, and they can more effectively resist (even with force) the efforts of others to coerce them into changing their

ways. No one fully succeeds, but the potential for resistance means that adult socialization is not as likely to change the individual in fundamental ways.

These differences affect the cost calculations of individuals or groups as to whether the investment necessary to change the adult is really worthwhile. The most extreme form of adult socialization is perhaps the political "brainwashing" of prisoners in some repressive nations.[53] By coercion, bribes, threats, and deprivations, prison authorities attempted to reduce the prisoner to a helpless, isolated child. They succeeded with some prisoners, but never on a large scale. Even when many prisoners bent somewhat to these forces, most resisted any full-scale change. Most importantly, however, the amount of personnel, time, and energy needed is too great to make these efforts worthwhile, except for temporary propaganda goals.

The investment is viewed as justified, by contrast, where the aim is to train selected, willing recruits for a demanding occupation. The more the norms and behaviors required of the occupation are different from those of average people, the more likely it is that recruits are separated from other social influences, taught by influential authority figures, and asked to live a time-consuming schedule—and are also informed of the high rewards that eventually await them. This occurs, for example, in training for the priesthood or religious orders, for the medical profession, and for a military career.[54]

[53]This was done, for example, in the Korean war by the Chinese, who attempted to persuade their Allied prisoners to become communists. They succeeded with some United States prisoners. On this process see Robert J. Lifton, "Methods of Forceful Indoctrination," in Maurice R. Stein et al., eds., *Identity and Anxiety*, New York: Free Press, 1960, pp. 480–492. For an analysis of the Nazi concentration camps, see Bruno Bettelheim, "Individual and Mass Behavior in Extreme Situations," *Journal of Abnormal Psychology*, 38 (1943), pp. 417–452.

[54]See Erving Goffman, "Characteristics of Total Institutions," in Stein et al., eds., op. cit., pp. 449–479. Of

On the other hand, most adult socialization requires much less investment from the individual or group. It focuses on learning technical rules, ways of carrying out tasks, or local customs of a group, or simply on the acquisition of a well-known role such as grandparent, neighbor, or retired worker. In any case, it is clear that when the adult willingly submits herself or himself to a program of social learning and thus resists less, the costs of socialization are less, and organizations or groups are willing to invest more in that training.

Adult Socialization in Primitive Societies

Critical readers will perhaps ask, What of adult socialization in most primitive societies? Although some were kingdoms (for example, the Ashanti or Dahomey in West Africa), in most the population was small, most social relations were determined by kinship and thus were not open to much change, and interaction was not specific or segmental but involved the whole person (see Chapter 6 on primary groups). Thus, adult socialization would appear to be different from that in industrial society. Yet adults did go through successive statuses as they grew older; some became magicians, priests, or chiefs, and almost everyone assumed the role of spouse and parent. That is, they did enter new roles in adulthood.

Adult socialization in most primitive societies differed from that in a modern society, and both differ from childhood socialization. First, there were far *fewer* new roles to enter than in an industrial society. Thus, there were fewer new positions to enter for which the individual had not been prepared by earlier socialization. Second, the *amount* of difference between one life phase and the next in primitive society was much less, so that the amount of social learning needed for changes in adulthood was much less. Since, moreover, there were few if any alternative or competing moral authorities, few situations for specialized, intensive socialization were created in which recruits were separated from outside influences.[55] That is, in general, it was assumed that any adult *was* adequately socialized, while the older people who were the keepers of wisdom were there to give additional advice or learning when necessary.

On the other hand, as in childhood socialization, other members of the primitive group or society had an interest in any person's development, since everyone interacted with everyone else. The behavior of anyone was visible to almost anyone else, and fellow members were concerned about the whole person, not simply his or her behavior in a narrow, specific role.

All those influences, without any alternatives for escape or any countercultural authorities, were once thought to produce (as the French sociologist Emile Durkheim believed) a kind of mechanical uniformity among members of a primitive society. That is, everyone fully accepted all the traditional norms, values, and customs, and everyone thought alike. In fact, however, everyone begins with a somewhat different personality potential, and every child's experiences are somewhat different, so that common pressures or influences in a primitive tribe did not have the same outcome.

More importantly, adults in primitive societies, too, always had personal resources of esteem, courage, or goods with which to resist others' attempts to mold them, while such societies had to eventually accept almost everyone as he or she was, or as he or she became. Thus, not everyone was shaped

---

course, mental patients are much less willing recruits, but many processes are similar. See Erving Goffman, *Asylums: Essays on the Social Situation of Mental Patients and Other Inmates*, Chicago: Aldine, 1961; Garden City, N.Y.: Doubleday, Anchor, 1961.

[55]Some notable exceptions were the witch-doctor training among the Azande, the teaching of genealogies among the Maori, or the male camps for warriors among the Zulu.

or molded into a mechanical likeness of everyone else. As adults, some had visions that changed their lives. Some became wise old women and men or successful rebels, while others became lazy and incompetent. In short, in primitive societies, too, some social learning took place in adulthood, and the individual made unique, personal adjustments to the new roles he or she assumed over the life cycle.

FINAL COMMENT: INTENDED AND UNINTENDED EFFECTS OF SOCIALIZATION

Primary groups and formal organizations devote some attention to the socialization of adults because they want new members to carry out their role obligations well, whether as factory manager or as new resident of an old-age home. However, as in all socialization, what people actually learn is likely to be somewhat different from what was intended. Children may learn some arithmetic in school, but they are certain to learn that the classroom is a *competition* and that losers are disesteemed; that children who are polite and seem middle-class get better treatment from the teacher; and that order is considered more important than creativity.

In adulthood, too, socialization may produce some unintended effects. Preparation for the role of teacher, for example, stresses the subject matter of the classroom (history, music), but some of the *by-products* of fitting that role are very different. A thoughtful sociologist of education has pointed out some of the unfriendly descriptions of what this experience does to teachers:

There is first that certain inflexibility or unbendingness of personality. . . . That stiff and formal manner into which the young teacher compresses himself every morning becomes . . . a plaster cast. . . . In his personal relationships the teacher is marked by reserve, an incomplete personal participation . . . and a lack

of spontaneity. . . . One who has taught long enough may wax unenthusiastic on any subject under the sun. . . . The didactic manner, the authoritative manner, the flat, assured tones of voice that go with them, are bred in the teacher by his dealings in the school room where he rules over the petty concerns of children as a Jehovah none too sure of himself.[56]

So, similarly, Waller suggests, adult socialization affects people in other occupations as well:

The lawyer and the chorus girl soon come to be recognizable social types. One can tell a politician when one meets him on the street. Henry Adams has expanded upon the unfitness of senators for being anything but senators; occupational molding, then, affects the statesman as much as lesser men. . . . Perhaps no occupation that is followed long fails to leave its stamp upon the person.[57]

Many of the effects of socialization in childhood or adulthood are unintended, and a high percentage of these are destructive. The ghetto child learns at an early age what the teacher did not intend, that is, that he or she cannot succeed. The underprivileged adult learns that he or she is not likely to earn much respect for anything he or she will do, and is thus not encouraged even to try very hard. A generally punitive environment does not teach precise lessons, but crude ones of avoidance. Similarly, the mental patient or an old person in a home for the aged is taught the rules for adjustment, but in addition comes to understand the hopelessness of trying to maintain his or her dignity and unique selfhood under those rules.

Adult socialization teaches people, then, to take on new duties and to embrace new opportunities as they mature and age. However, not all roles and social positions make

[56]Willard Waller, *On the Family, Education, and War,* William J. Goode, Larry Mitchell, and Frank Furstenberg, eds., Chicago: University of Chicago Press, 1970, pp. 287–288.

[57]Ibid., p. 284.

life pleasanter or richer. Much adult socialization requires people to learn the rules of demeaning positions—how to show appropriate respect to the better-off or how to reduce their poverty somewhat by solving the puzzles of welfare bureaucracy. Part of adult socialization is learning that one's high

hopes for advancement will never become reality, and that most others will not be much concerned about it. Any social system offers new positions and roles to adults as they go through life, but adjusting to those roles is often a trying rather than a rewarding experience.

READINGS

Diana Baumrind, *Early Socialization and the Discipline Controversy,* Morristown, N.J.: General Learning Press, 1975.

Nancy Bayley and E. S. Schaefer, *Correlations of Maternal and Child Behaviors with the Development of Mental Abilities: Data from the Berkeley Growth Study,* Society for Social Research in Child Development Monograph, vol. 29, ser. 97, Chicago: Child Development Publications, 1964.

J. A. Bowlby, *Attachment and Loss,* New York: Basic Books, 1969.

Orville G. Brim and Stanley Wheeler, *Socialization after Childhood,* New York: Wiley, 1966.

Urie Bronfenbrenner, *Two Worlds of Childhood: U.S. and U.S.S.R.,* New York: Russell Sage, 1970.

Ernest Q. Campbell, *Socialization: Culture and Personality,* Dubuque, Iowa: Wm. C. Brown, 1975.

John A. Clausen et al., *Socialization and Society,* Boston: Little, Brown, 1968.

Hans P. Dreitzel, ed., *Childhood and Socialization: Recent Sociology No. 5,* New York: Macmillan, 1973.

Glenn Elder, *Children of the Great Depression,* Chicago: University of Chicago Press, 1974.

Erik H. Erikson, *Childhood and Society,* 2d ed., New York: Norton, 1963.

John Flavell, *The Developmental Psychology of Jean Piaget,* Princeton, N.J.: Van Nostrand, 1963.

E. Z. Friedenberg, ed., *The Anti-American Generation,* Chicago: Aldine, 1971.

D. G. Gil, *Violence against Children,* Cambridge, Mass.: Harvard, 1970.

William J. Goode, "Force and Violence in the Family," in Suzanne K. Steinmetz and Murray A. Straus, eds., *Violence in the Family,* New York: Dodd, Mead, 1974.

———, Elizabeth Hopkins, and Helen M.

McClure, *Social Systems and Family Patterns,* Indianapolis: Bobbs-Merrill, 1971.

Mary Ellen Goodman, *The Culture of Childhood: Child's-Eye Views of Society and Culture,* New York: Teachers College, 1970.

Robert L. Hamblin et al., *The Humanization Processes: A Social, Behavioral Analysis of Children's Problems,* New York: Wiley, Interscience, 1971.

David R. Heise, ed., *Personality and Socialization,* Chicago: Rand McNally, 1972.

Ronald A. Hoppe, G. A. Milton, and E. C. Simmel, eds., *Early Experiences and the Processes of Socialization,* New York: Academic, 1970.

Jerome Kagan and H. A. Moss, *Birth to Maturity: A Study in Psychological Development,* New York: Wiley, 1962.

Melvin L. Kohn, *Class and Conformity: A Study in Values,* Homewood, Ill.: Dorsey, 1969.

Margaret J. Lundberg, *The Incomplete Adult,* Westport, Conn.: Greenwood Press, 1974.

George Herbert Mead, *Mind, Self, and Society* (1934), New York: Morris, 1962.

A. S. Neill, *Summerhill: A Radical Approach to Child Rearing,* New York: Hart, 1960.

Jean Piaget, *The Moral Judgment of the Child* (1932), New York: Free Press, 1948.

Martin P. M. Richards, ed., *The Integration of a Child into a Social World,* New York: Cambridge, 1974.

David A. Schultz, *Coming Up Black: Patterns of Ghetto Socialization,* Englewood Cliffs, N.J.: Prentice-Hall, 1969.

Arlene Skolnick, "The Construction of Childhood," and "Socialization: Generational Politics," in *The Intimate Environment,* Boston: Little, Brown, 1973, pp. 313–354, 355–394.

Melford Spiro, *Children of the Kibbutz,* New York: Schocken Books, 1965.

Edward Zigler and Irvin L. Child, eds., *Socialization and Personality Development,* Reading, Mass.: Addison-Wesley, 1973.

CHAPTER FOUR

PRESTIGE
AS A CONTROL SYSTEM

Machiavelli's sixteenth-century how-to-do-it book, *The Prince*, instructs the ruler when the cool application of force is useful; but it is often forgotten that much of that manual suggests many techniques for persuading subjects that their prince is honorable, righteous, and protective of his people, that is, *deserving of respect*.

On a less exalted plane, we can observe the importance of prestige or respect in daily life.[1] People who enjoy more respect are also more likely to become heads of their organizations, to elicit cooperation from others, to obtain desirable social invitations, or to be promoted earlier. Organizations that are widely respected can recruit abler employees. Consequently, people are likely to alter their behavior so as to accu-

mulate prestige, if the cost is not too great. For example, all of us refuse at times to engage in acts that would yield money but decrease our prestige. Indeed, most studies of social influences on productivity show that groups of workers set an output standard below and above which an individual is punished by a loss of group respect. If we feel we have earned some prestige by having performed well, but others have not shown it by the appropriate tokens of respect—such as promotions, leadership posts, medals and scrolls, or simply compliments or pats on the back—we feel hurt and indignant. A goodly part of our own conversations during the day consists in rating others with respect to their various acts and qualities, or stating how much respect or prestige we think they deserve. Some evaluation, to be sure, is not verbal but is shown in gestures or emotionally toned monosylla-

[1]This chapter is partly based on materials in my monograph *The Celebration of Heroes: Prestige as a Control System* (forthcoming).

bles; but it is clear that we are constantly observing and evaluating others by reference to our view of how people *ought* to act; and we alter our own behavior so as to gain or keep the esteem of others.

We can begin, then, with an easily available range of observations about the utility of having a higher rather than a lower rank in prestige or respect; costs and contingencies in obtaining it; how one can lose it; and how pervasively it shapes social action. However, before analyzing more systematically the processes of prestige allocation, we should note that ordinary social life does not offer an accepted rhetoric or vocabulary for talking about these processes. We can speak about getting a promotion or a raise, or about the accumulation of property over time, more easily than we can comment that our prestige has risen. We read of the President's "loss of popularity," when a moment's thought will tell us that it is more likely the nation's respect for his performance has dropped. We can perceive that the black chant of the 1960s *I am somebody* is not only a demand for more respect, but a claim that one has already earned it; yet common language has no accepted forms for talking about these processes. Ordinarily, if we use the term "prestige" we do so mainly with reference to very high posts or distinguished careers, great discoveries or works of art, or perhaps families of high distinction.

On the other hand, because the processes of prestige are pervasive, we have ample opportunity to observe them. Consequently, we shall refer to esteem or respect in ordinary experience. Let us note some common forms for such evaluations, before examining the process of prestige allocation more systematically.

Common Examples of Prestige or Esteem Evaluations

Dissident wife to husband: "Stop treating me like a servant!"

Principal's announcement to the school: "Our team has brought great honor to our school."

Clique member, discussing a possible political nomination: "What's he ever done for this community?"

Manager, considering a new person who might join the firm: "What's his reputation?"

Parent in solemn talk with child: "Our family has always been respected in this neighborhood; we don't do such things."

Informal leader, on being told to approach Mr. X for help: "I can't just call him out of the blue; he's a big shot and doesn't even know me."

Advice from older employee to young, ambitious one: "If you're pushing for that kind of job, you'd better prove yourself first, show what you can do."

From a close friend: "If your friends find out what you've done, they'll never speak to you again."

PRESTIGE ALLOCATION

An important foundation of all social action, and thus of both economic and prestige systems, is a set of group or individual evaluations that prescribe what anything is "worth," that is, how desirable it is. We can ascertain what these evaluations are, how intensely people feel about them, and whether there is consensus within a group concerning any of them, by straightforward observation or survey techniques.

As we noted in earlier chapters, to know people's values and norms is not an adequate basis for predicting what they will do, but it does at least tell us what they would prefer to do if they had the opportunity, or were not prevented from doing it. People may not act in conformity with a norm they hold, because they may give a higher priority to still other norms; or they may instead decide that other people will reward them more for an alternative course of action or punish them for following this norm. Nevertheless, if we know how much an individual or a group values a social pattern, a behavior, an action, a goal, or a response from someone, this does at least give us the direction the person or group would probably go if no other pressures entered.

Except for very short periods of time, no social system can be based upon the assumption that its members are saints and heroes; and as a consequence, an examination of the values and norms of any group will disclose that though the group may exhort its members to live up to an "ideal," in fact there is almost always an accepted average, or "working ideal," by which members are expected to measure their own behavior and that of others.[2]

Since all societies rank both ascriptive and achieved performances, they also grant prestige or esteem for both. Performances or qualities at the average, or working, level yield no more than the continued acceptance of the group; below that the individual will encounter negative approval or disrespect.

However, not all performances and qualities are *finely* ranked from denigrating to admirable. In some activities we are only roughly graded, and unless we are extreme in our behavior, most of us earn about the same amount of respect. These might be called the "small virtues," such as being a good parent or being a helpful or kindly neighbor.

Certain other qualities and performances are not graded very finely, either, but if one goes much beyond the working ideal, the performance or quality is no longer viewed as admirable, heroic, or saintly, but instead

as neurotic, obtrusive, or annoying. For example, any group has an acceptable level of cleanliness; below that, one is considered "dirty." Above the acceptable level, one may receive modest admiration; but at a still "higher" level, one is likely to be viewed instead as silly.

In some contexts it is necessary to note carefully *whose* ideal one is following. In many work groups, to perform much beyond the norm does not earn the admiration or approval of one's fellow workers, but their enmity and dispraise. By contrast, one's superiors may give praise. This is not, however, an important conceptual distinction; it is rather a significant empirical one. We are required, then, to specify at times *which* group ideals are being used as the criterion by which to measure prestige.

Thus, for the purposes of our analysis, *prestige* is the esteem, respect, or approval that is granted by a collectivity or an individual for above-average performances or qualities.[3]

These qualities and performances may take a variety of concrete forms. For example:

An individual may make a *contribution* to a group by sacrificing her or his life or by paying for religious rituals.

A person may generate respect or esteem for *achieving* an above-normal level of performance in an area that is highly valued by a particular group or collectivity: winning a track meet, splitting the atom, singing a Bach cantata brilliantly, or making a suitably inflammatory speech in the early stages of a successful revolution.

Prestige, negative or positive, may also be granted for qualities with which the individual is *endowed* by birth, such as mem-

[2]For the distinction between these types of ideals, see William J. Goode, "Norm Commitment and Conformity to Role-Status Obligations," *American Journal of Sociology*, 66 (November 1960), pp. 246–258. See also Marion J. Levy, *The Structure of Society*, Princeton, N.J.: Princeton University Press, 1952, pp. 157–166.

[3]We must also not forget that the definition ignores the obvious but theoretically trivial exception; for example, it could be argued that being born with six green legs is "above the norm" of two pink ones, but it is empirically ascertainable that this is not a desired or approved trait.

bership in an ethnic group, nobility, or perhaps musical genius.

Some qualities that are approved or disapproved may be *acquired* without achievement, such as age or various physical or mental disabilities.

Generally, to exhibit approved qualities or performances above the average overlaps to some degree with contributions to the group, since a group shares somewhat in the prestige that one of its members receives.

The conceptually acute reader will perceive that we have not presented a definition, but have postulated an empirical regularity. In its purely definitional form, it would be circular: A group pays prestige, that is, approval or esteem, for the things it respects or approves. The term is partly indefinable and primitive, like many other terms that ultimately refer to feeling tones ("hate," "love," "awe"). On the other hand, since these responses *are* part of our personal experience and *do* lie within our common observation, it is unlikely that we will be handicapped much in analyzing this social behavior.

That prestige is not merely an individual or idiosyncratic response is especially visible when awards, prizes, honors, scrolls, or trophies are handed out in formal ceremonies. The rhetoric of presentation clearly emphasizes these group consequences of high achievement:

1 Group values have been affirmed because members get some gratification from the achievement.
2 The performances prove that the ideals have not been set so unrealistically high as to make them illusory; that is, their relevance for actual behavior is confirmed.
3 The awards prove that if others will aspire and achieve, they too will be honored in the future.

4 Members of the group decide who will get the awards, and thus validate the prestige of the people being honored.
5 Those who get the prizes typically announce that lesser-ranked group members "all contributed their part" and thus have a right to share in the prestige.

Another group aspect of prestige as social control can be seen in the social pressures on the individual to respond with esteem to the *right kinds of achievements or qualities*. From our earliest childhood, people around us approve if we give the "right" evaluations, and they correct us if we are "wrong." If we like what others consider vulgar, ugly, immoral, or incompetent, then parents, friends, and teachers give us less approval. Thus, not only do we learn how we ourselves are supposed to act, or which norms we are supposed to obey, but we are also socialized to respond appropriately to *others'* behaviors, traits, and activities.

As in all social behavior, it is the individual who acts or responds, but these apparently personal responses not only are maintained by the groups within which the person acts and lives, but they initially were generated and created by such groups. In the socialization process during infancy, childhood, and even adulthood the individual was taught to respect such achievements or qualities—and to want approval itself.

It is useful to make a further distinction, that between a prestige *response* and the *act* of overtly paying prestige or respect. For various reasons an individual may hide the admiration felt for another person's work or performance. Similarly, we can and do sometimes pay more deference or respect than we actually feel. The empirical fact that the inner prestige response does not always correspond with the overt deference or respect shown underlines the possible importance of manipulation, or *subversion*. Since improving our performances may be tedious, difficult, or even impossible—a fact that does not reduce our wish to be respected by others—we may be tempted to engage in public relations techniques that range from oblique hints to outright lying in order to persuade others that we deserve more esteem than our achievements might justify. On the other hand, because everyone has a stake in who is respected more or less, others may expend some energy in penetrating our rosy presentation of self, or exposing our fraud.

In examining the allocation of prestige, we must also be alert to the *contingencies* or accidents in all moral and occupational careers. Some people's achievements or excellent qualities may not become known to others for various reasons. In contrast, the performances of other individuals may be given great prominence by design or by accident. In such instances the amount of respect or deference that is publicly expressed may correspond with people's inner prestige response, but it may be greater than the achievement would have obtained had it occurred under different historical circumstances.

Manipulation of Prestige

We are primarily concerned with the extent to which people alter their behavior in response to respect or disrespect, anticipated or actual. We have just noted that many contingencies affect the overt expression of esteem or disesteem, and there are many possibilities of manipulation and insincerity. It is therefore important to consider both the extent to which people are *conscious* in their efforts at controlling others and how widespread various forms of *manipulation* may be. Here is a summary of observations, subject to the later correction that empirical investigation may disclose:

1 Most expressions of respect are not only genuine but unthinking; that is, whatever esteem people express, they actually feel, and they do not express it with the conscious thought of influencing others.

2 Some individuals are frequently conscious or even Machiavellian about giving praise (or dispraise) to others as a way of obtaining their own goal, whether that is general approval from other people or some specific benefit.

3 At the opposite pole, there are very few true "innocents" who almost invariably respond spontaneously with praise or blame without being the least conscious about which of those statements have favorable or unfavorable effects on their own plans or others' behavior, because of the counterresponses of others.

4 All people are at times conscious of these effects on others, and thus all try from time to time to affect others' behavior consciously by giving or withholding praise or blame.

5 In some situations this consciousness is very salient, especially in anger or when an individual is disappointed. Then, people may indeed count up whether they have been paid appropriately, or whether they are giving more respect than the other person deserves. When people get about as much esteem as they think they deserve, they are less conscious of how they are themselves affected by praise; and the person who praises them is not forced to be as conscious about the control results of his or her praise. We can express this by saying that there is a "floor" to the level of praise that individuals feel is appropriate, below which they may become very conscious of how much they "deserve" or how much they are giving, but there is a much less firm "ceiling." That is to say, if people get a good bit more respect than they feel they deserve, they are much less prone to be guilty about deserving the praise than they are to be indignant when they get far too little.

6   Expressing approval or respect without feeling it—that is, dissimulation or insincerity—is likely to have some effect on others, just as failure to express approval will, whether or not that failure is intentional and actually hides a real approval. Both types of dissimulation will have some effect, though it is much less when the target is sure that the praise, dispraise, or nonpraise is not what the other person really feels.[4]

7   Similarly, as noted earlier, people may correctly penetrate the dissimulation, and they also have a strong motivation to do so. Experimental evidence suggests that false praise, even correctly perceived as false, may nevertheless have some control effect over the target person. Just how much is a question that still must be determined by empirical investigation.

8   Some social transactions will be unsuccessful unless people can to some extent penetrate others' conscious attempts at dissimulation. For example, one person may follow good form by openly stating his or her admiration but may fully intend that the other individual should know that this was merely correct form, and not sincere. For the smooth unfolding of some social transactions, the penetration of double dissimulation is required. For example, a common pattern of flirtation occurs when both intend that the other should know that each means the *opposite*, as when a woman and man engage in ironic verbal or other symbolic attacks on each other, both intending that the other should understand that this means each is attracted to the other.

The most crucial observation is, however, that the amount of consciousness or even calculation in the use of respect or esteem to control others does not usually determine whether others will conform. Individuals vary from one moment to the next in their alertness to how much effect their expressions of respect will have on others. People have a strong motivation to perceive respect or disrespect and are likely to respond to it (negatively or positively) whether or not the other person intended to affect behavior or feelings.

A Triadic Relationship

Our analysis up to this point leads us to the important conclusion that although people who hand out honors, medals, or awards include in their speeches some reference to "how much we owe" the person being honored, and people do feel indignant if they are paid less respect than they feel that they have "earned," the prestige or esteem relationship is essentially *not* dyadic. It is not a relationship in which one person does something for another, which the other then repays. What we do to earn esteem is not a "favor" to be compensated. It is thus different from the ordinary economic transaction, for it is not a contract, and it is not a purchase. It is also very different from the exchange of affection between friends.

The central relationship in the allocation of esteem or respect is most fruitfully seen as *triadic*, a relationship among Person, Other, and Group or Community. The individual does expect to gain some esteem or prestige if he or she performs very well, but no specific person "owes" that response as a "payment." The standards for payment are set by the community or group; and ultimately the respect or prestige that is handed out comes from the group as well, though a specific individual must be moved to give voice to whatever admiration (or disrespect) is felt within that group. Overpraise by an especially significant other person is welcome, as underpraise is unwelcome; but they are perceived and evaluated by refer-

[4]For some experimental data on these points, see especially Edward E. Jones, *Ingratiation*, New York: Appleton-Century-Crofts, 1964; and Elaine H. Walster, *Interpersonal Attraction*, Reading, Mass.: Addison-Wesley, 1969.

ence to both the specific person who voices that approval and the real or supposed responses of others.

This may be seen in the extreme form at the debut of a talented concert artist. The audience expresses admiration by tumultuous applause, the critics by favorable reviews, and the artist's coach in some personal way; but all are ranking the musician by reference to the group standards or norms they feel are appropriate for great performers.

All individuals engage in prestige processes if they interact with others at all. Everyone is constantly under judgment, being evaluated for qualities and performances, if only as a normal by-product of everyone's concern as to whether others are fulfilling their obligations. Though this pervasiveness appears to be similar to that of economic phenomena, the prestige processes differ in several ways beyond the fact that the central relationship is not dyadic.

First, we are all consumers in both systems (we must obtain goods, and we cannot avoid evaluating other people), but in the economic sphere some can avoid being producers. By contrast, no one can avoid doing some acts that will be evaluated by others and will be disesteemed or esteemed. Next, in the economic realm an individual producer can be a specialist, for example, growing only wheat; but in the area of prestige one produces not only whatever the job calls for, but a wide range of other acts and apparent feelings—friendly greetings, paternal behavior, neighborhood cooperation, and so on—and all will be approved to some extent, or not. One can leave the economic market (except for consumption), but one cannot leave the realm of prestige: From infancy to old age, one's behavior will be weighed and found acceptable or wanting by individuals and groups with whom one is in interaction.

It is useful at times to think of prestige as one side of an exchange, by which someone performs well and in return is given respect, because people do in fact often use that

rhetoric in analyzing what has happened. It is also fruitful to view the process in this way because its control effect comes from people's knowledge of how much prestige they will accumulate over time in return for their performances or qualities. Nevertheless, the "exchanges" that take place in prestige processes cannot be adequately analyzed by market or economic formulations.

At any given time, however, and within any specific subgroup, there is little haggling or making higher demands can do (as they might in an economic negotiation), since the terms for this kind of exchange are generally settled before any individual engages in a given prestige transaction. We cannot easily persuade others to give us more prestige than they spontaneously feel. But if an individual has some authority, or is in an advantageous economic position, she or he can demand more in overt deference than others would prefer to give; and one can easily observe such instances (husbands and wives sometimes make such demands; parents do; teachers often do; and so on).

Though the terms for a prestige exchange are typically already set, and individuals generally know what they are and must accept them, this does not mean that everyone is pleased with those terms. Much of the dissidence in any society is created precisely by the belief or feeling that the terms themselves are unfair, somehow "wrong." Less respected subsegments (overlapping in various degrees) of the society, such as artists, women, lower-class men, and blacks, not only want *more* esteem than they actually get, but a higher percentage of these who suffer from being in such disadvantageous social ranks feel that they do not get their *just* rewards for their special traits or behaviors. Correspondingly, a major revolution, when dissidents come to rule, typically proclaims that the criteria for earning rewards have been changed, that new terms have been set, especially for those who were formerly denigrated.

Figure 4-1 Though in many urban areas the salaries of teachers and garbage collectors are comparable, the prestige associated with the two positions is not. (Left: Hugh Rogers, Monkmeyer; right, Wide World Photos.)

People have been socialized to want the respect of others as an end in itself, as a direct pleasure. They also come to perceive the advantages of having esteem: jobs and promotions, membership in highly ranked social circles and clubs, deference, or the ability to elicit cooperation or help from others. Consequently, other things being equal, people prefer to gain more rather than less prestige, and they will alter their behavior to gain more, if the cost is not too great. However, they will also decide, as in all other choices and actions, whether the goal is worth the effort. Or, more specifically, since they will be evaluated whatever they do, they must decide whether a given allocation of skill or energy to one task is likely to yield more than a similar allocation to a different task.

Prestige Allocation and Social Control

In order to control others, people as individuals or as group members must somehow persuade those others that "virtue" *as they define it* is not only intrinsically better but more advantageous than "vice," and they must develop procedures or mechanisms for distinguishing between the two. *This is the fundamental problem of all social control processes.* Giving prestige for virtue and disrespect for vice is a major dynamic basis for social control in any society. In facing the problem of how to allocate our talent and energy so as to gain the esteem of others— as well as our own self-esteem, since we are likely to share the group norms about what is admirable—we obtain a continuing flow of "control messages" that shape our occupational and moral career. Here is a summary of the major regularities that can be observed:

1   If one kind of behavior is widely approved but there is a plentiful supply of it, then little prestige (but simple acceptance) is given for meeting that norm, and considerable disesteem results from its violation. For example, we strongly disapprove of murder and place a high value on our control over our own and especially others' murderous impulses. But since most of us do control ourselves (that is, the supply of this behavior is high), we gain no prestige from not murdering, even if we harbor an intense dislike for someone.

2   Some kinds of achievements are valued highly, but the supply is low; few can supply them, so the prestige given for them is much higher. For example, the evaluation of scientific discoveries is high in the modern era, and large investments of both money and prestige are made with the anticipation or hope that there will be some important developments in science.

3   If people or groups do not like the amount of esteem they get for what they do, they cannot simply stay out of prestige processes in order to increase the amount paid. They cannot use the device of manipulating the market by removing their own goods from it, in the hope that the reduced supply will raise the price or that the price will rise over a short period of time. Not only will the "prestige price" not increase, but dropping out will be disesteemed as well.

4   The control messages may inform some people there are better markets elsewhere, and so persuade them to offer their skills where the payoff will be better. If not encouraged by praise or approval to work hard

in mathematics, a student may decide instead to compete in athletics, where the applause is greater. And since these experiences occur mainly in local groups, the person may seek another group or even another region where the same investment of talent and work will yield a better outcome.

5   Groups try to manipulate other groups so as to get more esteem from them. Many occupational groups have made such attempts, and a few have succeeded in part.[5] Probably every major occupational group has attempted to upgrade the respect it enjoys from society by public speeches, brochures, advertisements, political lobbying, and so on. Typically, these efforts aim at improvement in both prestige and economic ranking, so their particular success in the prestige market is not always clear. This subject is explored in detail in Chapter 14.

6   Organizations may attempt to increase the esteem given to specific submembers or segments of the corporation, in order to motivate them to try harder or to achieve at a higher level. Thus, prizes and awards are offered to raise the performances of salespeople as well as janitors. Titles of jobs are changed to make the incumbents feel their jobs are paid more respect, to make others feel that the job deserves more respect, and to motivate job holders to do their work better.

7   It is not only formal organizations that face the problem of whether, by consciously paying more or less esteem than they now "feel," they could alter the behavior of employees; natural social groups and individuals also face a similar choice at times. Will the act of initiating praise (before it is earned) elicit enough improvement in an-

---

[5]For a comment on the problems that occupational groups face in that attempt, see William J. Goode, "The Theoretical Limits of Professionalization," in Amitai Etzioni, ed., *The Semi-Professions*, New York: Free Press, 1969; and William J. Goode, "Encroachment, Charlatanism, and the Emerging Profession: Psychology, Sociology, and Medicine," *American Sociological Review*, 25 (December 1960), pp. 902–914.

other person's behavior to make that technique worthwhile? Or, if we disparise another person when praise is expected—thereby giving a lower "price" than was hoped for—will that improve behavior?[6]

People in positions of authority are especially unlikely (unless they have studied the rules of sophisticated modern management practices) to use praise or esteem for improving the less than adequate achievements of lesser-ranked persons. By contrast, subordinates are much more likely to praise a superior even when they do not feel esteem, because overt disparise directed at a superordinate may cause some uncomfortable or awkward consequences; overt respect is also likely to be more successful as a control procedure. Note that in all class systems this pattern is observable: Members of the upper social strata are less generous in handing out more praise than they feel and are much freer in expressing disesteem; being in an advantageous position in social exchanges, they attempt to drive down the price. By contrast, people toward the lower social strata feel pressed to increase the price; thus they are more likely to hand out more praise than they feel and to feel constrained in criticizing social superiors. To reverse these patterns might well improve the performances of both, but the possible costs decrease the likelihood of either solution.

8   The likelihood of achieving a high level in any area of endeavor is low, because that is difficult; but it is even more difficult for women, blacks, the lower classes, members of most ethnic groups, and so on (again, note that these categories overlap in some degree). Members of such groups are not awarded additional esteem in recognition of

the hurdles they face; more commonly, they are given less. Many decide as a consequence that the investment in effort is too high for the likely yield in esteem, especially since even after a substantial achievement they may still be deprived of rewards in esteem that are equal to those given to others who begin from a higher social rank.

The disadvantages suffered by "outsiders" can be observed in every major nation, and in any organization. The insiders in any type of activity not only give each other more esteem for accomplishments than they give to outsiders; they also persuade the larger society to give them more than is given to outsiders who achieve at the same level.

The formal organizations and associations in most finely graded activities usually contain a more or less "inner" group who decide whose achievements should be given more esteem and which person may be considered an insider or an outsider. Such judgments are of special importance in the modern age of great specialization, since few people are competent judges of high achievement in any area. As a consequence, various kinds of gatekeepers, informal and formal judges, critics, reviewers, or opinion leaders may have great effect on who is to get how much esteem. One result is that those who have high aspirations will usually attempt to follow traditional modes of education, training, and membership in organizations in order to be treated as insiders.

9   The differences in prestige given for excellent or merely adequate performances of the "small virtues" are modest. Within wide limits, most of us get about the same amount of esteem, and we usually are not ranked by fine gradations. In technical terms, the distribution of respect is a very flat curve. This wide set of performances or qualities contrasts with achievements in the occupational sphere, where explicit rankings are much more common, and where many gradations of rank are either measured nu-

---

[6]The answers to these questions are much more complex than is stated in these pages, for they bear on the general question of *elasticity*, that is, whether raising or lowering the price of a commodity a certain percentage will lower or raise the amount purchased by that percentage or by a higher percentage. To explore these matters at greater length, see William J. Goode, *The Celebration of Heroes* (forthcoming).

merically or are implicitly made. We can infer here that any society will make much finer rankings in the activities viewed as more important. One might therefore assert that in general the activities that are most minutely graded in esteem are those the society as a whole considers more important.

In such activities it is possible for individuals to achieve greatly and to earn a great deal of prestige, while risking the possibilities of failure, lost social standing, or only modest achievement. Since those processes which determine the allocation of prestige are of great consequence socially and personally, we shall discuss them at greater length.

THE DISTRIBUTION OF PRESTIGE: WHO GETS HOW MUCH?

Societies differ from one another in the esteem they give to even the more finely ranked activities. Thus, the prestige that is earned and given within any society may be variously distributed to different areas of social action. Within each such sector, how is prestige distributed to individuals or to organizations?

We have already pointed out that in many day-to-day, informal roles—the arenas of the small virtues—only crude distinctions are made, and within wide limits most of us are given about the same amount of respect. By contrast, the leaders in more competitive fields seem to receive a large part of whatever prestige is given to these fields. Even when "winners" are marked off from "losers" by minute differences in performances (in Grand Prix skiing, sometimes by tenths of a second) or by very narrow differences in time of discovery (as in science), the differences in the amount of esteem given seem to be very large. At higher levels of achievement, *prestige payments appear to rise more sharply than increments in the level*

of performance. We will consider the causes of this distribution and then examine its likely results for social control. Next, since perhaps most people in an industrial society do not get as much prestige as they had hoped, we must look at the processes of sifting and adjustment that are to be found within any social system.

Two major patterns are widely observed: (1) Performances above the average become increasingly difficult to improve with each upward step, even if the reward is great; consequently, the number who can or will achieve such higher levels drops off sharply. However, (2) if a substantial number of people are engaged in the activity (because the rewards in fun, money, or prestige are high), there are likely to be *some* performers at the top level, separated by small differences, not merely one person who is unequivocally superior to all the rest.

To perform and be ranked at the highest levels, whether in saintliness or in shooting marbles, demands both talent and dedication that only a few can muster. Such "heroes" are given more prestige or admiration, because both the level and the type of performance are rare and are evaluated highly within the relevant group. Most admirers recognize that such performances are possible for only a few people. The supply is and remains low. Why does it remain low even when people try very hard?

Trees cannot grow indefinitely higher, even in the most propitious environments. The descendants of immigrants to this country do grow bigger, but the curve of increase flattens out eventually. Pressed by fast predators, antelopes have become fast runners over thousands of years of evolution, but they do not indefinitely increase their speed. This general phenomenon is doubtless created by fundamental relations of physics and chemistry, not by human will. Practice will improve the playing of an ordinary violinist, and assiduous training with great talent will lead to still finer playing, but the ultimate limitations of the human animal make the progress asymptotic. More and more of the same inputs will not continue to produce more output per unit input, and at some point even the absolute output will decrease.[7]

Thus, the few individuals at the highest levels of achievement where inputs are very high find that they, as well as their closest competitors, have approached their physical, mental, or moral limits. The person who wishes to achieve saintliness through asceticism and the punishment of the body cannot go beyond certain limits, or the result will be death.

Though there are few who are outstanding at the upper levels of performance, in activities where competition is keen the highest achievements are close in rank. Indeed, in perhaps most fields, from racing to piano playing to ditch digging, the most astute critics might argue instead that there is no "top" individual, but rather a handful of first-rate people, each distinguished from the other by complex differences of quality rather than by simple degrees of excellence. That is, the differences in excellence among the top performers are small. Nevertheless, the disparity in acclaim is large between a few leaders and those very close to them in accomplishment, or between the "winner" and those who fall short by microscopic differences.

This phenomenon can also be observed more generally in a technical trait of the curve of normal distribution (the "bell-shaped" curve), which appears to encompass most human abilities. The mass of human beings will cluster near the average, but toward the higher or lower levels the number drops off sharply, so that only about 5 percent will be found above or below the points where the curve begins to

flatten out. However, the curve does *not* drop rapidly after that. In concrete terms, in a large population there will be not one, but *some*, individuals at the upper (or lower) reaches of any such curve of quality or achievement.

Just how large are such increments of prestige at the higher levels? Since we have no measuring instrument that will give a numerical answer, we can at best ascertain the *rankings* of individuals, groups, classes, or occupations. Thus, since the 1920s, hundreds of studies have reported the prestige ratings of various ethnic and racial groups, based on some variant of E. A. Bogardus's Social Distance Scale. Since the 1930s, various investigators have used prestige indices (social acceptability, style of life, neighborhood, and so on) as elements in class rankings. Prestige rankings of occupations are widely used in research.[8]

We can, nevertheless, think of indices, or substitute measures, that give at least some idea of how great such increments are, and doubtless future research techniques will furnish much more adequate data. Let us consider an example from sports. The move from a .250 batting average to, say, .300 is a numerical increase of 20 percent, but that step eliminates almost all the batters in the major leagues in any given modern year. Then the smaller upward step of another 10 percent to .330 eliminates all contemporary batters except those on a batting streak or those who simply fail to complete a full year of play. With reference to recognition, it would be relatively easy to show that if a batter moves his average up by 20 percent from .250 to .300, he will receive a very

---

[7]This is one more illustration of what Kenneth Boulding calls the Law of Diminishing Everything: Nothing increases indefinitely; all real curves fall off as they rise.

[8]Good examples of occupational prestige studies are "A Comparative Study of Occupational Prestige," by Robert W. Hodge, Donald J. Treiman, and Peter H. Rossi; and "Occupational Prestige in the United States, 1925–1963," by Robert W. Hodge, Paul M. Siegel, and Peter H. Rossi; in Reinhard Bendix and Seymour M. Lipset, eds., *Class, Status, and Power*, rev. ed., New York: Free Press, 1966, pp. 309–334.

Figure 4-2 The differences in excellence among these sprinters are so small that special camera-timing equipment is needed to measure them. (United Press International Photo.)

large increase in the attention paid to him by fans, baseball analysts, managers, other players, and, of course, newspaper writers. The last of these affords us a possible numerical comparison, the number of column inches devoted to the player over a period of time when he becomes, say, a steady .300 or .330 hitter. The rise in attendance or in the size of the TV audience is also sharp when such a batter appears, or a correspondingly effective pitcher. The number of fans who seek autographs and the number of testimonial dinners or requests for public appearances are also possible measures of this increment.

If the distribution of prestige reward parallels that of money income in business, the top individuals receive far more than those below. We do not know how they rank in achievement—an imponderable; indeed, their salaries may well be determined more

by their esteem than by any quantitative proof of their productivity. For example, the president of a corporation is likely to receive 50 to 100 percent more than the second or third in command. We cannot unquestioningly assume that the prestige pattern is the same as the economic pattern, but in that sector the rise in prestige payment parallels very closely that of the economic at the upper end of the achievement curve.[9]

We have been looking at prestige rewards for achievements. Do these statements also apply to *ascriptive* traits? Ascriptive traits are differentially rewarded, but many are not *scaled* very much. Thus, while sex and race are differentially rewarded, they are

[9]For an analysis that attempts to calculate how large an increment in scientific productivity is required to obtain a given increment of reward, see Carl Shockley, "On the Statistics of Individual Variations of Production in Research Laboratories," *Proceedings of the Institute of Radio Engineering*, 45 (March 1957), pp. 279–290.

only minimally scaled because the socially recognized categories are few. It would be difficult to claim they have any "upward" end of the "curve" where there are sharp increments in prestige. Other ascriptive traits are scaled and differentially rewarded, such as age, nationality, ethnic membership, or family honor. But to the modern mind the most striking scaled, ascriptive trait is nobility. In an epoch in which those who reach the top may not all be the "best" or ablest, but have nevertheless usually fought or struggled to get there, the notion that some people were once believed to be born not only rich (as they can be today) but also endowed with innate refinement, courage, the ability to rule, and so on, seems nothing short of startling. Within that system placement was scaled, a matter of degree, and the curve of prestige rose greatly with each formal step upward—for example, from gentleman, baron, viscount, earl, marquis, and duke, to king. The separate quality of prestige is difficult to analyze out since the increases in ascribed wealth, income, and political influence were also very great. For wealth, the upward steps were especially steep.[10] That is to say, where the ascriptive traits are not merely dichotomous (for example, male-female, black-white) but are also scaled and admired, the same phenomenon is observed as for achievement: a rather sharp upward step in the amount of prestige paid for each step in the respected trait at the higher levels.

We have not fully analyzed the phenomenon of prestige allocation, and we cannot as yet be sure of the descriptive facts, since there is no easy way of measuring the *amount* of prestige (as distinct from the *ranking*) given to a specific person. Nevertheless, let us consider the processes that seem to create this type of allocation or distribution.

Patterns of Prestige Allocation: Peakedness and Contingency

The patterns of prestige allocation exhibit a process which can be thought of as typical of the economic market in a mass society but which appears to have a broader application: "The Failure of the Somewhat Less Popular." Perhaps the best illustration is the disappearance of good products from grocery shelves, fairly popular programs from radio or television, good automobiles from the market, and so on.[11] Grocery stores have only so much shelf space and thus only so much for each type of soap, cornflakes, or maple syrup. If the aim is to maximize profit on each item, obviously the most popular of any class of products will shoulder the less popular off, although in quality the products may be close and the less popular may be only slightly below the most successful in popularity. Similarly, the time and channels of radio and television are limited. When decisions are reached as to which programs are kept, those with higher ratings will be chosen, even if the difference is marginal. Again, at the upper levels of rewards, the payoffs may be more sharply graded than the apparent quality.

Different as these failures may be, they share at least one major process, the disappearance of a commodity from a *single* unified market because of marginal differences in consumer evaluations. Aiming at a single market, which will support only so much production of a given type of commodity— whether this is concert playing, scientific research, or becoming the governor of a state—and in competition with somewhat

---

[10]Lawrence Stone, *The Crisis of the Aristocracy, 1558–1640*, Oxford: Oxford University Press, 1965, Appendices VII, X, XII. Keith Hopkins also asserts the amount of wealth of the Roman nobility was strikingly higher than that of even the apparently rich nonaristocrats. See Keith Hopkins, "Elite Mobility in the Roman Empire," *Past and Present*, 32, (December 1965,) pp. 12–26.

[11]For mathematical treatments of this phenomenon, see William N. McPhee, "Survival Theory in Culture," Chapter 1 in *Formal Theories of Mass Behavior*, New York: Free Press, 1963.

similar products or people, it is not enough to be somewhat popular.

In turn, this gap is created by the commonsense unwillingness of most people to buy any worse commodity, to admire any less competent person, than the one they rate highest, *if the choice costs little.* If there are perceptible, evaluated differences, those marginal differences can be sufficient to drive the product with even slightly less desirable qualities from a given market, or at best to cause the product to yield a much lower economic or prestige return. Let us consider for a moment the matter of "choice without cost," for it is extremely important and it is one major process by which a favored few in a given field are ranked far above the rest.

If microeconomic explanations are correct, a choice can sometimes be without cost because the constant effort of producers to gain or control a market forces them to adopt the most efficient techniques, so that almost every producer is forced to sell at the same low level in order to survive at all. Alternatively, some analysts would hold that producers try rationally to avoid price competition among themselves, and constantly seek new markets by the proliferation of minute differences in the product, supported by heavy advertising expenditures. Consequently, competing products are not sold at a slightly lower price in order to dominate the market.[12]

Under either explanation the result is the same: With reference to a wide variety of mass products in the modern economic system, consumers are *not* faced with the choice of paying somewhat less for a product of lesser quality. Rather, they are faced with an array of products which are sold at roughly the same price, but which have somewhat different types of characteristics— and these are often not even real differences, but are imputed or claimed by advertis-

ing, and certainly these differences are not in any way known as facts by consumers.

Products in this category include a range of commodities such as cigarettes, gasoline, detergents, and breakfast cereals. The most attractive, pleasing, or funny performer on television costs no more to watch than one who is viewed as a lesser performer. The recordings made by the most admired musical performers typically cost no more. Even in commodities where there are supposedly some real correlations between quality and price, for example in automobiles, it is clear that the consumer cannot learn where a car falls on some technical scale of measured excellence, to set against its price, so that he or she can decide at exactly which point to make a purchase.

In any event, the basic prestige processes contrast with those of traditional microeconomics in that they are *typically* cost-free. That is to say, it costs no more to admire the best than to admire the worst.[13] Under most circumstances any individual or group is free to feel respect and deference for the best performances or the qualities held in highest regard. The fundamental hierarchy of evaluation and respect is not hampered much by the possibility that feeling more admiration is costly. (Of course, to *pay* deference to another may be costly, as many observers have remarked.)

One may suppose in a commonsense way, without an adequate theoretical formulation, that the principle of "limited space," with respect to ordinary commodities, also applies to the individual or group processes of prestige. That is, since it costs no more to admire the best performer than to esteem

[12]See John Kenneth Galbraith, *The New Industrial State*, Boston: Houghton-Mifflin, 1967, pp. 120–125.

[13]To attempt to mix *socially* with the most admired *does* cost, as a later section will discuss. And, as we noted earlier, publicly *expressing* one's admiration may cost something, if one's friends or superiors disagree; one may gain or lose some respect for admiring the "right" or "wrong" things. These areas of cost widen in a dictatorship. As Nadezhda Mandelstam has remarked (in *Hope against Hope*, trans. by Max Hayward, New York: Atheneum, 1970), under totalitarianism one is condemned to public enthusiasm.

a lesser one, the few top achievers or "the champion" will dominate the attention and interest of those who care at all, and will push the less esteemed to the sidelines of concern. Each person's investment of concern in a given field (even one's own) is limited. Most people are satisfied to know the names of a few baseball players, concert artists, scientists, automobile mechanics, sculptors, or political figures. Indeed, if we examine the conversations of any subgroup, whether a neighborhood gathering, a family dinner, or women, it is clear that only a few names come into prominence, and only those of high evaluation or notoriety are discussed at length. That is, in both a psychological and a temporal sense, people do not possess sufficient time and energy— enough "space," so to speak—to focus on every competitor and to evaluate each one carefully.

Although we can easily observe the extreme peakedness in the distribution of prestige that has been the focus of this discussion, we can also observe an apparently contrary phenomenon, or at least one that qualifies that general regularity. If we observe our own daily behavior or that of others, it is evident that at almost *any* level of competence, at any prestige level of occupation, people are paying *some* esteem to each other. The notion that those at the top get a high percentage of all the prestige granted might suggest that only a few people are evaluated in a detailed way and that most people receive little prestige. In fact, whatever the peakedness, everyone is constantly being rated; and most people receive some modicum of esteem for what they do and how well they do it.

Let us summarize here the several patterns that seem to be more relevant to this aspect of prestige allocation:

1 Since everyone who engages in an activity of any kind—and especially the activities that are occupationally important— is observed by *someone*, everyone is

rated. There is no getting out of the prestige market.

2 On the other hand, not everyone is rated by everyone. This is impossible because of factors such as time, space, and energy. At some point, everyone is rated by someone or some group, but those persons or groups are not in direct communication with everyone else who is also interested in the same field but who lives in a different place or is concerned with a somewhat different level in the total range of skill.

3 Perhaps the only apparent exception is sports, where performances can be measured to some extent, and a small industry has arisen to keep records of performances in national track meets, baseball, prize fighting, and so on. Though the published records do take account of thousands of performances, even people who are well versed in a given sport have not heard of most performers' names.

4 As will be noted later, many evaluative activities constitute a "national system" or even an international system— examples are the performing arts, show business, sports, politics, art, and scientific research—while many other types of skills are not structured as a national system (radio repairing, school teaching, plumbing, hairdressing). In the latter set of skills and qualities, people are not ranked on a single scale within a single social system.

5 As in class stratification generally, people make relatively refined evaluations of those who are important to them in daily interaction, who form part of their social system, but they do not continue these refined evaluations indefinitely beyond that point. For example, people in a given division of a corporation or in a science department within a university (*a*) make rather close evaluations of people about them, (*b*) beyond that, know or affirm a few evaluations of people still

further out in their social network, but (*c*) beyond that, will be able to list only the top people in their relevant activity or skill.

6   On the day-to-day level, people at modest levels of achievement contribute far more to our own immediate pleasure and comfort (or dismay) than do the heroes of the field, who nevertheless serve the important functions that we have noted before. People at every level of accomplishment must receive some daily esteem payoffs, or else they do not feel inclined to contribute much in that activity or even to perform adequately.

7   This pattern of some day-to-day esteem payments and responses for those at less than the top level is important because it (*a*) prevents most people engaged in that activity from simply eating their hearts out in futile aspiration, (*b*) contents them reasonably well for *that* level of performance, and (*c*) keeps them going in an activity that is approved by a group or by society.

Up to this point we have been examining the broad question of the impact of prestige allocation on the performance of people in a specific type of respected activity, with reference primarily to the problem of *peakedness*, the extent to which a few get a lot. However, we must also consider once more another variable that affects willingness to strive: the *contingency* of the payoff.

When people know that the chances of their obtaining some type of reward are low, they are less willing to strive harder and to accede to others' wishes, and it is sensible to be so.[14] They are likely to discount in advance the value and reality of that reward, and will invest less of their energy, work, and skill in any high endeavor. The amount

of contingency we face is a function both of our class and individual position and of the height of our aspirations: For example, a talented boy whose father is a physician will perceive much less contingency in aspiring to become a physician than will a girl or boy born in a slum family. Generally, in modern industrial societies the distribution of prestige at especially the upper levels is peaked and highly contingent for groups and individuals.

Our system may well create greater contingency than others do—higher for the higher levels of almost *any* kind of activity (not only do most of us never learn to sing brilliantly, but most of us never learn to polish shoes nearly as well as the best can; only a few have a "green thumb" for gardening; and so on). However, for those who are born with considerable disadvantages, such as being poor, living in a ghetto, or belonging to a denigrated ethnic or racial group, the contingencies are great even in aspiring to *middle* positions in activities that enjoy either high or middle amounts of prestige. Correspondingly, the actual impact of prestige allocation on striving will be affected not only by the general prestige level of the activity or occupation, but also by the contingency of the payoff.

Results of Peakedness and Contingency

We have seen that the prestige system in industrial societies is highly peaked and highly contingent. These facts create prob-

---

[14]With reference to the "rationality of dropping out," see Stephan Thernstrom, "Poverty in Historical Perspective" (in Daniel P. Moynihan, ed., *On Understanding Poverty*, New York: Basic Books, 1968, pp. 160–186). Thernstrom cites the work of Samuel Bowles, based on 1960 census data, and the investigation of G.

Hanoch, "Personal Earnings and Investment in Schooling" (Ph.D. dissertation, University of Chicago, 1967), as showing that "many legal school dropouts are in fact behaving in an economically rational manner in that for Negroes but not for whites the income lost by remaining in school will not necessarily be made up later." Well-educated blacks earn more than less-educated ones, but at some educational levels short of graduate school the gap is not large enough to make up for the additional years the educated remain outside the labor market. Bowles's argument is to be found in his "Toward Equality of Educational Opportunity?" *Harvard Education Review*, 38 (Winter 1968), pp. 88–99. This historical situation is changing, but in the early 1970s it had changed little.

Figure 4-3 Which child is more likely to become a physician? (Charles Gatewood.)

lems of both personal adjustment and social pattern. With respect to contingency, each individual may discount the risk at very different rates. If a young man grows up in a family network where there are several physicians, he is likely to consider as minimal the risk of not attaining a medical degree and making a fair success in medicine.[15] He has learned what he should do, which school he should attend, the kind of career line he should follow, and which kinds of sponsors he ought to gravitate toward as he advances in training. By contrast, a slum girl of equal talent may view the contingencies as nearly hopeless. Not only does she lack the relevant knowledge and the experience of seeing others attain such an eminence, but the chances against her seem far too great to be worth much investment. The first of these two individuals views the re-

wards as peaked but relatively noncontingent; the second sees them as peaked and contingent.

We may suppose that personality factors also operate to change the perception of contingencies. From research on the need for achievement, it appears that persons who rank high in that personality trait do not typically choose competitions in which the risk is high. They are much more likely to choose situations of moderate risk in which their extra efforts will pay off.[16] On the other hand, there are gamblers in every social stratum, people who are willing to take a considerable risk, as their peers see it, in order to aim very high. Thus, they discount the high contingency because they nevertheless have either some stubborn faith in themselves or a much more optimistic view of their chances, or they simply fear failure less.

[15]Even at present, that person is likely to be a "he"— another contingency to be considered by anyone choosing an occupation.

[16]Davis C. McClelland, *The Achieving Society*, Princeton, N.J.: Van Nostrand, 1961, pp. 211–225.

Modern industrial society, in its sermons, editorials, rhetoric, and propaganda, presents the contingencies of high achievement as being not only worth the effort and morally obligatory, but capable of being overcome by anyone with talent and the willingness to work hard. By contrast, the rhetoric of caste and estate societies urges that each person not aim at a higher rank, but instead adjust to the situation where fate has placed him or her, thus reducing the contingency by lowering his or her aspiration, and reducing the competition that more favorably placed people encounter.

Similarly, in most large societies the common rhetoric among those at a *lower* social rank, where there are many social pressures against striving very hard toward perhaps unscalable heights of achievement, emphasizes the importance of the small virtues and pieties—friendship, loyalty to kin, neighborliness, or parental virtues.[17] These attainments appear much less contingent.

Although these theoretical points have utilized class as a factor in the distribution of prestige, it should be emphasized that one major *structural* difference between class and occupation is observable: People do *not* typically have any great stake in protecting the less competent in any kind of special work, endeavor, or competition unless these are members of their *own* group. Far more people have a stake in maintaining class barriers, at various levels. The result is a peaked allocation of prestige. This distribution is not the most effective for pressing people to the highest performances possible, for these reasons:

1 Very likely a threat of prestige loss at the upper levels and prestige gain at the lower-class levels might improve performances or general social control.
2 People do not know that such a system

[17]See the relevant data in Herbert Hyman, "The Value Systems of Affluent Classes: A Social Psychological Contribution to the Analysis of Stratification," in Bendix and Lipset, eds., op. cit., pp. 488–499.

would elicit more desired behavior, but in any event the society does not want those at lower-class levels to compete more adequately, for those above would lose some of their own prestige.

By contrast, both societies and individuals exhibit very different attitudes and norms toward high performance than they do with reference to classes. Upper-class people would prefer to avoid equal-opportunity competition with individuals of a lower class ranking, and so would most individuals who are competing with each other *within* any given set of individual activities; but almost everyone would prefer that people in *other* types of activities perform at the very best level possible. All would prefer to be served well in a restaurant or shop, to purchase gadgets and commodities that have been made by dedicated workers, to be diagnosed and treated by the very best physicians, and so on. Indeed, it is for that reason that so much prestige is paid to those who are thought to be the best. Thus, though individuals *within* a given set of activities typically wish to protect *each other* (and thus themselves) from a high level of competition, they have every interest in obtaining excellent performances from all *other* role partners, if it is at all possible. Thus, again we return to the question of which kind of prestige allocation for individual types of performances or qualities will elicit the optimum performances, the optimum kinds of activities, from others.

PRESTIGE ALLOCATION AND PERFORMANCE

As we implicitly noted earlier, most people do not attempt to fulfill their role obligations as friends, relatives, neighbors, or civic-minded community members at the highest possible level, because they see that if they perform at a modest level they will get about as much as other people do, and even a performance at the highest level will not bring much public acclaim. Most people also understand that they can obtain only modest gains by simple haggling or even by subversion, hypocrisy, or cheating designed to convince others they should get more. They have received control messages that tell them that neither of these routes to the accumulation of prestige is very productive. By contrast, in the areas that are considered more important by the society, people are told that the chances of good payoffs are better. However, the extent to which people will improve their performances or maintain high ones will be determined for the most part by their perception of how likely it is that they *can* perform better, at how much cost, compared with the greater amount of esteem that they might (or might not) get. That perception, and therefore that response, will be different for people at different levels of performance, in differently ranked types of activities or skills. Let us consider these possibilities with reference mainly to the occupations.

At the highest levels, where the differences in rewards are very great between the top persons and those just below them, people do try to expend greater efforts to do their best, as hundreds of personal accounts, interviews, novels, and essays testify. People expect a "real champ" under pressure to rise to still greater heights. Being Number One yields a big enough reward differential to arouse still more effort when close competitors threaten to win. Both the close competitors and those who get the highest honor recognize to some degree that their accomplishments are similar in level, even though the last few increments may be difficult. All are aware that any one of them may be able to supplant the leader at some time, and perhaps soon. All must look to their laurels.[18]

The able person who is close to seizing the great rewards for yet another step upward is stimulated to sacrifice time, energy, and even social relations to make that last successful effort. Although one need not accept fully the time budgets reported by people in various kinds of activities, all such studies show that at the higher levels, in business, the university, or the arts, the leaders work long and hard.[19] Obviously, some at the top do not do their best, and some are protected from displacement by their money, class position, political influence, or friendship. Some worked very hard once to get to the top or near it, but now find that extra effort does not gain them much. A lesser effort is more comfortable, and they can avoid great loss by manipulating the system. Nevertheless, on the whole, to get to the top in almost any competitive activity or to remain there requires great effort, and this effort is at least in part generated by the marginally greater payoffs: A relatively small amount of additional achievement elicits a very large additional amount of esteem.

What of people in less esteemed occupations or people whose performances or qualities are ranked very low? They are not offered much increase in potential prestige for any likely improvements in their performances. By the time such people are adult, many have learned that the payoff will be hardly worth the effort. Lower-class children, for example, have relatively high "fantasy aspirations," but relatively moderate real expectations. As they grow older, they learn from the social realities that improving their various skills and competencies will

---

[18]An example of the awareness of the high-level competitors that new aspirants may be breathing on their heels is the prototypical and perhaps not entirely apocryphal story, told about any of several musicians,

which can be related in this version: When Menuhin made his New York debut in Carnegie Hall, the somewhat older Heifetz turned to Rubinstein and commented: "It's very hot in here, isn't it?" Rubinstein, secure in his métier, answered, "Not for pianists."

[19]For an example of time-budget data for executives, see Osborn Eliot, *Men at the Top*, New York: Harper, 1959, pp. 112–130.

FOCUS

WHITE COLLAR

The prestige enjoyed by individual white-collar workers is not continuously fixed by large forces, for their prestige is not continuously the same. Many are involved in status cycles, which, as Tom Harrison has observed, often occur in a sort of rhythmic pattern. These cycles allow people in a lower class and status level to act like persons on higher levels and temporarily to get away with it.

During weekdays the white-collar employee receives a given volume of deference from a given set of people, work associates, friends, family members, and from the transient glimpses of strangers on transport lines and street. But over the week end, or perhaps a week end once a month, one can by plan raise oneself to higher status: clothing changes, the restaurant or type of food eaten changes, the best theater seats are had. One cannot well change one's residence over the week end, but in the big city one can get away from it, and in the small town one can travel to the near-by city. Expressed claims of status may be raised, and more importantly those among whom one claims status may vary—even if these others are other strangers in different locales. And every white-collar girl knows the value of a strict segregation of regular boy friends, who might drop around the apartment any night of the week, from the special date for whom she always dresses and with whom she always goes out.

There may also be a more dramatic yearly status cycle, involving the vacation as its high point. Urban masses look forward to vacations not 'just for the change,' and not only for a 'rest from work'—the meaning behind such phrases is often a lift in successful status claims. For on vacation, one can *buy* the feeling, even if only for a short time, of higher status. The expensive resort, where one is not known, the swank hotel, even if for three days and nights, the cruise first class—for a week. Much vacation apparatus is geared to these status cycles; the staffs as well as clientele play-act the whole set-up as if mutually consenting to be part of the successful illusion. For such experiences once a year, sacrifices are often made in long stretches of gray weekdays. The bright two weeks feed the dream life of the dull pull.

Psychologically, status cycles provide, for brief periods of time, a holiday image of self, which contrasts sharply with the self-image of everyday reality. They provide a temporary satisfaction of the person's prized image of self, thus permitting him to cling to a false consciousness of his status position. They are among the forces that rationalize and make life more bearable, compensate for economic inferiority by allowing temporary satisfaction of the ambition to consume.

SOURCE: C. Wright Mills, *White Collar* (1951), New York: Oxford University Press, 1956, pp. 257–258.

Socially, status cycles blur the realities of class and prestige differences by offering respite from them. Talk of the 'status fluidity of American life' often refers merely to status cycles, even though socially these cycles of higher display and holiday gratification do not modify the long-run reality of more fixed positions.

Status cycles further the tendency of economic ambition to be fragmented, made trivial, and temporarily satisfied in terms of commodities and their ostentatious display. The whole ebb and flow of saving and spending, of working and consuming, may be geared to them. Like those natives who starve until whales are tossed upon the beach, and then gorge, white-collar workers may suffer long privation of status until the month-end or year-end, and then splurge in an orgy of prestige gratification and consumption.

Between the high points of the status cycle and the machinery of amusement there is a coincidence: the holiday image of self derives from both. In the movie the white-collar girl vicariously plays the roles she thinks she would like to play, cashes in her claims for esteem. At the peak of her status cycle she crudely play-acts the higher levels, as she believes she would like to always. The machinery of amusement and the status cycle sustain the illusionary world in which many white-collar people now live.

yield little increase in wages, stability of income, or prestige.[20]

Similarly, blacks and women[21] find that even when they have entered relatively prestigious occupations, they are likely to be fixed in subordinate positions, not given full opportunity to utilize their highest skills, and paid lesser rewards for what they actually do. Thus, they learn or come to believe that an increase in their output or a higher level of performance will not yield the higher level of prestige that males or whites in the same types of jobs would get. People in occupations that are generally paid lower esteem are motivated still less because they know how little prestige they will get from any improvement in output.

Up to this point, we have mainly compared the top performers in the most esteemed jobs with those at the other end of the scale. Now we can look more intensively at the middle ranges of esteem allocation in order to examine the impact upon people's willingness to contribute and to perform at a higher level. We concern ourselves now with the further categories of activities, jobs, and performances in which the best achievement does arouse some esteem but the activity itself is viewed as of only middling importance to the society—and this

[20]Roberta G. Simmons and Morris Rosenberg, "Functions of Children's Perceptions of the Stratification System," *American Sociological Review*, 36, no. 2 (April 1971), pp. 235–249. See also Elliot Liebow, *Tally's Corner*, Boston: Little, Brown, 1967.

[21]We noted earlier that these are not mutually exclusive categories. For a provocative hypothesis about those who are both, see Cynthia F. Epstein, "Positive Effects of the Multiple Negative," *American Journal of Sociology*, 78 (January 1973), pp. 912–935. The income discrepancy between whites and blacks is greatest at the level of college education; if a black comes from a higher *class* position, this gives him much less advantage in competing later on than it would give a white. See Otis Dudley Duncan, "Inheritance of Poverty or Inheritance of Race," in Moynihan, ed., op. cit., pp. 85–110.

includes most of the activities for which people receive wages, such as cooking in a roadside diner, operating a cash register in a supermarket, serving as a filling station attendant, or repairing radios. We wish to enlarge our scope so as to include not merely the extreme top and bottom performers, but also a wider range of *activities* and performances as well. An activity that is ranked may be viewed as generally deserving high, middle, or low prestige; in addition, however, the actual achievement reached by *individuals* within any one of those categories may also be viewed as high, middle, or low.

Thus, an individual may indeed achieve a very high performance in a high-ranking occupation such as medicine, but most do not. They have only a *moderate* or *low ranking* in that occupation, though the occupation *itself* has a high ranking in all nations. Correspondingly, there are middle-level occupations and activities in which one may make a high personal achievement, but even an excellent individual achievement cannot change the basic ranking of the occupation itself. In addition, there are many relatively low-ranking activities, from shining shoes to mopping floors, in which again some individuals may perform outstandingly while the fundamental ranking of the occupation remains low, and thus the possible yield of prestige is low.

Since many activities are not ranked very high by the society as a whole, they do not as a general rule generate much prestige that *can* be distributed. Thus, even the best performers are not likely to earn much by working harder, although they do earn more than the performers viewed as less able.

Here, however, we encounter again an important *structural* feature of prestige generation and allocation. Some occupations, like the professions and sciences and the higher levels of corporate life, contain both local and national or international figures.

Others, like carpentry and truck driving, contain people with only local reputations.[22] With respect to the purely local activities, those who occupy a *middle* or *low* position in a high-ranking activity do get some prestige from being there at all. A village physician may get no national prestige or rewards, but he or she *is* at the top of the local occupational ranking. Even in a town with several physicians, the lowest-ranking among them is likely to have a loyal clientele and to receive local deference for being "the doctor." One can make similar assertions about other professionals, scientists, academics, and heads of small corporations, who are not known beyond their local network.

It seems likely that most such people feel little or no social pressure to aspire high or even to live up to the highest standards of their professions. In part making up for this lack of pressure is a prior socialization during occupational training, which emphasizes dedication and whose aim is to persuade practitioners to feel less self-respect if they fall very low in their devotion to their job. Moreover, as editorials and speeches about each occupation constantly emphasize, if a high percentage of such people perform poorly over a long period, the prestige ranking of the occupation itself will begin to drop. It is likely that that process has already happened to some extent in the field of medicine.[23] Nevertheless, they are threatened with no loss of local respect unless

[22]For data on the local orientation of blue-collar workers as contrasted with managers, see Curt Tausky, "Occupational Mobility Interests," *Canadian Review of Sociology and Anthropology,* 4 (November 1967), pp. 242–249. For data on "cosmopolitans" and "locals," see Robert K. Merton, "Patterns of Influence: A Study of Interpersonal Influence and Communications Behavior in a Local Community," in P. F. Lazarsfeld and F. Stanton, eds., *Research in Communications, 1948–49,* New York: Harper, pp. 180–219.

[23]For the dynamics of this process, see William J. Goode, "The Theoretical Limits of Professionalization," pp. 266–313.

they flagrantly violate the occupational norms that the local society recognizes. This will be true both in the local network of a county or village and in a neighborhood of a large city. If they are inept, exposure is difficult and unlikely.

If our analysis of the prestige allocation patterns is correct, those in the middle-ranking types of activities (police officers, truck drivers, railroad conductors) do receive more for a modicum of extra effort than those in lower-ranking activities, although once again the highest performers cannot hope to be paid the same kind of esteem for each additional level of achievement that will be given to those in higher-ranking activities.

Those at high or middle levels of *achievement* in middle-ranking or lower-ranking types of *activities* can expect to receive, as a result of the prestige they earn, standard or somewhat better than average pay, stability in their jobs, some respect from their superiors and some from their peers, together with a slight amount of disesteem and annoyance from their peers who feel they are rate-busting. In addition, for those who perform very well in the middle-ranking activities, there is at least a chance of moving to still higher occupational levels where the payoff for added effort will be still greater.

In all these subcells except the highest, peers who are members of a working group (with the exception of professional sports, research teams, and music groups) make some effort to protect the lesser performers among themselves, since thereby they are themselves protected in their own jobs.[24] By keeping the working ideal relatively modest, the average performers are less threatened.

Indeed, only if there is a local shortage in economic demand or an oversupply of people available for such activities—so that a hard-driving competitor can garner most of

the available business or a slightly better job in an office—is a person in such positions likely to feel much pressure to improve her or his performance substantially, and then only if that person recognizes that the performance is not respected much and that as a consequence her or his economic position is in some danger. If demand is adequate, and if the normal social processes of protection for the less able operate well, moderate differences in performance do not change greatly the prestige rating of any individual. The payoff in money or social success is not likely to suffer much.

As a consequence, the normal pattern of prestige allocation does not motivate a substantial part of the people in these occupations to try as hard as possible. Note that at middle- and lower-level types of activities especially, even when the individual may recognize that he or she might gain some modest amount of esteem by trying harder, that amount may not seem much more rewarding than the continuing approval of peers for supporting their local work demands. The reward payoff from superiors is somewhat uncertain, but quite certain is the disapproval or annoyance from peers who feel threatened by the striver.[25]

OCCUPATIONAL AND SOCIAL SIFTING

Several secondary personal and social processes that arise from prestige allocation may be noted in this final section. They center about adjustment to failure at some level, and the sifting processes that affect both smaller social networks and the individual's place in them.

In modern societies people are encouraged to aim higher than most can in fact

[24]For this process see William J. Goode, "The Protection of the Inept," *American Sociological Review*, 32 (February 1967), pp. 5–19.

[25]For an example of the literature on rate-busting, see William A. Faunce, ed., *Readings in Industrial Psychology*, New York: Appleton-Century-Crofts, 1967, especially sec. 4, "The Industrial Work Group and Informal Organization," pp. 281–377. Rate-busting is not, of course, found only among blue-collar work groups.

achieve, and thus all but a few will have to adjust to a somewhat lower level of success. Few people in such societies manage to keep their aspirations as low as their achievements, at all stages of their lives. Doubtless, most could accomplish more than they do but are insufficiently attracted by the rewards offered for additional effort. Others are tantalized by the glittering prestige rewards that lie just beyond their reach. Still others attain great acclaim, but only for a brief time.

When the individual decides (earlier or later) that the payoffs in esteem are not likely to be as great as hoped, several choices are open. Most are included in these alternatives:

1 To remain in the same activity, but accept the lower rank or prestige given there.
2 To move into somewhat different activities where the rewards may be about the same or lower.
3 To use very different talents that may yield as high or higher rewards in esteem.

Cases in the first category include most employees, who finally learn that they will not indefinitely be promoted and must instead adjust to whatever level they do reach. Here, too, are many academics and concert artists, whose hopes of great fame were eventually dimmed. As noted, they may not leave the field entirely, but may adjust to lesser success. The persistent academic can eventually become a full professor at a lesser college and even continue to do some research. The person trained for concert work can become a member of a symphony orchestra or a music teacher. The person who once hoped to become governor may not leave politics, but may accept a modest position in the governmental bureaucracy.

Many people adopt the second choice: Some who wanted to become actors move instead into the activities behind the stage, from advertising and ticketing to handling costumes. An athletic club, whose main admiration is focused on the success of the athletes who represent it in competition, also needs coaches, publicity agents, secretaries, and the like. Voluntary organizations of all types need many different kinds of skills, and all pay some respect for those contributions.

By offering alternative positions, and alternative if lower amounts of esteem, groups and organizations move their members to accept positions that are within their capabilities but also contribute to the total prestige of the group. A college may well pay great prestige to its football stars, but the school as a whole receives far more prestige if it persuades some who fail to make the team to try their hand at academic honors, basketball, newspaper writing, and so on.

Many people who fail, or who are very successful but seek more prestige, may instead move into activities that are both different and highly rewarded. Some scientists move out of research and into the higher levels of university administration, or into advisory committees or planning councils for the government. An actor fading in acclaim may decide to enter politics or to direct plays. A plumber who is no more than adequate as a craftsman may become a plumbing contractor, and success in that business brings both money and greater esteem. It is especially those who have been successful in their first career steps who are given the most opportunities to enter new areas of action where the potential prestige rewards are as high or higher; but we should not forget that many great successes were achieved by people who first did poorly at other jobs.

The differential allocation of prestige at different stages generates processes of "social sifting" as well as career sifting. Because people in general want to interact socially with more-esteemed groups and individuals, those at the top are in high demand. Since

Figure 4-4 Ronald Reagan (left) moved from a career as a movie star to politician, where the rewards—at least in prestige—were higher. (United Press International Photo.)

they, too, have such preferences, we can expect a considerable amount of *homophily*; that is, people of roughly the same social ranking will be found together.[26] This pattern is also supported by the fact that they often encounter one another in the same geographical space.

Since people who do not themselves enjoy a high rank do prefer to be with those of higher prestige, some are willing to pay overt deference, gifts, hospitality, or services to associate with such people. In turn, some

[26]Robert K. Merton and Paul F. Lazarsfeld, "Friendship as a Social Process: A Substantive and Methodological Analysis," in M. Berger, T. Abel, and C. Page, eds., *Freedom and Control in Modern Society*, New York: Van Nostrand, 1954, pp. 18–66. On both subjective and objective measures of social distance, Lauman has shown that while same-status choices (people like people who are similar) and higher-status choices for friendship can be observed, the latter effect is somewhat stronger. (Edward O. Lauman, *Prestige and Association in an Urban Community*, Indianapolis: Bobbs-Merrill, 1966, chaps. 3 and 5.)

esteemed individuals are willing to take part in that kind of exchange, for it validates their rank while offering some additional inducements. These processes occur at almost all levels of prestige; it is not only the stars who can enjoy a coterie of admirers, retainers, or stooges. Some people will pay overt deference or lavish hospitality to a second- or third-rank person, for less personal esteem is required and other social costs are also likely to be smaller. Thus, in addition to the pattern of homophily at all levels (people of like rank associating with one another), there will be some sifting that places groups of lesser-ranked persons in social exchange relationships with people whom they admire.

We cannot ascertain whether the adjustment and sifting processes we are sketching were as widespread, or as fraught with hurt, in caste or estate societies of the past. According to classic descriptions, the social ideology of such systems persuaded most people that they should remain at the social rank where they were born. Thus, though the allocation of prestige was peaked and skewed in favor of those toward the top, most people knew early in life about what rank they would enjoy. Since most were trained for their tasks from childhood, and the contingencies of failure were lower, fewer people began with high aspirations that were later destroyed.

We have no such data for the masses in such societies or for the middle ranks. Since most people were peasants, obviously most people could not have risen high, and it seems likely they were not tantalized with the dazzling possibilities of high rank. On the other hand, the classic literature of the past, in both Oriental and Western countries, depicts the violent ups and downs mainly of people at the highest levels. Studies of mobility in the major dynasties of China show that turnover at the high rank of mandarin was substantial. Indeed, one might well argue that in most estate and caste societies of the historic past much of this turnover among upper-class families was caused by their own internecine battles, not by the rising masses. In any event, in estate and caste societies of the past, security of rank was not great at the highest levels.

What we cannot know, however, is whether families of the peasant and urban masses invested as much energy in small rises or declines of fortune and prestige, were as dismayed by failures, and in the process became more or less acceptable socially—just as people do today in industrial countries where the apparent amount of gain or loss seems so much greater.

Near the top in such societies, additional rewards were handed out, which may have reduced some people's resentment and increased their loyalty to the system. These include minor honors, estates, medals, or places of precedence in court functions. In our society they include corporation jobs with less authority but some prestige, counseling posts in a college, and so on. All societies emphasize, too, that everyone has the duty of serving the collectivity in whatever capacity, and thus deserves some esteem for doing it well. Finally, all societies contain some of the frustration that arises from all these contingencies, failures, and patterns of sifting by making it clear there is nowhere else to go. Social systems, if they are to continue, must persuade their members to avoid considering whether the system as a whole might be changed, and to focus their energies on doing as well as they can within the one they help to maintain.

CONCLUSION

One of the earliest bits of wisdom that infants acquire is an awareness that whatever they want must be obtained through other people. Adults view themselves as more independent than infants, but little they do

from making love to murder is accomplished without enlisting the aid of others. Although we often speak of *groups* "doing things," in fact whatever they do is done by specific people, and thus groups (as well as individuals) must command various techniques and resources for eliciting the cooperation of human beings. In this chapter we have focused on just one of those major resources, the giving or withholding of respect, deference, or prestige. Both people and organizations can lose or gain it, accumulate or expend it, and grant it to others or withhold it. These evaluations and acts are a pervasive part of our daily lives, and they thus shape our behavior both over the short and long run and within our careers and informal relations with friends and kin.

We have made several important distinctions that are useful in both observing and thinking about these processes: between prestige as a direct pleasure in itself (because we have been socialized to want the approval of others) and as a resource or utility (because we can use it to gain many of our ends); between an inner prestige response (how we internally evaluate another person or performance) and overt prestige payments or deference; and between working ideals and "ideal ideals." We have noted that people may withhold or give respect consciously, as a calculated manipulation, but that much or most of our evaluative behavior of this kind is spontaneous and unthinking. At most, we become aware that the other person has responded to our feelings of lesser or greater respect. Thereby, of course, we also perceive many possibilities of subversion, that is, actually manipulating the prestige processes in some way, so as to gain more or lose less esteem than our behavior or qualities would otherwise cause.

Most importantly, we pointed out that although people use the rhetoric of "exchange" in many social situations, asserting that others "owe" them respect, there are many structural differences between the prestige relationship and market exchange. The relationship is not basically dyadic, but triadic. One person does not do a "favor" for another, and in return get paid so much respect. Rather, the relationship is between Person, Other, and Community or Group. People do come to expect esteem from others for high performance, but in fact specific others do not "owe" esteem; rather, if there is any obligation, it is the group or community that owes it and sets the standards for what deserves esteem.

Since the main focus of the chapter has been on how giving and withholding prestige controls our social behavior, we examined at some length the skewed and peaked distribution of prestige (the top few get much of it), by first analyzing the several processes that create that distribution. We then considered how people at different levels of achievement, within different *ranks* of activities (from shoe shining to medicine), might be affected by more or less esteem. It seems likely that a different pattern of distribution might be more effective in shaping behavior toward the upper as well as the lower levels, but we noted some factors that reduce the likelihood of such an experiment.

Finally, we sketched some of the ways these processes affect the social and career sifting that goes on continuously throughout our lives. People who enjoy higher esteem are also socially more acceptable, both to one another and to others at somewhat lower ranks. On the other hand, those at lower ranks may be willing to pay various kinds of costs in order to engage in social interaction with more-esteemed people. In people's careers we observe a similar pattern of sifting, whereby—especially in an industrial society, where people are encouraged to aspire higher than they are likely to achieve—most of us must come to terms with the contingencies, costs, and rewards of various kinds of jobs. We may adjust to the rewards we do receive, move to different jobs with no great added reward, or instead attempt a very different kind of activity with equal or larger possible yields. We have noted in these cases the problems of contingency, failure, and opportunity. Finally, we have raised the question of how these sifting and adjustment processes might have operated in societies that have been labeled "caste" or "estate."

Related to these questions of sifting and adjustment is how the social system elicits loyalty in its members, a willingness to maintain it. We noted some of the patterns to be found, such as secondary or lesser prestige rewards, turning the attention of people from the inequities in the system itself to the smaller problems of day-to-day adjustments, and emphasizing everyone's duty to serve the group by doing his or her best at any level. However, the stability of most societies doubtless rests, too, upon the conviction of most members that there is nowhere else to go, that they cannot find or create easily an alternative social system with fairer rules for the allocation of esteem. Consequently, most people believe it is wiser to contribute as best they can to this one, and to adjust to the rewards that contribution yields, than to rebel or even pine over nonexistent utopias.

READINGS

E. Digby Baltzell, *The Protestant Establishment,* New York: Random House, 1964.

John K. Campbell, *Honour, Family and Patronage,* Oxford: Clarendon, 1964.

Frank Cancian, *Economics and Prestige in a Maya Community: The Religious Cargo System in Zinacantan,* Stanford, Calif.: Stanford University Press, 1965.

Jonathan R. Cole and Stephen Cole, *Social Stratification in Science,* Chicago: University of Chicago Press, 1973.

Peter Ekeh, *Social Exchange Theory: The Two Traditions,* Cambridge, Mass.: Harvard University Press, 1974.

M. I. Finley, *The World of Odysseus,* London: Penguin, 1972.

Erving Goffman, *Behavior in Public Places,* New York: Free Press, 1963.

William J. Goode, "The Theoretical Limits of Professionalization" in Amitai Etzioni, ed., *The Semi-Professions,* New York: Free Press, 1969.

———, *The Celebration of Heroes: Prestige as a Control System* (forthcoming).

Edith Hamilton, *The Roman Way to Western Civilization,* New York: Norton, 1932.

Robert W. Hodge, Donald J. Treiman, and Peter H. Rossi, "A Comparative Study of Occupational Prestige," in Reinhard Bendix and Seymour M. Lipset, eds., *Class, Status, and Power,* rev. ed., New York: Free Press, 1966, pp. 309–321.

Frederic C. Jaher, *The Rich, the Well Born, and the Powerful,* Urbana: University of Illinois Press, 1973.

Edward E. Jones, *Ingratiation,* New York: Appleton-Century-Crofts, 1964.

Suzanne Infeld Keller, *Beyond the Ruling Class: Strategic Elites in Modern Society*, New York: Random House, 1963.

Edward O. Laumann, Paul M. Siegel, and Robert W. Hodge, eds., *The Logic of Social Hierarchies,* Chicago: Markham, 1970.

Elliot Liebow, *Tally's Corner: A Study of Negro Streetcorner Men,* Boston: Little, Brown, 1967.

Kurt B. Mayer, "Social Stratification in Two Equalitarian Societies: Australia and the United States," in Bendix and Lipset, eds., op. cit., pp. 149–161.

Richard Sennet and Jonathan Cobb, *The Hidden Injuries of Class,* New York: Vintage Books, 1973 (Random House, 1972).

Edward A. Shils, *Centre and Periphery and Other Essays,* Chicago: University of Chicago Press, 1975.

James Silverberg, ed., *Social Mobility in the Caste System in India,* The Hague: Mouton, 1968.

Lawrence Stone, *The Crisis of the Aristocracy, 1558–1640,* Oxford: Oxford University Press, 1965.

Kaare Svalastoga, *Prestige, Class, and Mobility,* Copenhagen: Gyldendal, 1959.

Joel L. Telles, "Deference Processes in Intensive Care Units," Ph.D. dissertation, Columbia University, 1976.

Thorstein Veblen, *The Theory of the Leisure Class,* New York: Viking, 1931.

James D. Watson, *The Double Helix: A Personal Account of the Discovery of the Structure of DNA,* New York: Atheneum, 1968.

Max Weber, "Class, Status and Party," and "The Development of Caste," in Bendix and Lipset, eds., op. cit., pp. 21–36.

CHAPTER FIVE

DEVIANCE AND CONFORMITY

For decades the study of deviance has been marked by strong conflicts about the definition of deviant behavior; that is, what should be included in it, but also by continuing attention to very similar topics, for example, crime and juvenile delinquency, drug addiction, alcoholism, mental illness, sex offenses, divorce, and suicide.[1] Different terms, such as "social problems," "social disorganization," or "social pathology," have been applied to these inquiries, but all carry a somewhat negative tone, for all suggest that the behavior under study is disapproved.

[1]Although success in prediction is partly accidental, I cannot refrain from pointing out that I made a similar statement nearly thirty years ago and predicted that the situation would continue. See William J. Goode, "Conceptual Schemata in the Field of Social Disorganization," *Social Forces*, 26 (October 1947), p. 25.

DEVIANCE AND SOCIAL INTERACTION

The simplest definition of *deviant behavior* is that it is any action or statement the members of a group consider to be violations of the group norms; in short, deviance is nonconformity with the norms of the group. By that definition a burglar who returns stolen loot to the victim instead of sharing it with the gang is behaving in a deviant manner. However, the usefulness of that definition, as well as the difficulties it contains, requires further discussion, which will clarify some of the central social processes in deviant behavior as well as conformity.

First, note that the definition does not refer to people who are *called* deviants; it refers to acts or statements—to *behavior*. The definition merely states that what sets apart deviant behavior from any conforming behavior is how people respond to it. According to that definition, *no* specific kind of behavior can be classified as deviant in itself, without reference to the responses of other people. Thus, for example, killing another person may be praised if that person is an enemy soldier, or condemned as a homicide when it is done for personal revenge.

At a deeper level this applies to all other judgments as well: The social meaning of *every* concrete act is to be found in the responses of other people; it cannot be determined by merely examining the act itself. *Respect and blame are both transactional.* They are not simply what one person does to another, but are *at least* triadic. The process may include the person acting, one or more observers, people in the group who learn about what was done, people in the group who talk about the relationship between the norm and the supposed act, and some who judge the *secondary* response of the actor, when he or she perceives that others disapprove. Thus, the judgment that a deviation has taken place is an *interactional process.*

This definition is not, however, *subjective* in the sense that it depends on the attitudes, values, or personal responses of sociologists who study these processes. Whether a given behavior is classed as deviant can be decided quite objectively, by reference to how members of a group respond: *Their* interaction or judgment may be called subjective but as sociologists we can objectively determine by inquiry and observation what that response was.

The most central part of this process, then, is the interaction among the people (including, often, the individual who performs the act), who label any given act or statement as deviant.[2] The act or statement

itself is almost always of some importance, but primarily through the ways it is perceived and judged by other people. It is for this reason that the most acute analysts of deviant behavior now accept some version of *labeling theory*, the hypothesis that what distinguishes "deviants" from others is that they have been so labeled,[3] not that their behavior violates social norms more than that of others. That hypothesis (if true) poses a further problem: Why are *these* people, and not those, given that label? We shall analyze this issue later.

Social Judgment of Deviance

If we classify as deviant whatever the members of a group judge to be a violation of group norms, we encounter a problem that was considered in Chapter 2: *Which* group, and *which* norms? We pointed out that groups differ in their norms, some people within any group may not accept supposed norms and values or do not feel strongly committed to them, people change their norms and values over time, and some norms are viewed as important while others are not. All these facts apply to our definition and raise the question of how (if norms are variable and changing) some people's violations *are* judged as deviant.

[2]Here we follow the clear statement of this position in Peter M. McHugh, "A Commonsense Conception of

Deviance," in Hans P. Dreitzel, *Recent Sociology No. 2: Patterns of Communicative Behavior*, New York: Macmillan, 1970, pp. 152–180.

[3]Some prominent exponents of this view are Edwin M. Lemert, *Human Deviance, Social Problems, and Social Control*, Englewood Cliffs, N.J.: Prentice-Hall, 1967; Howard S. Becker, *Outsiders*, New York: Free Press, 1963; Edwin M. Schur, *Labeling Deviant Behavior*, New York: Harper & Row, 1971; and Jack D. Douglas, *American Social Order*, New York: Free Press, 1971. For a thoughtful critique see Carol A. B. Warren and John M. Johnson, "A Critique of Labeling Theory from the Phenomenological Perspective," in Robert A. Scott and Jack D. Douglas, *Theoretical Perspectives on Deviance*, New York: Basic Books, 1972, pp. 69–92. Thomas J. Scheff, "The Labeling Theory of Mental Illness," *American Sociological Review*, 39 (June 1974), pp. 444–452, makes a vigorous defense of this position against some current critiques.

Moreover, our example of a gang of burglars reminds us that though one may conform to the norms of one group, that same behavior may be condemned (1) by much of the society, of which we are *also* members, and (2) by various other groups of which we may or may *not* be members. This difference among groups is one we observe frequently. We recognize, for example, that some groups have more power than others to impose their labels; if the local police view our acts or statements as deviant, they may succeed in pinning that label on us, even if our friends continue to approve our behavior. Indeed, in the Prohibition era some people were put in jail for buying or possessing whiskey, even when a majority of the adults in that city or town did not consider that activity improper, and were themselves guilty of it. This emphasis on differing norms and different groups does not mean that all who are labeled deviant are innocent victims; it merely reminds us that we must be careful to specify *which* norms and *which* groups we are referring to when we analyze deviant activities.

With reference to many kinds of deviant behavior we can be fairly safe in referring to the "norms of the group or society," for there is widespread disapproval of some kinds of behavior, such as armed robbery, fraud, alcoholism, incest, rape, the use of heroin and cocaine, or juvenile delinquency. For many other kinds of behavior that are labeled deviant, however, we shall have to specify which groups do the disapproving.

In either case we must further examine the process by which that judgment is reached. We begin with the fact, discussed in Chapter 4, that the behavior of everyone is constantly being judged, although most evaluations are not openly expressed at the time. What is it we do when we judge some act or statement to be deviant?

The judging process focuses on the question, What is that person *doing*? However, a satisfying answer is not a simple description of the behavior. When we observe others, we are constantly (1) constructing a *whole* action sequence from the small part of it we witness, and (2) *creating*, guessing at, or assuming, the *intentions* or motives of the actors. Only rarely do we actually make a close investigation of an entire action sequence or test the accuracy of our guesses about what people think they are doing. We do not even have time to do that more than once in a while; we could not get on with our own activities if we did it often.

In this *social construction of reality* we make several judgments that determine whether an action or a statement is to be considered deviant. Here are three of the central ones:

1 At least on the surface, the act violates a norm.
2 Within that situation, the actor did not *have* to do what she or he did; alternative choices were possible, and the actor knew of them.
3 The actor was aware of what he or she was doing, was his or her own agent, and was not directed by others, that is, *did* "know what he or she was doing." Thus, children or persons thought to be drunk or insane may perform a forbidden act and escape much of the penalty for it, since others will usually agree they did *not* know what they were doing. A bank employee who locks another in the vault will escape penalty if a robber threatened them both with a gun.

Note that the consequences of the act are often less important than the intentions that are constructed by others. Perhaps every society tries to punish some "victimless crimes," that is, acts that are forbidden even though the actors harm no one else (such as drinking coffee or alcohol among Moslems, various kinds of sexual acts between adults not married to each other, many or most forms of taking drugs, or jumping off high bridges). Some of these acts are thought to offend the gods or spirits, and some can be traced to other deep-lying values (for example, to sex taboos relating to sex roles and to procreation). But such "causes" may be no more than guesses. What is certain is that in the eyes of the group, the religious sect, or the whole society, such behaviors are simply viewed as improper, wrong, or evil in themselves. That is, the *consequences* of such violations are less important than how group members feel about the actions.

Generally, then, morally grounded punishments are linked far more to people's supposed intentions than to their consequences. This is especially evident in the law, where the apparent motives of the accused have far more effect on how severe the penalty is than does the harmfulness of the original act itself. On the other hand, if the case is brought to a conclusion, court decisions are of two kinds—guilty or not guilty—while social responses are more complex. If the consequences are very harmful (death, crippling, the burning of a house), the culprit with even the best of intentions will be blamed by some people, and typically will blame herself or himself—whatever the court may say. In such instances the behavior itself, viewed in the abstract, may not be seen as "deviant," but the person is blamed just the same— very likely because others believe that somehow the person *could* have done differently.

A further step can be seen in social transactions that result in a decision that deviant behavior has occurred. Although accidents, evaluations, and guesses always shape such judgments, group members do not perceive their decision as arbitrary or simply as an evaluation. Instead, they feel they have merely followed a set of self-evident rules and have arrived at a factual, objective description or judgment.[4] They think that what was decided was determined in fact by what the other person did, not by a subjective social construction of reality.

The Process of Labeling People as Deviants

Everyone engages in some acts that others view as deviant. However, most people are not given the label "deviant." That is, though everyone has committed some crimes—almost every child has stolen something at some time, and most of the United States population takes drugs (alcohol, marijuana, amphetamines, barbiturates and other tranquilizers, aspirins)—few people are labeled criminals, juvenile delinquents, or drug addicts, by themselves or others.

That contrast between behavior and label seems to suggest that somehow a few people who are not at all different from others are caught by the labeling process. In short, people who are called criminals may be the same as other people, except that they have had the label "criminal" pinned on them. Thus, two labeling theorists assert that what produces the rates of various deviant behavior is the "actions taken by persons in the social system which define, classify, and record certain behaviors as deviant."[5]

Such assertions suggest that people who control police records are the only reality in criminality,[6] that people called mentally ill are as sane as the rest of the population, that those labeled criminals are as law-abiding as everyone else, and that alcoholics are no more prone to drunkenness than others. Yet, the author has not been able to

[4]For an application of this notion to the evaluation of scientific papers, see Peter McHugh, Stanley Raffel, Daniel C. Foss, and Alan F. Blum, *On the Beginning of Social Inquiry*, London: Routledge, 1974, pp. 76–108.

[5]John Kitsuse and Aaron Cicourel, "A Note on the Uses of Official Statistics," *Social Problems*, 11 (1965), p. 135.

[6]Commenting on this, Jack P. Gibbs scathingly asks how it is that United States police chiefs can manage (since they are "producing" the rates of deviance) to report just enough crimes from each size of city so that there is a neat rank-order correlation between the size of city and the number of crimes. (Jack P. Gibbs, "Issues in Defining Deviant Behavior," in Robert A. Scott and Jack D. Douglas, *Theoretical Perspectives on Deviance*, New York: Basic Books, 1972, p. 48.)

find any deviant researcher in sociology who actually makes those claims explicit,[7] though some focus more on the reactions or responses of others than on what the supposed deviant actually did. Indeed, if those absolute claims were made, they would point to a sociological puzzle of the first magnitude: population stigmatized and punished in various ways, but without any observable differences that would explain why those people are so treated. In subsequent pages we shall analyze the principal factors that affect labeling, but let us first consider an important subprocess in labeling, called *secondary deviation.*

Secondary deviation refers to the various processes set in motion when other people view someone as deviant and begin to treat him or her differently. Primary deviation (that is, the deviant act) has many causes, Lemert asserts, but only small consequences for the individual's social position or the individual's self-definition and inner life.[8] By contrast, when people see that person as deviant and stigmatize, punish, segregate, or control him or her, the person must adjust in various ways to this new social environment. It may be necessary to alter one's view of oneself as adequate, as socially accepted, as respectable. One may be forced to find new friends or a new place to live. One may be affirmed in the deviance, since other doors seem to be closed. That is, sec-

ondary deviation refers to all the *further* deviant actions and interactions that are set in motion by the primary deviation and people's initial response to it.

Without doubt, those processes increase the total amount of deviation in any society by making it more difficult for the labeled person to conform. For example, persons who have been officially labeled as criminals will find it hard to obtain a job, to establish friendships with law-abiding people, to move into a new area without being noticeable (they may have to continue reporting to probation officers), to obtain automobile insurance, or to take part in any political activities (felons lose their civic rights). For all these reasons, people usually resist when others try to pin such labels on them.

We should also be alert, however, to another aspect of these secondary processes: Some people seek or accept easily a deviant label for various reasons; that is, they assert their membership in a deviant category. They may feel loyalty to a group (such as a delinquent gang) that has been labeled as deviant. They may ease some social pressures in ordinary social relations by claiming the "rights" of deviance (alcoholics may tell others they are alcoholics and thus should not be pressured to take part in sociable drinking, or homosexuals may offer some cues to others about their status, so as to avoid problems in heterosexual encounters). Announcing or conceding deviance makes it easier to find or associate with others who face similar problems in respectable society. It is thus easier to neutralize or reject the disapproval of that part of society. That is, where the "deviant" label does not create great problems in ordinary living, some people may find some advantage in it.[9]

[7]After writing this statement I find that Erich Goode concurs; see *The Sociology of Deviant Behavior*, Englewood Cliffs, N.J.: Prentice-Hall (forthcoming). Erving Goffman, who so persuasively described the process by which asylums degrade the people they process, and elicit behavior that might be called "insane" or disorderly, reminds us that mental illness is not *only* a labeling process. See both "The Moral Career of the Mental Patient," in *Asylums*, Chicago: Aldine, 1961, pp. 126–169; and "The Insanity of Place," in *Relations in Public*, New York: Harper & Row, 1971, pp. 357–388.

[8]Edwin M. Lemert proposed this concept in his *Social Pathology*, New York: McGraw-Hill, 1951, pp. 75 ff., and suggests further elaborations of it in "The Concept of Secondary Deviation," an essay in his book *Human Deviance, Social Problems, and Social Control*, pp. 40–64.

[9]On this point see Ralph H. Turner, "Deviance Avowal as Neutralization of Commitment," *Social Problems*, 19 (Winter 1972), pp. 308–321. A common example is the person who at a party plays the role of being drunk, though not actually so, and thus is permitted a wider range of normally disapproved behavior, including open amorousness.

Most Deviant Behavior Does Not Lead to the Label "Deviant"

Much of our analysis has emphasized the fact that labeling occurs and also what happens afterward. We wish now to ask what factors cause that labeling to occur, or what factors increase or decrease the chances that it will occur?

We begin by repeating two seemingly contrary regularities. (1) People are constantly observing what others do and judging that some of their behavior is (or is not) deviant. (2) Very little of the total deviant behavior leads to an individual's being *labeled* deviant. The reader can test both of these observations through experience, but let us consider some evidence for the latter statement especially.

Each year, employees take $2 to $3 billion of property from the companies they work for. These range from tools or the goods they manufacture or sell, to summer homes built for a manager by subordinates on company time.[10] Few such employees are ever formally charged in court for these offenses. In his *White Collar Crime* Sutherland reported that all the corporations investigated, and *therefore* the corporate officers of those corporations, had engaged in various offenses defined as crimes, but almost none of these people were labeled as criminals even when a corporation was actually fined.[11] Although homosexuality is generally disapproved in United States society, most homosexuals do not have trouble with the police, and most cope fairly well with the daily problems of living.[12] Moreover, as we noted earlier,

most criminal acts do not become known and recorded, and the overwhelming majority of criminal acts do not lead to prosecution.[13] Many studies of supposedly law-abiding citizens have been carried out, which show that almost all these people admit that they have at some time committed various crimes (in one study, averaging about 18 per person) without ever having been arrested.[14]

Two sociologists who studied police encounters with juveniles in situations where either a citizen had made a specific complaint or the police had actually witnessed some deviant act found that only in about 12 percent of the cases were there any arrests at all, and most of these did not result in a court trial or conviction.[15] Shoplifting, fraud, and embezzlement—amounting to well over $2 billion annually—do not often result in imprisonment, and (especially when the culprit makes an effort to pay back or pay for what was stolen) typically the offender does not face any adverse publicity at all.

This is all the more true for behavior that is responded to with less severe attitudes. Outside Nevada, many forms of gambling are against the law, but tens of millions of United States citizens engage in gambling each year just the same, while the enterprise itself is estimated to handle as much as $2 to $3 billion a year.[16] Similarly, prostitution is widely condemned, and prostitutes are stigmatized; but its normative status is ambiguous, and customers are usually not

---

[10]The National Retail Merchants Association estimates that $2.7 billions of store goods alone "disappear" each year (*Newsweek*, Nov. 24, 1975, pp. 103, 107).

[11]Edwin H. Sutherland, *White Collar Crime*, New York: Dryden, 1949.

[12]John H. Gagnon and William Simon, "Homosexuality: The Formulation of a Sociological Perspective," in Mark Lefton et al., eds., *Approaches to Deviance*, New York: Appleton-Century-Crofts, 1968, pp. 353 ff.

[13]On this point see Austin T. Turk, "Prospects for Theories of Criminal Behavior," ibid., pp. 367–368.

[14]An earlier study was done by James S. Wallerstein and Clement J. Wyle, "Our Law-abiding Lawbreakers," *Probation*, 25 (March–April 1947), pp. 107–112.

[15]Donald J. Black and Albert J. Reiss, "Police Control of Juveniles," in Robert A. Scott and Jack D. Douglas, *Theoretical Perspectives on Deviance*, New York: Basic Books, 1972, p. 133.

[16]Some estimates were given a decade ago for various of these offenses, in *The Challenge of Crime in a Free Society*, Washington, D.C.: Government Printing Office, 1967, p. 33.

punished or labeled. Millions of people are estimated to be "problem drinkers," but few are viewed as real alcoholics. A majority of students cheat on exams at times, but that event is noteworthy only when someone is expelled for it.[17]

The list is long and could be extended, but the evidence is clear that the major social processes are not *primarily* aimed at labeling some people as deviants; their most important result is to label some *behavior* as deviant, and then to push people *back* into the ranks of those labeled respectable, in spite of their having engaged in some deviant act. In short, social processes press people toward conformity.

The reason for this difference in emphasis can be seen in miniature within our personal lives. In most families hardly a day goes by in which one or more members do not engage in acts that others view as irresponsible, wrong, or deviant in some way. Nevertheless, the others do not label the offender as deviant, as irrevocably or characteristically a person who does bad things. If they did, the family would quickly break apart. So it is in friendship networks, universities, corporations, associations, or societies. If everyone were labeled deviant who engages in any deviant behavior, almost everyone would soon fall into that category, and it would become meaningless. Putting some people into the category of deviant person is only a part of the total social control system; if that were the only technique that groups possessed, they would not last long. It is an extreme mode of control and cannot be used on most who deviate from the accepted rules from time to time.

For adequate social control a group, organization, or society needs to have effective means for learning who has violated a rule and a wide range of different *amounts* of censures or rewards for bringing those peo-

[17]William J. Bowers, *Student Dishonesty and Its Control in College*, New York: Bureau of Applied Social Research, Columbia University, 1964, p. 193.

Figure 5-1   This person's drinking patterns would be labeled deviant if she lived in Saudi Arabia, for example, or drank in the morning, or were a daily lone drinker. (Charles Gatewood.)

ple *back* to conformity. Sometimes political or religious groups are very preoccupied with ideological purity and are quick to impose severe punishments, from branding to casting the offenders out, but such groups are not successful in expanding their influence and numbers until they relax somewhat their procedures for social control.

Factors That Affect the Chances of Being Labeled as Deviant

An interactionist perspective is a part of any adequate theory of deviance, but it requires that we consider more than the primary and secondary consequences of being labeled. It is also necessary to go back to that set of processes and ask why some people are more likely than others to be considered deviant or, instead, conforming.

Unfortunately, we do not have satisfactory data on this point. Although there are some unofficial or official data on who are classified as drug addicts, criminals, or prostitutes, we cannot easily construct an adequate sample of all people who have ever engaged in a specific kind of deviant behavior, and thus we cannot follow them over time to ascertain why some are viewed as deviants and others are not. Nevertheless, we can use some data as well as our knowledge of how social processes work. Let us now consider the main factors that seem to influence the chances of being labeled as a deviant person. As must be obvious, those factors also increase the likelihood that any individual *act* will be responded to as a deviant one.

Visibility Here we refer to the common-sense fact that if persons are highly visible when they engage in any deviant act, they are more likely eventually to be labeled as deviants. This includes not merely the ability of officials to see what is going on, but also the capacity of ordinary people to observe what is being done.

Visibility is clearly a matter of degree. As we have noted before, it is not typically the case that we observe an entire sequence of actions or every part of a deviant act. On the other hand, people do make many inferences about what has happened. People learn or guess, although usually they do not take any steps to bring that information to the knowledge of officials. Nevertheless, they talk about such activities with one another. Such observations are worth gossiping about.

As a consequence, the alcoholism of secret drinkers is less likely to be known to others than the alcoholism of public ones. To operate an enterprise in gambling, prostitution or drugs *requires* being partly known, since otherwise customers will not know where to go. By contrast, people who engage in sex offenses take many measures to hide what they are doing, and it is a condition for successful swindling that the nature of the activity not be known until much later. In the ideal case the swindler tries to persuade the victim that there was no swindle at all. On the other hand, it is not easy to hide a murder or a suicide.

Intensity of disapproval How intense is the disapproval of the deviant activity, or how willing are people to overlook it? In all societies, including very violent ones, physical assault is viewed as a very serious act, and the murder of a group member is disapproved even more.[18] Crimes against property arouse somewhat less intense disapproval. Most people—and not only business people—do not become as indignant over the wide range of corporate crime as they do over acts that violate rules that are more a part of daily life. Most people do not even understand the rules involved and are not so strongly opposed to violating them, even when they do actually approve them.

We can draw upon our own observations of how other people respond to various kinds of deviations and thus note that people who violate norms that arouse great disapproval are much more likely to be labeled as deviant.

In general, there is more disapproval when the amount of loss is high rather than low. That is, if the violence was extreme or the amount of money was large, people are morally more upset. Theologically, it may be as sinful to steal something small as to steal something large, but in social life people feel different. In general, people who take larger sums of money, or cause greater damage, are more likely to be labeled as deviant.[19]

[18]The most useful study on this point is Peter H. Rossi et al., "The Seriousness of Crimes: Normative Structure and Individual Differences," *American Sociological Review*, 39 (April 1974), pp. 224–237.

[19]In a small-scale test of labeling theory, the most important variable determining whether a shoplifter

Frequency of violation The more frequently someone engages in an act that is defined by others as deviant, the more likely it is that they will begin to consider the person a deviant in the ordinary sense, that is, that such behavior is typical of that person, that she or he will do it again under various kinds of circumstances. This again accords with both common sense and observation. Everyone tells small fibs at times, but the person who frequently tells lies that are eventually exposed will sooner or later be labeled as simply a *liar*, and not like ordinary people. Certainly a higher frequency of violations will become known and will be viewed as typical.

Stakes involved How big a stake do people with resources have in labeling the supposed culprit? The stake may be political motives, political attitudes, public pressures, or private vengeance. For example, police officers have a very high personal stake in tracking down anyone who has killed another police officer. When newspapers report a high increase in the crime rate, police officers are under strong pressures to do something about it. The kidnapping or murder of an important person will arouse a goodly number of people, including political leaders and police officers, to bend their efforts to finding the culprit.

By contrast, the person who has been fooled by a swindler or a confidence man may well have a relatively low stake in pursuing the case, because typically the individual will be exposed as having been foolish. In addition, a considerable number of confidence games and swindles are successful only because the victims were tempted into

trying a swindle of their own (for example, purchasing a "money-making machine"), and thus they would prefer that their victimization not become widely publicized.

In general, members of any group have a somewhat higher stake in labeling as deviant those who are *not* members of their group than they do in labeling members of their own group.

Resources of offenders The resources of the people who are threatened with being labeled also affect the outcome. People who are well-to-do can hide their deviations more easily. They can also defend themselves more effectively if their deviations become known. An extreme case is murder. Rich and poor people are treated differently in the courts. Recently, some legal briefs have attacked the constitutionality of capital punishment, partly on the grounds that almost no one who is rich enough to pay for an elaborate legal defense ever gets sentenced to death. Most of the people who have been waiting on death row for some time are black and poor.

Those who have resources in power or money can sometimes influence officials, reporters, and others to turn their attention away from the deviation, or at a minimum to charge them with a minor offense. Corporate crime is typically defended by an elaborate organization of legal skills. Juvenile delinquents of upper-middle-class families are much less likely to be convicted and sentenced to a reform school. Such families can sometimes make restitution to others in money or other gifts, and they can utilize their own prestige and influence to persuade police officers or political officials to be less harsh in prosecuting the case. In addition, they are considered by others to command enough resources to be able to control their own children eventually, if given the chance.

In short, there are a variety of ways by which people with resources can reduce the

---

was prosecuted was simply how valuable the stolen merchandise was. See Lawrence E. Cohen and Rodney Start, "Discriminatory Labeling and the Five-Finger Discount," *Journal of Research in Crime and Delinquency,* 11 (January 1974), pp. 25–39; Black and Reiss (op. cit., p. 135) also report that the probability of juveniles being arrested increases with the seriousness of the crime.

publicity given to their deviation, divert other people's attention from it, reduce the severity of an accusation, or vigorously defend their innocence in open court. One consequence of this is that, in general, people with lesser resources are more likely to be labeled as deviant even when they commit the same offense. The unemployed, for example, are more likely to be prosecuted for shoplifting.[20]

In one study the chances of actually going to prison were shown to be much higher for people who are poor, black, and less educated.[21] It should be emphasized that this regularity does not mean that there are no differences in life patterns between those who are considered respectable and those who are considered deviant. It rather states that when the actual deviation is the same but the resources are different, the social response to the deviant or the deviation will also be different.

"Good excuses"   The previous factor overlaps somewhat with this one, because those with more political or economic influence will be able to contrive or to manufacture better excuses. We refer, in any event, to the fact that most people, when confronted by a charge that they have engaged in a deviant act, or that they are engaged in a general *pattern* of deviation, are likely to offer defenses of various kinds. These are excuses, explanations, or some type of interpretation that is aimed at reducing the amount of disapproval against them or sim-

ply the amount of punishment they are likely to undergo. They range from real *alibis* (proving that one was somewhere else when the violation occurred) and denials backed by weak proof all the way to offering *explanations* ("It *looked* like theft, but I was just borrowing it for a while"). This category includes offering additional information that makes the violation much *less serious* ("I did knock the old lady down and did not stop, but I was running home, where my child was sick"). Perhaps one should also include here the plea that one was under great *temptation* ("I stole, but I was starving") or *incapacity* ("I grabbed the cashier, but I was drunk and did not know what I was doing"). In some instances, the person being charged may even adopt the tactic of making a confession and asking for *forgiveness* or, instead, asking to be allowed to make up for it in some way (*restitution*).

Some of these attempts work, and some do not, depending on the artistry of the individual and the willingness of others to suspend disbelief. Very likely, many or most of these attempts at least reduce the severity of disapproval and weaken the other people's desire to label or punish. All have in common a focus on the individual's motivation, which we earlier noted as an important factor in the general social construction of what any person is doing when she or he is engaged in any kind of activity, deviant or otherwise. All have in common an assertion by the person accused that he or she did not defy the norm, did not intend to violate it, and wants to continue to be a member in good standing.

The Limits of Degradation

Whether only negative labeling has an effect on deviance, by pushing the individual into the social role of being deviant, or whether positive labeling presses people into a law-abiding role as well, has not been tested. However, even negative labeling is *limited*,

[20]See Cohen and Stark, op. cit., pp. 25–39.

[21]A Florida law permits judges the choice of *not* labeling a convicted person as a convict or "convicted felon." A study of who were actually given that label disclosed that people who were older, black, and poorly educated; had a prior record; and were unable to hire an attorney of their own were the most likely to be given that label. See Theodore G. Chiricos, Phillip D. Jackson, and Gordon P. Waldo, "Inequality in the Imposition of a Criminal Label," *Social Problems*, 19 (Spring 1972), pp. 553–572. However, the rank of occupation did not affect the outcome much (p. 559).

for the very factors that increase the chances of being branded as deviant are themselves limited.

For example, some people may have a stake in prosecuting a juvenile delinquent or an embezzler, but few have much stake in continuing to follow that person's career forever afterward. Moreover, at least some people will have a stake in overlooking past deviance. The reformed alcoholic or the ex-drug addict cannot easily live an ordinary life afterward, but if either pays his or her bills, there will be many sellers of commodities and services who will have some interest in that continuing reform. Most people have other things to do than to waste time in hounding the former deviant. The convicted adult criminal is most likely to have a hard time of it afterward, because he (most are male) has few resources with which to combat the label, fewer law-abiding friends than noncriminals have, and fewer legitimate job opportunities. On the other hand, some do have such resources, and again their employers or people who sell to them have a stake in helping the person to make a new career.

In any event, as Lemert has pointed out, with reference to many deviant acts the participants cannot be ignored afterward,[22] whether they have been punished much or little. The unwed mother, for example, cannot be either completely shunned or eliminated, and thus both private and public organizations as well as individuals must give her *some* position in the society. An individual is not likely to be discharged from a mental institution unless family or friends are available to be at least partly responsible for maintaining a reasonably stable social environment and for dispensing the usual tranquilizing drugs. Thus, several sets of people and organizations are likely to have a

stake in keeping the person on an even keel.

In short, there are some limits to the degradation of being labeled as a deviant, simply because there are competing interests that yield some benefit to persons who ignore that former label, and there may be no strong interests in reimposing it.

The Avoidance of Self-labeling

We noted earlier that most people wish to avoid the social costs of being labeled as deviant and thus use various techniques for hiding from others what they do, rejecting any accusations or offering explanations and excuses for it. In contrast, many people label themselves inwardly as deviant and suffer some pangs of conscience, even if other people do not know what they have done. Similarly, for various psychological reasons a high percentage of people who are accused of crimes by the police will eventually "come clean" and confess to the crime.

However, the much more common behavior is to avoid any recognition that one is deviant, that is, to avoid the self-label. Most people who break laws or who violate important norms avoid labeling themselves as deviant in any way. The list of deviant activities in which this is done is long. Indeed, the numbers of people who do that very likely include most of the population at one or more points in their lifetime.

For example, some lower-class males engage in homosexual acts for money and thus are technically "homosexual prostitutes" but do not think of themselves as homosexuals at all.[23] Since almost every male reader of these pages has at times engaged in some form of juvenile delinquency, but few ever label themselves as "delinquents," he can measure his own experience against this general assertion. In addition,

---

[22]Edwin M. Lemert, "The Concept of Secondary Deviation," in *Human Deviance, Social Problems, and Social Control*, pp. 48–49, 60.

[23]For a summary of one research on this topic, see Albert J. Reiss, "The Social Integration of Queers and Peers," *Social Problems*, 9 (Fall 1961), pp. 102–119.

however, juvenile delinquents utilize a wide range of techniques for explaining or excusing to themselves whatever law breaking they have engaged in: They may deny that they themselves were really responsible, since the situation was caused by social forces outside their control; they may deny that any real injury was done to anybody else; they may deny that the victim deserved any consideration, since he was a bad person anyway; or they may turn the possible accusations around and accuse the authorities of being hypocrites or disguised deviants. In addition, they can assert that they were simply being loyal to their own friends.[24]

Most shoplifters, whether adolescent or

[24]Gresham M. Sykes and David Matza, "Techniques of Neutralization: A Theory of Delinquency," *American Sociological Review*, 22 (December 1957), pp. 664–670.

Figure 5-2 Most shoplifters do not see themselves as criminals. (Mimi Forsyth, Monkmeyer.)

adult, do not view themselves as thieves or criminals, and indeed part of the arresting process may focus on the efforts of the arresting officer to bring home to the shoplifter that he or she is actually engaged in crime and is in fact a thief.[25] One might suppose that check forgery is so serious a crime that no one could commit it without being highly aware of the dangerous step being taken, but Lemert's study shows clearly that a high proportion of these people manage to engage in the crime without actually coming to admit to themselves that they are forgers.[26] Embezzlers, occupying positions of trust, often manage to tell themselves that they are not really stealing; they are only "temporarily borrowing the money."[27] One would expect that alcoholics would hide from themselves the steps they take toward alcoholism. Indeed, it is common for almost every one of the alcoholic's acquaintances to have labeled the individual long before the person has come to recognize this condition.[28]

We should add to our list most white-collar crime, not because corporation executives who violate a government for the benefit of their companies are unaware of the law, but because most are likely to view those regulations as nuisances or simply as barriers to get around if they can. This self-deception is especially easy, since typically the charge is brought against a corporation, and rarely do corporation executives go to jail for the violation.

Finally, most people who become mental-

[25]Mary O. Cameron, *The Booster and the Snitch*, New York: Free Press, 1964, pp. 159–166.

[26]See Lemert, *op. cit.*, chaps. 7, 8, 9.

[27]See Donald R. Cressey, *Other People's Money: A Study in the Social Psychology of Embezzlement*, Belmont, Calif.: Wadsworth, 1971.

[28]See Thelma Whalen, "Wives of Alcoholics"; and Joan K. Jackson, "The Adjustment of the Family to Alcoholism"; in William A. Rushing, *Deviant Behavior and Social Process*, Chicago: Rand McNally, 1969, pp. 301–306, 315–323.

ly ill are not themselves first aware of it, and come only reluctantly to that conclusion after they have experienced many stages of increasing disorientation or difficulty. Moreover, members of the family are likely to continue to interpret the behavior as merely a temporary episode, a mood, or an effect of some external cause ("Something is bothering him these days").[29]

The list could be extended to many other activities labeled as norm violations or crimes. These processes are relevant to deviance theory in several ways.

First, they give some emphasis to the general thesis that merely engaging in a deviant act does not usually result in the person's taking on a deviant role, either inwardly or socially. Second, they also underline our earlier assertion that most social processes serve to keep people within the group and in reasonably good standing. To place a person in a deviant social position and to keep him or her there requires that action to that end be taken.

Finally, these processes remind us that although some part of deviance does grow from a specific deviant subculture or counterculture—that is, a system of beliefs and values held by a small deviant (criminal, revolutionary, or political) group that supports its members in their deviance—most deviance is not a career that is fostered or affirmed.

JUVENILE DELINQUENCY

Much of the theory of crime has focused on the processes by which young people become juvenile delinquents, since it is esti-

mated that more than one-half of all Class I offenses (theft, burglary, stealing automobiles, and so on) are committed by persons under eighteen years of age. If we broaden the age grouping to twenty-four years and under, about four-fifths of all burglary, larceny, auto theft, arson, and vandalism is committed by people in that category.[30] The estimates will vary if somewhat different age groupings are used, and will vary by the type of crime (for example, adolescents commit only a small percentage of all crimes of fraud, forgery, embezzlement, or homicide); but the general relationship is clear: Young people commit much of the crime that makes law-abiding adults anxious and fearful.

If our previous analysis did not explain why some young people become juvenile delinquents, it did suggest who would be most likely to be haled into court or sentenced to reform school. Such people are more likely to be young, male, black, poor, frequent offenders, poor performers in school, and serious offenders. Obviously, there is much overlap among these categories. Black adolescents, for example, are more likely to be "committed at younger ages, for less serious crimes, and with fewer prior court appearances and institutional commitments" than whites are.[31] Crimes are more frequent in slum areas, and slum dwellers are more likely to be arrested and sent to reform school. In a study of a sample of boys born in 1945 in Philadelphia and residing there through age seventeen, only 6.3 percent of the boys committed more

---

[29]See Erving Goffman, "The Moral Career of the Mental Patient," in *Psychiatry*, 22 (May 1959), pp. 123ff.; Marian R. Yarrow et al., "The Psychological Meaning of Mental Illness in the Family," in Earl Rubington and Martin S. Weinberg, *Deviance*, New York: Macmillan, 1968, pp. 31–41; and Harold Sampson, Sheldon L. Messinger, and Robert D. Town, "Family Processes and Becoming a Mental Patient," in ibid., pp. 41–51.

[30]For comparable and more recent data, see the annual *Uniform Crime Reports*, compiled by the Federal Bureau of Investigation, U.S. Government Printing Office. See also *The Challenge of Crime in a Free Society*, chap. 3.

[31]See Albert K. Cohen and James F. Short, "Crime and Juvenile Delinquency," in Robert K. Merton and Robert Nisbet, eds., *Contemporary Social Problems*, 3d ed., New York: Harcourt Brace and Jovanovich, 1971, p. 109. Many studies have documented this general conclusion.

than half of all the serious offenses attributed to the entire cohort of boys.[32]

The problem that investigators have tried to solve is not why some boys commit a few delinquencies, but why some boys in poor urban areas seem to commit a great many serious delinquencies. Note what is omitted. First, rural and small-town delinquency is rarely viewed as a problem, because the delinquency rates are lower, and because informal social controls in such areas are more effective. Parents, kin, neighbors, teachers, and officials cooperate both to keep down the number who are actually haled into court and to press the violators toward conformity. Second, juvenile delinquents of middle- or upper-class families are not viewed as part of the problem for the same reasons.

Third, girls play only a small role in theories of delinquency, in part because most of their arrests are for sex-related offenses. Often they are arrested at the wish of their parents, who feel they are "out of control," which usually means that the girls are thought to be sexually promiscuous—that is, they are engaged in activities for which neither boys nor adults would be arrested. The ratio of boys arrested to girls arrested is about 4:1 in the United States, perhaps the lowest ratio in the world. This doubtless reflects the greater freedom given to girls in this country. As traditional societies modernize, the proportion of girls and women in crime increases.

This formulation of the problem of juvenile delinquency also omits the fact that most adolescents who engage in juvenile delinquency do not thereafter devote themselves to serious criminal careers. Most grow up to become reasonably law-abiding citizens. To be sure, many of these remain poor and frequently unemployed, because they suffer the handicaps of being black, school dropouts, and unskilled. Nevertheless, most do not go on to adult criminal careers.

Thus, theories of juvenile delinquency do not attempt to account for all aspects of youthful crime. Since the phenomenon itself is so complex and is defined in so many different ways, that is perhaps a wise restraint. At the present time, most theories try to explain the prevalence of juvenile crime among urban, slum-dwelling males[33] by a combination of several traditional hypotheses:

1 Juvenile delinquency is *socially learned* from intimate interaction with others who are already engaged in it. Thus, most juvenile crime is a group activity, and it is primarily the individuals who come to associate closely with such groups who learn to engage in it. They are rewarded socially by group members, who thus come to be important for those individuals' identity.

2 In areas and among groups where crime rates are high, there is likely to be a

---

[32]See ibid., p. 113; the data are from Marvin E. Wolfgang, Robert M. Figlio, and Thorsten Sellin, *Delinquency in a Birth Cohort*, Chicago: University of Chicago Press, 1972, pp. 247–248, and chap. 14 generally. Anthony C. Meade, "The Labeling Approach to Delinquency: State of the Theory as a Function of Method," in *Social Forces*, 53 (September 1974), pp. 83–91, presents contrary data; but the Wolfgang, Figlio, and Sellin findings seem fairly conclusive. Meade asserts that blackness, lower social class, school failure, and adult offense are not significantly related (or are *negatively*) to the young person's being subjected to a formal hearing or trial (p. 85).

[33]As suggested earlier, whether in fact the rate of juvenile delinquency is higher at lower class levels is still hotly debated. See in this connection Steven Box and Julienne Ford, "The Facts Don't Fit: On the Relationship between Social Class and Criminal Behavior," *Sociological Review*, 19 (February 1971), pp. 31–52; as well as the criticism by W. R. Bytheway and D. R. May, "On Fitting the 'Facts' of Social Class and Criminal Behavior: A Rejoinder to Box and Ford," ibid. (November 1971), pp. 585–607. See also Jay R. Williams and Martin Gold, "From Delinquent Behavior to Official Delinquency," *Social Problems*, 20 (Fall 1972), pp. 209–229, who in spite of their generally negative finding nevertheless found that black youths admitted to more *serious* crimes. On the other hand, black youths in their sample had no more contact with the police than did white boys, and were not more frequently picked up by the police.

subculture in which drug peddlers and dealers, pimps, hustlers, hoodlums, numbers runners, thieves, and gamblers are given some respect for their success, and the "outside" dominant society is partially rejected for its corruption, hypocrisy, and discrimination. Young people who grow up in those surroundings can thus avail themselves of a set of rationalizations and excuses for taking part in crime, from vandalism to robbery, and even the law-abiding see little advantage in cooperating with the police. Thus, the social pressures on the individual to avoid delinquency are not high.

3 Opportunity also plays a large role, especially in determining whether and when a young male will be accepted as a useful candidate for a delinquent or criminal career, or will instead find a satisfactory job. Many young toughs will not be accepted as recruits in a criminal subgroup, because they are not clever enough, reliable, or sufficiently cool under stress. That is, the *structure of opportunities* is important in determining whether a young man engages in serious delinquency, and continues that pattern, or goes on to an adult criminal career.

These explanations share one important insight that runs contrary to what many people believe—that delinquents are simply "bad kids" whose wild or evil character causes them to disobey the laws and who must be punished severely if they are ever to reform. Instead, these explanations assert that almost any young person might become a delinquent if she or he had the same social experiences as most delinquents. In short, it is *normal* to become delinquent under these social circumstances. Consequently, it is unfair to blame individuals for their delinquency, and mere punishment will not reform them. Only a change in the social structure of the slum will reduce delinquency.

The criminologist Sutherland, who viewed both delinquency and crime as the result of learning and differential association,[34] asserted that the motives, personality needs, learning processes, and psychological predispositions of both the law-abiding and the criminal are the same. Young people learn to be delinquents just as they learn to drive an automobile or eat hamburgers. This learning process follows the ordinary psychological principles of learning.

The two hypotheses—(1) it is social rewards and punishments that facilitate learning delinquent patterns, and (2) differential association, or the extent to which adolescents interact more or less with delinquents, determines how deeply persons get involved with delinquency—give little or no weight to *personality* factors. However, there need be no contradiction between these general explanations. It seems likely that psychological variables may increase or decrease the effect of either learning or differential association.

In general, psychological research on this point has not been persuasive. That is, no special "delinquency personality pattern" has been located. However, the same criticism could be made about sociological hypotheses as about psychological interpretations; that is, most young people in slum areas do *not* become seriously involved in delinquency, and most who do cannot be said to show any specific "juvenile delinquency" personality pattern.

A major study of the biological and psychological traits of delinquents asserted that adolescents who are *mesomorphic* (who have

[34]These notions were introduced by Edwin H. Sutherland in his 1939 edition of *Principles of Criminology* and are more recently presented in E. H. Sutherland and D. Cressey, *Principles of Criminology*, Philadelphia: Lippincott, 1970. See also Robert L. Burgess and Ronald L. Akers, "A Differential Association–Reinforcement Theory of Criminal Behavior," *Social Problems*, 14 (Fall 1966), pp. 128–147; as well as the more recent emendations in Reed Adams, "Differential Association and Learning Principles Revisited," *Social Problems*, 20 (Spring 1973), pp. 458–470.

a sturdy muscular physique) are more likely to become juvenile delinquents.[35] With reference to the personality that is associated with mesomorphs, two analysts comment that they are "aggressive, energetic, daring types of people; it is the stuff of which generals, athletes, and politicians, as well as delinquents, are often made."[36]

Moreover, even the nature of the causal relationship is open to question. One might claim, for example, that the active life of boys in slum streets may well produce more muscular types, or such boys simply compete more successfully (and thus are rewarded more) than boys who are skinny or fat, weak, and incompetent at physical skills.

Other studies suggest that close ties with parents (whether father or mother is most important is still debated) reduce the likelihood of juvenile delinquency.[37] There is some evidence, too, that young people learn aggressiveness or patterns of violence, rejection of school, or a general unwillingness to conform to law-abiding ways from their fathers; obviously, if a boy has *close* ties with a deviant father, this would doubtless increase the chances of delinquency. Most studies report, however, that delinquents are more likely than nondelinquents to feel that they experienced an unhappy home life or felt rejected by their parents.

The hypothesis that slum areas are characterized by a *lower-class subculture*, in which juvenile delinquency is fostered, does not require the assumption that most people in it accept fully a set of counternorms or values, for example, a belief that crime and violence are good,[38] or that slum areas are socially integrated about a deviant way of life. Most people in them are making desperate attempts, under great handicaps, to get and hold steady jobs, to obey the law, to give respect to others who do, and to keep their own children out of trouble.

Cautiously phrased, that hypothesis only asserts that at least *many* groups or gangs of boys in slum areas give respect to adults who are successful in deviant careers, and give disesteem to some of the conventional social behavior that is supported by schoolteachers and officials, such as care for others' property, politeness and the avoidance of violence, or obedience to authority. Even if slum boys do not completely reject conventional norms, these differences are enough to permit gangs to flourish, or young boys to form subgroups in which delinquent behavior is viewed as more rewarding than abiding by the law. These differences are also sufficient to make it rather difficult to put much informal social pressure or social controls on young people who seem to be heading for more serious delinquent activities.[39]

[35]Sheldon Glueck and Eleanor Glueck, *Physique and Delinquency*, New York: Harper, 1956.

[36]Cohen and Short, op. cit., p. 119.

[37]See Travis Hirschi, *Causes of Delinquency*, Berkeley: University of California Press, 1969. Hirschi claims that parental bonds have a stronger effect on reducing delinquency than does a higher social class position. For an application of Hirschi's findings to a male and female rural group, see Michael J. Hindelang, "Causes of Delinquency: A Partial Replication and Extension," *Social Problems*, 20 (Spring 1973), pp. 471–487.

[38]Walter B. Miller, in his "Lower Class Culture as a Generating Milieu for Gang Delinquency," *Journal of Social Issues*, 14, no. 3 (1958), pp. 5–19, does not speak of a counterculture, but of the "focal concerns of lower class culture" such as trouble, toughness, smartness, excitement, or being lucky. Albert K. Cohen, *Delinquent Boys*, New York: Free Press, 1955, describes in some detail the social relationships that help to generate, especially in adolescent gangs, a set of attitudes that run counter to conventional norms and values. The reader should, however, keep in mind the earlier paper by Gresham M. Sykes and David Matza on the various techniques of excuses, rationalizations, or mutualization, for they argue that delinquents do not simply *reject* the norms of law-abiding society.

[39]Aside from Albert K. Cohen, op. cit., on gangs, see James F. Short and Fred L. Strodtbeck, *Group Process and Gang Delinquency*, Chicago: University of Chicago Press, 1965, who claimed that delinquent gangs are not typically organized for specialized purposes, but engage in a wide variety of behavior. Some gangs seem to be more organized around gang conflict and narcotics, but not typically around theft. Nor should all "gangs" be

Perhaps most important, however, is that adolescents in slum areas simply do not perceive—and their perception is correct—great opportunities for good jobs, social mobility, or an adequate life when they survey their future. They are like other people in accepting such *goals*, but they feel the *means* available to them are not adequate. Some may withdraw or retreat from this problem of the discrepancy between means and ends, but many will accept deviant routes if they seem promising.[40]

Ohlin and Cloward have built on this scheme by pointing out that, as in other types of life choices, the slum dweller faces various opportunities, both legitimate and illegitimate, for achieving success or an adequate career.[41] In the more law-abiding areas legitimate opportunities for young people are greater, and they may be somewhat less attracted to the possibilities for continuing delinquencies or criminal careers. In some especially disorganized slum areas, neither organized crime nor legitimate job opportunities may be common, and youths are more likely to engage in violent, vandalizing delinquencies whose payoff is primarily in the excitement of aggression and an occasional theft. Where crime is more organized (narcotics, numbers, gambling, prostitution, rackets, or professional theft and robbery), the young punk or hoodlum who is irresponsible, foolishly violent, given to risky adventures outside the law, or unable to keep cool in emergencies is not likely to be given much opportunity to train himself for a criminal career. That kind of behavior may yield some respect from fellow members of a street gang, but it is not approved by professional criminals or organized criminal groups. Thus, many delinquents fail at the first steps toward either a legitimate or an illegitimate career. It is possible that some of these go on to become "jack-of-all-trades offenders," who try almost any kind of crime that tempts them at the moment. These people seem to have less contact with professional criminals, a lower degree of skill, and a higher chance of being sentenced.[42]

CRIME: ORGANIZED AND UNORGANIZED

Without aiming at a serious classification of criminality, we have been using an implicit one just the same. It is based on social responses to the crime itself and on who is most likely to engage in it. First, there is the huge volume of corporate crime, mainly the violation of one or more of the thousands of regulations that have been designed to curb the power of corporations: laws against price-fixing, interference with union activities, dangerous working conditions (for example, chemicals, asbestos), stock market manipulations, adulteration of foods or drugs, or contributions for the election of useful candidates. Most people do not know much about these laws, but would

viewed as well-organized groups, for many are temporary aggregations with no continuing leader. On this point see Lewis Yablonsky, "The Delinquent Gang as a Near-Group," *Social Problems*, 7 (Fall 1959), pp. 108–117; and *The Violent Gang*, New York: Macmillan, 1962. This observation has been made many times over the past fifty years, but the popular press rejects it in favor of the notion that all boys' gangs are delinquent gangs, and that all delinquent gangs are highly organized mini-armies.

[40]These alternative possibilities are based on the classic article by Robert K. Merton, "Social Structure and Anomie," in *Social Theory and Social Structure* (1949), rev. ed., New York: Free Press, 1968, pp. 185–213. Merton outlines the various likely responses of people in different types of situations, whether they have (or have not) come to accept the goals or ends of their group or society, and whether they have (or have not) the means for achieving them. A likely response to having accepted the goals but being without the facilities to achieve them is that of "innovation," trying a different solution, which may be legitimate or illegitimate.

[41]See Richard A. Cloward and Lloyd E. Ohlin, *Delinquency and Opportunity*, New York: Free Press, 1960.

[42]Julian Roebuck and Ronald Johnson, "The Jack of All Trades Offender," in William A. Rushing, ed., *Deviant Behavior and Social Process*, Chicago: Rand McNally, 1969, pp. 107–113.

FOCUS

THE SKID ROW ALCOHOLIC'S LOSS OF SOCIAL MARGIN

THE PROTECTORATE FUNCTION OF SOCIAL MARGIN

Social margin refers to the amount of *leeway* a given individual has in making errors on the job, buying on credit, or stepping on the toes of significant others without suffering such serious penalties as being fired, denied credit, or losing friends or family. Where a person is well known, and considered to have many likeable traits, there exists social margin to have some unpleasant characteristics as well. If there is a past history of good work on the job, a failure will be overlooked, although this may vary according to the stiffness of the competition.

Thus it is not only the act of "messing-up" (violating social norms) itself that gets a person in trouble. It is the number of times the breech occurs, the way it is accomplished, and the previous reputation (margin) that a person has at the time of any given act. In the same vein, it is not actually lack of cash that keeps a person from purchasing, nor merely public drunkenness that lands him in jail. It is the width (size) of his margin or social credit. Social margin also encompasses the human resources a person can call upon in case of disaster, such as an incapacitating accident, losing a job, or being arrested. A person with margin can get help from his family, employer, or friends at such times.

Social margin, then, is an attribute that must be ascribed by others, although its ascription can be manipulated by the social actor to some extent, and is, of course, influenced by his actions. Social margin is compounded of the good will of people within the actor's ambit of influence and the time, credit, or money they are willing to devote to assist him should the need arise.

Social margin is graduated somewhat like the possession of riches. The more one has, the more he can get. As a result, possession of margin is class-bound: the higher the social class one has, the greater margin one can draw on. This is not to say that the lower-class man has no margin, but he has less than the middle-class man and what he has is often dependent on his display of middle-class traits of dependability, responsibility, and future orientation. The increase and decrease of margin occurs in geometric ratio rather than arithmetic proportion. The term "my luck ran out" probably refers to the dramatic disappearance of social margin.

Consistent overdrawing of margin can result in its reduction to the point where a man is almost paralyzed, inasmuch as loss of this social

SOURCE: Jacqueline P. Wiseman, *Stations of the Lost*, Englewood Cliffs, N.J.: Prentice-Hall, 1970, pp. 223–224.

leeway makes every mistake increasingly serious until a small misstep can be "the last straw" and result in disaster. This is, indeed, the case of the Skid Row drunk.

Concomitant with the loss of social margin is the most serious loss of all—social grace and assurance in everyday situations. As a man is faced with increasingly serious definitions being assigned to his missteps, he is beset with "nerves" and paralyzed lest he reveal this. It is this loss of self-assurance that is most difficult to replace. Such a self-confidence gap can make the difference between being hired and not hired, kept and not kept on the job, treated as an insider or as an outcast.

Width of margin is historically determined by a person's known biography. This, in turn, affects the number of people willing to render aid in a tight spot. When an alcoholic acts in such a way that his wife divorces him, his in-laws and children avoid him, and his friends, associates, or employer sever relations with him, he has lost something besides their companionship or good will. He has lost the social margin their good will provides. By the time a man hits Skid Row, he has very little, if any, margin remaining.

At first, the drinker may not feel the loss, and may actually be relieved to be free of a nagging wife and disapproving in-laws, children, friends, or a dominating employer. He may even feel a sense of relief at no longer having to go to a hated job. As his money dwindles to a few pennies, and the hostile world intrudes, the protectorate role of these normal social connections becomes more apparent. At this point he must measure his margin in terms of today's companions, today's housing, today's economic power, which of course goes a long way to explain his "now" orientation.

In economic and power terms, there is no one from whom to borrow any substantial sum of money, regardless of the emergency. There is no credit from stores where credit has been abused, and no credit from stores that know of the abuse. There is no one to write a letter of recommendation so that a new job can be obtained. There is no one to handle bail in case of a drunkenness arrest, or to protest the loss of medicine or other mistreatment in the jail. There is no one to resist commitment to a mental institution or to offer an alternative to the Christian Missionaries.

Margin has other functions besides protecting the individual from the ultimate dire consequences of his actions or providing the basis for social assurance; social margin gives him reason for restraining himself from committing future deviant acts. That is, the possession of margin operates *to commit a person to protection of that margin*—a future-orientation, to be sure. Concomitantly, the loss of all or almost all margin means that the person has no stake that he need protect by conformity. In other words, margin is both protector and worth protecting. When the homeless male drunkenness offender starts drinking again, he usually has little margin to protect and can expect little protection in return.

approve of them if asked. On the other hand, people do not fear this kind of crime and do not become indignant about its volume. Business people who commit such crimes do not see themselves as criminals, and their colleagues in the business world share that opinion.

Such crimes can be distinguished, but not very sharply, from a second category— crimes of embezzlement or fraud on a large or small scale, committed by employees or by people in high business positions. When the crime is the ordinary theft of other people's money, committed typically by a white-collar employee who is in a position to enter false figures in the account books, it is taken very seriously, and the employee is severely stigmatized. It is unlikely that such a person will ever be given a position of financial trust again, though whether she or he is sent to prison may be largely determined by whether the money can be repaid.

Such crimes shade off toward much more complex crimes of corporate fraud; for example, a high official of an insurance company has subordinates write false insurance policies as a basis for corporate loans; another conspires to issue false documents certifying that goods exist in warehouses or olive oil in tanks, as a basis for sales or loan transactions; or still another corporate officer has the corporation buy, at a high price, some goods or property that the officer owns privately. In general, such crimes are more likely to be viewed as ordinary corporate violations (that is, our first category) if the officials execute them mainly to benefit the corporation. To the degree that they benefit a single individual, and can be viewed as something like simple theft, the condemnation is likely to be greater, and the criminal is more likely to be sent to jail.

These two somewhat overlapping types of white-collar crimes cause losses of billions of dollars annually. The total is impossible to calculate, since the untangling of some corporate frauds takes years even in the

courtrooms, and it is difficult to decide how to calculate who lost what. Sometimes a single case is estimated to cause losses of hundreds of millions of dollars. The losses from price-fixing, injurious work conditions, or illegal actions against unions are still more difficult to calculate.

Since crimes in these first two categories cannot be executed except by careful planning, we might speak of them as "organized," but in fact most people do not put them in that category. Two main explanations for this response seem plausible. The first is that these crimes, especially those in the first category, are not easily identifiable as "real" crimes like bank robbery or burglary. The second is that the primary activity of such business people is not violations of the law, but the ordinary work of the corporation. That is, they are *mainly* engaged in the insurance, oil, or electrical equipment business, and while doing so they break some corporate laws in addition. Thus, in the eyes of most citizens, they are at worst respectable citizens who were tempted by something shady. By contrast, *real* organized criminals are seen as engaging in crime as a *main* activity.

Competing with these two large categories in sheer dollar volume is what most people call *organized crime*, or syndicates of crime, and what newspapers mean when they write their recurring exposés of "the Mafia" or "Cosa Nostra."[43] In the popular view, based necessarily on little direct observation by participants but on many movies and news stories, that kind of crime is dominated by an extensive, tightly controlled organization, much like a corporation founded on violence.[44]

---

[43]For a good account of especially the generational changes in Mafia activities, see Francis J. Ianni and Elizabeth R. Ianni, *A Family Business: Kinship and Social Control in Organized Crime*, New York: Russell Sage, 1972; see also his *Black Mafia*, New York: Simon and Schuster, 1974.

[44]For details, see Donald R. Cressey, *Theft of the Nation: The Structure and Operations of Organized Crime*

Although thousands of hours of conversations among crime syndicate members have been recorded by various law enforcement teams, and dozens of investigatory commissions have attempted to analyze the operations of such syndicates over the past decades, in the author's opinion no really plausible account has been written as yet. Both the recorded conversations and news accounts reveal that discipline is not as taut as popular descriptions suggest, gangland "codes of honor" are frequently violated, crimes and legitimate business plans are bungled, and members sometimes cheat one another or do not live up to their agreements. There is no real national, integrated system; many of the rank and file do not have steady jobs in crime; and in spite of corrupt government officials, many syndicate members are sent to prison. It is dramatic journalism to claim that a fully organized underworld exists, with powerful, all-knowing rulers, but there is much evidence against it.

However, even if so romantic a version is not entirely correct, the most lucrative criminal activities *are* dominated by organizations of greater or lesser effectiveness, whose top leaders manage for much of their lives to avoid going to prison. It is not necessary to assume a neat, monopolistic corporate model to account for the patterns that can be observed in every major city. These can be summarized:

1   Criminal organizations control most illegal gambling, loan sharking, narcotics at the importing and wholesale level, and prostitution; and they have a hand in many other, legitimate enterprises.[45]

Figure 5-3   Senator Frank Church talks with Daniel J. Haughton shortly before Haughton resigned his chairmanship of Lockheed Aircraft Corporation during a Senate investigation of bribes given to foreign officials in order to induce them to make large investments in American products. (Wide World Photos.)

2   They are successful in extensively corrupting both police departments and other law enforcement agencies.

3   They furnish social "role models" for young men in slum areas; that is, they serve as visible examples of success in a world that seems *possible*—unlike the role models offered by schoolteachers in such areas.[46] They prove that crime pays very well indeed, even over the longer run, for one may follow a criminal career without being sent to prison for it.

4   They prove to slum dwellers that government generally and especially the law enforcement system (police, prosecuting attorneys, judges, and prison officials) are corrupt, and that most officials at high and low levels can be bought, from the police officer who permits narcotics

in America, New York: Harper & Row, 1969; and *Criminal Organization*, New York: Harper & Row, 1972. Cressey points out that ordinary street crime requires some planning or organization, but syndicates are like corporations in having specific positions for various tasks, and a continuing process of replacement so that the organization outlives the individual.

[45]On the extensiveness of this latter infiltration, see

Donald R. Cressey, "Delinquent and Criminal Structures," in Robert Nisbet and Robert K. Merton, eds., *Social Problems*, 3d ed., New York: Harcourt Brace Jovanovich, 1972, p. 165.

[46]For an account of this process, see Irving Spergel, *Racketville, Slumtown, Haulburg: An Exploratory Study of Delinquent Subcultures*, Chicago: University of Chicago Press, 1964, especially the account of Racketville.

peddling on the beat to the governor who grants an early pardon to a member of the crime syndicate. Thus, they undermine the efforts of law-abiding citizens to achieve an effective government or to convince each other they should cooperate in fighting crime.

5   Most importantly, it is evident that activities of organized crime are intertwined everywhere with those of legitimate businesses and with people who view themselves as respectable.

Let us consider this last pattern, which the crusading journalist Lincoln Steffens revealed in several United States cities at the turn of the century, before the Mafia was dominant.[47] Although members of organized criminal groups engage in violent crime—such as highjacking truckloads of cigarettes, liquor, or furs; or stealing goods from airports, warehouses, or the waterfront—the most profitable activities could not be carried out without the support of both officials and much of the law-abiding public.

This support takes many forms. It includes the failure of business people in slum areas to report many of the criminal activities they know about, including police toleration of narcotics. Of great importance are the many business people and private citizens who are willing to purchase "hot bargains" knowing they are likely to be stolen goods. Business people who hire arsonists to burn down their buildings, or thieves to ransack their warehouses, in order to obtain insurance payments must be added to this list. Corporate officials have connived with racketeers to help them infiltrate and dominate a union in order to keep wages low. Otherwise respectable citizens who buy the various illicit services of organized crime—many forms of gambling including the num-

bers game, loan sharking, narcotics, prostitution—are also part of that support system.

If this support did not exist, *creating a continuing demand for what the syndicate offers for sale*, corruption of officials and law enforcement systems would not even be profitable. Social analysts have pointed out these crucial links between respectability and criminality for decades.[48] That people should *organize* to gain profits from so lucrative a set of possibilities is to be expected. Organization yields some efficiencies that the lone free-lancer cannot achieve, especially in the area of paying off police officers and government agents for protection against arrest or conviction.

Our fourth type of criminality is what the average citizen thinks of as "real" crime (theft, robbery, burglary, assault, or murder) and thus disapproves of more than other crime. Learning that only about 3 percent of such crimes result in convictions and sentencing, the law-abiding citizen might suppose that a criminal career could be a rational choice for some people who have few skills or little education, and whose alternative is unemployment or wages too low to support a family. However, the chances of being caught eventually are very high even at that low rate if the crime is repeated. As a consequence, sociologists have gained most of their knowledge about criminal careers from men in penitentiaries or from men who have spent much of their life in prison.[49]

Such people include professional pickpockets, shoplifters, burglars, check forgers, and armed robbers. The first three of these

---

[47]See especially Joseph Lincoln Steffens, *The Shame of the Cities* (1904), New York: Sagamore Press, 1957.

[48]See, among others, Willard Waller in William J. Goode, Frank F. Furstenberg, Jr., and Larry R. Mitchell, eds., *On the Family, Education, and War: Selected Writings* (1938), Chicago: University of Chicago Press, 1970.

[49]For a classic account see Edwin H. Sutherland, *The Professional Thief*, Chicago: University of Chicago Press, 1937. See also John Irwin, *Felon*, Englewood Cliffs, N.J.: Prentice-Hall, 1970.

(as well as confidence men) are likely, if they are professionals, to have had extensive training, to work as a team, and to have a continuing relationship with one or more relatively respectable persons who can help with legal difficulties in case of arrest. In the days when money was usually kept in a company safe, blowing a safe was a highly technical task, and such men were honored for their skill. In several of these specialties, then, a small-scale organization may be encountered, some kind of continuing group. It is possible to engage in any of these crimes as a solo practitioner, but professional criminals consider that unwise. Some teams do not stay together long enough to be able to count on the help of a respectable outsider. Thus, even when practitioners agree that an effective organization is important, many do not achieve it.

Amateur or poorly trained criminals are common enough, as well as criminals who are not able to maintain a team. However, the better-trained are more likely to plan their careers and their crimes more carefully than others do. Their gains from any one job are likely to be higher than those of the less well organized criminals, because they plan each operation with more care. They are less likely to be convicted and more likely to receive lower sentences.

Though such professional or well-organized criminals enjoy more respect among other criminals, they are likely to share the same social backgrounds as less competent ones, just as they eventually share the same prison cells from time to time. To be sure, check forgers and to some extent confidence men are likely to have (or to claim) a middle-class background, because their victims must be persuaded they are either respectable or prosperous. But the bulk of crimes the public views as more serious are committed by young men from slum backgrounds.

Most of the criminals in this category were once juvenile delinquents who saw their best opportunity in crime and were encouraged in that ambition by the people they associated with on the street or in reform school. Having already been labeled as hoodlums or small-time criminals, seeing no chance of getting a well-paying job, and preferring the respect of fellow criminals to that of the law-abiding, these people could weigh a career in crime as a possibly rational choice.

Even if they do not *consciously* choose that career (and most do not),[50] they are likely to calculate the possible outcome of a particular crime—which becomes a step in a continuing career in crime. Both the criminal and the law-abiding citizen might decide that the chance of being caught this time is small, but the latter weighs the cost of the outcome differently. To the ordinary person with a steady job, even a tiny risk of going to jail is a potential loss that seems unbearable. To professional criminals, however, it is one of the harsh but unavoidable costs of doing business. Most of the other criminals they have known view it the same way. They will not lose much respect if they are convicted (but they will gain some admiration if they get away with it), while they take it for granted that prison will interrupt a criminal's career from time to time.

Even so crude a classification of crimes reveals how the different social responses to crimes as well as the varying resources of the criminal are related to differing types of organizations for crime, the later careers of criminals, the support the society gives to these activities, and the class backgrounds of those who engage in them. As can be seen, these differences are also related to more general factors, noted earlier, that af-

[50]Almost certainly people move into adult criminality, as David Matza reports they move into and out of juvenile delinquency, by a "drifting" process (*Delinquency and Drift*, New York: Wiley, 1964) that is nevertheless shaped by the opportunity structure and how much the person associates with delinquent or criminal groups.

fect who is more likely to be labeled as a deviant.

DRUG USE

In most societies at even a medium technological level, human beings have for untold centuries been clever enough to find out which substances in their environment could be used as drugs—any chemicals that affect the organism in ways the user perceives as desirable. These include coca leaves (one constituent is cocaine) in the Andes Mountains, alcohol (beer, wine, liquor, mead, kava), coffee and tea, tobacco, opium (from the poppy), marijuana, and various mushrooms. With modern chemistry hundreds of additional drugs have been created (amphetamines or "speed," barbiturates, LSD, methadone). Over the past three centuries

Figure 5-4 Many adults consume large quantities of dangerous addictive drugs, but do not consider themselves drug addicts. (John Briggs.)

all of these have been forbidden in one or more countries; and thousands of attacks on them have been published, often predicting both personal degradation and the decline of society if these drugs were not abolished.

Meanwhile, the citizens of this country have become the most voracious consumers of drugs the world has ever seen. In both volume and financial cost, the amount of prescription drugs that are legally purchased with permission of the physician is much greater than the amount of illegal drugs used.[51] If we add to this the social consumption of legal drugs—alcohol, tea and coffee (both containing caffeine), and tobacco—the illegal drug market pales into insignificance.

From a sociological viewpoint, we are most interested in the fact that most adults find no difficulty in consuming several kinds of drugs, while condemning the "drug user" or "drug addict." Here, especially, we observe some of the complex results of social definitions: That is, certain substances are called *drugs* and are thought of as dangerous or somewhat immoral. On the other hand, consumption of other substances, which are addictive and may actually kill or harm far more people each year (for example, tobacco and alcohol), is viewed as no more than a harmless vice.

These definitions vary from one society to another, and over time. Before World War I, opium and its various derivatives were widely used in this country, especially in medicines (paregoric, made from alcohol and opium, was a common household remedy for infant stomach aches until late in this century). Opium addiction was once most common among physicians. In the form of heroin (an opium derivative) it came to be widely used among slum youth and musicians much later, probably after World War II. In the nineteenth century opium use

[51]For a detailed critique of these practices, see Henry Lennard, *Mystification and Drug Misuse: Hazards in Using Psychoactive Drugs*, San Francisco: Jossey-Bass, 1971.

among the Chinese was encouraged by the British government. Though its use was deplored by many Chinese leaders, most opium smoking was a tolerated social vice among Chinese men. In rural Jamaica marijuana is widely used in cooking as well as in smoking. A majority of students in the more elite United States colleges have at least tried this drug, and associate with regular users of it.[52] In short, social definitions have a large effect on what is called a dangerous drug.

Precisely because these definitions are learned early and are little questioned, the social demand for valid data about the effects of drugs has not been high. Having already made their decision about various drugs, people have not seen any need for serious research on their real physiological consequences. Indeed, it was not until the youth rebellion of the 1960s, when the right to use "pot" came to be seen as a political issue, that many people began to understand how little was known about most of the common drugs and to question the various official assertions about their harmfulness. Until that time millions of people had (without publicizing it) smoked pot without becoming slavering drug addicts bent on rape or murder, as the Bureau of Narcotics had claimed they would. Nevertheless, few had actually made adequate experiments to test those official claims. One of the most important effects of the drug scare of this period, when middle-class youth especially experimented widely with many types of drugs, is that more people decided they wanted to know the real effect of various drugs.

A secondary effect of this set of investigations is that in most United States jurisdictions the legal enforcement of laws against

pot has weakened, and many old laws have been repealed. Those studies have generally shown that smoking marijuana is probably less harmful than drinking alcohol or smoking tobacco. On the other hand, the use of LSD dropped swiftly when some studies revealed that it may result in genetic damage.

Of all the addictive drugs, perhaps none has been studied more than opium and its derivatives or relatives (for example, morphine, heroin, methadone, codeine) because of their medical uses and people's fear of their harmfulness. They have been praised and damned for centuries, by poets as well as politicians. Little investigation is needed to learn of their destructive effects as they are now used by most addicts in the United States: ill health, dietary insufficiencies, infections from unsterile needles, deaths from overdosing, crimes committed in order to be able to support an expensive habit, the inability to hold a job when getting a drug supply becomes the dominant concern in the addict's life, or the agonizing experiences of withdrawal.

However, for opium as for most other addictive drugs (prominent exceptions are tobacco, alcohol, and coffee), little is known about the long-term effects of moderate use when getting the drug is *legal*. Both in this country and in China, many people once carried out their duties in responsible positions while using it over many years. Almost certainly, that use caused some impairment of function, as does tobacco and alcohol, but we are far from being able to prove that moderate use is too destructive to be tolerated legally.

Note that if its use were legal, its price would not be kept artificially high by governmental efforts to eliminate it altogether (this keeps supply too low for the demand). Then organized criminal groups would not command a profitable monopoly over its importation and wholesale distribution. Addicts would not feel they simply must engage in crime in order to support an expen-

[52]For a study of the *situations* that affect students' social definitions of how deviant is the use of either alcohol or marijuana, see James D. Orcutt, "Deviance as a Situated Phenomenon: Variations in the Social Interpretation of Marijuana, and Alcohol Use," *Social Problems*, 22 (February 1975), pp. 346–356.

sive habit, because the drug would not be expensive. Much governmental corruption would be eliminated, because the profits from its illegal sale would not be high enough to make bribery worthwhile.

In fact, that situation has existed in England for many years, where the addict can easily obtain the drug through a physician. With that example available, many reformers have proposed the legalization of heroin in this country.

However, precisely because the data come from another country and drug patterns have very different meanings in different cultures, it is not clear that all these improvements would result from that legalization—or, indeed, the legalization of other forbidden drugs, which has also been proposed.[53]

First, the sheer *size* of the problem is very different. Heroin addicts may well number more than two hundred thousand in this country, as against about one thousand in England. Second, a large-scale attempt *has* been made in this country to substitute an easily obtainable, addictive relative of heroin, methadone, which is cheap and permits the user to hold a job. It has not been very successful, as measured by the increase in the illegal methadone market, the number of deaths from overdoses, and the percentage of heroin addicts successfully rehabilitated by this substitute. Third, heroin addiction is primarily found in United States slum areas, while in England it is more commonly a middle-class pattern, as it once was in this country. Most of the United States heroin addicts who are young, male, and poor would not solve many of their life problems by merely being able to obtain heroin cheaply. Many would continue in crime and would not take a low-paying job, even if they did not have to obtain large sums of money for drugs. The factors that led them

into crime would remain strong even if heroin were free. That is, making heroin cheap does not improve the opportunity structure that young slum addicts face.

Fourth, and perhaps of most importance although its precise impact cannot be easily stated: With reference to many aspects of legality, the English culture is very different from that of the United States. The fact that the number of heroin addicts has never been very high in England suggests at least that its inner strains at lower-class levels are not as high as in the United States. The general crime rate in England is much lower, and so is the homicide rate. Police officers do not use guns, and few criminals do so, either. There are some criminal organizations in Great Britain,[54] but they are not comparable in scope or effectiveness with those in the United States. In short, it may well be that the English social patterns generate a lesser drug problem to begin with, and thus their solution will work for them and not for the United States.

The biological effects of the major drugs are *not* mere matters of social definition, although social definitions do shape part of human reactions to them.[55] For example, the heavy use of amphetamines (speed) or alcohol is biologically harmful, whatever the social definition.

Nor is it true that the social definitions of what is a harmful drug are entirely arbitrary or whimsical. Sometimes they are based on ignorance, for example, the belief that cof-

[53]The author does *believe*, however, that some version of the English plan would improve the drug situation in this country.

[54]See Cressey, *Criminal Organization*, especially chaps. 3 and 4.

[55]Note, for example, the wide variety of responses to marijuana, as reported in Erich Goode, *The Marijuana Smokers*, New York: Basic Books, 1970, especially chap. 7. Similarly, people may respond appropriately when they are told how a particular chemical or drug will affect them. (For ingenious experiments on this point, see Stanley S. Schachter, *Emotions, Obesity and Crime*, New York: Academic, 1971.) For this reason, many medical tests of drug effects are done in a "double-blind" manner. That is, neither the patient nor the person administering the drug knows which person gets which drug.

fee is very dangerous. Sometimes they are based on ignorance but are correct just the same, such as the early belief in the destructive effects of smoking tobacco.

Social disapproval of drugs is commonly expressed in the *rhetoric* or vocabulary of health. However, their biological harmfulness is not the major cause of that moral disapproval, and proving that a given drug is not very destructive will not change people's attitudes much. The heavily fat-laden United States diet is known to be dangerous, but little improvement in it is observable. In any event, people do not disapprove of being overweight in *moral* terms. Obesity is caused almost entirely by taking in more calories than one burns up in living, and is much more harmful than smoking pot, but few people view the fat, or obese, as "food addicts" or as moral deviants. Only a slight, recent trend toward moral disapproval of cigarette smoking is evident, though its dangers have been known for many years. Moreover, the disapproval comes almost entirely from the belief of nonsmokers that smoking will hurt *them* or that it befouls the air; the effect on the health of smokers is not what arouses their disapproval.

Much of the social disapproval of drugs is based on a judgment, in most cases correct, that the user withdraws either into his or her own world or into a world that is deviant in other ways, and thus rejects or is unable to discharge his or her role obligations. That statement applies as well to the United States drug of choice, alcohol. As part of the socialization process, most people in this country "learn to drink." That is, they learn to like the taste of one or more alcoholic beverages, learn what happens when they drink too much, learn how much they are permitted to drink in a particular social setting, and come to understand what their own tolerance for alcohol is. Thus, they eventually figure out how to control their drinking and acquire some ability to behave properly even if they have drunk a

bit too much.[56] When they step beyond those limits, others disapprove, for thereby uncontrollable drinkers cease to carry out their role obligations of guest, friend, date, driver, or fellow employee. "Drinking on the job" is frowned upon. Retiring into the very private world of alcoholism is viewed as a major role failure. Those who retreat to the company of the deviant and defeated alcoholics on Skid Row are viewed with repugnance.[57]

If that is true of a drug that has been well integrated into Western culture for thousands of years, the modern response to heroin, cocaine, pot, speed, and still more esoteric drugs is understandable. Fears about the harmfulness of pot can be based on ignorance, because it had not been widely smoked in this country (though the plant had been cultivated for over 200 years; its fiber was used to make hemp rope), and unsettling stories about its effects had filtered in from the Middle and Far East for centuries.[58]

It was also observable that its users were mainly middle-class youth who openly rejected much of respectable society or at best spoke ill of it, and retired into their own world of fellow smokers. Heavy users seemed to be "dropouts," hippies, or worse;

[56]For opinions of drinking in different settings, compared to those about smoking pot, see Orcutt, op. cit., pp. 352–353.

[57]For a sensitive portrayal of this world, see Jacqueline Wiseman, *Stations of the Lost*, Englewood Cliffs, N.J.: Prentice-Hall, 1970.

[58]Erich Goode has emphasized the *political* roots of the social disapproval of drugs, and I agree, but I believe that political forces are not directed arbitrarily or whimsically: The special, real or supposed, characteristics of some substances are much more likely to arouse political or social disapproval than others are. For a brief exposition of his opinion, see his *Drugs in American Society*, New York: Knopf, 1972, chap. 1, "A Sociological Perspective on Drugs and Drug Use." For a more general statement on this position, see Erich Goode, "Notes on the Enforcement of Moral Crimes," in Harvey A. Farberman and Erich Goode, eds., *Social Reality*, Englewood Cliffs, N.J.: Prentice-Hall, 1973, pp. 254–264.

they refused to accept the roles their family, school, or larger society had given to them.

That was, of course, a circular process. Respectable society labeled such people as deviants and put thousands in jail, thus reinforcing their tendency toward role rejection. Moreover, pot smokers openly proclaimed that the drug *did* take them out of this world and into another (and much better) world, thus confirming the widespread suspicion that the drug led people to reject "normal society." That is, though people did believe marijuana was biologically and psychologically harmful, that error was not the primary cause of the social disapproval directed against it and its users, or against any other drug. Far more important is the belief of ordinary citizens that some drugs cause users to reject or neglect their social obligations, to retire into another world (where they cannot be reached by ordinary social controls), in short, to cease being a full member of the society.

That set of self-reinforcing processes was very likely broken in the case of pot by primarily political factors: (1) the youth rebellion, which openly proclaimed the *right* to smoke pot and thus created a demand for factual knowledge about its real effects; and (2) the *class* impact of arrests for possessing or selling pot. Although parents of middle to high social rank were as indignant as any others about this new wave of drug use, it was after all *their* children who were being put in jail and labeled as criminals. They were not willing to tolerate that outcome, and eventually used their influence to modify both the pot laws and the administration of those laws, although that process of reversal has not yet been completed.

Where the society defines some occasions as appropriate for "getting high" for ritual or social purposes, so that many people see visions after eating certain mushrooms or get drunk, that *is* the appropriate role behavior. It does not interfere with normal,

day-to-day activities. That is also true *within* small groups of drug users whose actions are deplored by the outside, larger society. It is worth noting in this connection that drug users, themselves viewed as deviant, in turn view "speed freaks" as deviant, because any meaningful social relations with heavy amphetamine users are very difficult and erratic.

Thus, as in other labeling processes, there are underlying social and even biochemical realities in the disapproval of some types of drugs; that disapproval is not entirely whimsical or arbitrary, or as likely to be directed against chocolate bars as against LSD. Tea and coffee seem not to be very harmful biochemically, but in any event they do not interfere with ongoing social processes. Cigarette smoking does kill people, but even people who smoke heavily do not retire into a private world while in the land of the living. Drinkers who leave their social obligations because of their alcohol addiction are disesteemed, even though this drug is generally accepted. Moderate pot smoking, apparently harmless, is coming to be acceptable, because an increasing number of people have observed that it need not interfere with either work or ordinary social relations if (like drinking) it is used only on sociable occasions.

The use of heroin may be somewhat harmful even when socially tolerated, but at present much of its destructive effect in this country is caused by its peculiar legal status. That is, since it is defined as illegal, immoral, and dangerous, a monopolistic, mainly Mafia-dominated, highly profitable market in it has arisen. Prices are artificially high, and most addicts can buy it only if they steal, rob, pimp, or hustle. Since they are thus doubly deviant, it is especially difficult for them to lead normal lives. In turn, those processes prove, to most law-abiding citizens, that heroin addiction fully deserves to be condemned. Although some responsible people have proposed the legalization of heroin, that step does not seem likely at present.

ORGANIZATIONS OF AND FOR DEVIANTS

The sociologist views deviance and reactions to it as continuing social transactions. The person seen as deviant may proclaim and reaffirm her or his deviance, or instead deny or evade the charge. Others may in turn (depending on their stake in the issue and their influence) reject and punish the supposed deviant, or perhaps continue to view that person as a member in good standing.

However, these interactions occur not only between individual persons or between a person and one or more groups. They also occur *between groups*. As noted earlier, juvenile gangs affirm some values and norms that are different from those of the dominant, larger society, and may form at least quasi-groups. Political deviants also organize in order to support their political aims more effectively. Any large society contains thousands of formal or informal groups, circles, and networks, many of which have goals or norms that are opposed to those of other groups and of the society viewed as a whole.

The past decade has witnessed a blossoming of explicitly deviant groups, whose aim is explicitly to promote some activity generally thought of as violating social norms or laws, for example, organizations in favor of abortion, lesbianism, homosexuality, smoking pot, or general sexual freedom. However, their still more important aim is not the promotion of such activities, but the protection of those who engage in them; an example is COYOTE, the organization that demands better treatment for prostitutes.

Their aims are partly political, since typically they wish to change the laws that forbid the activities they support. Their aims

are also social and cultural, since they want others to stop discriminating against people now labeled as deviants. Indeed, they usually ask that people begin to approve their activities.

Are such organizations different from tens of thousands of organizations that have existed in the United States in the past—to save the steam railroad (surely a deviant goal!), to impose the prohibition of liquor, to promote the belief in astrology or the practice of witchcraft, or to discriminate against the Irish, the Catholics, or the blacks? *Legally* they are not, since almost anyone can organize with others to proclaim almost any belief whatsoever, whether it is some form of communism or fascism, or the healthfulness of chewing one's food thoroughly (Fletcherism).[59]

Socially they are different, however, for their members publicly affirm that they *are* deviants, that they do break certain laws, but they demand the right to be treated just as conforming citizens are. Organizations to facilitate abortion did just that, when abortion was against the law, and insisted that abortion was morally permissible. Organizations exist whose aim is to support the civil rights of homosexuals or lesbians, including the right to hold any job. To that extent

[59]Alexis de Tocqueville, in his classic *Democracy in America*, remarked on the astonishing tendency of Americans to create associations or organizations, and his comment has been repeated many times since then. Whatever may have been the situation in the United States at the beginning of the nineteenth century, compared with that in Europe, no modern research has disclosed any such social pattern. In fact, most people in this country do not belong to any organizations at all (other than some church). For data on this see S. M. Lipset, "Religion and Politics in the American Past and Present," in Lipset, *Revolution and Counter-Revolution: Change and Persistence in Social Structures*, New York: Basic Books, 1968; Robert Lee and Martin Marty, *Religion and Social Conflict*, New York: Oxford University Press, 1970; Henry Ehrmann, "Interest Groups and the Bureaucracy in Western Democracies," in Reinhard Bendix, ed., *State and Society: A Reader in Comparative Political Sociology* (1968), Berkeley: University of California Press, 1973.

Figure 5-5 Actress Jane Fonda (left) talks with Margo St. James, chairmadam of COYOTE, an organization promoting better treatment for prostitutes. (United Press International Photo.)

they are simply exercising their right to free speech. However, members are also (with few exceptions) proclaiming publicly that they are engaging in this forbidden activity, and that though they do violate the law as well as social custom, they refuse to accept the label of deviant, outcast, or criminal. Moreover, such organizations make public appeals to their many fellow deviants, demanding that they stop hiding or running, and instead proudly affirm what they secretly practice.

A second type of deviant organization does not try to *promote* deviant activities, but to help deviants live normal lives. A few of these overlap with the previous group, and the difference is mainly that of emphasis. Alcoholics Anonymous, Gamblers Anonymous, Weight Watchers, and suicide prevention organizations, among others, try to engage in *therapy* or prevention. They are much more sympathetic to the problem of avoiding the deviations they are concerned with, and claim to be more effective at such helping procedures than are government agencies.[60]

[60]Not all are as sympathetic, since members in some of these organizations use strongly punitive therapy, partly directed by their own contempt for their former

A third type of helping organization for deviants is again aimed not at promoting deviant behavior but at *restoring* the rights of deviants who cannot easily reenter the conforming society. One example is the various associations that are concerned with prisoners' rights, that is, the rights of both prisoners and ex-prisoners. These assert that the deprivations that vex prisoners are too harsh, for example, the loss of voting rights or the right to drive, or the difficulty of getting a job. Other organizations help unwed mothers escape the stigma of their past and make a new life for themselves. Such organizations also assert that their efforts help to prevent a recurrence of the deviant behavior. However, they mainly focus on the task of protecting former deviants from being further harried or rejected when they do try to live a conforming life.

These different types of organizations do not typically become large or politically influential, because not many people wish to be socially linked with such deviant activities. Not many who were deviant but who now conform want others to know about their past. People who might be sympathetic are not likely to be able to contribute large funds to help such organizations.

On the other hand, no previous historical period has been as willing to listen to the messages of such groups. None has offered them as much opportunity (through TV, radio, or newspapers) to present their claims to millions of fellow citizens, and thus to reach all who might give support. Although the federal government launched many programs in the 1960s and early 1970s to curb the freedoms of deviant groups, its efforts were ineffective. In fact, during that decade more of such organizations, with far more

deviations. The best instance is Synanon, whose aim is supposedly the cure of drug addicts and most of whose members are ex-addicts. Thus, they can reject the addict's "excuses and rationalizations," because they know how empty such rationalizations are. See Lewis Yablonsky, *The Tunnel Back: SYNANON*, New York: Macmillan, 1965.

radical proposals, worked publicly in favor of their aims; were later supported by favorable court decisions when they fought the efforts of government or private citizens to stop them; and received far more support from fellow deviants of various kinds as well as from conforming citizens, than at any period of the past.

In spite of such efforts, it seems unlikely that many of the deviations called victimless crimes will eventually be accepted as "each person's business" and that the laws against them will be repealed. It is easy to make that predictive error, because so many organizations of (or for) deviants receive much public attention, and their members seem to be widely tolerated. The tolerance occurs far more in the mass media than in concrete reality. Thousands of people are now in jails because they were convicted under existing laws against drugs (including marijuana), various laws against sexual deviations between consenting adults (of the same sex or different sex, married or not married, prostitutes or amateurs), drunkenness, pornography, and various political acts. Although a few such people may be helped by organizations of (or for) deviants, and some are aided indirectly through the effect of organizations on public opinion and existing laws, the processes of punishment are not stopped by those efforts to reduce the disapproval directed against most forms of deviant behavior.

CONCLUSION: PUNISHMENTS AND REWARDS IN DEVIANCE AND CONFORMITY

Social definitions of deviance and the efforts of people to press each other toward conformity are based on a set of folk assumptions and ideas about how individuals or groups will respond to various rewards and punishments. These ideas need not be in conformity with the best knowledge of sociologists or psychologists; commonsense assumptions are often wrong. Modern psychology has emphasized the usefulness of rewards, especially in acquiring a habit pattern, an attitude, or a predisposition in favor of some action. That is, if the individual is rewarded with each step toward an approved skill or behavior (walking, speaking, working hard), learning is likely to be much more rapid than if punishment alone is handed out for wrong moves. In general, if both are used, learning is *not* more rapid, whether it is a new technique or skill, or an attitude, preference, or norm which is being taught.

Nevertheless, all societies use punishments of various kinds to press members toward conformity. In Chapter 3, on socialization, we sketched out the effects of punishment and pointed out why all societies use it in various ways to get conformity from their members. (1) It gives quick results, especially in teaching avoidance or fear. (2) Learning through punishment is hard to undo or root out. (3) Punishment-learning is crude and *constrictive*; it keeps people within narrow limits. All those consequences of punishment fit rather well the goals of teaching the child to shun deviance: What is prohibited is learned early, deeply and crudely. With reference especially to important prohibitions, the individual is pressed toward general avoidance, not a precise calculation of how closely he or she may come to a violation without crossing the boundary. We are not taught to weigh carefully whether the costs of crime, sexual deviations, suicide, or rebellion might be less than the rewards. We are taught they are *bad*, and we should halt any approach toward them.

Both childhood and adult socialization offer rewards, too, for ordinary conformity as well as for excellent achievement. Material satisfactions, affection, and esteem support the processes by which people come to want to do what others want them to do or what the society needs to have done.

Consequently, in addition to any such inner commitment from socialization, all societies create systems of immediate or distant rewards and punishments that make it more profitable to conform. Thus, even if we inwardly deny we *should* obey our high school teacher or the policeman, we know that if we disobey we shall face some punishments, and if we are obedient we shall obtain some rewards. Simple rationality suggests that it is generally wise to obey people who combine legitimate authority and some threat of force.

These mutually supporting processes cannot operate well, of course, without adequate mechanisms for *observing* who has or has not conformed well or ill and for handing out rewards or punishments. In small societies, as in villages, mutual visibility is high. In a city it is much lower, though in many social situations (work, local neighborhoods, streets where many people gather or walk) there is considerable visibility. However, even where *some* people observe others' behavior, they may or may not report to others what they have seen; and those to whom they do report may or may not know the person who was observed. Thus, in a city much behavior remains unobserved or unreported, or others do not act on the knowledge even if reported.

In addition to those contingencies which reduce the effective visibility of deviations or weaken the mechanisms for handing out rewards and punishments, a much more important set of factors may reduce conformity: Are the rewards or punishments *enough* to ensure conformity? After all, what is forbidden is often desirable, or else it would not have to be forbidden. Losing one's freedom or the esteem of others is a serious threat, but the temptation of stealing, swindling, drugs, or sexual deviations may also be great. An individual may calculate the likelihood of getting caught as relatively low and the gain from success as high. Often,

that prediction is correct. Whether or not it is correct, different people will perceive those chances very differently and will perceive the relative gains or losses in very different ways.

The result is not at all that most people carry out all their role obligations and avoid all deviations, but that most do engage in various serious or trivial deviations from time to time. Daily social life exhibits a continuing tension between the pressures or attractions toward deviance and those toward conformity in this or that area of social behavior. In no society, in any area of living, except for short periods of crisis, will the pressures toward conformity be so overwhelming that almost everyone obeys the rules. If the leaders of a group set standards too high, they will lose their positions or people will simply not obey. Social patterns are constantly being undermined, and constantly being reconstructed, as people move from deviance to conformity and back again.

Although some extreme limits might be hypothetically suggested, at which the society begins to fall apart because too few people conform even to get the work of the society done, in fact we have no evidence that *any* whole society ever came apart because of widespread deviation. Short periods of disorganization or revolution occur in which many older patterns are no longer followed. However, new ones arise soon, or old ones are again accepted. Even during historical periods that seem very disorganized, most people do not rush to engage in general deviant behavior. Human beings experience a completely disorderly life as uncomfortable and unsatisfying, just as they cannot tolerate a life in which they are pressed to obey strict standards all the time. If everyone succumbs at times to the temptations of deviation, so do most people labeled as deviants prefer to live in a world that is generally orderly and nondeviant.

READINGS

Howard S. Becker, *Outsiders,* 2d ed., New York: Free Press, 1973.

Egon Bittner, "The Police on Skid Row: A Study of Peacekeeping," *American Sociological Review,* 32 (October 1967), pp. 699–715.

Donald J. Black and Albert J. Reiss, "Police Control of Juveniles," in Robert A. Scott and Jack D. Douglas, eds., *Theoretical Perspectives on Deviants,* New York: Basic Books, 1972, pp. 119–141.

Theodore G. Chiricos, Phillip D. Jackson, and Gordon P. Waldo, "Inequality in the Imposition of a Criminal Label," *Social Problems,* 19 (Spring 1972), pp. 553–572.

Richard A. Cloward and Lloyd E. Ohlin, *Delinquency and Opportunity,* New York: Free Press, 1960.

F. James Davis and Richard Stivers, eds., *Theoretical Perspectives on the Collective Definition of Deviance,* New York: Free Press, 1975.

Simon Dinitz et al., eds., *Deviance,* 2d ed., New York: Oxford University Press, 1975.

Jack D. Douglas, *The Social Meanings of Suicide,* Princeton, N.J.: Princeton, 1967.

Kai T. Erikson, *Wayward Puritans,* New York: Wiley, 1966.

Jack P. Gibbs, "Suicide," in Robert K. Merton and Robert Nisbet, *Contemporary Social Problems,* 3d ed., New York: Harcourt Brace Jovanovich, 1971, pp. 271–312.

Erving Goffman, *Stigma,* Englewood Cliffs, N.J.: Prentice-Hall, 1963.

———, "The Insanity of Place," in *Relations in Public,* New York: Harper & Row, 1971, pp. 357–388.

William J. Goode, "Violence between Intimates," in Donald Mulvihill and Melvin Tumin, eds., *Violent Crime,* Washington, D.C.: U.S. Government Printing Office, 1970, pp. 941–977.

Travis Hirschi, "Procedural Rules and the Study of Deviant Behavior," *Social Problems,* 21 (Fall 1973), pp. 159–173.

Edwin M. Lemert, *Human Deviance, Social Problems, and Social Control,* 2d ed., Englewood Cliffs, N.J.: Prentice-Hall, 1972.

Peter Maas, *The Valachi Papers,* New York: Putnam, 1968.

Peter M. McHugh, "A Common Sense Conception of Deviance," in Hans P. Dreitzel, *Recent Sociology No. 2: Patterns of Communicative Behavior,* New York: Macmillan, 1970, pp. 152–180.

David Matza, *Becoming Deviant,* Englewood Cliffs, N.J.: Prentice-Hall, 1969.

Peter H. Rossi et al., "The Seriousness of Crime: Normative Structure and Individual Differences," *American Sociological Review,* 39 (April 1974), pp. 224–237.

Earl Rubington and Martin S. Weinberg, eds., *Deviance: The Interactionist Perspective,* 2d ed., New York: Macmillan, 1972.

Thomas J. Scheff, "The Labeling Theory of Mental Illness," *American Sociological Review,* 39 (June 1974), pp. 444–452.

Edwin M. Schur, *Labeling Deviant Behavior,* New York: Harper & Row, 1971.

James F. Short and Fred L. Strodtbeck, *Group Process and Gang Delinquency,* Chicago: University of Chicago Press, 1965.

Jerome H. Skolnick, *Justice without Trial,* New York: Wiley, 1966.

David Sudnow, "Normal Crimes: Sociological Features of the Penal Code in a Public Defender Office," *Social Problems,* 12 (Winter 1965), pp. 255–276.

Edwin H. Sutherland, *White Collar Crime,* New York: Dryden, 1949.

PART THREE

FORMS OF SOCIAL
ORGANIZATION

CHAPTER SIX

FORMS OF SOCIAL ORGANIZATION: GROUPS LARGE AND SMALL

Human social life, as we note at many points in this volume, seems to take place between *individuals* because we mainly *see* individuals in social interaction. However, much of human interaction is shaped by our membership in one or more groups, and people respond to one another as group members, not just as isolated persons. The importance of groups is seen in another connection: The social organization itself, the structure of the society, is partly made up of groups, large and small, that direct human skills and aspirations toward various goals, from electing a president to rearing the next generation.

Human groups include, then, friendships and families, social networks and neighborhoods, country clubs and political party organizations, national veterans' associations and Masonic lodges, international stamp collectors and manufacturers' associations.

Much of what we do is related to groups in some way. This chapter focuses on the various kinds of groups we observe and their place in our lives.

GROUP TRAITS

As a first step, let us consider what a group is. The question is not trivial, because we rarely see a whole group all together, available for observation, and because sociologists use the term for so many kinds of apparently different relationships. Moreover, almost any relationship can, over time, *become* a group. As a consequence, the distinction between a real group and a mere huddle of people on a street corner on a cold day, or an audience, or several agricultural workers hired to pick grapes, may not be clear at times.

We can agree that a set of people is a group when it has the following traits:

1 Members continue to interact with one another.
2 Members expect to continue their social relations with one another.
3 Membership requires living by norms that are special to the group.
4 Members view each other as part of the group; that is, there is a social boundary between membership and nonmembership.
5 Accordingly, group members feel some sense of *identification* with the group and with one another.
6 Members are seen by others as a group (unless membership is secret, as in a ring of spies).

These traits reinforce one another and thus are not entirely independent. If people interact with one another for a long time (*duration*), they are likely to share both information and attitudes (*scope*). If members are viewed by others as a group, they are more likely to see each other as fellow members, too (*unity*). If there are *social boundaries* that set a group apart, others are more likely to treat members differently and to view them as a unit. Each of these characteristics, however, has a separate effect on the behavior of groups and group members.

The reader will note that none of these traits is defined *quantitatively* or precisely. The boundaries may be more or less distinct; there is no specification of how *much* interaction must be repeated to create a group. Just how "special" the group norms have to be is not stated. In short, in any concrete case, whether an aggregate or set of people should be called a group is a matter of "more or less." The more it exhibits such traits, the more definitely it is to be considered a group. Let us now examine the various parts of our definition to see how each of these factors may affect social behavior.

Duration and Scope

When we examine the first trait, the extent to which there is *continuing* social action among members, it is evident that it has many aspects having to do with *scope* and *duration*. If much of a person's *total* social activity (wider scope) takes place within the group, then it is likely that *repeated* or recurrent social interaction will take place. Examples would be families, a group of explorers, or a primitive society. If the scope of social interaction is broad, then members are likely to affect each other's behavior in many *different* ways.

How long the relationship continues has even more aspects. First, duration may be thought of as *real* continuity, as contrasted with *expected* duration. Second, we can ask whether either applies to membership (does the person's *membership* last?) or to the group itself (does the *group* last?). All four of these aspects may have some effect on people's behavior.

Groups may form for a specific purpose, such as fighting a superhighway that threatens to destroy their village or neighborhood or putting on an amateur show at a summer camp. Then the real and expected duration of both the group and the members' interaction will be short. Groups that last a short time, and are expected to do so, are less likely to accumulate much goods or money or to command deep loyalty from members.

Some groups are expected to last long and do so, but the *membership* is expected to change constantly. Thus, one may be a member of a campus club or swimming team this year, but not the next, while both groups continue through many generations of students. A group that is expected to continue may change its rules or goals to attract new members if membership drops.

Family lines are expected to continue for generations though individual members can enjoy only one lifetime. A specific family unit is *expected* to last only through the lifetime of its members, but in reality may break down through divorce. Note that even then we expect the relations of the parents with their children to continue through the parents' lifetime, and most do.

Norms

Groups vary greatly in the extent to which they develop a set of norms special to that group. A team of mountain explorers, dependent on one another and interacting with each other almost every hour of the day, is very likely to create special rules for a wide range of behavior (broader scope). So is a medical group working in an intensive unit of a hospital and steadily alert to the many dangers from which they must protect their patients. Here, however, the breadth or scope of activity covered is much narrower than that of a team of explorers. On the other hand, many special interest groups, organized to pursue a narrow goal such as collecting comic books or studying wild mushrooms, may develop only a few rules to facilitate that goal.

In addition, however, groups vary with respect to *how much conformity* they require from their members. Some religious sects are very strict, as the Pilgrims were. Secret revolutionary groups are also likely to be strict, while most social clubs are likely to be more tolerant of different kinds of behavior.

In either case some groups create an elaborate set of procedures and offices to deal with *deviations,* while others do not. In a modern hospital many systems of control over the general quality of medical treatment, the decision to operate, the correctness of diagnosis, and lines of authority are likely to be encountered. In a university research team almost all the rules are *informal;* that is, they have not been made by real votes or by the decision of an official leader, and they are not written down on paper. There are no special officers whose

duty it is to report violations of the rule or any official procedures to deal with them.

Boundaries

With respect to the *boundaries* of groups, we note that some have real lists of members, for example, the American Bar Association or a university swimming team. To find out the membership of other groups, however, we would have to carry out a special research project. Thus, if we wanted to know all the people who are in groups called "close friends" in the neighborhood, we would have to interview everyone. Whether a distant relative is to be thought of as a "member of the family" could not be decided by kinship charts alone. We would have to ask family members, for sometimes a distant cousin or uncle interacts frequently or is well liked and is thus counted a member.

The boundary may be sharp because entrance is difficult, as with professional associations and honorific groups (Nobel Prize winners, members of an elite club). Boundaries may also be sharp because, by contrast, the group is viewed as outcastes, as some people are in India and Japan. Parent-teacher associations may have lists of dues-paying members, but few or none make a sharp distinction between real members and those who simply come to meetings. Some fans or supporters of baseball teams may attend often enough to know each other, but again no attempt is made to define who is a "real" member.

Note that when the boundaries are fuzzy or indistinct, the group is less likely to make any rules about proper behavior or to enforce them.

Unity

Related to the sharpness of the boundaries is the *unity,* or cohesiveness, of the group, that is, how close members feel to one another, or how closely they identify with one another or to the group. The Pennsylvania Mennonites make a severe distinction between members in good standing and others. They "shun" the latter and will not engage in social relations with them. Members in good standing are cohesive; they stand together until erring members have repented. (Outsiders are not "shunned," but Mennonites restrict their social relations with such people to only the political or commercial activities that are necessary.) Groups that are more cohesive are likely also to be able to resist outside pressures or attacks. To the extent that they are cohesive, other people are likely to see them as a unit, or a group. Where boundaries are not distinct, this is harder to do.

The foregoing analysis reminds us of the wide range of relationships that can be seen or defined as groups, the extent to which a set of people can or cannot be properly called a group, and how the various traits used in our definition of a group actually do affect the behavior of both members and the groups themselves. In the following section we shall consider some types of groups that play a special role in social life.

KINDS OF SOCIAL GROUPS

Groups come in many sizes and shapes, and no system of classification does justice to their wide variety. Most groups number no more than two or three members, while others may contain millions. Some groups are secret, and others advertise their existence. Some are open to anyone who cares to join, while some clubs are so exclusive that neither the road to the clubhouse nor the building itself is marked by any sign at all: If you do not know where you are, you have no right to be there. Some are marked by affection and closeness, others by formality and reserve. Some have many formal rules, and some have no explicit rules at all.

Groups are more numerous than the people who belong to them, because almost every person in a modern society is part of several or many groups.

Though no one has succeeded in neatly classifying groups,[1] sociologists have chosen some kinds of groups to study more closely because their importance in social activities seems clear. That is, commonsense observation affirms their significance in day-to-day social activities. Indeed, under various labels these types have been a subject of study for many centuries. As we shall see, some of them overlap with one another, for they do not make up a complete classification. They are simply the kinds of groups that are most often discussed. The following groups will be analyzed in subsequent sections:

1 In-groups and out-groups.
2 Peer groups.
3 Reference groups.
4 Hierarchical triads.
5 Small groups and large groups.
6 Primary groups.
7 Friendships.
8 Secondary groups, or formal groups.

In-Groups and Out-Groups

Almost certainly, the oldest distinction between groups is that between "us" and "them," between friend and foe, between "those who try to eat *us*" and "ourselves, who kill and eat *them*." Members of groups, as noted before, think of each other as forming a social unit. They feel they share a common fate. They are more forgiving toward their own errors or wrongdoing and less forgiving toward those of out-groups.

[1]In his rewarding analysis of the important characteristics of groups (which I am following here), Robert K. Merton notes that over a generation ago the sociologist E. E. Eubank could locate thirty-nine different classifications of groups. See Merton's "The Classification of Types of Membership Groups," in *Social Theory and Social Structure*, enlarged ed., New York: Free Press, 1968, pp. 362–380.

As we noted in Chapter 2, we sometimes give the label *ethnocentrism* to such a set of attitudes; that is, *our* culture and social customs are the "center." Our system is *right*; theirs, by contrast, is evil, full of errors, or laughable. Ours is superior. Because ours is superior, we need not respect them much or apply the same standards of justice we use to evaluate our actions toward ourselves.

Although this social pattern is ancient, we can observe its influence in our daily lives. Student bodies in rival high schools or colleges may look on one another as traditional enemies, each viewing the other as inferior in many ways. Families protect their members even when that does an injustice to outsiders. An inner clique within a corporation may plot to advance their own interests, sacrificing other employees.

On the other hand, we can see some changes in the slow development of cities, large nations, and the industrial world, in which larger numbers of strangers are to be found who must somehow learn to get along with one another. First, larger social units necessarily create rules that impose the *norm of civility* toward people whom we do not care about or even know. Some tribes in the past felt free to kill strangers, whereas in modern societies, in many areas of social life, we are supposed to be both friendly and fair toward anyone else who at least behaves that way toward us. The creation of much larger social units, in which many different groups must work together, forces us to accept many strangers as members of a larger "we"-group, as fellow citizens.

A second cause of this process is *crosscutting statuses*, or the extent to which we occupy many different social positions, some of which we do not share with all the members of our most intimate "we"-group. For example, we may identify strongly with members of our family or neighborhood, but in other areas of life (on the job, in

Figure 6-1 This closely knit Italian family may squabble among themselves but form an in-group in relation to the nonfamily society around them. (Raimondo Borea, Editorial Photocolor Archives.)

college, in a political organization) we owe other allegiances that we do not share with the fellow members of our in-group. These crosscutting influences prevent the society from breaking up into warring subgroups, each seeking its own ends. By contrast, in some isolated societies or villages, members have no important social positions outside their own group.

In-groups and out-groups are not, therefore, simply holdovers from the past, a kind of ancient social pattern that will disappear as we become more enlightened.[2] The feeling of allegiance to one's groups, and the sense of identification with one's fellow members, is as natural as breathing. To the extent that interaction with group members

[2]For an elegant commentary on arguments as to whether "they" have a right to study "us," and whether we who are "inside" can analyze more objectively than "they who are outside," see Robert K. Merton, "The Perspectives of Insiders and Outsiders," in Robert K. Merton, *The Sociology of Science*, ed. by Norman W. Storer, Chicago: University of Chicago Press, 1973, pp. 99–138.

is satisfying, that the group rewards us in many ways, and we accept its norms and values as our own, we are more likely to judge it to be distinct from other groups, and superior as well—or at least more deserving of our support. Thus, though the social, political, and economic processes of modern society increase the number of groups we belong to, create more crosscutting positions, and in many situations require us to treat strangers as fellows, new in-groups are constantly arising.

Peer Groups

Peer groups are simply a form of in-group that is made up of peers, or equals. The term more frequently refers to *age* peers, and usually to "teenagers" or to play groups of children. Though the term suggests equals, we know that in almost all groups, including those with only two or three members, one or more individuals are leaders or are more dominant than others. Nevertheless, peer groups are likely to be informal groups, without any elected leaders, and the term conveys a reality; members view each other as roughly equal or at least *agree* to the norm that "everyone should be treated the same."

Peer groups have attracted much attention in recent years because the numbers of teenagers increased substantially as a result of the post-World War II baby boom. It also became a large specialized market because of the rise in national income of this and other industrialized countries. In addition, during that period the mass media gave considerable coverage to rock music and student rebellions, emphasizing the linkages among peers and the extent to which they look to one another for guidance. To many commentators these groups seem to form a world of their own with different costumes, language patterns, goals, and values from those of adults. However, the dramatic processes by which a younger age segment

comes to prominence should not hide the more *general* importance of peers in *all* classes, ages, groups, and historical periods. In some African societies, for example, peer groups began as a segment of young boys—called age groups—but instead of breaking up when the young men married, they continued through life as special segments of the society. In Japan, too, age peers among men are of great importance in both recreation and work. When school peers become adults, they may see a member off when he travels and formally welcome him when he returns. In industry it is common to promote by seniority, so that many groups of peers are not split apart by wide differences in job success.

We should not suppose, however, that even in the United States peer groups are confined to young people. Friendships are most likely to arise between people of the same age, sex, and general social rank. Intimate friends are likely to share much more. As we observe many situations, we often see that people who are different from one another in many ways seem nevertheless to enjoy each other's company if they have at least shared their own generation's experiences. Like their younger counterparts, people of more advanced years are not simply isolated individuals, but are members of peer groups. Parents were upset upon learning that peer groups seemed to have more effect on their children's behavior than did their elders or the authority figures in their lives. What they forgot was that they, too, are shaped in attitudes and norms by their own peer groups.

Reference Groups

Since this term was coined, the idea of reference group behavior has been widely used in sociology.[3] The concept of reference

[3]The term was created by Herbert H. Hyman in *Psychology of Status*, Archives of Sociology, No. 269, 1942. However, as Merton and Rossi have pointed out, the

group refers to one aspect of our earlier definition, the fact that a group is characterized by a special set of norms or values. Thus, a *reference group* is any group whose norms or values we use when we are deciding what is wrong or right, excellent or worthless. That is, we *refer* to that group when we are engaged in evaluations and actions. Usually, we are members of our reference group, for we are more likely to accept the values and norms of groups in which we play a role.

On the other hand, only a moment's thought will remind us that sometimes we accept guidance from a group of which we are *not* a member. Thus, a budding poet in a southern town might well reject not only the opinions of his or her own peers or friendship groups, but also those of teachers or fellow members of a literary circle. Instead, his or her criteria for excellence might be those proclaimed by the literary critics in *The New York Review of Books.* An Army private who aspires to become an officer is much more likely to use as a reference group the officers encountered or read about than other privates.

Reference group explanations have been especially enlightening in helping us to understand social behavior or attitudes that do *not* seem to fit commonsense or rational self-interest. Thus, in a famous comparison that was reported from World War II, in general people who were promoted felt that the chances of promotion were good. However, men in the Air Force (with a very high rate of promotion within the group) were generally less satisfied with the chances of

promotion than were members of the Military Police (who rarely got promoted). However, as soon as one understands that members of the latter group were simply making comparisons with fellow members (no one seemed to be doing much better) and not with other branches of the service, their greater satisfaction becomes more understandable.

Similarly, in a study in England, the better-paid manual workers were asked whether there were any other people who were noticeably better off than they, and only about half replied that there were.[4] This might seem surprising, since every day they read about people much richer and more privileged than they. On the other hand, their reference group was in fact other manual workers. By contrast to this case, even a talented young research scientist might feel very dissatisfied with quick upward progress, however much faster it might be than that of his or her fellows, if the reference group chosen is *other* historical figures who achieved greatly at an early age. Poets and musical composers are often plagued by the embarrassing fact that many great historical figures began to write important works before they were out of their teens. We can observe the importance of reference groups in the somewhat cynical remark made by a contemporary philosopher: "It is not enough to succeed; our friends must also fail."

Thus, whether an individual feels satisfied or instead feels deprived of success is likely to be more significantly determined by *which* reference group is chosen than by membership in a particular group. We note, too, that the group chosen as a reference group may be one that enjoys a higher rank, but sometimes it is not. For example, many contemporary literary figures as well as sociologists are defenders of the under-

---

general idea has been used widely in social analysis from time immemorial, and they point to numerous uses of it in previous research. Since the original article, Merton has developed reference group theory in a still more elaborate fashion. See Robert K. Merton and Alice K. Rossi, "Contributions to the Theory of Reference Group Behavior"; and Robert K. Merton, "Continuities in the Theory of Reference Groups and Social Structure"; in his *Social Theory and Social Structure,* pp. 279–334, 335–440.

[4]*Relative Deprivation and Social Justice,* Berkeley: University of California Press, 1966, p. 193.

dog, the deprived, and the disadvantaged. They would prefer to earn the respect of such people rather than that of the more respectable members of their occupations.

Further complexities in the choice of reference groups should be noted. We are all members of many formal and informal groups. Some are engaged in a wide range of activities, while some focus on a narrow segment of activities. It is at least conceivable that we might refer to the same group each time we make a comparison, no matter which activity we engage in, but common-sense informs us that we do not. For the most part we use the standards or norms of those groups that are most relevant to the activity we are engaged in at the moment. Thus, when writing an article, a university professor is likely to use as a reference group some respected leaders of the profession, but is much more likely to use the standards of *neighbors* if he or she makes a speech to the local parent-teacher association.

Nevertheless, for any particular activity, each individual must choose *which* reference group standards are to be followed in any given situation. Social rules will not always offer much guidance in this choice. Moreover, an individual's reference groups will change over time, as people alter their social positions, their occupations, or their residential location. People may use as their reference group the social clubs or groups to which they *aspire*; or they may instead continue through adulthood to hold the standards of the groups they associated with in childhood. The fundamental fact is that in many decisions we must *choose* which reference group to use, and these may support one another or be in conflict.

It is evident, however, that "the *distinctive* focus of reference group theory is that . . . [people] often orient themselves to groups *other than their own* in shaping their behavior and evaluations."[5] That is, tradi-

tional sociological theory has always focused on the importance of *membership* groups, and reference group theory does not deny that importance. It has especially illuminated the many instances in which people utilize standards or norms of groups of which they are not a member. Thereby, we are often able to understand behavior or attitudes that seem somewhat at odds with the apparent social position or membership of an individual or subgroup.

Although the number of reference group commentaries and explanations has multiplied over the past several decades, much less success has been achieved in what seems to be a central problem in reference group theory. That is, how *do* people choose their reference groups, among the wide range of groups about which they know something; and upon what basis do they choose a reference group of which they are not a member? We can think of very rough possibilities: Individuals are more likely to choose a reference group whose main focus of activity is the one they are now engaged in; groups with somewhat more prestige or other rewards to offer are more likely to be used as reference groups; if an individual has a belief that she or he is likely to be able to move to a higher-ranking group, and wants to do so, that group is more likely to be chosen as a reference group. However, these are no more than mere suggestions, and they cannot be viewed as adequate solutions to the question of which factors shape individuals' choice of reference groups.

Hierarchical Triads

In detective stories (and also in real life) detectives sometimes work in pairs in order to elicit a confession from a suspected criminal. One of them is rough, abusive, and threatening. The other, by contrast, plays the role of comforter and friend, explaining that he will try to protect the criminal from the bad behavior of the rough one, if only

[5]Merton, op. cit., p. 361.

the criminal will confess. This system has, in fact, worked again and again. Either detective working alone will not, however, be sufficient.

The foregoing may seem to be an oddity; but real life affords many examples of a triad in which two of the members have high rank, but one of them plays the role of authority figure while the other plays the part of a friend. Moreover, this is only one of *many* possible triadic combinations that ordinary social life affords. It is striking, however, that commonsense observation gives relatively little attention to them.

Let us first note the general importance of the triad in social life. Without at all agreeing to Theodore Caplow's assertion that "triads are the building blocks of which all social organizations are constructed,"[6] it must be conceded that common observation will disclose that triads are important in many social situations, and they may be made up of individuals, groups, or bureaucracies. For these reasons numerous analysts have attempted to lay bare the sometimes complex behavior of people or organizations in triadic relationships.

The beginning point to be noted is that as soon as any relationship between two people has expanded to include a third, the number of *possible relationships* increases three times. As a dyad, the relationship can be stated as A=B; but when the dyad is expanded to a triad, the possible relationships are A=B, B=C, and A=C. Obviously, each of these three persons or groups may have very different resources of prestige, influence, or wealth.

One of the more striking findings from numerous studies is that if we look for the coalitions among members of a triad in order to ascertain who will side with whom

in a conflict, most commonly it will be the *two weaker* members who side with each other against the *stronger* member. Although this would seem to create some risk, it is the more rational course of action. If either of the weaker individuals sides with the stronger, that weaker one is still in a position of subordination. If they side with one another, they may well overcome the stronger one.

It is this basic fact, Caplow asserts, that underlies the resistance of weak people to tyrants and the general inability of higher-rank persons to dominate completely any social group or even a society where their influence might seem to be overwhelming. Such coalitions have many ramifications. For example, one is that boys are more likely to develop a greater need for achievement if they early learn that they are not helpless before the environment; and in a male-dominated society they are especially likely to gain that understanding if they are able to make a coalition with the mother against the father.

We cannot explore fully the intricacies of coalitions in triads, for this literature is large, complex, and specialized. Here we shall only focus on some of the hierarchical triads that are most typically found outside laboratory research.[7]

A common triad to be found in primitive societies, and fairly frequently in our own, contains a boy, his father, and his mother's brother. It will be noted that two of these have high rank, but one of them represents paternal authority, while the other one more often plays the role of "older friend"; and thus the relationship of the boy to mother's brother is one of greater ease than fear. In a *matrilineal* society, where by contrast authority and wealth go through the mother's line, the mother's *brother* is the authority figure, and the boy has a different relation-

---

[6]Theodore Caplow, *Two against One: Coalitions in Triads,* Englewood Cliffs, N.J.: Prentice-Hall, 1968, p. 1. His well-written summary will serve as a basic introduction to both the technical literature and its possible implications for much larger issues of how social structures operate.

[7]An excellent analysis of this phenomenon is found in Morris Freilich, "The Natural Triad in Kinship and Complex Systems," *American Sociological Review,* 29 (August 1954), pp. 529–540.

ship with his biological father, who more frequently plays the role of adviser or helper of high rank.

In various smaller segments of a bureaucracy, a similar pattern may be found. For example, in a prison the warden plays the authority of higher rank, while the chaplain or social worker plays the role of friendly person of higher rank. Thus, the prisoner engages in very different role relations with each of them, and may make a profitable coalition with one or the other. In turn, as in the case noted before of the two detectives attempting to influence the prisoner, both of the ranking persons may attempt alternately to influence the prisoner by different means, thus supporting one another. In a university there is no special position that could be called the "higher-ranking friend," but some professors choose that role, while in some universities there are special advisers and counselors who may do so.

In such a naturally occurring triad, the higher-ranked authority is likely to be the person who *initiates* action for others and makes most of the major decisions, while also imposing discipline. Thus, the relationships of others with that person are likely to be reserved and formal, perhaps even hostile. By contrast, the lower-ranking person is more likely to take steps to talk with the higher-ranking *friendly* person, whether counselor, adviser, chaplain, social worker, or uncle.

We cannot suppose that societies have created such triads deliberately in the past, but we can at least note an important consequence of the higher-ranking *friendly* person being within that coalition. Essentially, that individual prevents the person of higher authority from using her or his position to further her or his personal interest or simply from ruling arbitrarily and without regard to what the society views as justice. In short, the higher-ranking friendly person helps to balance the power relations in the social structure.

It may also be suggested that the high-ranking friendly person helps to restore good feelings or harmony in a situation where some tension is created by the commands or wishes of the person in authority. Within the family this is often the role that is given to mothers, although in large families of the past the elder sister sometimes took that role. The reader will also remember that grandparents in the United States sometimes play the role of higher-ranking friendly person who intervenes to reestablish harmony or justice, or simply to reduce the severity of the rules that parents try to impose.

In a parallel fashion, numerous studies of groups in experimental situations have revealed that over time two kinds of leaders arise, one concerned with the solution to specific problems that have been posed and the other concerned with reducing social tension within the group, or restoring goodwill. In this instance, we may conceive the "triangle" as being made up of (1) the leader to whom the group looks for solutions to problems, (2) the leader who succeeds in restoring harmony or goodwill, and (3) the rest of the group.

We have emphasized the naturally occurring hierarchical triad rather than the experimental results of various coalitions to emphasize the fact that these are not artificial creations; they do not simply break down easily into other combinations. For example, various social rules prevent the person in authority from being seduced by the friendly overtures of the lower-ranked person, or from attempting to be a "good egg" simply to be liked better by others.

The organization, whether an isolated triad or a set of triads within a larger system, cannot operate effectively if there is no person with authority who can make decisions and coordinate efforts. Systems of formality develop to remind both the person of authority and those of lower rank that the high-ranked authority is in a different position, in case any two of the three members are tempted to deviate. Some of these formalities are military salutes or titles of address ("professor," "dad," "sir"). Rules of social systems do suggest that people believe too great a familiarity between high-ranking persons with authority and subordinates will lower the effectiveness of those who make decisions for others. It is as natural for groups to give authority to people who are responsible for initiating action as it is for groups to resent the authority when exercised.

Since people are constantly trying to get others to do something, and since it is unusual for those others to be simply delighted to do that very thing, there are likely to be pervasive tensions in any relationship. How these are resolved is likely to be determined by which *coalitions* exist among the individuals in a small or large group. Coalitions can form only when *more* than two people are in a relationship together. Thus, it is at least possible to argue that the most primitive, or fundamental, element in many social structures is some kind of triad. Following that insight, sociologists have attempted for many generations to ascertain the outcome of various coalitions under various types of social conditions. In addition, however, they have noted the existence of many naturally occurring triads. Triads in which all three members are exactly equal in resources are not common. Here we have especially focused on one subtype of triad, in which a lower-ranking person is in interaction with a higher-ranking person who represents authority and wish another higher-ranking person who is friendly or supporting. Readers will be able to test the usefulness of the ideas presented in this section by becoming alert to the many situations in which various kinds of triads are open to observation.

Small Groups and Large Groups

The definition of a group does not ordinarily specify size, and we have already noted that a group may contain as few as two members or, instead, millions. Whether a group is to be considered large or small might thus be decided by its aims. Friendships and love relationships, for example, seem to break apart easily when they expand to include even three persons (thus, a love group of four persons is large), but political groups may still be effective when they number in the hundreds of thousands (and are thus small). Here we wish to do no more than point out some of the *effects of size* on the behavior of groups and group members.[8]

We suggested one of these consequences in the previous section, when we wrote that the number of possible relationships, and thus the complexities in the group, increase much more rapidly than the number of members. Thus, the increase from two members to three increases the number of possible relationships from one to three. However, after that, the number of relationships grows astronomically.[9]

This does not mean that all these possible relationships will exist or become of any great importance, but the increasing potential complexity of a group with increasing size has many implications for social behavior.

One of these is easily observable at any party. If only three or four people are present, it is possible to hold a genuine group discussion, in which everyone waits for any other to finish speaking and every individual talks to everyone present. Beyond that number, it is likely that a group will break up into subgroups, dyads, or triads. Only a

---

[8]One of the early commentaries on the effect of numbers on groups is the work of Georg Simmel, "The Number of Members as Determining the Sociological Form of the Group," *American Journal of Sociology*, 8 (July 1902), pp. 1–46, 158–196.

[9]The relationship is expressed by a standard formula: Number of possible groups with two or more members

$$= \sum_{r=2}^{n} \left[\frac{n!}{r!(n-r)!} \right]$$

very forceful person will be able to speak to the entire group for any length of time if it numbers as many as eight or ten. In a *formal* group, such as a committee, where parliamentary rules are observed, a chairperson is designated precisely because without someone in charge the committee would break up into smaller groups. This occurs in part because with increasing size each individual has to wait much longer before getting a chance to speak and during that period may have to listen to a discussion of very little personal interest.

With increasing size, the group also takes on a *character of its own*, apart from any individual members. If a dyad breaks up, nothing is left. If a triad breaks up, two members may still maintain their relationship. If the group is much larger, an individual or several individuals may go, but the group can continue what it was doing. Again this is observable at any party, as people come and go during the course of an evening. If a group continues over a long period of time and develops its own norms and rules, the newcomer entering as well as the member of longer standing who leaves is likely to have little effect on how the group or its members act.

Another difference between large and small groups is that the great increases in the *potential number of relationships* as group size increases will not affect the general structure or social patterns of a *large* group. This may be seen by considering how different a group of 7 or 8 is from a group of 3 or 4, on the one hand, compared with the very small difference between a crowd of 5,000 and a crowd of 7,000, or between a city of 200,000 and one of 300,

Figure 6-2 A chairperson prevents a group of this size from breaking up into smaller groups. (M. E. Warren, Photo Researchers, Inc.)

000. As the group becomes fairly large, a much larger increase in numbers is required to change it very much.

It has also been observed that groups are likely to be smaller if their activity is making real decisions, or *taking some action.* If, by contrast, a committee is engaged in discussing issues generally, or exploring a topic, it may be much larger. Apparently, people find that the larger group is unwieldy if its goal is to make decisions. New England town meetings, which have often been extolled as an example of rural democracy, can work reasonably well until towns become large and it is no longer possible for everyone interested to be within the same auditorium or to explore topics adequately. The unwieldiness of large groups in taking action moves almost all large nations to elect *representatives* in some type of national parliament, simply because the nation as a whole cannot directly meet. Even there, it is necessary to adopt extremely formal sets of procedures and rules in order to permit group decisions. Moreover, the most important decisions are not made in such large meetings, but in subgroups or committees that are small enough to operate effectively.

Our frequent mention of formal rules suggests another regularity, that with larger size any group is likely to become *formally organized.* That is, a charter or constitution is devised, rules are written down, and new ranks or positions are created to facilitate action. The group names some people as leaders; that is, with a larger size, groups begin to display *hierarchy,* or rank differences of some importance. Some people are designated to make decisions or to coordinate the activities of subgroups within the larger group.

As the group grows larger, factions or subgroups with special interests begin to arise, which may oppose the policies of those in charge of the organization. In addition, specialists appear, who are given responsibility for dealing with particular kinds of topics such as relations with the public, keeping account of money, or informing the mass media of what is going on.

Communication within the group also becomes a problem, since it is not possible to know everyone or to inform everyone of what is happening. Only in isolated villages, where several hundred people live during their entire lifetime, is it possible for everyone to know everyone else reasonably well and to be informed of what is occurring within all the families of the village. Another way of saying this is that intimate relations among all members of the group will decline, and as a substitute, people will begin to develop intimate relations with a smaller number of people within the whole group.

Perhaps the most important generalization that can be derived from these various effects of size is that with increasing size a number of the emotionally satisfying experiences that are common in small groups are lost by all the members viewed as a *whole* unit, but they are recaptured through the development of numerous *subgroups,* in which personal relationships can be maintained. Thus, we can expect that numerous small subgroups will exist within even very large ones, and they will have the characteristics of small groups found outside those larger ones. It is as though human beings create large groups because of the advantages they bring, but with those gains come a host of losses because of the formality of relationships that is necessary for adequate functioning. In turn, human beings create *primary* groups within the larger organizations to make up for those losses. Because primary groups are important both as independent units and as parts of larger groups, it is to these we now turn.

Primary Groups

Primary groups are also likely to be small groups, but it is not their smallness that commands our attention. They are found in primitive as well as industrial societies. They play important roles in large corporations. They are the social arena in which people are most likely to express their emotions. The main activity of socialization—that is, getting the child to accept the norms, values, and customs of the group—takes place there. They are the source of much of our deepest satisfaction as well as of our sharpest anguish. That primary groups are a universal experience of human beings can be seen by the ease with which we can read folk stories and myths from the distant past, even though the larger culture itself has long disappeared and we can no longer feel at home in it.

The term itself comes from the writings of Charles Horton Cooley, who observed such social patterns in families, playgroups, and neighborhoods.[10] However, other social analysts from Confucius to the present have also noted the importance of primary relationships.

Although the exact wording of definitions will vary, most writers agree on the core meaning of the following concept. A *primary group* is any group in which social relationships, in reality or social expectation, are:

1 Emotional.
2 Diffuse; the breadth of the interaction or its *scope* covers many aspects of life.
3 Particularistic; that is, the relationship is specific to the persons within the group (*my* friend, *my* father), not just to a class of persons (clerks, police officers).
4 Collectivistic; people in it should guide their behavior by what is good for everyone in the group.
5 Enduring.[11]

[10]Charles Horton Cooley, *Social Organization* (1909), New York: Free Press, 1956, chap. 3.

[11]Here I am using the descriptive concepts (called the *pattern variables*) of Talcott Parsons, except for the last one. His fifth concept is ascriptive-achieved, but in primary relations there is no specification that relations

Each of these elements or aspects is related to some degree with the others, but no one of them determines any of the others. Now let us consider primary groups in further detail.

Three aspects of primary groups As Kingsley Davis has pointed out, Cooley (and many subsequent analysts) emphasize the *face-to-face aspect* in primary relationships, but in fact this is not a *necessary* part of any definition. It is simply one of three factors that increase the likelihood that such a relationship will develop.[12] Indeed, primary groups based on friendship or love have sometimes arisen between people who only correspond with one another, and in our generation many people view each other as close friends although they live far apart.

Moreover, the geographical closeness that permits face-to-face contacts is only one of three major conditions or factors that affect the chances that a primary group will *arise.* The other two are the *size of the group* and *how long it lasts.*

All three of these affect the development of a primary group, because they maximize the chances that some of the characteristics used in our definition will actually occur. Thus, in a face-to-face relationship it is at least more likely that we will come to know the other person well. Moreover, if the face-to-face interaction continues over time, it is likely to do so because we like the person more. Interaction with the other person makes it more likely that we will share our ideas and sentiments.

Granted, this may also mean that we will then reject a close relationship. However, face-to-face association at least permits us to

should be either one. For a discussion of these ideas see Talcott Parsons, *The Social System,* New York: Free Press, 1951, pp. 55–88. The terms are an elaboration of the concepts *Gemeinschaft* and *Gesellschaft,* to be discussed later in this chapter.

[12]Kingsley Davis, *Human Society,* New York: Macmillan, 1949, pp. 289–294.

make a positive or negative decision. We do not often become friends with people whom we do not interact with in a face-to-face manner.

We should also note that most of our social action is face-to-face, but that the social definitions of appropriate behavior prevent any great exchange of ideas or feelings. This is especially true in relations between people who are very different in social rank or between people in a merely commercial interaction, as when we buy or sell something or interact with a clerk in a public utility office. Note, too, that part of our socialization consists in learning with *whom* it is appropriate to have face-to-face relationships. Children are warned "not to talk with strangers"; young girls are taught to refuse to talk with strange men; and parents warn their children against associating with people from a lower social class.

Face-to-face relationships are also likely to be small (the second factor that may affect whether a primary group will arise). In a small group, it is easier to express emotions and easier to exchange ideas, tastes, and attitudes. It is difficult to ascertain the particular characteristics of other people if the group is large. We have already noted some of the differences between interaction in small groups and in large ones, and it is clear that in a small group the chances that a primary relationship will arise are greater—if the individuals come to enjoy one another's company.

We listed the *duration* of a primary relationship as part of the definition, although it can also be seen as a *condition*. This is not a paradox, for in our definition we mainly refer to the socially *expected* duration, while here we are referring to the *real* duration. That is, we would not consider a group or a relationship as primary if both individuals viewed the interaction as a mere episode, transitory, and without any likelihood of continuing. Many primary groups, such as friendships or love relationships, do not in

fact continue for long, but while the relationship exists both members *expect* it to continue.

On the other hand, the real duration of any relationship does affect the likelihood that a primary group will arise. The longer the interaction continues, the greater is the likelihood that individuals in it will know one another better and at least will have some basis for deciding whether they want to interact more intimately. Over a longer period of time, more different aspects of each individual's personality will become manifest, and again the persons involved will have a better basis on which to decide whether they care to deepen and widen their interaction. Put more succinctly, in face-to-face interaction, within a small group, over a longer period of time, the persons who take part are more likely to develop a primary group, because those who do not care to do so are likely to drop out or move away. Here, then, we see a reinforcing process if the relationship continues. On the other hand, these conditions permit individuals to decide instead that they do not want such a relationship.

Primary groups are emotional Whatever the factors that maximize or reduce the likelihood that a primary group will arise, *if* it *does* arise, the relations among members will be *emotional* in both fact and expectation. That is, a primary group is a set of relationships in which people are permitted to express their emotions, and are even urged to do so. This is so for the family, for play groups, for friendship and love relationships, and for intimate interaction among neighbors.

This also applies to many primitive societies in which almost everyone is in a primary relationship with almost everyone else. It is not merely that we are *permitted* to express our emotion, whether it is love or hostility; we are *supposed* to do so, in contrast to many of our economic work relationships, where the rule is that members or participants should be somewhat more reserved and should carry out their roles without intruding their personal feelings in them.

An important consequence of this factor is that even trivial things come to be important. We are likely not to care at all about the musical tastes of our waitress in a restaurant, but we may be troubled to learn that a close friend does not like Mozart or Bach, or indeed does not care for music at all. Within the family almost anything that anyone does, from the way a child washes dishes to how an adult dresses, may arouse comment, criticism, or praise.

Primary groups are diffuse We use the term *diffuse* to refer to the fact that much of an individual's personality, tastes, and activities is considered part of the relationship. That is, it is broad in *scope*. In a primary relationship there is little that anyone has a right to hide from others. In much of our interaction within a large city, by contrast, we deal with individuals only with reference to very specific goals that we have in mind, from buying a newspaper to purchasing a meal. A primary relationship is not so narrow as that.

In any primary group people may develop private rules about what they will share with one another. Younger members of a family may not wish to watch the same TV programs as their parents. Friends may decide that they will not talk about some subjects because they disagree too much. In addition, everyone has other social commitments, so that not all of one's time is free for friends, family, or neighbors. Nevertheless, compared to other kinds of relationships, the primary group is much wider in its concerns with all the various aspects of each individual's life.

Primary groups are particularistic The meaning of *particularistic* is quite specific. It means that our rights and duties with re-

spect to the other person are determined by our *special* relationship to that person, rather than to the *class* of roles or positions he or she occupies. An illustration is that married people are supposed to kiss their own mates, but *not mates in general*. We owe particular obligations to our own close friend and do not owe the same obligations to the larger category of people who are simply close friends to someone else.

In fact, our relations with people in a primary group contain two major components. One is a *set of norms* that relate to the general obligation that friends, sons, daughters, neighbors, or sweethearts are thought to owe to one another in a particular society. Thus, for example, friends should not betray one another, they should respect the confidences that each gives to the other, and they should help each other in difficulties. Nevertheless, those general obligations are not owed to all friends, sweethearts, or members of families, but only to our *own*.

Second, however, each relationship contains *unique elements*. For this reason some definitions of primary groups state that they are relationships in which the uniqueness of each person is important. In any United States family, the people within it accept generally the role obligations and duties that are part of being parents, spouses, sons, and daughters, but in addition the particular qualities of each person have gradually created a somewhat different definition of role behavior for each person than other families would accept. Thus, it may come to be understood that the daughter has a special interest in mathematics, while the son is especially interested in natural history, and the father is expected to take charge of cooking on specified occasions. Too, friends may accept all the general obligations of friendship, but they may also develop a specific understanding that one of them is to play the role of comforter and helper more often than the other, who in turn is more likely to make plans about their recreation together.

The particularism of social interaction

within a primary group is also expressed by saying that the people in it are not substitutable. That is to say, each person is viewed as unique, and thus no one in the world is quite like that. We may have many close friends over a lifetime, but our relationship with each one is likely to be different; no one is completely a substitute for the other. Similarly, each person with whom we have a love relationship is different from all others. Moreover, *while* the relationship is ongoing, no outside person could quite take the role of the person within our primary group. Thus, it is not possible for married people to delegate their marital responsibilities to someone else. They *are* permitted to delegate housekeeping responsibilities, but not the close affectional ties they are supposed to have with their spouses.

Primary groups are collectivistic   In a society that gives great play to economic interests, many relationships are viewed as appropriately self-interested. Thus, for example, we do not become indignant when we understand that a shopkeeper is looking out for profit, just as we believe it is an individual's right to try to obtain as good a salary as is possible. However, the primary group is expected to be *collectivistic*. Each member has the obligation of being concerned about not only the *other person*, but also the *group* itself. This is sometimes expressed in the folk observation that family members may fight among themselves, but when criticized by outsiders they stand together to defend their own.

This collective concern has more than one aspect. First, a primary group is viewed by its members as an *end in itself*. It is considered wrong to enter a primary group, or to continue the relationship, merely because we can make a profit from it for ourselves or can make a better bargain than we can get elsewhere. It is supposed to be satisfying simply to participate in the group. As social scientists we understand that in fact people do gain a great deal from their primary rela-

Figure 6-3   Members of the Ithilien religion, in an act of collective concern, work to convert a natural spring into a water supply for their private community. (Wide World Photos.)

tionships, or else they would not continue them. Nevertheless, it is understood that what one gains from the relationship is the pleasure of the relationship itself.

Another aspect of this collective orientation is that members of a primary group are likely to share very *similar ends*. Indeed, if they did not, the relationship would probably not continue. We are much more likely to share the same ends with people who are our friends, sweethearts, or family members than we are with outsiders.

Third, when the goals or ends of particular persons are somewhat different—and they always will be to some extent, because every person is unique—then individuals must feel that they have *shared goals*. That is, each individual must be able to say, "Your goals are also mine; I accept them and support them." Thus, friends do not always share each other's aspirations, but they are supposed to rejoice if the other person achieves them. What one person succeeds in doing, the other person can also enjoy. This collectivistic orientation is the basis for the strong feeling of primary group members that they constitute a "we," a social unit in which (ideally, though often not in fact) each person *wills* or desires what the other person wants.

Primary groups are enduring We have already noted the double meaning of *enduring*, that is, as a reality and as an expectation. We repeat: Many primary groups, especially love and friendship relationships, do not last long, but while they continue each person expects that their emotional commitment to one another will go on. Until a conflict arises, it is assumed that each has a normative obligation to continue. In general, we can say that we must *explain*, if we decide to drop out of or reject a primary relationship.

The family is a special case here, since it is the only type of primary relationship that is defined by law and that imposes many restrictions on who may enter or leave. Children, for example, cannot choose another set of parents, though doubtless many parents experience moments in which they wish their children would do so. Every society contains many rules about who may marry whom and what are the consequences of deciding to break up a marriage. Thus, the family as a primary group is likely to be more enduring than are friendships or love relationships. As to neighbors as members of primary relationships, United States families change their neighbors relatively often (on the average, at least once in five years).

Duration has many consequences for the depth and meaning of any primary group. These we have already suggested. First, if people do not care for one another, they are much less likely to continue the relationship. If they do continue over time, they are likely to share much more of their lives with one another and to come to agree in far more ways. In addition, the mere fact of having taken part in a relationship over

many years is viewed as a large investment of one's life. As a consequence, when it breaks up, people are more likely to feel hurt and a sense of loss.

Nevertheless, as already noted, it is not the *real* duration of a primary group that is a necessary part of its definition. People do *expect* it to endure, on the other hand (and this *is* part of the definition). Consequently, they feel freer to make emotional and economic investments in it. They can enjoy some emotional security in the thought that they do not have to check each morning to find out whether their close friend is *still* a close friend.

Emphasizing this set of expectations does not deny that friends do worry about whether the other continues to feel intimate or close. Moreover, precisely because the primary relationship is emotional and highly important to the individual, these concerns are understandable; the loss of the other person or persons would be hurtful. Nevertheless, we can observe that there *is* an expectation of the relationship continuing, because when anyone drops out of a primary relationship without any explanation, or arbitrarily and whimsically, the other person or persons in it feel that he or she has been violated and betrayed.

Other characteristics of primary groups Although we have used friendship and love relationships, families, and neighborhoods as illustrations to analyze primary groups, it should be emphasized that not all of the concrete cases in these categories should be called primary. In the United States, for example, we use the term "friend" in a very general way, to refer to almost anyone with whom we have continuing civil interaction. Some families stay together even though the members within them share very little with one another. Some neighbors isolate themselves from others, while in some neighborhoods primary groups are relatively common. We cannot assume that any apparently friendly relationship, or a family, or a neighborhood is to be classed as primary. We ascertain whether the group is to be classed as primary by the degree to which it fits our earlier definition. Readers should also keep in mind that our definition does not require that members of a primary group interact with one another harmoniously. Indeed, precisely because it is emotional, the primary relationship is often characterized by hostility and anger.

Usually, primary groups begin out of spontaneous liking or choice, and therefore some definitions include the characteristic of being *voluntary*. However, we have already noted some exceptions—for example, families, neighbors, and small primitive societies. Consequently, we cannot include this characteristic as an essential part of our definition.

On the other hand, choice *is* important in various ways even in these exceptions. For example, children and parents cannot choose one another, but spouses do. Moreover, who is included in the primary group of the family beyond the boundary of parents and children is to a substantial degree a matter of choice. We are very likely to choose as members of one or more of our primary groups *some* of our relatives, but we do not choose *all* of them who are equally close to us in kinship. Not only do siblings (brothers or sisters) sometimes maintain a merely civil or polite relationship when they are adults, but more distant kin may be included or not, depending on how we feel about them.

So, similarly, even in a small primitive society, not everyone maintains an intimate relationship with everyone else. Often the ties are closest between kin. Among neighbors, we establish close relationships with some and not others. Age groups in African societies are primary groups, and everyone in a given age group is a member; but once more, some relationships are closer than others.

To say that most primary groups are voluntary does not mean that they are purely spontaneous and are not affected by many social pressures, both negative and positive. Thus, as children, we are urged to treat our kin with both respect and affection, and primary relations among kin are encouraged. We have already noted in this chapter the effect of physical closeness or geographic factors on intimate relations. That is, we are more likely to choose our primary group memberships from people who are physically close to us, and thus interact with us more frequently and easily.

People do not choose either their sweethearts or their friends because they are of the same age, religion, ethnic group, or class background; but in fact most primary groups are relatively homogeneous socially, and *others* urge us to *consider* those facts. Once again, we are more likely to interact frequently and intimately with such people than with others, and thus we choose from among those people whatever primary group relationships we have. If we do not, we may be criticized.

For all these reasons primary groups play an important part in the larger social processes. We shall examine those more fully in the succeeding pages, but let us note here that much of the socialization and social control in the society is carried out by primary groups.

This is almost a truism, since most families are to be classified as primary groups, and children are largely socialized there. However, much *adult* socialization takes place in the society as well (as we have analyzed in our chapter on socialization), for as we grow older we learn additional or different norms, values, or social customs. The primary group is peculiarly suited to this purpose. The other people in it, whether they are friends, sweethearts, parents, spouses, or neighbors, are important to us, and we wish to keep their liking and respect. If they live by the norms of the group, we are likely to want to do so, too. We are vulnerable to their criticism, and they are in a position to know what we do.

For the same reason, even if we do not actually *change* our attitudes or values, we may be at least *controlled* by the members of our primary groups, because we want to keep the relationship harmonious and we need their respect and affection. Sometimes, primary groups are also deviant and members protect each other from being punished by members of the larger society who wish to make them conform. That possibility is intensified by the fact that each primary group develops a somewhat different set of role obligations or rights than other people in the society recognize.

On the other hand, such deviant possibilities are less common than might be supposed, because almost any member of one primary group is also a member of other primary groups, and in addition is affected by the threats of punishment or the hopes of reward that people in still other circles may present. Since individuals within any primary group are concerned about each other, but have a stake in the larger society, their more likely choice is to press each other toward at least an acceptable amount of conformity. Few primary groups are so positioned in the social structure that each member can reward every other member for deviance sufficiently to make up for the other pressures that each member feels from the larger society. Indeed, a common mode of social control in the society is for one or more *outside* persons to urge one or more members of a *primary* group to use their influence to bring an erring person back in line.

Friendships

Whether we expand the term "friendship" to include almost any relations in which people like one another a good deal or narrow it to refer only to one's "very best friend," friendship has a considerable effect on the quality of our lives and even on our material success.[13] If we do not confine our-

[13]Although I have studied this area of social behavior

selves to "best friends" and do consider the large number of relationships that we view as moderately warm and friendly, it is clear that friendship is a social resource. It can be used for many goals. As a consequence, we can ask many sociological questions about the conditions under which such relationships are established, and specifically what people do to begin and continue any kind of friendly relationship.

Social analysts have long noted that people who are friends exchange many things with one another: gifts, services, sympathy, and support, or directly instrumental help in obtaining some goal. It is especially among the lower classes that young people are likely to believe success comes from whom you know rather than from skills or achievement, for in their experience people who are more successful seem to be "lucky" in obtaining the help of people who are friendly to them. Thus, one can view friendships as systems of social exchange, and friendship itself as a resource that can be drawn upon for various purposes.

People reject this view of friendship, even while recognizing that such exchanges do take place. Indeed, there are many normative rules about appropriate behavior in a friendship, and the rules themselves specifically reject an exchange view of friendship processes. For example, it is understood that one should not continue to accept many gifts or services from someone if one is not willing to be a friend to that person, unless the person who receives such gifts is a person of much higher rank. In effect, the rule

and have been writing on it for some years, I have barely mentioned it here and there in my publications. My colleague Allan Silver is preparing a monograph on this topic, and I have learned much from him. By now, considerable social psychological research on friendship has been carried out. See especially the work of Elaine Walster, Ellen Berscheid, Kenneth J. Gergen, and E. E. Jones. For example, see Ellen Berscheid and Elaine H. Walster, *Interpersonal Attraction*, Reading, Mass.: Addison-Wesley, 1969; Edward E. Jones, *Ingratiation*, New York: Irvington, 1965; and Kenneth J. Gergen, *The Psychology of Behavior Exchange*, Reading, Mass.: Addison-Wesley, 1969.

states that to accept many gifts is to incur the obligation of friendship. Similarly, if one has been encouraged to make many friendly overtures, including gifts or services, but the other person has had no *intention* of becoming friends, that encouragement is viewed as a betrayal.

One can also observe that, as in the case of love, if an individual offers friendship to another person but the other rejects it, the person who offers not only feels hurt, but does not wish to continue the formerly merely civil relationship, either. People react in this fashion, even though they understand that others cannot simply *decide* to feel warm and friendly, and they also know that the person who rejects a friendship cannot explain without embarrassment why he or she has done so. One cannot, in any event, explain to another that one does not want his or her friendship simply because not enough is offered. Again, the exchange vocabulary is rejected.

Indeed, the most notable exception to this general unwillingness to think of friendship in exchange terms occurs when friends are angry with one another. Then it is likely that they will remind the other about all that each has done and give good reasons why the other person has fallen short in the obligations of friendship.

People are willing to grant generally that friendship is a useful resource, but typically will deny that *they* view their own friends in that light. By definition, the relationship is supposed to grow from spontaneous affection or liking, not from a careful calculation of the profit that can be derived from it. Precisely because people assert they have chosen their friends on a basis of simple liking, it is considered socially permissible to admit that one seeks friendships with others, or that one has many friends. By contrast, it is not considered socially permissible (unless one is a politician) to admit that one seeks power.

Ours is a bureaucratic society, in which people are supposed to be given promo-

tion on the basis of competence, to be given favorable decisions in courts or corporations if the rules are on our side, and to be protected by law from the harassment of public officials, but that ideal is often violated by the reality. As a consequence, now as in the period before the industrial revolution and the advent of large-scale, rational bureaucracies, people use their friendships not merely to get around the rules, and to further their self-interest at the expense of others who deserve more; they may also use their friendships to gain simple justice when it has been denied to them.

Since this possibility is well known, dozens of books have been written to give lessons to the reader on how to "win friends and influence people." Being friendly to others is perhaps the single most important technique for eliciting friendly feelings from others, or even real friendship, and thus people are taught to *show* friendliness when it will further their ends. Although this state of affairs has been widely deplored, as marking a great fall from a previous time in which true friendship was to be encountered and social relations were "authentic" and sincere, we may question that picture of the past.

Without doubt, the place of friendship in modern society is different from that in the past, but it does not lie in the fact that modern friendship is "false" because some people seek to use it for their own ends. Indeed, in other countries now and in past historical epochs when bureaucracy has been *less* developed—and thus "the rules" are not expected to apply to *everyone* without regard to *who* that person is—people are or were much more alert to the practical uses of friendship. In such societies people do in fact expect to be able to further their own interests through friends and to help them in turn. These friends are often *kin* as well, but the fact remains.

In the sixteenth-century Elizabethan court, people shamelessly flattered the mighty to gain their favor and friendship.

Wise advisers counseled their younger friends to follow that custom. Put more generally, where merit counts less and justice is handed out arbitrarily, people are more likely to feel it is *proper* to use their friends for their own goals, even if that creates an injustice for others.

We can observe that pattern in our own society: In activities where success depends far more on one's excellence (such as sports and scientific research) people are less likely to advise younger aspirants to cultivate friendships as a means to that end. Those who aspire would feel it detracts from their achievement to admit they succeeded through friendship. It is even possible that persons in modern society can more selflessly cultivate friendship, simply because in many kinds of situations they do *not* need to call on friends in order to obtain what they believe they should get.

How friendship affects daily decision and action has not been studied in depth, but common observation suggests that its importance is not to be encountered only in the pleasant hours of sociability but also in many political and market activities. It may also help to restore our emotional balance. Humanists support that notion by claiming that we need friendship even more in our cold, impersonal, threatening world than it was needed in the past. Bureaucracies do seem particularly unfitted to hand out love or friendship, and our world is dominated by such organizations. If it does not solve that problem, further study of this topic may at least disclose more clearly how friendship affects our daily lives.

Secondary Groups or Formal Groups

In industrial society the differences between one person and another are much greater than in rural or primitive societies, because people in different regions, cities, neighborhoods, social classes, religions, ethnic groups, schools, jobs, and political parties are subject to so many different social influences from childhood to death. That is, people are more *differentiated* and have very different interests, goals, tastes, and hobbies. Though people are internally more differentiated than in the past, a modern nation's population is so large that there may be thousands of people who are interested in some very special activity or goal, from collecting lacquered snuffboxes to promoting the use of an international language.

Thus, they may form a group of likeminded people in order to enjoy that interest or further those goals. The group may be as large as a political party, or as small as a neighborhood society devoted to singing eighteenth-century chorale music. People's relationships with each other and with those organizations are sometimes called *formal* or *secondary,* and we may apply the same terms to the group itself. That is, we speak of formal groups or of formal relationships. Relationships within such groups differ from the relationships in primary groups in all the traits we used earlier in that definition. That is, these relationships are expected to be:

1   Emotionally neutral.
2   Segmental, or narrow.
3   Universalistic.
4   Self-interested.
5   Not enduring (though the group itself may endure).

The meaning of these terms can be briefly stated. The norm of *emotional neutrality* does not mean that individuals are not supposed to be passionate about the activity they pursue in formal groups. It means only that people are not expected to express either love or hostility to one another, and in their formal activities as members they are expected to be relatively more reserved than in primary relationships. Their interaction is expected to be *segmental, or narrow*, for it is appropriately confined to the task at hand, that is, the purpose of the group itself. The

Figure 6-4 Town meeting. Even at this modest size, if everyone at the meeting made a speech, most decisions would take days.

individual who wants to talk about personal tastes in music at a meeting of stamp collectors is ignoring the purposes of the association.

Relations within a formal, or secondary, group are expected to be *universalistic,* which means that the same rules are supposed to apply to everyone in the same *office* or social position. This does *not* mean that everyone is treated exactly the same. After all, some persons have formal offices and may exercise some authority because of their positions. On the other hand, the chairperson who presides over a meeting is supposed to be treated as though she or he were chairperson. In some associations there are different rights or obligations. Again, however, everyone *within* that given class should be treated the same. No one should be given special privileges or should carry out special obligations because of the particular relationship that someone has with that person.

The relationship of the individual to the formal group or to other individuals is thought of as *self-interested,* in the specific sense that he or she is engaging in that activity for the gains that can be obtained from membership. Always, members are ex-

pected to further the goals of the group itself (and to this extent one can observe some *collectivistic* behavior); but in general it is not expected that individuals should sacrifice themselves for one another, and it is taken for granted that if the goals of the group or organization do not serve the interests of the individual, it is appropriate that she or he should leave the organization.

For these reasons it is not expected that individuals will continue indefinitely in their relations with the organization or its members. It is not so much that individual interests are thought to be transitory or do not sometimes last a long time in fact. On the other hand, there is no norm that requires individuals to continue if they do not care to do so. The group itself may continue for generations if it is successful in attracting new members over time, but when one joins the group one does not incur an obligation to continue in it beyond the time that it serves one's goals or interests.

The pursuit of common goals brings people in closer proximity and causes them to work together. As a consequence, within any formal group many primary groups are likely to develop. These may become small cliques that further their own private interests, or they may instead become friendship groups entirely outside the organization. However, there is no obligation to enter a primary group, as long as one continues to carry out the obligations that are prescribed formally. Many people are able to work together in formal groups who do not especially like one another and who disagree on many important issues. All that membership requires is that they shall help one another to pursue the narrow interests that the group officially announces as its own.

Members of a primary group may also pursue such special interests, from union activities to electing a Republican president, but they are handicapped by the small size of the group and their wide range of other goals. Secondary groups are specialty groups. Since they can officially ignore all the other aspects of individuals except their dedication to one main activity, they can persuade many people to contribute their resources to that end. They need not take account of the uniqueness of each person, as the primary group must.

Secondary groups are counted successful if they help individual members in their enjoyment or pursuit of a narrow range of goals. Many fail, but as they disappear still others are created by people who believe they themselves would be more effective if still others could be persuaded to join together in a formal group to serve their shared interests.

PRIMARY GROUPS AND BUREAUCRACIES

Since primary and formal groups are found throughout the society, and most people are members of both types of groups, we should consider some of the relationships between them. As noted in Chapter 7 on bureaucracies, formal organizations have become a dominant social trait of modern societies, just as machines are a dominant pattern in modern technology. Over the past hundred years both have expanded in size, numbers, influence, and the areas of life they control. Surveying this trend, commentators have wondered whether we shall all eventually become bureaucratic automatons (each with a serial number instead of a name) in a totally bureaucratized world, directed constantly by official rules, dominated by bureaucratic experts, and allowed only a few moments of joy or play at specified times when the computer permits it.

However, as Chapter 7 points out, formal organizations can do many things well, but fail miserably at other, very different tasks. Most fundamentally, bureaucracies work well on problems in which there are *economies of scale*, that is, when a solution can be used for large batches of *similar cases*, such as applications for telephone service, receiving income taxes, or mailing bills each month. However, bureaucracies are poor at precisely the kinds of tasks primary groups do. Formal organizations are relatively ineffective in giving love or friendship. They cannot pay much attention to the uniqueness or special qualities of individuals; that would be too costly in office time. Interested in their own narrow goals, bureaucracies do not concern themselves with the many goals of real persons, except when the two sets of goals are the same. If we do not believe that bureaucracies are actually hostile to us, we at least know that they are most unlikely to sacrifice their own interests to our personal ones. In all these ways they contrast with primary relationships.

Neither primary groups nor bureaucracies can function well without the other in modern society. The specialization and expertise of bureaucracies permit them to get more done, and more economically, than primary groups could, and the latter enjoy those benefits. On the other hand, bureaucracies are too narrow to function as total subsocieties. Human beings could not operate them, and thus these organizations could not exist,

if primary groups did not restore the wholeness of persons outside or inside working
hours.

Their relations are still more complex
than that set of comparisons suggests. Bureaucracies develop expertise of many kinds,
and thus we are dependent upon them in
many ways. This does not make them more
effective than primary groups in all ways.
After all, much of our knowledge is not
expert knowledge, but it is important just
the same. Second, bureaucratic expertise
may be useless when it cannot be applied
quickly. This is less likely to occur in primary groups, which have short lines of
communication. It does not take long for an
individual to learn what other members of
his or her primary group think, feel, need,
or want. Thus, if there is a sudden crisis,
members of primary groups, whether families or friends, can step in quickly to solve
the problem. This may be as trivial as giving
information where needed or picking up a
friend's child if a school bus fails to appear.
By the time a bureaucracy could be set into
motion, it would be too late.

Third, in some situations there is no real
expertise, anyway, and the cost is not worth
it, so that family members, friends, or even
neighbors can step in, as when a bedroom
needs to be prepared for someone returning
home from a hospital, or when we wish to
persuade a child to eat properly at the table.
Finally, some problems are simply unique,
and a bureaucracy is not easily fitted to
solve these either, as when an older member of the family needs special foods, or
when we must deal with the particular personalities of brothers and sisters who are
not getting along well for a brief time.

In short, there are many problems of life
where there are no special economies of
scale, and expert knowledge is either un-
available or unequal to the task. For all
these reasons we can be sure that bureaucracies will not continue indefinitely to expand in all the sectors of our lives.

On the other hand, these very different
modes of operation can sometimes be combined to help solve problems that separately
neither kind of organization or group could
handle as effectively.[14]

Neighbors who are part of a primary
group may help each other when one is ill,
but if the illness continues long or requires
very special kinds of care, it is likely that
family members will take part. In some
cases cooperation between the primary
group of the family and the bureaucratic organization of the hospital may be necessary
to care adequately for the patient. For example, many technical treatments can be
learned by a member of the family and applied to a patient. One of these is the home
"washing" of the blood when the kidneys
do not function adequately. Similarly, the
bureaucracy called the police has the duty of
preventing crime or arresting criminals, but
it is now well known that they cannot do
this job by themselves. People in neighborhoods must also act to supervise the streets
and to be alert to possible threats.

Aged people and mental patients are likely to feel at times that the staff in their
institutions are oppressors rather than helpers. The bureaucracy serves its own ends to
some extent, and thus the unique needs or
feelings of inmates are neglected. Consequently, future programs for enriching the
lives of older people may well have to in-

[14]Here we are following the line of analysis that has
been pursued by Eugene Litwak and his collaborators in
a series of papers devoted to the differences between
bureaucracies and primary groups, and the possible
modes of support or interaction between them. See, for
example, Eugene Litwak and Ivan Szelenyi, "Primary
Group Structures and Functions: Kin, Neighbors, and
Friends," *American Sociological Review*, 34 (August
1969), pp. 465–481; Eugene Litwak and Henry J.
Meyer, *School, Family, and Neighborhood: The Theory
and Practice of School-Community Relations*, New York:
Columbia, 1974; and Eugene Litwak, Henry Meyer,
and David Hollister, "Theories of Linkage between Bureaucracies and Community Primary Groups: Education, Health, and Political Action as Empirical Cases,"
paper presented at the American Sociological Association meetings, Montreal, 1974.

clude plans for either creating or supporting primary relations that could be of help to the aged both within and outside homes for the elderly.

Thus, primary groups and formal organizations are not simply antagonistic to one another, although the patterns of social behavior characteristic of each are very different. Each is more effective at somewhat different kinds of tasks. Although they often conflict, each contributes something to social life. Here we have also suggested some ways the two kinds of social organization can actually work together to solve social or personal problems.

We have moved from the analysis of specific kinds of groups or social organizations to a clearer understanding of their place in the larger social structure. It is therefore reasonable to take the further step of considering the social organization of societies viewed as a whole.

FOLK AND URBAN SOCIETY: *GEMEINSCHAFT UND GESELLSCHAFT*

From the earliest writings about social relationships to the present time, analysts have been occupied with a fundamental distinction between two types of societies. We noted this distinction in Chapter 1, and here we consider it in more detail. These types of societies have been given various labels, all referring to the same kinds of social patterns. Sometimes they are viewed as *rural* or *folk* societies as contrasted with *urban* social patterns. The great French sociologist Emile Durkheim focused on the kinds of social links among members of the society, using the terms *mechanical* and *organic solidarity*. He meant thereby that people in primitive societies cooperated and followed the rules together because everyone is very much alike and believes in the same values and norms (they are *mechanically* solidary); by contrast, in an urban or industrial society, people are linked together by virtue of their various dependencies upon one anoth-

er. That is, everyone is very different, but the differences mesh with one another, and as a consequence people can exchange profitably (socially and economically) with one another (they are *organically* solidary). A generation earlier, the British legal historian Sir Henry Maine spoke of the change in societies from *status* (people's rights and obligations flowed from their fixed social positions) to *contract* (the rights and obligations are *negotiated*). However, sociologists more commonly use the German terms *Gemeinschaft* and *Gesellschaft*, which were suggested by the German sociologist Ferdinand Tönnies in 1887.[15]

Basically, all these distinctions, under different titles, refer to the same thing: a society that is based on primary relationships, and especially kinship (*Gemeinschaft*), as contrasted with one based on formal, or secondary, relationships, and especially bureaucracies (*Gesellschaft*). Thus, at the one extreme end we would put most small primitive societies, and at the other we would place modern industrial societies. As in all such distinctions, we take for granted there are many concrete cases that will lie somewhere between these two extremes; that is, there are gradations between the two. European mountain villages in the past would, for example, be placed toward the *Gemeinschaft*, or "folk," end, and many agrarian kingdoms of the past (such as the monarchy of Louis IV) might be put somewhat toward the *Gesellschaft*, or "society," end.

This distinction seems so simple and obvious that, once stated, it appears to be hardly worth any further analysis. What, after all, can one learn about *modern* life from examining a *primitive* society? Why should we bother about comparing the two, when we can analyze each one separately?

We believe that the reasons why sociologists have continued to analyze these two types of societies together are the following. First, it seems clear that analysis of a folk

[15]Ferdinand Tönnies, *Community and Society* (1887), trans. and ed. by Charles P. Loomis, East Lansing: Michigan State University, 1957.

society tells us where we came from; and analysis of the industrial society tells us where we are going. Clearly, the two are linked together, and we are interested in how those origins gave rise to such an outcome. Second, it is a common experience in science that great apparent differences may conceal an underlying unity. Thus, we may suppose that the same social processes operate in both kinds of societies, and comparing the two will illuminate their operation.

Perhaps the most important reason is that modern industrial society poses a kind of puzzle, and we seek the answer to that puzzle in rural, or *Gemeinschaft*, societies. It can be stated easily: We can understand how people might conform to the rules of a *Gemeinschaft* society, or why such a society would hold together, and why people might even sacrifice for it, since presumably everyone believed in the values, norms, and customs of the group. Its members had seen only those social patterns, and no alternatives. There were no subgroups that rewarded people for rejecting the old ways. The socialization process made everyone feel a deep commitment to that society. In short, there was a *consensus*, or a set of common beliefs and attitudes about most important things.

By contrast, what holds a modern society together when everyone seems to be out for only their own material interest and decisions appear to be based on rational calculation—where there is no consensus, for many people do not accept, and many even reject, the supposed norms and values of the society? It seems likely, as Thomas Hobbes claimed in his seventeenth-century work *Leviathan*, that a society based on self-interest and careful calculation is not really *possible*, for soon everyone would turn to force and fraud as the most effective ways of obtaining what they want. It would be a jungle society, in which every person's hand is turned against every other. If conformity rested only on the individual's calculation of what he or she could get away with, by any means whatsoever, social order would be

fragile indeed, and no person's life would be safe. Under those conditions, as Hobbes argued, human life would be "solitary, poor, nasty, brutish, and short."

Sociologists may then continue to analyze the two together in order to understand why modern society, apparently based on contract and exchange, does not fall apart.

A final reason for sociologists' interest in both forms of society is that modern intellectuals feel some *nostalgia* for the lost solidarity of the past, the seemingly more ordered and integrated life that they believe people once experienced. Hundreds of essays are published each year that express this theme, deploring the loss of loyalty, affection, the wholeness of human beings, and their rootedness in a harmonious social existence. Whether or not the essayists are merely indulging in sentimental thinking about the past, they at least believe they are living in a modern world of high production and technical achievement that seems inhuman, with a past world where physical existence was chancy but human relations were more satisfying[16] Here we shall suggest a more useful comparison.

Gemeinschaft Social Patterns

In societies that are called folk, rural, or *Gemeinschaft*, the following social patterns are to be found. First, most relationships are ascribed and are based upon kinship. *Ascribed* means that most of the duties or rights that an individual has are determined by her or his position in the kinship structure, and thus are defined by birth. Consequently, most social exchanges, whether of services or of loyalty, are not *contracts*, but are set by tradition. That is, people do not choose the partners with whom they will engage in exchanges of services or goods. These are determined by kinship and tradi-

[16]For an insightful comparison see Peter Laslett, *The World We Have Lost*, London: Methuen, 1965; as well as the more nostalgic work by Robert A. Nisbet, *Twilight of Authority*, New York: Oxford, 1975.

tion. What each owes to the other is less determined by individual haggling than by custom. What each owes is not carefully calculated in a very precise way, as it would be in the modern contract, where people try to figure out how little they have to pay. On the contrary, the primary group gives honor to people who offer more in return or are generous in their gifts. Moreover, if someone obtains services or goods from another, there is no immediate repayment. Repayment is once again based on broad understandings of what each person's rights and obligations are.

In the legal system, too, punishments are not usually specified in great detail. Often there is no specialized agency or unit whose duty it is to pass laws, and often no system of judges. There are no prisons or penitentiaries. Much of the specialized governmental apparatus that we observe daily is absent in such a society. People are not divided into distinct churches, each with its own set of doctrines, but everyone takes part in communal religious ceremonies and festivities. There are no committees that engage in rational planning for the future, and the skill of planning plays a much smaller part in integrating food production or distribution, because that is also set mainly by traditional understandings. There are no experts on child rearing, because the transition from childhood to adulthood is not viewed as problematic. Children gradually learn what they are supposed to do and begin to do it when they are able, without feeling much need to rebel against their elders.

As readers can observe, in all these ways modern industrial society seems different. Not every primitive society, and not every agricultural or rural village of the past, would fit the foregoing description, but most would come closer to it than they would to the social patterns to be found in the urban western European countries or the United States.

Real *Gemeinschaft* Societies

The somewhat idyllic or ideal picture of real *Gemeinschaft* societies is not entirely correct. In many primitive societies and agrarian villages of the past, adults were acutely focused on economic exchange and material gain. Often they were concerned with increasing the advantages to their own family, at the expense of the larger group. Not all is harmony; bitter fights, feuds, and wars occurred at times. In both primitive societies and agrarian states, many chieftains and kings violated custom and oppressed their people, before industrial or bureaucratic systems arose.

More importantly, no society moves indefinitely toward formal or bureaucratic social patterns, toward contract and economic exchange, as its sole foundation. First, within all bureaucratic organizations, many primary groups arise that continually resist the pressure to make all social relationships secondary, or formal, in character. Second, within industrial society generally, important areas of social life are typically not contractual, such as friendship, family, and kin relations and interaction among neighbors.

Nationalism has been often deplored in modern times as the source of much human sorrow, but as social analysts we must recognize that people's loyalty to the nation—their willingness to sacrifice for it in time of war, and even their willingness to oppress others for the supposed good of the nation—is comparable in its emotional quality (and often, too, in its unfortunate consequences) to the group cohesion, allegiance, and ethnocentrism of *Gemeinschaft* societies. In addition, people in many sectors of social life create subgroups or networks in which they do not carefully calculate how little they have to give, and they contribute their energies generously to common goals, looking more to gain the respect and affection of their fellows than for material wealth. Almost everybody will have had

FOCUS

GEMEINSCHAFT AND PROCESSES IN A FACTORY

Although relations between factory workers are thought to be governed almost entirely by specific provisions in their work "contract," the organization is not likely to be efficient if that is so. In addition, the work experience is not likely to be pleasant for either workers or supervisors. Here Alvin W. Gouldner describes what workers "expect" from a lenient management, even when they understand that management has the right not *to do what they want.*

The selection of expectations to comprise the indulgency pattern was not an arbitrary one; for all the elements in it are particularly salient, referring to things reiterated by the workers themselves, and to which workers explicitly attributed significance as a source of their job satisfaction. Thus the indulgency pattern was a distinctively important factor motivating workers to fill the roles for which they had been employed, expressing a commitment to a set of beliefs as to how the plant should be run, and generating loyalties to the Company and management. While other elements also influenced work motivation, those in the indulgency pattern were at the center of the workers' daily attention and comprised the standards they most commonly used to judge the plant.

There were further ways in which the expectations incorporated in the indulgency pattern differed from others held by workers. It may be observed that workers did not define management as "lenient" when the latter gave "tit for tat." Specifically, workers did not tend to speak of "leniency" when they were given something that they already felt to be rightfully theirs. Instead, this approving judgment was reserved for management behavior which complied with expectations of tenuous legitimacy, and when management gave up something for which workers could make no compelling claim.

For example, workers never commended management, or spoke of its "leniency," when they were paid their proper wages; it is, in part, for this reason that wage satisfactions are not an element in the indulgency pattern. On the other hand, management would be within its *legal rights* if it kept workers busy every minute of the time for which they were being paid. Insofar as management did *not* do so, workers spoke of it as lenient.

The case of the sample room, and its use as the factory "hospital," further illustrates this. Management did not have to allow injured workers to earn money at the jobs in the sample room; it could have insisted that injured workers remain at home, collecting their compensation only, until they were ready to resume their regular jobs. But, here again, the Company did not "stand on its rights."

Similarly, management was not compelled to allow workers to punch

SOURCE: Alvin W. Gouldner, *Wildcat Strike*, New York: Harper & Row, 1954, pp. 21–22.

in early, or to punch out early; nor was it required to allow workers to use Company materials for household repairs. It was, however, primarily in these situations, when the Company did not appear to strive for a return on every cost, for a gain against every outlay, when management did what it was privileged not to do, that workers felt it to have a "proper attitude," and said they were being treated "humanly."

It is clear, then, that workers did not define "leniency" as a management *obligation*. Instead, "leniency" seems to refer to managerial compliances with workers' role preferences, rather than role prescriptions. Furthermore, "leniency" also involves managerial behavior which is tempered by taking into account the worker's obligations in his other roles, for example, his obligations as a family member to maintain the family's income, to fix broken things around the house, or to leave work early to take "the wife" on a special outing.

In other words, when workers judged the plant to be "lenient," they were utilizing standards that would be relevant in some other situation or relationship, criteria legitimately applicable to the relations among family members, friends, or neighbors. The "second chance" expectation is a clear indication of this. These expectations, however, were only of dubious validity in a *business* and *industrial* context, and it is in part for this reason that management's compliance with them was especially noted and commended. In sum, the expectancies incorporated in the indulgency pattern were a problematic part of the workers' total role expectations, differing from others which had a firm and unambiguous legitimacy.

such experiences at some time in life, and people are likely to remember them as being more satisfying than activities that yielded economic benefits. They may be encountered in research teams within universities and industry; in much of amateur sports; in the creative arts; in hundreds of voluntary associations devoted to helping the disadvantaged; in the publication of school newspapers; and in political activities. People who take part in them are not indifferent to the fact that they may gain thereby in even a material way, but their primary gains lie in the respect and affection of those who work with them. Often such groups are in conflict with others, but that is so in *Gemeinschaft* societies as well. The primary fact to be emphasized, nevertheless, is that there are numerous sectors of activity in any modern society that are thought to be *Gemein-* *schaft* in some characteristics, and people who take pride in them obtain some of their most satisfying life experiences there.

No Single Pattern

We must think of social life not as neatly divided into two main sectors, primary and secondary, folk and urban, or *Gemeinschaft* and *Gesellschaft*. Nor should we think of modern life as slipping mindlessly into an automated bureaucracy in which all our humanity is destroyed. Instead, we must think of social life as an arena in which people are constantly recreating different forms or patterns of social organization.

Sometimes people will create or support a social pattern in which they owe minimum rather than maximum obligations, that is, in which they know exactly what they owe.

They press toward a system in which they owe only *performance*, but not affection or loyalty. They wish to be rewarded—and to see others rewarded—for merit rather than family or friendship ties or favoritism. They wish, moreover, to be free to leave this relationship and choose new ones if others seem more desirable. In short, they prefer a system that is contractual, formal, secondary, or *Gesellschaft* in character.

Sometimes that system is imposed on them by others, and they resist. In fact, people do resist frequently, and even successfully, throughout modern society—but many others prefer it. Still others prefer some pattern that is partly both. This is not new. For over four hundred years, as an illustration, British lords and gentry attempted to establish *contractual* relations with their tenants, who bitterly fought that step. That is, landowners wanted (as part of the land enclosure movement) to confine their relationships with tenants to specific, narrow obligations and rights: to be free to get the best price possible, to change tenants each year if that seemed wise, and to discard any traditional duties they owed to farmers on their land. Employees in a modern bureaucracy, too, like peasants of several centuries ago, may form a "community" of fellow union members in order to protect themselves from the insecurity, weakness, and impersonality of jobs in a *Gesellschaft* system.

In short, at any given time we can observe social processes moving in both directions: toward "community" or *Gemeinschaft* patterns, or toward secondary or *Gesellschaft* patterns. At a specific time, as a consequence, a system may seem bureaucratic at first glance but may contain many primary or community patterns in it.[17]

SUMMARY

We do not often see all of a group together, and thus we have little opportunity to ob-

[17]Such primary relationships will be especially common toward the *upper* ranks of management, among people who would prefer to have their *employees* live under a system of *formal* rules. Similarly, large corporations unite with one another to form a "community," again in order to avoid the insecurities of a contractual system, but they do not wish their customers to do that. Some of these processes are analyzed in William J. Goode, "The Protection of the Inept," in *Explorations in Social Theory*, New York: Oxford, 1973, pp. 121–144.

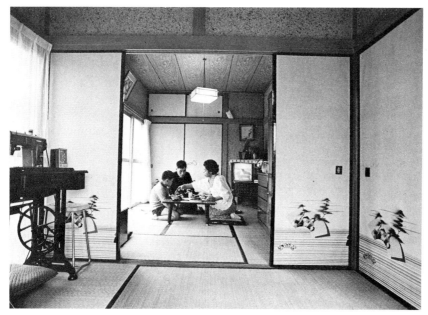

Figure 6-5 A Japanese family in two worlds: Lunch is served in the traditional manner before a television set. (Wide World Photos.)

serve one in action. We especially do not see *two* groups in interaction with one another (except for athletic teams on television). Nevertheless, much of what we do with others is shaped by our membership in one or more groups. We do read or hear of groups in interaction with one another—for example, two factions in a political conflict, a union fighting with a grape growers' association, or a residential group that has organized a patrol to reduce the threat of a local boys' gang. We also become aware at times that others are reacting to us in a certain way because they consider us a member of some group. Indeed, people commonly think of others in certain social *categories* (blacks, Catholics), when, strictly speaking, those are not real groups at all.

The importance of groups can be seen, then, in much of our personal interaction with others. That importance can be seen in still another connection: The larger structure of the society, the major goals that the government pursues, or the broad efforts of people to get things done are all determined in part by groups large and small.

Whether a given set of people can be called a group depends on whether it exhibits certain traits, among them group norms and a feeling of unity. Even so, most "members" do not view themselves as living by an agreed-upon set of norms and would prefer *not* to be treated by others as a special group. What such examples show is that persons who share some social trait may not be a real group, but under some conditions they do exhibit some grouplike social behavior.

We have noted that a group may have a short or a long life, and its members may expect to remain in it for shorter or longer periods. Various aspects of group duration may have different effects on group members. We have shown how each element in our definition of a group has some consequences for group and individual behavior.

Many sociologists have tried to work out a neat classification of groups, but none of these has been generally accepted by the

field. Accordingly, we have considered a wide range of different kinds of groups. Which classification we use is likely to be determined by the problem we are analyzing.

The effects of reference groups on individual behavior and attitudes are especially striking, for they may be observed even when the individual is *not* a member of the group, but simply uses their standards or norms as his or her own. These effects remind us to be alert not merely to a person's "objective" situation, but also to how his or her reference group views that situation. For example, someone may feel poor while receiving a substantial income, if his or her reference group considers that income inadequate.

We gave particular attention to the *triad*, which has no special label in ordinary talk, but which many analysts believe is the basic building block of large and small social structures.

Social scientists and philosophers have long devoted much attention to small, primary groups and to large, formal ones, and to the two kinds of societies in which one or the other type of group predominates:

Gemeinschaft and *Gesellschaft.* To many social analysts, the history of Western society for hundreds of years is a movement (often *not* viewed as progress) from *Gemeinschaft* to *Gesellschaft.* However, we suggested a more dynamic and contingent view of these types of societies. Observation of this most *Gesellschaft* of societies discloses that we cannot always apply the distinction neatly, for within many societies of the past there were movements and pressures that should be labeled *Gesellschaft* in type, and there are many within modern industrial society that are *Gemeinschaft.* That is, in a wide range of societies there have been some people or groups that preferred a system that was contractual, formal, secondary, or *Gesellschaft* in character. And by contrast, even in modern industrial society there are widespread counterpressures against the dominance of just those social patterns. *Neither* type of pattern is more "natural" or "wholesome" than the other, and few people can truly claim that they would prefer a society in which either would be followed *exclusively*.

It must be emphasized that neither is *necessarily* more exploitative than the other. Both are systems of social exchange, but what is viewed as more valuable differs between the two (loyalty, deference, personal ties, efficiency, freedom to act as an individual, high productivity). How much exploitation occurs under either is likely to be determined by which groups command more political influence or force, wealth, or prestige, rather than by which kinds of social relations are considered preferable. Groups that command little—serfs, peasants, old people, sharecroppers, colonial natives, migratory laborers, outcasts—may gain some small advantages from a change at some specific moment in history, but neither type of society will improve their position by much.

READINGS

Ellen Berscheid and Elaine H. Walster, *Interpersonal Attraction,* Reading, Mass.: Addison-Wesley, 1969.

Theodore Caplow, *Two against One: Coalition in Triads,* Englewood Cliffs, N.J.: Prentice-Hall, 1969.

Charles Horton Cooley, *Social Organization* (1909), New York: Free Press, 1956.

Kingsley Davis, *Human Society,* New York: Macmillan, 1949, pp. 289–294.

Morris Freilich, "The Natural Triad in Kinship and Complex Systems," *American Sociological Review,* 29 (August 1954), pp. 529–540.

Kenneth J. Gergen, *The Psychology of Behavior Exchange,* Reading, Mass.: Addison-Wesley, 1969.

Erving Goffman, *The Presentation of Self in Everyday Life,* Garden City, N.Y.: Doubleday, Anchor, 1959.

William J. Goode, "The Protection of the Inept," in *Explorations in Social Theory,* New York: Oxford, 1973, pp. 121–144.

Edward E. Jones, *Ingratiation,* New York: Irvington, 1965.

Rosabeth M. Kanter, *Commitment and Community: Communes and Utopias in Sociological Perspective,* Cambridge, Mass.: Harvard, 1972.

Peter Laslett, *The World We Have Lost,* London: Methuen, 1965.

Elliot Liebow, *Tally's Corner: A Study of Negro Streetcorner Men,* Boston: Little, Brown, 1967.

Eugene Litwak and Ivan Szelenyi, "Primary Group Structures and Their Functions: Kin, Neighbors, and Friends," *American Sociological Review,* 34 (August 1969), pp. 465–481.

——— and Henry J. Meyer, *School, Family and Neighborhood: The Theory and Practice of School-Community Relations,* New York: Columbia, 1974.

Robert K. Merton, "The Classification of Types of Membership Groups," in *Social Theory and Social Structure* (1949), enlarged ed., New York: Free Press, 1968, pp. 263–380.

———, "Continuities in the Theory of Reference Groups and Social Structure," op. cit., pp. 335–440.

——— and Alice Rossi, "Contributions to the Theory of Reference Group Behavior," in Merton, op. cit., pp. 279–334.

Theodore M. Newcomb et al., *Persistence and Change: Bennington College and Its Students after 25 Years,* New York: Wiley, 1967.

Robert A. Nisbet, *Twilight of Authority,* New York: Oxford, 1975.

Talcott Parsons, *The Social System,* New York: Free Press, 1951.

Georg Simmel, *The Sociology of Georg Simmel,* trans. and ed. by Kurt H. Wolff, New York: Free Press, 1950.

Gerald Suttles, "Friendship as a Social Institution," in George McCall, ed., *Social Relationships,* Chicago: Aldine, 1970, pp. 91–135.

Ferdinand Tönnies, *Community and Society* (1887), trans. and ed. by Charles P. Loomis, East Lansing: Michigan State University, 1957.

Benjamin D. Zablocki, *The Joyful Community,* Baltimore: Penguin, 1971.

CHAPTER SEVEN

(United Nations/M. Tzovaras.)

FORMAL ORGANIZATIONS

Technologically, modern society is distinguished from all prior civilizations by its high development of science and sophisticated machines. If we venture into a remote village of Mexico and imagine the problems of living there, or if we talk with others about their experiences in less developed nations, we are likely to note that "their machines don't work," or that they simply do not have many machines.

Sociologically, however, modern society is distinguished from past civilizations by the widespread use of *formal organizations*, or bureaucracies. Over the course of the day in an urban society we may see hundreds or even thousands of human actors, but we are less likely to be very conscious of the many bureaucracies that inhabit every office building. If we talk with others about our explorations in out-of-the-way places, we do not usually mention that a great many bureauc-

racies were missing. In short, we are more conscious of *human* actors and of machines than of "corporate actors," although these may have more effect on our social life than do machines.

THE PROBLEM OF DEFINING ORGANIZATIONS

Social science has hardly begun to describe adequately just how much of modern life is shaped by large formal organizations, and therefore much research on this topic remains to be done. However, let us consider this peculiarity of industrial society.

It is not easy to define a "formal organization" or "corporate actor," although we can all point to numerous examples: utility companies, universities, trade unions, foundations, churches, country clubs, the American Medical Association, banks, city governments, or the Boy Scouts. Some sociologists define them by stating they are agencies that have been organized for a *specific purpose* (for example, irrigation or telephone service), unlike families or friendship networks, which are likely to have many different goals. However, most large organizations were created for a multitude of purposes, not just to make a specific product or only to make money.

Some definitions focus instead on the *hierarchic* aspect of organizations by noting that some people in such agencies plan the activities of others; that is, there are higher and lower levels of authority, and the people in charge decide what others will do. However, that is also true for many informal groups, such as friendship networks or families, mass demonstrations, and (in the past) warlike invasions or raids carried out by a chief and his loyal followers. Moreover, as Max Weber pointed out half a century ago, bureaucracies of the past themselves have been of many kinds. Some were like modern ones, but others could be classified as simply the servants of the king, or part of a great extended household.[1]

Two main traits characterize the modern collective or corporate actor, usually called a *formal organization*: (1) All are formally created; that is, their structure, aims, ownership, management, location, and rules are spelled out, as in a charter or the constitution of a nation. (2) Once organized, they take on an independent existence. Laws apply to organizational behavior that do not apply to human beings; a corporation can go into bankruptcy or be sued without its managers or even its owners being personally liable. Many organizations can survive

beyond the life of the people who created them.

By contrast, the rules that govern a specific family or a family system are not created by the people who begin a particular family unit. Those who begin an organization or a corporation do set the rules for it when they begin it. The laws and regulations for families exist before a couple marries, and they continue to exist after that household breaks up.[2] And when the members of a family die, that is the end of the family; whereas formal organizations are continued by replacing their members who leave or die. The newcomers do not create the rules of the organization; they must abide by the rules in operation when they enter. Generally, people who are in charge of organizations think of the organization as existing independently, and they are simply obeying its rules. The owner of a small shop may feel this, too, although he or she is responsible for the rules of that business. On the other hand, the head of a government agency or the president of a public utility would not agree that the rules of that formal organization are of her or his own making. In short, members of an organization are likely to see it as having a life of its own.

Though these two traits—formal organization and independent existence—are the most important in defining the corporate actor or formal organization, like most definitions they do not permit us to place every enterprise neatly in one category. There are always some cases that cannot easily be classified. For example, both the Japanese and the Chinese family were ideally *corporate* or collective; the family head was only a temporary representative of a supposedly

---

[1]For what is sometimes called the classic description of bureaucracy, see Max Weber, *Economy and Society* (1922), ed. and trans. by Guenther Roth and Claud Wittich, New York: Bedminster, 1968, vol. 3, pp. 956–1005.

[2]For an extended analysis of the traditional elements in a legal marriage that are imposed by the state, and the barriers to making one's own marriage contract, see Lenore J. Weitzman, "Legal Regulation of Marriage: Tradition and Change," *California Law Review*, 62 (July–September 1974), pp. 1169–1288.

perpetual family line. He was the custodian, not the owner of its property, just as the president of a corporation does not own its property.[3] The family existed independently of the eldest male, who was its head.

Another borderline case might be neighborhood clubs or gangs that have definite rules about the duties of each member and a clear authority structure, but we would not view such groups as formal organizations. Doubtless, the reader can think of other borderline cases. In a society where people quickly think of forming an organization as a way of solving problems, thousands are created each year, and not all can be fitted into any simple classification or definition.

A loose definition does not prevent us, however, from considering (1) the impact of organizations on social life, and (2) the social patterns within those bureaucracies. These considerations raise two questions: How are human beings affected when some of the "actors" in their social environment are large "corporate" actors? And how do human beings act when they work within such organizations?

An Ancient and Modern Invention

We do not know when the notion of a formal organization was first implemented. There were factories in Athens as well as Rome. Corporations were not publicly chartered in Rome until the third century A.D., but they existed before that. In the Islamic world it has been possible since ancient times to set up a "trust fund" land whose proceeds were given to a family line until it died out, whereupon the land itself became the property of some pious enterprise such as a mosque.[4] The Christian church became

a bureaucracy at an early stage in its history, reaching from the exalted rank of pope at the top to minor church and monastery job holders in remote regions of the Western world. Apparently, some form of bureaucratic organization was created in every great civilization.

Nevertheless, in no other type of society has bureaucracy flourished as in modern industrial society, East or West. In the modern era armies are great bureaucracies, not simply a mass of loyal warriors following an especially magnetic leader. Most entertainment is arranged by large organizations—television, radio, theater, and sports corporations—in contrast to the spontaneous impulse or traditional theater of people in primitive tribes. Food production, preparation, and distribution (except for the final stages of cooking, if any) are carried out by companies rather than by a single family or several in cooperation. Education at the highest and lowest level is organized by large bureaucracies and is not the primary responsibility of the family or tribe. Finally, our political system consists of an array of state and national bureaucracies ranging from the local police department to the FBI, from the village council to the U.S. Congress. No other society has ever before given so much of its work to corporate actors. Formal organizations control or shape far more of our daily lives than in any society of the past.

Size and Numbers of Organizations

We can get some idea of the importance of formal organizations by considering these gross data: In 1970 there were over twelve *million* businesses of all kinds, including 1.7 million corporations and over half a million local governments. These organizations encompass most of our economic and governmental transactions. We cannot easily avoid face-to-face encounters with their

---

[3]For an extended analysis of these family systems, see William J. Goode, *World Revolution and Family Patterns*, New York: Free Press, 1963, chaps. 6 and 7.

[4]Ibid., p. 136.

representatives—teachers, police officers, filling station attendants, office managers, bridge toll takers, sales clerks—from one hour to the next if we venture out of our homes, while their activities affect much that we experience within them. By contrast, even a century ago a farmer could confine most social interaction to people who were not serving as members of an organization.

The sheer *numbers* of formal organizations give some hint of their importance. However, it is their *size* that sets the modern world apart from all societies of the past, and indeed creates social and personal problems for which the modern world is not prepared. If all bureaucracies were like, say, the town government of a New England village of a century ago, ordinary people might be able to watch what they do and even to control them. When, however, an ordinary person confronts the U.S. Department of Defense or General Motors Corporation, neither is possible. A small sample of figures will illustrate the size of organizations:

Various governmental units in this country spent over $450 billion (1974).

These governmental units had 13.6 million employees (1973).

One of the largest bureaucracies, the defense forces, had 3.2 million military and civilian personnel on their payroll (1973).

Of the 1.6 million corporations, the *top 100* industrial corporations enjoyed 62 percent of the total sales (1973).

The top 100 manufacturing corporations owned 48 percent of all the assets owned by all such corporations (1972).

In 1973, 124 United States manufacturing corporations owned $1 billion or more in assets; these corporations earned more than half of all the profits made by all such corporations, and they owned more than half of the total assets.

The top 100 industrial corporations employed 60 percent of all the people working for all such corporations (1973).[5]

We can immediately see at least one reason why any abstract definition of "corporate actor" or "formal organization" is likely to fail. It is required to cover a tiny corporation as well as Exxon and General Motors, whose combined revenues exceed those of the state of New York.[6] It must cover both a small village government and the U.S. State Department. Evidently, if we wish to understand the modern industrial society, whether socialist or capitalist, we shall have to focus on these great bureaucracies rather than the smaller ones. The influence of the great ones is large, and it is growing. The part of social life that is controlled or affected by the larger ones is increasing, and they make modern society different both from the ancient past and from even a century ago.

The Success of Organizations

Why do bureaucracies flourish, in both size and number? A beginning answer is that they are a social invention, like the division of labor in manufacturing, which yields much *greater efficiency and lower costs* for everything from ball-point pens to typewriters than a system in which each worker makes the whole product.

Perhaps no individual now exists who could make an automobile from start to finish, but no one has to do so. Each step is broken down into smaller, *specialized processes*, at which most people can quickly become expert: screwing on the wheel nuts or radiator caps, supervising a machine that

[5]All figures from U.S. Bureau of the Census, *Statistical Abstract of the United States.*
[6]John K. Galbraith, *Economics and the Public Purpose*, Boston: Houghton Mifflin, 1973, p. 43.

presses the curved rooftop from sheet metal, or attaching a fender. If the whole labor of making a car is divided into many smaller tasks, people can become excellent at their specialties, the factory can use people with no great talent, and machines can be created to carry out those simple tasks.

That is also what a bureaucracy can do. Whenever a complex task can be broken into smaller steps, and the task must be done again and again—sending out electricity bills, taking in money at the bank, keeping records of which farms have used how much irrigation water, or issuing automobile licenses—people with *modest training* can learn to do them well and quickly. "The modern system is more productive because its social structures utilize the inept more efficiently, rather than because it gives greater opportunity and reward to the more able."[7]

Organizations are especially efficient if the task is a repetitive one, so that the same simple procedures or rules are followed for thousands upon thousands of cases. Thus, a few people can handle a large volume of cases. In addition, it is easier to supervise people who are carrying out simple tasks. Although the cost of integrating all those tasks is high and people who manage get good salaries, the cost per task is low. The costs of labor turnover are also lower: If an employee leaves, that is no great loss, since new ones can easily learn the job. Since such organizations are more efficient, they can win out in any competition with small ones in which several people try to do the whole job—whether it is making a pair of shoes or delivering the mail.[8]

[7]See "The Protection of the Inept," in William J. Goode, *Explorations in Social Theory,* New York: Oxford, 1973, p. 142.

[8]On the other hand, see Paul Goodman's cogent argument that there are various situations in which the large-scale solution is not even efficient: *Communitas* (with Percival Goodman), New York: Vintage, 1960; and *Utopian Essays and Practical Proposals*, New York: Random House, 1962.

Figure 7-1 The original Ford Motor Company assembly line, where individuals performed specialized tasks for greater efficiency and lower costs. (Ford Motor Company.)

Some tasks become so huge that a bureaucratic solution is almost required. For example, it is unlikely that the daily garbage output of New York City could be gotten rid of at all on an individual basis, for it would be much too costly. If every inhabitant of that city had to carry his or her own garbage to the city dumps, the cost per pound would be prohibitive, many people could not do it (lacking transportation), and many others would decide the cost would be too high and so would clog the streets with it. If a small team of experts were to try to build a modern bomber or a giant dam, it is likely they could not do so within their lifetime, without the help of a bureaucratic organization.

All these tasks require organization, integration, and supervision (that is, *management*), and that is a cost; but since the cost is divided over thousands of specific tasks, the amount per task is low. There are likely to be, then, some *economies of scale*: The cost per unit is less when the output is large.

Again, however, it must be repeated: These advantages occur when the problem to be solved is, or can be made to be, repetitive, so that there are large numbers of similar cases. Organizations are *not* effective, by contrast, when the problem is very individual (such as soothing the anger of one's own child or making hot soup just to please one's grandfather) or is nonrecurring (such as the death of a close friend.)[9]

ORGANIZATION REQUIRES PLANNING

We noted that if a complex task is broken down into smaller parts, then these must be reintegrated. People must be hired who will supervise and manage. Repairing street potholes is technically simple, but the bureaucratic steps for doing so may be many: processing complaints from various sources; mapping the holes in the streets of a city; sending requests for bids to supply asphalt, gravel, and equipment; processing of job applications and keeping records afterwards; meetings of supervisors to determine how much to spend on given neighborhoods—the reader can see that the list could be rather long. All those additional coordinating or managerial steps would be wasteful if the work unit did not fill large numbers of holes.

Organizations, then, require investments in talent for planning, for skill in coordinating the parts of a bureaucracy, and for buildings and equipment. Consequently, they are most likely to flourish in societies that have enough wealth available for that investment. As in so many other economic situations, it is those who already have assets who can achieve the efficiencies of specialization, expertness, organization, and even innovation that will come from creating a modern bureaucracy.

These investments range from the tens of thousands of dollars the society pays to educate a physician or a scientist to the millions of dollars required to invent and perfect modern computers or to design and build the machines that will form an assembly line for the latest model car. They include the training of middle- or higher-level managers within a corporation and the testing of a system for routing mail within the organization.

Some machines make physical products, and some (typewriters, computers, telephones) facilitate the social processes within the organization; but neither can do without the other. Without the bureaucratic apparatus, the work of machines would never be coordinated. Materials would not be bought, and the output (whether toothpaste or divorce decrees) would not be delivered to those who want it.

Planning and Control

Planning is required if such large investments are to pay off and if the system is to deal effectively with thousands of similar cases—whether the problem is educating children, assessing property taxes, or manufacturing radios. The large bureaucracy cannot adjust daily to important changes in its tasks, rules, and procedures, or even its social environment. Its size gives it the capacity to hire experts who will plan, and "planning makes it more likely that the purposes will be achieved."[10] So large an investment requires a long time between the initial decisions and the beginning of some output, whether it is soap or loans to businesses. Consequently, organizations need secure sources of money (sales or taxation) and a

---

[9]Eugene Litwak has developed this notion with special reference to the family, which may be seen as a primary group that handles several tasks more effectively than formal organizations: "Technical Innovation and Theoretical Functions of Primary Groups and Bureaucratic Structures," *American Journal of Sociology*, 73 (January 1968), pp. 468–481.

[10]Arthur I. Stinchcombe, "Formal Organizations," in Smelser, op. cit., p. 23.

steady demand for their services. If they take risks by offering a new product or setting up new rules for pensions, those must be planned long in advance. Even when bureaucracies innovate, their experts strive to make them low-risk operations, protected as much as possible from a harsh, changing social environment.

In the industries where large corporations are dominant (steel-making, communications equipment, airplanes, computers, automobiles, electrical goods, chemicals, farm machinery, or soap, to name a few), they control both the sources of their raw materials and the prices at which they will sell. Prices do not change much in response to supply or demand. These are the most innovative corporations that are viewed as most typical of the modern industrial enterprise. They plan their products well in advance and persuade their customers to buy even when the new items are not notably superior to the earlier, now-outmoded products. They develop close relations with the government where necessary, to guarantee prices, control markets, and avoid any skeptical or unfriendly examination by regulatory agencies. In short, they are relatively successful in avoiding the rigors and unpleasant surprises that are to be found in the severe market competition faced by small shopkeepers, farmers, or building contractors, that is, by small and less influential organizations.[11] Controlling the market is as crucial as controlling production, and large corporations have mastered the techniques for both.

The Goals of Management

The managerial staffs of these large organizations try to create a secure environment for those firms. To do that, they seek (1) growth, (2) independence from outside con-

[11]On these and related points, but especially regarding the differences between businesses in which competition is severe and those which arrange their situation differently, see Galbraith, op. cit., especially chaps. 1 and 2.

trol, and (3) profits. Those goals are much more central than altruistic service to the public or to customers at large. That is not surprising, since the managers of those firms are rewarded to the degree that they succeed in achieving those goals.

The beliefs and observations of the ordinary citizen are in agreement with the foregoing description, although both run contrary to the analyses in economics textbooks. Textbooks continue to assume that the fate of the corporation, like that of the small business, is determined by the free decisions of ordinary customers when they go out to shop. Similarly, most political science textbooks assert that the policies of *public* corporate actors or bureaucracies are ruled by the votes of ordinary citizens at periodic elections. At these times public servants learn what their masters, the citizens, really want, and quickly take steps to carry out their requests. As the reader knows, however, few citizens believe that the U.S. State Department, the CIA, the Atomic Energy Commission, the Corps of Engineers, or the Department of Transportation will quietly adjust their actions in accord with the latest wishes of the average citizen. It is difficult to make a serious claim that ordinary people are incorrect in viewing their influence as modest.

HUMAN BEINGS IN CONTEST WITH ORGANIZATIONS

The citizen in an industrial society is in a peculiarly oppressive situation. It is new in its magnitude, and few are unaware of it. Ordinary citizens, and even those who hold relatively higher positions, feel they live increasingly among large organizations whose activities they can neither learn about nor control effectively. Since many industries are in the hands of a few large corporations, and most governmental agencies are monopolies, private citizens cannot go it alone. Individual citizens cannot manufacture automobiles, steel, or electricity; create a public utility; begin a school system on solid foundations; or establish their own State Department for making peace with foreign countries.

They cannot easily *resist* the influence of such large corporate actors because the discrepancy in influence is great. In addition, the discrepancy in *information* is especially great. Coleman has noted in this connection that universities or colleges get much information from applicants, but do not furnish comparable data about *themselves*: How good *is* their performance?[12] The corporation can hire expert salespeople (TV writers and actors, advertising companies, salesclerks), but the individual cannot easily hire an expert buyer to evaluate an ordinary purchase.

Some part of the feeling of powerlessness in our epoch, even among people of relatively higher positions, comes from an awareness of this reality: We do not have much influence; large corporate actors determine much of our lives; it is difficult or impossible to compete with them; and it is difficult to avoid taking a job with one, since that is where the jobs are. If one becomes part of a corporate actor, as member of a union or employee of a corporation, one may well gain in some ways but lose in total personal influence.[13]

How Government Organizations Avoid "Outside" Challenge

The management of a large corporation can avoid any serious outside challenges to its independence if profits and growth are reasonably high. In public agencies, by contrast, that test cannot be used. Government agencies do not make a "profit," and

growth is no proof that they are doing their jobs well.

Indeed, most people have no clear judgment at all as to whether various governmental units are efficient. Consequently, few specific challenges arise. For example, most state governments contain a Department of State, but it is likely that few readers even know what such departments do, much less whether they do it well. People do decide whether some officeholders are worth re-electing, but most people in the governmental bureaucracies hold relatively permanent jobs, unthreatened by such an evaluation.

Precisely because the administrative staff of most public organizations know that those who run for office, and thus the political appointees who get the *top* jobs in such agencies, will come and go, they can resist most political pressures for improvement. Such outsiders who become chiefs of governmental organizations can create some temporary, local discomfort; but only rarely can they alter the organizational goals, tasks, or procedures by much—any more than the president of a corporation can.

Public bureaucracies gain some security and autonomy because there is often little agreement as to what they should achieve, and thus no easy way of proving their ineffectiveness. In a Department of Defense, many generals will lose their commands (but will not be discharged) if a war is lost, but how can one measure whether the employees of the Department of Health, Education, and Welfare are accomplishing their purposes? The staffs of boards of education are supposed to see to it that schools teach children successfully, but since it is understood the task is difficult, if not impossible, no general test of performance has ever been worked out. Sanitation departments in most cities are likely to be evaluated by an obvious criterion: Does the garbage disappear? However, not many governmental units are measured by whether they accomplish some definite goal.

Perhaps the two most important addition-

[12]James S. Coleman, *Power and the Structure of Society*, New York: Norton, 1974, pp. 65–66.

[13]James S. Coleman has presented a mathematical demonstration of "loss of power" when one joins an organization, in "Loss of Power," *American Sociological Review*, 38 (February 1973), pp. 1–17.

al factors that help governmental agencies keep "outsiders" from intruding into their affairs are (1) avoiding any obvious personal corruption (for example, the acceptance of bribes), and (2) keeping good records and a clear set of rules.

Governmental organizations can also protect themselves from citizen interference by cultivating influential clients. Regulatory commissions have been especially adept at this, since their day-to-day relations with the corporations they are supposed to regulate are very close, or even intimate. The Federal Power Commission, the Federal Communications Commission, and the Federal Aeronautics Authority are good examples of this pattern.

Public agencies also protect themselves by controlling information about themselves. It is often impossible to ascertain just what they are doing, or why, simply because no outsider even knows how to find out where the data are concealed amidst thousands of filing cabinets. It was only long after the events that we could learn what messages and reports (*The Pentagon Papers*) were sent from whom to whom, when decisions about the Vietnam war were being made. Consider how even more difficult it was to know how well the CIA, the FBI, or the Atomic Energy Commission were performing until some of their files were opened because of political scandals or new laws that permitted citizens to learn what an agency has done.

A few governmental agencies are in the happy situation in which their task is to dispense largesse to influential people or corporations, and they have some control over who shall get it. Both in the federal government and in all state governments there is some type of Highway Department. Over the past generation they have dispensed tens of billions of dollars in contracts. Although they have destroyed a large part of the country in so doing, they have also been able to enrich the corporations that built the highways, as well as large landholders whose property values were

raised because of access to the new highways. Because they have enriched others, they have enjoyed much support, intensified by the backing of trucking companies and automobile manufacturers.

The U.S. Corps of Engineers, engaged in thousands of small and large projects from building canals and dams to swamp drainage and flood control, has been in a similarly pleasant position. So was the Triboro Authority under the leadership of Robert Moses, who may have had substantial control over some $27 billion of construction in his lifetime.[14] Some few people have objected to all these activities, but their resistance has been mostly ineffective. Specifically, in this country as in socialist countries, that kind of "progress" is approved, and few can agree on how to test the wisdom of building, say, a canal or a highway at all.

Two Types of Actors: How Do They Treat Each Other?

Thus, in a world whose inhabitants include large corporate actors as well as human beings, interaction seems to take place between and among human beings. However, some of these persons are not seeking their own goals or expressing their own opinions, but those of the organization of which they are members. Thus, sometimes we see two human beings who really are interacting with one another as persons, but sometimes that interaction is between one human being and a corporation. Or perhaps the interaction is really between corporations.[15]

We can draw on our own experiences to note the different forms of interaction between two persons, between a person and a

[14]For an especially enlightening detailed analysis of Moses' influence-trading, see Robert A. Caro, *The Power Broker: Robert Moses and the Fall of New York*, New York: Knopf, 1974.

[15]For further analysis of the consequences of these different types, see Coleman, *Power and the Social Structure*.

Figure 7-2 Army Corps of Engineers projects, such as this lock and spill in the Florida Everglades, have frequently been attacked by environmentalists as destructive of natural beauty and resources. (Army Corps of Engineers.)

corporation, and between two corporate actors. One is that in early childhood, both within the family and in school, we are told how to conduct ourselves with other *people*, but *not* with formal organizations. We do not learn how corporate actors "ought" to behave or what to do if they do not.

A second observation is again drawn from our personal experience. As people, we prefer to interact with other human beings and to favor them in our evaluations; but corporate actors favor their own kind, too! Human beings prefer news and television reports about persons to news about corporate actors; they feel more sympathetic toward people than toward corporations. In court cases they give higher awards to people in lawsuits against corporate actors.

Similarly, corporate actors favor one another: That is, people who protect the interests of the corporations they work for are rewarded by those corporations. Newspapers favor their fellow corporations by not calling attention to price comparisons of different stores. Corporations give better interest rates, discounts, and service to corporate actors. They give credit information about people to other corporations. Governmental organizations favor corporations in many ways, some of them already noted: by not regulating corporate behavior adequately, by an income tax policy that permits many expense deductions not permitted to human persons, and by granting interviews to heads of corporations more generously than to individual citizens.

Before leaving the broad topic of how the

presence of large corporate actors affects social life in modern nations and turning to the social patterns to be found *within* such organizations, let us note briefly a few additional differences in the behavior of human and corporate actors:

Those who make policies in a corporation typically do not carry them out, unlike the usual human-human interaction. Thus, if the corporation hurts people, those who are responsible do not have to witness that.

Information about corporate failure does not easily flow upward to the higher management levels, so that errors can be quickly corrected. Employees are not rewarded for bringing bad news. Human beings are quicker to point out each other's errors, since the chain of information is much shorter; knowledge is more difficult to avoid when people interact with people.

The employees or agents of corporate actors must justify their actions by the rules or purposes of the corporation, not by ordinary human rules. But the goals of the corporate actors need not coincide with the public good or with that of customers.

These relationships have not been adequately charted by social inquiry. Equally importantly, little systematic attention has been given to ways of altering the balance of influence so as to give more weight to the needs of human beings. Specifically, what structural changes can be made in modern societies that would increase the chances of serving the needs of human actors more than those of corporate actors?

SOCIAL PATTERNS IN A BUREAUCRACY

To this point we have been focusing on large formal organizations as corporate actors and how they affect the larger society. Let us now examine the *inner* structure of the organizations called *bureaucracies.* In ordinary English usage the term refers to the many white-collar workers and their managers who sit in offices and move pieces of paper from one desk to another. It also carries a negative tone, referring to rigidity, red tape, lack of concern for individual problems, and dead rules from the past. In this as in many other situations, sociology uses the term descriptively rather than evaluatively. It simply refers to any type of social organization (factory or office) in which the work is divided into specialties, jobs and promotions are supposed to be based on merit, the enterprise is coordinated by successively higher levels of management, and rules and procedures are worked out more by rationally calculating the most efficient ways of doing things than by whim or tradition. The foregoing is a complex statement and deserves a fuller exposition.

The Rules of Modern Organizations

First, let us translate the statement above into concrete terms by considering some of the *norms* of life in bureaucracy, that is, the rules that its members believe *should* be followed.

1. Employees should not let feelings about someone affect how well they work with that person.
2. The boss should not give favors or promotions to those who are liked or penalize those disliked.
3. The organization has no right to inquire into employees' private life or opinions, unless that private life can be shown to have a clear connection with how well they do their jobs. Employees owe the organization a good performance on the job, and very little off the job.
4. Employees should carry out the boss's orders not because the boss is more

competent, but because that job or post has the authority, or the right to give the orders (in the armed forces, you salute the uniform, not the person).

5   The boss does not have a *general* authority that comes from being "higher up." If the boss asks for things she or he has no authority to request (tools, supplies, money, special services), employees should refuse. Even supervisors cannot give orders to someone in another department.

6   Everyone doing the same job should be treated the same, and the same rules apply to everyone in the same category.

7   If one employee is better than another on the job, that employee should get the promotion.

8   If the boss wants to communicate with people at different levels above or below, those messages should "go through channels," that is, through every lower supervisor on the way down and through every supervisor on the way up. If an employee wants to send information to someone in another department, he or she should send it all the way up to the supervisor who has responsibility for *both* departments, who will send it back down to that person: Properly, the message goes up, over, and down so that everyone concerned will know about it.

9   If one wants to be promoted, one should aim at doing the job well, not simply calculating how little one can get away with or how one can exploit the job for personal advantage. On the other hand, the organization has no right to ask an employee to work longer or harder than the rules call for.

10   If an employee possesses skills that are not part of the job definition (he or she can take dictation but is a file clerk), the corporation should not ask him or her to do those things. An employee is responsible only for his or her own job.

11   Promotion should be based on achievement or merit (with a varying weight given to seniority), that is, how well someone might be able to do the job, and not "irrelevant" traits such as class background, race, age, sex, religion, beauty, or being the boss's nephew. For some jobs it may be believed that one or another of such traits might affect how well the person could do the task.

These are all rules or norms, in the sense that members of the organization will object or feel indignant when they are violated. If asked, employees will say that those rules ought to be followed. Violations do occur, as is true of all norms.

These norms are applied within a system that places great emphasis on keeping *records*. Almost any transaction of any importance is marked by a memorandum, list, letter, form, or punched card. Many copies are made of most such data, so that departments or units with some eventual concern for the event that is recorded will be able to "prove" that that event actually took place (such as checking out tools, completing a project, hiring an individual at a particular salary level, or transfer of goods to another warehouse). By and large, the rule is to *trust the documents, not the person*; for example, what "proves" that the tools were returned, or the goods were actually shipped, is not an individual's memory but the proper forms and signatures.

Bureaucracy in Less Industrialized Countries

Although most people in industrialized countries work at some time within such an organization and take it for granted as a normal social structure, it should be emphasized that one of the most difficult tasks of modernization in a new country is to develop this type of discipline. People who have traveled in countries without a developed bureaucratic system are mostly aware of the fact that so many things "don't seem to work" there, but they do not often have much direct experience with the specific bureaucracies that keep things from working.

When they do, they observe that the typical bureaucratic patterns of industrial societies work only partially, or not at all. For example, one of the common complaints in many underdeveloped nations is that employees do not focus on the job itself, but attempt to figure out how to exploit it for their personal profit or that of their family. They may use a position of bureaucratic authority to hire as many members of their family as they can, with little regard to competence.

We should not suppose, however, that the social norm in our own society is not to hire friends or kin. It is only the formal, *official* rules that forbid such favoritism. In fact, although employees may feel some envy if the boss's brother or nephew is hired, they are typically not indignant, and within their own social circles they would be dismayed or indignant if a friend or family member would not help them get a job. Note, nevertheless, that the informal social rules seem to be these:

1 You should not ask your friend or family member to hire you for a job that is beyond your competence.
2 The higher the job level (and thus the greater the costs of a mistake), the less should family or friendship connections play a role in a personnel decision.
3 Part-time or lower-level jobs are often filled through the friendships or family connections of the people already working at those jobs.
4 To avoid criticism, officials and bosses often do not hire their own family members, but ask their own friends who are fellow managers or bosses to hire them.[16]

Even when the external forms of bureaucracy are well established in a less industrialized country, as in India, those at higher positions will not easily delegate authority to subordinates, and subordinates are afraid of making decisions that lie within their jurisdiction. Consequently, a trivial matter may have to go through many levels of authority before it is finally decided, thus wasting much time and energy.

In less developed countries another rule that is difficult to learn—or perhaps to believe in—is that the supervisor has a limited jurisdiction or authority, not a general right to command. Where the supervisor is of a higher social rank (as is typical) in countries without a long bureaucratic discipline, that person may assume the right to give orders to almost anyone below in the bureaucracy, without going through channels. Correspondingly, it is difficult for subordinates to learn that the bureaucratic rules protect them from that type of personalistic authority or from exploitation generally, just as it is difficult to teach superordinates they do not have that right.

A further difference should be noted. It was earlier pointed out that the Western form of bureaucracy permits *strangers* to work efficiently together. It is not necessary that we have much personal trust in our fellow employees, since the records and documents are there to check whether a given event has taken place, a task has been finished, money has been removed, and so on. Personal trust is not as necessary, for we can quickly check whether the record corresponds with the actual fact. By contrast, in less industrialized societies, one of the most important aspects of all business and governmental transactions is to know whom one can trust. From the Greek countryside to Guatemala, ordinary people feel

---

[16]That some managers have not learned these norms in all countries can be inferred from a March 14, 1975, Associated Press dispatch from Argentina, reporting

that several thousand employees of the Parks and Public Works Department engaged in a sit-in protest because the Director had hired four of his sons, a brother, and a brother-in-law (*San Francisco Chronicle*).

most comfortable when transacting business through close friends or kin.[17] If a petition or request has to go through channels to higher levels, they feel safer if they can obtain the help of a go-between or broker who is on close personal terms with their family. In such a system bribery is a frequent occurrence, because once a problem has to go beyond the circle of friends and kin, it is assumed one must buy the cooperation of strangers. These people do not assume officials will follow the rules unless they are given a persuasive reward.

Pressures of the Bureaucracy versus Needs of Employees

Thus, we should keep in mind that bureaucracies, now existing by the tens of thousands and utilizing the work of hundreds of millions of people in different parts of the world, have not been typical in the history of the world, and people in modernizing countries do not accept them as "natural" patterns of social behavior. On the other hand, modern bureaucratic discipline is harsh, and people resist it to some extent in all societies. New employees have to be socialized and pressured to follow its rules, because the rules do not seem to be "sensible" or "natural." If the rules are followed, the bureaucracy is likely to be efficient, but constant supervision is required to avoid the threat of breakdown. Indeed, most of the energy of supervisors is not devoted to technical tasks requiring a high knowledge about the product being manufactured or the specific task being performed by subordinates, but to coordinating and integrating human relations. Let us examine this matter further.

The modern bureaucracy is an officially created social system. Like many attempts at consciously forming a social organization, this one accomplishes some purposes very

[17]For Greece, see John K. Campbell, *Honor, Family, and Patronage*, Oxford: Clarendon, 1964.

well, but omits other factors that are socially necessary if it is to continue functioning. This type of bureaucracy has one central aim or purpose: to make the human worker as much like a machine as possible and the organization as a whole as much like an interlocking set of machine processes as possible. All rules are to be made by reference to whether the task will be more efficiently done, with little regard for the wishes of the unique people who constitute the organization. Only that part of the person is relevant, or is to be utilized, which will facilitate the job itself. Friendship and kinship links, or likes and dislikes, are not supposed to affect how well people work together, and the individual is supposed to bring to the workplace only competence and willingness to work. The organization itself is not supposed to inquire much into the person's life off the job. New, more efficient techniques are constantly being worked out by research units. People are supposed to be able to change their procedures when better ones are worked out, even though they were comfortable with the old system.

If those "ideal" rules were followed, the organization would do its job well; but since the people in it would be very dissatisfied, it would fall apart just the same. That is, the system as created in this ideal form is not in fact viable; it cannot continue to exist. The human material that is needed for it has many other needs of its own, and these must be satisfied.

"Approved" Violations of Bureaucratic Rules

Consequently, all efficient bureaucracies develop a wide range of social patterns that partly violate bureaucratic rules and partly exist alongside the rules without violating them. Since human beings require a continual flow of friendly social interaction with those who occupy the same social space, informal social relationships come to play a large part in ordinary work life.[18] If there are rules against talking (because talking might distract workers from their jobs), those rules are violated, and the wise supervisor takes care not to observe the violations as long as they are within some limits. Work is supposed to go on at a fast pace, except for official coffee breaks; but employees develop informal standards of what a fair amount of production is for a given time, and they hold one another to that standard.

Information and memoranda are supposed to go through channels, but if normal work requires two people in different departments to interact with one another, they will work out their own rules for informing others about what they do. Wise corporate managers, recognizing that office or factory bureaucracies do not furnish much satisfaction, have typically encouraged the development of social activities off the job, such as bowling leagues, hobby clubs of all kinds, special charter trips available to employees, and cafeteria or coffee services. Recognizing as well that wages alone do not give adequate social satisfaction, effective managers have tried to develop competitions of various kinds for prestige, and to give special recognition to outstanding employees through periodic meetings at which prizes are announced. Honorific titles, rewards for cost-cutting ideas, letters of commendation for making an office attractive—all of these are ways by which effective managers bring into the bureaucracy some social elements that are missing from it in its official form.

The Inefficiency of Organizations

Thus, even with respect to total organizational efficiency, the bureaucracy that tries to follow the official rules closely incurs some losses as well. Without examining these losses in great detail, let us take note of them briefly:

1 Limiting the employee to a narrow set of tasks makes him or her expert in that task, but the organization fails to use all the other knowledge and ability this subordinate possesses.

2 If the organization focuses on the task alone, the work may go relatively smoothly, but the individual has little emotional commitment to the job and not much enthusiasm for it, especially at lower job levels.

3 Following detailed rules and procedures gives predictability and order, but it encourages individuals to follow those rules for job security even when those procedures do not solve the problem and they do not fit the needs of the customers or clients of the organization.

4 An efficient division of labor and an adequate flow of communication make it possible to create very large bureaucracies; but because the work alone does not satisfy the social needs of human beings, an even larger percentage of managerial skills must be devoted to integration, cooperation, and the solution of interpersonal conflicts, that is to human relations problems that are not taken account of in bureaucratic rules.[19]

The foregoing comments are not meant to suggest that the development of formal organizations in modern life is a vast error. Neither government nor industry could function at all without an elaborate bureaucracy. Rather, we are pointing out the sources of efficiency in modern bureaucracy, while noting the points at which such a social system cannot be viewed as self-

---

[18]For a set of hypotheses about clique formation in a bureaucracy, see Noel Tichy, "An Analysis of Clique Formation and Structure in Organizations," *Administrative Science Quarterly*, 18 (June 1974), pp. 194–208.

[19]Robert K. Merton's graceful analysis of this process will supplement the reader's personal experience; see "Bureaucratic Structure and Personality," in his *Social Theory and Social Structure* (1949), enlarged ed., New York: Free Press, 1968, pp. 249–260.

enclosed. It is a system that requires many other inputs and adjustments if it is to continue to function effectively.

Maoist and Western Theories of Management

As it has been depicted in newspapers and popular articles, modern Chinese bureaucracy seems remarkably irrational for a nation whose social ideal for over two thousand years has been a calm realism. We read of high government officials rejoicing that managers or technical experts are not supervising the steel furnaces, but are shoveling manure on North China farms. Factory managers are told they cannot simply order changes in production techniques or office rules, but must discuss them with, and take advice from, lowly workers and clerks. Generals are not to wear dazzling uniforms, but essentially the same clothing as do privates. Swarms of young people (Red Guards) shut factories down, and all workers and managers must be harangued about politics, endure denunciations, or engage in lengthy confessions about their own misdeeds. People may not simply go home to rest after the day's work, but must attend long lectures or indoctrination sessions that deal with both work and political attitudes. Nor is their private life exempt from intrusion. Fellow employees and neighbors feel free to ask about each other's sweethearts, wives, kin, or friends with reference to personal problems and work as well as their general political philosophy. Higher-level managers may well be removed from their jobs after years of active contributions to the nation.

Much of this seems to run so contrary to Western bureaucratic patterns, both socialist and capitalist, that one may wonder how the Chinese society survives. On the other hand, even if we set aside the claims of Maoist supporters in this country, or the boasts of Chinese officials in their own nation, most United States and European visi-

tors to that country attest to the impressive accomplishments the regime has achieved, especially by contrast with the stagnation and corruption of the period between World War I and the final Communist victory in 1949.[20]

However, social reality is more solid than general theories. If, as seems evident, the Chinese bureaucracy is working well, then the Maoists have made important social science discoveries about how to manage human beings—or the reports of their actions are misleading. Our own interpretation is that, allowing for different vocabularies or rhetoric and a somewhat different culture, the Chinese have been attempting to put into practice some of the human relations principles that the most sophisticated Western analysts of management have suggested for years. Although they do conflict with the traditional bureaucracy described by Weber, as analyzed earlier in this chapter, they also take into account some of the human elements that Western bureaucratic theory has sometimes ignored. So we have noted in some detail that "ideal" bureaucracy cannot exist without numerous adjustments to the human problems it creates or attempts to ignore. Doubtless, the ideal Chinese bureaucratic form creates its own problems, which in turn require adjustments of its bureaucracy, too.

Traditional Mandarin Bureaucracy

Let us first examine the *traditional* Chinese bureaucracy, for China once possessed the oldest continuous bureaucracy in the world. The Mandarin bureaucratic system survived several Chinese dynasties and at least two complete conquests by outsiders, for well over a thousand years. High posts in it were given more prestige than any other occupations in Chinese society. Unlike

[20]A good review of these achievements is that of Ross Terrell, *800 Million: The Real China*, Boston: Little, Brown, 1972.

Figure 7-3 Hundreds of Chinese mobilize to clear the streets of Peking during a snowstorm to supplement the mechanized equipment available. (Wide World Photos.)

Western bureaucrats, high-level Chinese officials got most of their income from some share of the taxes in the area under their jurisdiction, rather than from salaries. According to official ideology, almost anyone could aspire to the education that was necessary to become an official, although the poor typically could not afford it. Appointment in the bureaucracy was based on merit, not on family connection.[21] Every study of social mobility in China from the T'ang dynasty (609–918) shows that the percentage of "new men" in the upper social stratum was always high; that is, about 40 to 60 percent of the top people rose from other class levels. Merit was measured mainly through civil service examinations, which did not test anyone's skills as a manager or engineer, but as a philosopher, scholar, calligrapher, or poet.

In contrast to the bureaucratic ideal, nepotism, or "helping one's relatives," was

[21]For an excellent analysis of mobility through the bureaucracy, and especially the limitations on mobility, see Robert M. March, *The Mandarins: The Circulation of Elites in China 1600–1900*, New York: Free Press, 1961.

viewed as a moral duty in traditional Chinese society. A man who failed in this family obligation was viewed as lacking in Confucian virtue. Some rules were worked out to reduce its effect—for example, governors were not allowed to serve in their own native region. But duty to the family was never seriously attacked, and nepotism was common among officials.

Officials were not supposed to encourage new solutions or procedures, technical inventions, or social improvements. They were supposed to keep things in harmony, unchanged if possible. Officials were blamed, however, for famines, catastrophes, natural disasters, and military defeats, because these were an index or proof that the official (or in some instances, the emperor himself) had lost the Mandate of Heaven, and was no longer in harmony with the universe. His technical or managerial efficiency or expertise was not considered an excuse if such great events occurred.

The bureaucracy did reach from the emperor to the lowliest official, but it stopped short of the village level of administration, where local families decided matters according to traditional rules. Unusual occurrences could bring imperial officials into village problems, but in general the system depended upon informal interaction, customs, and traditions that local organizations and family clans followed.

The New Chinese Bureaucracy

Modern China rejected both the Western and the Confucian ideals of bureaucratic structures. In part, that rejection stemmed from Mao Tse-Tung's and Chou En-Lai's belief that political indoctrination was at least as important as increasing production. This emphasis is in harmony with our assertion, in the chapter on political sociology, that a central problem in the industrialization of new nations is the creation of legitimacy, the moral commitment of the citizenry to the regime.[22] Without this, the program and the leaders themselves will eventually be rejected.

Consequently, if more energy was invested in successfully persuading the Chinese populace to believe in the system, the result has justified the investment. If the duty of every Chinese is to watch everyone else, in public or in private, so that no one is given any opportunity to oppose the system, then few people are likely to oppose whatever program is carried out. Therefore, even modest projects are likely to work at some level of effectiveness, and everyone can observe that progress is being made. Cooperation is likely to be at a maximum, because everyone has the obligation of supervising everyone else, and no one can claim that "it is nobody else's business." Thus, the modern Chinese bureaucratic system places a

high importance on political indoctrination and purity. This in turn has contributed to both the stability of the political system and the effectiveness of its economic system.

The Western bureaucratic ideal is to supervise only how well the job holder performs the task. In this the two systems are very different. However, before looking at other differences, we should emphasize that both share fundamental traits:

1   Both have specific goals of production.
2   There is a division of labor.
3   There is a hierarchy of supervision, and the upper levels have authority over lower levels.
4   Those at the upper level are more experienced and educated, and they are better paid.
5   Criteria of competence are used to select who will get which jobs.
6   Records, rules, and written memoranda are of central importance.
7   The office or job, not the person, has authority.[23]

As against those similarities, the differences seem rather profound. Let us note the most important of these. As was already pointed out, political purity, not just competence, is the basis for respect and other rewards. Those rewards are greater for people who are at the top of the bureaucracy, but in China these differences are narrower; the official ideology proclaims that the differences in reward should be kept to a modest level.

As could easily be inferred from our earlier discussion or from newspaper reports, no clear line is to be drawn between "on the

[22]For some data on the problem of authority see Chalmers Johnson, "The Changing Nature and Focus of Authority in Communist China," Institute of International Studies, University of California, Reprint no. 382 (reprinted from John M. Lindbeck, ed., *China: Management of a Revolutionary Society*, Seattle: University of Washington Press, 1971).

[23]Martin King Whyte, "Bureaucracy and Modernization in China: The Maoist Critique," *American Sociological Review*, 38 (April 1973), pp. 156–157. See also G. William Skinner and Edwin A. Winckler, "Compliance Succession in Rural Communist China: A Cyclical Theory," in Amitai Etzioni, ed., *A Sociological Reader on Complex Organizations*, 2d ed., New York: Holt, 1969, pp. 410–438; and A. Doak Barnett and Ezra F. Vogel, *Cadres, Bureaucracy and Political Power in Communist China*, New York: Columbia, 1966.

job" and "private life." Everyone's actions at all times are to be supervised and publicly judged.

Next, lower levels of the workforce are pressed to participate in a wide range of political and production decisions. Higher levels can be called to account by lower levels and subjected to public criticism. It should not escape notice that it is the upper officials who are encouraging these public examinations, and it is especially political officials, or indoctrination leaders, who call for public scrutiny and report on officials in factories or offices. Consequently, just as they can call for those discussions, so can they also call them off. On the other hand, at times popular enthusiasm for these open confessions can get out of hand.

Personal ties, kinship links, and neighborhood associations are all to be used to generate commitment to both political and production goals. This means in turn that informal and formal social pressures are widely used, in the form of giving esteem or public shaming. Giving and withholding respect are utilized widely as supports for whatever economic rewards or losses may be part of the control system.

Finally, traditional rules and procedures are not viewed as sacred. Indeed, people are told to be suspicious of bureaucratic rigidity, and instead to be open to rapid change and to adjust to new situations constantly.

Capitalist Bureaucracy at Executive Levels

Stated without the drama of newspaper writing, these rules do not seem so alien, although they are different from those of most large bureaucracies in industrialized countries. Indeed, some of these Chinese patterns are, ironically enough, in harmony with many of the ideals and some of the practices of what is sometimes called "participative management," one of the more modern philosophies of capitalist administration. The Chinese system also exhibits some parallels to the practices and social rules in the most advanced sections of industrial bureaucracies, that is, the research and development units in both universities and industry and the executive levels of corporations.[24] Let us analyze these similarities.

First, at the higher management levels of modern bureaucracies—both socialist and capitalist, in both government and industry—ideological or political purity, commitment to the established system, or belief in the programs being carried out is considered indispensable. The cynic, the political dissident, the social rebel, all have a hard time of it at such levels. This is a political fact, not a bureaucratic rule.

Second, at such levels it is assumed (and social pressures translate that expectation into reality) that higher-level officials will devote almost all their time and energy to the programs and the enterprise. No sharp line separates "work" from "private life." It is expected that almost everything that is done outside official work hours will contribute to the task. Even spouses have an obligation to contribute to the effectiveness of the office program.

Third, especially in research and development units, but also at the higher levels of military and industrial management, it is not true that the top official gives orders and the others simply obey. Rather, everyone is encouraged to give suggestions. Decisions are likely to be made after much discussion. There are persuasive data, for example, that the modern president of the corporation is

[24]For various statements about modern management theory (often less descriptions of current practice than assertions about what are the best techniques), see George E. Berkley, *The Administrative Revolution: Notes on the Passing of Organization Man*, Englewood Cliffs, N.J.: Prentice-Hall, 1971; E. H. Schein and W. G. Bennis, *Personal and Organizational Change through Group Methods*, New York: Wiley, 1965; Warren G. Bennis, *Changing Organizations*, New York: McGraw-Hill, 1966, especially pp. 18–19ff. and chap. 8; D. McGregor, *The Human Side of Enterprise*, New York: McGraw-Hill, 1960; and John G. Maurer, ed., *Readings in Organization Theory: Open-Systems Approaches*, New York: Random House, 1971.

Figure 7-4 Role playing is one of the tools taught at management training sessions. (Charles Gatewood.)

ence discrimination. They are exposed to psychodramas in which they are severely criticized, or they take part in experiments in which their own management techniques are embarrassingly dissected.[28]

Fourth, for over a generation experiments in social psychology have shown that decisions reached after much group discussion are more likely to issue in changed *action*, not in just lip service.[29] That social fact has been widely used in planning the introduction of new techniques and procedures in large United States bureaucracies.[30]

Next, at higher bureaucratic levels in industrial society, both esteem and social pressures generally play a much larger role in controlling members than even material rewards do. People who consistently earn more respect will also eventually be paid more money as well, but the esteem of the group is the most important day-to-day reward of its members. Moreover, ever since the World War II studies of soldier morale, we have known that the respect of one's

not a "boss" in the traditional sense, but is a leader within a group of officials who *together* have far more influence on policy than the president does.[25]

Bureaucratic rules are less likely to be followed at the executive level.[26] Consensus is viewed as a more effective technique in the long run.[27]

In modern corporations, executives are likely to be offered, or given, considerable training in understanding how subordinates feel and how minorities or women experi-

[25]See Galbraith, op. cit., chaps. 2–5.

[26]Richard H. Hall, "Intraorganizational Structural Variations," in William K. Graham and Karlene H. Roberts, *Comparative Studies in Organizational Behavior*, New York: Holt, 1972, pp. 141–150.

[27]Andre L. Delbecq, "The Management of Decision Making within the Firm: Three Strategies for Three Types of Decision Making," in James L. Gibson et al.,

eds., *Readings in Organizations*, Dallas: Business Publications, especially pp. 166ff., on "creative" and "negotiated" decision making. See also Jack H. Holder, "Decision Making by Consensus," in ibid., pp. 173–185.

[28]Paul C. Buchanan, "Laboratory Training and Organization Development," in ibid., pp. 351–375; Herbert A. Shepard, "Changing Relationships in Organizations," in James March, *Handbook of Organizations*, Chicago: Rand McNally, 1965, especially pp. 1128ff.; Chris Argyris, "T-Groups for Organizational Effectiveness," *Harvard Business Review*, 42 (March–April 1964), pp. 60–74; E. H. Schein and W. G. Bennis, *Personal and Organizational Change through Group Methods*, New York: Wiley, 1965; Harold J. Leavitt, "Applied Organizational Change in Industry," in March, op. cit., especially pp. 1153ff. These sessions do not usually take place within the organizational setting, but over a period of days in an isolated resort setting. It is professors who direct these programs.

[29]Much of this work was originally stimulated by Kurt Lewin in the 1930s. See Kurt Lewin, *Field Theory and Social Science*, New York: Harper, 1951; and "Group Discussion and Social Change," in Eleanor E. Maccoby, T. M. Newcomb, and E. L. Hartley, eds., *Readings in Social Psychology*, New York: Holt, 1958, pp. 197–211.

[30]Matthew B. Miles, ed., *Innovation in Education*, New York: Teachers College, 1964.

buddies is fundamental in maintaining the fighting effectiveness of combat units.[31] Considerable discussion within the most industrialized nations has also focused on the need to decentralize bureaucracies in order to gain efficiency, and also to give workers more control over how they will integrate the steps in production. Some attempts have also been made to break up the assembly line, and to permit small teams to put together all or most of a complex product, such as an automobile.[32] Managers are frequently reminded they should elicit ideas and suggestions from workers.

It is thus clear that the major emphases of the modern Chinese bureaucratic system are not so alien to Western experience as they seem at first to be. Not only are they supported in part by research and experimentation by Western social scientists; they also are to be found in a modified degree at the higher levels of management in Western bureaucracies.

BUREAUCRACIES AS SOCIAL SYSTEMS

It is unlikely that the Western or the Maoist bureaucratic rules can be used exclusively. Neither alone could create an adequate, functioning social system. The Chinese pattern may be wasteful by encouraging people to spend much of their energy on political zeal and on the moral examination of others as well as oneself, and by paying lower attention to experts. Some Western social scientists have reported that when Chinese po-

litical leaders relax their vigilance, bureaucrats revert to a more Western style. The Chinese system also grants to the individual a much smaller area in which to relax, to have personal pleasures, and to be protected in his or her peculiarities—in short to recuperate from the rigors of work or politics.

The Western system also exhibits many pathologies, as we noted at some length: for example, the blind acceptance of rules and authority, the low concern with the real task of the organization, a neglect of the needs of the larger society, and an insufficient utilization of the talents and knowledge of people at lower levels. Both systems help us to understand how people can successfully cooperate in carrying out large programs. However, the resistance of individuals within each system also tells us that the organization cannot satisfy fully the needs of the human beings that run it, and that inevitably there will be other informal or formal adjustments made to take those other needs into account.

Line and Staff Relationships

Many nineteenth-century capitalists began with an idea for a service (telegraphy, telephone communications, hauling goods) or a product (lead pencils, wood stoves, ice) and then used personal savings or loans to form a company to make and sell the output. At first, owners not only supervised all aspects of production; they purchased raw materials, sold the produce or service, collected bills, and kept the company accounts as well. They might also do a stint as a laborer if that was needed.

In bureaucratic language, every employee was part of the *line*, that is, the chain of command from top to bottom that embraced everyone in direct production. Probably the first specialized employee hired who was *staff*, that is, not directly producing the service or the goods but giving a specialized service to the company itself, was a

---

[31]The data in S. A. Stouffer et al., *The American Soldier*, Princeton, N.J.: Princeton, 1949; and Robert K. Merton and Paul F. Lazarsfeld, eds., *Continuities in Social Research*, Glencoe, Ill.: Free Press, 1950; have been widely cited as proving that the respect of buddies was more important than war propaganda. However, the ideals of being a "good soldier" as well as the leadership of the unit were also important. On this point see Amitai Etzioni, *Complex Organizations*, Glencoe, Ill.: Free Press, 1961, p. 58.

[32]In this connection see the set of reports in Gerry Hummius et al., *Workers' Control*, New York: Random House, 1973.

bookkeeper-treasurer. Few small companies had any *staff* at all. There were no separate units of the company that devoted themselves to hiring (personnel), advertising, public relations, market research, or legal work. If new machines or technologies were needed, the owner or a supervisor developed them or bought them elsewhere. No specialized staff was hired for research and development. Indeed, many companies were begun by people who were inventors, or who had made some improvement in a product, such as revolvers (Colt), harvesting machines (McCormick), electric generators (Edison), or the steamboat (Fulton).

The bureaucratic organization of nineteenth-century government agencies was equally simple, though an immigration official or the head of a state railroad commission did not have to borrow money to begin operations. Heads of bureaus hired their employees with governmental taxes, but without the aid of a personnel office. They had no press officer whose duty it was to write up the news about that agency and feed it at appropriate times to the journals or newspapers of the day. They hired no social scientists to evaluate a governmental program or to do a study on the impact of railroads on social life. Almost everyone was part of the line; almost no one was hired as staff, that is, to carry out specialized functions that were not directly part of the service offered by the agency.

There were some specialists and researchers scattered here and there in the government. In the Department of the Army, both the Signal Corps and the Engineers discharged specialized, staff functions and were not in the regular "line of command." For example, the Signal Corps set up communications systems but did not command battalions of fighting men. The Bureau of American Ethnology did studies of American Indians. The Bureau of the Census hired staff specialists to plan censuses but did not carry out governmental programs

aimed at changing citizens' lives. Mainly, however, government agencies were operated here, as in other countries, by people who began their careers essentially as amateurs, learned on the job, and did not feel they needed the help of specially trained experts. There were almost no conflicts between the staff, made up of specialists, and the line, made up of the managers and subordinates directly engaged in the governmental activity—because few agencies had any staff at all.

The Growth of Staff in Modern Organizations

However, the past century has witnessed a vast expansion in scientific knowledge, the increased application of science to practical problems, and thus the employment of research and development staffs in both industry and government. In addition, as bureaucracies become larger and take on more tasks, they increasingly need specialized staff to feed information and advice to the managers in the line, or chain of command. Managers who are occupied with supervision, with getting cooperation from subordinates, with decision making, cannot be experts in all specialties. For example, even if a manager is an expert at accounting, he or she cannot supervise the intricacies of those operations as well as employees in the chain of command. No manager can be an expert in the details of purchasing the thousands of machines and products any large corporation buys each year; it is thus more efficient to have a purchasing division. Even if the manager was trained as a lawyer, he or she may need a legal department to advise on the legal aspects of new policies. A manager cannot interview all job applicants, and once a corporation becomes large, it is useful to add a personnel department. Without a research and development unit, either there will be no new products or they will not work well. Thus it is that although a president, or a president in consultation with his or her vice presidents, will make decisions, that person can do so only with the technical or specialized information that staff people furnish.

Consequently, although diagrams of a governmental or corporate structure may look like a pyramid, with the person at the top supervising a next level of managers who supervise a next level of supervisors, on down to the filing clerks or assembly line workers at the bottom, the reality is very different: Several specialized units are likely to be responsible to the top officials for their staff services (legal advice, research, accounting), but they are not part of the direct chain upward. More often, all the supervisors of staff units will report to the executive vice president, but in either case each such unit is "shallow," unlike the "tall pyramid" of the line organization.

As Organizations Grow, They Differentiate

Several social patterns can be observed within (1) this general process of differentiation, that is, the splitting of any organization into various types of specialized units; and (2) the relationships between staff people and the line organization.

The most fundamental pattern is that as the organization grows in size, it becomes more differentiated. That is, the number of parts becomes larger. There is a more minute division of labor, both in staff and in line. There may be people who only put the handle on the automobile door, or people who only invest the pension funds of the company, or people who only keep the dictating machines in good repair.[33] As might

be supposed, as organizations become larger and larger, this process of an ever-increasing division of labor slows down; the number of subunits, job titles, or special functions does not increase at the same rate.[34]

Since there are more differentiated units, each with its own demands, needs, and special personnel, management itself becomes more difficult. Consider why this is so. As organizations get bigger, *continuity* is more important: Since a factory cannot simply be started up and shut down either quickly or easily, it is better to plan effectively so that it will continue to function more or less smoothly through the year. As there are more and more subunits and people to be considered, the cooperation or integration of those separate subparts is less likely to happen through accident, friendship ties, or spontaneous harmony: Managers have to ensure that harmony. That is an integration among people, but an integration of the *production process* itself is a management problem: As organizations become larger, there is a longer period of time between the idea or plan itself and the final output. To be sure that tires are ready for the car when it comes off the assembly line, someone may have to plan a rubber plant years in advance; to be sure that someone can keep the dictating machines in repair, someone may have to arrange for special factory training in another city, months in advance.

Nevertheless, since as agencies or corporations become larger they do not continue to differentiate at the same rate, this means that each supervisor oversees a somewhat larger number of employees. This is called a larger *span*. Obviously, a larger span costs less in managerial overhead, that is, a smaller managerial cost per subordinate employee.

---

[33]These propositions, with some modification, are conclusions from a study reported by Peter Blau and Richard A. Schoenherr, *The Structure of Organizations*, New York: Basic Books, 1971, pp. 301–310. The research examined fifty-three employment security agencies with 1201 local offices. Some further testing of these ideas is reported in Paul Goldman, "Size and Differentiation in Organizations: A Test of a Theory,"

Pacific Sociological Review, 16 (January 1973), pp. 89–105.

[34]I remind the reader that this is one more illustration of Kenneth Boulding's Law of Diminishing Everything: Nothing gets bigger indefinitely.

FOCUS

THE NEW INDUSTRIAL STATE

The modern business organization, or that part which has to do with guidance and direction, consists of numerous individuals who are engaged, at any given time, in obtaining, digesting or exchanging and testing information. A very large part of the exchange and testing of information is by word of mouth—a discussion in an office, at lunch or over the telephone. But the most typical procedure is through the committee and the committee meeting. One can do worse than think of a business organization as a hierarchy of committees. Coordination, in turn, consists in assigning the appropriate talent to committees, intervening on occasion to force a decision, and, as the case may be, announcing the decision or carrying it as information for a yet further decision by a yet higher committee.

Nor should it be supposed that this is an inefficient procedure. On the contrary it is, normally, the only efficient procedure. Association in a committee enables each member to come to know the intellectual resources and the reliability of his colleagues. Committee discussion enables members to pool information under circumstances which allow, also, of immediate probing to assess the relevance and reliability of the information offered. Uncertainty about one's information or error is revealed as in no other way. There is also, no doubt, considerable stimulus to mental effort from such association. One may enjoy torpor in private but not so comfortably in public, at least during working hours. Men who believe themselves deeply engaged in private thought are usually doing nothing. Committees are condemned by those who have been captured by the cliché that individual effort is somehow superior to group effort; by those who guiltily suspect that since group effort is more congenial, it must be less productive; and by those who do not see that the process of extracting, and especially of testing, information has necessarily a somewhat undirected quality—briskly conducted meetings invariably decide matters previously decided; and by those who fail to realize that highly paid men, when sitting around a table as a committee, are not necessarily wasting more time than, in the aggregate, they would each waste in private by themselves.[1] Forthright and determined

---

[1] Also committees are not, as commonly supposed, alike. Some are constituted not to pool and test information and offer a decision but to accord representation to diverse bureaucratic, pecuniary, political, ideological or other interests. And a particular committee may have some of both purposes. A committee with representational functions will proceed much less expeditiously, for its ability to reach a conclusion depends on the susceptibility of participants to compromise, attrition and cupidity. The representational committee, in its present form, is engaged in a zero sum game, which is to say what some win others lose. Pooling and testing information is nonzero sum—all participants end with a larger score.

SOURCE: John Kenneth Galbraith, *The New Industrial State* (1967), Boston: Houghton Mifflin, 1971, pp. 63–64.

administrators frequently react to belief in the superior capacity of individuals for decision by abolishing all committees. They then constitute working parties, task forces or executive groups in order to avoid the one truly disastrous consequence of their action which would be that they should make the decisions themselves.

Thus decision in the modern business enterprise is the product not of individuals but of groups. The groups are numerous, as often informal as formal, and subject to constant change in composition. Each contains the men possessed of the information, or with access to the information, that bears on the particular decision together with those whose skill consists in extracting and testing this information and obtaining a conclusion. This is how men act successfully on matters where no single one, however exalted or intelligent, has more than a fraction of the necessary knowledge. It is what makes modern business possible, and in other contexts it is what makes modern government possible. It is fortunate that men of limited knowledge are so constituted that they can work together in this way. Were it otherwise, business and government, at any given moment, would be at a standstill awaiting the appearance of a man with the requisite breadth of knowledge to resolve the problem presently at hand.

Consequences of Larger Staff Units

The more important point, however, is that consequently each subunit is somewhat larger in bigger bureaucracies, and thus the specialized *staff* units will be larger. What consequences will that have for any organization? The most important is that people in staff units begin to support one another in their special definitions of the world and the agency itself. If the bureaucracy contains only one lawyer, that person is likely to focus only on the needs of the organization. If five or ten lawyers (with their subordinates deferring to them) form a subunit, the chances increase that they will form a little "subcommunity," concerned with their own problems. Consequently, even though larger organizations gain some advantage from *economies of scale* (the unit costs of management are somewhat smaller because the number of employees in a subunit is larger), some additional problems are created by the likelihood that some *staff* units will become large enough to create a separate small world of their own.[35]

Although we focus here on staff-line problems, it would be emphasized that *any* subunit of an organization will develop its own point of view and will attempt to some degree to protect itself from the demands of a larger organization. Workers in any unit will try to control the flow of work, against the wish of management to speed things up.

[35]Alvin W. Gouldner analyzes this problem, found in all larger organizations, in "Reciprocity and Autonomy in Functional Theory," in L. Gross, ed., *Symposium on Social Theory*, Evanston, Ill.: Row, Peterson, 1959, pp. 241–270. See also Melville Dalton, "Conflicts between Staff and Line Managerial Officers," in W. Richard Scott, ed., *Social Processes and Social Structures*, New York: Holt, 1970, pp. 356–365.

Typists are likely to feel that other employees do not understand their needs. Supervisors complain to one another about the latest orders from above, and work out techniques for seeming to conform while doing things their old, more reasonable way.

However, it is especially in the staff units that contain professionals (lawyers, physicians, cost accounting specialists) or scientists (in research and development units) that problems between the line and the staff are more likely to arise.[36]

The Different Viewpoints of Staff and Line

One potential for conflict is to be found in the background characteristics of staff and line people. Staff people are likely to be younger, to have more formal education, and to know more about certain specialized topics than do the managers in the central chain of command. But they also have less experience in this or any other bureaucracy. Supervisors and executives are likely to feel that although these "experts" know a great deal, they do not know what is important or how things really work.

The executive who gets advice from a staff unit is in a difficult position. The fact that the organization has asked for help from staff shows that he or she *could* do better but is not expert enough to solve the problem. To reject the advice may be unwise, but staff units (focusing on problems from *their* special viewpoint) may well not know

the important facts. Their solution may simply create other problems. A new computer program for keeping track of how many radios are stored in the warehouse or for billing customers sometimes creates bizarre errors.

Staff people, in turn, feel that a problem they have worked on for months, with their special expertise, is now basically *solved*, and all that is needed is to put the solution into effect. For that, they need the cooperation of the manager or executive, for he or she is in the line, and the line makes those decisions. People in the basic chain of command, not the special staff, typically have the authority to implement the decision. Set against the specialized staff knowledge, then, are the experience and authority of the management.

Staff units are often in the pleasing position of reporting *to* higher-level executives about deficiencies *of* lower-level supervisors of employees. The chief accountant reports that one supervisor is using up supplies at a high rate, or that one unit turns out too little production. The legal staff warns an executive vice president that the branch manager will be liable to a lawsuit if a proposed advertisement is published. Doubtless, these bringers of bad news contribute to the efficiency of the organization, but they arouse resentment by doing so.

Finally, staff people are less likely to conform to the minor rules of social life in a bureaucracy. This is especially true of scientists and of the research and development unit generally. They are less willing to keep regular hours. They spend more time talking among themselves while presumably at work. They do not like to report frequently to their supervisors, and are likely to be somewhat careless about paying deference to their superiors.

They are able to get into these ways because they are not as dependent on the organization as other employees are. Profes-

[36]These problems were discussed extensively in William J. Goode, Mary Jean Cornish, and Robert K. Merton, *The Professions in the United States*, 1956, unpub., a monograph written for the Russell Sage Foundation. See the analysis by Wilbert E. Moore, *The Professions: Roles and Rules*, New York: Russell Sage, 1970, chap. 9. An empirical study is Harold L. Wilensky, *Intellectuals in Labor Unions: Organizational Pressures on Professional Roles*, New York: Free Press, 1956. See also the analysis of professionals in William J. Goode, "The Theoretical Limits of Professionalization," in Amitai Etzioni, *The Semiprofessions*, New York: Free Press, 1969, pp. 266–313.

sional people and scientists are likely to belong to some type of association of their peers by whose standards their work will be judged. A chemist may wish to please the executives in the company, but she or he will also prefer to do research that is publishable in a chemistry journal and that will arouse the admiration of fellow chemists. A staff lawyer may well do whatever the president or bureau chief asks, but she or he will also be aware that fellow lawyers will use professional standards to evaluate what is done. The professional or scientist wants to maintain her or his "outside" reputation, not simply to make a successful career in the organization. Indeed, over the longer run that strategy is likely to pay off: *Other* organizations will offer good jobs, too, having heard of her or his work.[37]

Thus, within large organizations some conflicting social processes are at work, creating problems for both employees and the executives who attempt to integrate the inputs and outputs of the bureaucracy. Each subunit must achieve some autonomy, some independence, if it is to function well—even the stationery supply room employees or switchboard operators feel they must do so. However, each unit depends for its existence on all the other units as well. With increasing size, these problems also become larger. Professionals and scientists especially demand autonomy, and their expert contributions are essential for the modern organization. Executives in the line cannot be well informed about everything. On the other hand, they must guess whether the information or new policy suggestions from a

specialized staff unit will actually work well, or instead turn out to be so narrowly conceived as to guarantee disaster. There are, after all, an infinite number of ways to make mistakes, and managers sometimes feel that the insulation of staff people from reality permits them the luxury of suggesting every one of them.

CONCLUSION

For well over two thousand years people have "reinvented" some kinds of bureaucratic systems in many forms. Some were no more than large numbers of retainers or loyal servants who discharged official duties under a great lord or king. Others were genuine formal organizations, that is, defined by specific rules and having a life more or less independent of any given leader. These have been especially effective when the problems they solve are repetitive and can be handled in much the same way each time. Bureaucracies work well as a kind of social machine when problems and solutions can be standardized in some fashion.

What distinguishes a modern society from all previous ones is the enormous size, number, and social influence of its formal organizations. Because organizations range from tiny neighborhood corporations to bureaucracies that control tens of billions of dollars each year, it is difficult to formulate propositions that apply to all of them. We have therefore focused primarily on the impact of large organizations.

Large bureaucracies are characterized by much planning and control, because the investment in them is huge, and the time span necessary for creating one is long. Thus, all large organizations, and especially corporations, attempt to control their environment to a high degree. In effect, the managerial staff of a corporation tries to create a secure environment, primarily by

[37]And, correspondingly, professionals change jobs more frequently than do the executives in the line (Moore, ibid., p. 203). Sociologists sometimes use the term "cosmopolitans" to refer to staff or line people who seek the approval of colleagues outside the organization, and "locals" to refer to those who are mainly focused on the organization as their little world. Clearly, the former are more likely to move than are the latter.

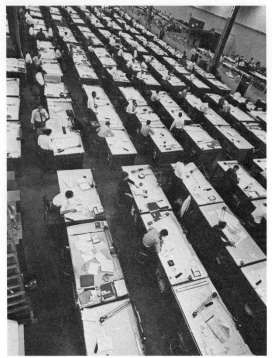

Figure 7-5 Large corporations are characterized by order and control—especially control of the corporation's environment. (Elliott Erwitt, Magnum Photos.)

growing, keeping independent of outside controls, and showing reasonable profits. Governmental organizations also attempt to maintain barriers against intervention by ordinary citizens.

In this chapter we have noted that in our world we see many interactions which seem to occur between human beings, but which are in fact interactions between two organizations, or between a human being and an organization. We have observed that people are taught appropriate role relations with other human beings, but not with corporations. It is equally obvious that large organizations have not been "trained" to interact in humane ways with people. Large formal organizations give far more support to one another and pay more attention to each other's needs than to those of human beings.

We have explored in some depth the rules

of behavior that workers in modern organizations are *supposed* to follow. In general, these rules are adhered to, and those who violate the rules are criticized. However, we have also pointed out some expected violations of the rules, such as talking when that is disapproved. More importantly, we have shown that the modern Western bureaucracy is not and cannot be a complete social system, fully satisfying the needs of its members. Consequently, at many points the rules must be bent to satisfy those human needs. The "human relations" approach in modern management theory has given much attention to this problem, since it is widely believed that bureaucracies will be more efficient if human needs are better satisfied.

The molding of people to fit such a social machine is difficult, as evidenced by the problems of introducing bureaucracy into less developed nations. We have considered, however, an unusual instance, the development of the modern Chinese bureaucracy. This system rejected the older Confucian bureaucracy, which endured through many invasions and changes of dynasty. It also rejected Western bureaucracy. We have examined this case in some detail, because it throws light on both the problems of formal organizations generally and Western bureaucracies in particular.

A closer analysis of the modern Chinese bureaucracy suggests that they have many social patterns similar to those of Western bureaucracy (a division of labor; hierarchy of supervision; higher rewards for the top jobs; the use of records; authority residing in the office, not the person). On the other hand, because the Chinese leaders felt the need to generate much authority in order to stabilize the revolution, they have emphasized the interpenetration of work and private life, political purity as a necessary duty for all members, the use of personal ties or neighborhood association to gain more moral commitment and production, and a considerable amount of public criticism and even confession at high and low job levels.

The more dramatic newspaper reports would lead the reader to believe that the Chinese bureaucracy is irrational, but clearly it has been effective. Our closer examination has disclosed that it has utilized some of the more sophisticated versions of modern Western management theory and practice, especially at higher management levels and within research and development units.

The Chinese resist the pressures of their bureaucratic system, just as Western bureaucrats resist somewhat different pressures, because neither system can exist without other kinds of social inputs. The Chinese system doubtless creates waste by encouraging people to be politically zealous rather than productive, or to ignore expert advice because it is politically tainted. The Western system, as we noted, also exhibits many pathologies. Both systems remind us that formal organizations cannot satisfy fully the needs of the human beings that run them.

Finally, we have considered a type of interaction that is to be found in almost all modern bureaucracies, the differentiation of the larger system into numerous smaller units, each concerned with rather specialized tasks. As organizations grow, they differentiate. In addition, each subunit grows in size. This produces some inevitable strains, conflicts, and adjustments in the relations between staff units (engaged in specialized tasks) and the line (engaged in the direct processes of management and production). We have analyzed the social backgrounds of staff and line people: They differ in education, age, and experience. In addition, however, they are in different social *positions*, see problems from a very different perspective, and measure success by different criteria. In the large organization, they are dependent upon one another, and both manage successfully to cooperate. But the tensions and conflicts that we have noted will nevertheless erupt from time to time.

READINGS

Chester I. Barnard, *The Functions of the Executive,* Cambridge, Mass.: Harvard, 1938.

A. Doak Barnett and Ezra F. Vogel, *Cadres, Bureaucracy and Political Power in Communist China,* New York: Columbia, 1966.

Morroe Berger, *Bureaucracy in Modern Egypt,* Princeton, N.J.: Princeton, 1957.

George E. Berkley, *The Administration Revolution: Notes on the Passing of Organization Man,* Englewood Cliffs, N.J.: Prentice-Hall, 1971.

Peter Blau and Richard A. Schoenherr, *The Structure of Organizations,* New York: Basic Books, 1971.

Paul C. Buchanan, "Laboratory Training and Organization Development," in James L. Gibson et al., eds., *Readings in Organizations,* Dallas: Business Publications, 1973, pp. 351–375.

Michel Crozier, *The Bureaucratic Phenomenon,* Chicago: University of Chicago, 1964.

Melville Dalton, "Conflicts between Staff and Line Managerial Officers," in W. Richard

Scott, ed., *Social Processes and Social Structures,* New York: Holt, 1970, pp. 356–365.

Louis E. Davis, "Job Satisfaction Research: The Post-industrial View," in Gibson et al., eds., op. cit., especially 227ff.

Andre L. Delbecq, "The Management of Decision Making within the Firm: Three Strategies for Three Types of Decision Making," in Gibson et al., eds., op. cit., especially pp. 166ff. on "creative" and "negotiated" decision making.

Amitai Etzioni, *Complex Organizations,* Glencoe, Ill.: Free Press, 1961.

Eliot Freidson, *Professional Dominance: The Social Structure of Medical Care,* New York: Atherton, 1970.

John K. Galbraith, *Economics and the Public Purpose,* Boston: Houghton Mifflin, 1973.

William J. Goode, "The Theoretical Limits of Professionalization," in Amitai Etzioni, ed., *The Semiprofessions,* New York: Free Press, 1969, pp. 266–313.

Alvin W. Gouldner, "Reciprocity and Autonomy in Functional Theory," in L. Gross, ed., *Symposium on Social Theory,* Evanston, Ill.: Row, Peterson, 1951, pp. 241–270.

Oscar Grusky and George A. Miller, eds., *The Sociology of Organizations: Basic Studies,* New York: Free Press, 1970.

Richard H. Hall, "Intraorganizational Structural Variation," in William K. Graham and Karlene H. Roberts, *Comparative Studies in Organizational Behavior,* New York: Holt, 1972, pp. 141–150.

Jack J. Holder, "Decision Making by Consensus," in Gibson et al., eds, op. cit.

Seymour M. Lipset, Martin A. Trow, and James S. Coleman, *Union Democracy,* Glencoe, Ill.: Free Press, 1956.

James March, ed., *Handbook of Organizations,* Chicago: Rand McNally, 1965.

Robert M. Marsh, *The Mandarins: The Circulation of Elites in China 1600–1900,* New York: Free Press, 1961.

John G. Maurer, ed., *Readings in Organization Theory: Open-Systems Approaches,* New York: Random House, 1971.

Wilbert E. Moore, *The Professions: Roles and Rules,* New York: Russell Sage, 1970.

Arthur E. Morgan, *Dams and Other Disasters: A Century of the Army Corps of Engineers in Civil Works,* Boston: Porter Sargent, 1971.

Robert Presthus, *The Organizational Society,* New York: Vintage, 1962.

Philip Selznick, *The Organizational Weapon,* New York: McGraw-Hill, 1952.

———, *TVA and the Grassroots,* New York: Harper & Row, 1966.

David Sills, *The Volunteers,* New York: Free Press, 1957.

G. William Skinner and Edwin A. Winckler, "Compliance Succession in Rural Communist China: A Cyclical Theory," in Amitai Etzioni, ed., *A Sociological Reader on Complex Organizations,* 2d ed., New York: Holt, 1969, pp. 410–438.

Martin K. Whyte, "Bureaucratization and Modernization in China: The Maoist Critique," *American Sociological Review;* 38 (April 1973), pp. 149–163.

Karl Wittfogel, *Oriental Despotism,* New Haven, Conn.: Yale, 1957.

CHAPTER EIGHT

GEOGRAPHY AND SOCIAL LIFE

Essayists of our time are fond of proclaiming our proud dominion over space and therefore time: Once a trip to Japan took months, and now it takes hours; we can telephone almost any city on the planet; we can travel over the North Pole in a commercial flight from the Pacific Coast to Europe. Similarly, we are told, technology has conquered the problem of poor resources: Without enough local water, Los Angeles drinks from mountain streams hundreds of miles distant; we grow tomatoes in water troughs under plastic, in the Arctic or in the desert; we produce nutritious food from sea plankton.

Over the past generation sociologists have largely ceased to entertain hypotheses about the influence of geographical factors on social life, in the conviction that the reverse influence is much more significant. That is, social organization determines whether a river is a political barrier or a roadway; whether the land is to be ridden over by horse or by camel, or to be cultivated; whether the moon is an object of religious worship, or a rendezvous stop on the way to Mars or Jupiter. Sociologists have therefore argued that there is nothing fixed and determinate in geographical factors; they are whatever human society makes them.

To buttress their position, sociologists can note that Indians once roamed where Pittsburgh now stands—which at least suggests that geographical factors did not determine the form of social life to be found at that site. One can argue, similarly, that over time the geography of a region does not change much (though it may vary a good deal), while societies may change radically or even die out.

However, that argument merely denies that geography can explain everything. It puts a greater burden on geographical factors than they—or any other variables—can carry. In social explanations no factor seems to explain very much, unless it is almost identical with the variable to be explained. No single factor explains very much because most social situations or behaviors are caused by a multitude of forces. In addition, when we locate some factor that seems to "explain" another one, both of them are likely to overlap a good deal (for example, urbanization and population density, industrialization and the use of telephones). Therefore, we should instead ask, with reference to any form of social behavior, whether any geographical factor affects its form or frequency.

It does not detract from the explanatory power of sociology to concede that geographical factors also may affect social life somewhat. At a minimum, we should be alert to their possible influence in both social planning and research. Ignoring them may be costly. If geographical variables are not so prepotent in determining human fate as some social analysts once asserted, sometimes their cumulative effects can nevertheless improve or undermine the effectiveness of a social system. Arguments about the relationship of society to its physical environment have typically claimed too much for either side. Let us look at them before attempting to state more precise descriptions of the interaction between the two.

SOCIETY AND ITS PHYSICAL ENVIRONMENT

The Athenian Greeks often discussed the inviting question of why they were so superior to other peoples, and some thought that their geographic position helped to explain that high rank. In the fifth century B.C. the philosopher Parmenides postulated the existence of five major temperature zones. One was an extremely hot, or torrid, zone, which people of that time would have heard about: the tropics. Two were extremely cold zones, our present polar regions. The other two were the intermediate, or temperate, zones, north and south.

Then as now, people saw that people of the colder zones were different from those of intermediate regions. Both Hippocrates and Aristotle contrasted the wild Europeans, living in a variable climate, with the clever but docile Asians, who lived in a more constant climate. The Asians lacked spirit and therefore (so Aristotle thought) always lived in subjection—because of the steady climate. Aristotle was also perceptive enough to declare (to a Greek audience) that because the Greeks lived in an appropriate intermediate zone, they remained both free and intelligent.

The historian Thucydides also offered a geographical explanation of the Athenians. The rise of Attica, the region encompassing Athens, was not due to its being a geographical Eden, but the reverse. He argued that it was an undesirable place, with poor and rocky soil, so that no one else wanted it. It was free from invasion because it was worth little, and so became a place of refuge. While the richer areas of Greece were rocked by strife and raids, the Athenian region was permitted to develop.

Thoughtful people have often rediscovered the aphorism "There is always a South," and it is often supposed that climate causes the difference. Parallel to Greek thinking, travelers see that Northerners are slow, deliberate, strong; they talk little; they are less gracious and sociable; they work hard; they are less bending and flexible in their moral codes; and so on. Southerners contrast with them in all these ways. We now would call these images stereotypes and would express our skepticism, but in fact they do correspond to some of our experience. The sociologist, familiar with religious and ethnic stereotypes, is skeptical of such judgments, though it would be a rare analyst who would never indulge in them in the course of an informal conversation. The social researcher would also be tempted to ask why people hold such beliefs about one another. A social geographer might also expand such an inquiry by pointing out that what is north in one nation is south of still another nation or group—and people there, too, express such stereotypes.

Although such sociogeographic stereotypes are now viewed as unscientific, distinguished social scientists of the recent past made similar claims. For example, it has often been asserted that great civilizations did not arise in northern regions because life was too harsh to generate the surpluses necessary for art and science; or in the tropics because life was too easy; but only in temperate zones, where a moderate climate and stimulation were encountered. Both India and the Central American Maya are a slight embarrassment to such hypotheses, while the Inca and the Aztecs are not because at such altitudes the climate is temperate. Few, if any, modern social geographers would make such sweeping claims for the dominant influence of geographical factors.

In a classic study one of the founders of modern sociology helped to undercut geographical determinism by attacking the widespread notion that climate was a cause of suicide. Emile Durkheim brought data together that showed there is a correlation between the geographical variable of the season and the rate of suicide. However, he pursued his analysis to a deeper level; and he demonstrated that an even closer correlation existed between the length of day and suicide, and that the underlying variable was not daylight itself or the season, but the amount of *social* activity. At periods of maximum social activity the social links and supports will differ most among people in different situations. That is, those who have many such relationships are actively engaged in social activity; and those who do

not will be most lonesome. Whatever social differences there are among people will be at their greatest when the social activities are most intense. Thus, the social factors that increase suicide rates will be at their strongest. Therefore, there will be more suicides among those in situations that generate suicide.[1]

Sociologists have long followed the dictum of W. I. Thomas that if things are defined as real, they are real in their consequences. Applied to social phenomena, sociologists have fruitfully utilized this general orientation by considering social definitions as more central variables than factors that might seem to be more "objective." Thus, people who are poor but define themselves as middle-class are likely just the same to try to behave as much as possible the way members of the middle class do.

We can apply the same notion to both time and space. It is obvious that people with money view great distances as smaller than do poor people. Those with more education and money view long-distance telephone calls as lesser events and are much more likely to cross geographic barriers to find jobs, friends, spouses, or recreation. Though time and space are not absolutes and are in fact perceived and created by social interaction, they cannot be created out of whole cloth. Thomas was, after all, wise enough to understand that if things are real, they are likely to be real in their consequences, however we may try to misperceive them or socially define them out of existence.

At the most trivial level, the realities of geography make human society possible because they make life itself possible. The more we learn of other planets, the more striking are the peculiarities of our own. Its temperature range permits the kinds of chemical exchanges that are necessary for

[1]Emile Durkheim, *Suicide* (1897), trans. by John A. Spaulding and George Simpson, Glencoe, Ill.: Free Press, 1951.

the life of all organisms, including our own. Its resources of air and water create the basis for the food chain by which plants furnish nutrient for animals, which are eaten by other animals, the death of all leading to the life of others who will die in turn. Its daily revolution on its own axis has, over millions of years of evolution, created the night and day patterns of sleep and wakefulness, quiescence and social activity, that we have built into our social structures. Its angle and distance from the sun determine our seasons. Its mineral and organic resources are used by human beings to build great civilizations as well as tribal life.

However, though without such geographical foundations no human society could exist at all, they do not determine what kinds of social systems (hunting societies, a monarchy, a caste system) will arise or endure. Nevertheless, they may have a continuing, small-scale effect on how these systems operate and the kinds of social decisions people make—even when we are not aware of them. Therefore, we should not totally discount geographical factors. Changes in geographical conditions (extreme cold, tidal waves) have at times destroyed just those bases of human activity we have been considering.

The voyage of Columbus neatly shows the interaction between a society and its physical environment. Part of European culture at that time included a long tradition of seafaring; without it, the exploration would not have been attempted. Missing from that tradition was the knowledge that in fact the Vikings had already crossed the Atlantic Ocean. Had the Spanish or Portuguese been aware of those trips, they would have made the attempt sooner. At least some opinions within the European heritage asserted that the world was round (as the Greeks had known) and that one would not simply fall off the edge if one kept sailing. That tradition also set a high evaluation on trade and on the national glory that might come from

a successful voyage. All of this, it can be argued, shows clearly the overwhelming importance of social and cultural factors. They are surely of greater importance than the simple geographic position of Portugal and Spain, at the tip of Europe and closest to the African waters that were the most efficient first step in a westward route across the sea.

Nevertheless, a blunt geographic reality did prevent Columbus from reaching the wealth of the Far East: North and South America barred his way, and he discovered the New World instead.

Examples of Geographical Factors

If we consider the range of factors that may be thought of as geographical, as part of the environment not made by human beings, we can see how unlikely it is that all social life could proceed without being affected to some extent, indirectly or directly, by some of the following:

1 The motions of Earth itself in relation to the sun, and thus the daily cycle of sunlight and darkness as well as the seasons of the year
2 The physical features of the seas and mountains as well as the minerals and chemicals within them
3 The movements of wind and tides, the variations in rainfall and heat, and all the great changes in weather over time
4 The natural vegetation and the animal resources of the earth—without forgetting the microorganisms that flourish in some regions more than in others, such as those which cause sleeping sickness, malaria, or yellow fever

If we consider some of these differences, we can perceive the important truth that geographical factors are not a constant within the same region, even when they do not change much in themselves. The ocean has been a highway for some peoples and a frightening chaos to others, but that is not because the ocean is a constant and is passive, simply being transformed by social variables. Rather, the behavioral outcome is changed by *both* the sea and the society, just as the sea itself is very different to different societies and cultures.

Modern citizens ski down the mountains in the winter; or they vacation in an area, the Caribbean, that was once thought to be a graveyard for white people (as it was indeed for all races) because of its many tropical diseases. Rain is a nuisance in a city, although it may temporarily cleanse the air of carcinogenic gases. Summer heat can become intolerable, but most United States citizens escape much of it each day with the help of air conditioning at their workplace or home. In short, for the affluent nations and especially the well-to-do classes, "climate" does not appear to have many serious consequences for daily life. For the Indian farmer, however, a great delay in the arrival of monsoon rains can mean starvation. A drought at the southern edge of the Sahara has resulted in the death of many tens of thousands of people. Extremes of heat and cold, rainfall or drought, do not absolutely prevent social life from proceeding, but they can exact a great cost. As one geographer remarked ironically, it is possible to grow potatoes at the North Pole, if only one can put a professor of agronomy beside each plant to take care of it.

With modern technology tunnels can be driven through mountains and airplanes can fly over them, but again at a substantial cost, while the present patterns of settlement, communication, and transportation still reflect the historical barriers or opportunities created by steep or easy slopes, the presence of snow at high altitudes, river valleys that cut through mountains, or passes at lower altitudes. For example, if we put the dates of early settlements on a map of Pennsylvania, we see that the waves of migration pulse outward from eastern centers, and at any given time period (say, 1797,

1801, 1807) the wave is much farther advanced along the river plains. These were geographically more accessible and more fertile. The curving mountains and valleys still affect social patterns: For example, marriages are more likely to occur within the same valley than across the mountain chain that defines the valley, even though the trip across the mountain may be physically much shorter.

Sea and wind currents may also affect social life in various ways. The Gulf Stream is a vast, warming "ocean river" that flows through the Atlantic Ocean a few miles off the East Coast of the United States and then curves northeast toward Iceland and Norway. It creates a delightful climate in Bermuda and keeps the northern settlements of Iceland and Norway far warmer than they would otherwise be. Before its effect was understood, it reduced the efficiency of sailing ships on the voyage from Europe to New England.

Other factors to be considered are the diseases that are endemic to one geographic area or another, the animals and plants that flourish here rather than there, or the minerals, oil, and timber resources more easily available in one region than in another. When, in short, we draw up a list of even the large categories of geographic forces that might affect our decisions and actions in some way, directly or indirectly, it seems apparent that our understanding of social order would be illuminated somewhat if we became alert to the geographic setting in which social interaction unfolds.

Boundaries and Social Systems

Most *informal* social systems (families, friendship networks, bowling teams, political parties, and so on) are not marked by a geographical boundary, but they are delimited from other systems by social boundaries. Most *formal* social systems (corporations, governmental agencies, universities, social

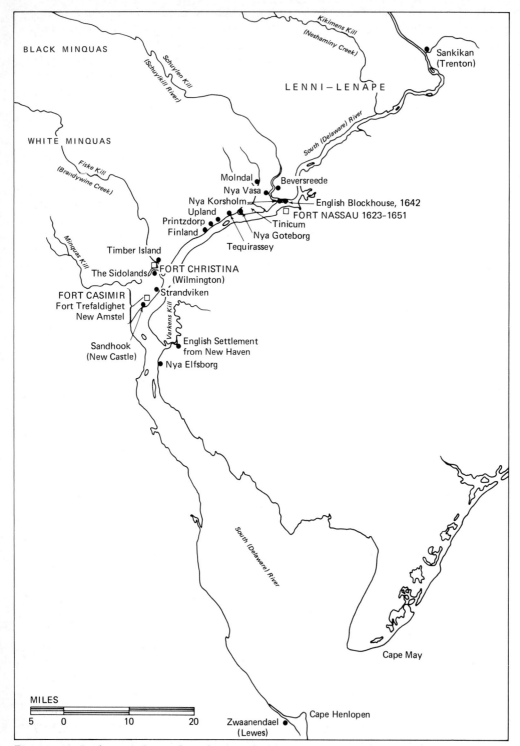

Figure 8-1 Settlements began first along navigable rivers. Between 1631 and 1664, the Dutch, Swedes, and Finns settled along the Delaware River. (After Adams, 1943.)

clubs) are marked by geographical boundaries as well. The boundaries may be determined by law (who is a state citizen, who is a "member" of a university or a private club) or by informal agreement ("He is not one of our friends"; "Jones is not a real member of the Republican party"). If pressed for a definition of a social system boundary, the sociologist will sometimes point to observable behavior: If we wish to ascertain whether and where a boundary between two systems really exists, we find out whether, with reference to a given kind of social activity, one set of people interacts more frequently with one another than with people in the other system.

We apply this operational definition in daily observation, without concerning ourselves much with its complexities. We decide that a group of boys *is* a group, with a social boundary, because we see them interact more with one another than with other boys who seem very much like them in many respects. We separate spectators from players by the same criterion: Players interact more with one another than with spectators, and in fact the social (and even legal) rules often specify that spectators must not interact with the players except by applause, encouraging shouts, or jeers.

The idea of a social boundary is widely recognized, but ordinary language does not give it a label. By contrast, we are familiar from childhood with the term "geographical boundary," though it is a misnomer: In fact, it refers to a *political* boundary, mainly determined by social factors but marked along a geographical line of some kind. Historically, when small or large societies organize themselves into political states, they set rather exact geographical boundaries that proclaim everyone inside them to be subject to the authority of that state. And the social consequences of those boundaries are many.

Whether by war or by amicable exchanges, geographical boundaries are mainly determined by social, not geographical, factors. Granted, a river or a mountain chain always affects the amount of social interaction between the populations on either side of it, but that geographical fact does not require the middle of the river to separate them into different political units. The Mississippi River, for example, divides the United States physically, but it is fully incorporated within the nation and unites it in many ways; by contrast, the Rio Grande is so little a physical barrier that people can walk across it most of the time, but a large governmental apparatus is employed to keep it as a political boundary between Mexico and the United States.

To concede that social factors are more important than geographical factors should not obscure the considerable weight of geographical elements. Let us consider some examples of this influence. One large category is made up of situations in which it is precisely the *geographic resources* that determine where the political leaders will draw the boundary. For example, victories and defeats in war have several times determined whether the line between France and Germany puts Alsace-Lorraine inside the former or the latter country—because this tiny region contains a vast metallurgical complex based on its iron and coal reserves. Similarly, the political boundary between Colombia and Panama was drawn there precisely to take away from Colombia the strip of land that contained a potential Panama Canal, a geographic resource that could not be duplicated elsewhere.

Another category of geographical influences on boundaries is *natural defenses*. Military experience over many centuries has shown that it is easier to defend against attacking forces that are crossing a river, climbing a hill or mountain, penetrating a swamp, or going through a narrow pass. Consequently, postwar decisions about where to put new boundaries have often utilized one or more geographical lines where defense (by one or both sides) would be easier, on the grounds that if attack is more difficult, peace is more likely. Al-

Figure 8-2 The Rio Grande (top), though a small physical boundary, is a political barrier, while traffic moves freely along and across the Mississippi River. (Top: Alex Webb, Magnum; bottom: Wide World Photos.)

though such factors might appear to play little role in modern warfare, with its airplanes and nuclear bombs, ground fighting has continued to determine success in war for the past thirty years.

Similarly, the widespread folk knowledge that people separated geographically reduce their rate of interaction and begin to go their own way persuades most boundary commissions to place all the people in a nation, a county, or other unit within a unitary or *contiguous territory*. The most extreme violation of this understanding in recent history was the attempt to create the new nation of Pakistan from its two major parts, East and West Pakistan, which were separated from one another by the subcontinent of India—and then, of course, separated politically by a civil war.

Thus, even when we are certain that it is the social definitions or political forces that determine both informal and formal boundaries, whether drawn with geographical precision or by rates of social interaction, we should also take note of the possibility that geographical factors have shaped social patterns in the past and continue to do so in the present. Let us now consider some social behavior that is affected by geographical variables and that is open to daily observation.

Microgeography

Even if we remain convinced sociological imperialists, certain that only social factors determine whether great geographical factors like climate, the seas, or natural resources will affect social behavior, we must at least concede the impact of space and time within the smaller compass of day-to-day interaction: whom we meet, who are our friends, how closely we stand to others, the spatial organization of discussion, and so on—in short, the microgeography of social interaction.

We all exhibit the effect of space and time, or the costs of either, in our daily lives. Indeed, over the past generation many observers have uncovered numerous "rules" that most of us follow in our spatial relations with others, even when we are not aware that the rules exist. That some are genuine rules—for example, not facing to the rear of the elevator; eating with one's family at mealtimes rather than carrying one's food to the bedroom; standing at an appropriate distance from a friend while talking, rather than, say, ten feet away—can be tested by violating them. In that case, others are uncomfortable, hurt, angry, or puzzled, unless we can offer an acceptable excuse or explanation.

Some sociologists view these regularities, too, as caused only by sociological factors, because it is social groups that define them. However, people cannot simply define space as they choose, and they do not. Even if they wish to, people cannot socially define a distance of six inches between conversationalists as being farther away than two feet.

A more fruitful view of these relations is that social behavior results from an interaction between both social and physical variables, and that human beings define spatial variables in certain ways because some kinds of behavior are more likely to occur at one distance rather than another. For example, physical closeness is socially defined as meaning "somewhat more emotional interaction," but that definition is not simply arbitrary. In fact, physical closeness does maximize the chances of a more emotional interaction, whether of anger or of affection. If we want another person to respond affectionately, we are likely to try to move closer to the other person, because we are aware of that consequence—and the other person may draw away for the same reason. But in a situation of anger, people will define a movement toward greater physical closeness as threatening. Turning or moving away is not only a social signal to the other that we are less motivated to fight—or to engage in a warm embrace; that move also makes either outcome more difficult.

Social definitions of space stipulate that living in an upper-class neighborhood yields some prestige, but it is also a sociogeographic fact that living there will maximize the chances of informal interaction or friendship with the people in that neighborhood. Similarly, parents "protect" their children from "inappropriate" friendships by controlling their movements in space and time, not merely because social definitions fix the meanings of space and time, but also because of the reverse relationships. Those social definitions exist at least in part because people have observed that the relations of space and time do affect our social behavior. Thus, social definitions may ultimately determine the meaning of space—and therefore of time as well—but those definitions begin with physical realities that are not infinitely malleable.

Physical location may also affect the interaction of an individual with several others simultaneously. Consider the response of students if a teacher enters the classroom at the usual time, but sits in the middle of the classroom, side by side with the students. If a person is placed so that he or she sits facing others during a discussion that is created for experimental purposes, that person is more likely to receive leadership nominations than will those who sit side by side.[2]

Needless to say, this relationship may be created by persons who want to become leaders (by placing themselves in that position), or it can arise after an informal leader has become apparent. That is, if someone *not* seated so as to face the others emerges as a natural leader, it is likely that that person will change his or her position, either at the first meeting or at subsequent meetings—but note that this, too, still suggests a relationship between geographic position and social position.

A city map will disclose how human life has adjusted to the curves of a river, hills, and valleys or to the presence of much rock underground as the foundation for buildings. We can make a similar mapping of our own history as it was shaped by microgeographic factors. As children in elementary school, we were more likely to become friends with others who sat close to us, and as adults we are more likely to make friends with people whose spatial movements bring them more frequently into contact with us. Friendships are less likely to continue if one person moves farther away. As Robert K. Merton has commented, how spatially close

people are, or how easy it is to encounter each other in the same area, affects "the formation of social relations, the types of social control, and the degree of involvement of members with the group. It is presumably related also to the observability of role-performance."[3]

These regularities have been reported in several studies of housing projects, where everyone lives within a short distance from one another but differences in physical convenience—"functional distance"—still affect social relations. For example, two families may share the same wall along the length of their apartment, but their entranceways open on different streets, so that they do not frequently encounter each other while going and coming.

Let us consider a few of these findings from one study. In a suburb called Park Forest, people were more likely to become friends with another couple if their driveways were close together, rather than separated by an expanse of lawn; people were less likely to become friends with people across the street or across the back fence than with others who lived next door; people who lived in the middle of the block were more likely to be popular or socially central than were those who lived at either end of the block; and where the housing units were formed around a parking area, and the back entrances faced onto that area, people were more likely to interact with one another than if they lived across a wide street from one another.[4]

Such findings illustrate the impact of space on social relations as well as how social interpretations alter the meaning of space. At any given time, then, we can ob-

[2]L. T. Howells and S. W. Becker, "Seating Arrangement and Leadership Emergence," *Journal of Abnormal and Social Psychology*, 64 (1962), pp. 148–150.

[3]"Reference Groups and Social Structure," in *Social Theory and Social Structure* (1949), enlarged ed., New York: Free Press, 1968, p. 376. See also Leon Festinger, Stanley Schachter, and Kurt Back, *Social Pressures in Informal Groups*, New York: Harper, 1950, especially chap. 3.

[4]William H. Whyte, *The Organization Man*, New York: Simon and Schuster, 1956, pp. 330 ff.

serve various geographic distributions of social patterns, mostly the result of social factors, but also partly caused or maintained by geographic forces. Once they exist, however, these geographic relations continue to affect the later social interaction of human beings. They affect not only economic transactions or markets; they also help to determine friendships and marriages.

That general finding, now corroborated for more than a generation, is partly a function of class: People of the same class are more likely to marry, and people who live close to one another are more likely to be of the same class. It is also a function of propinquity, for propinquity promotes interaction and interaction facilitates both friendship and marriage. Indeed, we can state this relationship in a somewhat more sophisticated way: The likelihood of a man or woman marrying each other, if we control for class, is a *positive* function of their residential propinquity and a *negative* function of intervening opportunities for interaction with someone else instead. We shall later consider again this pattern of interaction at a distance.

In the United States, mapping by race will reveal a strong geographic clustering or segregation; most blacks live in neighborhoods where few or no whites live. Mapping will show a lesser concentration for nationality, religious affiliation, or class. These social differences among neighborhoods are usually known to the longtime residents in any city of the world. Tourists or strangers sometimes wander into the "wrong neighborhood" out of ignorance. Because of concern or suspicion, police officers will often question anyone who seems to be in an inappropriate area. Thus, the geographic distributions express many social realities.

Some of those distributions seem to be affected only slightly by any obvious geographical factors. For example, as housing deteriorates in a given area, people of a lower class level move in, but the geograph-

ical factors that once caused the area to be desirable may not have changed at all. In New York City, 110th Street crosses Manhattan Island at the north end of Central Park, and this socially black area is as attractive geographically as it was at the turn of the century when it was defined as a very exclusive residential location.

Geographical factors do, however, influence to some extent the maintenance of ethnic enclaves in a large city. Greeks, Armenians, Italians, Ukranians, or other groups who wish to be close to their own church, speak their own language of origin, obtain specialty foods, or seek fellowship in clubs and lodges can do so more easily if all those facilities are close together. Such neighborhoods offset other disadvantages by the convenience they offer. If a large enough number of people with similar goals live in the area, organizations to serve their needs can flourish. If they do flourish, people will cluster there to avoid the time and energy costs of traveling from more distant residences.

On the other hand, it should not be supposed that the mere costs of distance determine housing choices. Within any cultural system some types of geographic locations are viewed as simply more desirable. More commonly, the well-to-do buy and develop the areas that seem geographically attractive from the beginning: water views; areas that are not subject to flooding or close to swamps; residences that are insulated from noise, dirt, and smells; locations accessible to beaches, scenic hillsides, and ski slopes; and so on. They not only spend their own money to take over and maintain such neighborhoods or regions; they also use public influence and money to create zoning laws, restrictions as to who may buy and what may be built, or more efficient transportation systems, all toward the same end: the maintenance of a geographically desirable residential area.

These variegated ways in which microgeographic factors affect or interact with social variables do not exhaust the research findings of sociologists and geographers. They do, however, alert us to the possibility that time-space-distance costs, or location in a spatial structure, may shape our social behavior somewhat. Even this sample of findings underlines, however, the extent to which sociological analysis might fruitfully utilize a somewhat systematic view of geographic forces.

Modern theoretical geography as a discipline has developed a considerable body of knowledge that sociologists could exploit, especially with reference to problems of social planning. These data and theoretical formulations range from the microgeographic relationships we have been discussing in this section to propositions about the entire world as a sociogeographic system. In the following section let us turn to a historical case that falls between those two extremes.

ENCOUNTERS BETWEEN CULTURAL SYSTEMS AND GEOGRAPHY: THE SETTLEMENT OF THE WEST

To speak of human beings "conquering" the environment implies that the environment has some independent effect, for otherwise there is nothing to conquer. When any group of people enter a new geographic region, they will have to adjust more or less, depending on how different the new geographical conditions are from the old. Settlers in a new country bring with them all the old cultural patterns their ancestors worked out in a very different environment, utilizing very different resources. Some of these beliefs and assumptions are simply irrelevant under the new conditions, while others are actually destructive. Some tools and techniques remain useful, while others must be discarded.

The key principle to be observed in such encounters between human beings and a new country is not that geography imposes

a specific set of solutions, a particular social and cultural pattern. It is rather that people who wish to maintain intact much of their old systems must work out new solutions for the problems created by the new geographic forces they confront. A large-scale example of this type of encounter is the slow settlement of the Great Plains of the United States. Extending roughly from the ninety-eighth meridian to the Pacific slope, a line that nearly bisects the country and thus covers much of what we have come to call the West, it is the land of the mythic cowboy and cattle ranches, Indians and the buffalo, the six-shooter and the personal avenging of injustice. Although much of that cultural complex has disappeared, Westerners still feel that they are very different from people "back East." Since the people who settled that land and created the Western patterns were Easterners by origin and culture, the case may be instructive.

The social quality of the West was the outcome of an encounter between the Eastern migrants and settlers and the peculiar geographical reality of the Plains. That reality can be seen in the total failure of the Spanish to keep it under control, to colonize it, or even to exploit it, from the sixteenth century until it was lost or sold to the United States; or in the failure of United States emigrants to settle it until after they had crossed it repeatedly to establish communities on the more hospitable Pacific Coast. It can be seen in the inability of the Southerners to extend their cultural patterns to the Plains states, even though most of that region was legally open to slavery by the 1850s. Neither the Eastern nor the Southern farming patterns could survive intact, and for many decades their social and legal patterns too were modified in the new setting.

Referring to this encounter with the Plains region, the historian Walter Prescott Webb wrote:

The ways of travel, the weapons, the method of tilling the soil, the plows and other agricultural implements, and even the laws themselves were modified. . . . East of the Mississippi civilization stood on three legs—land, water, and timber; west of the Mississippi . . . civilization was left on one leg—land.[5]

The most fundamental of these geographical factors is aridity. Most of the Great Plains is subhumid; its annual rainfall is twenty inches or less, and its rate of evaporation is high because of winds and high temperatures. Years of adequate rainfall may be followed by successive years of drought, so that an initial farming success was often ended by complete failure. Rivers are not navigable for any great length. When in flood from rare cloudbursts they are dangerous, and in normal times it is possible to wade across many of them. After a rain, the runoff is rapid, so that little water is stored in the ground or in lakes. In the eastern part of this region, rainfall is adequate, and the land is level but treeless; in the western part the land is not level, but it is treeless and subhumid; on the High Plains, the land is treeless, subhumid or semiarid, and level.

None of these geographical elements created any problems for the various Plains Indians. Taking over the Spanish horses that had spread throughout the Plains, they became magnificent riders. They did not engage in agriculture, but lived mainly from hunting the wandering buffalo. Having no fixed dwelling, they needed no timber for houses, forts, or fences. Within its territory each tribe wandered as did the buffalo, with no desire to acquire possessions. Social prestige was far more important than wealth, and it was earned by excellence and bravery in war, hunting, and stealing the horses of other tribes. Since the Plains peoples had no need to accumulate a large surplus of anything except horses, the problem of transporting heavy loads long distances without navigable streams did not concern them.

[5] *The Great Plains*, New York: Grosset & Dunlap, 1931, p. 8.

Not wishing to follow the Indian cultural pattern, the United States migrants at first saw no easy solution to these geographical problems. Instead, they simply rode or drove across the plains to the Pacific. Many even chose to make that trip by sea (a fifteen-thousand-mile voyage at that time!). Over the latter half of the nineteenth century, however, settlers gradually began to solve the difficulties they faced on the Great Plains.

Many of these adaptations were primarily technological and economic, though they led to various social effects as well. The invention of barbed wire made it possible to fence vast tracts of land cheaply. (Large land units were necessary, because the productivity per acre is low in subhumid regions—for example, in many areas, one acre could support no more than four cattle.) The ease of fencing with barbed wire led in turn to innumerable violent conflicts and lawsuits, as people tried to bar others from water or to take over land whose title was obscure.

Adjustments to the lack of water were many. Most important was the development of cattle and sheep ranching, hardly to be encountered in the eastern United States. This development essentially accepted the fact that much of the land was best suited for grazing. Thousands of settlers attempted traditional farming but eventually failed, and this land also reverted to grazing. The windmill was perfected to yield water for at least the ranch stock and a small garden where rainfall was inadequate. Irrigation was begun where streams permitted that more complex adjustment. A new development of an old practice, dry farming (plowing to facilitate the absorption of rain, and harrowing to make a light dust cover that would prevent evaporation) became the basis of wheat farming in many subregions.

The Plains could not develop an internal waterway system made up of canals and rivers, and thus lacked the cheap Eastern system for transporting bulk cargo over long distances. The transcontinental railroads were begun in the 1860s to solve that problem, though initially their main goal was not to serve the Plains, but to link the Pacific Coast with the East.

It should be emphasized that none of these and other adjustments were absolutely required by the new conditions on the Great Plains; they were necessary, however, if the settlers were to earn their living from the soil in any way and to maintain as much of their tradition as possible. Most of the adjustments noted so far were technical and economic, and social life was somewhat different because of them. Let us now take note of further effects.

English common law relating to the rights of people whose land bordered on a stream was also changed in this region, where access to water was much more crucial and irrigation was profitable. In general, the ancient legal tradition held that only the border properties could utilize the water of a river, with the restriction that landholders must return the water to the stream. Although the water in any stream obviously drains from lands lying well away from the stream, people in humid lands do not see much injustice in the principle that only the property owners on the banks are to enjoy the use of the water. Since there is enough water for wells and enough rainfall for everyone, access to the stream is useful but not crucial.

By contrast, that principle was contested on the Plains and was modified or changed in most of the Western states, along with the notion that the user of stream water must return it to the stream. People far from a stream might demand some rights to the water in it, since it contained water that flowed from a large drainage basin that included their land. Water became a collective commodity, in which the state law had a keen interest. If some people were simply to consume the water through irrigation, as was not contemplated in the English law,

those downstream would receive little of it and would protest, for their land would then be worth less. Here again, a new body of legal tradition arose in the arid states.

The dramatic case of the United States West, which has colored so much of our literature, illustrates the general principle that although geographical factors do not dictate technological, economic, or social patterns, they may cause some solutions and adaptations to appear more attractive than others. Around these, in turn, still other secondary social patterns may be created. In this case they range from trivial ones such as the commercial rodeo performance and cowboy films to more important ones such as the populist and radical political movements of the Western states and the development of a new set of legal traditions centering on the problems of allocating water. Basically, this case illustrates how geographical factors may make it difficult to maintain some older traditions that settlers bring to a new region.

SOCIAL INTERACTION AT A DISTANCE

Once we become alert to the pervasive social aspect of distance, we can observe its effects in almost everything that people do, from buying a newspaper to visiting friends. No movement is without cost in time, energy, or money. Thus, interaction at a distance costs more than interaction nearby.

This fundamental *friction of distance* shapes our actions even when we do not think of it in making our decisions. Very few people—perhaps only geographers and experts who work out communication or shipping routes—spend much time at computing the most efficient ways of interacting at a distance. Nevertheless, the attractiveness of a "least effort" solution can be seen in the actual shape and frequency of any communication or trade between two more places, whether it be the spread of gossip, the flow of information, or migration.

Interaction and Distance

Let us begin with the simplest formulation, which we can then improve by introducing additional variables: $I = f1/D$, or the rate of interaction (I) between two places (or corporations, or people) is a negative or inverse function (f) of distance (D). Plotted as a curve, this general relationship exhibits a negative slope; that is, it moves downward to the right. The greater the distance, the lower the rate of interaction, whether the social activity being charted is murder or war or is instead retail trade or shipping.

However, we perceive a further regularity: The line that describes that decrease in interaction, or *lapse rate*, with distance does in fact *curve*; that is, the rate of *decrease* slows down. It falls off rapidly at first and then falls off less rapidly. In technical terms, it is a "negative exponential relationship." Figure 8-4 shows an ideal version of this curve.

This corresponds to our daily observations. For example, most people who commute to work do not travel far, so that if we plot their residences on a map, we can see that they become very sparse only a few miles from their workplaces. However, if we continue farther out on the map, we shall still find *some* courageous, energetic, or wealthy few who will pay that cost.

The curve also corresponds to our intuitive feelings about *how* costly those additional costs are. Most people would prefer not to commute at all, if they could obtain pleasant residences close to their work. If they must commute, most would prefer not to commute far. Within the typical commutational radius, a difference of even ten minutes will loom large; after all, if the trip homeward takes forty minutes, an additional ten minutes is an increase of 25 percent. On the other hand, most of us will also feel that with increasing distance, *another* 10 or

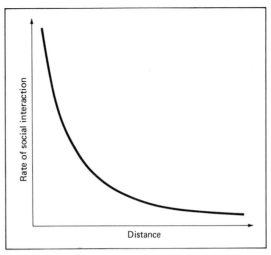

Figure 8-3 A negative exponential relationship.

15 miles more entails a much smaller additional cost. If we plan to fly to a ski resort several hundred miles away, and learn that an equal or better one is a hundred miles further, the additional cost seems small.

If we continue to explore our own memories of how distance affects the common varieties of social interaction, we see additional regularities: The lapse rate will vary a good deal, depending on the *kind of activity* we plan. That is, the decrease of interaction with distance will be very sharp for some kinds of social behavior and less so for others. Thus, if we want no more than a quart of milk, we are likely to be unwilling to travel more than a few blocks in the city. If we map the customers of a local store who bought only one quart of milk, few will have traveled, say, 2 miles to get it. By contrast, if our aim is to enjoy a splendid meal at a fine French restaurant, the *Guide Michelin* informs us that some are worth a long automobile trip with only that goal in mind. Correspondingly, if we map the geographic origins of diners at La Pyramide in Vienne, we can expect that they will have come from all parts of the world (though most will nevertheless have come from nearby cities in Europe).

The crude variable of distance conceals some of its subtle constituents that are often more powerful than mere *lineal* distance. Indeed, as we shall continue to emphasize, modern geography as a discipline typically translates physical distance into other variables that are socially or psychologically much more crucial. If it is the friction of distance that reduces the rate of social interaction, then as analysts we need to know the costs of traveling a given distance. Obviously, if we must travel by foot, the lapse rate of any kind of social interaction will be sharper. Most people in this country would, if faced with the prospect of walking a mile for a loaf of bread or a conversation with a casual acquaintance, simply do without it, or wait until better transportation is available. A trip that could be made by bus or automobile could be longer for the same "cost," and thus the drop in interaction at greater distances would be more gradual along the routes of easy transportation.

We can observe this pattern in the first years after the opening of a new highway or (in the past) a new railroad line: Settlement was thicker along the new route and toward the two ends of the route, that is, the cities of origin and destination.

The crude variable of distance contains another important subvariable, noted before, the number or *density of intervening opportunities* between one place or person and another. People will not travel to a distant pharmacy for a common item if they can get the same thing closer at hand. And most love relationships that face the barrier of great distance will end, because one or both persons are likely to find another desirable person within that intervening social space. If the social landscape contains many job opportunities, people will not travel as far to seek a good job. More bluntly, since movement costs something, people will not in general travel any farther than they have to

in order to get what they want; if there are many intervening opportunities between point X and point Y, they are less likely to make the entire trip.

Interaction and Basic Attractiveness

However, we have been focusing on distance and the subvariables concealed within it, and neglecting the *basic attractiveness* of the two places, persons, or agencies in interaction. Although distance in general attenuates that potential for interaction, basic attractiveness may nevertheless be large enough to overcome the costs of distance. Spices were shipped from the Far East to Europe in the Middle Ages, and some people have entered a happy marriage after a long, successful courtship though separated by a continent.

Sometimes, social analysts introduce this general notion of attractiveness by lumping it under the general category of *population* (numbers of people), which is a crude substitute for wealth, for example, how much they ship, how often they use the telephone, and so on. That is, the likelihood of interaction, or the potential for interaction between two groups, will be greater if each of the two populations is independently wealthy, or the members of each population generally engage in much interaction within their group (telephone messages, shipping, purchases, writing books, publishing research articles).

Since the crude variable of population, or numbers, is only an index of other subvariables such as wealth, let us explore further the underlying forces that may generate more or less social interaction at a distance. Some geographers put these factors under three large categories: *complementarity, intervening opportunities,* and *transferability* (the friction of distance).

The first of these is defined by the extent to which people's needs in one place are *complementary* to those in another, that is, each wants what the other has. It is not enough that some places lack an important commodity, while others possess it. Complementarity must be *specific*; the bananas, information, or personal attractiveness that one person possesses must be desired by someone else, whose qualities, activities, or possessions are desired *in turn* by the first person. The complementarity in immigration is clear: For example, for most of United States history, millions of people in Europe wanted the social and economic opportunities that this country offered, while political leaders here believed that an additional labor supply was needed. For other activities the complementarity may be less obvious. For example, when scientific information is "exchanged," it is rare that the complementarity is specific, for scientists do not offer to trade one bit of information for, say, a specific solution to a problem. There is, instead, a more general presentation or offer of information through journals and conferences. Even in that generalized exchange process, however, it is apparent that the greatest amount of interaction occurs between scientists whose informational needs complement each other.

As was already noted, the density or amount of *intervening opportunities* reduces the distance people are willing to travel or communicate, for if there are many such opportunities for a wanted kind of social interaction, there is no need to go far.

Although *transferability* refers to the real costs of movement or social interaction, in time, energy, or money (how easily something can be transferred elsewhere), these costs are altered by technology and they vary by income level. Throughout most of human history, water transportation has been the cheapest mode of communication and transportation over the longer haul for both goods and people. It is still the cheapest transportation for goods, but not for people. In addition, planes, trucks, and trains are now so cheap that their additional cost is small for goods that require a quick delivery. Telephones, radios, telegraph and cable lines, and television have reduced the cost of communication. In a technologically advanced country, the transferability of goods and messages is high, because the costs of sending either are low.

However, how "low" a cost is will vary by income as well as by the value of the commodity or message sent. The cost of a transcontinental telephone call to a close friend is the same for the rich as for the poor, such is the democracy of high technology, but the former call is a tiny fraction of the wealthy person's income. For this reason, the lapse rate of telephone calls made by the more affluent classes will fall off much less sharply with distance than for calls made by the less affluent. Similarly, people with more money are more likely to enjoy friendship networks that extend over wide distances, to marry people from more distant regions, and generally to engage in more social interaction at a distance.

On the other hand, it should be kept in mind that even with the best of technology, kisses have a low transferability. Telephones are a poor substitute for an embrace. Similarly, personnel managers and interviewers want to "see" the person they are considering for a job, and a face on a television screen does not seem adequate. In short, though technology increases transferability of both people and communications, for human beings that transferability cannot be reduced indefinitely, and for some aspects of communication and interaction only the person will do.

Interaction Potential

The impact of all these variables may be seen both statically and dynamically. At any given time if we chart who is interacting with whom, with reference to the flow of friendship, spouses, goods, or information, we can see that places or groups that are

FOCUS

POOR TRANSPORTATION IN THE MIDDLE AGES: THE COSTS
OF GOING THERE ONESELF VERSUS OTHER SOLUTIONS

Compared with what the world offers us today, the speed of travel in that
age seems extremely slow. It was not, however, appreciably slower than
it was at the end of the Middle Ages, or even the beginning of the
eighteenth century. By contrast with today, travel was much faster by sea
than by land. From 60 to 90 miles a day was not an exceptional record for
a ship: provided (it goes without saying) that the winds were not too
unfavourable. On land, the normal distance covered in one day amounted, it seems, to between nineteen and twenty-five miles—for travellers
who were in no hurry, that is: say a caravan of merchants, a great
nobleman moving round from castle to castle or from abbey to abbey, or
an army with its baggage. A courier or a handful of resolute men could by
making a special effort travel at least twice as fast. A letter written by
Gregory VII at Rome on the 8th December 1075 arrived at Goslar, at the
foot of the Harz, on the 1st of January following; its bearer had covered
about 29 miles a day as the crow flies—in reality, of course, much more.
To travel without too much fatigue and not too slowly it was necessary to
be mounted or in a carriage. Horses and mules not only go faster than
men; they adapt themselves better to boggy ground. This explains the
seasonal interruption of many communications; it was due less to bad
weather than to lack of forage. The Carolingian *missi* had earlier made a
point of not beginning their tours till the grass had grown.[1] However,
as at present in Africa, an experienced foot-traveller could cover astound-
ingly long distances in a few days and he could doubtless overcome
certain obstacles more quickly than a horseman. When Charles the Bald
organized his second Italian expedition he arranged to keep in touch with
Gaul across the Alps partly by means of runners.[2]

Though poor and unsafe, the roads or tracks were in constant use.
Where transport is difficult, man goes to something he wants more easily
than he makes it come to him. In particular, no institution or method
could take the place of personal contact between human beings. It would
have been impossible to govern the state from inside a palace: to control
a country, there was no other means than to ride through it incessantly
in all directions. The kings of the first feudal age positively killed
themselves by travel. For example, in the course of a year which was in
no way exceptional, the emperor Conrad II in 1033 is known to have
journeyed in turn from Burgundy to the Polish frontier and thence to

[1]Loup de Ferrieres, *Corréspondance,* ed. Levillain, I, no. 41.

[2]*Capitularia,* II, no. 281, c. 25.

SOURCE: Marc Bloch, *Feudal Society,* trans. by L.A. Manyon, Chicago: University of Chicago
Press, 1964, vol. I, pp. 62–63.

Champagne, to return eventually to Lusatia. The nobleman with his entourage moved round constantly from one of his estates to another; and not only in order to supervise them more effectively. It was necessary for him to consume the produce on the spot, for to transport it to a common centre would have been both inconvenient and expensive. Similarly with the merchant. Without representatives to whom he could delegate the task of buying and selling, fairly certain in any case of never finding enough customers assembled in one place to assure him a profit, every merchant was a pedlar, a 'dusty foot' (*pied poudreux*), plying his trade up hill and down dale. The cleric, eager for learning or the ascetic life, was obliged to wander over Europe in search of the master of his choice: Gerbert of Aurillac studied mathematics in Spain and philosophy at Rheims; the Englishman Stephen Harding, the ideal monasticism in the Burgundian abbey of Molesmes. Before him, St. Odo, the future abbot of Cluny, had travelled through France in the hope of finding a monastery whose members lived strictly according to the rule.

Moreover, in spite of the old hostility of the Benedictine rule to the *gyrovagi*, the bad monks who ceaselessly 'vagabonded about', everything in contemporary clerical life favoured this nomadism: the international character of the Church; the use of Latin as a common language among educated priests and monks; the affiliations between monasteries; the wide dispersal of their territorial patrimonies; and finally the 'reforms' which periodically convulsed this great ecclesiastical body and made the places first affected by the new spirit at once courts of appeal (to which people came from all parts to seek the good rule) and mission centres whence the zealots were despatched for the conquest of the Catholic world. How many foreign visitors came to Cluny in this way! How many Cluniacs journeyed forth to foreign lands! Under William the Conqueror almost all the dioceses and great abbeys of Normandy, which the first waves of the 'Gregorian' revival were beginning to reach, had at their head Italians or Lorrainers; the archbishop of Rouen, Maurille, was a man from Rheims who, before occupying his Neustrian see, had studied at Liege, taught in Saxony and lived as a hermit in Tuscany.

Humble folk, too, passed along the highways of the West: refugees, driven by war or famine; adventurers, half-soldiers, half-bandits; peasants seeking a more prosperous life and hoping to find, far from their native land, a few fields to cultivate. Finally, there were pilgrims. For religious devotion itself fostered travel and more than one good Christian, rich or poor, cleric, or layman, believed that he could purchase salvation of body and soul only at the price of a long journey.

mutually marked by high values of transferability and complementarity and low intervening opportunities will engage in far more interaction than do others with opposite values for those variables. Over time, or viewed as a process, we can also see that if by historical accident two people, organizations, or cities happen to interact intensely for a brief time, and thereafter one or more of these three variables run in the "wrong" direction, the interaction rate will begin to decline.

We should take note, however, of various *barrier effects*, notably those created by political boundaries and language. In effect, they increase the friction of distance. Telephone calls, letters, or travel will be much less frequent across such boundaries than would be predicted by the physical distance alone. In one study of telephone calls between Montreal and (1) English-speaking cities in Canada, (2) French-speaking cities in Quebec, and (3) United States cities, it was ascertained that, for a given *physical* distance, telephone calls to English-speaking cities in Canada drop off as though they were five to ten times farther away than the French-speaking cities, and calls to United States cities drop off in frequency as though they were fifty times as far away.[6]

These cases are instructive, for though distance still plays a role in them, social barriers and definitions also stretch or shrink the perception of the friction of distance. We would predict that a study of marriage patterns would exhibit similar patterns.

DISPERSAL AND AGGLOMERATION: THE CITY AND ITS HINTERLAND

Archaeologists and geographers were convinced, not so long ago, that urban life began about eight to ten thousand years ago when agriculture improved enough to produce a surplus that could feed the inhabitants of a town, who could then devote themselves to other kinds of production. That reasoning cannot be entirely wrong, since a surplus of *some* kind (agricultural or hunting) is obviously necessary if some people are to be fed by others.

However, alternative views are possible. For example, the members of a goodly number of hunting and gathering societies, as well as agricultural societies at a low level of technology, work very little to produce an adequate living, and some members work hardly at all. They could easily produce the surplus necessary for small towns, but do not. Or a conqueror may require subjects to produce a surplus even when the agricultural yields are low, simply by forcing them to live on less.

More importantly, urban living may have gradually evolved as a social invention that itself produced a new kind of surplus, and indeed may have given an impetus to the innovative agricultural technology of the Neolithic Age. Since at the earliest stages of urban settlements most or all the inhabitants continued to be farmers, hunters, or herders, it is as plausible to suppose that the initial surpluses came from the economic and social advantages of urban life.[7]

Although it has been charged that sociology for two thousand years can be viewed as an extended commentary on urban-rural differences, and thus it has much to say about cities, it may also be profitable to look at certain aspects of cities from a geographical perspective. Some regularities can be noted, which may be useful for a sociological view as well.

Geographical Aspects of Urban Living

One of the more obvious geographical aspects of urban living is that it yields some

---

[6]J. Ross Mackay, "The Interaction Hypothesis and Boundaries in Canada: A Preliminary Study," in Brian J. L. Berry and Duane F. Marble, eds., *Spatial Analysis*, Englewood Cliffs, N.J.: Prentice-Hall, 1968, pp. 122–129.

[7]For example, most of the important technical or chemical innovations that improved farming output were *urban* in origin.

advantages of scale: With greater numbers of people in the same area, the unit cost for various services and products will be lower. A well that would be beyond the economic or physical capacity of a single family can be paid for by a very small village or hamlet. Even at a primitive level of technology, as Adam Smith pointed out, if a person devotes his or her energies to a single task, production is likely to be higher than if everyone were to produce his or her own shoes, clothing, or plows—but that specialization is not possible until a sufficient number of potential customers exists. Conquerors have often found that the unit costs of keeping their subjects under control were lower if they kept them within city walls, especially at night.

Such advantages are partly based on sheer *numbers*; that is, for some enterprises and some services, some minimum number of people is needed. They are also based on the geographical variable of density, or number of people within a given area. More precisely, urban settlements yield some economies of scale because the *friction of distance is less.* Customers or clients and the producers of services are closer together. Materials and skilled hands need not travel far to meet each other. Social and political decisions can be made more expeditiously. One can argue, then, that the social invention of cities would have been accomplished sooner or later because agglomeration yields some advantages over dispersal, or cities yield advantages over the countryside; and that cities would have arisen even if human beings had initially lived in a homogeneous plain, with no obvious, particular place to build towns or cities.

Whether in the earliest period of urban settlements the town was parasitic off the farmers, living off their surplus, or the little towns themselves produced the surpluses that permitted farmers to make the innovative steps toward plowing and the continuous cultivation of grains or other crops, we know that those urban populations were more *dispersed* than they are now. Let us consider this fact for a moment.

Unlike farmers in the United States and some parts of England, agriculturists in most societies have lived in hamlets or villages and have walked to their fields each day. That geographical solution gave them some protection against marauders, bandits, or even small parties of invaders. However, it also imposed a parallel geographical problem: How large can a hamlet be if most people must walk to their fields? Clearly, whenever the population grew beyond some point where the friction of distance began to be a heavy burden, new hamlets hived off. If the soil was extremely fertile, a large number of settlements could be supported within a smaller area. If enemies abounded, people would be less eager to found a new village. Of course, if everyone had had a horse or bicycle five thousand years ago, the area surrounding a village could have been larger. Nevertheless, at any given level of technology there would be some upper limit to the size of such villages. Consequently, over thousands of years of settlement, as the space gradually filled with the tillers of soil in any region, settlement was relatively dispersed. Only with the development of more specialized towns, in which the urban production was great enough to permit many people to avoid farming altogether, could there by much larger and denser cities. Very likely, the first ones were administrative towns, the residences of kings, whose "production of surplus" was the simple confiscation of both urban and rural goods.

Though agricultural settlements were relatively dispersed—in medieval England, about a mile apart—the people who made them were adjusting to the geographic scale of the human *walk*. Every mile walked to the field requires a physiologically longer walk home, because one is tired at the end of a day's work. If a new hamlet hives off the older one, the new settlers will want to visit their friends and kin in the old one, and again the friction of distance limits how far they will go in order to establish that new place. Thus, the relatively dispersed settlements of the past would appear to our modern eyes, accustomed to travel by automobile, as very close together.

Whether people both farm and reside in the country, as in the United States, or live in a hamlet and farm in the surrounding fields, as in most of the historical past, some part of the produce must be carried to the urban center, and people must go to the center to purchase or trade. Here we can see that two sets of variables work against one another in determining how many such settlements per square mile a given region will support. In general, people would prefer to travel a shorter distance for trading purposes, and this factor would cause settlements to be very close together; that is, the larger the number of hamlets per square mile, the shorter the distance anyone has to travel to arrive at one of them from any given farm. On the other hand, the *shorter* that distance, the *smaller* the farming area that is served by a given hamlet. Beyond some point in diminishing size, the area will simply be too small to produce enough to support an urban settlement. If the land is especially rich, a smaller area will support a village of a given size, and as a consequence the number of settlements per square mile will be larger.

Competition among Land Uses

Implicit in the paragraphs above is the notion that urban settlements compete with one another for both the population and the produce of a given geographic region. Thus, beyond some distance from one village a new settlement can arise, because people who must now travel that far would prefer instead to go a shorter distance. This is the exact analogue of the market or social patterns of individuals: For example, in spite of the bankruptcy of many local stores in large cities, they are constantly being started in

response to the desire of the people to avoid traveling far to get common services or goods. Similar pressures can be observed that support the establishment of local elementary schools, banks, newspapers, lodges, libraries, or post offices.

The cost of producing goods must include the cost of distance, and this affects not only the modern economic market, but a simple village trading system as well. Specifically, it helps to determine how successful different *land uses* are in competing among each other, at different distances from the town or city. Such apparently economic variables have, in turn, many social and political consequences. They affect political pressures concerning pollution, water supply, zoning, price controls, and the land values of suburbs. Moreover, they have at times, as economic factors are likely to do, created even more dramatic consequences. One of the most famous is the Whiskey Rebellion, noted in many high school history textbooks.

In 1794 farmers in Western Pennsylvania rose in armed revolt against the federal whiskey tax, and United States troops were sent to quell them and thus to affirm the legal authority of the newly fledged Republic. These farmers were aggrieved because at that time they were far beyond the zone in which grain could be profitably grown for shipment to distant markets. However, whiskey was (as it still is) a *concentrated* form of grain, and the cost of shipment was low relative to its value per barrel. Unfortunately, the new tax was so high as to wipe out their profits, an economic change that the farmers viewed as an affront to justice and thus an adequate reason to challenge the national government. They failed in the protest, and ultimately the rise in whiskey prices and a drop in transportation costs removed their grievance, while the whiskey profit zone moved still farther west. Thus, as so frequently occurs in economic relationships, problems of justice and authority erupt, while the case illustrates at least the potential impact of seemingly unspectacular geographical variables.

The Effects of Urban Competition

Having considered briefly the competition among land uses, let us return once more to the *competition among urban settlements*. An index of this silent process may be found in the startling fact that although the United States population has more than doubled since the late nineteenth century, and the nation has become highly urbanized, few new communities have been founded, while many have disappeared.[8] This process has changed substantially the social life of this and many other settled countries. While we cannot examine it fully, let us consider this competition for a moment.

We noted earlier that the distance between communities is partly a function of purchasing power or of other variables that make social interaction more likely. Population thins out where the land becomes less productive, and thus the distance between communities increases. Correspondingly, the distance between *large* towns is also larger if population density or purchasing power is low.

Cities also compete with one another. Over time this means that if there are two towns or cities that are growing in size toward the rank of "central places," and they are close together, they will compete with one another, and one of them will eventually decline (other factors being equal). Over time within a given area there will come to be *one* central place rather than several close together. The weakest will decline to a smaller size in the *ranking* of size of cities, even if the weakest does not actually drop in absolute numbers. In dynamic terms, we sometimes say that cities "push each other

away"; that is, as cities grow, some will decline and others will rise, but big cities will be farther apart.

However, we must keep in mind the importance of *purchasing power* in reducing the friction of distance. In modern times Western nations and especially the United States have become richer. Thus, between any two central places, the higher the purchasing power, the greater the growth of small towns lying between the big towns. More places will come into being, or existing hamlets will become villages or towns, so that the distance between places of a similar size will *decline*. That is, with increased purchasing power the larger cities can be closer together.

Thus, in the spacing of cities these two factors work *against* one another; the actual distance between cities is a function of *both* variables, size and purchasing power.

One final geographical aspect of cities should be noted, the fact that although cities have continued to grow, their *internal density*, or population per square mile, has declined. The development of the streetcar at the end of the nineteenth century, the subsequent spread of the automobile, and the growth of telephone service allowed people to live farther out and lose no more time than before in getting to work, in interacting with one another across town, or in maintaining the flow of information among persons and organizations at a distance. The central business district is no longer the most accessible place, for many other locations have become about as accessible, with reference to the cost of interaction. Organizations and corporations may now choose their site with reference to geographical *amenities*—trees, water, landscape, quiet—instead of geographic *accessibility*. Thus, social, technological, and geographical factors interact to reduce the density of population in the modern city, even though the nation as a whole has continued to become more urbanized.

[8]Ronald Abler, John S. Adams, and Peter Gould, *Spatial Organization*, Englewood Cliffs, N.J.: Prentice-Hall, 1971, pp. 515–517.

THE HUMAN CREATION OF GEOGRAPHY

Compared with the awesome size and power of physical nature, human beings and their works seem puny indeed. In its energy a run-of-the-mill hurricane dwarfs by far even the megaton explosions of the largest hydrogen bomb; all the human beings in the world could be put into the Grand Canyon; the sun produces more power each day than the annual output of all the electric generators of the world; the sea can destroy any ship ever built; and so on.

On the other hand, we have become increasingly aware that the work of human beings is neither so inconsequential nor so benign as observers once believed. Our achievements may, it is true, be gradually swallowed up by jungle or desert and overwhelmed by geological forces, but we may be likened to microorganisms such as bacteria, whose cumulative effects can destroy a giant tree or a whale. The drama of Person against Nature has excited people for thousands of years, but it is only recently that we have come to see that to be against Nature is to act against ourselves, for we are Nature, too.

Our work in controlling Nature is often destructive. Timber cutting and cattle raising may bring some temporary benefits, but they also destroy the fertility of millions of acres of land. With each passing month we are making the earth's envelope of air less able to sustain animal life. Even the oceans, once thought to be limitlessly capable of absorbing industrial or personal sewage, are rapidly becoming a dead cesspool.

In a general way, those facts are well known. What is worth underlining is that once we have changed the gross features of our environment, we must live in the new, *humanly created geography*. The world's societies must then adjust to their new geographic environment. They may adjust poorly or well, but the geographical problems will not disappear if people ignore them. We are surely a very interesting animal, but other equally interesting animals have preceded us and disappeared. To put the problem bluntly, the oceans can do very well without whales, which we are killing off, but both the oceans and the earth as a whole can do without human beings, too.

One of the most important environmental changes that human beings have caused is the efflorescence of their species, *Homo sapiens*. We are part of earth's fauna and must therefore be considered part of its geography, like starlings and English sparrows in the United States, rabbits in Australia, or ferrets in the Hawaiian Islands. From the time the first small urban settlements were made, about 8000 B.C., to the middle of this century, the population increased about fifty times, that is, from about 5 million to about 1.5 billion. At present, it is *doubling* every thirty-five years, and the year 2000 may well see a world population of over 6 billion.

So great an expansion of any large animal, even one with a mild temperament, would have created a new geography for all other living things. That we are omnivorous and predatory and make machinery only magnifies the effects. We must adjust to the fact that much of the physical space is occupied by members of our species and their habitations; to the fact that there are few fertile areas not yet occupied by people; to the fact that comembers are rapidly consuming the earth's resources; and to the fact that the wastes from fellow human beings affect our own lives.

As we have noted, one of the most striking peculiarities of the human animal is our ability to shrink space and therefore time: We move faster and farther and communicate over greater distances. Increasingly we all live within each other's environments and are part of one another. Phrased differently, we are in the process of *creating one geography for all*—perhaps the ultimate democratization of our era. Since nothing really disappears, the pollutants from one region are the environment of another, and vice versa. When there were fewer human beings, they could be relatively unconcerned with their own waste and destruction, or with that of others, for both the quantities and the rate of exchange were low. Now, by contrast, the farm pesticides that are used today may appear in next week's soup, while tomorrow the farmer may have to breathe in today's urban air pollution.

Human beings have also made their own geography by draining and filling in marshlands. While this creates new dry land for building, it also destroys a major source of marine food, since the early stages in the life cycle of many fish and shellfish take place there. Similarly, pesticides increase agricultural productivity at one point; but because they are poisons, they reduce other kinds of productivity (fish, birds, shellfish) at another. And the amount of sewage sludge is so great in the city that it would inundate the local inhabitants; it is therefore carried out to sea. However, there it causes large areas of the ocean bottom to die, while slowly spreading—in some cases back toward the seashore, where it contaminates the environment of still another population.

These effects occur in capitalist as well as socialist countries, and have occurred in the past, too. East or West, humankind has never "lived in harmony with nature," except by accident, that is, when the population was small, or its technical achievements were too low to destroy the environment very fast.

Though the geographical limitations and threats of the immediate future are less rosy for our species as a whole than in any period in our short history on this planet, our technical ingenuity and economic resources are also greater. Consequently, it is at least possible that the insects will not soon take over the earth, but that in simple self-interest human beings will learn more adequate social behavior for living wisely with their geographical reality.

CONCLUSION

In any consideration of social interaction we should, as the founders of sociology have argued, focus on sociological variables, just as in the analysis of biological problems we focus on biological variables. That injunction applies to all sciences. On the other hand, our aspirations should not lead us to assume burdens that are too great for our intellectual tools. With only its own skills, sociology cannot explain all of social behavior, because some of that behavior is more parsimoniously explained by biological or physical variables, and we should not expend much of our talent where other variables are

Figure 8-4 Our humanly created geography now includes shopping centers and the access routes to them. (Photo Trends.)

more powerful. Reciprocally, very little of consequence for sociolinguistic theory can be explained by biological variables.

Thus, we have avoided the grandiose socio-geographic speculations that were common half a century ago, when almost any social or cultural phenomenon could be confused with its geographic distribution and ascribed to "the geographic factor." On the other hand, we have traced through a series of social and political relationships in which it seems reasonable to suppose geographical factors play a larger or smaller role. We have noted a wide range of geographical factors in order to alert the reader to the many junctures at which they might have some effect—often silent, unnoticed—on the frequency and form of social behavior. Whether in the microgeography of friendship or the macrogeography of pollution, we never observe any one type of factor as the sole "cause," but we have repeatedly noted

how social and cultural variables interact with the geographical to shape the patterns of social behavior we encounter.

In these initial chapters, then, we are taking account of some of the foundations on which social life is built. Like foundations generally, they do not determine fully the shape of the edifice. They do limit the range of variation that is possible. They impose heavy costs on social experiments that ignore those foundations. To speak of costs and limits is merely a loose way of saying that with respect to some social patterns the geographical, biological, or psychological factors may well explain some of the variance in social behavior that the sociologist seeks to understand. It is intellectually thrifty to attempt to explain only as much as is necessary and not to scorn the help of other fields in trying to understand why human beings and their groups act as they do.

READINGS

Ronald Abler, John S. Adams, and Peter Gould, *Spatial Organization,* Englewood Cliffs, N.J.: Prentice-Hall, 1971.

Ian Burton and Robert W. Kates, "The Floodplain and the Seashore," *Geographical Review,* 54, no. 3 (1964), pp. 366–385.

Melvin R. Cox, *Man, Location, and Behavior: An Introduction to Human Geography,* New York: Wiley, 1972.

Emile Durkheim, *Suicide* (1897), trans. by John A. Spaulding and George Simpson, Glencoe, Ill.: Free Press, 1951.

Leon Festinger, Stanley Schachter, and Kurt Back, *Social Pressures in Informal Groups,* New York: Harper, 1950.

L. T. Howells and S. W. Becker, "Seating Arrangement and Leadership Emergence," *Journal of Abnormal and Social Psychology,* 64 (1962), pp. 148–150.

Ellsworth J. Huntington, *Climate and Civilization,* New Haven, Conn.: Yale, 1924.

Terrence Lee, "On the Relations between the School Journey and Social and Emotional Adjustment in Rural Infant Children," *British Journal of Educational Psychology,* 27 (June 1957), pp. 101–114.

J. Ross Mackay, "The Interactance Hypothesis and Boundaries in Canada: A Preliminary Stu-

dy," in Brian J. L. Berry and Duane F. Marble, eds., *Spatial Analysis,* Englewood Cliffs, N.J.: Prentice-Hall, 1968, pp. 122–129.

Robert K. Merton, "Reference Groups and Social Structure," in *Social Theory and Social Structure* (1949), enlarged ed., New York: Free Press, 1968.

Nancy Jo Felipe Russo and Robert Sommer, "Invasions of Personal Space," in William B. Saunders, ed., *The Sociologist as Detective,* New York: Praeger, 1974, pp. 142–153.

Thomas F. Saarinen, *Perception of the Drought Hazard on the Great Plains,* University of Chicago, Department of Geography, Research Paper no. 106, 1966.

J. K. S. St. Joseph, *Medieval England: An Aerial Survey,* Cambridge: Cambridge, 1958.

Pitirim A. Sorokin, *Contemporary Sociological Theories,* New York: Harper, 1928.

Eugene J. Webb, Donald T. Campbell, Richard D. Schwartz, and Lee Sechrest, "Physical Traces: Erosion and Accretion," in their *Unobtrusive Measures: Nonreactive Research in the Social Sciences,* Chicago: Rand McNally, 1966, pp. 35–52.

Walter Prescott Webb, *The Great Plains,* New York: Grosset & Dunlap, 1931.

PART FOUR

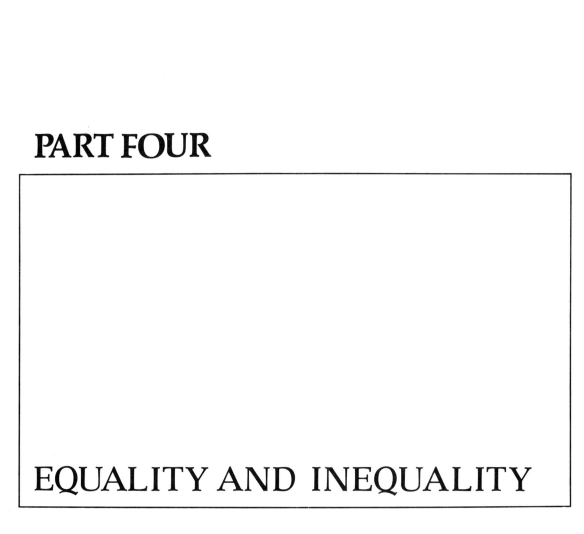

EQUALITY AND INEQUALITY

CHAPTER NINE

THE STRATIFICATION SYSTEM

Two powerful regularities are observable in most societies: (1) Resources and rewards are unequally distributed. The few have much; the many have little. (2) Parents pass on their benefits to their children. The ways in which resources and rewards are distributed and passed on is called the *stratification system.*

This system is usually experienced, and described, as a pyramid, with the upper "classes" at the top and the great masses at the bottom. The shape of the pyramid may be steep or flat. In some societies this pyramid is not very steep, because the distance between top and bottom is not very great. In others the pyramid is steep, and those at the top are very privileged, in some cases even holding the power of life and death over those at the bottom.

Within the system we speak of *social stra-*ta, or various "layers" that enjoy different amounts of resources and rewards. Unlike rock strata, where the lines between layers that touch one another are definite and easily visible, adjacent layers of *social* strata are not usually very distinct.

We give the label "classes" to these social strata, though whether there is a specific number of definite, distinguishable classes is debatable. The term is warranted, however, because those at the top *do* enjoy more wealth, esteem, and political influence than those lower down. If we rank or classify people by resources and rewards, we observe that most other human traits are also ranked in the same way. That is, a correlation is observable—modest or high—between how much money, prestige, and political influence people enjoy, on the one hand, and almost any other characteristic that people exhibit. Thus, people whose rankings are at far extremes are likely to live very different lives.

For example, toward the upper ranks people are taller, live longer lives, have higher IQs, exhibit lower rates of schizophrenia, read more books, are more likely to approve of modern art, engage in sexual intercourse at a later age but then are more likely to indulge in a wider variety of sexual variations, belong to more organizations, have lower divorce rates, are more likely to vote in elections, and participate more in outdoor recreation (except hunting and fishing). This list does not make up a distinctive style of life for each class, but the sum of class differences does at least set apart the people who occupy very different rankings on the scales of prestige, income, and political influence.

Though there are great differences between extreme positions or ranks, there are no large differences between ranks that are close together. In fact, sociologists debate what a class *is*. For over two thousand years analysts and philosophers have also debated whether that unequal distribution of income and respect is *just* or *necessary*. Thus, the traditional questions in the analysis of stratification are (1) What is a class? and (2) What theories can account for the class systems we observe? In addition, because *social mobility* (the movement upward or downward in wealth, esteem, or political influence) changes who gets what, a third traditional topic focuses on the causes and consequences of those upward and downward moves. It is so significant we shall give it separate attention below.

WHAT IS A CLASS?

The traditional question "What is a class?" implies that each class is a definite, distinctive thing, with traits that can be listed easily. But if we ask "How *should* we define a class?" the question suggests, by contrast, that we can define class position or a class as a separate entity in *many* ways, depending on the kind of sociological problem we want to study.

Most research on class differences does not aim at creating a definition of class but instead simply takes it for granted, by using a particular *index* of class ranking, such as income, education, occupation, or prestige. Each of these indexes will place some people on a slightly different level—for example, if income alone is used, international airline pilots will rank above university professors; but if occupational prestige alone is used, they will rank lower. However, *class-linked findings will be almost the same*. For example, if we use income as our class index, we will learn that toward the upper-class levels a higher percentage of young people will complete a B.A. than toward the lower strata. However, we would get the same result if instead we use occupational level, prestige ranking, education of parents, total value of property, political influence, or even self-reports of class membership as our index of class. There would still be a positive relationship, or a *correlation*, between class and completion of a specific number of years of education.

Changing the index does not, then, make a large difference in the relationships between class and some other pattern of behavior. While this important fact does not prove we can neatly separate each class, it does suggest at least that class *ranking* or level is *real*. Position in the stratification system seems to affect much of our social life.

The most common measures of class ranking utilize one of three techniques:

1 The most frequently used ranking system includes *indexes* of income, wealth, education, occupation, or residential location. These indicators carry the unfortunate label *objective measures*, presum-

ably because they could in principle be obtained from official records. In fact, they are no more objective than the other types of ranking systems.

2   A second system relies on asking people how they *rank others* with respect to esteem, social acceptability, political influence, or class level. Such rankings are often called *subjective* (because they report people's opinions), but they are also objective in that they reveal what a person's or family's ranking is, and they are the social reality to which people must adjust.

3   A third type of ranking, also subjective, consists of *self-reports* about class position; people are simply asked to which class they belong, for example, working, lower, middle, or upper class.

All these measures can be criticized for weaknesses and biases. If we use the first ranking technique and divide families according to the index of annual incomes, those divisions are completely arbitrary; we could divide the population into three, five, or even fifty classes if we wanted to. Second, these divisions do not correspond to *distinctive*, separate classes. If we wish to separate the upper middle class from the upper class, we might wish to set the dividing line at, say, family incomes of $40,000 and over, but clearly some families would be very close to the line, and there would be no sociological reason to exclude or include a given family in any group. Obviously, the same comments could be made about wealth, education, or indeed any other "objective" measures.

If we use the second ranking technique and ask people to tell us what are the classes they *perceive*, they are likely to place most people in one of three classes, upper, middle, and lower; but we can see that that ancient form of classification is just as arbitrary as a dividing line between $4,999 and $5,000. While it is usually easy to distin-guish between the "highs" and the "lows," unfortunately the "middles" are simply everything in between, and there may be nothing distinctive about them at all. Most importantly, people (especially in cities) often do not know one another well enough to assert what class a family belongs to, and researchers are forced once again to return to *external* measures or indexes of class.

The third ranking technique, self-reports, has the advantage by contrast, that at least the respondents know themselves and presumably know where they rank in the whole system. However, some people have exaggerated or pretentious notions of how high they rank, while others rank themselves more modestly than their position justifies. In addition, self-reports will yield different results, depending on how a question is asked. For example, in the United States few people place themselves in the category of "lower class," but about half will agree they belong to the "working class." Different people respond somewhat differently to different labels, and so the results will be different.

Thus, the problem of neatly defining a class is plagued by the arbitrariness of the lines between classes as well as by the somewhat different placement of people, depending on which index is used. In addition, it is a principle of all classification systems that the more measures are used, the greater the amount of overlapping of classes, and thus the greater the difficulty of placing every individual in a definite class. Thus, if we divide people by income, we can have a simple set of arbitrary divisions. If, however, we add accumulated wealth, not everyone who is middling in accumulated wealth will be middling in income. Some people make very high incomes, but spend it all and save little. If we use education *in addition*, this will coincide roughly with both income and wealth, but again not exactly: Some people with much education will have only modest incomes. If we use prestige rankings, these will again correlate with wealth, but not exactly; again, there is much overlapping, while the distinctness of any class division is blurred still more. Some people are very well-to-do, but enjoy little esteem from the society. Thus, the use of several measures together blurs the division between classes.

Some analysts solve the problem by simply asserting that wealth or income "ultimately" determines all other aspects of stratification. That is, if someone has a great deal of money, that will eventually override any other social variable, and thus that person must be classed as "upper." However, that assertion is empirically weak and fails to recognize the complex processes that link esteem, political influence, and money. In fact, if one has only high prestige and little money to begin with, one will obtain not merely invitations to dinner, but job opportunities and promotions as well. Political influence can also be used to obtain wealth. Similarly, if a person has a relatively high income but does not enjoy much esteem, it is likely that he or she will attempt to gain esteem. Thus, newly rich people who recognize that they are not very acceptable socially may engage in a wide variety of actions designed to increase their social esteem and to acquire the external social polish of the more secure members of the upper class. In short, all those variables are interlinked, and it is difficult to assert that any one of them "ultimately" determines the others.

One practical research consequence of several decades of debate about the distinctness of class is that at the present time most stratification analysis uses the simple measure of *occupational level* as a class index.[1] Among all societies for which we have data, occupational rankings are extraordinarily similar. The variation from one nation to

another is very small. The utility of this measure is that it combines several other stratification indexes. People at higher occupational levels enjoy higher incomes; typically, they have more education; they have more political influence; and they receive more esteem from others. Thus, instead of using separate measures for each of these various dimensions of class, many researchers use occupation instead as a rough measure of class position. While this still does not yield neat, distinctive classes, it does yield definite class *rankings* that correlate with a wide variety of social patterns.

Class Consciousness

The most important reason for attempting to ascertain whether there is a distinctive set of classes is the possibility that people may act in a concerted way to further their own class interests. This claim has been made by many analysts, notably C. Wright Mills and, more recently, G. William Domhoff,[2] who wish to explain how it is that the people at the top are able to manipulate the system to their own advantage. Marx's analysis (see the next section) also asserted that the lower classes would eventually become *class conscious*[3] and would further their own interests by organizing a revolution.

It seems likely that there is more class consciousness at the higher and lower class levels, and where social interaction within the group is more intense. Thus, black workers who have experienced much unemployment, people who work in more isolated settings where they interact with one another frequently (loggers, fishermen, miners), or members of more militant un-

[1]For cogent reasons in favor of this procedure, see Peter M. Blau and Otis D. Duncan, *The American Occupational Structure*, New York: Wiley, 1967, chaps. 1 and 4.

[2]C. Wright Mills, *The Power Elite*, New York: Oxford, William 1956; and G. William Domhoff, *Who Rules America?*, Englewood Cliffs, N.J.: Prentice-Hall, 1967; as well as *The Higher Circles: The Governing Class in America*, New York: Random House, 1970.

[3]That is, they would perceive their own class is distinct, would feel solidary with fellow class members, and would be politically active for the goals and interests of their class.

ions are likely to be somewhat firmer in their belief that they are exploited by the system.[4] Class consciousness is also more likely to be greater among the upper classes. In the upper social strata the people are fewer in number and the possibilities of interaction are greater, while their shared economic and political interests are more obviously different from those of the society as a whole. Consequently, the people at these two levels are certainly linked more closely with one another than the vast segment of the population that might be called middle-class.

In general, however, the data on industrial nations do not reveal a high degree of class consciousness. On the other hand, no assumption of class consciousness is needed for most analyses of class-linked behavior. Almost any measure that we use will *rank* people at different levels in the class system. At that level, they will perceive most social problems differently and will take different political positions, usually to help their own interests.

Although class level will not predict exactly how people will vote or behave, we can nevertheless observe a general correlation between class level and almost any kind of important social behavior. In some stratification systems of the past, it was possible to place most people in an identifiable category—serf, peasant, baron, or member of a particular trade. That seems to be no longer possible, but it does not undermine the importance of class position for social life; people at different class rankings behave differently just the same.

Marxist Class Analysis

Although the Marxist analysis of how capitalism developed and how its future history would unfold rests fundamentally upon a particular conception of class relations, Karl

[4]John C. Leggett, *Race, Class, and Labor: Working-Class Consciousness in Detroit*, New York: Oxford, 1968.

Marx himself did not complete a systematic theory of class. He derived his view of class from the historians and economists of his own time period, the middle of the nineteenth century. The distinctiveness of his own view was to argue that:

1 The particular classes we now observe arose only at one great historical phase in the development of the economy, that is, capitalism (in other times, there were other classes).
2 The conflict among classes in modern capitalism will inevitably lead to a polarization of the whole society into two great groups, owners and workers.
3 This conflict will then end with a victory of the working class.
4 When that happens, a totally new type of society will arise, a socialist society without classes.

According to Marx, a person's class position in any society is determined by his or her relationship to the system of production—primarily whether the person owns the means of production, or instead offers his or her own labor on the free market. That relationship determines the kinds of social experiences individuals have, their legal rights, the level and stability of their wages, and even their beliefs about art or social reality.

Basing his analysis on the best economic theory of his day and a detailed study of many empirical reports, Marx argued that capitalists were forced to exploit workers because of competition. He prophesied that small businesses would be increasingly absorbed by owners of large companies, who would acquire more and more wealth. An increasingly larger part of the work force would become laborers receiving low wages, as machinery took over more tasks of the economic enterprises. More and more members of the middle class would be forced to become workers, while a smaller part of the population would become extremely rich. As this polarization of the society developed,

Figure 9-1   Leisure interests of different social strata vary from the highly formal horse show to the informal bowling alley. (Top: Sam Falk, Monkmeyer; bottom: George W. Gardner.)

the working class would develop a consciousness that their miserable condition was not created by their own failure, but by the system itself. Radical intellectuals would help them to that consciousness. Finally, there would be a revolt of the workers.

After the workers' revolution a classless society would be established in which everyone would own everything. Much or most of the state apparatus would simply disappear, since much of the government and legal system in the capitalist era is designed to keep the workers in their place as exploited masses. A new era of harmony and justice among human beings would result.

Marx was one of the greatest social analysts of the nineteenth century. He was also a leader of the socialist movement, and both his revolutionary doctrines and his work as a social scientist came to be accepted as faith by communist parties in many countries. Consequently, his work has been fiercely attacked and defended. It is, indeed, difficult to do either without being accused of partisanship. Let us nevertheless consider his analysis of socioeconomic processes.

It is unfortunate that Marx laid such stress on predicting the future, since it is much more difficult to predict the future before it happens than afterwards. Clearly, the fate of a prophet's words is a hard one, unless the prophecies predict what will happen far, far in the future.

First, in contradiction to Marxist prophecy, modern communist revolutions have occurred in rural, agrarian societies, not in the most advanced capitalist systems. Second, capitalist societies have not split into two warring classes, in part because nationalism has proved to be an enduring basis of solidarity among classes during periods of war. Third, Marx failed to predict the rise of a new type of middle class, the strata of technical employees in large governmental or business bureaucracies that are very different from the middle classes he knew, that is, small producers, craftsmen selling their own goods, self-employed professionals, or farmers. Thus, though a good part of the middle class that he knew in the mid-nineteenth century *has* gradually been reduced to some extent, the middle class of white-collar and technical workers at high and low levels has grown.

More importantly, the position of the worker has improved over the past century. Workers have acquired civil and political rights, and through both independent collective action and their voting threat they have changed their economic bargaining position. Thus, as against the "progressive immiseration" Marx predicted for most of the population, workers now enjoy more political influence as well as more economic benefits.

Finally, and perhaps of greater analytic significance, especially in the communist countries but to a considerable degree in all nations, the political apparatus of the state has come to have far more influence over the economy itself. Far from being the dominant and ultimately overwhelming factor in social life, the economic system is determined to a large degree by the decisions and actions of political authorities. New forms of conflicts may become important, but the simple economic class antagonism of the nineteenth century does not seem to be as prominent.

Nevertheless, if the chief predictions that Marx made are not in fact correct, this does not mean that all of his analysis of the active forces in capitalist society should be discarded. Much of Marx's social analysis of the processes at work in industrial society can still be useful.

For example, it remains true, as Marx insisted, that people in different class positions perceive social reality differently. Almost any belief about society will vary among different classes. This includes attitudes about art, pollution, or war, as well as other political issues. If we want to understand how people will behave in a political conflict, a primary question to ask is, How will it affect their class interests? As Adam Smith commented slyly a generation before Marx was born, we can infer from the recent Quaker decision in Pennsylvania to free the slaves that the Quakers do not own very many slaves.

If the capitalist societies did not produce a mass of poverty-stricken workers who would take over the state through armed conflict, as Marx predicted, it was to some extent because conservative leaders themselves recognized the cogency of Marx's analysis and took steps to improve the lot of the workers. Thus, they reduced the revolutionary potential that Marx proclaimed. Pioneer welfare and social security programs were inaugurated by a right-wing Bismarck in the latter part of the nineteenth century, precisely because he wished to undermine that threat. In the 1820s the threat of possible revolution led even conservative British leaders to extend the vote—if not to workers themselves, to at least the lower middle classes. In the 1960s the threat of race-conscious militancy among blacks in the United States persuaded many white people that some efforts toward increasing their opportunities would be wise. Consequently, the absence of polarization does not prove that the Marxist analysis of class conflict was incorrect. On the contrary, such conflicts have been visible in every major society over the past century, and have often failed to issue in revolution because leaders took steps to improve the condition of workers.

Moreover, although it is difficult to locate a neatly delimited "ruling class" which owns all the means of production and whose economic dominance gives it overwhelming political power, the upper social stratum has managed to retain enough influence to protect its own interests. For well over half a century thousands of regulations and laws have been passed whose aim was to reduce the vast inequality between the wealthy and the poor, between those of high income and low, and between those with vast political influence or little. Each year efforts are made to create a genuine progressive income tax, so that people with large incomes will pay a far higher percentage of their income than those with less income. Inheritance taxes attempt to reduce the accumulation of wealth between generations. Antitrust and antimonopoly legislation has attempted to curb the oligopolistic tendencies[5] in corporate life.

Nevertheless, the overwhelming descrip-

tive fact is that the changes over many decades have been small and without any apparent trend. If the concentration of wealth or economic dominance is reduced for a brief period, it reasserts itself soon. Thus, even if we cannot demonstrate a conspiracy or organization among a delimited group of people who are the "rulers" of modern capitalist societies, it is at least apparent that those at higher class levels have managed just the same to defend their own interests very effectively. Thus, again, if the specific details that Marx predicted do not occur, nevertheless, some of the forces that he saw at work in the nineteenth-century capitalist societies can still be observed.

THE "CAUSES" OF INEQUALITY

Traditional sociological theory, instead of focusing on the interaction of classes as actors, attempts to explain why the stratification system exists at all.[6] In addressing this problem social theorists have, for over two thousand years, considered it from the perspective of justice: That is, is it *just* that some people should get so much more than others do? The problem to be considered is not why certain *people* manage to get into certain positions, but why *societies* pay very

---

[5]As noted in the chapter on formal organizations, oligopolies—a small number of companies that make the important decisions within an industry—are prominent in the advanced sector of the economy: for example, oil, rubber, steel, aluminum, automobiles, communications, and computers.

[6]For extended commentaries on this question, see Kingsley Davis and Wilbert E. Moore, "Some Principles of Stratification," *American Sociological Review*, 10 (April 1945), pp. 242–249; see also Kingsley Davis, *Human Society*, New York: Macmillan, 1949, pp. 366–368. For critiques of this earlier version, see Dennis H. Wrong, "The Functional Theory of Stratification: Some Neglected Considerations," *American Sociological Review*, 24 (December 1959), pp. 772–782; and Melvin M. Tumin, "Some Principles of Stratification: A Critical Analysis," *American Sociological Review*, 18 (August 1953), pp. 387–393.

For further contributions by Davis, Moore, and Tumin to this debate, see Reinhard Bendix and Seymour Martin Lipset, eds., *Class, Status, and Power*, rev. ed., New York: Free Press, 1966, pp. 47–63. It seems useful, for example, not to use the term "functional importance," not merely because it is extremely difficult to measure that variable, but also because the use of the term generates much heat but little light.

different rewards to different *positions* in the occupational system.

We begin with two fundamental facts: (1) A division of labor is to be observed in all societies, but especially in large ones. This creates some efficiency but does not in itself cause occupations to be ranked high or low. (2) People evaluate tasks and rank some of them as more valuable than others, no matter what society we examine, past or present. In all societies, for example, people give considerable respect to the job of medicine man, and far less respect to people who dig ditches or carry burdens. Ordinary economic analysis, too, begins with evaluations of services and products. In the vocabulary of economics, this is the basis for what is called *demand*.

Economic theory does not focus much attention on *why* demand is high or low, or why some things are evaluated as more desirable. Sociology has that task; yet there is no generally accepted explanation for these evaluations. On the other hand, the *general* patterns of evaluation do not differ so radically. For example, every cross-national study that asks people about the prestige of various occupations shows that people in all countries seem to rank occupations in a strikingly similar way. This suggests that the demand for different kinds of skills is not so variant from one society to another as has been supposed. However, we do not have an adequate explanation for these regularities.

Nonetheless, it is observable that people do evaluate some achievements and qualities more than others. However, to understand *how much reward* a society pays for a specific achievement, it is also necessary to consider the *supply* of such achievements or the possible supply of people who can furnish them. If everyone values medical skills highly, but in fact everyone is capable of furnishing them, the reward or price for those services will be low. Serving as chief group leader or manager (that is, getting

people to work on a common task) is a highly valued task, but apparently not everyone commands that ability. When the supply is somewhat limited, the rewards paid will be higher.

A General Formulation

The most general formulation to explain social stratification simply asserts that a society will offer higher or lower rewards (of all kinds) to people who enter different occupations, depending on (1) how highly they value those occupations, and (2) how big the supply is of people who might be willing or able to do them. Where people are permitted to make choices of occupations, they will enter those which pay better in one way or another, *if they have no superior alternative.* That is, (1) not everyone has the choice of all occupational levels; (2) not everyone is attracted to every occupation equally, even without regard to the rewards paid; and (3) each person will be motivated differently by the different mix of political influence, money, or prestige that is paid to each occupation.

Such a general formulation accepts as a fact that there are very great differences among potential job candidates in their talents, their desire for one kind of activity rather than another, their perceived chances of doing well, and the resources their families are willing to invest in them. Not everyone with talent is willing to study long and hard to become a lawyer. Not everyone with military talent is willing to risk her or his life. In all societies, families with greater resources can see to it that their sons (and in modern times, their daughters as well) are permitted a wider choice of occupations.

Such a general formulation accepts as a fact that in all societies different occupations are ranked differently. That is, people believe that it is right for some occupations to get more money, esteem, or political influence than other occupations. How much each occupation gets cannot be manipulated much by its occupants, although they try to do that in every society. However, it is not possible to manipulate generally the values or opinions of the whole society about the worth of jobs in it and thus how much they should be rewarded. Even with vast budgets at their disposal, it would not be possible for electricians, business people, accountants, or nurses to persuade the whole society that they should be given more prestige than, say, physicians or university professors. By limiting entrance and thus creating scarcity, an occupation can increase its income higher than it would otherwise be; it is much harder to raise its prestige that way. Even with vast political influence, as we shall note later in this chapter, leaders of socialist countries have been unable to persuade their fellow citizens that being a worker should be honored as much as being a professor.

So far, the formulation is relatively simple, and it corresponds with both common sense and daily observation. However, we now must introduce two further variables: (1) the social or legal limitations on *supply*, and (2) the social or legal limitations on *demand*.

Supply, Demand, and Rewards

With respect to supply, it is clear that a truly open market does not prevail in any economic system. As Adam Smith remarked two centuries ago, whenever members of the same occupation get together, it is likely that they will discuss plans for taking advantage of the public. Great warriors will teach their sons the tricks of their trade to give them advantages over sons of peasant or scholarly families; in the high Middle Ages a peasant's son was not allowed an education without the lord's permission; millions of brilliant lower-caste children in India are typically prevented from entering occupations where they would distinguish themselves; until fairly recently a large seg-

ment of lawyers were excluded from Wall Street because they came from disapproved ethnic or social backgrounds. These wide-ranging examples make the general pattern obvious: Numerous regulations and social patterns prevent free access to positions that pay high rewards. In no society is talent or achievement given no weight at all, but in no society will all the potential applicants, or supply, be encouraged.

Demand is not free, either, but is shaped by the social and legal systems. For example, in socialist countries the political order and the official ideology determine in part how much will be paid to people in different positions. In fact, political leaders will attempt to control both supply and demand in an effort to shape the development of the country. In such countries special incentives and opportunities are given to people who are willing to be trained as engineers, with the result that the percentage of engineering students is likely to be as high in less-developed socialist nations as in the most industrialized societies of Europe. By contrast, in Latin America no special inducements are offered to engineering students, and the overwhelming majority of university students in Latin America are in law and the humanities.

Note, too, an additional limitation on the reward structure in socialist countries. There is almost no room for *legal* free enterprise activities. In capitalist countries, by contrast, there are no legal limits on the income that can be made in nonsalaried activities, such as developing new and profitable enterprises, manipulations of the money or stock markets, or buying and selling anything that will yield a profit.

In every society there are social limitations on *salaries* paid. Many individuals in the United States make several million dollars annually in *income* (for example, rock and film stars, boxing champions), but *no one receives that much in salary*, in part because people in an organization cannot easily be persuaded that even the top person in it actually deserves that much more income than those at lower levels. The limitations are even sharper on the salaries of government officials.

We must now introduce a set of variables that complicates the analysis of stratification even more: Which *kinds* of rewards are paid to which kinds of occupations? In some occupations (for example, selling insurance) the top earnings are extremely high, but the prestige given is relatively modest. Salaries given to the clergy and to professors are somewhat modest, but their prestige rewards are high. Many political offices pay salaries in middle ranges, but their political influence is substantial. Thus, upper *salaries* are limited, but people are willing to take those jobs because the *total rewards* are high. No society has ever given its highest prestige rewards to people in business, but there the money rewards may be high. All countries have given high prestige to people in the medical professions, in academic learning, and in law. The position of the warrior has varied; in some societies the prestige given to excellence in military activities has been very high (Rome, Tokugawa Japan, Imperial Germany). No one has worked out an adequate statement of how people come to feel these different "mixes" of rewards are appropriate for the various occupations.

Family Patterns and the Stratification System

Although the foregoing analysis helps us to understand why different occupations are ranked higher or lower than others, a further step is necessary to transform those job rankings into a stratification *system*. The building block for this transformation is the link between such occupational levels and family patterns. What distinguishes a simple occupational ranking from a stratification system is the fact that the *family*, not the

individual, is the basic unit of class systems. It is the families in all societies that attempt to pass on whatever advantages they possess to their children, and it is therefore the families that try to maintain their class position for their children. When we speak of class rigidity, or barriers to mobility, we are referring to the successful efforts of higher-level *families* to create social networks and systems of influence, so that they can maintain their own position from one generation to the next, against the attempts by low-level families to rise.[7]

There is no society in which families do not attempt this. When social philosophers attempt to imagine new kinds of improved societies, invariably they attempt to change the family system somewhat, so that talent and hard work will be rewarded but family influences will be reduced or eliminated. In Plato's *Republic*, for example, children were not to know who their parents were, and parents would not know their own children. As a consequence, the link between occupational level and the family itself would be severed. Although every revolution attempts to move in this direction, even successful revolutions cannot go far along this course, for after the new regime has become established, the new families at high levels want to pass on many of their social advantages to their own children.

VARIATIONS IN CLASS SYSTEMS

Stratification systems differ from one another in many ways. If we could visit a highly advanced society of the past, such as China in the sixteenth century, we would observe that almost everyone was rather poor, and a peasant. In the United States, by contrast,

[7]For comments from Russian sources on this problem, see S. M. Lipset, "Social Stratification Research and Soviet Scholarship," in Murray Yanowitch and Wesley A. Fisher, eds., *Social Stratification and Mobility in the U.S.S.R.*, White Plains, New York: International Arts and Sciences Press, 1973, pp. 355–391.

Figure 9-2 One way that higher-level families attempt to maintain their position is by trying to ensure that their children marry into the "right" families. (Yoram Kahana, Peter Arnold.)

farmers make up only about 4 percent of the population. In most great historical societies, men in the upper strata took for granted their right to use physical force on men of the lower strata, without being called to account for it; but that was not so in fifth-century Athens. Until the eighteenth century in Europe, gentlemen had the right to wear a sword. Until late in that century, many kings and their noble supporters believed in the divine right of monarchs to rule, and thus to condemn or free others by their own decision, but in many other societies there were no monarchs.

In short, stratification systems differ substantially. And although this chapter focuses on class systems in industrial societies, which are very similar to one another, here we broaden our perspective to consider many other kinds of systems.

What variables or factors differentiate among class systems? Perhaps one of the most obvious is, How rich and politically powerful is the topmost class compared with the bottom? That is, if one thinks of the population as a giant pyramid, how much distance is there from the top to the bottom? Is the pyramid tall or flat? This image cannot easily be translated into exact figures, but it is clear that in many small tribal societies even kings had relatively little wealth or authority, whereas in almost all large-scale societies the topmost stratum has been so rich as to challenge our ability to think about it.

By contrast, legal restrictions on both ownership and inheritance prevent the development of such a wealthy stratum in socialist countries as well as in the Scandinavian nations. With reference to political influence, the rulers of modern societies believe that they must govern with the consent of their people, even in communist countries where free elections do not exist. Although Stalin had as much political authority as any czar of the past, in neither Russia nor any other great modern nation can one find a stratum of nobles or political rulers who can capriciously decide the fate of their subjects without consulting them or the head of the government. Thus, in some countries from top to bottom is not as great a distance as in others.

The imagery of a pyramid suggests that we also can compare class systems by reference to how widely prestige or political influence is *distributed*. That is, of the total available, how much do people at different class levels get? Is there a large middle class, or are most people found at the bottom of the pyramid? Thus, we can consider how *high* a pyramid is from top to bottom, and we also can consider its *shape*, that is, whether it bulges at the bottom or in the middle.

One way of doing this is to ask how much of the total income is received by each fifth of the families in a given country. That is, does the topmost 20 percent get only 20 percent of the total income, or much more? For the United States at the beginning of the 1970s, the highest fifth of all families received about 41 percent of the total income. That is, they received about twice as much as their proportionate share. By contrast, the bottom fifth of all families received approximately 5 percent, that is, about one-fourth of their proportionate share.[8] The middle 40 percent received about that share of the income, 41.5 percent. Such figures are only approximate, since a great number of fringe benefits such as lavish expense accounts, corporation services, automobiles, and vacations are not included in the incomes of the top stratum.

A contrast may be made with India, although the statistical data are less easy to obtain: The great bulge is at the bottom. In one survey, a simple tabulation was made of the percentage of Indian households that were below the poverty line. According to

that calculation some 95 percent fell below that line as defined by Indian standards. At approximately the same time period, about 18 percent of United States households fell below the poverty line, as it was defined in this country. (In 1974 that figure was approximately 10 percent.)[9]

It is perhaps even more difficult to measure the extent to which societies differ in the amount of *respect* they pay to people at different class levels. However, we can at least perceive great differences when we read of past monarchies whose nobles demanded and received great amounts of deference from those whom they considered lesser beings. In many Eastern countries it was expected that people at lower levels should approach a court officer only after prostrating themselves to the ground. Although European gentry did not expect this type of deference, Western nobles required other signs of respect, such as bowing, taking off one's cap, and making way for persons of high degree.

In India, for well over a thousand years, lower-caste people were viewed as so polluting that they could not touch food that was to be eaten by the high-caste group of Brahmins. A few outcaste groups at the bottom were not supposed even to allow their shadow to touch a Brahmin. The liberating constitution of 1949 officially abolished such caste privileges, but since then many murders and riots have occurred when members of lower castes did not pay the traditional deference or entered temples that were forbidden to them, or even drew water from wells that were socially defined as available only to the upper castes. In the southern United States until recently, most public

---

[8]*Current Population Reports: Consumer Income,* ser. P-60, no. 97, January 1975, p. 43. The data are for 1973. The differences are greater for individuals than for *families.*

[9]Nathan Keyfitz, "Privilege and Poverty: Two Worlds on One Planet," in Edward O. Laumann, Paul M. Siegel, and Robert W. Hodge, eds., *The Logic of Social Hierarchies,* Chicago: Markham, 1971, p. 699; and U.S. Bureau of the Census, *Statistical Abstract of the United States,* 1973, Table 548. The 1974 United States figures assume a poverty line of $4,000; see *Consumer Income,* p. 3.

places had water fountains marked "Colored" or "Negro" as well as "White," and restrooms were similarly marked.

Achievement and Ascription

All the foregoing differences in class systems are correlated with a traditional sociological distinction between *ascribed* and *achieved* rank. In an ascriptive society, people's rank or position is given to them by birth. In an extreme form, in India a child born to a Sweeper caste was expected to be a Sweeper throughout his or her life. In most monarchies the eldest son of a king was designated to be king eventually. By contrast, in some societies the person's *achievement* determines whether she or he is permitted to occupy a given post, take a particular job, or be treated with more or less respect.

All industrial societies officially proclaim that only *achievement* is to count and that anyone may rise who can. Most traditional societies of the past asserted that rank was *ascribed* and that people should remain in the rank where they were born. Thus, we speak of most modern societies as *class* societies in contrast to both *caste* systems (no mobility permitted) and *feudal* or *estate* systems (where some mobility was permitted, but not officially approved).

However, that distinction is not clean-cut. In no society is achievement irrelevant to the income, influence, or prestige of the individual. Kings have been deposed because they were incompetent or corrupt. A monarch *might* choose only nobles to be foreign ambassadors, but he *could* choose the most competent among them to do that job. In Tokugawa Japan the ideology of fixed social position was strong, but a father with incompetent sons, or no son, might well adopt an able boy from a somewhat lower class ranking. Sex is ascribed, but in every society there have been women who were given high position because their achievements overrode that ascriptive rule.

The distinction is not clean-cut on the other side, either. We have but to look about ourselves in the United States to see in turn that ascription has great weight in an achievement-oriented society. Wealth is inherited. Initial class position is inherited. The well-to-do family sees to it that its children get a better education and greater opportunities than others do. Family connections influence almost every aspect of life. Ascription by race continues to weigh heavily, and it is often more important than achievement.

Nor is this situation confined to the United States. It applies as well to socialist countries. It was also observable in Chinese society in the past, which was perhaps the only Eastern country in which an open-class ideology was publicly accepted. There, at least as an ideal, any young man could attain the highest posts if he was brilliant and worked hard and could afford so expensive an education.[10]

Moreover, we must distinguish between the *ideology* of ascription and the laws that support it, and the *reality*. Every careful study of societies of the past discloses that the social rule of rigid ascription did not prevent people from rising or falling just the same. As we note later, the same *class* may continue to rule, but the *specific* families who are in that class change constantly. If 95 percent of the population is made up of poor peasants, and only 5 percent is made up of well-to-do merchants or nobles, obviously it is not possible for 95 percent of the population to move into the higher class in one generation. On the other hand, it is common for a substantial percentage of that upper stratum—from 20 to 40 percent—to be made up of "new people" from other social strata, even when official ideology denies that possibility.

Caste systems are much more rigid than

[10]For an analysis of these patterns in Ch'ing China, see Robert M. March, *The Mandarins: The Circulation of Elites in China, 1600–1900*, New York: Free Press, 1961; as well as Yung-Teh Chow, *Social Mobility in China*, New York: Atherton, 1966.

FOCUS

HOW MUCH DOES BEING SOUTHERN, BLACK, OR IMMIGRANT HANDICAP A PERSON'S SOCIAL MOBILITY?

The situation of southern whites provides an interesting contrast with that of Negroes. The chances of occupational success of Southerners are inferior to those of Northerners, both whites and Negroes, whether the Southerners remain in the South or migrate north to pursue careers there. Southerners have lower social origins than Northerners, they are less educated, and they start their careers on lower levels. Although the differences between Southerners and Northerners are not so great as those between whites and Negroes, there are parallel differences in respect to every variable under consideration. However, the handicaps of Southerners do not have cumulative effects on their occupational chances, whereas those of Negroes do. When social origins, education, and career beginnings are controlled the occupational level of southern whites is, on the average, no longer any different from that of northern whites. In other words, the inferior background and education of southern whites fully account for their limited occupational chances, and there is no evidence of discrimination against Southerners once these initial differences have been taken into consideration; whereas the chances of Negroes remain inferior to those of whites under controls, which probably is the result of discrimination. Moreover the occupational chances of southern Negroes remain inferior to those of northern Negroes under controls, in contrast to the case of southern whites, which undoubtedly reflects the more severe discrimination against Negroes in the South. Southerners have many competitive disadvantages in the struggle for occupational success, just as Negroes do, but the handicaps of southern whites do not produce cumulative impediments for their careers, while those of Negroes do. It may well be that ethnic discrimination is at the root of such cumulative adverse effects on careers and that without discrimination there is no vicious cycle of poverty.

The case of a third minority—sons of immigrants—differs from that of Southerners as well as that of Negroes. The background of all three minorities creates hardships in their occupational lives. The initial handicaps do not fully account for the inferior occupational chances of Negroes but do account for the inferior chances of southern whites. However in both cases the initial handicaps are accompanied by inferior subsequent achievements, whereas the occupational achievements of the second generation, despite its initial handicaps, are not inferior to those of northern whites of native parentage. That is, sons of immigrants have lower social origins and less education than the majority group of

SOURCE: Peter M. Blau and Otis D. Duncan, *The American Occupational Structure*, New York: Wiley, 1967, pp. 406–408.

northern whites with native parents, yet their occupational achievements are on the average as high as those of the majority group, not only if initial differences are controlled but also without such controls. Although these results seem to indicate that white ethnic minorities do not suffer discrimination in the American labor market, a possible alternative interpretation is that some white ethnic groups are disadvantaged in their careers but the effects of these disadvantages are neutralized, and hence obscured in the data, by the overachievement of selected members of the white minority groups. There is some evidence in support of this interpretation. Thus second-generation men of northern or western European descent have slightly more successful careers than those with less prestigeful origins (primarily southern and eastern Europe). Besides the data on education show that the second generation has initial disadvantages, but those men among them who overcome these disadvantages are exceptionally successful.

Minority group handicaps are challenges for as well as impediments to achievement. They create obstacles to success and simultaneously provide a screening test of the capacity to meet difficulties, with the result that those members of the minority who have conquered their initial handicaps and passed the screening test are a select group with high potential for continuing achievement. The background handicaps of the second generation are evident in the finding that fewer of them than of the majority group complete eight years of schooling, go on to high school, and remain in high school until graduation. In order to graduate from high school sons of immigrants had to meet more serious challenges than sons of native parents. High-school graduation, consequently, is a particularly effective screening test for the second generation, which is manifest in exceptional rates of proceeding to higher educational levels once the initial handicaps are overcome. The proportion of high-school graduates who go on to college is larger among the second generation than among the majority group, and so is the proportion of college entrants who graduate and the proportion of college graduates who proceed to professional or graduate school. Men who had to overcome competitive disadvantages progress to higher levels subsequently than those never confronted by such difficulties, partly because having to pass through this screen selects men with high initiative or ability, and partly because success in meeting challenges steels men in further competitive struggles. For hardships to be such a spur to achievement, however, requires that those members of minorities who have conquered their initial handicaps are then permitted to enjoy the fruits of their success and that persisting disadvantages and discrimination do not rob them of these hard-won benefits. At least, this conclusion is suggested by the findings that Negroes, whose occupational chances remain inferior when education and background are controlled, do not have exceptionally high probabilities of continuing their education on advanced levels, whereas white minorities, whose occupational rewards for given educational investment are not inferior, do not have such high rates.

class systems. However, two processes are observable. In India, at least, some sub-castes succeed in raising the social rank of the caste itself over a period of time, typically by imposing new rules of ritual purity on themselves (for example, becoming vegetarian) and inventing a more respectable history. In addition, members of a caste may become well-to-do in a given locality or may achieve considerable political influence.[11] In many local communities members of the middle caste levels (warriors and merchants) may well be *dominant* because there are no Brahmins on the local level.

Other Variations in Class Systems

Implicit in the foregoing discussion is an important difference among class systems, that is, *the amount of social mobility* they allow. We are convinced that all societies have exhibited more social mobility than has been believed, but clearly some are more "open" than others. Modern socialist countries, especially immediately after the revolution, are far more open than other societies and give great encouragement to members of the lower classes. In the United States there is considerable upward mobility, and more upward mobility from the working class to the upper occupational levels than in other industrial countries. Nearly 10 percent of the sons of manual workers move into top occupational levels in the United States.[12] The processes by which this social mobility occurs will be discussed further in the succeeding section.

A further important variation, though again one that is correlated with the differ-

ence between ascription and achievement, is whether the classes or segments of the society are *distinctive*, that is, whether there are sharp boundaries setting each off from the other. In many past societies these distinctions took a legal form. People of a given rank might be forbidden, for example, to have any silverware or to own a carriage or to bear arms; people at the lowest levels might be forbidden to receive an education or to learn certain trades or skills.

Such legal restrictions attempt to *support* social distinctions, but they cannot be made unless people already recognize the distinctiveness of particular occupations or classes. Furthermore, social and legal definitions of classes or occupations could exist only in a society where classes and occupations did not change rapidly, and where they were few enough to permit everyone to know about all of them. By contrast, it is not possible for people in modern countries to have different expectations about the tens of thousands of occupations that now exist. Moreover, these change constantly. At best, our expectations can focus only on large categories, such as classes, or on traditional occupations with which we have some continued experience, such as carpentry or operating a pharmacy. Since, in any event, there are no sharp separations among adjacent classes with respect to income, prestige, or political influence, people disagree about where they belong in the class rankings, and even more about what kinds of behavior to expect from people at different levels.

Class systems vary from one society to another as well as historically. Over the past several hundred years, a worldwide movement toward a greater *openness* of class systems can be observed, though upper-class leaders have stubbornly resisted this change in every country.

Much research remains to be done on classifying different stratification systems. As we noted earlier, we do not have precise

[11]See M. N. Srinivas, *Social Change in Modern India*, Bombay: Asia Publishing, 1966. See as well James E. Blackell, *The Black Community*, New York: Dodd, Mead, 1975, for a description of class differences in the black community.

[12]Blau and Duncan, op. cit., p. 435. This percentage is the highest of the ten countries being compared; see Table 12-1.

data about the past, and even modern comparisons about the distribution of money, prestige, or political influence are difficult to make. More importantly, we do not have adequate knowledge of what are the *consequences* of different class systems; for example, how do they affect the utilization of talent, the potential for revolution, or even national production? A satisfactory classification of stratification systems will probably not be made until we understand both the causes and the consequences of stratification systems.

SOCIAL MOBILITY

The income and prestige rankings of occupations change little from one decade to another, and changes in the United States over the half-century from the 1920s to the present have been minor. In fact, the minor differences that have been observed in public opinion polls are probably caused by differences in how researchers phrased their questions, and not by changes in rank. Moreover, the prestige rankings of occupation are remarkably similar in other countries.[13] Similarly, the income and prestige rankings of identifiable classes or castes are relatively stable. Unless a revolution occurs, a class of nobles remains at the top for generation after generation. In Western industrial societies, the middle class has become more numerous and its aggregate wealth and political influence have grown, but this has taken place over a period of several centuries. Even if caste discrimination is outlawed, as in India and the United States, the upper caste retains most of its political influence, wealth, and prestige; in short, it stays at the top. If the nobility is

driven out, killed, or absorbed, a new revolutionary elite arises that again keeps control over its privileges for a long period of time.

However, individuals and families do not experience as much stability as social classes. As Schumpeter comments, "For the duration of its collective life . . . each class resembles a hotel or an omnibus, always full, but always of different people."[14] The landed nobility in England continue, but few of them are the direct heirs of the dukes, earls, or barons who held those titles in the seventeenth century. Most of the titles now held have been granted to new families over the past several generations. Individuals and families try to move upward in whatever ways they can. But some fail and stay where they are or drift downward. To change the whole system seems difficult or impossible.

Thus, when we speak of social mobility, we typically refer to the movement of individuals or *families*, rather than of whole classes or castes. However, here we do not focus on how one person moves upward or downward. Instead, we are concerned with *rates* of mobility, that is, whether many or few people rise or fall over a generation or more.

As was already noted, that emphasis on aggregate measures is of fundamental importance for the continuing worldwide social and political conflicts about stratification systems. Why are such facts important for political debate? Suppose the data show that in industrial societies the *long-term* class movement is not generally downward. If most people in the middle class are not becoming impoverished workers, and if the stratification system is *not* moving toward a two-class structure of rich owners and poor

[13]Robert W. Hodge, Paul M. Siegel, and Peter H. Rossi, "Occupational Prestige in the United States, 1925–63," *American Journal of Sociology*, 70 (November 1964), pp. 286–302. See also Robert W. Hodge, Donald J. Treiman, and Peter H. Rossi, "A Comparative Study of Occupational Prestige," in Bendix and Lipset, eds., op. cit., pp. 309–321.

[14]Joseph A. Schumpeter, *Imperialism and Social Classes*, trans. by Heinz Norden, New York: A. M. Kelley, Publishers, 1951, p. 165. For historical data on these changes, see Bernard Barber, *Social Stratification*, New York: Harcourt, Brace & World, 1957; and B. Barber and Elinor G. Barber, eds., *European Social Class: Stability and Change*, New York: Macmillan, 1965.

workers, then Marxist theory is incorrect. Political leaders in every country believe that one important technique for lowering political discontent is to increase social mobility, so that able people in the lower social strata can rise. Much of the attack on existing social institutions focuses less on how much income or prestige each class enjoys, and more on the barriers to equal opportunity that individuals and families must face. Thus, it is important to know how much mobility there is in different countries, and whether there is more or less than in the past.

This research is highly technical and cannot be carried out by simply summarizing governmental data, because it is necessary to know the specific job history of individuals, as well as the occupational levels of the specific families from which those individuals came. Errors in classification as well as in memory or knowledge increase the difficulty of this kind of research. Comparisons among countries are difficult, because the occupational structure in each country is different, and it changes over time. Complex problems in statistics are also encountered. For example, if white-collar jobs are expanding rapidly in one country but not in another, then the percentage of people who move from a blue-collar family background to white-collar jobs may be the same in both countries, but the class structure in the second country is somewhat more open. However, it is not easy to standardize for that large difference in the occupational structure.[15]

From the wave of comparative research done in the 1950s, many analysts concluded that the amount of social mobility to be found in most industrial nations was about the same.[16] Later analyses, which correct

some errors in the earlier research, yield a somewhat different conclusion by separating *upward* mobility from *downward* mobility. In most of these industrial countries about 20 to 30 percent of the sons of fathers who did manual labor ended up in nonmanual occupations, and between 20 and 40 percent of the sons of white-collar workers moved into manual labor.[17] In those comparisons the rate of upward social mobility in a few countries were higher than those in the United States.

If the finding of greater mobility in some other countries were correct, it would be puzzling, because of the general belief among European observers for generations that opportunities in the United States were higher. However, more recent analysis does correct the earlier findings in part: In the United States the rate of upward mobility of working-class sons into white-collar occupations is 37 percent. This high rate is exceeded by only two of the nine countries in earlier comparisons.[18] However, with reference to movement into the *highest* occupational levels, upward mobility from the *working* class into the top levels is *higher* in this country than in other countries. The chance that sons of the middle class (white-collar workers) will move into the top occupational levels is topped only by Sweden and Italy; it is at about the same level as for West Germany.[19]

Perfect Mobility

The comparisons above help us understand how much social mobility exists. However,

[15]The most sophisticated discussion of this and other related problems is to be found in Blau and Duncan, op. cit., chap. 4.

[16]Seymour M. Lipset and Hans L. Zetterberg, "A Theory of Social Mobility," in Bendix and Lipset, eds., op. cit., pp. 561–573.

[17]See S. M. Miller, "Comparative Social Mobility," *Current Sociology*, 9, no. 1 (1960); see also the tables cited from Miller in Celia S. Heller, ed., *Structured Social Inequality*, New York: Macmillan, 1969, pp. 327–330; and Thomas Fox and S. M. Miller, "Intracountry Variations," in Bendix and Lipset, eds., op. cit., pp. 574&581.

[18]These are France and Switzerland, though the Swiss data may not be reliable.

[19]For statistical reasons, a high mobility ratio for sons of manual laborers reduces somewhat the ratio for sons of the middle-class fathers. For this analysis see Blau and Duncan, op. cit., pp. 433ff.

we must take a further step, which requires some understanding of a technical concept, what is sometimes called *perfect mobility*. Let us start with its opposite, the notion of perfect rigidity. If there are 100 workers divided into 10 occupations, and in each generation the fathers in those occupations produce one son each, and that son inherits his father's occupation, then we would say that such a system is perfectly rigid, or immobile. If we take a next step and observe that 10 workers out of the 100 are professionals in one generation, but this number doubles in the next generation to 20, then obviously 10 must have come from somewhere else. There will therefore be *some* amount of mobility in the system. However, it is unlikely that all of them would come equally from each of the occupations, since manual or farm laborers at the bottom are less likely to give that much education to their sons. Very likely, many of those new recruits would come from fathers in the somewhat higher occupational levels.

However, if we have a system in which *all* the people who enter any given occupation have about as much chance (allowing for the number of people in the occupation) of coming from fathers in one occupation as from those in any other occupation, so that the sons in *every* job category are distributed exactly as was the work force of that previous generation (for example, if 10 percent of all the work force in the father's generation were skilled artisans, then they furnish 10 percent of the sons in *each* job category in the next generation); and if that same pattern or distribution *also* holds for the origins of the fathers, then we have a condition of perfect mobility. In common-sense terms, *no one has any advantage or disadvantage simply because he or she had a parent in a high- or low-level job.*[20]

<hr>

[20]In more technical terms, when the category of sons in the "destination group has the same distribution of origins as the total population, each origin group has the same distribution of origins as the total population," and all the ratios or indices are 1.0 (p. 35).

Social Mobility in the United States

If now we develop a large matrix or cross-tabulation made up of 17 occupational levels of fathers and 17 occupational levels of sons, we have a matrix of 189 cells, or a total of 189 possible combinations. In the United States system about 100 of these show an excess flow of manpower from one cell to other cells. Several regularities can be observed in this flow and are summarized as follows:[21]

1 At all occupational levels there is more occupational *inheritance* than would be found in the case of perfect mobility; that is, the jobs of sons *are* affected by their father's jobs.
2 However, as just noted, there is considerable mobility just the same.
3 There is more *upward* mobility in the United States than *downward* mobility; that is, in each generation, more sons move to jobs that are higher than those of their fathers. The ratio of upward movement to downward movement is about 5 to 2.
4 Short-distance movements are more common than long-distance ones. In general, the closer any two occupations are to one another in occupational level, the greater is the amount of manpower that is exchanged between them. However,
   a Working in one industrial line (such as heavy manufacturing) is a strong barrier to mobility into another (for example, mining or insurance), even at the same beginning job level.
   b Sons of skilled workers or craftsmen are more likely to move into higher white-collar occupations than into lower ones, in part because a movement into lower-level white-collar jobs such as file clerk yields little improvement in income.
5 Every occupational group has, in the

<hr>

[21]The calculations are analyzed in Blau and Duncan, op. cit., especially chaps. 2 and 4; see also pp. 418 ff.

Figure 9-3 At all occupational levels children's jobs are affected by their parents' jobs. (Dan O'Neill, Editorial Photocolor Archives.)

past, received more than 10 percent of its members from sons of farmers, though that relationship cannot continue in the future since the percentage of farmers is now so low.

6   Lower-level occupations are more likely than any others to send most of their sons to other, higher levels; that is, the two lowest white-collar levels, the two lowest blue-collar levels, and farm laborers send more of their sons into other occupations than do other occupational levels (if they move at all, they will move up).

7   Most occupational inheritance or self-recruitment is found in the category of self-employment: independent professionals, owners of businesses, and farmers. These occupations have not changed much in recent years, and certainly have not expanded, so that there has been less opportunity for recruits to enter.[22]

These findings partly corroborate previous analyses. In addition, they can now be stated with more quantitative precision than in the past. More importantly, however, it is now possible to state how much total mobility there is. In the United States "the amount of intergenerational mobility between census major occupation groups is [about] seven-eighths as much as would occur if there were no statistical association between the two statuses whatsoever."[23]

This is a strong refutation of the common notion that family background determines everyone's occupational level. If this were so, it would lead to a kind of "vicious circle," by which the disadvantages of the lower classes are intensified or at least continue from one generation to the next.

Perhaps of equal importance as a quantitative statement is the fact that if we weigh the total effect of what appear to be three most important factors in determining occupation—(1) the father's education, (2) the father's occupation, (3) the son's

[22]For these general findings, see ibid., pp. 26–43. Wilensky has pointed out that "the decline of self-employment has been exaggerated." Most of the apparent drop is simply the decline in farming. "The proportion of self-employed in the non-agricultural labor force has remained steady at about 10 percent for almost a quarter century." See Harold L. Wilensky,

"Measures and Effects of Mobility," in Neil J. Smelser and Seymour M. Lipset, eds., *Social Structure and Mobility in Economic Development*, Chicago: Aldine, 1966, p. 133.

[23]Blau and Duncan, op. cit., p. 200.

education—we find that these powerful variables explain only about *42 percent of all the casual influences that measurably determine the son's occupation.* That is, there is an unexplained variation of nearly 58 percent that can have nothing to do with the impact of the family on the job of the son. Note that within these calculations are included the prestige ranking of the family, the educational advantages that are passed on, and the many indirect effects that flow from those overlapping factors.

Two important qualifications should be noted here. One is that these data may not apply to women. We do not know the facts because adequate research on women's mobility remains to be done. Second, although the *general* patterns of mobility noted above are also found among blacks, the data prove clearly that barriers to mobility among blacks are very great. Most importantly, with every step in the white person's job career, *family background plays a lesser role;* it has less explanatory power. By contrast, as Blau and Duncan have pointed out, the family background of blacks continues to play a role, for the disadvantages of blacks continue through their lifetime. At the same socioeconomic levels of family origin, blacks get worse educations. However, even if we compare only blacks and whites with similarly poor educations, blacks still get worse jobs when they are first hired. Finally, if we compare blacks and whites with similarly poor initial jobs and education and low socioeconomic origin, the blacks still do not enjoy comparable success. There are, in short, *continuing* disadvantages in the mobility experiences of blacks, but typically not for whites.

What of changes in social mobility over *time?* It is even more difficult to obtain such data for past generations than it is for the present, since those records are usually not available. A careful examination of the studies that have been made, however, suggests that there has been little change over the past half-century, in contrast to the convic-

tions of both the pessimists who believe that the system has become increasingly rigid and the optimists who believe that social mobility has increased.[24] Although the system has certainly become less rigid for women and for blacks, on the whole it has not changed much.[25]

The same conclusion of "no great change" is equally true of two other important class variables, the distribution of income and the distribution of total assets, or wealth. In spite of numerous laws whose official aim was to reduce the discrepancy between top and bottom economic classes, little change has resulted. The very top economic stratum may now receive or own a slightly lesser percentage of the total than it did a generation ago, but even that conclusion has been questioned.[26]

STRATIFICATION IN COMMUNIST COUNTRIES

Social science research in communist countries, and especially the study of social stratification, has been hampered by political constraints. Political leaders of these countries have consistently taken a Leninist position with reference to social science inquir-

[24]For a careful study of an earlier period, see Natalie Rogoff, *Recent Trends in Occupational Mobility,* Glencoe, Ill.: Free Press, 1953. See also Kaare Svalastoga, *Prestige, Class, and Mobility,* Copenhagen: Gyldendal, 1959; and Blau and Duncan, op. cit., chap. 3.

[25]For some data on the position of blacks, see Reynolds Farley and Albert Hermalin, "The 1960's: Decade of Progress for Blacks," in Lee Rainwater, ed., *Social Problems and Public Policy,* Chicago: Aldine, 1974, pp. 225–240; Thomas F. Pettigrew, *Racial Discrimination in the United States,* New York: Harper & Row, 1974; and *Current Population Reports: The Social and Economic Status of the Black Population in the United States,* 1973, Special Study Series P-23, no. 48, July 1974. See especially Sar A. Levitan et al., *Still a Dream,* Cambridge, Mass.: Harvard, 1975.

[26]See in this connection Herman P. Miller, *Rich Man, Poor Man,* New York: Thomas Y. Crowell, 1964; and Gabriel Kolko, *Wealth and Power in America: An Analysis of Social Class and Income Distribution* (1962), rev. ed., New York: Praeger, 1964; as well as our later section on reducing inequality.

ies, that is, that all intellectual work should further the tasks of the revolution. Consequently, they believe, the publication of embarrassing facts should be forbidden. Valid sociological investigations do expose the failings of any system. At the same time, Western social scientists, themselves barred from access to the necessary data on communist countries, have been politically opposed to those regimes, and have not been conspicuously objective in their own analyses of those countries. In addition, only one communist regime, Russia, has been in existence for more than one generation, long enough to permit us to observe how it works over the longer run.

Nevertheless, examining communist systems can be sociologically fruitful because they are the first nations in the history of the world (although France of the 1790s may be a temporary earlier case) whose aim was simply to abolish the class system, at least eventually. Indeed, Soviet spokesmen frequently claim that that has already been done. They claim that a class is defined by whether its members are owners or workers, and since every Soviet citizen has the same relationship to the means of production—all are workers and there are no individual owners—the class system has already been abolished. Any surplus or profit belongs to everyone and does not go to the individual capitalist. The official Soviet position is that there are no exploited workers, that factory and farm work is honored as much as white-collar work, and that sex discrimination has been eliminated as well. Social scientists in Yugoslavia and the central European countries are somewhat more willing to concede that the new system has its problems but that their aim remains that of creating a classless society.

Dissidents in both Russia and Yugoslavia, as well as those who have been expelled or have escaped, assert that the new system is at least as class-ridden as the old, because now the party officials and higher managerial authorities constitute a "new class" who

reap great economic rewards and stifle all objections by their control over the police apparatus.[27]

Three Phases of Stratification

To understand these class systems, it is important to distinguish (1) the period immediately after the revolution from (2) a later period of stabilization, and possibly both of these from (3) a still later period when new requirements in the economy or the political system begin to affect the rewards given to people in different occupations. In all these countries, there was a very high rate of social mobility in the period immediately after the regime took over.

In this first stage the political authorities made an attempt to remove almost all the former elite from their high position through simple demotion, exile, imprisonment, or death. Next, factory and farm labor was praised as the most honorific set of tasks. Steps were taken to improve working conditions on the farms and in the factories as well as the economic rewards both classes of laborers received.

Third, a special effort was made to open both high schools and universities to the children of workers, almost none of whom had been given that privilege under previous regimes. Often this meant enrolling students who had not yet had the formal education that was officially required. Quotas were set to reduce the number of children from families of former officials or the rich and to increase the number of children from rural, lower-class, and different ethnic backgrounds. Thus, some of the family influences on class position were reduced.

Fourth, the state took over private land and companies, thus further diminishing the economic bases of class position. The accu-

[27]For comments on this, see Milovan Djilas, *The New Class*, London: Thames and Hudson, 1957; Alexander I. Solzhenitsyn, *The Gulag Archipelago*, trans. by J. P. Whitney, New York: Harper & Row, 1974; as well as Nadeszda Mandelstam, *Hope against Hope*, trans. by Max Hayward, New York: Atheneum, 1970.

mulation and the inheritance of wealth were made much more difficult.

Finally, the rhetoric and ideology of equality ("All are comrades") emphasized that though a factory manager or party chairman has the duty of commanding, everyone deserves respect as well as a voice in all decisions. That theme was emphasized by the leaders' dedication to hard work, an austere style of life, and the imposition of punishment on those who slipped into the old, corrupt ways. To emphasize this change, the external insignia of rank were rejected; and titles of nobility, special ranks, and imposing uniforms were abolished.

The description above applies, it must be emphasized, to the countries that have been relatively successful in establishing their authority. Without question, those leaders did prove that it is possible to reduce inequality drastically, even if they did not achieve overnight a completely equalitarian society.

However, some of these equalitarian tendencies are likely to be halted or even reversed at a later period, once the government has been established. In the Soviet Union this process began in the 1930s when a strong campaign against "equality-mongering" was launched by Stalin, who also ordered that disparaging public remarks about administration and white-collar employees should cease.[28] Whether or not an official move toward greater inequality occurs, that effect may occur from time to time just the same, because of the greater authority and resources of those who are in higher positions. That process took place in Yugoslavia; and the pressures toward a return to inequality can be discerned in China as well, in recurring phases when the economic experts, more interested in production than political purity, are in charge.

The move toward greater inequality, how-ever, is not likely to be permanent. Recent data from Yugoslavia, Poland, Hungary, and the U.S.S.R. suggest that the larger differentials of the early 1960s have again been somewhat reduced in this third phase.

It is at least fair to say that in the communist countries (as in the United States) many categories of blue-collar workers receive wages that are about as high as, or slightly more than, the wages of lower white-collar workers. In addition, the prestige they receive may not be as different from that of white-collar workers as it is in capitalist countries.[29] Typically, blue-collar workers in capitalist countries are much less likely to receive paid vacations, guaranteed pensions, or paid time off for personal or domestic crises, and they are under much tighter supervision in their time schedules.

Until the most recent return toward some-what greater equality, higher-level factory managers in the Soviet Union made about twenty to thirty times as much as lower-level manual laborers, a differential that was very similar to the income differences in capitalist industry. It is not clear whether that difference remains as large. On the other hand, even today the upper occupational levels in Russia continue to enjoy many privileges that do not appear as wages, such as the use of cars and chauffeurs, cheap vacations, tickets to entertainments that most people could not attend, and so on.

Two other special aspects of the class system in the Soviet Union should be noted. First, certain types of occupational positions receive much more esteem and perhaps even greater economic privileges than in Western countries: ballet dancers, chess players, poets, and other practitioners of the

[28]Frank Parkin, *Class Inequality and Political Order*, London: MacGibbon and Kee, 1971, pp. 1433ff.; as well as Thomas Bottomore, *Classes in Modern Society*, 2d 3d., London: G. Allen, 1966, pp. 47ff.

[29]Parkin, ibid., pp. 146–147. However, see also chap. 6, especially pp. 172–178, which show less unemployment among white-collar workers in Yugoslavia and fairly high wage differentials. Because job categories differ among countries, it is not always certain that precise comparisons are being made.

fine arts. Second, a small number of deviants enjoy much *underground* esteem. That is, they are engaged in activities that are widely disapproved by the political authorities, but enjoyed by people whose political attitudes are somewhat dissident. These include many poets, popular singers, jazz players, and the like.

Command Economy and Capitalism Compared

Let us now consider the class system in communist countries from a more general point of view. Stratification processes take place within what might be called a *command economy*, that is, an economic system where political decisions can override the goal of higher production if it will serve political purposes. In such an economy the differences in wages and other income advantages (subsidized housing, food allowances, working conditions, bonuses) can be set at rates that may or may not be what a free market would pay. If the political leaders want to keep more workers on farms, they can nevertheless pay them less than urban workers, but reduce the flow of people to the city by refusing living quarters or even jobs in the cities. If they wish to encourage the economic development of a harsh region such as Siberia, they can offer an attractive total income package, along with greater political freedom. That is, they can pay more or less than the free market does, depending upon which sectors of the economy or which geographical regions the leaders wish to favor.

This artificial manipulation of the economy makes it more difficult to determine the true prestige of occupations in communist countries. Thus, if some categories of skilled or unskilled blue-collar workers are paid more in communist countries than lower-level white-collar workers, we cannot conclude that the public praise of the worker has somehow persuaded the population that manual labor should be esteemed more than white-collar work. Those pay differentials may simply be the result of a political decision to encourage one type of manpower flow, as against another.

It is, however, equally important to note that there is a substantial overlap in both the esteem and the wages of white-collar and blue-collar workers in *both* communist and capitalist countries. Researchers in Poland and Yugoslavia have reported that some skilled occupations rank higher in prestige than some routine white-collar jobs. However, it should not be forgotten that this is true in the United States as well. For example, systematic studies of the prestige ranking of occupations in this country show that the occupations of railroad engineer, electrician, and machinist all rank higher in prestige than the following white-collar occupations:[30]

Welfare worker

News columnist

Reporter

Radio announcer

Bookkeeper

Insurance agent

Manager of a small city store

Traveling salesperson for a wholesale concern

Clerk in a store

Moreover, the average 1973 earnings of craft and kindred workers are higher in the United States than those of clerical and kindred workers by a tiny amount (both being slightly over $10,000); and those of clerical workers are only slightly higher than those of "operatives" (assembly line workers) and

[30]Robert W. Hodge, Paul M. Siegel, and Peter H. Rossi, "Occupational Prestige in the United States: 1925–1963," in Bendix and Lipset, op. cit., pp. 324–325.

transportation workers, that is, semi-skilled blue-collar workers. Thus, in both communist and capitalist countries, people in professional managerial and administrative positions are paid much more prestige and higher wages than those in lower-level occupations. Similarly, the higher levels of blue-collar work overlap to some extent with those of white-collar work in both systems.

In both, too, the evidence is clear that the children of higher-level managerial or official families receive many educational advantages that help them to maintain their class position.

In contrast to these similarities, a set of social differences between communist and capitalist countries should be noted. First, it seems likely that the very high emphasis on equality in communist countries creates a high awareness among the poor of how much the advantaged groups get. There is very little counterpropaganda that asserts the privileged classes have an inalienable right to their "property." The official ideology asserts no one should have special privileges.

Second, there is a widespread understanding in communist countries that the leaders have *created* their system, and are directing it. By contrast, in capitalist countries the most widespread conservative ideology asserts that the system was not actually created, but simply grows out of "human nature." At higher and lower class levels in Western societies, it is difficult to know who is in charge. "The system" seems to function autonomously, whether it functions well or ill. Political leaders in this country would emphatically deny that they are responsible for the inequality of the United States class system. However, writing of communist countries, one analyst asserts: "In a command system by contrast there is much less of a problem about whom to shoot."[31] Without question, people believe

those at the top are in charge and should be held responsible for any observable inequalities.

A further difference should be noted: In capitalist countries both the working class and political dissidents generally have access to a radical ideology that is sharply opposed to the normative or political system of the upper class. In Western countries, there is a long tradition of socialist and communist analysis, empirical inquiry, and propaganda that offer a complex and persuasive reinterpretation of the capitalist system, as well as a strong attack on it. No such weapon is available to the working classes of the communist countries. After all, the rulers themselves also affirm a socialist or Marxist body of teaching. This situation weakens to some extent the potential attacks by dissidents on communist leaders. However, those leaders in turn become much more vulnerable to the charge of failure if they attempt to seize special privileges, engage in unofficial, capitalistic profit making, or accumulate wealth. Precisely because such leaders, whether factory managers or party officials, have accepted an ideology that disapproves such activities, the scandal is much greater when they violate those norms.

THE REDUCTION OF INEQUALITY

World history has seen many opulent societies, in all of which the miserable poor eked out a scanty existence. That situation was generally taken for granted but was not viewed as ideal. Indeed, some philosophers presented a contrary view, that riches were spiritually impoverishing. In Christian history there has been a continuing line of preachers who argued that the simple life was best.[32] However, it is only in the past century that a few social analysts—mostly

[31]Parkin, op. cit., p. 163.

[32]For the importance of this theme in peasant rebellions, see Rodney Hilton, *Bond Men Made Free*, London: Temple Smith, 1973, especially chap. 3.

socialists, until recently—have argued by contrast that we should not reduce the level of living for the well-to-do (so that they can be virtuous, too), but raise that level for the poor. Industrial productivity is so great that no one need suffer. It is wise and just to increase the equality among human beings, to assure a comfortable life for everyone, even if that reduces the wealth of the rich somewhat.

That view does not seem radical now, and in fact it is much more widely accepted than is commonly supposed. As long ago as 1965, when few people had heard of a guaranteed annual income, two public opinion polls reported widespread United States support for proposals to give the federal government the responsibility of ending poverty, to spend more on urban renewal, and to establish a national system of health insurance.[33]

To be sure, those same polls reported that most people thought the welfare rolls were loaded with chiselers, that we should rely more on individual initiative and less on welfare, and that any able-bodied individual who really wants to work can earn a living. The contrast between the two sets of attitudes may indeed be the heart of the political problem: People believe in reducing inequality, but they also believe no one should get something for not working. In addition, they object to paying very much for any improvement in *other people's* level of living.

However, such dilemmas are common in politics, as they are in our personal lives; all of us value contradictory things. Political decisions and actions are typically aimed at resolving conflicts, while all resolutions are costly for some people and some goals.

The Extent and Distribution of Inequality

Let us note once again the extent of inequality in the stratification systems of modern

[33]Harold L. Wilensky, *The Welfare State and Equality*, Berkeley: University of California Press, 1975, p. 37; as

industrial societies and then point out why this situation has come to be increasingly challenged in our generation. Here is a selection from the voluminous data that demonstrate the inequality of wealth in the United States (the facts are not very different in other industrial nations):

1   For the past generation the poorest 20 percent of United States families have received 4 to 5 percent of the income, while the highest 20 percent received 40 to 43 percent.

2   Since in the aggregate the wealthy *save* a higher percentage of their income than do the poor, the concentration of *wealth* is even greater. From the 1920s through the 1960s, .05 percent of the United States population owned 20 to 30 percent of the wealth.[34]

3   At the upper levels a higher percentage of income derives from property or company profits, rather than from wages and salaries: Two-thirds of United States incomes over $100,000 annually come from stock ownership or profits, while only 15 percent comes from salaries.

4   The richest 20 percent of the United States population owns about three-fourths of the total wealth, which includes about 95 percent of the corporate stock that is owned by individuals.[35]

5   Moreover, the presumably "progressive" income tax rates, which are higher for upper incomes, reduce inequality very

well as Richard F. Hamilton, *Class and Politics in the U.S.*, New York: Wiley, 1972, chaps. 3 and 5.
[34]Bottomore, op. cit., pp. 34–35. All such figures are estimates; it is difficult to know who owns what. In England wealth is even more concentrated.
[35]Internal Revenue Service, *Statistics of Income, 1966: Individual Income Tax Returns*, Tables 7, 11, 19; and Frank Ackerman et al., "The Extent of Income Inequality in the United States," in Richard C. Edwards et al., eds., *The Capitalist System*, Englewood Cliffs, N.J.: Prentice-Hall, 1972, pp. 211–213. For uncorrected but recent figures on income, see the relevant tables in current editions of the *Statistical Abstracts of the United States.*

little. Taxes generally are *regressive*; that is, the poor pay a higher percentage of taxes. Even if we focus only on *federal* income taxes, which are somewhat less regressive, there is little difference in the percentage of taxes paid at various income levels from the lowest group of $2,000 annually up to the $15,000 level.[36]

6 To be sure, at the lowest levels many counterpayments are made by social security and welfare systems, which partly offset those high taxes. For the lowest income group, these payments, called *transfer payments*, are *larger* than the taxes, although these payments do not help everyone at that level, since the transfer payments do not necessarily go to the same people who pay the taxes.

7 Many loopholes and exemptions benefit the wealthy far more than the poor, for example, capital-gains tax rates, deductions for expenses of home ownership, oil depletion allowances, and the like. These tax advantages reduce the taxes of the rich to levels that are comparable to those of people at the middle class levels.[37]

Despite the evidence of little change, a major change *has* occurred in the *distribution* of poverty in modern societies, and especially in the United States. The changes generally reduce the political threat of poverty. Today the poor do not constitute to the same extent as a century ago a relatively homogeneous mass of poor workers. In the modern United States, they constitute "pockets," or segments, of people with very different characteristics—the *rural* poor,

large families, broken families, the unemployed, blacks, the aged, or families without a male head. And most of the people in these sometimes overlapping categories have few political resources with which to exert influence in order to change their condition. They do not form an organized political threat. Nevertheless, an increasing number of people have challenged this situation as being unjust or at least undesirable. Why has that challenge arisen?

Shifting Social Attitudes

Perhaps the most important factor, which has affected political action in all industrial nations, is the spread of a common United States attitude, that the rich are *only* rich; as a class, they do not have any special qualities that merit any deference. This attitude is one that de Tocqueville remarked on in the 1830s' that is, the United States upper classes can buy services and even overt deference, but ordinary people generally feel that the rich are not a genuine elite.[38] The attitude was expressed succinctly in Ernest Hemingway's response to F. Scott Fitzgerald's assertion that the rich are "different." Hemingway said, "Yes, they have more money." The financial success of the rich proves that they are good at making money, and that yields some esteem, but not much. After all, they are already rewarded amply by their wealth; to get more respect, they must contribute to the community or achieve in other ways. It is not generally believed that they are nobler in character, braver in battle, finer in their manners, more virtuous or creative, or even better educated. In most large nations of the past, the nobility or elite made all these claims,

[36]*Economic Report of the President*, 1969, p. 161.
[37]An eloquent case of this kind is made by Philip Stern, *The Rape of the Taxpayer*, New York: Random House, 1973. A more sober analysis is that of Richard M. Titmuss, *Essays on the Welfare State*, London: G. Allen, 1962. See also Kolko, op. cit.; Robert J. Lampman, *Ends and Means of Reducing Income Poverty*, Chicago: Markham, 1971; and Joseph A. Pechman and Benjamin Okner, *Who Bears the Tax Burden?*, Washington, D.C.: Brookings, 1974.

[38]Alexis de Tocqueville, *Democracy in America* (1835), trans. by Henry Reeve, New York: Schocken Books, 1964, vol. II. book 3, chap. 1. This enduringly fresh analysis of the United States in the early nineteenth century contains many acute observations on the class system.

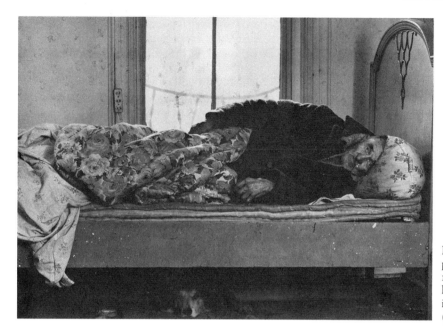

Figure 9-4 Many elderly people, living in "single-room-occupancy" hotels, have been segregated into pockets of poverty. (Bruce Davidson, Magnum.)

and lesser folk could see that nobles seemed superior in many ways.

In the 1960s those claims were widely challenged in every industrial nation, and the rich as well as the heads of major governmental and private organizations were asked to prove their right to rule. Even now, when that revolutionary impulse has abated, people in modern societies are less willing to pay as much deference as their ancestors did.[39] Consequently, there is much less political or social support than once existed for the privileges of the upper class. The middle classes do not agree to the notion of pure equality, but they no longer feel (if they ever did) that the upper classes should have as large a fraction of the total wealth and income as they now do.

Second, there is a growing recognition that most poverty, unemployment, the inability to pay for necessary medical services, or the economic and social problems of old

age are not mainly caused by incompetence, laziness, or weak character. Here the impact of sociological knowledge is evident: A larger number of people understand that these problems are caused, at least in part, by large-scale social and economic dislocations, and that it is difficult to claim that the victims are somehow at fault. It is harder to make that claim when white-collar or managerial workers lose their jobs, when persons over sixty-five form 10 percent of the population and need support,[40] or when the public learns that many rich individuals pay no income taxes at all. All these facts intensify the feeling that it is the "system," not individual incompetence, that causes inequality and poverty.

In the United States the working class does not participate as widely in politics, in workers' organizations (clubs, unions, cooperatives), or in the administration of welfare

[39]On the decline of deference, see Edward A. Shils, "Deference," in Edward O. Laumann, Paul M. Siegel, and Robert W. Hodge, *The Logic of Social Hierarchies,* Chicago: Markham, 1970, pp. 420–448.

[40]Wilensky, op. cit., pp. 12, 26–27, and especially Table 6, which reports a correlation of .87 between the percentage of the *aged* in the population and the percentage of the *gross national product* that is spent for social security.

programs as in many European countries. However, in industrial countries where they do participate more, there is a stronger movement toward reducing inequality by social security measures as well as by heavy taxation.[41] That is, a strongly organized working class perceives inequality through its own experiences and thus exerts some political pressure toward increased equality.

It is also possible that the mass media have played a large role in the growing objection to the presence of widespread poverty amidst riches. It is more difficult than in the past to avoid knowledge of one's poorer fellow citizens, for newspapers, radio, and television force these facts on our attention.

Finally, in contrast to most of world history, fewer people now believe, especially in rich countries, that poverty is *necessary*. The economy is productive enough to support everyone at an adequate level. A nation that spends over $10 billion annually for cosmetics and other toilet goods, and approximately $200 million for advertising those products, can hardly claim that improving the condition of the poor somewhat is simply impossible.

Equal Opportunity versus Equal Results

In the United States social debate has begun to shift in the past ten years away from the simple issue of equal *opportunity*, (that is, whether the poor, black or white, should be given an equal *chance* to *compete* for all jobs). More people, though still a minority, turn that question aside and ask instead about the equality of *results*. A philosopher once phrased the difference between equality of opportunity and of result by pointing out that the law in its majesty punishes the rich and the poor alike for stealing a loaf of bread, and forbids both to sleep under bridges. A recent social analyst asserts:

Rich and poor, for example, have an equal opportunity to work as common laborers but the poor rarely obtain the education and social contacts that provide access to executive positions. Equality therefore cannot be defined solely in terms of opportunity. It must be judged also by results. [42]

That is, the debate shifts to how we can guarantee more equality in the goods and services people *actually get*, not merely how we can ensure more opportunity to compete for the available jobs.

The key sociological fact that is the answer to whether a move toward more equality is possible is that in all systems of allocation, whether capitalist or socialist, agrarian or industrial, totalitarian or democratic, *who will receive a high income* or enjoy great wealth is always *determined by traditional rules and regulations* that have grown up within the society. That is, particular definitions of property, economic access to education, legal systems that decide who may obtain benefits from which kinds of property, inheritance rules, import and export restrictions, and social understandings as to what are public and private rights—all these arrangements largely determine who will be rich or poor. These distributions all were created and maintained by human beings, and correspondingly they can be changed, if people want to change them. It is sociologically impossible to eliminate inequality, but it can be reduced.

Some of the suggestions that have been made toward this end can be noted here as indications of directions the society may move in the future, following the lead of other advanced nations. One of these is simply the expansion of various forms of *social security measures*—unemployment insurance, national medical systems, health insurance, old age systems, and so on—

[41]Ibid., p. 65.

[42]Herbert J. Gans, *More Equality* (1968), New York: Vintage, 1974, p. xi.

in which the United States lags behind all of the twenty-two richest nations with the exception of Japan. (The Soviet Union is lowest among the large European nations.)[43]

A second set of major proposals has been widely debated in Congress, the *elimination of tax privileges* and loopholes that favor the well-to-do. It was estimated for the year 1972 that such a change would increase the average income per United States family by approximately $6,000.[44] Needless to say, these proposals are vigorously opposed by influential people.

A more far-reaching set of proposals centers on *political structures* of various kinds, specifically the development of rules that would permit the participation of disadvantaged people, white and black, in business as well as government decisions. Corporations have a large economic influence, and all the major ones are closely intertwined with government. Consequently, the proposal has been made that far more *corporate decisions* should be made by its employees, and those decisions should also be subject to some review by representatives of the citizenry. The same suggestion has been made with reference to large *labor union decisions*. If working-class people are given more right to participate in social security programs of all kinds, it is likely that their decisions will favor the disadvantaged somewhat more. Another suggestion is directed toward giving *minorities* a greater voice in such political decisions, since at present they remain permanently outvoted, while their interests are not being served.

One type of proposal has been widely offered by both conservatives and liberals, that is, some type of *guaranteed annual income*. We shall not review these various schemes, since they are all rather complex, and it is not possible to guess which one of them is most likely to be enacted in the future. However, it does seem likely that some such program will eventually be put into effect. In one version, called the Credit Income Tax, everyone is taxed on all income, and at the same rate, with no loopholes. The scheme then gives people a different tax rebate or credit, depending upon their income. If their income is very low, the rebate would be more than the tax they paid, the aim being to assure everyone an adequate income. A more commonly proposed scheme is to pay people the difference between some minimum level—whatever is defined as "adequate"—and what they actually earn during the year. Typically, one criticism of this system is that at the upper level of that income bracket, some people might be tempted to avoid work, for as soon as their income rises to minimum level, they will get no added income from the government.

This and other proposals have as their aim the construction of a floor, or basic level, below which the society has some responsibility to help the individual or family. All of them run counter to the traditions of the past that emphasize personal initiative, responsibility for one's own fate, and the belief that hard-working people can earn enough to support themselves. Clearly, the trend of world history is toward a weakening of that ideology. To some observers, the change is proof that the moral fiber of this and other nations is disintegrating. To others, it is viewed as an increase in human compassion, a belief that even the stranger may be viewed as our brother or sister, for whom we have some responsibility.

[43]Wilensky, op. cit., Table 4.
[44]Gans, op. cit., p. 42.

READINGS

E. Digby Baltzell, *Philadelphia Gentlemen: The Making of a National Upper Class,* New York: Free Press, 1958.

———, *The Protestant Establishment: Aristocracy and Caste in America,* New York: Random House, 1964.

Bernard Barber, "Social Mobility in Hindu India," in James Silverberg, ed., *Social Mobility in the Caste System of India,* Comparative Studies in Society and History, Supplement III, The Hague: Mouton, 1968, pp. 18–35.

Reinhard Bendix and Seymour Martin Lipset, eds., *Class, Status, and Power,* rev. ed., New York: Free Press, 1966.

Peter M. Blau and Otis Dudley Duncan, *The American Occupational Structure,* New York: Wiley, 1967.

Thomas Bottomore, *Classes in Modern Society,* 2d ed., London: G. Allen, 1966.

Richard Centers, *The Psychology of Social Classes,* Princeton, N.J.: Princeton, 1949.

Phillips Cutright, "Inequality: A Cross-national Analysis," *American Sociological Review,* 32, no. 4 (August 1967), pp. 562–578.

Ralf Dahrendorf, *Class and Class Conflict in Industrial Society,* Stanford, Calif: Stanford University Press, 1959.

Man S. Das and Gene F. Acuff, "The Caste Controversy in Comparative Perspective: India and the United States," *International Journal of Comparative Sociology,* 11 (March 1970), pp. 48–54.

G. William Domhoff, *Who Rules America?,* Englewood Cliffs, N.J.: Prentice Hall, 1967.

———, *The Higher Circles: The Governing Class in America,* New York: Random House, 1970.

Saul Feldman and Gerald Thielbar, *Life Styles: Diversity in American Society,* Boston: Little, Brown, 1972.

George Gallup and S. F. Rae, *The Pulse of Democracy,* New York: Simon and Schuster, 1940.

Celia S. Heller, ed., *Structured Social Inequality,* New York: Macmillan, 1969.

Robert W. Hodge and Donald Treiman, "Class Identification in the United States," *American Journal of Sociology,* 73 (March 1968), pp. 535–547.

Gabriel Kolko, *Wealth and Power in America: An Analysis of Social Class and Income Distribution* (1962), rev. ed., New York: Praeger, 1964.

Robert J. Lampman, *The Share of Top Wealth-Holders in National Wealth,* 1922–1956, Princeton, N.J.: Princeton, 1962.

John C. Leggett, *Race, Class, and Labor: Working-Class Consciousness in Detroit,* New York: Oxford, 1968.

Seymour Martin Lipset and Hans L. Zetterberg, "Social Mobility in Industrial Societies," in Seymour Martin Lipset and Reinhard Bendix, *Social Mobility in Industrial Society,* Berkeley: University of California Press, 1959, pp. 60–64.

Herman P. Miller, *Rich Man, Poor Man,* New York: Thomas Y. Crowell, 1964.

———, *Poverty: American Style,* Belmont, Calif.: Wadsworth, 1969.

S. M. Miller and Pamela Roby, *The Future of Inequality,* New York: Basic Books, 1969.

C. Wright Mills, *The Power Elite,* New York: Oxford, 1956.

Frank Parkin, *Class Inequality and Political Order: Social Stratification in Capitalist and Communist Societies,* New York: Praeger, 1971.

Natalie Rogoff, *Recent Trends in Occupational Mobility,* Glencoe, Ill.: Free Press, 1953.

Joseph A. Ryan, ed., *White Ethnics: Life in Working-Class America,* Englewood Cliffs, N.J.: Prentice-Hall, 1973.

Arthur B. Shostak et al., *Privilege in America: An End to Inequality?,* Englewood Cliffs, N.J.: Prentice-Hall, 1973.

——— and William Gomberg, eds., *Blue-Collar World: Studies of the American Worker,* Englewood Cliffs, N.J.: Prentice-Hall, 1964.

James Silverberg, ed., *Social Mobility in the Caste System in India,* Comparative Studies in Society and History, Supplement III, The Hague: Mouton, 1968.

Neil J. Smelser and Seymour Martin Lipset, eds., *Social Structure and Mobility in Economic Development,* Chicago: Aldine, 1966.

M. N. Srinivas, *Caste in Modern India, and Other Essays,* Bombay: Asia Publishing, 1962.

———, *Social Change in Modern India,* Berkeley: University of California Press, 1966.

Kaare Svalastoga, *Prestige, Class, and Mobility,* Copenhagen: Gyldendal, 1959.

E. P. Thompson, *The Making of the English Working Class,* New York: Pantheon, 1964.

Melvin M. Tumin, *Social Stratification: The Forms and Functions of Inequality,* Englewood Cliffs, N.J.: Prentice-Hall, 1967.

W. Lloyd Warner and Paul S. Lunt, *The Social Life of a Modern Community,* "The Yankee City Series," I, New Haven, Conn.: Yale, 1941.

Michael Young, *The Rise of the Meritocracy (1870–2033),* New York: Random House, 1959.

CHAPTER TEN

(United Press International Photo.)

RACE AND ETHNIC RELATIONS

Strictly speaking, human beings interact with one another, but races or ethnic groups do not, for they are not actors. They are not even real *groups*, since people who belong to the same race or who have similar national background (Americans of Puerto Rican, Polish, Italian, or Chinese descent) are not organized as a collectivity, do not live in the same area, have no formal leaders, do not share a set of customs or social rules, and may not even feel they *are* a group.

Nevertheless, in much social interaction between two *individuals*, each responds to the other as a *member* of a racial or ethnic *category*. When a white person meets a black person, much of their behavior is shaped by the awareness of both that they belong to different races and thus have had different experiences. So, to a lesser degree, do gentiles when they interact with Jews, Italian-Americans with German-Americans,

Americans of Chinese descent with New England Yankees. The social interaction between customer and clerk, patient and physician, army recruit and drill sergeant, or pupil and teacher is shaped by the demands of those social roles, but it may also be affected by their ethnic or social class memberships.

The importance of racial and ethnic factors in day-to-day social interaction is intensified by the typical pattern of dominance by one ethnic segment or group; normally, one group has more social or political influence and enjoys greater economic advantages, while other ethnic or racial groups object to that arrangement. Consequently, race and ethnic relations are shot through with hostility and misunderstanding. Moreover, racial and ethnic clashes have been mounting in intensity for decades in most parts of the world, so that they must be considered a "social problem," a difficulty that people view as a problem for society to solve.

For all these reasons, this topic is of pressing importance politically and socially. It affects our personal and collective lives. Racial and ethnic discrimination is very costly to the nation and to the individuals who are its victims. It therefore deserves as adequate an analysis as we can give it, just as it is worth the personal investment that individuals make in order to reduce it.

THE EXTENT OF ETHNIC AND RACIAL DISCRIMINATION

If ever there was a time of harmony when all the different peoples of the world viewed each other as equally meriting friendship and respect, we do not know of it. Certainly, as long as nations have existed, they have included people of different tribal, ethnic, or racial backgrounds, who at best have typically lived with one another in troubled peace. People have lumped together all the members of each other's group and have perceived them not only as "different" but also as *inferior* (or, much more rarely, as superior). For example, some Romans thought their English subjects were handsome, but by nature not very intelligent. Whites thought the Plains Indians were warlike, cruel, and able to bear torture. Italian, French, and Hispanic peoples have for generations claimed that they were more passionate than other Westerners, who by and large were persuaded by that claim.

These claims and the consequent patterns of interaction are neatly exhibited in one small area of East Africa where three separate tribes live in close interaction—the Watutsi, the Bahutu, and the Pygmies. The Watutsi could see for themselves that they were tall, strong, aristrocratic-looking, and warlike, and thus fit to rule over the Bahutu, who were better at menial agricultural and clerical tasks. In turn, the serious Bahutu felt they were right to demand services from

the Pygmies, whose childlike, gay, and irresponsible nature made them unfit for any task requiring concentration or a long attention span, but excellent for hunting or finding wild honey in the forest. Similarly, in the United States, Southern whites felt that blacks were better at agricultural work in the fields because their bodies could stand higher temperatures than those of whites and their brains were not fitted for study.

Thus, we already can observe two regularities in racial and ethnic relations. First, they are widespread, to be found in almost any nation.[1] Second, conquering nations and societies are never content merely to exploit their victims, and dominant ethnic groups and castes are never satisfied merely to enjoy their privileged position. They add insult to injury by proclaiming those subordinate people to be inferior, and they assert a right to rule over such inferior people. In the nineteenth century, when the sun never set on the worldwide British empire, some English leaders took a further step: They asserted that it was the White Man's Burden to rule over the darker races and to guide them toward enlightenment.

Such attitudes are not merely the superstitions of the past. The supposedly enlightened European countries still act in similar ways. The British view the Gypsies with suspicion, and the Nazis tried to exterminate them. Swedish-speaking Finns feel they are superior to the Finnish-speaking Finns, and both discriminate against their fellow citizens the Finnish Lapps. Russians proclaim the brotherhood of all "nations" within their Republic but see to it that almost all political influence is withheld from the Asiatics.

In short, the racial and ethnic relations

[1]For a cross-national analysis of race relations, see Michael Banton, *Race Relations*, New York: Basic Books, 1967, especially chaps. 6, 8–10, 11; Minako Kurokawa, ed., *Minorities Responses: Comparative Views of Reactions to Subordination*, New York: Random House, 1970; and Heribert Adam and Kogila Adam, eds., *South Africa: Sociological Perspectives*, London: Oxford, 1971.

that plague the United States can be observed almost everywhere else in the world. Moreover, the present is shaped by a past that was equally hostile, discriminatory, and exploitative. People have rarely treated as equals those whose language was different, whose physical appearance was different, who worshiped different gods, or whose customs were different.

Such "inferior" people were sometimes enslaved. Some were forced to live separately in ghettos, forbidden to own land, and required to engage only in certain occupations. Some were considered outcastes.[2] Others, like the Irish in the mid-nineteenth century, were viewed in the United States as dirty, drunken, and irresponsible—until later immigrants from southern and eastern Europe (Poles, Russians, Russian Jews, Sicilians) arrived, whereupon the Irish could feel superior to *them.* The United States then, has not been different from other past or present nations, except in one major respect: This country has had greater difficulty in keeping ethnic and racial groups "in their place," because its public philosophy has asserted that the true and rightful place of such groups was *equal.*

SOCIAL SCIENCE AND RACE

In the modern world racial and ethnic relations are increasingly shaped by two new factors. First, there is a spreading belief in the equality and dignity of all peoples and a concurrent decline in respect for traditional rulership by any dominant ethnic group. Second, there is a continuing intellectual attack by social scientists on racism, and even on the idea of "race" itself. These two factors are closely connected. Let us, then, consider briefly the recent history of the social science ideas about race.

Although dominant races and ethnic groups have not needed any additional reason for disliking or mistreating subordinate groups, they obtained considerable help from social scientists in the past century. This came from the nineteenth-century Darwinian notion of the "survival of the fittest"[3] (not Darwin's phrase) and from "scientific" studies of the abilities of different races of the world. However, by the 1930s, social science research had amassed enough data to reject both theories.

Survival of the Fittest

Charles Darwin was not himself responsible for extending the idea of the survival of the fittest to human races and societies, although the notion itself was his invention. Darwin proved that new animal species arose because every species produces more offspring than the environment can support, and thus the unfit do not survive to pass on their traits to the next generation. The animal species that could not develop traits for survival in desert conditions simply died out if an area became very dry. Deformed, sickly, or slow antelopes were quickly killed off, and only superior specimens remained. Over thousands of generations, each animal species gradually developed traits to fit its environment or died out.

When Social Darwinist theories were applied to human racial groups, it was assumed that since the Anglo nations were in power, they obviously were fittest to survive. Social Darwinists did not see that "survival" in that situation simply meant "the ability to wage war." It did not imply superiority in any intellectual, moral, or artistic sense. The Anglos also overlooked the "superiority" of other races in different historical periods. For example, it is likely that until about the seventeenth century the

---

[2]See George De Vos and Hirochi Wagatsuma, eds., *Japan's Invisible Race,* Berkeley: University of California Press, 1967, for analyses of the Japanese outcastes, the Eta.

[3]For an examination of the Darwinian notions as they were applied to societies, see Richard Hofstadter, *Social Darwinism in American Thought,* Boston: Beacon Press, 1955, chap. 9.

technical and artistic achievements of China were superior to those of Europe. Most nineteenth-century social scientists simply ignored that fact or viewed it as merely one historical phase of the vast upward evolution of humanity toward Anglo domination. That is, just as dinosaurs were dominant at one point but then died out, or the dodo was once widespread and then died out, so each nation might have its period of dominance. Nevertheless, the fact remained that at the end of the nineteenth century the dominant nations were the Anglo countries and Germany, and both felt their rulership proved that they were the fittest.[4]

Physical Traits and Race

Separate from this nationalistic behavior was a serious scientific attempt to classify all races *physically* and to correlate or link racial traits with the cultural and social patterns of those races—just as one might classify all birds or plants. It is not worthwhile here to summarize the efforts mainly of anthropologists to locate the various traits that distinguish one race from another in physical terms (length of head, curliness of hair, color of skin and eyes, length of leg in relation to height), or the ingenious efforts that were made to show why those particular *races* had developed their special *cultures*. What is important is that these were dedicated scientists, whose conscious aim was not to support racism but to answer what seemed to be a significant scientific question: How can the human races be classified, and why did they develop those particular cultural traits?

The effort to link physical and cultural traits was one of the most spectacular intellectual failures in the history of social science. After thousands of studies it became clear that there are *no significant connections* between the *physical traits* that define race

and the *cultural or social behaviors* that distinguish one society from another. Normal infants of any race can acquire the cultural behavior of any society. Blacks can become great chemists, Jews can become daring warriors, and Japanese can learn to play the music of Mozart. The effort to interpret social and cultural patterns by supposedly racial traits had been discarded by the 1930s except in racist political propaganda and in some German anthropological journals.

Modern Thinking about Race

Not all the early research was totally wasted. It led to a still more radical hypothesis, whose implications have not even yet been fully explored: the possibility that there are no adequate scientific techniques for distinguishing races *even in physical terms*.[5] Readers may find this idea difficult to assimilate, since it may seem obvious that there *are* real races; that is, blacks are physically different from whites, orientals from either, Scandinavians from American Indians, or Pygmies from all the rest. Let us examine the notion that races cannot be distinguished physically, for it is coming to have an increasing political effect in the worldwide attempts by various nationalities and ethnic groups to achieve equality.

The problem is essentially one of *scientific classification*: Where do we draw the line between and among the various biological stocks of humanity? If we select only one trait, skin color, we can divide the world's population simply by arbitrarily deciding that beyond a certain degree of darkness we shall call people Negroid. However, then we must include in that Negroid race the southern population of India, many Arabs in North Africa and Arab countries and many island people of the Pacific, although an-

---

[4]See Banton, op. cit., chaps. 2 and 3, for further data on Social Darwinism.

[5]For a brief, clear statement of this notion, see Leonard Liebman, "The Debate over Race: A Study in the Sociology of Knowledge," in Ashley Montagu, *Race and I.Q.*, New York: Oxford, 1975, pp. 19–41.

thropologists have always classified the first two of those groups as Caucasoid, or white. Moreover, many supposedly Negroid subgroups have relatively light skin and thus might have to be classified as Caucasoid.

If instead of skin color we use straight, black hair as our racial index, we find that it is common among Mongoloid races; but then we must also include American Indians, tens of millions of Latin Americans, most of the population of India (as noted above, "properly" classified as Caucasoid), and tens of millions of Europeans. Again we run into trouble.

No matter which physical traits we choose, two important findings emerge from such attempts at classification. First, any trait that roughly distinguishes most of the traditional races will also be distributed widely among *other* groups that have been defined as belonging to different races. In short, every such trait is widely distributed, and there are no sharp differences among the various populations of the world. All shade off toward one another. The Mongoloids of China may seem to be "obviously different" from other races, but these shade off into the people of southeast Asia, and these link in turn with Javanese and other peoples who inhabit the Pacific islands; the Mongoloids also shade off into the people who live in Tibet, Mongolia, much of Russia extending westernly to the Ural Mountains, and all of North and South America where Indian populations live.

The second great finding is that even when *one* trait seems roughly to capture a population that has been traditionally viewed as a race, as soon as we use two, three, or four additional traits, the overlap becomes much more extensive, and it becomes still less possible to separate clearly one race from another. This overlap is a general property of all concrete systems of classification. Moreover, it applies to the traditional "racial traits" such as skin color, color of eyes, curly or straight hair, or

Figure 10-1 Any physical trait that we pick to distinguish one "race" is found widely among others. (UNATIONS.)

roundheadedness versus longheadedness as well as it applies to the more modern traits such as different kinds of blood groups. The greater the number of traits used, the greater the overlapping, and thus the difficulty in distinguishing neatly any traditional race from another.

Thus, the scientific investigation of the links between race and culture led first to the conclusion that no such links existed; this gradually has led to the more radical proposal that it is not scientifically justified to assume the existence of any clear-cut races either.

However, the main body of early social science was less concerned with race than with a description and appreciation of the world's hundreds of cultures. Its contribution to a reduction in racism is more profound. Both anthropologists and sociologists increasingly tried, especially after World War I, to analyze society through the eyes of the natives or subordinate ethnic groups, that is, with understanding of and respect for their achievements and wisdom: the arts of many societies, their cleverness in exploiting the environment, their tragic resistance to European conquest and domination. Moreover, in scientific monographs, textbooks, and popular accounts social scientists have passed on their findings for several decades to all who are willing to read. In addition to their scientific reports, they have written numerous political tracts designed to persuade people that all groups should be respected.

Thus, although we would now classify most social scientists who wrote before World War I as racist in some sense, in recent decades almost every responsible social scientist concerned with these problems has asserted (1) that race can no longer be defended as a significant variable for interpreting social or cultural patterns, (2) that even the idea of classifying human beings by race seems to be suspect or impossible, and (3) that there is no way to demonstrate scientifically that one group is in fact superior to any other. No one can evaluate any group in that fashion except by imposing his or her values upon that group.

Consequently, a new set of factors in the racial and ethnic relations of the world has been the increasing body of scientific information discovered by social scientists. The three conclusions just noted in the previous paragraph have come to be accepted more and more by many world leaders, who at least publicly must proclaim the equality of all mankind. Those findings have steadily undermined traditional superstitions or folk beliefs about the nature of race and the inherent superiority of any group over another.

Since, however, current political and social debates continue to speak of "races," we shall use that term in this chapter, simply to designate people who are *socially* defined as belonging to one race or another.

STEREOTYPES

The social processes of race and ethnic relations contain some interesting (though yet unsolved) puzzles: Why do people seize on certain traits and not others when they think of a particular social or ethnic group? How do people maintain their image or stereotype about a race or group when their day-to-day experience with *individual* members of that group does *not* fit their image? And why do such images or notions *change* over time?

These questions all assume a fact that readers have experienced throughout their lives, that is, that people hold *stereotypes* of various groups, classes, races, and even organizations. These are images or descriptions, like cartoons, which do not change quickly even if new data are produced and which are recognized and accepted within a given social network. Stereotypes have appeared in popular literature (the Western sheriff), radio and TV serials (the dedicated physician), cartoons (the henpecked husband), political propaganda (the rich Republican club member), and vaudeville (the neighborhood drunk).

It is an index of change in these stereotypes that it is now considered bad manners in the United States to use most racial and ethnic stereotypes in films (the evil Fu Manchu, the sly Mexican who stabs someone in the back, the lazy and good-natured Southern black) or in any public entertainment. In more informal settings such as nightclubs, private clubs, social organizations, or friendship groups, ethnic and racial stereotypes are still widely used in both comedy and hostility. Vaudeville died in the 1930s, but for decades its common themes of humor depended on audience recognition and acceptance of stereotypes: the dumb Swede; the thick-headed German (before they came to be cruel Nazis); the drunken, singing Irishman; the stingy Scot; the avaricious and sly Jew; and the irresponsible, lazy Mexican. These stereotypes found their way into all popular art forms, because in fact they were widespread in American culture for many generations.

Many factors help to shape such stereotypes. The most important is one group's wish to present another in negative ways. Whatever traits are utilized in its formation, the stereotype derogates or deprecates the group being symbolized.

Note, then, what is absent from such stereotypes, but what even in the 1920s *could* have been used on the basis of the knowledge *then* available: not the dumb Swede, but the sophisticated, clever, sexually liberated Swede; not the sly Jew, but the great Jewish scientist or humanist; not the drunken Irishman, but the great Irish writer (Oscar Wilde, George Bernard Shaw, James Joyce). Second, note which traits in an ethnic group are seized upon within a given culture: All these negative stereotypes were images of *immigrants*, complete with foreign accents. Third, they are all images of *lower-class* ethnics. The use of foreign accents or "broken English" is socially significant in such stereotypes, because all peoples find the awkward or inappropriate use of language somewhat funny—perhaps because of the incongruity between the person's claim to adult status and a language pattern more appropriate for a child.

Fourth, because reality cannot be completely denied, some traits are used that *could* be positive, but they are given a negative twist. For example, it was difficult to use stupidity as part of the Scots stereotype, for they seemed clever enough; however, that trait was given a negative twist by being expressed as stingy calculations about small amounts of money.[6] So, similarly, blacks could be presented as cleverly frustrating the plans of whites, but unable to carry through a plan on their own.

Traits that are chosen to make up stereo-

types have another element in common: They cannot require much knowledge about the group or its real values, thoughts, and aspirations. The characteristics chosen must be *easily visible* to outsiders, and they must appear in ordinary interaction with members of that group. This is sociologically necessary, since stereotypes are most important for the dominant group, whose members do not have any motivation to be concerned about the details of living within another ethnic group. Stereotypes are crude descriptions, blocked out in large letters or gross strokes; they are socially unusable if detailed and subtle knowledge is needed for their creation or if such knowledge is included in them.

It is equally important, however, that learning such stereotypes does *not* require *direct interaction* with members of the group. Most people learn stereotypes about *other* groups from members of their *own* group or from cartoons, literature, or political propaganda. This was strikingly illustrated in the 1920s, when the first research was done on *social distance*, that is, the extent to which people would be willing to permit members of some ethnic group to marry within the family, live next door as a neighbor, be a friend, be a fellow worker, and so on. Toward the bottom of that list were some ethnic groups with whom the respondents were likely to have had some contact: for example, Mexican-Americans and Negroes. However, Turks, Koreans, and East Indians were almost at the bottom of the list, too, and it is safe to say that few people who answered those questions in the 1920s had had any contact at all with members of those groups.[7]

A still more dramatic regularity in the public, widely used stereotypes of the past is an omission: In such a gallery of stereotypes *one is conspicuously absent*, the White Anglo-Saxon Protestant (or WASP), though

---

[6]As Robert K. Merton has eloquently shown, the very traits that would be given a complimentary phrasing if applied to the dominant group are given a negative tonality when used in the stereotype of a subordinate group. See his article "The Self-fulfilling Prophecy," in *Social Theory and Social Structure* (1949), enlarged ed., New York: Free Press, 1968, pp. 475–490, where he reminds us of the folk recognition of our stereotypical biases, to be found in the old verbal formula: "I am *firm*; *you* are stubborn; but *he* is pig-headed."

[7]This research, done in the 1920s, is presented in a more recent analysis by Emory S. Bogardus, *Social Distance*, Yellow Springs, Ohio: Antioch Press, 1959; see especially p. 33.

in fact each of the ethnic or racial groups discussed above held then and still holds a stereotype of that ethnic group, too. In popular literature as in vaudeville that stereotype almost never appeared. Among Jews, for example, the WASP is seen as thin-lipped, without humor or irony, lacking in warmth or spontaneity, a poor sexual partner, uninterested in the joys of food, and not very clever. They are (but especially WASP *women* are) blonde, blue-eyed, and athletic (that is, they generally are not interested in books or culture, but in sports). Moreover, again within intimate gatherings, Jewish humor makes fun of those WASP traits. Chicanos accept the above stereotypes but add the WASP characteristics of being forever driven by work and always rushing to get somewhere on time.

Nevertheless, American audiences of vaudeville, radio, TV, film, and popular literature—made up of those same ethnic and racial groups—took those many ethnic images for granted, laughed with and at them, and contributed to them as writers and actors. They did not demand their removal until recently and did not create similar skits or stories that publicly exhibited WASPs as objects of fun, roguery, or debasement—although in recent years WASPs have been written about in this fashion.

It seems likely that the absence of stereotypical WASPs is partly a tribute to their dominance in American life: It is not usually safe to make fun of or to deride those who rule. Much more important is that ethnic groups themselves saw much truth in those images about themselves and indeed used them within their own circles. The stereotypes would have failed as humor or as popular literature if they had not done so. Moreover, the approved *standard* of behavior was that of WASPs. Ethnic or racial behavior was seen as deviant, amusing, or odd because it did not live up to that standard.

Finally, as a principle that has wide appli-cation, the dominant group *does not usually see itself as a stereotype*. Just as men, for example, see themselves as just people, each very different from all others, but "Women are all alike," so have WASPs not viewed themselves until recently *as a group*. It is *others* who are groups. All Chinese may look alike, according to WASPs, but WASPs do not look alike. Educated WASPs can *now* turn that joke against themselves, but they did not in the recent past. As a consequence, it was only within the sheltered circles of ethnic or racial groups that the stereotypical WASP was created. Real WASPs would have been bewildered had they encountered such a figure.

Changes in Stereotypes

Although stereotypes like those described above cannot be changed easily merely by public relations campaigns, they do change. Moreover, although the old images are only cartoons or caricatures of real ethnic or racial groups—*distorted* bits of reality presented as *typical*—*new* realities can change them. College professors and students whose main contacts with Italian-Americans are with people like themselves, and who think of Italy as a repository of great art, a source of delightful operas, a center for high-fashion clothes, and a producer of serious films (the Italian "spaghetti Westerns" rarely come to these shores), are offended by traditional Italian jokes and do not find them funny. In fact, when stereotypes seem so far from reality that even as cartoons they are not recognizable, they lose their effect. Similarly, the tiny, buck-toothed, grinning Japanese-American using *r*'s for the English *l* sound ("Rotsa ruck!"), clever at imitation but not creation, a sweatshop worker, and sly in dealing with Americans,[8]

[8]For various aspects of prejudice and discrimination against this group, see Harry Kitano, *Japanese-Americans*, Englewood Cliffs, N.J.: Prentice-Hall, 1969.

is hardly recognizable in the modern Japanese-American professional or business person whom most people are likely to encounter. Again, the older stereotype becomes inapplicable and even embarrassing. New realities do alter stereotypes.

It should be emphasized that in each of these instances we are also observing a *class* change, as more members of an ethnic group enter into higher-level occupations and become less distinguishable from the WASPs who are gradually being displaced. This point needs special emphasis, because at the present time many analysts, struck with the insistent demands of many ethnic groups that they be treated with respect, have asserted that the United States is no longer a "melting pot" in which descendants of immigrants continue to be assimilated into the dominant culture. Instead, they claim, people are returning to their ancestral heritage, secure in their knowledge that by doing so they cannot be accused of being "foreign."

In fact, however, Armenians, Greeks, and many other ethnic groups have no intention of resurrecting the culture of their ancestors. In major cities there are small ghettos, or islands, where some descendants of former immigrants still live (along with a few new ones), and within them some remnants of ancestral culture are maintained. Some ethnic leaders gain political influence by asserting those cultures should be maintained. Nevertheless, the overwhelming majority of the descendants of all ethnic groups have moved out from such ghettos, and continue to be assimilated into the dominant American culture. Those local islands of ethnicity within large cities are maintained in part because they become marketing areas for specialty foods, and sometimes tourist sites as well. In addition, they offer a home to those who wish to live in traditional ways. We should not, however, confuse this peripheral phenomenon with the massive process of assimilation that has been going on

for generations, and continues in the present as well.[9]

With reference to the place of traditional elements in the lives of United States ethnics, note that while members of all ethnic groups are being *assimilated*—that is, they are taking on the traits of the dominant ethnic group—they now have more influence and rank. Consequently, they are able to retain various minor ethnic cultural patterns if they choose to do so. They can demand that respect be given both to their group and to some of its traditional customs. For example, a Lubavitcher Hasidic Jewish manager can insist that he be served only dairy or vegetarian food in Gentile homes; a Japanese-American physician may perform the tea ceremony for admiring Anglo friends; or a black professional may display an African art collection and may even attempt proudly to trace his or her ancestry into the African period.

In considering these partly contrary changes in stereotypes, we can observe several processes that affect them.

First, it becomes both more embarrassing and more offensive to use derogatory stereotypes about another group if one's conversational group *contains* members of that ethnic or racial group. In modern life they *are* likely to be in it. Second, the stereotypes themselves seem inapplicable or foolish if they do not correspond with some visible reality. Third, since those members are part of one's own group (that is, they are *peers*), they may well be equal in influence. Consequently, they can *retaliate*. People are less likely to use negative stereotypes when their victims are there and can hit back.

At the beginning of this section we noted that one of the important questions to be

[9]For an excellent analysis of this point, see Herbert J. Gans, "Foreword," in N. Sandberg, *Ethnic Identity and Assimilation*, New York: Praeger, 1974. An earlier study of the maintenance of such islands is to be found in Daniel Moynihan and Nathan Glazer, *Beyond the Melting Pot*, Cambridge, Mass.: M.I.T., 1963.

You don't have to be Jewish

to love Levy's
real Jewish Rye

Figure 10-2 Advertising campaigns such as that for Levy's Jewish Rye do much to debunk ethnic stereotypes. (Henry S. Levy & Sons, Inc.)

raised about stereotypes is why the individual's direct interaction with members of an ethnic group does not change or alter very much the stereotype that a person holds of the group as a collectivity. Before dealing with that question, we analyzed how the stereotypes themselves change as a step toward understanding how people can remain "satisfied" with the stereotypes they have acquired from their own group, even when they conflict with the reality they actually experience. Since this special question is related to the *general* question of prejudice and

discrimination against ethnic or racial groups, it is to these topics we now turn.

Stereotypes, Prejudice, and Discrimination

Stereotypes are images that people hold about some group or collectivity. Most of them are originally acquired in childhood socialization, and they are maintained by the individual's social network and groups. Since people perceive *individuals* of another group as fitting that stereotype whether or not they actually do fit it, such stereotypes are made up of *prejudices*, that is, "pre-judgments." People *begin* an interaction with members of another ethnic or racial group with a set of judgments they have made or accepted *prior* to that encounter. As is obvious, people acquire such prejudgments about all kinds of groups and organizations, not only about ethnic or racial groups. It is rare that human beings enter into social relations with any person without any preconceptions whatever.

Thus, prejudice is the more general phenomenon. We can have prejudices about almost anything, for we have many kinds of such prejudgments, but not all prejudices are used to create the unified images called stereotypes. When W. C. Fields remarked that a man who hates children can't be all bad, he was expressing a prejudice, but not a stereotype. The prejudgment of many blacks that "only blacks have soul" *is* part of a stereotype, but the prejudice of whites (fading fast) that blacks should not sing "white" roles in classical opera is not part of a stereotype. It is only a prejudice. That is, the popular "picture" whites had of blacks did not contain any specific denial that they could sing opera.

Most prejudices take the form of *evaluative descriptions*; that is, they seem to portray the traits of an ethnic or racial group but use evaluative words in that portrayal ("X group are all dirty"). Few people simply say, "I don't like them." Instead, they give reasons: Such and such a group is dirty, lazy, irresponsible, prone to crime, immoral, or clannish.

Prejudices are *attitudes* and are likely to lead to the *action* we call *discrimination*, that is, barring people from opportunities and rewards they deserve or punishing them, simply because they are members of a racial or ethnic group (even when we cannot really differentiate a Polish-American from a Scotch-American, or an American Indian from a Chicano). Prejudice and discrimination are distinguished, then, by whether we are referring to attitudes or to action. A building contractor may, for example, discriminate against blacks without being prejudiced, because he wants to avoid trouble from a white labor union; or he may *not* discriminate, even though prejudiced, because he feels that a government-guaranteed loan will be withdrawn if he does.[10]

Prejudices, like the stereotypes that are created from them, are sociologically interesting because almost everyone harbors them and because they seem to be descriptions but are not quickly changed by better information. People also find no difficulty at all in holding diametrically opposed prejudices about the same group. Prejudiced whites who read of distinguished black lawyers, professors, or writers do not then alter their beliefs that blacks are not very intelligent. Instead, they simply believe that those cases are "exceptions." WASPs can simultaneously assert the contradictory stereotypes that Jews are clannish (they keep to themselves) but that Jews are trying to push in where they are not wanted (thus they are not clannish). Whites can believe that blacks are not talented or educated but can erect barriers to prevent their being educated

without seeing that discrimination would not be necessary: If blacks were so untalented, they would fail anyway.

When we encounter such sociopsychological or social resistances, we are wise to look for the profit—social or economic—that can be made from prejudice and discrimination. We need not travel far in that search, although our understanding is not then complete. Clearly, discrimination has widespread uses for those who can impose such barriers, and it diminishes when such people see their profit from it is being reduced.

For generations the successful attempts by United States Southerners to prevent blacks from moving into skilled or office jobs maintained a large reserve labor force that cost almost nothing when jobs were scarce and that kept farm wages low even at the peak phases of the farming year. White businesses could enjoy a virtual monopoly, because whites would not buy from black businesses. By barring blacks from the vote, whites could more easily control politics and the patronage that officials could hand out. By viewing black urban districts as deserving only inadequate public services ("They live like animals anyway"), they could keep white taxes low. Inadequate schools for blacks also kept white taxes low. By holding all blacks, uneducated and educated, skilled and unskilled, in a lowly caste, even poor whites could feel they deserved more respect than *some* people. In addition, higher-ranking whites could maintain their social, economic, and political influence by manipulating racial feelings. Progressive legislation or candidates could be voted down because any threat to the political or social system could be made to seem a threat to the racial system; maintaining the racial system outweighed everything else.[11]

[10]For a general explanation of these processes, see Hubert M. Blalock, *Toward a Theory of Minority-Group Relations*, New York: Wiley, 1967.

[11]A summary of these advantages may be found in Norval Glenn, "White Gains from Negro Subordination," *Social Problems*, 14 (Fall 1966), pp. 159–178. See also Robert Blauner, *Racial Oppression in America*, New York: Harper & Row, 1972.

Moreover, Northern whites also enjoyed those advantages, and only to a slightly lesser degree. Although many Northerners have viewed the racial superstitions of Southerners as quaint, amusing customs from a bygone past, suitable for caricature,[12] the occasionally violent resistances of Northern communities to any changes in housing, schools,[13] political offices, or jobs should prove that their supposed enlightenment was a sham.

As in other cases of colonial prejudice and discrimination, white racism was not profitable for the nation as a whole or even for the South over the long run. Since the Civil War, hundreds of billions of dollars of production were lost because blacks were barred from an adequate education or training, from high-level jobs, or from ownership of businesses. Cheap labor is profitable for the specific people who exploit it, not for the whole nation, since cheap labor is almost invariably less productive labor and its costs must be borne by everyone.

If blacks had earned more income, South and North, business would have flourished still more, but possibly not the same business people.[14] The specific system of discrimination hurt blacks and hindered the development of the nation while benefitting some specific categories of whites. If the caste system of prestige permitted lower-class whites some small measure of respect at least by reference to blacks, the system as a whole kept those whites at a lower posi-

tion, too, than they would otherwise have had. This relationship between discrimination and costs can be much more widely applied: For example, the colonies of Vietnam and Algeria were certainly a *net burden* to France, as was India to Great Britain, although specific categories of people did profit greatly (plantation owners, civil servants, army officers, and some corporations).

Thus, resistance of whites to any attack on their racial prejudice and discrimination grew partly from the advantages they got—and still get—from that system. Correspondingly, as more whites have become convinced that the total costs of discrimination (in employment, health, productivity, civic allegiance to the nation, combat effectiveness, or diplomatic relations with foreign countries) are simply too great to tolerate, private and governmental pressures have combined to reduce discrimination somewhat.

Nevertheless, prejudice and discrimination cannot be fully explained by the easy formula of "gains to the dominant group." The white racist system also grew from still more primitive sociopsychological and sociological pressures, which fed those prejudices directly and offered moral and pseudofactual justifications for both prejudice and discrimination.

Immigrants to this country were typically poor when they arrived, and a high percentage of those people moved upward only a little for many decades afterwards.[15] Visitors to immigrant districts could see that many lived in squalor. The first blacks did not come as slaves, but most did, and after the Civil War most blacks were poverty-stricken in both urban and rural areas.

However, it is typical that people who are

[12]For a balanced inquiry into Southern racial behavior and prejudices, see Lewis M. Killian, *White Southerners*, New York: Random House, 1970.

[13]For a description of the processes by which Northern public schools can have destructive effects on black children, see Jonathan Kozol, *Death at an Early Age: The Destruction of the Hearts and Minds of Negro Children in the Boston Public Schools*, Boston: Houghton Mifflin, 1967.

[14]For data on the extent to which blacks form a monopoly market for white merchants, see David Caplovitz, *The Poor Pay More*, New York: Free Press, 1963.

[15]On the social mobility of lower-class, mainly Irish immigrants in the nineteenth century, see Stephen Thernstrom, *The Other Bostonians*, Cambridge, Mass.: Harvard, 1973.

better off are *not* aroused to help those whose condition is much worse, or even to admit that the misfortune was an accident of birth or personal history or was caused by an exploitative socioeconomic system. Instead, people are more inclined to believe that somehow the misfortune was the fault of those born poor.[16] In short, people who are poor are likely to be blamed for it. Thereby human beings can make sense of a puzzling world. The misfortunes in it no longer seem meaningless.

Consequently, the prejudice that dominant Americans have felt against successive waves of immigrants, and especially against blacks, was partly a blaming process, and thus an "explanation" of the poverty and discrimination the racial and ethnic groups suffered in this country. If they were poor, it was, after all, their fault. It should be emphasized that this sociopsychological process of blaming the victim is a human pattern, common to people of high and low degree. It is not simply the evil trait of some few exploitative people. Analyses in other chapters—on prestige, political processes, and stratification—provide further support for this point.

Note, then, how neatly interlocked are prejudice and discrimination with such processes: Discrimination helps to perpetuate poverty, but poverty persuades the better-off onlookers that the victims are poor *because* of their traits. Therefore, the members of any racial or ethnic groups who suffer social or economic indignities do not *deserve* much help in fighting against discrimination. Discrimination profits those who discriminate and thus rewards people who have such prejudices and who therefore support discrimination with "good" reasons. Considering how these processes bolster one another, we can wonder that any progress at all

has been made against prejudice and discrimination.[17]

A final source of prejudice is a set of universal social processes by which people draw lines between us and them (ethnocentrism) and condemn or hate them for *their* strange, ridiculous, stupid, or evil ways. *Our* ways are right, honorable, just, aesthetically good, and reasonable; *theirs* are not. The greater the differences between any two groups, the more likely it is that they will make such judgments about each other. The greater those differences are, the less likely it is that the two groups will interact much with each other. The exception to this generalization is in black-white relations because the blacks had no such choice. They were forcibly brought to this country. They were not given the political and social right to organize their own communities or governments or to maintain any social customs that might have been a threat to white domination.[18]

Consequently, blacks in this country were not able to resist effectively the social and cultural domination by whites or to create an effective system for maintaining their own customs and beliefs. Whites were bent on justifying their slave system, and more broadly their racist system, but blacks were not in a position to develop and publish their own view of whites. As is obvious, dominant groups are *typically* able to proclaim their own superiority and the inferiori-

---

[16]For an analysis of this process, see William Ryan, *Blaming the Victim*, New York: Random House, 1971.

[17]In these respects the position of blacks has been that of a caste. On this see Oliver C. Cox, *Caste, Class, and Race*, Garden City, N.Y.: Doubleday, 1948.

[18]Music is one of the few cultural patterns that did not interfere much with white rule, and thus the African influence persisted much more strongly in that activity. For an analysis of the persistence of music over time and space, see Allan Lomax, *Folk Song, Style and Culture*, Washington, D.C.; American Association for the Advancement of Science, 1968. With reference to the cultural destruction, see "Illegitimacy, Anomie, and Cultural Penetration," in my *Explorations in Social Theory*, New York: Oxford, 1973, pp. 261–286.

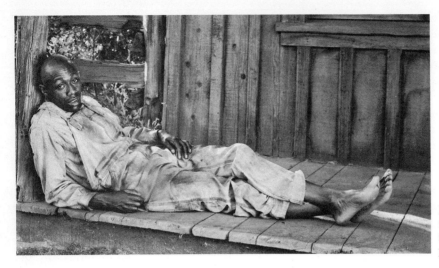

Figure 10-3 "Boy, I'se ti-ahd"—Stepin Fetchit, in a stereotypical action photo. (Culver Pictures.)

ty of subordinate groups, while denying that freedom to other racial or ethnic groups.[19] Thus, even though differences in customs and values will generate some feelings of suspicion, hostility, or contempt in groups that live with one another, the whites have been able to discriminate and to justify it by their race theories, while most blacks until recently had to confine their views to their own circles.[20]

In analyzing some of the processes that create stereotypes, prejudice, and discrimination, and some that sustain stereotypes and prejudices even when the facts run counter to those prejudgments, we have left for last the influence of an ideology of equality—a factor that was noted before as weakening the racial and ethnic pattern of

discrimination. Only a few leaders who contributed to the development of the U.S. Constitution thought that equality should be given to blacks or women. Nevertheless, that commitment to equality has not only survived every onslaught; it has increased in scope and intensity over the generations.

Thirty years ago the Swedish economist and sociologist Gunnar Myrdal labeled this conflict An American Dilemma: That is, people do believe in racism, but also strongly affirm the ideal of equality.[21] It is especially in the last two decades that one could claim equality has begun to weigh more heavily than racism (or sexism). Thus, the processes we have been describing are weakening under the pressures from racial and ethnic groups, but they are also being increasingly undermined by a deep commitment to the ideal that it is *morally wrong* to discriminate against any racial or ethnic groups. Every such group should be given equal rights.

---

[19]For some late attempts to remedy that lack, see Malcolm X, *The Autobiography of Malcolm X*, New York: Grove Press, 1966; James Baldwin, *Nobody Knows My Name*, New York: Dell, 1961; Frantz Fanon, *The Wretched of the Earth*, New York: Grove Press, 1963; and Claude Brown, *Manchild in the Promised Land*, New York: Signet, 1965.

[20]Much humor among blacks focuses on the oddities and injustices of white people. For one commentary on the special role that blacks evolve to cope with white behavior, see Langston Hughes, *The Ways of White Folks*, (1933), Vintage, 1971.

[21]Gunnar Myrdal et al., *An American Dilemma*, New York: Harper & Row, 1944. For a report on whites who object to black progress, see Peter Binzen, *Whitetown U.S.A.*, New York: Vintage, 1970.

PERSONALITY AND PREJUDICE: AUTHORITARIANISM

Many social scientists have attempted to explain racial and ethnic prejudice by reference to personality factors. This view seems to fit commonsense observation. When we encounter persons whose hostility or contempt for members of other nationalities, races, or religions is very strong, they do appear to be psychologically different. They seem to be afraid of any changes in social patterns and thus against what one might see as progress. They view political issues as clearly right or wrong, and they deny the various shades of possible opinion between the two. They look back to "the good old times" when everyone knew his or her rightful place (the Nazis used symbols associated with the time of mythical heroes). They view both children and younger adults as wild, irresponsible, and destructive of all that is socially valuable, besides being immoral. Their hates lie close to the surface, and they see punishment as the best solution for social problems. In short, they seem to have the psychological patterns that we associate with Nazi leaders.

Dozens of scientific inquiries have by now studied this phenomenon. The general personality pattern described has been given the label *authoritarianism* because one of its central factors is a need or wish to impose authority or commands on others, and also to submit to leaders because they have a position of authority, not because they are right. Authoritarianism has been linked with *anomie* (a feeling that there is little order or regularity in social life, or little sense in it); a sense of *futility* or *helplessness* (that is, the individual cannot influence her or his own fate); *alienation* (feeling one is a stranger in one's own group, or feeling cut off or estranged from others); conservatism; right-wing political beliefs; a concern with one's social rank; and many other variables.

Essentially, these studies ask the question, Is the personality pattern of authoritarianism an important cause of racial or ethnic prejudice?[22] To answer that question, researchers created a set of questions that were thought to measure the person's degree of authoritarianism, that is, his or her score on the "F scale." These scores were then correlated with many different measures of prejudice.

The findings from these studies do reveal that a high score on the F scale is correlated with ethnic and racial prejudice. People who have a sense of being powerless, of being unable to influence others, are more prejudiced. Those who are anomic—who feel isolated emotionally from others or socially unattached to others, and who perceive the social world to be without order—also show more prejudice. Similarly, people who feel uneasy in a competition with *equals* are more prejudiced.

It would be comforting if the personality pattern of authoritarianism could explain much of the prejudice we observe or experience. We could "explain" the bigot by referring to her or his unattractive personality. However, the personality approach to prejudice sheds only a small light on the complex processes we discuss in this chapter. Let us examine some of its failings.

Perhaps the most important is stated by

[22]The first major publication in this area is a series of studies in T. W. Adorno, E. Frankel-Brunswik, D. J. Levinson, and R. N. Sanford, *The Authoritarian Personality*, New York: Harper & Row, 1950. Several criticisms of this work have since appeared, notably Richard Christie and Marie Jahoda, *Studies in the Scope and Methods of "The Authoritarian Personality*," New York: Free Press, 1954. For summaries and bibliographies see John P. Kirscht and R. C. Dillehay, *Dimensions of Authoritarianism: A Review of Research and Theory*, Lexington: University of Kentucky Press, 1967. For a critical analysis from a personality approach, see also Milton Rokeach, *The Open and Closed Mind*, New York: Basic Books, 1960. A more sociocultural approach is to be found in Charles Y. Glock and Rodney Stark, *Christian Beliefs and Anti-Semitism*, New York: Harper & Row, 1966.

one analyst who notes: "One reason why the F-Scale turns out to be related to a wide variety of variables is that it contains a little bit of everything."[23] It is a general finding in sociology that when we use a very broad variable made up of numerous subvariables (such as urbanization, industrialization, or class), many social factors are correlated with it. The F scale contains, for example, some elements of personality rigidity, helplessness, aloneness, resentment, hostility, a dislike of ambiguity, and even the feeling of persecution. Attempts to "hold everything else constant" in order to test the "pure" effect of authoritarianism yield confused or contrary results because of the mixed character of this scale.

Almost as important is that people with such personality problems may not "solve" them by hating or despising different racial or ethnic groups. They may instead express or resolve their insecurity by turning to religion or even to anti-authoritarian activities, in which they challenge the right of people in high places to rule. Instead of becoming *right-wing* bigots, they may become bigots of the political *left*.

Finally, this general hypothesis suffers from cultural blindness. Societies vary considerably in their tolerance of ethnic minorities, foreigners in their midst, or even moral deviance. A variable that does not take these cultural differences into account cannot have wide application. In some societies, such as the Deep South prior to World War I or modern South Africa, the people who are prejudiced include almost everyone. In such cultures it is "normal" to be prejudiced; children are socialized to be prejudiced, whatever their personalities. By contrast, in a society like Hawaii or Brazil, people are more tolerant of all races and ethnic groups—to be sure, in part because a large part of the population has a racially mixed ancestry.[24] A prejudiced person may not be at all deviant within his or her own prejudiced culture and society. Since so much prejudice is determined by the cultural assumptions of the society, it seems unlikely that personality variables would independently cause more than a small part of prejudice when we look at this phenomenon in many societies. That is, societies *socialize* children to become prejudiced, and that can be accomplished without at all distorting their personalities.

In any event, as we noted earlier, although prejudice and discrimination are correlated, they are not the same. It is easier to change people's behavior than it is to rid them of all their prejudices or to make everyone psychologically healthy. In fact, those who are discriminated against often see a clear benefit from action alone. Many blacks have announced they do not care any more whether white people love them; they only want white people to get off their backs. People's actions may change if they are offered rewards or threatened with punishments when they discriminate, but it is more difficult to alter their attitudes. Similarly, it is easier to change behavior than to change people's inner feelings, though these too are somewhat easier to change if we can first make it profitable for them to improve their behavior. If, however, we were to try to first make everyone psychologically healthy in order to reduce prejudice, we should indeed despair, for the difficulties of such a task would be nearly insuperable.

REDUCING RACIAL DISCRIMINATION

Many conservative critics have charged that sociologists try to be social engineers, work-

[23]Blalock, op. cit., p. 7.

[24]See Andrew W. Lynd, *Hawaii: Last of the Magic Isles*, New York: Oxford, 1969; and Melvin M. Tumin, ed., *Comparative Perspectives on Race Relations*, Boston: Little, Brown, 1969.

ing out ways of manipulating the opinions and behavior of ordinary people. In the area of minority group relations, this accusation is correct, for sociologists have generally tried to persuade others that prejudice and discrimination are costly and bad. Sociologists could equally be charged with muckraking: For decades, they have published data that revealed the discrepancy between democratic ideals and the grim reality of racial and ethnic discrimination.

However, sociologists have borne such charges with serenity, for they have enjoyed the smugness of having been right all along. In contrast, the "practical, hard-nosed men of the world" and especially those who "knew the colored people well" were wrong. So were those whose kindliness and optimism led them to believe that "things will keep on getting better if we don't rock the boat and make everyone angry." (To the contrary, the economic position of blacks was actually worse in the early 1960s than in the 1950s, relative to whites.) Perhaps the prize for being most wrong should go to those who supposed that blacks were content with the progress being made, simply because the U.S. Supreme Court ordered schools to be desegregated, or because blacks were finally allowed to sit anywhere in public buses.[25]

However, the studies and experiments of both social psychology and sociology have disclosed that reducing prejudice or discrimination is not a simple matter. The racial patterns of this and all other countries are deeply embedded in every social institution and process from childhood socialization to the church, and only major changes can root them out. Let us consider some of the techniques that seem useful. To do so adds to our understanding of society, for good social engineering must rest on good sociology.

Wise social engineering must begin with the realities. Four of the most important realities are:

(1) Various groups derive profits (money, job monopolies, political influence, or social esteem) from ethnic and racial discrimination. They will not give these advantages up easily.
(2) Prejudiced people will pay for indulging that prejudice. That is, even if discrimination costs money and work or lowers the efficiency of the organization, some people may still be willing to discriminate and to pay the price.[26] Prejudice is a set of real preferences. People will abandon them about as willingly as they give up their favorite drugs, tobacco and liquor.
(3) Change is often painful, not only because habit is more comfortable, but because to change is to reject one's old self.
(4) Almost every area of social behavior is affected by racial aspects. Even when *no* members of another race are present in a given social setting, one must ask *why* they are not there, or which social pressures have excluded them.

It is difficult to locate areas of social interaction in which racism does not play any role; to eliminate racism means altering almost

---

[25] In the early 1970s a program was developed for periodic measurement ("Social Indicators") of the progress, or lack of it, in many areas of American life, among them race relations. Although useful data often appear in newspaper reports as part of a national survey, few surveys attempt to analyze the factors (such as fear of violence, education, type of occupation, or age) that affect the intensity of prejudice. An excellent study of this kind is that of Angus Campbell, *White Attitudes toward Black People*, Ann Arbor: University of Michigan Press, 1971, chaps. 4 and 5. See also Raymond A. Bauer, ed., *Social Indicators*, Cambridge, Mass.: M.I.T. Press, 1966, for comment about such plans.

[26] For an analysis of the variables that affect discrimination at the supervisory level, see Robert P. Quinn, J. N. Tabor, and Laura K. Gordon, *The Decision to Discriminate*, Ann Arbor: University of Michigan Press, 1969, which focuses mainly on anti-Semitism.

FOCUS

STRATEGIES FOR SURVIVAL IN A BLACK COMMUNITY

The structural adaptations of poverty described in this study do not lock people into a cycle of poverty preventing the poor from marrying, removing themselves from their kin network, or leaving town. But if such opportunities arise (and they rarely do), these chances only are taken after careful evaluation based on both middle-class standards and the experience of poverty. Like many white, middle-class women, black women are likely to evaluate a potential husband in terms of his ability to provide for a family. For example, Julia Ambrose estimated the man she married to be a good provider, a reliable risk. After her husband was laid off his job, Julia was forced to apply for welfare benefits for her children. Ruby Banks returned to The Flats without her husband, within a year of her marriage, embarrassed, disappointed, and depressed. Her pride was injured. She acquired a bitter resentment toward men and toward the harsh conditions of poverty. After the separation, Ruby's husband moved into his older sister's home in a neighboring town. His spirit and optimism toward family life also had been severely weakened.

Many people, politicians, social workers, urban planners, psychologists, and social scientists, have suggested remedies within the existing social system designed to alleviate poverty, and to provide the poor the opportunity to share in the economic benefits of our affluent society. Programs such as increased educational opportunities, public housing, a negative income tax and welfare reform have been proposed. These programs appear to be designed to increase social-economic mobility. Such programs are doomed to failure. This is because within our economic system these inequities are not unfortunate accidents. They are necessary for the maintenance of the existing economic order.

Two necessary requirements for ascent from poverty into the middle class are the ability to form a nuclear family pattern, and the ability to obtain an equity. Close examination of the welfare laws and policies relating to public assistance show that these programs systematically tend to reduce the possibility of social mobility. Attempts by those on welfare to formulate nuclear families are efficiently discouraged by welfare policy. In fact, welfare policy encourages the maintenance of non-coresidential cooperative domestic networks. It is impossible for potentially mobile persons to draw all of their kin into the middle class. Likewise, the welfare law conspires against the ability of the poor to build up an equity. Welfare policy effectively prevents the poor from inheriting even a pitifully small amount of cash, or from acquiring capital investments typical for the middle class, such as home ownership.

It is clear that mere reform of existing programs can never be expected to eliminate an impoverished class in America. The effect of such programs is that they maintain the existence of such a class. Welfare programs merely act as flexible mechanisms to alleviate the more obvious symptoms of poverty while inching forward just enough to purchase acquiescence and silence on the part of the members of this class and their liberal supporters. As we have seen, these programs are not merely passive victims of underfunding and conservative obstructionism. In fact they are active purveyors of the status quo, staunch defenders of the economic imperative that demands maintenance of a sizable but docile impoverished class.

SOURCE: Carol B. Stack, with John R. Lombardi, *All Our Kin: Strategies for Survival in a Black Community*, New York: Harper & Row, 1974, pp. 126–128.

every part of the social structure to some extent.

Consequently, to reduce racial discrimination calls for a wide variety of techniques, applied to different aspects of both behavior and prejudice.

Techniques to Reduce Discrimination

Propaganda campaigns It is commonly supposed that some kind of "massive propaganda campaign" would create a fundamental improvement in race relations in this country. This is as erroneous as believing that everyone will flock to buy Catclaw nail polish or Haystack cigarettes if only the sellers could purchase enough TV time. To the contrary, most advertising and propaganda campaigns are failures for the simple reason that they compete with other sources of persuasion or knowledge. Not even totalitarian governments, with complete control over the mass media, can convince subjects that the world is rosy, because people trust their own daily experience more than the governmental information.

Of equal importance are the questions raised by two distinguished analysts of race relations. Pointing out that exhortations against racism are like sermons, they ask, "Are the sinners in the pews; are they listening?"[27] The most fully documented fact

about all propaganda and election campaigns is that most of the people who pay attention are believers already. They would not bother to come or to listen if they were not. People's commitment to equal rights may be strengthened by such sermons, but the indifferent or the hostile are not affected, because they do not come or they do not listen.

Even if unbelievers do hear the message, most of them can easily deny that it applies to them. If the message is, Don't be anti-Semitic, they can assure themselves that they are innocent by saying, "Some of my best friends are Jews." If the advice is that police officers should not be brutal to blacks, they can agree, for they have never clubbed a black. In short, they can agree with a general democratic plea to be fair to blacks, without agreeing they themselves have ever been unjust to any member of another race or ethnic group.

On the other hand, to drop all efforts at education, persuasion, and propaganda would be unwise, if only because racist information abounds and it cannot be allowed to dominate the attention of the public. Since some people will proclaim that blacks are inferior to whites, it is useful to point

[27]George E. Simpson and J. Milton Yinger, *Racial and*

Cultural Minorities, 4th ed., New York: Harper & Row, 1972, p. 668. Their chaps. 21 and 22 contain the best evaluations of different techniques for reducing ethnic and racial discrimination.

out the intellectual achievements of blacks in poetry, playwriting, science, or music; to note that Southern black children who migrated to the North in the 1930s increased their IQ; to note that Northern blacks made higher IQ scores than Southern whites as long ago as World War I; and to note that many black youngsters with poor scholastic records have entered special college programs and have gone on to do fine work.[28]

It is also useful to point out the racist content of many common practices that grow from unthinking prejudice: school textbooks whose illustrations contain almost no one who is not white and middle-class; identifying criminals as black but not as white, in newspaper stories; omitting the important part that blacks have played in the history of this country from the Revolution on; or failing even to consider blacks for promotion to supervisory jobs because white employees might be annoyed. In short, both factual information and sermons serve at least the minimum goal of offering some competition against the racist information that is widespread in this society.

Here we are labeling as propaganda a wide array of messages, which range from emotional appeals to cool factual data. We do so because we realize that what is one person's "education" is another person's "propaganda." In addition, the purpose in all cases is persuasion, and those who do not like the facts presented will call them propaganda just the same.

[28]For earlier data, see Otto Klineberg, ed., *Characteristics of the American Negro*, New York: Harper, 1944, especially his "Introduction—Early Studies—The Results Obtained." For arguments against the equal capacity of blacks, see William Shockley, "Racial Studies: Academy States Position on Call for New Research,", *Science*, 158 (November 1967), p. 82; and Arthur R. Jensen, "How Much Can We Boost I.Q. and Scholastic Achievement?" *Harvard Educational Review*, 39 (Winter 1969), pp. 1–123; as well as H. J. Eysenck, *The I.Q. Argument*, New York: Library Press, 1971. See also the answers to Jensen's argument in *Harvard Educational Review*, 39 (Spring and Summer); as well as the summary of the issues in Simpson and Yinger, op. cit., pp. 203–204.

Consciousness raising   Perhaps, however, we should note that some efforts at persuasion are not directed to just anyone who might care to listen, but are presented to a specific "captive audience" such as a classroom, a summer camp, or a group of corporation managers. These efforts take many forms. Some are films, in which the evil effects of bigotry are shown, or the achievements of a racial or ethnic group are portrayed. In some, groups from different ethnic backgrounds are brought together to express their fears or hostilities openly. In others, people of one background are asked to take the role of another; for example, a *white* manager plays the role of a *black* employee being fired by a white boss or being turned down for a supervisory job. Thereby individuals learn something about their own racist feelings and also go through the humiliating experiences of a subordinate group member.

Thousands of such experiments or programs have been carried out. These efforts at persuading specific sets of persons are likely to be somewhat more effective than general propaganda campaigns. However, as social engineering they suffer from two main defects. The first is that although the subjects of those experiments do express less prejudice later, the effect is likely to be modest, and it does not last long. Afterwards, people return to their ordinary life, where their social networks give little support to their new enlightenment.

Much more important is the simple economic fact that at best such programs can reach but a tiny percent of the whole population, while the cost for each person who takes part is high. They may be useful as a way of learning which kinds of appeals will work best for which kinds of people, but they offer little hope as a solution for a nationwide problem.[29]

[29]For continuing summaries of the research conducted by social scientists on prejudice and discrimination, see

Social interaction   The politically liberal person is likely to believe that *social interaction*, especially in informal situations, will lead to understanding, tolerance, and reduced discrimination. When each person sees that the other, though of a different ethnic or racial background, is similar in important ways, both will become less prejudiced. Then, neither will discriminate, for each sees the real worth of the other. *In general*, that is a correct sociological insight. *Other things being equal*, the more social interaction, the more people like one another.[30] Unfortunately, other factors do enter, and they may prevent that happy outcome. What are some of these variables?

One is that coming to know the other person well may give us even more reason not to like her or him. Interacting with WASPs in their native habitat may convince us that they are even more intolerant, smug, and cold than we had believed.

Second, our interaction may instead let us *sympathize* with their problems, but may only strengthen our rejection. For example, after intimate association with blacks we may understand better why blacks feel hostile toward Whitey, but that hostility may arouse our fears just the same.

Third, our prior evaluations may prevent us from perceiving anything except what we believed all along. Let us not forget that literally millions of Southern white children had *some* intimate contact with blacks over the generations, but were able to see only what their white elders and peers had taught them to see. Even when they liked some blacks, they were still likely to see them all as lazy, irresponsible, dirty, and superstitious. If their intimate contacts were unpleasant, that strengthened their prejudic-

es still more. If those contacts were _ and seemed to disprove their traditi_ stereotype, most people would simp_ ceive their friends of another race as _cep-tions."

The most penetrating analyst of prejudice and discrimination emphasizes how complex the results of social contact may be by suggesting the range of variables that might or might not reduce discrimination. Here are some of the factors suggested by Gordon Allport in *The Nature of Prejudice:*[31]

> As to the *quantitative aspects of contact*, what is the frequency, duration, number of persons involved, and the variety? It seems likely that if contact is frequent, lasts longer, involves more people, in a wide variety of situations, social interaction would be more likely to reduce prejudice.
>
> With reference to the *social rank of the people in social interaction*, we would ask whether the member of an ethnic or racial minority has an equal, inferior, or higher rank than the member of the dominant group.
>
> Equal-rank interaction is more effective in reducing prejudice, though it is likely that when a minority member has a higher rank, this may serve to break up the stereotype that is typically held by a member of the majority group.
>
> In the social interaction, are the people engaged in competitive or cooperative activity? And is their relationship one of master and servant, teacher and pupil, or employer and employee?
>
> It seems clear that when the minority member is serving in a subordinate capacity, the dominant person is less likely to change his or her feelings of prejudice, or patterns of discrimination.
>
> As to the *social structure* within which the interaction occurs, it is important to know whether *segregation or discrimination* is *widely practiced* within the social structure, or is uncommon; whether the persons in interaction

the *Research Annual on Intergroup Relations.* These have been edited by Melvin Tumin and others.

[30]For the social conditions under which different forms of interracial housing will decrease prejudice, see Morton Deutsch and Mary F. Collins, *Interracial Housing,* Minneapolis: University of Minnesota Press, 1951.

[31]Gordon W. Allport, *The Nature of Prejudice,* Reading, Mass.: Addison-Wesley, 1954, pps. 262–263.

planned or desired to be there, or were forced into the social interaction; whether the social interaction is perceived as simply aimed at an artificial kind of "interracial interaction" or is part of an activity that *has other goals* (such as entertainment, or willing a contest).

Needless to say, of course, the prejudice with which each individual enters the interaction will play a large role as well.

These are not all the factors Allport suggests, but they do serve to underline the complexity of the total situation in which racial and ethnic interaction occurs and to emphasize how many factors may affect whether prejudice is reduced.

Separatism   At present, a minority of blacks, containing, however, some of the ablest of militants, outspokenly prefer separatism to social interaction. Politically, that position has yielded great influence within the black community and has served to strengthen its resolution to fight for equality. Arguments in favor of separatism have also helped to convince many whites that discrimination is becoming too costly.

On the other hand, that political position may lead to unfortunate consequences as well. A keen analyst of race relations has suggested that it may result in still more avoidance of any social interaction between the races:[32] (1) If blacks and whites separate still more, their norms, values, and attitudes are likely to diverge even more than they do now. (2) They are less likely to communicate with each other, and thus their misunderstandings will increase further. The less communication, the greater the number of distortions about what the other wants or feels. (3) The greater the amount of separatism, the greater the development of *vested interests* in each group who find it profitable to exploit the monopoly that develops with separatism. At present, many prejudiced

whites would welcome a move toward separatism, but the majority of both blacks and whites do not perceive it as a solution for prejudice or discrimination.

The Need for Cooperation

The more effective programs are aimed, not at altering *directly* the inner feelings of individuals, but rather at altering the *social structure* in which blacks and whites interact. Even the prejudiced will discriminate less if it is in their interest to change their behavior, and if people around them support that change. When blacks actually register to vote, Southern and Northern politicians do change their public words and their deeds. If corporations place blacks in supervisory positions and then help them to function effectively, employees are quick to conform.

Any "stereotype-breaking" situation (that is, where a minority person is permitted to show he or she does not fit the stereotype) lessens both prejudice and discrimination. However, the most effective social structure combines that situation with the *need* for cooperation. That is, when members of different groups *must* work together to achieve a *collective* goal they desire greatly, prejudice and discrimination are reduced. When an air force crew's survival depends on cooperation as a unit, they are much less likely to discriminate against their black gunner. If a neighborhood association is fighting an encroaching freeway, their shared political action is likely to make each person's contribution more important than his or her race. Sports teams are more likely to judge a member by his or her performance and less by race, because they want to win. In such situations, members of all types of backgrounds have a stake in the outcome and can then focus on the important issue of the goal itself, rather than on the race or ethnic backgrounds of their fellow members.

[32]Thomas F. Pettigrew, "Racially Separate or Together?" *Journal of Social Issues*, January 1969, pp. 58–59.

Figure 10-4 The fight for equality has eliminated segregated facilities, but some blacks press for more extreme segregation: total separation of the races. (Danny Lyon, Magnum.)

Legal Means and Organizations

Allied to this possible procedure—which occurs with *increasing* frequency as more blacks actually become important members of "interracial groups" (corporations, universities, opera and dance companies, or clubs)—are the quiet but continuing *legal* fights for equality. Some of the most important *foundations* for success in overcoming discrimination have been laid by such organizations as the American Civil Liberties Union, the National Association for the Advancement of Colored People, and the American Jewish Congress, which have won numerous Supreme Court cases.

Such events seem undramatic, but they have gradually destroyed much of the racist legal structure of the United States. This did not change people's attitudes by much, nor did it create a *positive* program. Nevertheless, those laws which restricted the vote, supported the exclusion of non-WASPs from houses in desirable neighborhoods, permitted all-white juries, supported segregated schools, and defended employers who wished to discriminate against black employees were eventually abolished. These laws made up a set of rewards and punishments in favor of traditional racism. It was *necessary to destroy* them in order to develop any *positive alternatives.*

In addition, hundreds of national and local, governmental and private, organizations have developed a wide range of other programs. Some of these train blacks to cope better with job opportunities or political problems. Many attempt to persuade whites to become less prejudiced. Others have engaged in both private and public campaigns to reduce discrimination in corporate life. Others have created new opportunities for blacks who have had little encouragement in their career aspirations.

The diverse goals and programs of these organizations inform us of the many areas of social life in which discrimination can be found and the considerable planning and energy needed to make any substantial changes in the larger society. They are, simultaneously, a symbol of hope. They suggest that this country is at last, reluctantly, being forced to confront its own racism and to take responsible steps toward eliminating it.

VIOLENCE, RACE, AND THE POLICE

Although the most important social forces that affect race relations are the competitive economic processes and the struggle for prestige or respect, the problem of violence probably plays a larger role in the day-to-day emotions of blacks and whites in this country as well as in other countries. This may be specified still further: Blacks fear encounters with the police and violence from fellow members of their ghettos; the police fear blacks; and whites fear both black riots and criminal violence.[33] One result of these fears is hostility on all sides. Since crime rates continue to rise, police treatment of blacks does not change radically; and since crime rates among blacks are higher than among whites, not much improvement can be predicted for the future.

For every category of criminal behavior, blacks are more likely to be arrested than whites. They are about fourteen times as likely to be arrested for robbery or murder, about nine times as likely to be arrested for assault, about eight times as likely to be arrested for forcible rape, about four times as likely to be arrested for burglary. Even after considering the possibility that whites "escape" arrest for such serious crimes simply because they *are* white, almost certainly the crime rates for such categories are higher among blacks. Needless to say, the black rates for white-collar crime, and especially for large-scale corporation violations, are lower than white rates—but these crimes do not typically lead to arrests and are not violent.[34]

As to the growing fear of crime, since the social science surveys of the late 1960s, it is also known that a very high percentage of crimes are not reported at all, especially crimes of assault, rape, and burglary. Thus, the rising crime rates do not accurately state how widespread these *experiences* are. In general, the rates obtained from social science surveys are about twice as high as those obtained from the *Uniform Crime Reports*. In almost every city people are willing to express concern about "crime in the

street," and whites are likely to express some concern about possible black riots.

As one can easily predict from elementary sociology, most crimes are committed against members of his or her own race, simply because these are the most convenient victims. Consequently, blacks are, if anything, far more concerned about crime than are whites. They are, after all, the chief victims of crime in United States cities.[35]

Whites do not, however, give blacks much sympathy for this situation, since they blame the collective black population for the violence of a minority. In addition, they combine their own *fears* of black violence with the traditional *stereotype* of blacks as prone to crime, to create a set of emotions that color the relations between blacks and whites in both official and informal interaction. In turn, law-abiding blacks are resentful because they know whites are not much concerned with the violence that blacks use on each other. They are aware that whites do not distinguish between black criminals and the black majority who do obey the laws and who would prefer security in their own lives.

A further factor in this tension-ridden situation is the racial prejudice of some police officers, which every study of police behavior reports. In addition, the police know that crime is rampant in the ghetto, and they are in danger. As the novelist James Baldwin comments:

The only way to police a ghetto is to be

---

[33]See David H. Bayley and Harold Mendelsohn, *Minorities and the Police: Confrontation in America*, New York: Free Press, 1969.

[34]The classic work on this type of crime remains Edwin H. Sutherland, *White Collar Crime*, New York: Holt, 1949.

[35]See the summary by Simpson and Yinger, op. cit., pp. 451ff.; Jerome H. Skolnick, "The Police and the Urban Ghetto," *A Research Contribution of the American Bar Foundation*, no. 3, 1968, pp. 7–9; Irving Piliavin and Scott Briar, "Police Encounters with Juveniles," in Richard Quinney, ed., *Crime and Justice in Society*, Boston: Little, Brown, 1969, pp. 247–249; and *Report of the National Advisory Commission on Civil Disorders*, New York: Bantam, 1968, chap. 8. See also Peter H. Rossi, Richard A. Berk, and Bettye K. Eidson, *The Roots of Urban Discontent*, New York: Wiley, 1974, chaps. 5 and 6.

oppressive. . . . Their very presence is an insult, and it would be, even if they spent their entire day feeding gumdrops to children. They represent the force of the white world, and that world's criminal profit and ease, to keep the black man coralled up here, in his place. . . . [The police officer] is facing, daily and nightly, the people who would gladly see him dead and he knows it. . . . There are few things under heaven more unnerving than the silent accumulating contempt and hatred of a people. He moves through Harlem, therefore, like an occupying soldier in a bitterly hostile country.[36]

Blacks know that police officers are not controlling crime adequately, and yet they fear constantly the possibility that they will be insulted, roughed up, dragged to the police station, or treated generally with contempt. The police protect each other in their delinquencies perhaps far more than the members of any other occupational group. Police officers typically feel that "law and order" are much more important than procedural or legal regularities. As Skolnick has commented, the very development of police work as a "profession," with its military-technological orientation, avoids the recognition that to violate the rule of law, to deny constitutional rights to a citizen, while putting down suspected disorder undermines the very social structure police officers are paid to protect.[37]

By and large, whites support police in this behavior, since the American population gives only mild support to the constitutional rights of people who are suspected of criminal activities. Knowing this, however, black citizens react to the latest newspaper report of police violence being used on a juvenile or adult black person by taking for granted

that the force was illegally used and by doubting that the victim was indeed a criminal. Almost every black in the large cities of the United States knows someone who has been victimized or insulted by a police officer when he or she was innocent. Moreover, since black citizens are aware of many of the criminal activities in their own neighborhoods, they are convinced, correctly, that the police must be involved to some extent and must derive some benefit from the crime that is taking place. They believe that the police not only are failing to protect them but are corrupt as well.[38] That these relationships support one another in a kind of vicious spiral is noted by Skolnick, who comments,

> Accordingly, the police come to be seen not as protectors of those who need assistance against the depredations of gang activity, but rather as those who fail in their essential task of maintaining public order. . . . Thus the police are mistrusted in the ghetto. To the extent that police are bigoted and manifest prejudices in the daily performance of their duties, to the extent that they employ different standards, to the extent that they insult black people . . . they receive the hostility and hatred of the black man. . . . This hostility and hatred, in turn, reinforces the policeman's bigotry, the policeman's hatred, the policeman's fear, and the social isolation of the policeman.[39]

Since few whites are willing to agree that it

---

[36]Baldwin, op. cit., pp. 65–67.

[37]Skolnick, op. cit., pp. 9–12. For additional analyses of both police violence and the occupational rules of police work, see William A. Westley, "Violence and the Police," in Quinney, ed., op. cit., pp. 206–216; and Arthur Niederhoffer, "On the Job," in ibid., pp. 217–238.

[38]For other aspects of police-minority relations, see Jerome H. Skolnick and Thomas C. Gray, eds., *Police in America*, Boston: Little, Brown, 1975, chap. 5. With reference to general police *corruption*, see the analyses in chap. 9.

Blacks have witnessed or read about numerous incidents in which the police have overreacted to riots, by shooting at or manhandling almost any black who was visible. Blacks are also aware that the police have been especially harsh in their attacks on politically militant blacks. Consequently, they both resent the specific police behavior they have observed or heard about and view it as one more mechanism by which whites oppress them.

[39]Ibid., p. 9.

is white racism that maintains the conditions (lack of adequate job opportunities, ineffective schooling and job training, economic and social barriers against leaving the ghetto) that generate much of black crime, they continue to blame the blacks for the threats of daily living and to blame the police for not controlling those threats. They themselves feel innocent in these matters, since they did not create the ghettos by any *direct* act of their own. Consequently, they feel justified in their fear of black violence. That fear in turn supports the prejudice they already feel against blacks.

A SUMMARY OF RACE PROGRESS

The decade of the 1960s was one in which blacks expressed their anger and despair through riots, increased political participation, nonviolent resistance, sit-ins, and demonstrations. Many whites supported that movement, and numerous governmental programs attempted to erase the inequalities of the past.

Increasingly during that decade many whites, especially in the working and lower middle classes, began to object that blacks were "trying to move too fast." News commentators often asserted that the rapid changes caused a "backlash" among whites. That is, it was claimed that whites became even *less* willing to support equality than they had been, although clearly the whites who were "lashing back" had never shown much enthusiasm for black rights at any time.

Since United States whites generally assume that the social and economic position of blacks has risen very rapidly during the past ten years, while blacks generally disagree, it is useful to consider how much social change has occurred within the recent past. Let us then look at a wide range of facts in order to gain some perspective on this matter. Here we shall simply summa-

rize the results—a kind of report to the nation—from several social, political, and economic areas, as a way of judging how much change has occurred.[40]

Economic Position

In job level blacks improved somewhat relative to whites in the fifteen years between 1958 and 1973: Their ratio to whites nearly doubled in the categories of professional, managerial, and craft jobs, while the percentage of blacks relative to whites dropped by about one-third in service or domestic work and unskilled labor.

About half as many blacks as whites (proportionally to their numbers) received incomes of $15,000 or over in the early 1970s, but this is an improvement over 1960, when one-quarter did so.

The percentage of *both* blacks and whites owning their own homes has increased by about one-fifth since 1920, so that the *gap* in ownership is as great as it was over fifty years ago.

The black unemployment rate remained twice that of white unemployment from 1950 to the early 1970s. In August 1975, black unemployment was 13 percent, and that of whites was 8 percent.

In the late 1940s black males had a median income approximately 54 percent of that of white males; this rose to 77 percent in 1974, an improvement of 23 percent in about twenty-five years! Black *women* have, however, made a dramatic improvement: Their income has risen from 43 percent to over 94 percent of the income of white females.[41]

---

[40]All the data in this set of comparisons over time comes from official United States sources, such as the P-Series of the Bureau of the Census, the *Statistical Abstract of the United States*, publications of the Civil Rights Commission, or *Current Population Reports*. Many are summarized and analyzed in Sar Levitan, William B. Johnston, and Robert Taggart, *Still a Dream*, Cambridge, Mass.: Harvard, 1975.

[41]U.S. Bureau of Labor Statistics news release, Sept. 1, 1975.

Figure 10-5 Among the influential black elected officials are, from left, mayors Maynard Jackson of Atlanta, Georgia; Richard Hatcher of Gary, Indiana; and Kenneth Gibson of Newark, N.J. (Edward Hausner, NYT Pictures.)

If we look at the younger age categories, the gap between white and black wages is somewhat less.

Although the total percentage of the whole population below the poverty line decreased from the late 1950s to the early 1970s, blacks made up a larger percentage of all those people, rising from about 25 percent of all the poor in 1959 to about 32 percent in 1972.

Education

The largest improvements have occurred in education, but they too have been exaggerated somewhat.

Between 1960 and 1974 the gap in median education between whites and blacks declined from 2.7 years to 1.3 years. The median education of blacks rose from 6.9 years in 1950 to 11.1 in 1974.

The education of blacks in Southern and in rural regions lagged, but in suburban and Western regions it came closer to the levels of white education.

The percentage of whites with four years of high school or more education increased from 26 percent in 1940 to 63 percent in 1974; that of blacks increased still more,

from 8 to 44 percent, thus narrowing the gap. Of young blacks, twenty-five to twenty-nine years of age, more than two-thirds have a high school education or more.

Most of this improvement, however, has come from a decline in *black high school dropouts.* By now, the school attendance of blacks and whites *below* college is very similar.

The gap in college graduates *has* narrowed, but very slightly: From 1940 to 1974 the percentage of whites who have had four or more years of college education rose threefold, from less than 5 percent to about 14 percent; that of blacks six times, from 1.3 to 8 percent.

The *reading* gap between blacks and whites continues to be very large. It increases from the elementary grades through high school. By the senior year blacks lag 3.2 years below the reading level of whites.

Political Influence

In one of the most important contact-jobs between white authority and blacks—the police—blacks continue to have a low percentage of posts in relation to their population: For example, in Atlanta they make up half the population, but 10 percent of the police; in Detroit, 44 percent of the population, but 13 percent of the police; in New York City, 21 percent of the population, but 9 percent of the police.

From 1960 to 1974 the number of black elected officials doubled, rising to a total of just under 3,000. However, the *number of such posts is well over* half a million! *After* that rise, black elected officials constituted 0.5 percent of the total.

In the decade 1964–1974 the number of black senators rose from none to one, a large percentage increase surely; and the number of U.S. Representatives from five to sixteen. However, they constitute 1 percent of the Senate and 3.5 percent of the U.S. House of Representatives, while blacks make up 11.5 percent of the population.

Voting among blacks has improved substantially and has begun to affect the political climate, both North and South. In 1960 twenty-nine percent of Southern blacks of voting age were registered, but 59 percent were registered by 1971 (whites: 65 percent). In 1972 the difference between whites and blacks in actually voting was about 10 percent, in both the North and the South.

School Segregation

In the past decade, in the cities with the largest black populations, few have become much less desegregated. Of those that have done so, most are in the South; the number of Southern cities that improved is about as large as the number of Northern cities that got worse (for example, New York City, Newark, Los Angeles, Boston). Generally, black pupils are less isolated racially in the South than in the North, but school desegregation has almost stopped. It has done so because of white resistance to busing (though the practice of transporting students some distance to school began generations ago and was taken for granted everywhere

until the late 1960s), the white flight from the city to the suburbs (so that there are few "white" schools that *can* bring in more black pupils), and white enrollments in private schools (from 40 to 60 percent in one sample of large United States cities). Less than 10 percent of whites favor busing as a way of reducing segregation, while the existing segregation by *housing* or residence has hardly been changed—that is, if blacks cannot easily move into "white" areas, the schools cannot be desegregated.[42]

Attitudes of Whites

Here the changes have been larger. Many standard questions about white racial attitudes have become obsolete, since new laws or practices give blacks many rights that once were strongly resisted: the use of hotels, public parks, streetcars and buses, and restaurants; and the right to intermarry with whites. Overwhelmingly, white attitudes are in favor of these rights. In 1974 almost 70 percent of whites say they "would" vote for a black for President.

In answer to the question of whether "it would make any difference to you" if a black moved into the same block, and had a similar education and income, the white attitudes changed from 35 percent saying "No" in the 1940s, to 85 percent saying "No" in 1972.

In answer to the question of whether blacks "should" have as good a chance as whites to get any kind of job, 47 percent said "Yes" in the 1940s, but even by the late 1960s almost *all* whites said "Yes."

Whites were questioned about sending their own children to a school under these three conditions: (1) where there are a few black children; (2) where half the school

[42]It can also be argued that busing and desegregation were both programs that avoided trying to solve the problem of how to educate ghetto blacks; that is, the "solution" was to bus them to better schools, rather than to make better schools. And no program seriously tackled the problem of *residential segregation*.

population is black, or (3) where more than half are black. In the 1940s there was substantial opposition to these options. By 1974 in the North only a token percentage (3 percent) would object to the first option (a *few* black children), and Southern whites who would object amounted to only 11 percent. To the *second* option (*half* black), one-fourth of whites in the North and 29 percent of those in the South would object. Overall, 47 percent of whites North and South would object in 1974 to sending their own children to schools in which more than half the pupils were black.[43]

Where Are We Going?

Not all the opinion data above are equally credible, but the mass of data over the past generation yields a firm conclusion that white attitudes are changing, and have been changing rapidly during the past ten years. Even when the poll results seem unlikely at best, as in the data above on attitudes toward one's own child attending a school half of whose pupils are black, the changing percentages inform us of an important fact: The expression of prejudice in these areas *is no longer viewed as socially appropriate.* Even to a public opinion pollster, most United States whites are unwilling to exhibit a prejudiced set of attitudes. That is at least a small step forward. At a minimum, such changes in racial attitudes make it easier to put into effect a program that yields some

practical results, such as training or hiring blacks for higher-level jobs or making better housing available. White prejudice is at least somewhat less intense against such moves when they are made.

Another set of opinion data should be noted, since we have been focusing mainly on white attitudes.[44] In general, surveys have shown that blacks perceive somewhat *less* bias and discrimination against them than in the past with reference to treatment by the police, wages paid, prices paid in stores, getting into labor unions, housing, or the respect given to them as human beings. On all these points a *higher percentage of whites perceive that blacks have not been getting fair treatment.* That is, the perceptions of blacks and whites have been coming together. If, however, as seems likely, there has been little genuine improvement since 1970, the gap between black perception of national trends and the reality will widen, and doubtless will cause more trouble. It remains to be seen whether the growing white recognition that blacks have been discriminated against will actually persuade them to support programs aimed at equality for blacks (or for any other minority group).

FINAL COMMENT

These fact-studded summaries cannot be assimilated fully by the casual reader, but they can be used as reference material in thinking about the race relations of the coming decade. Clearly, the long-delayed confrontation between the American ideal of equality and American racism has finally begun to take place. The conflict about race over the past decade is evidence of growth and development, not of pathology. Deeply embedded prejudices do not change easily, or without anger and hurt. Well-entrenched

[43]Trend data from the 1940s to the present are difficult to put together, because so many questions are not repeated later, especially when they become "out of date," that is, when almost everyone disagrees or agrees, and thus the figures are no longer considered news. The data above are from successive National Opinion Research Center studies and from Gallup reports. For sources see Hadley Cantril, *Public Opinion 1935–1946*, Princeton, N.J.: Princeton, 1951; Herbert H. Hyman and Paul B. Sheatsley, "Attitudes toward Desegregation," *Scientific American*, 211 (July 1964), pp. 16–23; *Gallup Opinion Index*, 1973; *NORC Codebooks*, 1972, 1974; *Harris Survey*, 1972. 1974 data by courtesy of James A. Davis and A. Wade Smith.

[44]From *Harris Survey*, Jan. 15, 1973.

patterns of discrimination cannot be rooted out unless organizations are willing to change their habits. Whites who resist equality for blacks will not alter their behavior until they see that others do not approve what they do, and until they see that their behavior is really costly. It is a difficult road this country has chosen to follow.

These data prove that the much heralded "dramatic improvements" in the economic, political, and social position of blacks have been vastly overrated. Both the optimist and the prejudiced are likely to mistake a few isolated cases for a massive trend: For example, a black vice president is hired by a corporation, or the family of a black professional moves into a heretofore white-only suburb. In some instances a large *relative* change has occurred (up from zero to one U.S. Senator), but the absolute amount of improvement is minimal. In many areas, as we have noted, the improvements are visible, but the gap between blacks and whites has narrowed only slightly.

In short, we are but at the beginning of the road toward equality. We shall not move backward in the decade ahead, but to move forward any great distance will require much organized effort. It seems likely that this country will in fact make that effort.

READINGS

Heribert Adam and Kogila Adam, eds., *South Africa: Sociological Perspectives,* London: Oxford, 1971.

Gordon W. Allport, *The Nature of Prejudice,* Reading, Mass.: Addison-Wesley, 1954.

James Baldwin, *Nobody Knows My Name,* New York: Dell, 1962.

Michael Banton, *Race Relations,* New York: Basic Books, 1967.

Peter Binzen, *White Town USA,* New York: Vintage, 1970.

Hubert M. Blalock, *Toward a Theory of Minority-Group Relations,* New York: Wiley, 1967.

Robert Blauner, *Racial Oppression in America,* New York: Harper & Row, 1972.

Angus Campbell, *White Attitudes toward Black People,* Ann Arbor: University of Michigan Press, 1971.

Current Population Reports: The Social and Economic Status of the Black Population in the United States, 1973, Special Study Series P-23, no. 48, July 1974.

George De Vos and Hirochi Wagatsuma, eds., *Japan's Invisible Race,* Berkeley: University of California Press, 1967.

Frantz Fanon, *The Wretched of the Earth,* New York: Grove Press, 1963.

Nathan Glazer and Daniel P. Moynihan, eds., *Ethnicity: Theory and Experience,* Cambridge, Mass.: Harvard, 1975.

Charles Y. Glock and Rodney Stark, *Christian Beliefs and Anti-Semitism,* New York: Harper & Row, 1966.

Lewis M. Killian, *White Southerners,* New York: Random House, 1970.

Harry Kitano, *Japanese-Americans,* Englewood Cliffs, N.J.: Prentice-Hall, 1969.

Minako Kurokawa, ed., *Minorities Responses: Comparative Views of Reactions to Subordination,* New York: Random House, 1970.

Sar Levitan, William B. Johnston, and Robert Taggart, *Still a Dream,* Cambridge, Mass.: Harvard, 1975.

Andrew W. Lynd, *Hawaii: Last of the Magic Isles,* New York: Oxford, 1969.

Malcolm X, *The Autobiography of Malcolm X,* New York: Grove Press, 1966.

Ashley Montagu, *Race and I.Q.,* New York: Oxford, 1975.

Gunnar Myrdal et al., *An American Dilemma,* New York: Harper & Row, 1944.

Milton Rokeach, *The Open and Closed Mind,* NewYork: Basic Books, 1960.

Peter H. Rossi, Richard A. Berk, and Bettye K. Eidson, *The Roots of Urban Discontent,* New York: Wiley, 1974.

William Ryan, *Blaming the Victim,* New York: Random House, 1971.

N. Sandberg, *Ethnic Identity and Assimilation,*
New York: Praeger, 1974.

George E. Simpson and J. Milton Yinger, *Racial
and Cultural Minorities,* 4th ed., New York:
Harper & Row, 1972.

Jerome H. Skolnick and Thomas C. Gray, eds.,
Police in America, Boston: Little, Brown, 1975.

Melvin M. Tumin, ed., *Comparative Perspectives
on Race Relations,* Boston: Little, Brown, 1969.

CHAPTER ELEVEN

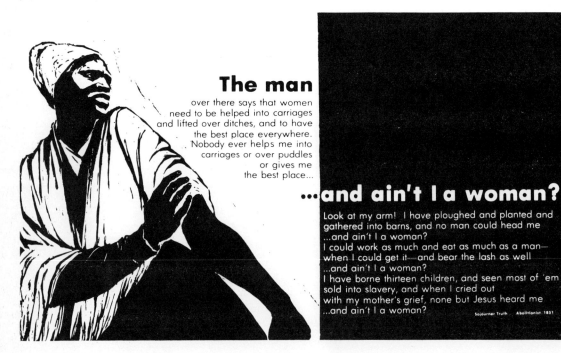

The man

over there says that women
need to be helped into carriages
and lifted over ditches, and to have
the best place everywhere.
Nobody ever helps me into
carriages or over puddles
or gives me
the best place...

...and ain't I a woman?

Look at my arm! I have ploughed and planted and
gathered into barns, and no man could head me
...and ain't I a woman?
I could work as much and eat as much as a man—
when I could get it—and bear the lash as well
...and ain't I a woman?
I have borne thirteen children, and seen most of 'em
sold into slavery, and when I cried out
with my mother's grief, none but Jesus heard me
...and ain't I a woman?

Sojourner Truth   Abolitionist 1851

(Ann Grifalconi.)

WOMEN AND MEN

Radically or moderately, social movements seek to alter traditional ways of acting or believing and thus raise a political challenge to the existing social order. One of these, the feminist movement, is part of a world-wide freedom movement that has destroyed almost every monarch, aroused the natives in almost every colony to throw out their foreign rulers, and stimulated ethnic and minority groups within nations to demand greater equality. Both freedom and equality have a universal persuasive appeal; and as each rebelling group gains somewhat greater political and economic influence, its members become more effective in implementing their demands.

Progress in the feminist movement has been necessarily slow, for many reasons. Most important is that even men who accept the general principle of equality nevertheless resist any loss of their own influence

or dominance, and they object even more vigorously when the principle of equality may cause them to lose rewards, opportunities, or prestige in their work.

A BRIEF VIEW OF THE FEMINIST MOVEMENT

At the beginning of the nineteenth century in England, and in the 1840s in the United States, a few women began to form a small social movement aimed at overthrowing men's domination. In this country it made alliance with the antislavery movement, and its leaders even agreed to support full civic rights for blacks after the Civil War, without insisting on equal rights for themselves as a condition for support. Until the 1960s the movement's high point was the achievement of women's suffrage after World War I; its history has been sporadic, fitful, and marked by periods of relative inaction and even setback. Although at present its impact can be observed in almost every major country, we cannot yet be certain what its long-term results will be. The author has commented elsewhere that women will be the last disadvantaged group to be given equal rights (the young and the old will never be). Yet it seems likely that the present movement will not die in spite of considerable male resentment and resistance, and the movement toward greater equality will continue over the next generation.

Thus, it is only since the beginning of the industrial revolution, and until recently only in relatively industrialized or socialist countries, that any substantial number of people have come to view women's equality as a defensible issue. We shall later ask why this change occurred, and more specifically why it accelerated in the 1960s.

However, the vitality of the women's movement rests on its challenge to the traditional division of labor by sex. That division has always generated an obvious inequality in the rewards allocated to the two sexes. To what extent is the sexual division of labor based on biological factors? That is, can women perform all of "man's work," and vice versa, except those functions which are specifically biological; or do biological forces limit sharply the kinds of social roles that each sex can carry out most easily? Similarly, are the psychological differences between the sexes caused by socialization? Let us then examine the sexual division of labor, as well as its rewards, for it is a fundamental organizational principle in all societies.

THE SEXUAL DIVISION OF LABOR

If we look at how societies divide work, we encounter two general regularities, which seem somewhat at odds with each other: (1)

In all societies some tasks are deemed specifically masculine and some specifically feminine; but (2) the divisions are not the same in all societies. Let us consider one such tabulation. Table 11–1 is a tabulation of sex allocations of forty technological activities of 185 societies (not nations) studied in recent times. Note that small tribes such as the Arunta in Australia count as one society, and are given as much weight as large ones.

Consider the first few tasks in Table 11–1. We can see that they do seem "masculine." At a minimum, they might require strength for especially dangerous situations. However, why should the manufacture of musical instruments (item 8) or making objects from horn (item 12) be given almost entirely to men? Similarly, those who have tried to handle the dead body of a large animal may understand why butchering is almost exclusively left to males, and so for the clearing of land; but why are bonesetting and other surgery, the collection of wild honey, and fishing?

Traditional Symbolism of the Sexes

If we do not assume that the tasks listed in Table 11–1 are allocated for maximum efficiency, allowing the most competent to carry them out, and if we keep in mind the traditional meanings of "masculine" and "feminine," more of the differences seem understandable as a result of the symbolisms that are part of our cultural heritage. For example, we expect honorific posts or occupations to be given to men, and boring and repetitive tasks to be considered appropriate for women. On the other hand, this second category cannot be the exclusive domain of women, because it comprises too much of the daily life of humanity everywhere: weaving, dairy production, water carrying, planting rice, getting firewood, spinning, or laundering. Within the less glamorous activities we would again expect

TABLE 11-1 SEXUAL DIVISION OF LABOR
sex allocation of 40 technological activities in 185 societies

	Task	Exclusively Male	Mainly Male	Equal	Mainly Female	Exclusively Female	Index
1	Hunting large aquatic fauna	48	0	0	0	0	100.0
2	Smelting of ores	37	0	0	0	0	100.0
3	Metalworking	85	1	0	0	0	99.8
4	Lumbering	135	4	0	0	0	99.4
5	Hunting large land fauna	139	5	0	9	0	99.3
6	Work in wood	159	3	1	1	0	98.8
7	Fowling	132	4	3	0	0	98.3
8	Manufacture of musical instruments	83	3	1	0	1	97.6
9	Trapping of small land fauna	136	12	1	1	0	97.5
10	Boatbuilding	84	3	3	0	1	96.6
11	Stoneworking	67	0	6	0	0	95.9
12	Work in bone, horn, and shell	71	7	2	0	2	94.6
13	Mining and quarrying	31	1	2	0	1	93.7
14	Bonesetting and other surgery	34	6	4	0	0	92.7
15	Butchering	122	9	4	4	4	92.3
16	Land clearance	95	34	6	3	1	90.5
17	Fishing	83	45	8	5	2	86.7
18	Housebuilding	105	30	14	9	20	77.4
19	Soil preparation	66	27	14	17	10	73.1
20	Preparation of skins	39	4	2	5	31	54.6
21	Gathering of small land fauna	27	3	9	13	15	54.5
22	Crop planting	27	35	33	26	20	54.4
23	Harvesting	10	37	34	34	26	45.0
24	Crop tending	22	23	24	30	32	44.6
25	Milking	15	2	8	2	21	43.8
26	Basketmaking	37	9	15	18	51	42.5
27	Burden carrying	18	12	46	34	36	39.3
28	Preservation of meat and fish	18	2	3	3	40	32.9
29	Loom weaving	24	0	6	8	50	32.5
30	Gathering small aquatic fauna	11	4	1	12	27	31.1
31	Fuel gathering	25	12	12	23	94	27.2
32	Manufacture of clothing	16	4	11	13	78	22.4
33	Potterymaking	14	5	6	6	74	21.1
34	Gathering wild vegetal foods	6	4	18	42	65	19.7
35	Dairy production	4	0	0	0	24	14.3
36	Spinning	7	3	4	5	72	13.6
37	Laundering	5	0	4	8	49	13.0
38	Water fetching	4	4	8	13	131	8.6
39	Cooking	0	2	2	63	117	8.3
40	Preparation of vegetal foods	3	1	4	21	145	5.7

SOURCE: G. P. Murdock and C. Provost, "Factors in the Division of Labor by Sex," *Ethnology*, 12, no. 2 (April 1973), p. 207.

men to predominate when the products have an honorific character, as do pottery or articles fashioned for high officials or nobles, for religious use, or as art objects. An obvious similarity within many jobs can be noted in our own society; for example, cooking is "woman's work," but kings, nobles, and fine restaurants have always hired chefs, and they are men.

Again keeping in mind the traditional

symbolism of the two sexes, we would expect tasks that permit time-and-space freedom to be masculine. With few exceptions, men will be in charge of any tasks that permit or require long trips or periods of time away from the hearth. Missing from the tabulation in Table 11–1 is how much *time* is spent at these tasks. Many masculine activities are sporadic (killing large sea or land animals) or regular but infrequent (clearing land). By contrast, many feminine activities, such as taking care of children or preparing food, demand long hours of work. However, we should not suppose that this rule generally distinguishes men's work from women's.

Table 11–1 omits, too, the structure of rewards that accrue to those who engage in the activities listed. However, we need only scan the list to perceive what we know already, that in general the more masculine tasks are also more highly esteemed. The higher the rewards paid for any activity, in money, prestige, or political influence, the lower the percentage of women doing it. Moreover, within any special activity or job the higher levels of honor and money are given to men.

For example, after more than fifty years of ideological and political pressure to give women equality in Soviet Russia, about three-fourths of the physicians are women. Yet the higher the medical post, the lower the percentage of women; and at the level of professors of medical specialities in the higher academies, women are rare. In some university departments in the United States, from 15 to 25 percent of the instructors or assistant professors are women, but it is uncommon to find any department at a major university in which more than 10 percent of the full professors are women.

Percentages and Distributions of the Labor Force

Let us consider these differences further by analyzing the percentage of women and men in modern nations who are in the labor force (Table 11-2). We see that nations do not differ much in the percentage of men who are in the labor force: Almost all are. Men have no choice. By contrast, the percentage of women holding jobs varies considerably. (Keep in mind that a woman who receives wages for housekeeping is in the labor force; a wife who does the same tasks without pay is not counted.) The ideology of communist countries emphasizes opportunities for women, and in fact a high percentage of their women are in the labor force. At the other extreme is Egypt, where in spite of much Westernization, there is little encouragement for an adult woman to continue a career after marriage.

Women in the labor force who receive wages independently of the family will have more esteem and influence than women who stay at home and take care of their families (other things being equal). However, it is clear that this variable—independent wage work—does not explain adequately the differences in the position of women in different societies. The position of women is much higher in Sweden, for example, than in Japan, but the percentage of women in the labor force is lower. In many countries women's wages have not been "independent," because decisions about whether a woman worked and where, as well as what her wages were used for, were all decisions traditionally made by family elders. Moreover, in most countries it is still taken for granted that even women who work are not to consider their jobs as steps in a career, and they must be responsible for the home as well. If women are mostly kept in less challenging, low-paying jobs, those jobs do not seem very attractive as alternatives to involvement in family life.

Table 11–3 gives the general distribution of women and men among various occupations in the United States. The only surprise is a superficial one: Women are as well represented as men in the large census category of "Professional and technical workers."

TABLE 11-2 PERCENTAGE OF MEN AND WOMEN IN THE LABOR FORCE FOR SELECTED NATIONS

Country	Year	% Men	% Women	Age Range
Canada	1974	76.5	40.0	14 and over
Czechoslovakia	1970	72.9	54.1	15 and over
Egypt	1966	81.1	5.8	15 and over
Finland	1970	74.3	48.8	15 and over
Germany (Fed. Rep.)	1970	79.7	37.9	16 and over
Great Britain	1971	81.5	42.8	15 and over
Hong Kong	1971	84.7	42.8	15 and over
India	1971	85.5	18.5	15 and over
Israel	1973	68.3	31.3	14 and over
Japan	1970	84.3	50.9	15 and over
Mexico	1970	80.8	18.2	15 and over
Morocco	1971	80.0	12.6	15 and over
Poland	1970	79.9	62.0	15 and over
Spain	1970	80.1	17.7	15 and over
Sweden	1971	69.4	37.3	15 and over
Switzerland	1970	84.3	41.9	15 and over
United States	1970	74.7	40.5	15 and over
Yugoslavia	1971	77.9	40.7	15 and over

SOURCE: *Yearbook of Labor Statistics*, International Labor Office, 1971 and 1974; Central Bureau of Statistics, *Statistical Abstract of Israel*, 1974; *Statistics Canada, The Labor Force*, October 1974; and country reports.

However, as we shall see later, this does not mean that they have equal access to the more esteemed and lucrative occupations. Most women in this category are auxiliary technical aides of various kinds, such as laboratory technicians, ancillary workers in chemistry laboratories, statistical clerks, schoolteachers, and the like. Otherwise, Table 11–3 shows with more precision what we observe daily: that women are more likely than men to be engaged in service work (which for women is usually domestic work, while the men classified as service workers are watchmen, guards, and some janitors); that those in skilled crafts are mostly men; and that most women are engaged in clerical and sales tasks of various kinds. Women are not common in the managerial ranks; and if we select an arbitrary level of, say, "Managers earning $20,000 annually," almost no women will be found in it.

Table 11–4 takes a more microscopic view, focusing on the single category of profes-sional workers over time. Since we are all likely to believe that women have steadily been improving their position since the early 1900s—and a good argument in favor of that belief can be made—we may be surprised to see how little change has occurred in many of these professions over the past half-century. During that period women have not improved their positions by much in the academic world, in medicine, or in dentistry, and they have hardly changed their near-monopoly of the "women's professions," that is, nursing, social work, and librarianship.

We are accustomed to such data. Thus, when someone refers to a lawyer, we expect that professional to be male. And while we do encounter a few women physicians, we expect them to be pediatricians, psychiatrists, and gynecologists: These are the "women's specialities." However, a view of other nations will warn us that such distributions are socially created, and are not the outcome of an open competition among the

TABLE 11–3   DISTRIBUTION OF WOMEN AND MEN WORKERS IN THE LABOR FORCE

Job Category	Percent of All Male Workers	Percent of All Female Workers
Professional and technical	14.3	15.8
Managers and administrators	14.3	4.8
Craft and kindred workers	20.5	1.5
Operatives	12.4	12.6
Sales	6.0	6.6
Clerical	6.4	34.9
Service workers	8.1	21.1

From *Employment and Earnings*, vol. 20, no. 9 (March 1974), p. 37.

talented of both sexes. In Table 11–5 we can see, for example, that, in contrast to the 3 percent of dentists who are women in the United States, 21.8 percent are women in Sweden; as against the approximately 9 percent of physicians who are women in the United States, one-fourth of West German doctors are women.

To be sure, these large differences conceal other differences. For example, in perhaps no other country has dentistry developed so elaborate a scientific and technological base, required so much education, or achieved such high earnings as in the United States. In addition, in many countries dentistry in large part is not a "free profession," in the sense of independent practice. Rather, the laboratory and office equipment are part of a governmental or corporate enterprise. Given this difference, it is not surprising that dentistry is almost exclusively a male occupation in this country.

Similarly, there are far more official levels of "being a physician" in the U.S.S.R. than in the United States, while the lowest level requires far less education and more supervision. Though nearly three-fourths of Soviet physicians are women, only a small fraction of professors of medicine are women. As in dentistry, where the necessarily heavy

TABLE 11–4   WOMEN IN SELECTED PROFESSIONAL OCCUPATIONS: UNITED STATES
(% in each category who are women)

Occupation	1900	1910	1920	1930	1940	1950	1960	1970
Lawyers	—	1.0	1.4	2.1	2.4	3.5	3.5	4.7
Clergy	4.4	1.0	2.6	4.3	2.2	8.5	5.8	2.8
Doctors	—	6.0	5.0	4.0	4.6	6.1	6.8	8.9
Engineers	—	—	—	—	0.3	1.2	0.8	1.6
Dentists	—	3.1	3.2	1.8	1.5	2.7	2.1	3.0
Scientists	—	—	—	—	—	11.4	9.9	13.1
Nurses	94.0	93.0	96.0	98.0	98.0	98.0	97.0	97.4
Social workers	—	52.0	62.0	68.0	67.0	66.0	57.0	58.6
Librarians	—	79.0	88.0	91.0	89.0	89.0	85.0	81.5

SOURCES: All data prior to 1970 from *Women's Place* by Cynthia Epstein, Berkeley: University of California Press, 1971; for 1970, calculated from U.S. Bureau of the Census, Subject Reports: Occupational Characteristics, PC (2) 7A, Table 38, pp. 582–592, 1972.

TABLE 11–5   WOMEN IN SELECTED PROFESSIONS BY COUNTRY

Country	Doctors	Dentists	Lawyers	Judges	Architects	Engineers	Scientists
U.S.	8.9	3.0	4.8	5.1	3.7	1.6	13.1
U.S.S.R.	[70.0[a]]		—	[32.5–49.6[b]]	—	—	40.0
Great Britain	17.9	19.0	[5.3]		3.4[c]	0.8	9.0
Germany (Fed. Rep.)	25.0	18.8	7.6	7.7	2.8	2.2[d]	7.4
Canada	10.1	4.7	4.8[e]	5.5	2.8	1.6	16.3
France	18.2	18.0	16.4	6.6	2.8[c]	2.6	27.3
Yugoslavia	[37.1]		[23.4]		[14.7]		—
Sweden	17.3	21.8	4.2[f]	11.6[g]	[2.0]		14.4
Japan	9.4	10.8	[1.7]		0.2[c]	0.3	—
India	8.4	11.1[h]	1.4	0	2.3[i]	0.4	4.1

Brackets indicate combined or detailed categories; dashes indicate data not available:
[a]"All types of doctors."
[b]People's Courts National—People's Courts District and City.
[c]Includes city planners.
[d]Includes categories of architect, civil engineer, and town planner.
[e]Includes notaries.
[f]Includes some executive government officials.
[g]Includes some lawyers.
[h]Dental surgeons only.
[i]Includes civil engineers.
SOURCES: Data on the following countries are based on the national census for each country: Sweden (1970), Japan (1965), India (1971). The following countries' data are based on personal correspondence with officials in each country: U.S., Jerome A. Mark, Assistant Commissioner for Productivity and Technology, U.S. Department of Labor, Bureau of Labor Statistics, based on 1970 census (Mark also supplied data for Great Britain from that country's 1971 census); U.S.S.R., L. M. Ilbina, Central Statistical Board, Council of Ministers (1975); Federal Republic of Germany, Mortl, Statistisches Bundesamt, from 1970 census; Canada, Nancy Friedman, Librarian, Canadian Consulate General, New York, from 1971 census; France, André Arnaud, Director, Service de Presse et d'Information, Ambassade de France, New York, confirming figures provided by 1968 census; Yugoslavia, Vojislav Balaban, Acting Chief, International Division, Federal Institute for Statistics, 1975.

investments in both education and equipment are made by the state, women are more likely to be given greater opportunities. Thus, where national systems of medical care exist, a higher percentage of women physicians is likely to be observed. Moreover, *within* a profession, that part of it which is contained within the governmental bureaucracy, where rules of equal opportunity are more likely to be approximated, will also include a higher percentage of women.

Whether these differences are to be explained by women's seeking a more "protected" occupational environment or by the application of equalitarian rules that permit fair competition, they prove that the low percentages of women in the highly esteemed professions in most countries of the world are not caused by an inability of women to do the job: They are created by social rules, both formal and informal.

Education and Earnings

The relationships described above are reciprocal: If an occupation pays well in respect and money, it is likely to require higher education and training, to gain its recruits from slightly higher class levels, and to be predominantly male. The higher the investment, the higher the rewards, but also the higher the percentage of men. If education leads to a modest position, such as elementary school teaching, men do not compete very strongly; but if it leads to higher-level jobs, such as school administration, a higher percentage of male students are to be encountered. A lower percentage of women

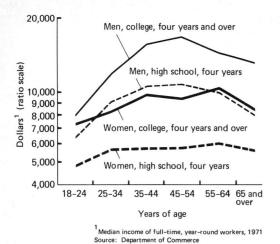

^{1}Median income of full-time, year–round workers, 1971
Source: Department of Commerce

Figure 11-1 A demonstration of the disparity in wages between men and women with equivalent education.

get the higher-level professional jobs because fewer of them take higher degrees; but they have been socialized, persuaded, and to some degree barred from those higher degrees.

The stepwise loss of women competitors is shown in Table 11–6. (In the West European countries the percentage of women receiving college or graduate degrees would be much lower than in the United States; in the socialist countries the percentage would

be higher.) In all, women drop out at the higher levels of education. Thus, they are less likely to be well represented in the higher professions. However, the women who do obtain college or graduate degrees do not obtain comparable wages. Figure 11–1 summarizes this important regularity. Perhaps the most striking fact to be noted from Figure 11–1 is that women with college degrees begin at only a slightly higher income level than men with only a high school education, and for most of their work lives they will earn less than men. Women do not achieve income equality simply through education.

However, level of education does not explain fully the distribution of jobs. For example, having a higher degree is poorly correlated with success as a corporation president, or for that matter, as a clerk or a supervisor. Education does not explain the substantial differences between men and women *within* all large job categories that are seen in Table 11–7.

As has often been pointed out, these crude differences in earnings are accounted for to some extent by "nondiscriminatory" factors: Women have less seniority and work experience; within the same large category of workers (for example, clerical),

TABLE 11–6   WHO GETS EDUCATED? MALE-FEMALE DIFFERENCES IN THE U.S.

	Female	Male
Percentage of population aged 3–34 enrolled in any school (1973)*	50.9	56.1
Median school years completed (1973)†	12.2	12.3
Earned degrees conferred (1971)‡		
B.A. and first professional degree	366,538	511,138
Percent of B.A.'s	41.8	58.2
Master's	92,363	138,146
Percent of M.A.'s	40.1	59.9
Doctorates	4,577	27,530
Percent of Ph.D.'s	14.3	85.7
Percent of population 25 years or older, completing college (1973)§	9.6	16.0

*U.S. Statistical Abstract, 1974, Table 177, p. 113.
†U.S. Statistical Abstract, 1974, Table 188, p. 117.
‡U.S. Statistical Abstract, 1974, Table 233, p. 139.
§U.S. Statistical Abstract, 1974, Table 188, p. 117.

TABLE 11-7 WOMEN'S AND MEN'S EARNINGS COMPARED: U.S., 1973

	Median Earnings		Women's Earnings as Percent of
Selected Occupations	Women	Men	Men's
Professional and technical	$9,095	$13,945	65.2
Managers, administrators (nonfarm)	7,998	14,737	54.3
Sales workers	4,674	12,031	38.8
Clerical workers	6,458	10,619	60.8
Craft and kindred workers	6,315	11,308	55.8
Operatives	5,420	9,481	57.2
Service workers (except private household)	4,745	8,112	58.5
Laborers (nonfarm)	5,286	8,037	65.8

SOURCE: *The Earnings Gap: Median Earnings of Year-Round Full-Time Workers, by Sex,* U.S. Department of Labor, Employment Standards Administration, Women's Bureau, Washington, D.C., March 1975.

they are less likely to have the more skilled and better-paid jobs; and so on.

On the other hand, such relationships are circular: Women have worked for a shorter time in most jobs because they had difficulty getting the job; they have the less skilled jobs because other jobs have been barred to them; and so on. In any event, when all such major factors are held constant, every inquiry has shown that the practice of paying women less for the same job has been widespread in the United States as well as in other societies. In this country the Equal Pay Act (1963) and many subsequent acts and judicial decisions will make that practice less likely in the future. If we examine the changes in the position of women and men during the recent period, in which it could be supposed that governmental and other social and economic pressures in favor of women would have improved their lot substantially, we find that no such change occurred. Table 11-8 shows that for two decades the trend (if any) was downward.

To ordinary common sense, however, those large differences in earnings do not prove injustice. Women are not given equal money rewards, it is argued, because the tasks they perform and the jobs they hold are not as important. Women university

teachers do not earn, on average, as much as men do, because far fewer of them are full professors, and it is only right that full professors get higher incomes. "Women managers" as a category receive lower incomes because very few of them occupy high corporate posts that pay high salaries. Women in "skilled labor" are only rarely journeymen in the skilled jobs that form the core of the unionized construction trades, where wages are higher. In short, women get less because their jobs are worth less.

However, we must probe that state of af-

TABLE 11-8 ARE WOMEN RAPIDLY CLOSING THE EARNINGS GAP?

Year	Women's Median Earnings as Percent of Men's
1955	63.9
1960	60.8
1965	60.0
1968	58.2
1969	60.5
1970	59.4
1971	59.5
1972	57.9
1973	56.6

SOURCE: *The Earnings Gap,* U.S. Department of Labor, Employment Standards Administration, Women's Bureau, Washington, D.C., March 1975.

fairs, too. Granted, performance at a higher level will be valued more, and thus rewarded more. But is there any evidence that at all these levels men have actually won those higher posts, jobs, or opportunities in an open, fair competition? In more analytical terms, can it be proved that at each succeeding stage of the process from infancy to ultimate job, boys and girls are given equal rewards for equal achievement, are encouraged equally to go on to higher, better-paid tasks (doctors or nurses, chemists or dietitians, store managers or sales clerks), and are selected at each level or type of work with regard only to the objective data about their individual skills or talents? Whether we consider a strongly male-dominated nation like Saudi Arabia or a self-proclaimed equalitarian one like Sweden or Soviet Russia, it is clear that no nation has ever achieved that kind of equality.

Moreover, although the public philosophy of "equal opportunity" has been spreading in the United States for at least the period since World War I, and by the turn of the century many women had already entered the higher professions, from the beginning of the century until about 1970 the percentage of women in law and medicine did not change. Nor did the percentage of women who were full professors increase substantially. In spite of the great expansion of the female labor force, especially in business, the percentage of women at higher-level managerial posts showed almost no change. From the 1950s to 1970 women's wages in relationship to men's wages did not improve and may well have dropped slightly. Thus, in spite of a widespread impression to the contrary, even during a long period in which the general skill level and education of women rose substantially, their share of the more rewarding positions did not increase measurably.

In short, men receive greater rewards because they have higher-level jobs, but it is also possible that they command higher-level jobs—and the opportunities that lead to them—because of their sex.

BIOLOGICAL DIFFERENCES BETWEEN THE SEXES

Given the differences found between women and men, we must continue to explore the sociological question that began this chapter: What are the foundations of the sexual division of labor? The question becomes even more puzzling if we discard assumptions about the two sexes and look at the earlier years of a child's life. A persuasive case could be made that female children are superior in many ways. Indeed, if the sexual division of labor were the reverse of what it is now, and women were actually in command, we might well find that in all the standard textbooks some of these biological and sociological advantages in favor of girls were presented scientifically as the ultimate foundation of that allocation of the best posts to women.

The biological superiority of the female begins in the womb, where far more male fetuses die than female fetuses. Far more male children are born dead, and far more boy infants die in the first year of life. More boy than girl infants suffer injuries at birth; more exhibit congenital malformations or circulatory diseases; more die of diarrhea, influenza, and pneumonia. More boys than girls die in accidents, even in the first years of life when they are presumably fully protected by their parents.

Apart from their higher susceptibility to disease and death, male babies are inferior in several neurological ways. More of them have poor hearing or deafness, color blindness, and limited vision. Girls begin to speak earlier and more frequently, and they retain this ability to handle the symbolism of language (which is, after all, the basis for the higher levels of human achievement) throughout the educational process. Boys also suffer more from reading problems, including dyslexia. Needless to say, in the United States (though not in all countries) their school performance is consistently worse. Although any simple statement about which sex "grows faster" would be treacherous—because the rates of growth vary by age and depend on which aspect of growth one considers—in general, girls remain somewhat more advanced physically than boys until after puberty.[1]

If we view "intelligence" as innate and ultimately biological, we must at least state cautiously that the thousands of efforts that have been made to ascertain the superiority of either sex disclose almost no basis for the higher occupational rewards for males. Since girls are verbally more able than boys, and since intelligence tests rest heavily upon verbal facility, girls have a slight edge in IQ tests. In the earlier years, at least, the differences in spatial or mathematical talent are minor. These do not become substantial until after puberty, when girls are increasingly shunted from both course work and life situations that might develop those skills. At a minimum, it must be conceded that if there are differences between the sexes in these talents, they are very small. For various reasons, there are probably more United States male underachievers, that is, males who show greater talent on their intelligence tests than competence in classroom performance. The overall result of more than fifty years of intensive work on this large problem of sex differences yields no evidence that males have any measurable talents that would create the patterns of allocating jobs by sex that are encountered in our society or any other society.

The past half-century of research has not settled the question of male-female biologi-

Figure 11-2 Contradicting the notion that girls are biologically ill-equipped for baseball, this Little League pitcher struck out sixteen batters and gave up four hits in a recent six-inning game. (United Press International Photo.)

cal or physical differences. The problem of proof is difficult, and new research continues to demonstrate how complex the problem is. As in other research on the interaction between biological and social factors, the fundamental problem is that we cannot easily measure or observe most of the traits or behavior that are important for social roles until a child has matured somewhat, by which time both family and society have shaped much of the child's behavior to fit the traditional sex role definitions.

It seems probable, for example, that male children have *on average* a higher propensity toward aggression (or dominance, if not ag-

[1]See Ashley Montagu, *The Natural Superiority of Women*, rev. ed., New York: Collier, 1970, especially chaps. 2, 5, 8; see also Patricia Cayo Sexton, *The Feminized Male: Classrooms, White Collars and the Decline of Manliness*, New York: Random House, 1969, chap. 1.

gression), a higher level of physical activity, and more exploratory behavior; but it is even more certain that in almost all societies female children are pressed more than males to be passive, obedient, and circumscribed in their physical movements. Cross-cultural studies show that boys in most societies are given more training to be self-reliant and to achieve, while girls are given more training to be nurturant, responsible, and obedient. Moreover, these differences are stronger in societies where males are more dominant—where large animals are hunted, war is important, the herding of large animals is common, grain rather than root crops are grown, or social life is nomadic. However, male-female differences appear in all societies, whether or not men are more dominant than in the average society.

With reference to almost any biological, psychological, or behavioral characteristic, female and male children overlap a good deal, even when their *averages* differ, and even though they have already been subjected to sex-typing socialization experiences. That is, many girls will rank above the average for boys in motor skills, space perception, strength, and aggressiveness or dominance, even though they have been trained not to be so. Moreover, almost all such differences are smaller the earlier in the child's life they are observed—thus suggesting again the weight of differences in socialization.

Finally, societies differ in how much respect and influence women enjoy, how much physical strength and aggressiveness they show, how creative they are, and so on. In short, one might argue that if all the male-female differences were really biological we would not encounter so much variation in sex role behavior among different societies. Moreover, just as sociological theories would predict, women are less like the passive, docile, nurturant, uncreative, home-bound, feminine stereotype where they are

permitted to choose different social roles. They have greater freedom where they have great control over property, where the family line is traced through them (that is, in matrilineal societies), where the husband lives with his wife's relatives, and where (as noted above) the main substance is gardening rather than grain growing and both war and hunting large animals are less important.

Nevertheless, the facts are not so easily discovered as these comments suggest. Most fundamentally, social variation does not fully prove that a given trait, say, aggressiveness or dominance, is not partially or even mainly caused by biological factors. Many biological forces are not so prepotent that they are completely resistent to social pressures, even when they have considerable influence on social behavior. Almost certainly, for example, the sex drive is mainly biological; but severe social training (in animals or human beings) can distort or even repress it, to the point that millions of biologically healthy female human beings have engaged in sexual intercourse without any desire for it or any pleasure in it. In a parallel argument Margaret Mead has stated that Balinese women and men are more alike than in the United States and that men do not even exhibit the characteristic male trait of showing sudden bursts of energy.

Thus, the variations among societies in the position of women do not prove that the biological or psychological potential of the two sexes is completely malleable, with no propensity in favor of traditional sex roles. It may well be that at least some part of the traditional allocation of sex roles is favored or facilitated by the greater or lesser ease that societies have encountered in putting females and males in those positions.

It should be reemphasized, however, that even if it were true that some biological differences make it easier for males, on an average, to exhibit command or leadership, that is largely irrelevant to the policy question of contemporary society. Even if women were, on the average, innately somewhat less comfortable in leadership roles, *some* women are clearly superior to *most* men in ways we deem important. To note the parallel in terms of class, to argue that able women should be kept back because women's *averages* on any trait are different from men's averages, is like arguing that a talented lower-class boy should not go to college because, on the average, lower-class boys do less well on intelligence tests than upper-middle-class boys do.

PSYCHOLOGICAL DIFFERENCES BETWEEN THE SEXES

Far more effort has been directed toward showing how psychological differences between the two sexes shape the social roles that males and females fill. Here again, however, the problem of proving that psychological patterns are not socially imposed remains difficult to solve. First, almost any psychological trait that one can think of differs between males and females. This creates very complex problems of research, since it is then difficult to separate the independent effect of any single factor. Second, an implicit line of logic runs through such research that differences that appear earlier in life are more likely to be biological in origin. On the other hand, since many behavioral or psychological traits simply do not appear until some years of maturation have elapsed, once more it becomes difficult to separate the influence of social, psychological, and biological factors. Next, many traits do not seem to have much connection with sex role definitions. Thus, for example, boys suffer more from dyslexia, color blindness, and hearing difficulties than do girls, but these do not seem to be related to any differences in the social roles that are given to the two sexes. Finally, and more importantly, it is not possible to measure these differences before socialization influences have already shaped the individual's responses.

Psychological Differences and Socialization

Let us consider just a few of these psychological differences that are linked to social roles and note how they might arise from socialization.

1 Even at early ages, boys are physically more aggressive and active and engage in more exploratory behavior.

It is easy to observe, however, that parents applaud such behavior in boys more than they do in girls, and the pressure on girls to be docile or passive continues throughout life.

2 Boys are more inclined to believe that their own abilities and action determine how much they achieve, while girls are somewhat more inclined to believe that what they succeed in doing occurs by chance or luck. Boys are also more realistic than girls about the level of their own abilities.

We can again observe that boys are constantly being told that their future success depends on themselves, not on their relationships with others, and that they cannot count on chance or being liked as a way of mastering the environment. Girls, by contrast, learn to manipulate the environment by manipulating people.

3 The motor skills of girls are not inferior in the earlier years; but not only do they lose ground in their later years compared to boys, but also these skills are actually worse in girls at age sixteen than at age thirteen.

This difference hardly needs much comment, since boys continue to be urged to acquire more complex and higher levels of motor skills, while girls are given relatively little encouragement.

4   Girls are not inferior to boys at mathematics in their earlier years, but they fall increasingly behind from puberty on.

Boys are pressed far more to acquire mathematical skills and to take courses in the physical sciences and mathematics, partly because they are told that these skills will aid them in adult success and partly because these are viewed as appropriate male activities.

5   Girls are quicker to speak, are more fluent verbally, and in addition remain superior in both grammar and spelling. Although boys are slightly behind in the earliest years, they quickly catch up in both vocabulary and reading comprehension.

These differences seem to reflect the training that girls are given in achieving their ends through persuasion, cajoling, and argument, as well as in acquiring the ability to "talk nicely," a mastery of the linguistic etiquette of the society. If boys are not encouraged to talk less, they are encouraged to solve their problems by their own actions rather than by social relations. Their equal mastery of vocabulary and reading comprehension suggests no fundamental differences in capacity, but a difference in what the language mastery is used for.

6   Boys who are better at impulse control do better in school, while girls do better who are nonphysically aggressive and are somewhat less than average in impulse control. The less dependent girls are brighter. Girls who have been permitted to wander and explore exhibit higher IQs.

These differences suggest, but do not prove, that boys have a greater propensity to be aggressive, impulsive, and uncontrolled. Thus, when these impulses are somewhat better controlled, the boys perform better in school. By contrast, girls come to school with greater docility and passivity and with less drive to explore. Thus, the girls who are more like boys in these respects are more likely to perform well. One illuminating finding in this respect is that girls who are poor in perceiving spatial relations are more likely to have mothers who control their explorations and intrude in their attempts to solve space problems.

7   Although the differences seem to be small or nonexistent at the earlier years (perhaps prior to school), boys are generally superior in "set breaking," that is, seizing upon some factor or factors in a total situation and analyzing them without being distracted by the social or physical context, at least in tasks that are visual-spatial. An example is the ability to tell whether a rod is upright in a situation where, say, the room itself is tilted, or where the chair on which the child sits is tilted. Presumably, this type of trait, which appears in many experiments, would aid males in the analysis of complex problems.

It is obvious that societies do not train boys and girls to be different in this respect, since parents at the earliest years would hardly know how to punish or reward the appropriate behavior. However, it is clear that girls learn to accept far more the contextual influences that are external to the problem itself, especially to be dependent on others for help or information in solving the problem, to take account of the whole situation rather than its parts, and to focus on whether other people are pleased rather than on the problem itself.

Neither these findings nor our commentary proves unequivocally any fundamental psychological differences in females and males that are both independent of social pressures and important in sex role definitions. It is at least clear that the differences that begin to appear are also reinforced and on the whole give very substantial advantages to boys in preparing themselves for adult male roles, while they prevent girls from competing successfully with boys or achieving the full potential of their talents.

Psychological Differences and Superiority

It has been argued that even if many or most psychological differences are minor at the earlier years and are possibly imposed by socialization, the innate psychological superiority of males is nevertheless exhibited in their production of geniuses. This notion is especially attractive to those who believe that genius will somehow appear, no matter what the hardships or difficulties that oppose it.

If we adopt any of the various psychological measures of creativity, such as being gifted or producing extremely high IQ scores, geniuses are common enough among women, perhaps about as common as among men. If, instead, we use the more pragmatic definition that genius is as genius does—that is, that we do not care about scores and grades and only ask whether someone has produced a creative work in the arts or sciences—then we must once again concede that though the number of women drops substantially compared to the large pool of apparent talent, there are still many women in that category. Especially in recent decades, an increasing number of women have made important discoveries or produced fine works of art. If, however, we move to the still more restricted class of great geniuses of the caliber of Bach or Beethoven, Rembrandt or Botticelli, Newton or Einstein, we do not find women in that class—and, it should be added, almost no men either. There have been women novelists of the first rank (for example, Jane Austen and George Eliot), but no woman writer in the rank of Shakespeare or Aeschylus.

Figure 11-3 Conditioning begins early, with male infants and toddlers being given mechanical toys. (Erika, Peter Arnold.)

The evidence is strong that the production of geniuses is in part a function of social factors. For example, Periclean Athens produced an astounding array of great artists, but no Beethovens; the modern world produces creative scientists at a higher rate than did the medieval world, for such opportunities and encouragement are given to young people who show scientific talent; countries differ greatly in the frequency of Nobel Prize winners they produce, but there is no evidence that they differ in potential geniuses; Jews in seventeenth-century Europe and blacks in eighteenth-century America contributed little to the physical sciences when both were mostly barred from competition, but in the twentieth century they have contributed substantially. At a minimum, it should be conceded that talented young men in Western culture have been exhorted for over two thousand years to aspire to the stars, have been supported in that endeavor and given teachers who could help them master their craft, and have been promised dazzling honors if they could create some work of genius in science or the arts—but women have not been so treated. It would at least be surprising if all these differences had had no effect on how many women geniuses have appeared over this long period.

In any event, no society rests on the presence or absence of geniuses, and the day-to-day operation of the social structure is not in the hands of geniuses. If males had to prove their genius in order to assume leadership, they would have to retire disgruntled to the hearth. The fact that Beethoven was a male should not be confused with the notion that only males are competent to manage a shoe store. It is possible that because of some hitherto undiscovered neurological or psychological factors males will always produce somewhat more geniuses than women will, but that difference is largely irrelevant to the general allocation of tasks by sex.

The almost dramatic evidence for the *social* creation of sex role definitions may be observed more precisely in the fact that women do not receive equal rewards for equal mediocrity. It is much easier to locate men of quite modest talents in command of university departments, businesses, philanthropic agencies, or offices of state governments and corporations than to find women of equally modest abilities in those posts.

SOCIALIZATION AND SEX ROLES

The apparently objective data on biological and psychological differences between the two sexes seem less clear in their implications than the observations we can make each day about how the two sexes are socia-

lized. From the earliest years onward, as we have already noted, social training aims at fitting boys and girls into the sex roles that have been prescribed by their society, whether or not their individual biological and psychological capacities are in harmony with those social pressures. Moreover, if the differences are innate, presumably they are the same in other societies; but in societies where the sex role distinctions are much sharper (for example, where men are very dominant, and try to keep women in seclusion), the socialization pressures on each sex are stronger still. That is, where people insist most firmly that "girls are different," they make sure that is so by more distinctive patterns of social training.

Whatever differences there may be in the "innate tendency" of boys to be more aggressive, independent, exploratory, and daring, one can at least observe that from the earliest weeks onward boy and girl infants are treated differently. Parents show hurt feelings or indignation if a stranger does not immediately observe that the infant is a little boy or a little girl. If the boy shows more resistance to being held (of which there is some evidence), he is given praise or approving exclamations, because it shows his strength and self-assertiveness. A crawling girl infant is kept within narrower bounds. She is constantly rewarded for being docile, sweet, and sociable. It is not only expected that boys are "more trouble," but even in the earliest months boys who are not placid, who exhibit more temper or aggressiveness, and who show more independence are given respect for being "a real boy."

It can be argued that since very young children do not yet understand the words, they do not get the message. However, modern theories about the "body language" of socialization suggest the opposite, that is, that approving and disapproving murmurs and noises, holding and restraining, and fears and joy are communicated. Indeed, modern work on the language of gesture, stance, and movement suggests that a considerable part of even adult communication is conveyed independently of verbal communication.

At a slightly later stage, certainly beginning with the child's command of language, children are told that they will become women and men and what that means. Boys are asked about job choices long before that question can have much intellectual content. Girls are told that they will grow up to be mothers and wives. In the earliest school and preschool textbooks boys are told they can become doctors and lawyers, pilots and steamship captains, plumbers and truck drivers; girls are told they will be housewives and mothers. If job options are presented to girls, they are women's jobs: elementary school teaching, nursing, school librarianship, and secretarial work. The pictures in many textbooks reinforce these inner and outer messages: Boys do, while girls watch; boys solve problems, while girls applaud; girls get into difficult situations, not by daring, but by foolishness or inadvertence, and boys save them.

In short, if we look at the socialization messages from the earliest months onward, it is easier to understand why women do not control a single major social institution in almost any society and why the highest command posts are given to men.

However, socialization is not entirely efficient, and thus all societies develop a wide range of barriers that prevent the as-yet-undefeated young woman from pushing through to better opportunities just the same. Since the late nineteenth century some determined women have managed to enter medical schools in this country, but until the last few years medical schools have had a quota system that kept women students at a low percentage of each class. So have law schools. In the university itself doors have been somewhat open at the lower levels, but almost closed at higher levels. Until very recently the police forces have barred women, and at present there are strong political pressures to close that gate or to remove the new recruits from police activities. Women have been almost entirely barred from the skilled construction trades. In short, the doors have been opened to permit women to go into "feminine" jobs; but even when their talent and aspirations seemed suitable for "masculine" jobs, the barriers against entrance have been strong.

Needless to say, the few women who have pushed past those barriers continue to encounter additional ones. Those who managed to become members of a law firm are not typically treated as equal colleagues but are often put at routine tasks, ancillary work, or library research in the preparation of briefs; in short, their opportunities are limited to various supportive activities that do not lead to wider opportunities for professional development. The pattern can be observed in any comparable occupation or profession. What we observe, then, is a set of self-fulfilling social defenses. From infancy on females are told that their capabilities and talents are not suitable for the more challenging and rewarding types of occupations, and an elaborate set of socialization pressures and barriers are organized to ensure that result. The consequence is that most women are not as competent as men in activities defined as masculine; and if they could have been, or are, it is unlikely that they will be permitted to demonstrate it.

This general process is an illustration of a widespread set of social arrangements to be found in all large-scale societies, by which one class, group, grouping, or social stratum is defined as unsuitable for a set of skills or jobs, but that result is not left to chance or choice. The people in such categories are not only socialized to be inept at those activities; they are also barred from them. It is clear that if such people were in actual fact untalented, no such socialization pressures or barriers would be necessary. They would fail without any additional social effort. However, no society is willing to undertake that risk.

THE BASES OF MASCULINE DOMINANCE

If the innate biological or psychological superiority of males could be demonstrated—and thousands of studies show that it cannot—then no one would wonder at the universal dominance of males. As was already noted, their command of high posts, of honors and rewards, of dramatic tasks, could be taken for granted since they would simply be better fitted for such activities.

However, men's social and economic advantages seem greater than can be accounted for by present evidence about biological or psychological differences between the sexes. On the other hand, common sense points out that one overwhelming evidence of men's superiority is the pragmatic one: Whatever their original, innate capacities, they have managed to be in charge. Why did they seek command, and how did they manage to succeed in that endeavor?

Let us put the first question more sharply, in defense of men. Why did men burden themselves with the dangers of killing large animals, risking their lives in war and raids, lifting heavy loads, exploring, defending their homes and societies by force, sailing the high seas for fish or trade, and earning enough at hard labor to support a family? In short, why did men venture outside the hearth and bear the risk of failure or death? Even if we grant the advantages of subordinating women, we must concede that it was not all profit.

We can speculate that in stratified societies the rules were largely constructed by the high-level rulers, not the lower-level ruled. In smaller, less stratified societies we would have to consider what advantages went to all men. Thus, in class-dominated societies we must search out the gains the upper-class men obtained from the sexual division of labor. But the gains must be partly shared by lower-class men, for they would not have followed that lead if they themselves had found such rules repugnant. Sex role definitions are not easily manipulated; people do not quickly emulate upper-class family or sexual patterns as they might follow a new fashion.

The Advantages of Controlling

Among the advantages that men, and especially men in the upper social strata, obtained are these. First, and perhaps most fundamentally, subordination means control; if members of one group can reduce another group's scope of decision or freedom, then they can also gain their own ends more easily. Controlling women gave greater control, for example, over who is to be father of a woman's offspring. Having authority over their daughters and wives, they could keep them close by, ensure surveillance over them, and guarantee the purity of the family line. They could thus arrange family alliances for money, honor, or political influence. By controlling their wives and daughters, men could prevent the dissipation of family property. Adult men have controlled younger men for these reasons, too; but the biological fact that women could become pregnant and thus frustrate family plans, while men could not, made it efficient to focus more attention on the behavior of females.

These advantages are especially important for upper-class men in large-scale societies, and for all men in primitive societies, but they are not trivial for men in any society.

Next, men at any class level simply cannot get done all that needs to be done in their small family economy without the help of a wife. These tasks include planting and herding, maintaining appropriate standards of hospitality, taking care of the children who are at once the adults' insurance for the future and their guarantee of family continuity, personal services, and validation as an adult. In most societies a man without a wife is deprived of much that gives meaning to a social existence, but men control women and thus can obtain these advantages from them. Almost universally, to men it has seemed obvious that since women were frequently pregnant or nursing children, they had to stay close to the hearth; and since they were there anyway, it was more sensible for them to carry out the range of tasks to be encountered there: gardening, preparing and cooking food, caring for children, sewing or repairing clothing, entertaining visitors, and so on.

A set of rules that defined all these as "women's tasks" would simplify daily living. By teaching young girls that this range of activities would be their destiny, men avoided arguments about who ought to do them, while they could also claim that only women were capable of doing them. Meanwhile, men were too busy at their own tasks to bother with women's work. Such a system or arrangement, once established, seems self-validating and is hardly open to challenge. It does work, and boys and girls are smoothly moved into their respective world without questions about alternatives. Grown women and men have generally believed, throughout the history we know, that the two sexes were almost as different as two species; it was as natural for women and men to follow traditional tasks, to acquire and exhibit sex-appropriate behavior, as it would be for a horse to behave in a horselike fashion. Consequently, few men or women would have believed the charge that the two sex types are socially created, that sex role definitions are imposed, manipulated, and controlled.

Thus, in asking what are the advantages that men have obtained from the subordination of women, we cannot assume a plot or plan, a deliberate male program to achieve that goal. On the other hand, the question, Whose advantage? certainly gives direction to the inquiry. It would be difficult, for example, to suppose that women aimed at being subordinate and also had the influence or ability to force men to be superordinate. Let us continue, then, with a consideration of these advantages.

Being in control gives more freedom. Men could go off for longer periods of time, farther, more often, and with less excuse, than women. By contrast, women were always on a shorter time-leash. The tasks of hearth and children cannot be neglected for more than a few hours. Men could, as they still can, refuse requests at less personal cost by claiming that urgent matters call them elsewhere.

These advantages do yield some satisfaction, some ego-enhancement: The male has commanded the center of the stage, while women have been busily engaged in the work going on behind the scenes. However one may argue that women's work was crucial and deserved equal respect, that the play could not go on if these auxiliary tasks were not carried out properly, people give most esteem to those who occupy the central roles and posts, not to helpers and aides. At present, too, men feel far less threatened by the possibility that women will gain in an open competition for jobs (in part because they do not believe women are equal in ability) than by the possible loss of their centrality, their higher evaluation as persons.

Such evaluations cannot be imposed simply by force or, for that matter, easily introduced by persuasion. A male head of a family could always demand and get overt deference by threat of force, but the society will not pay general respect for a set of tasks unless people actually feel or believe it contributes more to the collective good, is more dangerous, or requires more skill or strength—in short, that it is worth more by

FOCUS

THE OBJECTIVITY OF SCIENCE TEXTBOOKS:
HOW THEY VIEW THE SEXES

Science

In science, the most male-oriented series, three out of every four pictures are males. Throughout the science series the textbooks seem to imply that females have no place in the world of science.

For example, when we open the first grade science textbook, on the very first page we are told that we are going to learn about making things move. Immediately we learn it is boys who make things move. The next few pictures show boys riding bicycles and pushing objects. The following page contains a picture of a girl and movement, but here we find that the *wind* is propelling her balloon. It is clear she has *no control* over the movement of the balloon. The boy on the same page is *throwing* his basketball. This contrast continues throughout the series. When boys are shown, they are actively involved in experiments; looking through microscopes; pouring chemicals and experimenting. Boys control the action, and it is they who demonstrate scientific principles of motion, growth, energy and light.

In contrast, when girls are shown, they observe. They are shown smelling soap and perfume, and looking at rocks, thermometers and their sunburns. In some pictures girls are used as the objects of experiments, being injected or having balls thrown at them.

Adult women fare even worse than girls do in the science series. As Figure 10 shows, while girls are only 20% of the total illustrations, adult women are a mere 6%. In some grades, such as the 2nd grade science book, the percentage of adult women is as low as 1%. This means that in the 2nd grade science book, there are no adult women in 99 out of every 100 pictures.

Although our knowledge of women in science is very incomplete—because of the burdens they have had in gaining recognition for their work—at a minimum the science books could mention Madame Curie or Mary Leaky. Instead, science textbooks give children the impression that no woman has—or can—play a role in building our scientific knowledge. The scientific world is presented as a masculine domain: all scientists are male; only men do scientific work. The epitome of the male prototype in science is the romantic emphasis on the astronaut. But, once again, it is only boys who are shown in astronaut costumes and in the text only boys are told to imagine that they can explore the moon.

Mathematics

In the mathematics textbooks most males are shown as mathematically competent, but some of the females have difficulty with simple addition and are shown as baffled by counting to 3 or 20. These "dumb girl" images are not only derogatory and insulting to a girl student trying to learn mathematics—but they clearly contradict reality, for girls do better than boys in mathematics in elementary school. Adult women are also stereotyped: they deal only with math problems of dividing pies and shopping, and some are portrayed as mathematically incompetent. It seems ironic that housewives—who use so much math in balancing bank accounts and managing household budgets—are shown as baffled by simple addition.

Another feature of the mathematics textbooks is the frequent use of sex as a category for dividing people. For example, in explaining set theory, girls are set off as people who sew and cry. When sex is used as a category, girls are told that they can be classified as different—as typically emotional or domestic.

SOURCE: Lenore J. Weitzman and Diano Rizzo, *Biased Textbooks: A Research Perspective,* The National Foundation for the Improvement of Education, Washington, D.C., 1974.

their own criteria. The higher evaluation of men's tasks was not, and is not, a mere matter of fiat or convention.

Why were (and are) men's tasks given more esteem? We do not have a full answer to this question, but we can point to some important factors that shape such social judgments. Some are obvious: For example, people who work for the group are given more respect, and so are such social positions (chieftains, leaders of raids, shamans and witch doctors). The scarcity of a valued skill, and the marginal value of higher levels of skill, will ensure greater esteem. For example, the Polynesian navigator had rare skills, and an excellent navigator could save a group's life; by contrast, it has generally been assumed (and still is) in most societies that almost anyone could learn most of the traditional female tasks, and doing them less than excellently would not be so costly.

Thus, even in societies in which women produce most of the daily food by gathering roots, seeds, and fruits, that activity is esteemed less than hunting. Women, children, and men can all do the former reasonably well, but women and children are not substitutable for men on the hunt. The preparation of food is a skill, and so is the management of children. But neither women nor men believe (in most societies) that only women can do those tasks, while almost universally it is believed that women cannot substitute for men as warriors, raiders, and defenders; that is, to give over the latter tasks to women is to risk the destruction of the society as a whole.

Male physical attributes—greater height, weight, strength, speed, or endurance at running—did not alone create those scarcer, nonsubstitutable skills; they were, rather, a biological foundation on which the social training of males was erected. *Because* boys were to become hunters, builders, and plowmen, they were given an education toward those ends. As a consequence, even an unusually strong woman would not have had the opportunity to show that she *could* substitute for a man. The gross, powerful result is that men and men's activities have been ranked higher, not because of clever manipulation, but because their contributions have been viewed as crucial.

Given those initial advantages, which existed long before we have any written history, men used them to consolidate their position further with beliefs, rituals, myths, legends, specialized child training, and above all with the eternally available social technique of *categorization,* that is, applying the same rules to everyone in the group to prevent the deviant from raising awkward questions about what is male and female. Negatively phrased, since it is not obvious that women had superior judgment or greater wisdom in politics, war, and hunting, or a deeper clairvoyance in spiritual affairs, the masculine advantages we have already noted would have given men a dominant voice in determining who would rule, which rules would be made, and which legends and myths would bolster those arrangements. Women would have had to be clearly superior in other valued ways to overcome those advantages that men possessed as far back as we can trace the record of the species.

Nor is it at all trivial that those nonsubstitutable masculine traits and skills, which yielded greater respect in the society, permitted almost any man to dominate physically almost any woman. Pound for pound, men can fight better and on the average can whip their wives in a fair fight. Again, if women had been obviously superior in judgment or knowledge, they might have achieved more equality, but they were not and did not. As in any other animal grouping, the ability of the mature human male to outfight all other family members does not lead to pervasive exploitation and cruelty, but it does raise the likelihood that males can command greater respect and dominance. In human societies it also increases the chances that beliefs and values will be created to justify that dominance.

There is almost no possibility, then, that in some idyllic primeval period the two sexes were looked upon as equal, or that men conspired to impose an exploitative system on women. Nor is it enough to assert that a division of labor arose by which the two sexes worked at the tasks at which they were most suited biologically. *Most* tasks could be done by either sex.

However, some highly valued, necessary tasks could be done well enough only by men, and they could utilize that set of advantages in claiming the dominant posts in the society. Both men and women gave assent to the evaluations, and upon that dominance the leaders (men) could erect or maintain a set of social arrangements that solidified their position. Lacking any skills that were both crucial for the society and special to their sex, women could not oppose those arrangements, and almost certainly did not perceive any alternatives.

Moreover, that alternative male life was also perceived as hard and sometimes dangerous. For women, socialized from infancy to perceive only women's roles as appropriate, no serious choice arose. They already *had* their tasks to perform. And women did gain some small rewards from the position. They were defended by their men, they did enjoy some autonomy in their own household, and men did bring home their spoils of war, the hunt, or the market. That is, men have been as surprised by the feminist movement as Southern whites were to discover that "their" blacks were not contented.

In most societies, the male alternative would not have seemed a desirable life of ease. In all large-scale societies, and perhaps in most small ones as well, both men and women have had to work hard and long in order to support themselves. Although European travelers have remarked that men in Greek, Latin American, or Arab rural society talk comfortably with one another while the women are gathering firewood or carrying water, a longer observation would have disclosed that the men also engage in hard labor. In plain economic terms, aside from one's feminine or masculine biases, few women are so productive in any society that their husbands can indulge in much loafing at women's expense. Whatever one's definition of "exploitation," men have not been clever enough to make sufficient profit from women's labor to reduce their own workload by much. Where some men were able to enjoy life without devoting much energy to production, they did so by exploiting another *class*—serfs, slaves, colonials, or a proletariat. They could not, except rarely, live off their wives' labor.

MEN AND WOMEN IN TRANSITION

It is only very recently in world history that the major elements in these relationships have changed sufficiently to permit a major challenge to male domination. Until the turn of this century most people worked on farms even in the Western nations; and at numerous phases of agricultural work, a male's contribution was essential. Only since World War II has almost every lifting and loading job been given to machines that anyone can operate. Since World War I the percentage of the population in agricultural work has dropped, while the main expansion of the work force has occurred in management, clerical and office machine work, and professional jobs, which are not "masculine" in any obvious sense. Even in our recent wars millions of foot-soldiers were used, and they carried heavy packs that most women could not have handled. It was only during the twentieth century, too, that most women came to have about as much education as men.

Those changes did not themselves cause women to become restive, to object to their position in society. They did, however, weaken all the traditional arguments in favor of men's *necessary* domination. It has become increasingly difficult to point to any kind of task that "women can't do," in part because some woman is doing it, somewhere.

Against that possible relaxing of traditional restrictions, however, are settled customs, strong traditional attitudes, a complex body of law that supposedly protected women by placing them (as well as some or all their property) under men's control, a worldwide pattern of sex role socialization, restrictions on hiring and on wages paid, and so on. Consequently, even the changes in the technological, economic, and managerial systems that created jobs either sex could do reasonably well would not have been enough to cause the growing conviction that women should be given equality. Those changes were necessary, but not enough. Additional forces were needed to create the recent movement in favor of women's rights. Knowing those forces, could we have predicted that set of events?

Sociological principles, created to understand recurring or general patterns, cannot predict any unique historical event. Indeed, science typically has no tools for predicting unique events. Rather, it focuses on the abstract or universal conditions under which certain classes of events take place. Those general principles can be used to understand what has happened, but they cannot predict particular occurrences. Let us, however, at least attempt to illuminate to some extent why the feminist movement took on added dimensions and urgency in the 1960s.

The Forces of Change

Perhaps the most important relationship to be discerned in the resurgence of political and social pressure in favor of women's equality is this: the contrast between the steady rise in education, qualifications, and work experience of women over the past half-century and the lack of improvement or actual decline in the occupational and economic position of women through the 1950s and indeed continuing through the 1960s. Whatever index may be used, decades ago women began increasingly to catch up educationally with men at least through the level of high school. Almost all women came to have some work experience and to discover that they could carry out a range of jobs that, if they had been men, would have led to still higher jobs.

Equally importantly, the experience of World War II labor shortage proved that women could quickly master even jobs that had been traditionally reserved only for men, such as riveting, welding, ship building, and highly technical scientific jobs. Thus, the evidence was clear that almost any job could be discharged responsibly by a woman, if she were asked to do it. Men became substitutable as never before.

There is also some possibility, not fully demonstrated as yet, that the period of the 1950s, after women had been dropped from wartime jobs, was one of considerable home-centered propaganda. Women's magazines, as analyzed by Betty Friedan in *The Feminine Mystique*, were replete with exhortations to view the home as a creative challenge, to devote more time to children, and to find satisfaction in being a homemaker, wife, and mother. The persuasion was especially directed to the more educated women; and during the 1950s it became almost fashionable, especially among upper-middle-class and professional families, to have three or four children, which required considerable attention to home and family. However, many women who tried this route to self-fulfillment found it disappointing and hollow. Those who were most affected were women with more education and talent, and if they were momentarily persuaded by it, they became equally unsatisfied. As their own children matured, such women found in themselves little capacity for continued growth, as they might have had if their choice had been a profession instead.

Perhaps of greater importance, however, is the continued spread of the ideology of equality, applied not merely to women, but also to blacks, other ethnic groups, and indeed all ascribed statuses. The American population as a whole, in all strata, has been told that the doors are open to talent and hard work. In spite of the obvious fact that doors are not fully open, few people challenge that ideological position in public: If they are not open, at least they should be open. Thus, women's negative experiences revealed a discrepancy between what they were promised and what they could actually obtain. Consequently, an increasing number of women came to feel that the system itself was fraudulent, just as blacks in the 1960s began to express that notion more publicly and insistently.

Less attention has been devoted to a factor that may be of still more central importance: No matter what women achieved, in school or in their work experience, they were given less respect than men were given for any level of attainment. This occurred both in informal social relations and in work. Women were, as they still are, patronized even when they demonstrated their ability to perform at a high level.

In effect, then, women came to perceive that the promise held out to them was false. They had been told that since they were inferior, they earned less respect, and that if they only performed at the level of men, their work would be rated as highly as that of men. But that promise was broken in the real world. One type of experiment demonstrates this neatly. An article is presented to two sets of people, both women and men, who are asked to evaluate it. One group is told that the author is a man, the other that the author is a woman. A higher percentage of readers evaluate the article as superior when they are told that it was written by a man.

The rule that members of one ascriptive status are not given the same respect for the same achievement as members of other statuses is general throughout all societies. Not only does the exceptional person from a lower-ranking group not change the respect or rank of his or her own membership group; but rarely will that person be given as much individual esteem for any achieve-

Figure 11-4 The labor shortage during World War II dispelled many of the myths about the kind of work women could do, and "Rosie the Riveter" became a common sight. (Culver Pictures, Inc.)

ment as a person in the dominant group would be given. In Chapter 4, on prestige, we analyzed this general pattern more fully. It should also be noted here that this pattern supports the more general social arrangements by which people in an ascribed, subordinate social position are told that they do not have the innate ability to achieve, but are also prevented from even trying to achieve in a way that would prove that assertion to be false.

REGULARITIES OF REBELLION   *social*

The feminist movement over the last decade exhibits many of the social regularities that can be observed in almost any attempt by a social category or group to improve its position relative to a dominant group or stratum. It is too extreme to call this a women's revolution, but these patterns are also to be found in the interaction of whites and blacks over the past two decades, in radical revolutions, and in colonial rebellions.

A most important social regularity is that those who were oppressed redefine their social situation. Specifically, they begin to perceive that the discontent or complaints they felt before are not simply a personal or individual problem, but that the whole social category of which they are a member suffers in a similar fashion. That is, they begin to perceive themselves as a group or class, and the problem as a social or systemic one. That problem, therefore, cannot be remedied mainly by individual effort or personal bargaining. The society itself must change if their lives are to be improved.

Second, although that perception is at first confined to a small group of leaders who are mostly in a superior position and hardly to be classed as downtrodden, soon the perception extends to a large number of people who themselves may not even take an active part in the movement. Nevertheless, they share that new definition of their social situation. Typically, this includes a large number of people who were not even aware before that they were suffering greatly or were very discontented.

Third, those who have been dominant—in this case, men—are surprised at the outbreak. They had supposed that women were content. If they were aware of complaints, they simply viewed that as characteristic of women anyway. It had not occurred to them that women as a group felt their entire social situation was unjust.

Consequently, men are both hurt and angry. They are hurt because they feel that they have always taken care of their women (and similarly, colonial administrators felt that they were taking good care of "their" natives); they feel that they have sacrificed themselves or worked hard for their women. They are also angry because they feel somewhat betrayed. Before, their relations seemed to be happy or at least relatively content. But now they discover that that behavior was false, and a mere facade. Underneath it, women were resentful. Moreover, men are angry because the challenge is a threat to their position. Their centrality is under threat. They are asked to prove their good intentions, their fairness, and their right to rule and be served. Since in all situations of deference and respect behavior rests upon relatively unquestioned assumptions that are difficult to justify, such a challenge arouses anger.

A further source of men's anger should be noted. Since they do not take women's career aspirations seriously to begin with and do not believe in women's commitment to work, they feel that the entrance of women trivializes their own work. They have to work; women do not. Like factory workers and laborers who resent the rich boy who takes a summer job in order to experience "what real work is like," many men feel that women are essentially playacting the role of a job holder. Women can get the rewards of the occupation, but (like the boss's son working in the stockroom or the lawyer's son working on the assembly line) can escape at any time and thus avoid the anguish of a life that always depends on job holding.

Next, women (or natives) who come to sympathize with the movement discover that they harbor within themselves a great reservoir of hostility and resentment, which is now unleashed. They are able to express anger and animosity that were repressed before, and begin to remember and to dwell upon events, processes, and relationships that they had not previously questioned much. That is, it is not merely that they

have changed their mind and from now on begin to perceive injustice where they had not done so before. In addition, they discover within themselves that they had always felt resentment at the injustice and that they have been collecting injustices in their memory.

Since those who now feel oppressed come to view themselves as a category or class, they begin to seek each other out, to talk a great deal, to "raise their consciousness" about their problem. Those who take an active part feel a sudden growth in energy and capacity. They are no longer apathetic, and they feel that they can accomplish great tasks.

Parallel with that, they begin to support one another in these new plans and enterprises. In graduate school women encourage one another to drive directly toward the doctorate instead of subordinating their career goals to those of their husband or dropping out of school for a while to have a child. They are willing to take part in supporting the complaints by women against employers on an informal or formal basis.

This support also takes another form, which is that women begin to find each other far more interesting than before. It has been characteristic in informal social gatherings that men and women separated into one-sex groups in order to talk about common interests; women felt that they were being excluded and believed that the most interesting talk was going on in the men's group. Now it has become somewhat more common for women to take the trouble to find out what other women are thinking about and doing. Since they are in fact doing more interesting things, women find this talk more worthwhile. They discover that women whom they had viewed as having nothing to say are in fact more substantial and worthwhile as human beings than they had supposed.

Finally, in the development of any movement, organizations and counterorganizations spring up. Ideological splits create additional organizations and caucuses. Such organizations become a vehicle for political pressure, administrative influence, and the development of plans for additional propaganda, fund seeking, research, investigation, and mutual support. Individual women come to be thought of as representatives of the movement because they are officers in one organization or another. People who seek political offices consult them in the hope of gaining additional votes. Since most people do not join such organizations, their numbers typically remain small. Their influence is not illusory, however, because millions of women support the general aims of these organizations, even when they are not active members.

THE FUTURE OF THE FEMINIST MOVEMENT

Just as social science could not predict the feminist movement would happen when it did (as it cannot predict any other unique event), so it is difficult to predict the continuing impact of this movement on the society. It is at least speculatively possible that a retrogressive movement might set in, opposed to any further movement toward equality for women. But at the present time that seems highly unlikely. If change comes slowly for the reasons listed at the beginning of this chapter, we must also note that the problem is fundamental to the establishment of any new social system. That is, new social arrangements have to be created and supported precisely by the people who have maintained the older system. They cannot easily change their habits, and they have a high material and emotional stake in the older system. Even when the new principles are generally acceptable, people's older patterns of behavior continue to mold the younger generation in traditional ways.

Finally, no society has as yet worked out

adequately the social problems that would arise under a system of complete equality. Many solutions for these problems have been proposed, but most people find them all unacceptable. The fundamental problem is that most human beings take for granted the existence of a family system, living in individual homes, and rearing children of their own. It is difficult to work out any arrangements that would permit both husband and wife to have continued full-time careers without special social arrangements that would accomplish all these home-centered tasks in an equalitarian way. That is, even if it is not assumed that women will perform these tasks, someone has to do so, and we have not worked out an alternative system by which they will be taken care of.

Let us now point out some changes that may well occur in the near future, as this and other societies both recognize the problem of equity and inaugurate some ways of giving greater opportunities to women.

Several changes that relate to marital behavior are likely. Women will almost certainly marry later, and that trend has already begun. The divorce rate will continue to be very high, and women will become much less anxious about quickly returning to marriage after a divorce. That is, although they will eventually remarry, they are likely to spend a greater amount of time between marriages than in the past. At the present time and in the near future, an increasing number of women will use that period to try to reorganize their lives and to consider what kind of occupational future they can create for themselves.

Another change that is already occurring is a higher divorce rate among women who have been married more than ten years. In the past and at present, the divorce rate is the highest for the first few years of marriage. In the past very few divorces have occurred beyond about the fifteenth year of marriage. However, many women have come to have a feeling in their later years that opportunities are still available to them and that the home no longer can provide a satisfying life. Thus, what had been a marriage with a modest amount of discontent comes to be viewed as intolerable (although a higher percentage of men than women still want a divorce first).

A high percentage of women will become part of the labor force and will come to view their careers as central to their lives, not merely as a way of supplementing family income. Correlative with that change will be a continued low fertility. If this country achieves zero population growth in the next few decades, almost certainly two elements in that change will be the lesser willingness of women to have several children because of their career interests, and the lesser willingness of husbands to have several children because they know that they will have to assume more responsibility for them than in the past.

Aside from divorce itself, there will be an increase in the amount of argument and even hostility between wives and husbands about these issues. It is precisely when social norms are in flux, and have come to be widely questioned, that conflict about them is likely to be high. People can avoid much argument if both sides recognize that the situation is nearly unchangeable. However, both men and women are increasingly forced to work out their own personal solutions, often through heated bargaining, when the society no longer offers clear models for behavior.

At the present time surveys show that only a slight majority of adult Americans are in favor of efforts to strengthen or change women's position in society, and somewhat less than half are sympathetic with the efforts of feminist groups to improve women's opportunities. As might be expected, the young, the educated, blacks, and the urban population are somewhat more in favor than those who are married, older, less educated, white, and rural. At the end of 1971, for example, half of the respondents in a national poll agreed that women should take care of running their homes and leave running the country up to men. These figures will certainly change, but it should not be forgotten that a general agreement with the principle of equality is very different from willingness to yield one's own specific rights and privileges.

READINGS

Jessie Bernard, *The Future of Motherhood*, New York: Dial, 1974.

Jonathan R. Cole and Stephen Cole, *Social Stratification in Science*, Chicago: University of Chicago Press, 1973

Cynthia F. Epstein, *Woman's Place*, Berkeley: University of California Press, 1970.

Jo Freeman, *The Politics of Women's Liberation: A Case Study of an Emerging Social Movement and Its Relation to the Policy Process*, New York: McKay, 1975.

Betty Friedan, *The Feminine Mystique*, New York: Norton, 1963.

Judith Hole and Ellen Levine, *Rebirth of Feminism*, New York: Quadrangle, 1971.

Leo Kanowitz, *Sex Roles in Law and Society*, Albuquerque: University of New Mexico Press, 1973.

Anne Koedt, Ellen Levine, and Anita Rapone, eds., *Radical Feminism*, New York: Quadrangle, 1973.

Eleanor E. Maccoby and Carol N. Jacklin, *The Psychology of Sex Differences*, Stanford, Calif.: Stanford University Press, 1974.

Margaret Mead, *Male and Female*, New York: Morrow, 1967.

John Stuart Mill and Harriet Taylor Mill, *Essays on Sex Equality,* ed. by Alice S. Rossi, Chicago: University of Chicago Press, 1970.

John Money and Anke A. Ehrhardt, *Man and Woman, Boy and Girl,* Baltimore: John Hopkins, 1972.

Ashley Montagu, *The Natural Superiority of Women,* rev. ed., New York: Collier, 1970.

F. Ivan Nye and Lois W. Hoffman, *The Employed Mother in America,* Chicago: Rand McNally, 1963.

Rhona Rapoport and Robert Rapoport, *Dual-Career Families,* Baltimore: Penguin, 1974.

Alice Rossi and Ann Calderwood, eds., *Academic Women on the Move,* New York: Russell Sage, 1973.

Sheila Rowbotham, *Hidden from History: Rediscovering Women in History from the Seventeenth Century to the Present,* New York: Pantheon, 1975.

Patricia Cayo Sexton, *The Feminized Male: Classrooms, White Collars and the Decline of Manliness,* New York: Random House, 1969.

Ezra F. Vogel, *Japan's New Middle Class: The Salaryman and His Family in a Tokyo Suburb,* 2d ed., Berkeley: University of California Press, 1971.

Lenore J. Weitzman, "Legal Regulation of Marriage: Tradition and Change," *California Law Review,* 62 (1974), pp. 1169–1288.

Virginia Woolf, *A Room of One's Own,* New York: Harcourt, Brace, 1929.

PART FIVE

SOCIAL INSTITUTIONS

CHAPTER TWELVE

(George W. Gardner.)

THE FAMILY
AS A SOCIAL INSTITUTION

THE END OF THE FAMILY?

In this era of apparent breakdown in major social institutions, conservative doomsayers join with radical critics in agreeing that we are witnessing the demise of the family. The conservatives report that great civilizations like classical Rome and Greece became decadent because their family systems fell apart: People sought sexual pleasure where they could find it, the young no longer obeyed their elders, women abandoned their family duties, divorce and adultery were rampant, the birthrate fell, and everyone lived for himself or herself. The radical critics tell us, instead, that the family is simply out of date, like the gaslight and the horse-drawn wagon. They see the family as awkward when not painful, serving no human needs very well, and an instrument of oppression. Indeed, much research on the seamy side of family life claims that ancient institution to be a kind of swindle, which has now been exposed: No one got much pleasure from it, while everyone was subjected to propaganda that extolled it as a wise and excellent arrangement.

Consequently, while conservatives deplore the disappearance of the family, radicals and many liberals rejoice that this curious holdover from the past is rapidly slipping into limbo. Critics have also chided family sociologists for viewing "the normal family" as being always made up of two married parents and their children. When tens of millions of people now live under other arrangements, those other forms should be considered normal, too. About 12 percent of all family units are "headed" by a woman; perhaps another 10 to 15 percent of couples never have children; about 5 percent of the United States population will not marry at all; about 6 percent of the population is living alone at any given time; and so on.

According to the radical accusation, sociologists have been writing as though almost all analyses of family life could be confined to a traditional, "approved" form of the family, the *conjugal* type, which they believed to be universal. As against this bias, in the real world a wide range of family patterns can be observed, from homosexual unions to mothers living with their illegitimate children, from open-sex communes to the Shaker total rejection of sexuality, from living together without any ceremony to living separately in spite of a ceremony—the list is nearly endless.

All these lamentations, rejoicings, and descriptions suggest that the period of "the family" is rapidly passing. We now have many options open to us, and in the new world to come, people will choose whatever living arrangements suit them best. In short, critics imply that there is no such thing as "the" family, and that the future will offer us a smorgasbord of family styles among which to choose.

The author is as content as anyone else to prophesy a future no one can yet see. His position is strongly opposed to both conservative and radical views, but it is not cautious at all: Long after the last reader of this volume has moldered into dust, the vast majority of human beings will continue to be born into a family unit with two spouses, male and female, with or without another child already there. They will live most of their lives entwined closely in family relations and will experience much of their anguish and happiness because of what takes place there. Almost all people will marry and will live most of their adult lives within marriages. Children will learn their elementary social skills within a family unit and will also acquire there the desire to become spouses and parents when they grow up. Whatever the tragedies of family life, people will *not* create new, satisfactory arrangements that will substitute for the family. Great nations will lose or gain power, new music and other art forms will arise, and

people will even invent some new ways of taking care of some tasks the family now discharges, well or poorly, but most human beings will not be persuaded that any new family forms are preferable.

They will also continue to complain about the family. At the turn of the next century, assuming human beings are still alive then, sons and daughters will still be reduced to tears by parental authority, parents will continue to despair at their inability to mold their children in desirable ways, and spouses will continue to feel that their pleasures in living together are meager. People will still be arguing violently about what should be done about the inadequacies of the conjugal family. Few people will live in "open marriages," in which both spouses generously allow each other the right to engage in affairs with others; instead, adults will still be like teenagers, jealous when their partners flirt with someone else. In short, the changes now occurring within the family will not inaugurate a totally new system, and present trends will not continue in the same direction indefinitely.

This view seems to reject much of the modern commentary on the family and much common experience. Nevertheless, there are sound theoretical and empirical reasons in its favor—not the least of which is that human societies are not likely to give up easily an instrument so useful as the family. What it does must be done by someone or some agencies if society is to exist at all. However, no society as a whole has as yet been willing to assume collective responsibility for family tasks. To examine the seeming paradox between a widespread and even growing belief in the demise of the family and the powerful forces for its maintenance, let us consider further the place of the family in human society.

The Problem of Defining a Family

No known society has ever existed without family structures, but the keenest students of such structures, the anthropologists, have been unable to agree on a satisfactory definition of what a family is. This is not so surprising when we think of the many forms of unions that are "like marriages"— where should the line be drawn? For example, almost all the unions we call families are given recognition by a public ritual, but millions of unions in the Caribbean and in Latin America have begun without a legal ceremony. In almost all societies the two spouses live together, but in many polygynous unions the husband has slept with one wife for a few days at a time, and then with his second wife, or third, in succession. In almost all, the husband and wife enjoy mutual sexual rights, but in at least one society the official husband had no specifically sexual rights after the ceremony. Most unions are entered into with some notion of permanence, but in many societies the divorce rate is known to be high.

If we are determined to call all *unions* families, then no formal definition will cover every concrete case. Fortunately, we can study family behavior without making a neat verbal definition. After we have considered a wide range of variation in concrete cases, it still remains true that the overwhelming percentage of all people in all societies, past and present, have been born and reared in a *family* made up of a total of three to five members, belonging to only two generations, containing two adult spouses who are female and male and who are (and who define themselves as) the biological parents of the children in it, and who make economic contributions to the unit. Most family rules, and thus the social pressures to obey those rules, specify how those children, spouses, and parents should act and feel within that kind of social unit. Courtship rules specify how potential members of such a social unit should act and feel as they move toward establishing that kind of family. Or, putting the situation negatively, although some people in every society will not be included in such a unit, all societies create a variety of rules and social pressures that make it difficult for people to live comfortably outside the family, whether or not they can exist happily within it.

Even today, when it is easier than perhaps at any other time for persons to live alone outside the family, most adults go home to families at the end of the day and remain there the rest of the evening. We are such creatures of our society that few of us simply decide to reject completely the idea of eventually marrying. In a period when young women are moved by the ideology of the feminist movement, the aspiration of independence, and even of zero population growth, less than 1 percent assert that they will not become mothers.[1]

The Tasks of the Family

The pervasiveness of the family may be seen in cross-cultural perspective. Although many societies have been described as having no formal market system, legal system, or even political system, all have formally recognized family structures. In all societies the social placement of children is determined by their positions in specific families; they are socialized and fed there; and all members socially control each other. Thus, textbooks speak of the tasks of the family as these:

1 Reproduction of the young
2 Physical maintenance of family members
3 Social placement of children and adults
4 Socialization and emotional support
5 Social control

A moment's thought will tell us that all these tasks could be separated. For example, various utopian philosophers have suggested that young people be trained, not according to the social rank of their families, but according to their capacities; that adult males

[1]See Judith Blake, "Can We Believe Recent Data on Birth Expectations in the United States," in *Demography*, 11 (February 1974), p. 28. However, 13 percent of college women in 1971 said they wanted only one child, or none (p. 33).

Figure 12-1 On this Israeli *kibbutz* babies are put to bed by their mothers in the communal nursery where the children will spend their early years. (Hilda Bijur, Monkmeyer.)

and females not be permitted to unite as a couple, but that everyone should live communally; that parents not socialize their own young; or that only the best human stock be allowed to breed.

Some efforts (such as the Chinese commune, the Israeli *kibbutz*, and the Russian *kolkhoz*) have actually been made toward separating those tasks and giving a few (feeding and care, socialization, and social control) to the group. Regarding those possibilities, we can say that (1) in no society have these tasks been separated as a natural, steady historical development; (2) when they have been separated, it is the result of considerable special planning and much ideological fervor; and (3) invariably, the members of the society gradually fall away from the new ideal and return to a more traditional system in which family tasks are considered the joint responsibilities of individual family units. However frail and unstable any *individual* family unit may seem, then, the family as a *system*, or a set of processes, is extraordinarily persistent and tough. Even if it is not necessary, as some critics insist, people are not easily persuaded that there are obviously satisfactory substitutes for it. Let us consider why this is so.

It is unlikely we shall ever know much about the beginnings of the family. Each year discoveries about early humankind tell us more about the bone structure, the size of brain, and even the diet of people who lived more than a million years ago. However, courtship practices, the relations of fathers and sons, the quarrels and embraces of spouses, indeed whether the very idea of "spouse" existed (with its suggestion of marriage and legitimacy)—all this leaves no physical trace that can be read by Geiger counters or chemists. And while it is fun to guess about early family life, we should not take our speculations very seriously.

The Interaction of Biology and Culture in the Family

In any event, we need not search far in the past for the special place of the family in society: It is the only social institution that assumes the burden of transforming the infant human animal into a human being. Without it, the unique biological heritage of homo sapiens would end in disaster.

The human infant is not the most helpless animal at birth. Many other animals are even less mature biologically at that stage.

Nor is it true that all other animals are well endowed with instincts and can grow up normally without any social experience. For example, monkeys reared in isolation are incompetent at sex, parenting, and even ordinary social skills with their fellow monkeys; and wild birds will not respond to the songs of birds reared in laboratory isolation. However, human infants are helpless longer than other animals. Herbivore infants (deer, goats) need their mothers' milk, but they can graze well enough shortly after birth. Carnivores (wolves, lions) must learn to hunt, but by their second year they can usually manage to survive. Human beings mature more slowly and need years of social interaction to become even adequate adults. As a species, the human animal evolved away from biological solutions toward social and cultural ones and developed a flexible brain capable of learning almost anything that human society judged to be necessary. If the animal ancestors of this species ever had any genuine instincts (that is, automatic biological mechanisms that were solutions to its problems, such as the nest building of birds or the dam building of beavers), they are lost now. Instead, this animal cannot survive infancy or early childhood at all without the care that families give.

Thus, family patterns and our biological heritage are closely linked. The two sets of factors interact to support or to conflict with one another. For example, since family members transmit the culture of the society to the child, the two sets are mutually supportive; but since that culture typically contains many rules that *violate* biological impulses, the two sets of factors are in conflict. Societies have forced their members to submit to physical pain (circumcision, subincision, scarification); to control the occasions for defecation, urination, belching, or coughing; and even to sacrifice their lives in war or religious rituals.

All societies also *harness* biological drives or impulses in various ways. Sexuality is harnessed to both marriage and the desire

to become a parent by pressures that range from subtle advertising and film models to (in some societies) prods with a shotgun. Even so simple a drive as hunger is harnessed, beginning with the early infant lesson that feeding is an occasion for parental cuddling and proceeding to the more general experience that eating is most pleasant when it is social. For most children home is not only where, if you go there, they have to take you in; it is also where the food is. In fact, in most large-scale civilizations the satisfaction of most physical needs, from cuddling to protection, is closely associated with family living.

This complex set of links between the biological and the sociocultural also makes it easier to carry out other tasks ordinarily given to the family. If the home is where food is prepared and other biological and biosocial needs are satisfied, it is also likely that family members will encounter one another there, so that both *socialization* and *social control* can occur more easily there. The family is and has always been an agency of economic distribution, which can occur more easily if members are likely to be found in some central location. Constraints of time and space make it easier to link all these tasks together, rather than dispersing them throughout the whole society or handing them over to separate agencies. Other arrangements for these tasks have been made in the past and will continue to be made. It is nevertheless clear, when we contemplate the vast range of possible forms of the family, that some variant of the conjugal family has been the most common pattern.

BIOLOGICAL BASES OF THE FAMILY

Whatever the family may be socially, it is a biological unit. Indeed, many modern commentators still suppose that biological patterns determine much of family behavior. This has seemed obvious to many analysts, since so many important biological events take place in this social arrangement: sex, feeding, care of the young, and reproduction.

However, the claim that biology determines social structure does not sustain close examination. It is difficult to locate any important characteristics of human families that are clearly determined by biological factors, even though it is obvious that if the human animal were radically different, the forms of the human family would also be different.

For example, if human babies typically were born in large litters of five to ten for each pregnancy, caring for them would create an entirely different problem than does the arrival of a single infant. If there were four or five sexes, rather than two, the problems of courtship and mating would be very different. And if all of the four or five sexes were necessary for the production of one infant, clearly the form of the family would be different. We can also speculate that if males had been given the biological task of bearing the infant, the evolution of the family would have taken a different turn.

Such speculations can alert us to the general fact that family patterns are not likely to vary at random without regard to our peculiar human biology. Human biology does not determine our social behavior, but it does pose one set of problems, and not another. Moreover, without determining family patterns, it does make some of them more costly or more difficult than others— for example, even the sexually puritanical societies have seen to it that their sexually mature adults were married and thus not deprived of this natural delight.

Analysis of the relationship between biological and social factors is fraught with difficulties. Modern studies of animals in the wild and in laboratories show that adult behavior of even lower animals is more affected by social factors than was once thought. At the same time biologists have been detailing the exact physiological changes that induce or trigger various social responses. Knowing more, we can no longer state a set of simple relationships between these two great sets of factors. Our analysis is handicapped by a fundamental barrier, noted before: It is simply not possible to find out what "natural biological human beings" are like. If we try to rear a human being in isolation, in order to prevent the social factors from having effect, that person will not be normal. But by the time human beings are old enough to be tested or studied, their responses have been greatly shaped by social influences.

A second handicap should be repeated: We have no firm knowledge about human family life before the historical period, that is, before the beginning of writing some four thousand years ago. Thus, we cannot state that at some specific time, say half a million years ago, the family was shaped in a particular way by biology. Nor can we use field data on the family life of our anthropoid cousins—gorilla, orangutan, chimpanzee, and gibbon—for they all branched apart from human evolution as long as thirty-five million years ago. In addition, we cannot suppose that if we study living "Stone Age peoples" (recent or modern societies that used only stone implements before contact with Europeans) we are in the presence of the natural human family; they have as many years of evolutionary change behind them as do modern Europeans. There is no reason to assume that they are like the human beings who lived in the Paleolithic period or indeed in any other distant period in human evolution.

We are left with some interesting speculations but no precise evaluation of how much the biological set affects the social. But we already have noted three important facts of biology that affect the family to some degree:

1   The very late maturation of the human animal

2 A lack of instincts to guide the animal in solving environmental problems

3 A complex brain that creates a wide range of solutions to problems and thus can create numerous cultural or social forms that may or may not be in harmony with biological needs

The human being has a sexual drive, but it is far more social than in other animals, far more dependent on learning. In addition, the human sexual drive comes to have a social meaning that is far more complex than its biological significance: It is shaped, channeled, and restricted in all societies. The sexual drive in the human animal is relatively constant in that there is no specific rutting season. However, people in all societies are taught to feel a wide range of prohibitions with respect to who is a possible sexual partner, which situations permit them to express sexuality, and the kinds of stimuli that are likely to arouse them. There is no evidence at all of a *paternal drive*, and it is not clear that there is any maternal drive, either: Such behaviors are *socially* acquired.

An obvious point at which the biological affects the familial is that the female menstruates, bears the children, and lactates. But human societies were not forced by this to keep women close to the hearth and to put them in charge of the children. Menstruation does not prevent women from working in most societies; women are not perpetually pregnant; and they can and do carry out most productive tasks even when they are. Indeed, one might instead argue that since pregnant women are not as effective on a hunt as men are, they might well have been given the headship of the family during pregnancy—though this solution was not tried.

It does seem likely that the male's greater strength and endurance have helped to give him a dominant position in all family systems about which we have adequate data. We have no historical records of any *matri-*

archy (a society ruled by women). Even in *matrilineal societies* (where inheritance goes through the female line), males are in charge of the lineage and of the society itself. The more interesting biosocial fact is that in no society does the authority of the male rest upon his ability to win in a fair fight with women.

A widely disseminated view holds that the later physical maturation of males creates the typical family pattern of earlier marriages for women than for men. However, at present there is little evidence that girls produce a viable egg any earlier than boys produce a viable sperm cell. Certainly, males are harmed less by mating at early ages than girls are. Without question, a girl of fifteen to seventeen years is not ready for childbirth in a biological sense, as is a boy of the same age capable of reproduction. It is the *social definitions* of the appropriate adult tasks of the male that label him as too immature for marriage at an early age; he cannot discharge adult male tasks fully, while a young girl can discharge the traditional female tasks of childbirth and housekeeping. Similarly, we must not take seriously the currently accepted view (based on Kinsey's data) that males reach their fullest orgasmic or sexual potential at age eighteen, while females do so much later, at about thirty-five. This is simply a product of modern psychosexual conditioning. Women are taught to be much more inhibited sexually than men are, and thus do not respond freely until later.

One biological difference between the sexes may have some slight effect on family patterns. The female can become pregnant without sexual pleasure or desire, while the male must experience some sexual desire and an ejaculation to impregnate the female. This difference may have influenced the lesser emphasis in most societies on female sexual pleasure in or out of marriage. It may also have had some effect in creating another social difference, the somewhat greater freedom in mate choice given to males than

Figure 12-2 "Playing house" socializes children to adopt and eventually pass on to their own children the family system. (Lew Merrim, Monkmeyer.)

to females in most large civilizations. Where there has been a difference, women's choices have been much more controlled by their elders' wishes.

Note that none of the biological factors so far mentioned creates any family system at all. The sex drive of adults would ensure conception, in the absence of contraceptives, and thus the birth of infants. However, we do not yet have firm evidence that human beings are pressed by biological factors to care for their young. Indeed, the biological fact that requires the creation of some type of family system is the *absence* of specific biological forces to ensure the continuance of the species. The human animal is peculiarly dependent for its continued survival on the role relations imposed by the culture. It is the aim and result of socialization to engender in human beings the wish not only to become parents but to teach their *own* children in turn to want to become parents

when *they* grow up. Lacking this crucial link, the species could not have survived. The necessary link between the cultural or social heritage and the biological is precisely a three-generational tie, by which the adult generation teaches a second to want to socialize a third.

In turn, the peculiar character of the family itself permits this fixing of responsibility on the adult male and female. Since helpless infants need a long period of care, the family must and does last a long time (even in the United States, with its high divorce rate, far more marriages with children end in death, not divorce). This permits a longer period in which to give children the necessary training for their culture. The mother-infant tie is emotionally intimate, in part because of a relatively lengthy period of lactation, and this also facilitates socialization. In addition, the pattern of social dominance of children by adults, which arises in part from the adulthood of the parents and their much greater knowledge, gives added force to this socialization.

Still more fundamentally, all societies develop many rules that prescribe rewards for parents who live by these norms and punishments for those who do not. No society leaves its biological continuation to chance; that responsibility is not given to adults in general, but to the *specific* parents of specific children. The socialization process is bolstered by rewards and punishments for adherence to the parental norms, and the discharge of those responsibilities guarantees the continuation of the society.

THE SOCIAL DEFINITION OF LEGITIMACY

The interlocking relationships between biological and cultural factors make the Rule of Legitimacy important in human societies.[2]

[2]This rule was enunciated by the anthropologist Bronislaw Malinowski in "Parenthood, the Basis of Social

According to that rule, children must be the issue of parents who have been married by the customs of their group or society. Alternatively, people will be punished if they become biological parents without public recognition that they have accepted family responsibilities for their children. It must be emphasized that the rule cannot *prevent* illegitimacy; it can only punish those who violate it. However, like other important social rules, this one is bolstered by numerous social customs that make its violation less likely. These include the efforts of elders to see that their children get married, to choose mates for their children with or without their consent, and indeed to intrude in the lives of their married children and their grandchildren indefinitely—all because of parental concern about the continuity of the family line.

More specifically, some societies have prevented illegitimacy by chaperonage, and others by arranging marriages at such early ages that previous conception was not likely. All societies attempt to make of courtship a public relationship, watched by many interested people, so that even if conception does occur prior to marriage, the responsible male is known, and an early marriage can be forced. By watching courtship, societies and the families within them can also prevent unions that are disapproved. These include unions that cross caste, race, or class lines; incestuous unions; and, in many societies, unions between people who belong to inappropriate lineages.

As might be inferred, where there is a full-scale stratification system, middle- and upper-class families will be most concerned about family lines and illegitimacy, and they will put more pressure on their offspring to marry before having a child. Toward the lower strata in all societies, there is some-

what less concern about these matters. Even in societies where there are very high rates of illegitimacy, such as in Caribbean and Latin American countries, children born outside legal marriage still suffer some disadvantages. While the disapproval they face is much less than in societies with low illegitimacy rates, it is notable that even in such societies most adults do eventually marry. And when socioeconomic conditions improve so that adult men can make an adequate living, they are also more likely to marry. As these lower-class populations are integrated more into the dominant cultures of their nations, the rate of illegitimacy is likely to drop.[3]

In short, and contrary to much popular commentary, it is not true that such societies or lower-class strata, dominated and undermined for centuries by an alien culture, have worked out some type of substitute for marriage, which they support with a counterculture that simply rejects the alien forms of marriage. Marriage is not a bourgeois invention that has been imposed upon happy native cultures. It is rather a social instrument by which the responsibility for children is ensured through ceremonials and continuing social pressures. Where a culture or a society is undermined for a period of time, illegitimacy rates are likely to be higher; but when groups or social strata have a stake in their own sociocultural system, they reimpose the Rule of Legitimacy to publicly fix the responsibility for offspring on the parents.

Modern Ideology and Illegitimacy

Here we must consider a modern phenomenon, the rise of illegitimacy rates among a

Structure," in V. F. Calverton and Samuel D. Schmalhausen, eds., *The New Generation,* New York: Macaulay, 1930, pp. 137–138. His formulation was: No child should be born without a "sociological father."

[3]For an analysis of this widespread pattern, see William J. Goode, "Illegitimacy in the Caribbean Social Structure," *American Sociological Review,* 25 (February 1960), pp. 21–30; and "Illegitimacy, Anomie, and Cultural Penetration," in *Explorations in Social Theory,* New York: Oxford, 1973, chap. 10.

class stratum that in the past has shown a low rate. A tiny but increasing percentage of educated middle-class people now assert their right, not merely to live together without marriage, but to have children as well. A still smaller but increasing percentage of women proclaim their right to have a child without living with any man. These phenomena have been most notable in the United States and in Sweden. (An enlightened public policy in Sweden offers considerable assistance to women who wish to bear and rear children outside marriage and independent of a man.) Will this pattern become widespread? Even if it does not become widespread, how does it fit with the Rule of Legitimacy?

With respect to the first question, we can predict that the percentage of women who independently bear and rear their children will continue to increase; but it will never be more than a tiny percentage of the total middle-class population, simply because the costs in time, energy, and money are great under any likely social arrangements of the future. As all parents learn, children tire rapidly, but have a much faster recovery rate than adults. Trying to care for even one child without the aid of another adult is difficult. Children or adults do become ill, and at such times the burden is even heavier. One person can earn enough for the care of one or more children, but when one parent must both earn an adequate salary and pay for additional domestic services, the economic difficulty increases. There are, then, many factors that make it unlikely that any large percentage of adults will choose to be a single head of household caring for his or her children, if the alternative of an additional spouse is available.

The continued force of the Rule of Legitimacy will also make it unlikely that a high percentage of adults will choose to bear their children without marrying. Though our generation has become more tolerant, we think it unlikely that the disadvantages

that illegitimate children suffer, and the disapproval that their parents bear, will die out completely. At present, social circles that do not disapprove of living together without marriage nevertheless do approve of marriage, and they are especially likely to disapprove of having children outside marriage. To the extent that such couples seem to have made a permanent choice and to work regularly at an occupation, their social circle is likely to make it known that they expect a marriage to take place.

However, we should entertain an alternative hypothesis, even though we do not suppose the future will support it. The Rule of Legitimacy states that parents and children will be punished somewhat if there is no public ceremonial that fixes responsibility for the offspring on the parents. Future government services and individual economic security, coupled with an inability to disappear and thus abandon responsibility, might increase to the extent that having a child outside a family would not be disapproved, because under those circumstances the responsibilty for its care would be socially recognized just the same. We view this as unlikely, even though from time to time the prophets of the future suggest that the notion of illegitimacy will simply disappear.

LOVE AND COURTSHIP

It is notable that those who joyfully await the society of the future, in which that bourgeois relic of the past, the family, will have disappeared, do not suggest that we should also abandon love and courtship. Through them the continuity of family honor, estate, occupation, and power have been maintained or destroyed. Thus, elders in most societies of the past have viewed these processes as much too important to be left to the whims of children, and they have tried to control them in many ways. Although present Western societies express the norms of free courtship and legally permit almost anyone to marry almost anyone else, parents continue to try, with considerable success, to shape the mate choices of their adult children.[4] Indeed, most of us are unaware of the extent to which our choice of mate has actually been determined by what our parents have done.

To assert that others (both kin and friends) influence the courtship process, even in a society that proclaims great freedom, suggests that our system is as restrictive as other systems. We note that there have been many marriage systems in which choices were very narrow. For example, in many societies tradition dictated that people in a certain kin relationship to one another should marry: In Arab Bedouin tribes the ideal was that a young man and his father's brother's daughter should unite (patrilateral parallel cousin marriage). This would keep both political control and property within the family line of the male head of the family. Much more common is matrilateral cross-cousin marriage, which usually means that a boy is supposed to marry his mother's brother's daughter.

In most great civilizations it has been common for adults to arrange the marriage of their offspring, with or without consulting them. This was the approved pattern in most Western societies in the middle and upper classes. It was especially common among royalty, where it was considered wise to use marriages as a way of cementing friendly relations among the rulers of different countries.

In all these systems, even very restrictive ones, mate selection is like a market system. Whether a groom price or a bride price was demanded, the elders typically sought the best possible choice for their children. This meant a union with another family of

[4]An early study of this parental intervention was done by Marvin B. Sussman, "Parental Participation in Mate Selection and Its Effects upon Family Continuity," *Social Forces,* 32 (1953), pp. 76–81.

slightly higher wealth, political power, or prestige. But since other families sought the same goals, all mate selection systems have pressed toward homogamous marriages, that is, marriages between equals. The pattern of "like marries like" is supported not merely by norms and values, such as the belief that one should not marry outside one's ethnic or religious group. It is also supported by essentially market processes.

Within a commodity or a monetary market, people may seek the best bargain possible; but since other people are also seeking the best bargain, no one needs to accept less than the market affords. Thus, a family of high rank with an attractive daughter need not accept a marriage with a modestly talented son of a low-ranking family. In a marriage system in which a groom price or a dowry is paid, a family may marry their daughter into a somewhat higher-ranking family, but their dowry will have to be higher. A young man with exceptional talents who seems to be rising rapidly may be able to move upward somewhat through marriage because his *future* rank can be matched against the somewhat higher present rank of the young woman's family.

In any society an older man is worth more on the marriage market than is an older woman, but typically he cannot obtain as desirable a wife as a young man might, unless he also possesses some additional advantages such as money or prestige. Similarly, in our society, and in an epoch in which some part of the political rebellion of young people takes the form of sneering at adult materialism and praising affectional relations and free choice, the overwhelming percentage of all dating occurs within the same class or between two adjacent social classes. Moreover, when young people date someone of a lower class, in most cases those who are chosen have some special advantages such as popularity, attractiveness, school leadership, or success in athletics. In short, the qualities of those who date or go on to marry are likely to be about equal in value on the marriage and courtship market.

The Importance of Love

"Like marries like" (homogamy) may be stated still more specifically. Most marriages take place between people who are similar in age, who live very close to one another, who belong to the same racial and religious groups, and whose education is very similar.[5] These facts can be duplicated in all countries and seem to suggest that love does not control courtship and marriage. They suggest, too, that in Western societies, where love is proclaimed as a driving force, courtship and mate choices are simply the crude, crass outcome of market calculations.

Love is given great attention. In Western societies, and to some extent in other societies, people are socialized to believe that eventually they will fall in love. Children are teased about whom they "love" and are taught to recognize the feelings and symptoms of love. They are told that love is important in dating and marriage. They are bombarded, through high or popular culture, with thousands of stimuli and suggestions about love. One result is that most people in Western societies believe they should not marry unless they have fallen in love, although generally they agree that this is not enough.

What role, then, does love play? The answer may seem paradoxical. Love is a universal human potential, but it is highly disruptive of existing social arrangements.[6] Consequently, family systems attempt to limit its influence, and they contain a wide

range of social processes by which its power is reduced. More specifically, even in a society where love is praised, people fall in love mainly with the people they meet in informal social relations, and family processes limit the number of intimate social encounters with people who might be "inappropriate."

Parental Control over Mate Choice

All nations contain many "marriage pools of eligibles" within which much of our intimate social interaction takes place. It is within these, where the eligibles are socially very similar, that we are most likely to date and marry. If parents are well-to-do, they control the social choices of their children even more, because then (1) their motivation is greater (a wrong choice by their children would be more costly), and (2) their resources are larger. If possible, they send their children to private schools where children from lower social strata are rare. They and their children's own peer group constantly express class evaluations about dates or marriage partners from lower social strata. Especially at middle- and upper-class levels, young people often entertain in each other's homes and thus are exposed to still further streams of approval or disapproval about the people they should choose.

Thus, even when young people assert a philosophy of free choice, based on the personal qualities and not the social class of their dates or potential spouses, they are most likely to associate intimately with people of similar backgrounds. Even when they do experiment for a while with dates from different backgrounds, with each step that they take toward a serious emotional relationship, or marriage, their choices also move steadily in the direction of people who are very much like themselves.

Contrary to the helplessness that parents express when asked about their ability to control the mate choices of their adult chil-

---

[5]For an extended analysis of this process, together with some critical comments on the "exchange model," see F. Ivan Nye and Felix M. Berardo, *The Family,* New York: Macmillan, 1973, chaps. 5 and 6.

[6]For a cross-cultural analysis of the "love pattern," see Goode, "The Theoretical Importance of Love," in *Explorations in Social Theory,* pp. 245–260.

dren, most parents intervene more or less strongly if they disapprove of the marriage choice being made, and a substantial percentage of them are eventually successful in their opposition.[7] But this does not prove that parents are dominant in their influence; it is rather that parents are likely to be in the same class position as neighbors, friends, and peer groups, who also share similar attitudes and thus are likely to support the parents' opposition.

It should be emphasized, however, that the degree of control is not necessarily the same in the modern system as in the past. Upper-class families still control the marriages of their adult children more than lower-class families do, but parental control has generally eroded. Today education is as important as economic capital, and parents encounter disapproval if they attempt to withhold education as a means of controlling the dating or mate choices of their children. By contrast, in the past parents were supported by kin or friends if they withheld landed property and inheritance as a way of influencing the mate choices of their children. Today most people do not obtain their jobs or promotions through the direct intervention of parents; and parents would not be given social approval for any attempts to control their children by hurting their occupational success. Women, especially, are for the first time able to obtain jobs or promotions independently of the males in their family. Thus, they can oppose the wishes of their parents if they want to do so.

Both economic bases and social norms give far less direct power to parents now than in the past. One consequence of this should be noted. Wherever marriages were stable and elders controlled mate choice, they were far more willing to invest in that marriage through substantial dowries or groom prices, as well as later handing over the accumulated family capital. In our own

[7]Sussman, loc. cit.

system, where both the control by elders and marriage stability are much lower, elders are much less willing to put that much investment into a child's marriage.

THE DYNAMICS OF HOUSEHOLDS

When people marry, they bring with them an accumulation of family information and skills as well as norms about how they should act as spouses or parents, what to expect from each other, and their resources of character, energy, or skill. Typically, they find that living together in marriage is different either from living together unmarried or from dating: A lifetime of observing and acquiring the internal roles of parent and spouse, along with expectations from others, leads people to behave differently in marriage. Unanticipated problems are likely to develop. For example, some parents are appalled to perceive that in conflicts with their children they are acting just as their own parents once did, although they had intended to be warmer and more understanding. The supportive, seemingly equalitarian date may begin to assert his husbandly "right" to be cared for; or the sweet, attentive woman becomes a mother who ignores her husband in favor of her children.

The complexity of all these processes of adjustment and conflict is too great to be encompassed within a brief section, but let us examine some aspects of family dynamics.

Family Statistics

For well over a decade in the United States the age at marriage has been slowly rising, though it is still much lower than in most European countries. In 1974 in the United States the average age at first marriage was twenty-one years for women and twenty-three years for men. The percentage of single women aged twenty to twenty-four years has increased substantially since 1960, to about 40 percent in 1974.[8] The trend toward later marriage is likely to continue in the near future. In the past, women with graduate school education or with a high salary were most likely to marry late and least likely to marry at all. While that relationship continues, the difference between this group and women with less education has been steadily dropping. It can also be noted that the 1960s witnessed an eightfold increase in the number of "household heads who live apart from relatives but shared living quarters with an unrelated adult partner (roommate or friend) of the opposite sex," a cool, gray Census Bureau category that is more commonly described as "They're living together now."

On the average, the interval between first marriage and the birth of the first child is relatively short, not much more than one year. However, total fertility declined from the end of the 1950s to the beginning of the 1970s.[9] At the present lower *fertility rate* (number of babies born each year per 1,000 women), we can expect that the average number of children born per woman will be just under 2. In the modern urban family the period in which children are born is relatively short, and the average age of the mother when the last child is born is about twenty-six years, that of the father about twenty-eight.

Note the important demographic effects of these patterns. If a woman has completed her childbearing by about age twenty-six, and her life expectancy is about seventy-three years, she has nearly a half-century of life after becoming a mother. If her children go away to college, she will still have about thirty years left. The combination of a rela-

tively early age at marriage, low fertility, and an extended life in a society that does not give high-prestige rewards simply for taking care of a husband would seem to be of no small consequence in affecting the growing aspirations of women toward achievements other than housekeeping.

It is characteristic of our marriage system that few married couples set up housekeeping in their parental homes or share a house with others. This percentage has steadily declined for the past two decades, and now only about 1 percent of all couples double up with others. Independent living arrangements have become common in the United States, and at the present time about one-sixth of all households are made up of one person living alone.

Most women work outside the home at some time, but at any given time only about 45 percent (in 1974) of all women are in the labor force, the smallest percentage being mothers of young children (33 percent of women with children under six).

The divorce rate in the United States has been rising for some years. It is now higher than ever and higher than that of any other major nation. For example, a woman of about thirty years of age has about one chance in three of either having already been divorced or of being divorced in the future. The divorce rate for people in the upper socioeconomic strata continues to be *lower* than in other strata, but recent data show that professional women in that group have exhibited a very slow increase in their rate of divorce (it was relatively high before). Men in the higher socioeconomic category have exhibited a very fast rise since 1960.[10]

Size of Household

The evidence is clear that no family system *as a whole* can be called *nuclear* if by that we mean that the individual household ex-

[8]Many of the figures in this section come from Paul C. Glick, *Current Population Reports: Some Recent Changes in American Families,* Special Studies Series P-23, no. 52, 1975, pp. 1–17.

[9]However, as the number of women in the more fertile ages (twenty to twenty-nine) increased because of the "baby boom" of the 1950s, the *total number* of babies born increased.

[10]Glick, op. cit., p. 6.

members of one's family, relations by blood

ists in social isolation from its kin. All data show the contrary. On the other hand, it is equally clear that the conjugal family household, made up of parents and their children, was far more typical of the past than has been supposed. It is a myth that some time in the indefinite past the average Western household was made up of several generations under one roof. In fact, as far back in Western history as we can now penetrate, this has never been common. Moreover, almost no other family system in any major civilization has been typified by great extended households. For hundreds of years most of the population of the world, even in societies where polygyny was permitted, lived in some type of conjugal family unit, which only rarely encompassed more than two generations, and whose average size rarely went above five or six members.[11] Possibly large families were the ideal, but they were not the reality.

Although this fact runs contrary to widespread belief, a few moments' analysis will suggest why it is likely to be correct, even if the data from the past two decades of research did not prove it fairly conclusively. We can first consider the matter in *demographic terms*. Large polygynous households (one man married to two or more women) are not statistically likely to be common under most historical circumstances, simply because only rarely are there enough women to permit more than a few well-to-do or powerful men to enjoy that delight or burden. Only slightly more boys than girls are born, and by the age of marriage the ratio is about 1 to 1. Thus, most men must be content with one wife and thus one household. Second, the facts of mortality in

most societies prior to the modern world made it very unlikely that several generations could live under one roof, simply because the older generation died out fairly soon.[12] Only a few grandparents or great-grandparents would be fortunate enough to preside over a vast household of several generations.[13]

We can also consider the problem with reference to what is *needed* sociologically to maintain a large household. Any large social organization requires considerable managerial skill within it and substantial socioeconomic inputs from the outside. Only a few well-to-do or powerful families could ever command sufficient resources to support several generations, which would necessarily include older people incapable of much productivity. Traditionally, it required at least a strong, competent older woman (in addition to the traditional patriarch) who could run the household, considerable land or a substantial business to support a large family enterprise, and enough resources of various kinds to maintain control over rebellious members or young people who wanted to break away in order to become independent.

The conjugal family is potentially somewhat more fragile than the extended family household, because if one adult member

---

[11]For an analysis of this major correction of myth, see William J. Goode, *World Revolution and Family Patterns,* New York: Free Press, 1963, pp. 2, 22–24, 123ff., 188ff., 238ff., 371ff.; and *The Family,* Englewood Cliffs, N.J.: Prentice-Hall, 1964, chap. 5. The most important empirical summary is to be found in Peter Laslett and Richard Wall, eds., *Household and Family in Past Time,* Cambridge: Cambridge, 1972, though Laslett also doubts that large households were the ideal.

[12]These demographic calculations have been made. Moreover, under reasonable assumptions about mortality and marriage, computer analysis shows that most kinship systems will *not* work in their ideal form: Some kinship positions will not be occupied, some women will not have an "appropriate" man to marry, there will be no younger brother to "inherit" an older brother's wives, and so on. That is, if the computer follows the correct kinship rules through several generations, eventually the society will die out. People make rules for many reasons, but they are much too sensible to follow them. See Marion J. Levy, "Aspects of the Analysis of Family Structure," as well as "The Range of Variation in Actual Family Size: A Critique of Marion J. Levy, Jr.'s Argument," by Lloyd A. Fallers, in *Aspects of the Analysis of Family Structure,* Ansley J. Coale et al., eds., Princeton, N.J.: Princeton, 1965.

[13]Large, extended households are still rare in modern societies, but far more grandparents now enjoy the privilege of playing with their grandchildren than in the past.

dies, a substantial percentage of its social resources has been destroyed. If there is conflict between any two members, that conflict cannot be easily isolated from the unit, since two people make up a large part of the unit. On the other hand, the percentage of such great multigenerational households has been small in any great civilization, simply because a family could only rarely muster all the resources and skills necessary for its creation or maintenance; and even fewer could keep such an organization going for several generations.[14]

having to do with a husband or marriage

MARITAL ADJUSTMENT PAST AND PRESENT

Perhaps the most important difference between the modern family system and that of the past is the peculiar faith that marriage should make a couple happy, even when neither person had been graced by happiness while single. In all systems an unhappy marriage has been viewed as a curse, about as easy to ignore as an aching tooth. However, no society has asked so much of marriage as ours.

In most societies of the past the bride and groom were not expected to be in love when they married, and so spouses would not have supposed they should be unhappy about *not* being in love or about not being loved after a few years of marriage. Most husbands and wives began with similar role expectations about their duties, which were strongly supported by their kin and neighbors; thus, marriage brought fewer unpleasant surprises. Marriage was expected to endure; trivial or temporary conflicts were not viewed as a justification for divorce even if it was possible. Typically, there was no pool

of the already divorced, or of unhappy spouses willing to divorce, as potential alternative wives and husbands. Being mostly agriculturists, men needed their wives, and wives could not easily make a living as independent workers. It is not then surprising that spouses might be relatively contented and did not aspire to more.

In all these respects our society differs; but it differs most radically in the belief that if marriage does not bring happiness, it is a failure, and that perhaps another dip in the marriage pool will yield the desired transformation. Partly for this reason social scientists have done much research on what makes people happy in marriage, an inquiry that poses some interesting methodological problems in measurement as well as causation. Unfortunately, the instruments that have been developed have not been impressive in their achievements. While they may be somewhat better than common sense, they hardly justify using marital adjustment prediction scores as a basis for choosing one's spouse.

The most general finding is that people who come from a more traditional background are either more contented in marriage or more likely to say that they are contented. For example, if the husband and wife both come from contented families, and had a long acquaintanceship and engagement, they are more likely to report that they are contented or happy in the marriage. Unfortunately, a high percentage of the United States population does not fall into that category, but it needs to make a choice just the same. No single factor or set of factors has been shown to have great predictive power, and successive researchers do not confirm one another's findings.

Adjustment is easy if the other person will only do it. Unfortunately, in most marriages both persons feel the same way. Few of us are willing to adjust cheerfully to the needs of others or are blessed with a spouse who is able to do it. Consequently, as Jessie

---

[14]Since the modern commune must also face this range of organizational problems, we cannot be surprised that so many of them fail to become established even when motivated by the noblest of intentions.

Bernard argues, in most unions there are two marriages, that of the husband and that of the wife.[15] Each perceives different problems and prefers different solutions. Each is likely to feel she or he contributes a bit too much and is not adequately praised for it. Both spouses are likely to feel they do more of the "garbage work," the tedious, necessary tasks.

Analysts of the family have noted for generations that in general the wife does more adjusting than does the husband. The family is likely to relocate if that will make *his* job easier, or if a better job appears, but it is not typical for families to move simply because a better job is offered to the wife somewhere else. The friendship network of the family is more likely to be shaped by the husband's wishes and acquaintanceships than by the wife's.[16] He is likely to have a far more dominant voice in all major purchases and indeed in any other major economic decisions. One consequence of men having their needs met in domestic life more than women is that marriage decreases the suicide, disease, and general mortality rates of men more than those of women.[17]

External Influences on Adjustment

The feminist movement has affected these adjustment and decision processes. However, such changes are likely to occur slowly within the population as a whole, because

wives and husbands continue to adjust to one another on the basis of habits and customs which they have acquired over a lifetime and which are not easily changed. The contrast between ideology and action may be observed in a cross-class comparison: In middle-class circles, where the impact of feminist rhetoric is stronger, men are likely to express *equalitarian* sentiments, while their patterns of adjustment are more *traditional*. By contrast, working-class husbands are more likely to feel free to proclaim that they have special rights simply because they are males, whereas in fact their wives have more authority within the household than middle- or upper-class wives enjoy. The same contrast between ideology and action may be observed in a striking fashion in Soviet Russia, where the vocabulary of equalitarianism is perhaps stronger than in any other industrialized nation. Nevertheless, Russian husbands have been extremely slow to accept a fair share of household duties.

The adjustment of husband and wife is also affected by the social networks of which they are a part. These are not likely to be *groups* in the narrow sense that are closed circles. They are likely instead to be linkages of people, not all of whom enjoy frequent interaction with one another. However, to the extent that family relations are visible to those people, who express their evaluations about how the husband and wife treat each other, those comments affect marital adjustment.

In addition, contrary to much popular discussion, the modern urban family is not isolated from kinship networks. They too affect relations in the family. A generation ago, it was taken for granted that families within cities could be contrasted sharply with the traditional rural family, since urban people cut off their ties with kin upon marriage and were no longer dependent upon kin for help or social relations. However, in the 1950s a succession of research studies in several in-

[15]Jessie Bernard, *The Future of Marriage*, New York: World, 1972, chaps. 1–3.

[16]Nicholas Babchuk and A. P. Bates, "The Primary Relations of Middle-Class Couples: A Study in Role Dominance," *American Sociological Review,* 28 (1963), pp. 377–384.

[17]Jessie Bernard in *The Future of Marriage*, chap. 15, summarizes these data. (Emile Durkheim in his classic work *Suicide* [1897] proved long ago that the difference in suicide rates between married and single men was greater than the difference in rates between married and single women.) Bernard's attempt to prove, in addition, that single women are generally healthier than married women is not, on the other hand, persuasive.

dustrial countries, including Holland, France, England, and the United States, showed that almost all families maintain relations with a large network of kinfolk, typically numbering more than one hundred.[18] Some of this continuing interaction takes place only by letter or telephone, and sometimes people see their kin only rarely. Nevertheless, some type of contact is maintained. Moreover, there is a recurring flow of exchanges of various kinds among at least part of that kin network, including babysitting, loans, entertainment, and help in getting jobs. The network is larger and more active toward the upper social strata, among rural people, and among families engaged in small businesses. However, few families are genuinely isolated.

Moreover, we must not view this phenomenon as merely a residue of an older rural tradition. In fact, the network of kin furnishes a range of social services and exchanges that the modern urban bureaucracy cannot as easily achieve.[19] It is more flexible in its response to family needs, it can adjust more easily to idiosyncratic or special needs of individuals, and it can respond more

swiftly. Indeed, one could argue that the kin network is of even greater importance in an urban setting, precisely because urban living creates problems that the bureaucracy of social sciences cannot solve as easily.[20]

The Effect of Women's Employment

The relationship of women to career or job also affects household dynamics in many complex ways. Although women have worked in all societies, this is the only society in which women have been able to obtain jobs and promotions independently of the men in their families. Consequently, they have achieved a basis for greater social independence, and thus influence within the family as well as in other social relations. On the other hand, since their incomes have been kept low and their entrance into important jobs made extremely difficult, and because it was expected that the role of wife and mother would take precedence over job or career, that increase in influence and independence has been far more modest than most commentators suggest. At present the evidence suggests that marital conflict is somewhat higher when women work, but the general level of happiness within the marriage is not very different, because of the somewhat greater satisfaction that

[18]See, for example, W. Bell and M. D. Boat, "Urban Neighborhoods and Social Participation," *American Journal of Sociology,* 62 (1952), pp. 391–398; Elizabeth Bott, *Family and Social Network,* London: Tavistock, 1957; M. Axelrod, "Urban Structure and Social Participation," *American Sociological Review,* 21 (1956), pp. 13–18; Marvin B. Sussman and Lee Burchinal, "Kin Family Network: Unheralded Structure in Current Conceptualizations of Family Functioning," *Marriage and Family Living,* 24 (1962), pp. 231–240; and Gerrit Kooy, "The Traditional Household in a Modernized Rural Society," *Recherches sur la Famille,* 3 (1958), pp. 183–204; as well as G. A. Kooy, "Urbanization and Nuclear Family Individualization: A Causal Connection?" in *Current Sociology,* 12 (1963–1964), pp. 13–24.

[19]Eugene Litwak, "Geographic Mobility and Extended Family Cohesion," *American Sociological Review,* 25 (1960), pp. 9–21; and "Technical Innovation and Theoretical Functions of Primary Groups and Bureaucratic Structures," *American Journal of Sociology,* 73 (1968), pp. 468–481; see also Marvin B. Sussman, "The Help Pattern in the Middle Class Family," *American Sociological Review,* 18 (February 1953), pp. 18–28.

[20]For readers whose imagination or experience does not furnish them with satisfying examples, consider the young mother whose young children want or need to play outside, at a time when she must do some work in her apartment (such as writing a TV script or cleaning up the mess). Urban parents do not feel safe in sending young children out to "play on the street," but rural parents have never felt it necessary to guard their children when they were outside. If pet dogs and cats are also to be permitted that luxury, they must be accompanied. In rural settings most jobs were done at home; transportation was more difficult, but also less needed. In urban and suburban living more opportunities for a wide range of activities can be found, but to use them requires baby-sitting or transportation services. In cities people must interact with more bureaucracies, and they cannot both take care of home duties and deal with organizations. For all these activities people call on kin for help.

women obtain through the job itself. As one might expect, that satisfaction is likely to be greater when wives hold jobs at higher levels, where job satisfaction is generally higher.

Since this is a dyadic (two-person) relationship, the attitude of the husband makes a difference, too. If the husband disapproves of the wife's working but she works just the same, then marital adjustment will be lower; it will also be low, however, if he approves of her working and she does not work.[21] The level of the husband's income also affects the relations between husband and wife: Toward the lower socioeconomic levels, where the wife's salary is likely to be closer to that of the husband's, she gains more influence in family decisions when she works than she does toward the upper strata, where the husband is likely to make much more money than the wife.

With reference to the effect of maternal employment on children, at present no *general* conclusion can be made, for the effect depends on the kind of work, the age and sex of children, class position, and other variables. If the mother feels guilty about working, she may attempt to make up for her absence by consciously planning to be with her children or preventing difficulties in her children's lives. Where, by contrast, the wife feels that she is forced to work primarily for money (and thus feels little guilt about working), she is more likely to insist that the children, especially daughters, take on fairly heavy home responsibilities.[22]

Figure 12-3 When a woman begins to pursue a career, the household dynamics change. (Mimi Forsyth, Monkmeyer.)

PARENTS AND CHILDREN

The family sociologist Willard Waller once commented that parents enjoy their infants until they discover that even small children have a will of their own. Modern parents constantly deplore their loss of authority and the resistance of their children to becoming civilized. All this, they proclaim, is very different from *their* childhood. In fact, however, every historical epoch discloses the same complaints. Apparently, as far back as we have any historical evidence, children of that generation were much worse than children of the previous generation.

Moreover, among the children of the world, it has been generally agreed, American children are the worst, exhibiting poorer manners and less obedience than any others.[23] In the judgment of foreign adults that may be true, but this observation has been made for at least one hundred fifty years.

[21]F. Ivan Nye and Lois W. Hoffman, *The Employed Mother in America*, Chicago: Rand McNally, 1963, chaps. 15, 19, 20.

[22]See Louis W. Hoffman, "Mother's Enjoyment of Work and Its Effects on the Child," ibid., pp. 95–105; and Elizabeth Douvan, "Employment and the Adolescent," ibid., pp. 142–163.

[23]For a comparison between Russian and United States school children, see Urie Bronfenbrenner, *Two Worlds of Childhood: U.S. and U.S.S.R.*, New York: Russell Sage, 1970.

Travelers to the United States not long after its founding also noted that children were given greater freedom here than in Europe, went around unchaperoned, made their own choices as to whom they would marry, and enjoyed a free and easy relationship with their parents.[24]

Some parent-child conflict is inevitable in any society, since parents are engaged in the difficult process of attempting to make adults like themselves from infants whose potentialities are probably very different. Those tensions increase during any period of rapid social change. First, parents and children face different daily problems because they are twenty to forty years apart, and thus have different experiences, occupy very different positions, and have a very different stake in the social system. These differences exist even where there is little social change. Where social change is rapid, the two generations simply grow up in different worlds. Even at the *same* age they do not share the same experiences.[25] To make an obvious comparison, modern children have grown up in an age when the contraceptive pill is easily available, when the hydrogen bomb threatens the existence of the world, when the use of both prescription and street drugs has become widespread, when major catastrophes suggest that the older generation cannot solve the problems of their epoch, and when the constant threat of war has created for the first time in American history an immense, continuing

defense force and very close ties between the military establishment and the economy.

Consequently, what is surprising is not the amount of conflict between parents and children, but the extent to which children gradually come to share the opinions and attitudes of their parents as they mature. As one index, perhaps the best predictor of how a person will vote is how his or her parents have been voting over their lifetime. The revolt of young people against the older generation in the past decade has been more widespread and radical than at any other time in our history; but up to now every public opinion inquiry suggests that, aside from matters of taste and clothing, the rising generation will share to a remarkable extent the attitudes and even the behavior of the previous generation.[26]

Socialization

Far more than the parents of any other nation, United States parents have looked to supposed experts for guidance on how to rear their children. For over half a century tens of millions of parents have been avid readers of government pamphlets, magazine articles, and books on feeding schedules, toilet training, cuddling, breast or bottle feeding, the use of punishment, and other aspects of parent-child relations. That advice has changed from one decade to the next. At present it appears to be moving toward the approval of more parental authority; but in the generation after World War II it suggested less punishment and more loving,

[24]Frank F. Furstenberg, "Industrialization and the American Family: A Look Backward," *American Sociological Review,* 31 (June 1966), pp. 326–327.

[25]The classic analysis of this *generational* difference under conditions of rapid social change is that of Kingsley Davis, "The Sociology of Parent-Youth Conflict," *American Sociological Review,* 5 (1940), pp. 523–536. See also William J. Goode, "Family Disorganization," in Robert K. Merton and Robert Nisbet, *Contemporary Social Problems,* 3d ed., New York: Harcourt Brace Jovanovich, 1971, pp. 529–532.

[26]For some data showing that youthful attitudes do not diverge so radically from those of the older generation, once younger people have become adults themselves, see S. M. Lipset and E. C. Ladd, "College Generations —From the 1930's to the 1960's," *The Public Interest,* no. 25 (Fall 1971), pp. 99–113.

flexible feeding schedules, later toilet training, and much permissiveness.

It is not clear that these changes were based on real proof that one specific pattern of child-parent relations would make children happier, better able to cope with the world, or finer human beings. It is even less clear how much effect all this advice had on the actual behavior of the parents who read it so attentively. It seems likely that parents did change their behavior with respect to many minor items of child rearing, such as feeding time, letting the child cry between feedings, and toilet training. On the other hand, there have been relatively few adequate studies of the minute-to-minute behavior of parents toward their children with respect to much more fundamental things that may convey parental attitudes much more powerfully. It is easier to change some kinds of behavior than others, and the ones that are easiest to change are likely to be least significant in the socialization of the child. For example, for well over a generation it has been argued that physical punishment should not be used or should be used only rarely. In fact, it is likely that parents have changed their behavior somewhat, but it is much more difficult to control one's anger than it is to change feeding schedules. Unfortunately, it is likely that parental anger is more important in the process of socialization than feeding schedules are.

Similarly, parents have been advised to treat their children not only fairly, but in a relatively equalitarian fashion. Unfortunately, most parents have found this advice difficult to follow, since not only are they sure that they are right in their conflicts with their children, but they do not really believe that children should be given the same rights as parents. Nor do they believe that girls should be given the same rights as boys. Differential treatment of boys and girls is so ingrained in almost all parents that it becomes an automatic part of their training.

Finally, people can only be as good as they are. Parents cannot, even with the advice of experts, transform themselves into sensitive, warm, and understanding human beings. They carry into the parent-child relationship all their own problems derived from a childhood one generation earlier, and remain just as selfish and thoughtless after reading hundreds of pages of good advice as they were before.

There is some evidence that the child-rearing practices of the middle classes and those of the working classes have gradually been converging somewhat over the past twenty-five years.[27] Middle-class families, or at least educated families, have attempted, doubtless at times with some success, to use less physical punishment and more reasoning and explanation as a mode of controlling their children than lower-class families do. In deciding whether to punish, they have been more concerned about *why* a child did something than have lower-class families, who have been more concerned about the consequences of the act. Middle-class parents have also been reported to use more frequently the threat of withdrawing love.

Although most readers will doubtless feel more sympathetic toward the middle-class orientation and its accompanying rhetoric, the fact is that we do not have good data about the exact consequences of such differences. Our biases run against the use of physical punishment and in favor of giving reasons to the child. But the threat of with-

[27]Urie Bronfenbrenner, "Socialization and Social Class through Time and Space," in Eleanor E. Maccoby, T. M. Newcomb, and E. H. Hartey, eds., *Readings in Social Psychology,* New York: Holt, 1958, pp. 400–425. See also Daniel R. Miller and Guy E. Swanson, *The Changing American Parent,* New York: Wiley, 1958.

FOCUS

ECONOMIC AND MARITAL INSTABILITY AT LOWER-CLASS LEVELS

One of the major points of articulation between the inside world and the larger society surrounding it is in the area of employment. The way in which the man makes a living and the kind of living he makes have important consequences for how the man sees himself and is seen by others; and these, in turn, importantly shape his relationships with family members, lovers, friends and neighbors.

Making a living takes on an overriding importance at marriage. The young, lower-class Negro gets married in his early twenties, at approximately the same time and in part for the same reason as his white or Negro working- or middle-class counterpart. He has no special motive for getting married; sex is there for the taking, with or without marriage, and he can also live with a woman or have children—if he has not done this already—without getting married. He wants to be publicly, legally married, to support a family and be the head of it, because this is what it is to be a man in our society, whether one lives in a room near the Carry-out or in an elegant house in the suburbs.

Although he wants to get married, he hedges on his commitment from the very beginning because he is afraid, not of marriage itself, but of his own ability to carry out his responsibilities as husband and father. His own father failed and had to "cut out," and the men he knows who have been or are married have also failed or are in the process of doing so. He has no evidence that he will fare better than they and much evidence that he will not. However far he has gone in school he is illiterate or almost so; however many jobs he has had or hard he has worked, he is essentially unskilled. [1] Armed with models who have failed, convinced of his own worthlessness, illiterate and unskilled, he enters marriage and the job market with the smell of failure all around him. Jobs are only intermittently available. They are almost always menial, sometimes hard, and never pay enough to support a family.

In general, the menial job lies outside the job hierarchy and promises to offer no more tomorrow than it does today. The Negro menial worker remains a menial worker so that, after one or two or three years of marriage and as many children, the man who could not support his family from the very beginning is even less able to support it as time goes on. The longer he works, the longer he is unable to live on what he makes. He has little vested interest in such a job and learns to treat it with the same contempt held for it by the employer and society at large. From his point of view, the job is expendable; from the employer's point

---

[1] And he is black. Together, these make a deadly combination and relegate him to the very bottom of our society.

of view, he is. For reasons real or imagined, perhaps so slight as to go unnoticed by others, he frequently quits or is fired. Other times, he is jobless simply because he cannot find a job.

He carries this failure home where his family life is undergoing a parallel deterioration. His wife's adult male models also failed as husbands and fathers and she expects no less from him. She hopes but does not expect him to be a good provider, to make of them a family and be head of it, to be "the man of the house." But his failure to do these things does not make him easier to live with because it was expected. She keys her demands to her wants, to her hopes, not to her expectations. Her demands mirror the man both as society says he should be and as he really is, enlarging his failure in both their eyes.

Sometimes he sits down and cries at the humiliation of it all. Sometimes he strikes out at her or the children with his fists, perhaps to lay hollow claim to being man of the house in the one way left open to him, or perhaps simply to inflict pain on this woman who bears witness to his failure as a husband and father and therefore as a man. Increasingly he turns to the streetcorner where a shadow system of values constructed out of public fictions serves to accommodate just such men as he, permitting them to be men once again provided they do not look too closely at one another's credentials. [2]

[2] This "shadow system" of values is very close to Hyman Rodman's "value stretch." Members of the lower class, he says, "share the general values of the society with members of other classes, but in addition they have stretched these values, or developed alternative values, which help them adjust to their deprived circumstances" ("The Lower-Class Value Stretch," p. 209).

I would add at least two qualifications to Rodman's and other formulations that posit an alternate system of lower-class values. The first is that the stretched or alternative value systems are not the same order of values, either phenomenologically or operationally, as the parent or general system of values: they are derivative, subsidiary in nature, thinner and less weighty, less completely internalized, and seem to be value images reflected by force or adaptive behavior rather than real values with a positive determining influence on behavior of choice. The second qualification is that the alternative value system is not a distinct value system which can be separately invoked by its users. It appears only in association with the parent system and is separable from it only analytically. Derivative, insubstantial, and co-occurring with the parent system, it is as if the alternative value system is a shadow cast by the common value system in the distorting lower-class setting. Together, the two systems lie behind much that seems paradoxical and inconsistent, familiar and alien, to the middle-class observer from his one-system perspective.

SOURCE: Eliot Liebow, *Tally's Corner: A Study of Negro Streetcorner Men*, Boston, Little, Brown, 1967, pp. 210–213.

drawing love can create psychological problems that may be more serious than those resulting from being spanked. The preferred form of middle-class rearing may create far more conscience-ridden adults than does the lower-class pattern.

Perhaps the most important fact is that all societies manage somehow to produce a next generation that seems about as capable and as mature as the prior generation, no matter what child-rearing techniques were used. Whether childhood experiences are loving or distant, whether the child is given adult responsibilities early or late, parents in all societies seem to be effective in passing on the content of their culture and the social roles that are appropriate to their socieites.

Are Both Parents Needed?

The socialization process was somewhat easier in the primitive societies of the immediate past, where only one major set of beliefs and practices was visible. In modern societies young people are exposed to a wide range of customs and styles of life that are extolled by one authority or another. Parents give their children one set of principles; teachers may give very different advice; and much of that is contradicted in turn by what children see around them. If children and adolescents are sometimes confused as to what they ought to do, so are the adults who are trying to shape their attitudes and beliefs.

Among the many issues that analysts of the parent-child relationship have posed is whether it is necessary for adequate child rearing and adult psychological health that the child be reared in an intact household, with the role models of mother and father present throughout their earlier years. This issue has been raised with special force with respect to the black family, where so often the father is not the head of the household.[28] It has also been an issue in the feminist

movement, for so many people believe that the child needs the constant attention of the mother in order to become a healthy adult.

Unfortunately, even on this point the data are not definite. In 1973 approximately 8.3 million children were being reared only by their mothers. There were approximately 6.6 million households in which a woman was the head. A higher percentage of black families than of white fell into this category, and some part of the controversy about black families has focused on whether this living arrangement might be inadequate for effective socialization. As might be supposed, there is a substantial correlation between poverty and the mother-headed family. Approximately two-thirds of the families in that category fell below the poverty line. When we consider only these poor families, that is, when we compare only the families below the poverty line, the black and white family patterns are not so very different.[29]

In any event, a summary of literally hundreds of studies has reported that they yield no definite conclusion about whether the absence of the father has in itself any great effect on the adult capacities of the children.[30] The children who are reared in mother-headed families certainly suffer many deprivations, but these flow largely from poverty, from the lesser educational resources of the home, and from the social problems the child encounters in such neighborhoods, rather than from the simple absence of the father.

Our society is the first in human history to assume that motherhood is a twenty-

---

[28]For discussions on these issues, see Daniel P. Moynihan, *The Negro Family: The Case for National Action,*

Washington, D.C.: U.S. Department of Labor, Office of Planning and Research, 1965; Lee Rainwater and William Yancey, *The Moynihan Report and the Politics of Controversy,* Cambridge, Mass.: M.I.T. Press, 1967; and Andrew Billingsley, *Black Families in White America,* Englewood Cliffs, N.J.: Prentice-Hall, 1968.

[29]For the similarities between black and white families that are poor, see Herbert H. Hyman and John S. Reed, "Black Matriarchy Reconsidered: Evidence from Secondary Analysis of Sample Surveys," *Public Opinion Quarterly,* 33 (Fall 1969), pp. 346–354.

[30]For a brief summary of these data, see Nye and Berardo, op cit., pp. 397–401.

four-hour-a-day job. In most societies women have continued to work while being mothers, and children were not supposed to be the center of attention. Motherhood filled in the interstices of work here and there, but was not supposed to be a full-time occupation. Here too the data do not support a definite conclusion. Modern studies on the collective care of infants in the Soviet Union, Israel, and other countries make it very clear that children can grow up to be both intellectually and psychologically adequate human beings, even if their own mother did not care for them constantly during the first years of life.[31] There is little evidence at present that the child's own mother will necessarily do a better job at socialization than will professionally trained surrogate mothers. Moreover, the data are definite on at least one point: Maintaining an intact but conflict-ridden home "for the good of the children" does them little good. Studies show fairly conclusively that children of such homes are likely to suffer more problems later on than children whose parents broke their unhappy union apart.

DIVORCE

For the past hundred years, the divorce rate has been rising in the United States. The rate has been higher during prosperity and lower during depressions, but has climbed upward every decade. In the year ending August 1974 an estimated 2,233,000 marriages occurred, and 948,000 divorces.[32] (Keep in mind that most of those divorces happened to marriages a period of one to many years earlier; the figures *do not* mean that about forty-five percent of all marriages now end in divorce.) Although some nations and societies have exhibited high rates of divorce in the past, at present the United States has the highest rate among contemporary nations. On the other hand, some four-fifths

of all people who divorce get married again, showing a continuing, touching faith in this ancient institution. We should also remember that in other societies with high divorce rates (for example, Arab society) those family systems also continued to function generation after generation just the same.

Divorce must be seen as an escape valve for the inevitable tensions of marriage itself. In a family system in which divorce is not permitted, other kinds of marital dissolutions occur. People desert, or live apart from one another. They establish separate homes with other people or even live in the same household for years with little social contact. At present, most people in this country marry in their early twenties and enjoy a high likelihood of living until their early seventies. Thus, they can expect to live half a century with each other. It should not be surprising, therefore, that the rate of dissolution would be higher than in societies where the expectation of life was much shorter.

Earlier, we pointed to some forces that supported greater marital stability in the past, such as the need of both spouses for the services that each could contribute on a farm, the smaller number of alternative spouses if the union should break up, the likelihood that husband and wife shared the same definitions of their appropriate social roles, and the support of kin and neighbors. In all these respects modern society is different.

We can also observe the operation of these factors in the class differences in divorce rates. About two decades ago it was ascertained that where a substantial freedom to divorce exists legally, there is a higher divorce rate toward the *lower* social strata.[33] That study also showed that the divorce rate among blacks is greater than that among whites.

[31]Ibid., pp. 394–399.
[32]Glick, op. cit., p. 2.

[33]See William J. Goode, *Women in Divorce* (originally: *After Divorce*), New York: Free Press, 1956, chaps. 4 and 5, which seems to be the first to present a sociological analysis of this pattern.

One factor that creates these differences is the greater material difficulty of life toward the lower social strata, for at least some couples will displace their irritation about economic matters onto other areas of the marriage. The discrepancy between the potential income of the wife and the income of the husband is much greater toward the upper social strata; so that wives can easily perceive the greater costs of leaving the marriage. In addition, the kin and friend network is stronger toward the upper social strata; and the possible consequences of dissolution are likely to be greater. Data also show that toward the lower social strata divorced husbands are much more likely to escape paying child support. Indeed, within a few years very few men in the working classes continue to make their payments regularly. By contrast, divorced men in the middle and upper social strata cannot escape their obligations so easily. Thus, the costs are greater for men in these strata. Desertion is also more common toward the lower social strata, where a man can more easily disappear. Thus, a number of pressures combine to create a higher divorce rate toward the lower classes.

Norms for Divorce Adjustment

About one-third of all marriages in the United States will eventually end in divorce (the total was 948,000 in the year ending August 1974). Each year over 900,000 children under the age of eighteen are involved in those divorces, so that an extremely large percentage of the population, as spouse or as child, has been touched by divorce.[34] However, our society has not developed a set of social roles and expectations that adequately handle the problems that result from divorce. In most primitive societies there were clear rules as to whom the child should live with, the conditions under which a

bride price had to be returned, where the spouses went after divorce, and how new marriages would be contracted.

In our own society there are many *regularities* that can be observed in divorce processes, but these do not have the status of norms or role expectations. For example, there are few *social supports* that specify precisely how divorced persons *should* act. We are not sure whether we should congratulate them or sympathize. It is not clear whether anyone has a responsibility to help either spouse enter a new marriage. Moreover, the new philosophy expressed in the feminist movement subjects all these matters to even more scrutiny and debate in our time.

This situation can be contrasted with that of losing one's husband or wife by death. Then the social rules are fairly clear. Friends should rally around and help the survivor, both by sharing the grief and by solving some immediate problems. The friend and kin network is not broken by this event, but is likely to be temporarily stronger. There is no problem of divided allegiance. Far more social services are available. In short, all communities have fairly well-established rituals, customs, and role definitions for mourning and adjustment to the death of the spouse.

Many proposals for divorce reform have been made. One of the more radical ones to be put into action is the "no-fault divorce law." Although many proposals have been given that name, a genuine no-fault divorce law neither requires nor permits the spouses to accuse one another, nor to refuse to divorce on the grounds that they are the "innocent party." Under this type of law neither party can use that refusal as a way of gaining additional advantages. Its aim is to eliminate the notion of the "guilty party" who should "pay" for her or his faults.

The underlying philosophy of such a legal arrangement is essentially equalitarian. Neither party should obtain support from the

[34]See Glick, op. cit., p. 10.

other, unless put at some special disadvantage by the dissolution of the marriage. Under this view it is not taken for granted that custody will be awarded to the mother. It is assumed that women should begin to support themselves, for there is no reason they should not be in the labor force. On the other hand, until women do achieve equality with men in the socioeconomic world, the advantages that this reform brings must be weighed against the problems that it poses, especially for older divorced women.

to forbid.

CONCLUSION: THE OLD TABOOS AND THE NEW RADICAL ROMANTICISM

Sociology has long asserted that much of the influence of values and norms comes from their being unquestioned; they have the most power over our lives when we simply take them for granted, without even perceiving alternative ways of feeling and acting. If this is true, then the family is changing more rapidly than almost any other part of modern society. Almost every traditional taboo has been challenged publicly. Radically new family models are proclaimed as solutions for the oppression and evil the old system caused.

In rural areas as in cities, communes of various types have been established, in many of which "group marriage" is practiced. That is, anyone may enjoy sex with anyone else. Lesbian couples as well as male homosexual couples not only assert their right to a marriage ceremony; many also insist on their right to adopt children, so as to become parents as well. Couples who may have been married for years, and who do not intend to get divorced, may decide on an "open marriage," in which each party has the right to affairs with others, under the understanding that all parties will communicate fully with each other about their feelings. Other couples join networks of

Figure 12-4   Mike McConnell (left) and Jack Baker were married in a private ceremony in Minneapolis after a series of legal hassles contesting the validity of same-sex marriage. (United Press International Photo.)

"swingers" for temporary or longer-lasting periods of husband and wife swapping.

As some sober fact finders have asserted, there may be much more talk than action. Several studies have suggested, for example, that the amount of premarital sexual intercourse may not have risen as much as the mass media might suppose.[35] People have been heard to complain that though wild orgies seem to be occurring on every block, they never seem to be invited to them, so that once again there may be more rhetoric

[35]The changes in action seem certain; see Morton Hunt, *Sexual Behavior in the 1970's,* Chicago: Playboy Press, 1974.

than consummation. Nevertheless, most readers of this book can observe that action moves steadily in conformity with rhetoric.

Along with many changes has come a radical new romanticism that erodes still further the stability of the family and creates new problems for almost everyone who is tempted by its seductive promise. It is an implicit theme in most of the contemporary challenges to the old taboos. It is to be found as well in much of the feminist literature. It is also proclaimed in numerous books on how to improve one's psychological health and attain happiness.

Essentially, the new romanticism asserts the unlimited possibilities of choice in the sphere of intimate relations. It is perhaps a modern version of the old view that one should wait until one's true love appeared, whereupon life would be transformed, and (after marriage) one would live happily ever after with that unique person. The new romanticism is perhaps more radical, for it suggests that our fate is really not dependent upon any particular other person. Life is a series of self-discoveries, in which we proceed from one type of relationship to another, as we grow and develop.

Like all romantic views, this contains a core of truth. Jessie Bernard has suggested that in the marriages of the future we can ask for stability or monogamy, but not both. That is, we can ask for a temporary monogamy, while we are in an intense, possessive relationship; or we can opt for stability, and permit our partner to wander from time to time. There are in fact more options open to us now than in the past. We can indeed join a commune. If we are unwilling to commit ourselves to marriage, we may be able to find a partner who will share our lives for a while without that commitment.

The modern human being has grown accustomed to much change, and recognizes correctly that he or she may possess many potentialities that life has heretofore not developed or encouraged. Moreover, it is likely that at least some part of the population will experience a very different "marital career" than in the past. That is, some will experiment with a sequence, or succession: living together for a while with someone, marriage, divorce, a new period of searching for options, and even perhaps a period of communal living.

On the other hand, at the risk of seeming to be both conservative and pessimistic, it must be said that for most people these options are more illusory than real. Doubtless, our potentialities are typically greater than our achievements, but it is not true that we can easily rearrange the outside world so as to bring those potentialities to fruition. To avoid permanent commitments gives some freedom; but if our partners remain equally uncommitted, then the freedom is once more illusory. Few of us are so secure inwardly that we can live comfortably from day to day in relationships where the other person feels no great obligation to continue giving us support or affection beyond the whim of the moment. For that matter, few of us are so attractive, or attractive over many years, that we can be sure there *will* be another partner who will become available when we need her or him.

The author strongly favors the existence of these options. Nevertheless, we must also regard them with an objective sociological eye and not be deluded by their apparent promise. Social change brings great costs, which most people are not willing to pay over the long run, and indeed cannot pay. Precisely because we have been shaped and molded by a lifetime of experience in our own society, we cannot suddenly transform ourselves into different persons. And even if we could, the world will not treat us differently just because we proclaim our transformation. Although we do not believe the next few decades will witness a strong reassertion of traditional values, and we believe many alternatives to traditional conjugal unions will remain as options for some, most

people will—even after much experimentation—settle for the lesser delight but
greater steadiness of marriage as most of us
know it. In spite of the modern rhetoric of

the new romanticism, most will not find
fulfillment through an indefinitely variegated set of unions of all types, to which individuals feel no great commitment.

READINGS

Bert Adams, *The American Family,* Chicago:
Markham, 1971.

Jessie Bernard, *The Future of Marriage,* New
York: World, 1972.

Andrew Billingsley, *Black Families in White
America,* Englewood Cliffs, N.J.: Prentice-
Hall, 1968.

Elizabeth Bott, *Family and Social Network,* London: Tavistock, 1957.

Harold A. Christensen, ed., *Handbook of Marriage and the Family,* Chicago: Rand McNally,
1964.

Bernard Farber, *Family: Organization and Interaction,* San Francisco: Chandler, 1964.

William J. Goode, *Women in Divorce* (originally:
After Divorce), New York: Free Press, 1956.

———, *The Family,* Englewood Cliffs, N.J.:
Prentice-Hall, 1963.

———, *World Revolution and Family Patterns,*
New York: Free Press, 1963.

Kathleen Gough, "Is the Family Universal?—The
Nayar Case," in Norman W. Bell and Ezra F.

Vogel, eds., *A Modern Introduction to the Family,* New York: Free Press, 1960, pp. 76–92.

Reuben Hill et al., *Family Development in Three
Generations,* Cambridge, Mass.: Schenkman,
1970.

Morton Hunt, *Sexual Behavior in the 1970's,*
Chicago: Playboy Press, 1974.

Mirra Komarovsky, *Blue-Collar Marriage,* New
York: Random House, 1964.

George P. Murdock, *Social Structure,* New York:
Macmillan, 1949.

F. Ivan Nye and Lois W. Hoffman, *The Employed Mother in America,* Chicago: Rand
McNally, 1963.

——— and Felix M. Berardo, *The Family,* New
York: Macmillan, 1973.

Irving Rosow, "Intergenerational Relationships:
Problems and Proposals," in Ethel Schanas
and G. F. Streib, eds., *Social Structure and the
Family: Generational Relations,* Englewood
Cliffs, N.J.: Prentice-Hall, 1965, pp. 341–378.

Robert F. Winch, *The Modern Family,* 3d ed.,
New York: Holt, 1971.

CHAPTER THIRTEEN

(Jean-Claude Lejeune, from Black Star.)

THE POLITICAL PROCESS

WHAT IS POLITICAL?

A shipwrecked sailor, attempting to survive on an island, is isolated from his fellow beings and thus no longer needs to obey their customs. He does not have to engage in *political* action. That is, he does not have to develop or enforce rules about who gets what, since there is no one else to make any claims. Nor does the lone individual need a government to decide *how* to change the rules when that is desired.

But the arrival of even one more human being initiates political processes, whether or not anyone is conscious of them, for two people will have disputes about what each owes to the other or what rules they are to follow. They must therefore make an informal or formal charter, constitution, or set of "laws" if they want to avoid a fight every time they disagree.

Note that immediately we see how differ-ent is *economic* calculation from this, for even the lone person must engage in economic processes: Should that person gather only the food needed to get through the day, or should the food be stored for possibly more barren days ahead? Should time be invested in contriving fishing or hunting equipment, or should the individual simply eat what is found? Should time and energy be put into making fire, or will the food taste good enough if eaten raw? That is, the lone survivor must weigh alternative costs and rewards in allocating limited resources.

The problems that Robinson Crusoe faced each day alone are stated and solved more elegantly in formal economics; for example, he will spend more of his limited resources to get something he values highly (say, goat meat) than he will to get something he values less (sea urchins, clams, acorns), even if the latter are very nutritious. He is more likely to invest time and energy in making equipment if he already has a surplus of food. And when the payoff for additional work is small, he is less likely to make the investment.

For centuries social scientists have engaged in thought experiments, such as imagining an individual on an island, in an effort to locate the great sets of variables that shape social life. By thinking about human beings in simple situations, before complex societies arose, they hoped to perceive what the minimum requirements of any society were. In the case of Robinson Crusoe we can see that economic behavior is so elemental that it exists even without social life. By contrast, as soon as his man Friday appears, some types of political rules appear, as they work out their agreements about who should command or obey, how disputes are to be settled, or what they should do cooperatively.

Another thought experiment of the past was to imagine several human beings living alone or in isolated groups or families. If they decide to form a society, they will have to agree upon political rules. As soon as other people bring divergent goals and interests, disagreements will arise, and some way must be found to settle them. In short, people in groups must begin to make *political* decisions.

If they decide to live apart, but fight to ambush one another, that warlike existence is included among the traditional political processes we study. If they decide not to form a unitary society, but engage in peaceable trade, still there must be some rules about what to do when the inevitable conflicts or disagreements arise. Indeed, in some remote parts of the world, tribes who put little trust in each other engaged in "silent trade." One group left the goods for trade and then retired, and the other group left what they considered equal goods in exchange. However, either side could reject the exchange or take too much, and thus trading would break off. They could also take the goods by force. If they stopped their interaction and ceased to trade, no rules were necessary. But when people with divergent goals, interests, or values continue to occupy the same social space, they will contrive rules for handling their inevitable disagreements.

Although these situations seem unreal, similar ones have occurred. And even imaginary situations can be fruitfully used in thinking about real political systems. They are not all unreal: Shipwrecked sailors *have* had to work out procedures for getting along with each other or with strangers. Explorers, travelers, and migrants *have*, under great stress, abandoned traditions, customs, and values and turned to force as the ultimate resource to settle disputes. After the mutiny on *H.M.S. Bounty,* Captain Bligh maintained his authority by threat of death as he bullied his crew to survive a three-thousand-mile ocean voyage in an open lifeboat. Many travelers or migrants faced with starvation have killed one another for the remaining food or have eaten their dead comrades.[1]

In short, from time to time human beings have fallen into extreme situations where traditional social customs, values, and norms have little effectiveness. In such cases people have had to work out new ways of cooperating, solving disputes, or exploiting one another.

Social analysts of the past have also imagined the human situation before the invention of governments in order to think about what the basic political rights of human beings might be. The tough-minded Thomas Hobbes (1588–1679) argued that people did not have to give up much when they formed

[1]Many books have been written about the tragic fate of the Donner Party in California. For a recent account of cannibalism under such conditions, see Piers Paul Reed, *Alive! The Story of the Andes Survivors,* Philadelphia: Lippincott, 1974.

governments, since in the "state of nature" life was "solitary, poor, nasty, brutish, and short." Therefore, he asserted, people would willingly give up some of their "rights" to a monarch, in order to enjoy the benefits of security and order and to keep the goods they produced.

The English philosopher John Locke (1632–1704), whose thinking shaped the creation of the United States Constitution, believed that people in a state of nature, that is, before societies were formed, in fact led peaceful and contented lives. Consequently, it would not have been sensible for them to give up their basic rights unless guaranteed a great deal of freedom and voice in government, justice in the courts, choice of religion, and a rule of law rather than the whim of a despot.

Imaginary cases can help us think more clearly about elementary factors in political life, but once we turn to the complexities of modern society it is difficult to separate *political* processes from sociological ones. If we want to grasp how the leaders of any society manage to obtain more rewards than others and yet elicit obedience, we must ascertain to what extent both groups share the same values, what *economic* rewards followers will get for their obedience, how much *esteem* the leaders will enjoy, and how much *force* or threat of force the leaders could command if challenged. That is, individuals' control over others, the acceptance of rules for solving conflicts, and the ways of making new rules are affected by *all* and *any* resources that people can muster. Which resources should we call political?

The simplest solution is to be led by ordinary language: *Political* encompasses all governmental actions and, thus, the efforts of people to gain control of governments. Indeed, governmental activities do aim at solving the problems we have noted. Governments decide between parties in conflict, impose peace, or make new rules about who

may govern or how decisions shall be reached.

However, if we seek the underlying resource, or set of factors, that distinguishes the machinery of government from, say, that of a church, a university, or even a corporation, it is that (as Max Weber put it) *government claims a monopoly of legitimate force within its territory.* Governments can command other resources as well, but force is their ultimate basis of control when all else fails. Almost everyone uses force or the threat of force at times, but no one (not even a parent) has the *authority* to do so unless he or she has been delegated that right by the state. This holds even in the many primitive societies with no formal, distinguishable governmental agencies such as judges and courts, councils and parliaments, kings and chieftains, or lawyers and the police. For even in such societies there are traditional ways, backed by publicly organized force and its threat, for deciding the issues that governmental agencies handle in more bureaucratized societies.[2] In all societies social custom disapproves of individuals imposing their definitions of justice on others. That is left to government.

FORCE

Political sociology and political science as special fields have overlapped comfortably for several decades in their shared concern with how people decide to vote, change their political beliefs or parties, gain or lose

[2]For a wise discussion of whether such societies have a legal system, see E. Adamson Hoebel and Karl Llewellyn, *The Cheyenne Way: Conflict & Case Law in Primitive Jurisprudence* (1953), Norman: University of Oklahoma Press, 1967; and E. Adamson Hoebel, *The Law of Primitive Man* (1954), Cambridge, Mass.: Harvard, 1964. See also Geert van der Steenhoven, *Leadership and Law among the Eskimos of the Keewatiu District, Northwest Territories*, Rijswijk, Netherlands: Excelsior, 1962.

political influence and office, form protest movements, and make revolutions. What do these events or processes (except for revolution) have to do with force or even the threat of force? Before examining the sociological aspects of those concrete political activities, let us consider what force can and cannot do.[3]

The Strength of Force

Throughout history philosophers, kings, and brave people have denied the importance of force or its threat while disapproving its use. Philosophers have deplored its use because they correctly saw that using force suggests that an unjust demand has been made. As social analysts, they have noted that tyrants can take whatever wealth is available but cannot force their subjects to give them affection: After all, we cannot will another person to love us. While an absolute monarch can force subjects to kneel, to erect monuments in his or her honor, and to offer public praise, no ruler can force subjects to feel respect or esteem. Organizations that rest on force (slave systems, prisons, concentration camps, conquered colonies) are fragile in spite of their protective guns. Why? Because the people in them feel little or no commitment to the imposed group goals, do not believe the system is just, are eager to escape if they can, and are unwilling to work well unless they are watched constantly.

Rulers who have deplored force have also denied its usefulness. Even despots are likely to claim that force is of no great importance, because most have believed that their reign was just. They reasoned that since their subjects were happy, they did not need to use force, except perhaps on the misguid-ed few; ordinary subjects would be pleased to obey. Such rulers may also have wanted to persuade their subjects that the use of force is wrong so that the citizens would be easier to command.

The Weakness of Force

In speeches and acts brave people have denied that force could control them, and now and then they have pulled great emperors from their thrones. It is indeed such heroic examples that have taught social analysts how weak force really is. According to that belief, human resistance to tyranny is sometimes mute, but remains staunch; the will to freedom not only endures, but eventually prevails. The past five centuries in Western nations and the recent history of most nations illustrate the slow triumph of human rights over the swords and guns of dictators and despots.

Sociologists, too, have pointed out the weakness of force in asserting that the cultural and social systems of people are likely to survive even lengthy conquests. The Chinese absorbed their Mongol and Manchu rulers, the Indonesians evicted their Dutch rulers, and indeed only rarely in history have conquerors succeeded in imposing their way of life on their subjects.[4]

Against the optimistic view that force is weak and will finally be overthrown is the observation that the eventual overthrow of a tyrant, a dictator, or a colonial ruler will be of little help to the millions of people whose lives are shorter than those political systems. Other realistic comments can be elicited (though not always publicly) from people who are deprived of some of a society's advantages: slaves, children, dissidents, women, lower-ranked ethnic groups in all na-

---

[3]For a fuller theoretical analysis of force and force-threat, see William J. Goode, "The Place of Force in Human Society," *American Sociological Review,* 37 (October 1972), pp. 507–519.

[4]On the other hand, there are a few spectacular ones: the Roman Empire, the Mohammedan conquests, and the Anglo-Iberian takeover of the Western Hemisphere.

Figure 13-1 The victims of force may see it as the foundation of rule. (Fred Ward, Black Star.)

tions, and the lower social strata generally. Compared with people in higher positions, a greater percentage of such groups believe that the foundation of rule is force. Perhaps because they are most likely to be the victims, they more often observe force and its threat being used. Further proof of how important force is can also be seen in the fact that those in high positions exert much energy in trying to control the apparatus of the state: After all, the state is capable of using force to shape and determine people's behavior.

Traditional social analysis has argued that no regime or society can be founded on force alone. However, few societies have ever had to do so. Police and army officers, husbands and colonial rulers, and teachers and parents have enjoyed other resources as well, including the social approval of leaders and followers, financial rewards, and social esteem.

Sociological analysis has focused less on the threat of force and more on other bases of social control. Sociologists have explained social action by showing how people have been socialized to believe that rules are moral and good, not merely profitable, and how they have been pressured by others who also believe those rules are right. They have agreed that any society must be able to command enough force to kill or constrain any member who cannot be controlled by social or moral pressures, but they have supposed that force is used only in unusual cases.

However, as we understand modern society more fully, we become aware that *consensus,* or shared commitment to most norms and values, is not enough to guarantee adequate social control. People disagree about many important values. Therefore, we must examine more closely how other kinds of social control work. As suggested earlier, *economic* factors form one major set of controls. Another set is the processes by which people and groups give *prestige* or disesteem to each other. In more informal settings giving or withholding *affection* influences how people behave. In considering the effects of *force* and its threat here, we suggest that this set of controls is to be observed in much of social action, not only in deviant and unusual situations.

The Threat of Force

Much more important, however, is that people in positions of command do not have to use *overt* force when they are challenged. Teachers, for example, are now much more civil than fifty years ago, when their right to paddle pupils was generally conceded. Nevertheless, they still retain the threat of force. If students challenge their authority and disrupt classrooms, police officers will come and evict them. The courts, again backed by the threat of force if challenged, will support their eviction or expulsion. Similarly, business people obey governmental regulations they disapprove of, divorced parents obey custody arrangements they dislike, and defeated officeholders turn over their posts to winners they detest, not because *overt* force is used, but because they know that if they disobey, it may be used. The *threat* of force is sufficient, if people know that the threat is likely to be carried out when challenged.

Thus, although every social system is also a system of force, overt force is not commonly observed in daily life. We obey both the laws and the people in command because we know, or believe we know, that most others would approve the use of force if it became necessary. We are taught as children that it is both wrong and foolish "to disobey the law" or to disobey people who have been given the authority to command. It is wrong because we *should* obey. But it is also foolish because we will not get away with it; at some point in our rebellion or disobedience we may encounter overt force. This is true in nations with low rates of violence, such as Sweden or England, as well as in those with high rates, such as the United States.

Correspondingly, countries with a strong tradition of freedom are not those in which citizens carry guns to protect their rights. Rather, they are the Anglo and Scandinavian countries, where governments understand that to keep people in jail without trial, to censor newspaper criticism, to prevent free speech, or to violate religious freedom will not only arouse some immediate physical resistance, but will lead to court attacks on governmental officials who engage in such acts—and they will have to obey the courts, for ultimately they are backed by overt force, too. If we rank a citizenry by the force it commands, we do so, not by how many guns it owns relative to the government, but by whether its members can eventually count on each other for support against violations of their freedom, and by their collective determination to resist.

In the short run, that will be measured by the actions of courts, but in the longer run, by citizens' threat to use force on those who will not obey a court order to cease those violations of civic freedom. If defeated officeholders believe that their fellow citizens will very likely not use force to support a court order directing them to give up their positions, they might well decide—as they have done in dozens of countries, generation after generation—to ignore the results of the election. If they have no fear that sheriffs, marshals, courts, and the citizenry will eventually use force in demanding free elections, they might—as they have done—avoid elections or arrange controlled ones.

It must be emphasized that that support *is* based on a strong moral consensus and a set of shared values, for without consensus people would not run such risks. But, in turn, if that belief in the value of civil rights and in freedom is not ultimately backed by force or its threat, political leaders can violate those rights. Indeed, they have done so in every country from time to time, and only collective vigilance can preserve that willingness to resist tyranny with the threat of counterforce.

AUTHORITY AND MODERNIZATION

As we have seen, societies create a political apparatus to impose order, peace, and methods for settling disputes. The political system mobilizes group support for those goals, and it can also organize the energies of people for other collective goals that could not easily be accomplished by one person or a handful. These include war and defense against attack, where most people share the same value or goal. They also include many other enterprises whose benefits will flow more to one set of people than to another: canals, docks, and railroads; airports; opera houses; prison buildings; a new energy program.

Governments can also try to mobilize their people to support the still grander enterprise of *modernization*—to develop a modern industrial system with all its benefits and costs, such as better health, longer lives, more education, more murderous military equipment, more automobiles, space programs, and a higher income per capita. To do this, governments must compel or persuade people to change their old customs, to contribute in taxes or property, to obey the new laws and regulations, and to give up old privileges.

The Right to Command

Since World War II dozens of new governments have used force to mobilize civic energies for modernization, but force is successful for only a short while. People do not wish to cooperate much with a regime that prods them with bayonets. Instead, to be truly successful, a government must somehow achieve *authority*, that is, *the right to give orders*, or the public support of its commands. These new governments have typically failed to gain authority; in fact, *more political regimes have fallen during this past generation than during any comparable period in the past.* For example, hardly a

month passes without a newspaper report of another military coup in one of the new African nations. Although most of those leaders promised large benefits to the masses—such as land redistribution, freedom from political repression, participation in important decisions, better health, and even national glory—their citizenry did not continue to grant their right to give orders. Why were they unable to arouse continuing support? Why did these new leaders fail to attain the *right to command*?

The failure of authority has been a key factor in the incapacity of most revolutions even to establish a stable government, much less to fulfill their glowing promises. Of the many recent attempts to build new societies, only a few have achieved a continuing authority; some notable exceptions are China, North Vietnam, and Cuba. The modern era with its high political instability almost suggests that making a revolution is much easier than creating a political system that commands authority. Since most people seem to desire the modernization that revolution and colonial revolts promise, why do they withhold precisely the support that is necessary for the success of that kind of mobilization?

We have given a short definition of authority as the *right* to command, but let us analyze that notion more deeply. If we say that a government enjoys authority, we do not mean that it is powerful or even competent. What distinguishes a government with authority is that its citizens not only obey its commands (for example, to pay taxes, to appear for military service, to comply with a court order), but they believe they *should* do so and believe their fellow citizens ought to do so, too—even if they do not believe those commands are very wise.

Similarly, if we argue that the telephone company has no authority to cut off the tops of trees in front of our house, that a police officer has no authority to come into our apartment without a search warrant, or that a teacher cannot legitimately fail a student simply out of dislike, we do not mean that those events cannot *happen,* for we all know that they occur frequently. What we mean is that when those facts are known, others (both courts and our fellow citizens) will not agree that those people had the *right* to do those things, and we will be supported in our efforts at redressing those wrongs. So, similarly, we say that a general does not have the authority to give orders to a civilian or that a bank does not have the authority to cash a check signed by an unauthorized employee of a corporation.

What all these instances point to is an agreement (or denial) that (1) individuals acquire special posts or offices according to the socially approved rules and laws; (2) those offices have a socially approved right to issue certain commands; (3) at some point those commands will be backed by the law, the courts, and, if necessary, a governmental use of force; and (4) the citizenry in turn will back that compulsion.

One sociologist has suggested these definitions:[5]

Authority is institutionalized power (that is, it is the threat of force, backed by a social agreement that its use is legitimate).

Power is latent force (that is, it is the *threat* or possibility of force).

Force is manifest power (that is, the threat or possibility of force now brought into action).

Power is more often defined by sociologists as the ability to gain compliance from one or more others even if they do not want to give it. However, if we accept this definition, *power* would simply refer to any situation where one person gets his or her way, whether the other person yields because of love or friendship, economic rewards or losses, or even the possibility of losing or gaining esteem. It is much better to use the term, if we use it at all, to apply to the threat of possible force; and to use the term *authority* when we speak of *legitimate,* or *socially approved,* commands that are ultimately backed by the threat of force.

Supporting the Right to Command

That slight digression sharpens our problem somewhat, for then we see that although many revolutionaries and colonial rebels have been able to muster enough military force to *overthrow* the existing government—often that government was not even supported by its own troops—they have not been able to command their citizenry to carry out necessary civic or collective actions. Aside from war, what are these civic actions? Among them is the elementary duty of paying taxes and defending the new government. Others include contributions of work, obeying the laws against hoarding and profiteering, not using the revolution as an occasion for private family vengeance, giving up family or personal interests in favor of the nation as a whole, giving up one's family land for redistribution if that is called for, or backing the government in its new laws and regulations for the collective good. All these may be needed for a broad modernization program. Instead of doing these things, and thus agreeing that the government is legitimate, leading citizens over time are likely to oppose their own personal or group power to that of the state, and eventually to undermine or overthrow, that is, to deny its authority, its right to command. Consequently, the new government's aim of mobilizing its citizens in a

[5]Robert Bierstedt, *The Social Order,* 4th ed., New York: McGraw-Hill, 1974, p. 357.

grand program of modernization is likely to end in bankruptcy and disorder.

Such modernizing regimes face three especially sharp dilemmas. First, to keep power, they must elicit the support of the families, cliques, and groups in the society who traditionally enjoyed power and influence. On the other hand, if they do that, they cannot move ahead on any program of land redistribution, taxes on the rich, giving influence to the peasants or masses, or taking possession of factories or mines owned by foreigners or by the rich, for the traditional power holders will oppose these programs and thus the regime itself.

Modernizing regimes face a second dilemma, which becomes more serious with time. To gain support, they often have to paint utopian pictures of what glorious things the new leaders can accomplish when freed of the old colonial rulers or the former authoritarian regime. If they do not offer glowing promises, they are likely to be defeated by aspiring leaders who do. If they do make such promises, they will inevitably arouse much disappointment, because modernization, industrialization, the construction of an effective economic system, and the establishment of democracy are all difficult tasks. Grand promises with only modest success will lower public support.

Of equal importance is a third dilemma, generated by fundamental processes of political *socialization;* that is, the regime must convince the citizenry to believe in the political institutions of their society and to become morally committed to it. But the new group has had to gain power by *denying* legitimacy or authority to the old system, especially to the traditional procedures for getting into office and settling disputes among conflicting groups. However, no one has actually been reared under the new system. No one has, since childhood, come to feel an unquestioning obedience to its commands or any commitment to its rules. Consequently, at first it will be judged only by

Figure 13-2 Ho Chi Minh's programs for reform and modernization enhanced the support of his right to command in North Vietnam. (United Press International Photo.)

its *effectiveness,* or its ability to muster *force.* Since people do not feel much moral stake in it, they will not support it for long if, in their view, it begins to make many errors. People have little faith in the new rules, and thus will not be patient in the expectation that the rules will fairly give them their turn at an appropriate time. Thus, a regime that began by rejecting the legitimacy of a previous set of rules is challenged by a new set of aspiring leaders because it cannot generate its own legitimacy.

If no one else *begins* with a deep moral commitment to the new system, then the military does not either. Consequently, the new nations have been especially vulnerable to military take-overs. It should be emphasized that these military rulers are often *not* conservative, right wing, or fascist in their policies. The military leaders in most new nations do not come from the traditional upper strata, but from the newly educated middle class or even the lower class; and many of their programs have been liberal or socialist.[6] In any case, few regimes in any of the new nations have been able to count on the unswerving political commitment of their military officers.

How Fast Social Change?

As a final comment on the problem of modernization and authority, we should consider the possibility that if the new program is genuinely socialistic, fast social change may be less disruptive than slow change.

In the Anglo and Scandinavian countries democracy, political authority, and industrialization were all established over several centuries and were accompanied now and again by some civil strife. By contrast, present data strongly suggest that rapid socioeconomic change is accompanied by political instability.[7] Aside from the problems already noted, rapid socioeconomic change or modernization is also likely to make the rich richer and thus to increase the political tensions among classes.

However, in the modern epoch of greater political instability, the masses in almost all peasant societies have typically believed, correctly, that they were exploited by the rich and powerful families of the traditional ruling strata. When they see that under the new regime they do not benefit, there is more strife. By contrast, a more rapid pace may work better.

Quick removal of such rich and powerful families and cliques from power generates mass support that is in striking contrast to the resentment encountered where attempts at rapid industrialization simply make those few families still richer, with little improvement for the poor and powerless many. New regimes cannot, as we noted before, count on much traditional authority, and thus they must furnish continuing proof of their effectiveness. However, where the masses can easily observe that they are the immediate beneficiaries of any gains that are achieved, their support will be strong. That has happened in China, Cuba, North Vietnam, and Yugoslavia, as thought-provoking cases. Or, phrasing it more bluntly, if the gains from rapid socioeconomic change benefit most citizens, they are likely to adjust more easily and to support the new regime.

LEGITIMACY AND COMPETENCE

In our explorations of the relationships between social and political processes, we have stressed the importance of the citizens' self-interest by noting that people are more likely to grant authority to governments that seem effective at serving these interests. Even if a government comes to power in traditional ways or by free election, if it fails to cope with the problems of its day or if its citizens feel they are worse off, it is likely to lose some of its ability to command. Governments are especially likely to be radically changed or overturned by force during a depression or a famine or at the end of an unsuccessful war, when governments fail in providing traditional benefits to their citizens. In contrast, governments can more easily maintain their claim to legitimacy under steady prosperity or even during long periods of relative poverty, if no new problems arise that demonstrate governmental incompetence. The legitimacy of governments seems to rest on the twin pillars of

[6]For analyses of these factors, see Samuel P. Huntington, *Political Order in Changing Societies,* New Haven, Conn.: Yale, 1968, especially pp. 219ff.; Morris Janowitz, "Civil-Military Relations in the New Nations," in *Political Conflict,* Chicago: Quadrangle, 1970.

[7]See Seymour M. Lipset and William Schneider, "Political Sociology," in Neil J. Smelser, *Sociology,* 2d ed., New York: Wiley, 1973, pp. 415–416; Seymour M. Lipset, *Political Man,* New York: Doubleday, 1967, pp. 52–58; and Huntington, op. cit., pp. 32–59.

(1) traditional or folk beliefs in what is fair or just, and (2) the material and social benefits the leaders can produce for the nation—or for the important social strata within it.

Working-Class Conservatives

A brief look at Conservative party voting in England will aid our understanding of how competence relates to the legitimacy of authority. As in other nations, there has been a strong relationship between class position and conservative voting in England: Workers are more likely to vote for the Labour party (in the United States, for the Democratic party) and business people and professionals are more likely to vote for the Conservative party (here, the Republican party). Since about a century ago, when the vote was given to almost the entire British population (amidst dire predictions that the rude poor would destroy the fabric of civil life), about two-thirds or more of the electorate has belonged to the working classes. Some predicted that the workers would simply take over the government and rule for their own benefit.

Yet the historical facts confound that simple prediction of self-interest. Over the long period from the 1880s to the 1960s, there were fifteen general elections in which one party won a decisive victory and could claim a working majority in Parliament. In *eleven* of these instances, that victor was the Conservative party.[8] Although the Conservative party did not bring workers into its leadership (to be sure, only rarely did the Labour party do that, either), decade after decade it drew about half of its support from the working class.

As might be expected of a party that believed in the traditional system, Conservative propaganda played on nationalist and patriotic themes. The leaders could, as defenders of ancient tradition, assert that their party represented the best of England—its military and naval glory, its rule of law, and the quiet rural virtue of peasants and landed gentry. Labour leaders could attack those traditions, but they could not easily point to equivalent traditions that would evoke similar emotions. People who denied the legitimacy of the old ways could not easily link their party with feelings of nostalgia and folk sentiments associated with religious ritual, the monarch, pomp and pageantry, and monuments to celebrate British heroes.

Great Britain has been, and to some extent remains, a "society of deference," one in which the ideology and norms proclaimed that people both high and low merited esteem for what they were and did.[9] According to that belief, lords deserve more respect, but butlers and blacksmiths deserve some esteem, too. Consequently, individuals in most social strata could feel, even while doffing their cap to a social superior, that they were not being humiliated; they were also respected in their place. Indeed, European visitors sometimes expressed astonishment at the easy familiarity between English people of different social ranks. That apparently mutual respect did not threaten the class system, since both the well born and the less fortunate did not suppose that talking about shared interests, or for that matter even hunting and dining together, implied equality at all.

Thus, the Conservative leaders could assert (as the Republican party in the United States cannot) that the gentry of great families who were running for office *were* superior to workers by birth and training—and still not offend many people in the

---

[8] For a thoughtful analysis of these processes, see Robert McKenzie and Allan Silver, *Angels in Marble,* Chicago: University of Chicago Press, 1968.

[9] For an analysis of this factor in working-class votes, see ibid., pp. 16–17, 164–165, 183–191, and 225ff. Also, see the analysis of equalitarianism in Seymour M. Lipset, *The First New Nation,* New York: Basic Books, 1963, chap. 7.

working classes by that claim. Moreover, those leaders were able to link the deference for the upper classes with two equally important themes: (1) Because such lords and gentlemen in past centuries had taken care of the collective destiny of their people, they could be *trusted* to do so in the future; they would not only look to their own interests. (2) Because they were superior by endowment and training, they were simply more competent than Labour party leaders.

Finally, to emphasize the link between legitimacy, self-interest, and competence, the Conservative party could in fact claim much credit for a wide array of legislation and programs that would have been viewed as socialistic in many other countries, and certainly were in the interest of the working classes. Among these were the right to form trade unions and to strike; the many improvements in working conditions in factories, railroads, and mines; free education; unemployment and health insurance; and old age pensions. The Conservatives seemed able leaders, and they claimed by their achievements that they could be trusted to look out for the welfare of ordinary people.

This is not to say that Labour governments would not, or did not, support such improvements, and in fact most workers were not convinced by Conservative party claims. Enough of them were persuaded, nevertheless, to combine with Conservatives in other classes, so that over the course of a century this party was able to play a dominant role much of the time. Thus, many people whose class interests the Labour party claimed as its own gave their vote instead to the Conservatives who asserted that leadership should be left in the hands of the well born. These leaders, in turn, continued to gain support because they could lay claim to the legitimacy of ancient tradition and of competence, but in addition they continued to support programs that did help the common citizen.

AUTHORITY AND ELECTIONS

Because governments in all nations claim a monopoly over the use of legitimate force and command many resources for changing the economic and social opportunities of both individuals and organizations, control over the governmental apparatus can yield high payoffs. Aside from military coups and forceful take-overs, those efforts to control government are primarily directed at (1) winning elections, (2) influencing legislators, and (3) affecting the acts and decisions of governmental agencies that deal with more specific problem areas such as regulating airlines, the stock exchange, public utilities, railroads, oil and gas, or industrial health and safety.

Corporations spend far more money on the second and third of these three than do private citizens, and they hire people to be constantly vigilant about any corporate interests that might be affected by legislatures or by executive agencies. Even apparently minor changes in the phrasing of a law, or a ruling by bureaucratic agencies, will sometimes increase corporate profits by tens of millions of dollars. Private citizens do not possess the resources for protecting their own interests and do not usually see great rewards in being attentive; a legal or regulatory change that yields millions for a corporation might increase consumer costs by only a few cents per person.

Nevertheless, corporations, private citizens, and a wide range of voluntary organizations are concerned about elections. Elections are dramatic events, and a high percentage of the population is interested in them. Unlike the processes of influencing legislators or regulatory commissions, elections are scheduled and listed as "events to occur." They are public and ritualized as great competitions between opposing sides, following a complex body of rules that aim at creating a type of *game*. That is, both

FOCUS

THE EFFECT OF FORCE AND FORCE-THREAT

Abnormality

Almost every official riot commission has pointed out that riots are abnormal and useless:

The problem will not be solved by methods of violence.

The avenue of violence and lawlessness leads to a dead end.

[There] can be no justification in our democratic society for a resort to violence as a means of seeking social justice.

[Unless] order if fully preserved, . . . no meaningful, orderly, and rational physical, economic or social progress can occur.

Violence cannot build a better society.

This "violence doesn't pay" argument is misleading on two counts. First, it refers only to the domestic violence of disaffected groups, while ignoring the fact that systematic official violence for social ends is widely upheld in other spheres. Thus, the commissions of 1919, 1943, and 1968 do not even mention the possibility of a connection between war and domestic violence. It is a matter of moral judgment to attribute "normality" to one kind of violence—such as overseas war—but not to another. And it may be a glaring example of motivated obtuseness to ignore the possible connection between the public celebration of heroic military violence "over there" and the sporadic appearance of rebellious violence "back home." The breakdown of peaceful restraint during periods of war is among the most firmly established findings of social science.

Second, whether or not violence is "useless" is a problem for historical analysis, not a certainty. In any event, rioting has not been a particularly novel or unusual technique for expressing grievances. Instances of such rioting by both the respectable and disreputable poor in eighteenth- and nineteenth-century Europe have been well documented by historians. As Hobsbawm has noted, the preindustrial city mob "did not merely riot as a protest, but because it expected to achieve something by its riot. It assumed that the authorities would be sensitive to its movements, and probably also that they would make some sort of immediate concession." Like the modern riot, the classical mob was composed of a cross section of "the ordinary urban poor, and not simply of the scum." Moreover, one need not be fond of revolutions to observe that riots are sometimes the preface to an even more organized overthrow of existing arrangements with the substitution of new regimes. And one need not admire the consequence of the Russian Revolution to appreciate those of

America or France. All three began with rioting. There is no intention here of making dire predictions. Our only point is that the viewpoint that holds that rioting is "useless" lacks a certain foundation in reality. At the same time, rioting is a "primitive" form of political action, which may lead to consequences undesired by the rioters.

Collective violence by powerless groups acts as a "signaling device" to those in power that concessions must be made or violence will prevail. Hobsbawm gives the example of the Luddites, whose "collective bargaining by rioting was at least as effective as any other means of bringing trade union pressure, and probably *more* effective than any other means available before the era of national trade unions." Similarly, Rimilinger notes that those involved in the development of European trade unionism were "convinced of the righteousness not only of their demands but also of the novel means proposed to enforce them."

The available evidence, then, suggests that contemporary urban riots are participated in by a predominantly youthful cross section of the lower-class black community, that they are supported (usually passively) by other segments of that community, that they are often instrumental and purposive, and that they are not a historically unique form of social protest.

SOURCE: Jerome K. Skolnick, Director, *The Politics of Protest: A Task Force Report Submitted to the National Commission on the Causes and Prevention of Violence,* New York: Simon and Schuster, 1969, pp. 340–342.

sides play at being enemies, but they also promise to "play fair"—not to cheat, lie, steal, spy, and so on. Granted, the parties are likely to violate the rules here and there if they can, but it remains true that people believe the rules should not be violated and are indignant when they are. All parties also agree to abide by the election, that is, not to use force if the results are not pleasing.

The Importance of Elections

Elections determine who the legislators will be, and they are the ones to influence. Obviously, if we can elect officials who agree with our values and norms to begin with, we need not work as hard later in order to obtain laws we desire. Elections also determine to a considerable extent who will direct the governmental agencies that are concerned with more specific aspects of local and national life: pollution control, atomic energy, the defense forces, construction of highways and canals, leasing of offshore oil lands, street cleaning, and pensions. If a political party can win several elections in a row, it can gradually achieve control over several levels in a bureaucratic agency, as the older officeholders retire. In a more general way, in addition, governmental officials make some of their decisions partly by viewing an election as a message, a directive, an expression of what the citizens feel or believe. They may not obey that mandate, but they do take it into account when planning political strategies.

In nations where elections do decide who wins control of the government, organized political parties typically compete for citizens' votes. Thereby, party leaders face a problem that pervades all democratic processes: People organize parties in order to make their values, ideologies, or principles the policy of the government. To do that, they must proclaim their policies and support candidates who claim to believe them. Unfortunately for that purity of aim, they must also try to win the election. To do that, they must persuade a majority of the electorate that their policies and candidates are more desirable or attractive. Then they encounter a cruel choice: If they appeal to most voters, they cannot put forth a program that is very extreme in any direction.

That is, if they believe in their own policies, they wish to proclaim them in all their clarity; but to appeal to most voters, they must support programs that are middle-of-the-road, not extreme, perhaps even a grab bag of mixed proposals to attract one or another special group.

This is a key process in all clubs, organizations, or governments that attempt to pay attention to the wishes of the membership. To the extent that a minority group has some resource that the leadership wishes (in this case, votes), the desires of that group will be allowed to affect policy somewhat, even if in a modified form. One might say that in an adequately functioning democracy, people with extreme views must always water down their principles in order to gain office; and people with moderate views must move toward more extreme views to gain a few votes, or else their competitor for the office will gain them instead.

With *proportional representation* (where parties win seats in the legislature corresponding to their percentage of the vote in the total election), many small splinter parties can indulge in ideological purity, but they do not win elections, either. At most, they can win a few seats, and sometimes a minority voice in a working coalition, while the parties closer to the political center share most of the power.[10]

The Limitations of Party Politics

There are major consequences of the party process of changing policies to win the vote. The first is often cited as the hollowness or

---

[10]Douglas W. Rae, in *The Political Consequences of Electoral Laws,* New Haven, Conn.: Yale, 1971, shows how various types of electoral arrangements can affect who gets elected.

falsity of the claim that the United States (or any other nation) enjoys "free" or "democratic" elections: What freedom is there in a system that offers only a choice between two samenesses, Tweedledum and Tweedledee? If the fight for election is really between the parties of the center because parties move there to win the votes, and there is no difference, then there can be no real choice of freedom.

We have just seen one answer to that accusation. Even where small extreme parties do exist, from communist to neofascist, and thus real choice is encountered, the outcome of elections is not very different. There, too, the parties of the center appeal to more voters. A second answer is that in the usual two-party system the choices are very narrow, but that is because both parties constantly absorb some of the extreme opinions, where a few extra votes might be picked up: What was an extreme proposal in one decade becomes a diluted, mild version of that policy ten years later; and often, a stronger version of that proposal another ten years later. Thus, election choices do count: They change the political programs of the parties.

In the United States politics has moved steadily leftward over the generations since the Civil War, and both of the major parties have absorbed many of the radical or socialist policies that appealed to some voters. Sometimes emasculated or watered down, to be sure, such policies nevertheless attracted many people who would otherwise have been persuaded to vote or work for a genuine left-wing party. Some of those "radical" political planks now seem very tame, but that is precisely what the market competition among parties accomplishes over time. That is, party leaders who want to win elections must move to where the votes are, and a minority or extreme demand is transformed into a program that is viewed as ordinary common sense: The center, too, is moved thereby. Consider some of those "extreme" views of the past: the right of blacks, women, and the poor to vote; a progressive income tax (a higher rate for higher incomes); inheritance taxes; free elementary and high school education; governmental ownership of many utilities; or equal job opportunities for women.

Nevertheless, it would be naive to suppose party politics, or the attempts to manipulate legislators or government officials behind the scenes, are only a matter of a "free market," a market competition among leaders who will move in any direction to pick up votes. Indeed, the very assertion of a free competition should make any sociologist suspicious. In any social as in any economic competition, it is likely that supposed competitors will at times get together for their own goals, if these are different from the goals of their customers or the general public. From Adam Smith onward, economists who describe real behavior have pointed out that people believe in free competition primarily as an ideal for others, not for themselves. In the governmental regulation of corporations or in legislative maneuverings, this "getting together" often takes the form of "logrolling," not competition. One group that wants to lower the tax rate for oil companies will agree to vote with another that wants to increase the import duties on manufactured steel goods, both getting their wishes thereby, and both helping to increase corporate profits. Logrolling can work in liberal directions, too, but less often, simply because far more resources are available for influencing legislation or regulations in favor of the well-to-do.

A second limitation of the party process is that almost all party systems contain some version of a conservative party, so that the more liberal party does not have to move *far* to the left in order to appeal to a large number of voters. In the United States leaders of the Democratic party are themselves well-to-do and prefer not to move even as far toward liberal or left positions as the

population as a whole would accept.[11] On the other hand, they do not have to do so, because the Republican party does not support these positions either.

Of equal importance in day-to-day politics is a third fact: Leaders are not engaged *only* in winning elections. They have many other goals as well. For example, they are likely to have strong political views, and they may not be willing to discard them in order to capture votes. After all, one reason for winning elections is to put one's own policies into effect, and abandoning one's principles is a poor way of doing that. For example, if political leaders believe that people on relief or out of work for a long time are basically a shiftless and sorry lot, they will not be likely to vote enthusiastically for legislation to help such people, even if a majority of the population is in favor of it. Congressional representatives who have grown up in small towns and are homeowners are somewhat less likely than most of the United States population to feel much sympathy with city dwellers, or to want to spend vast sums of money to improve life in urban ghettos. Such people are not likely to change their minds when they learn that a "majority" of the population approves of such efforts.

Fourth, parties, candidates, and national leaders need not responsively tailor their promises or actions to the wishes of the electorate if they can turn people's attention to some other issue, such as the foreign enemy and war, domestic rebellion, the Red Scare of communism, or even corruption and immorality. Candidates have even won by supporting the prohibition of drinking, accusing their opponents of secretly swigging at the bottle. Political polls for more than two decades have shown that domestic communism has not been a daily concern of more than a tiny percentage of the popula-

[11]The data on this point seem certain: See Richard F. Hamilton, *Class and Politics in the United States,* New York: Wiley, 1972, chaps. 3 and 5.

tion. It is rarely mentioned as a central problem.[12] Nevertheless, a substantial number of candidates have been able to whip up some fear about this matter, to convince their fellow citizens that their opponent was sympathetic toward communists and therefore unpatriotic. If an opponent was truly "guilty," then he or she did not deserve office, no matter what the other issues might be. Rulers have always understood that one way of quieting domestic criticism is to locate a foreign threat. Thus, a free competition among parties and candidates about the issues and concerns of the populace does not always take place.

In addition to the four major factors that *reduce* the efforts of parties or candidates to gain votes by supporting policies the citizens want are these minor ones:

Many officeholders at the local levels are serving because of duty, not high political ambition; they do not intend to make a career of it. They may therefore not be moved to change their decisions or actions by the threat of losing the next election.

Within a party organization struggles for influence are going on constantly. Consequently, some local or national leaders may not work very hard for a candidate, because if she or he wins, they may lose some political strength. Consequently, who is nominated or elected may not be decided by whether the candidates are trying to follow the wishes of the larger populace.

Candidates and officeholders do not use scientific polls to find out what people want and then to obey their wishes. Experienced politicians believe they already "know how the people feel." Polls are ignored when they are available. They are often used to find out *which* candidates

are more appealing, but not why, and only rarely to locate the real concerns of the people in order to carry out their wishes.

Doubtless, the reader can think of other factors and processes that might prevent the party system from being a free competition among candidates who can win the vote only by supporting programs the people want. Free elections guarantee *some* responsiveness, but many social processes limit it substantially.[13]

Party Preference

Finally, however, some choice does exist, even if it is narrow, and voters do register their preferences. In all fully developed party systems, whatever other political cleavages exist, some version of a Republican or a conservative party is found, whose support of property and capitalist interests and the status quo generally is stronger than that of the Democratic or the liberal party. The differences are small, but they are real and they partly reflect the class divisions in the society. Moreover, when both parties do not take into account some important issues of the day, a higher percentage of the voters reject both parties.

Toward the lower classes, support of the Democratic party has been stronger for many decades. People who are out of work or have been unemployed, blacks, blue-collar workers, owners of small farms, Catholics, and Jews have traditionally voted more heavily for this party. These are not all "poor," but they are more likely to feel they suffer some socioeconomic disadvantages. By contrast, people who enjoy more advantages are more likely to vote for retaining the status quo and thus for the more

[12]On this point, see ibid., pp. 112–116 and the polls reported from time to time in daily newspapers.

[13]For further commentary on these limitations, see ibid., chap. 1, "Introduction: Responsive and Not-So-Responsive Parties."

Political Affiliation

Question: "In politics, as of today, do you consider yourself a Republican, Democrat, or Independent?"

	Republican	Democrat	Independent
Latest (March-May, 1976)	22%	46%	32%
July-Oct. 1974	23	47	30
June-Oct. 1972	28	43	29
(26th Amendment enacted)			
Sept.-Oct. 1970	29	45	26
Jan.-June 1968	27	46	27
Jan.-Feb. 1964	25	53	22
1960	30	47	23
1954	34	46	20
1952	34	41	25
1944	39	41	20
1940	38	42	20
1937	34	50	16

Figure 13-3 Republican, Democrat, and Independent political affiliation, 1937–1976. (The Gallup Opinion Index, Report No. 131, 1976.)

conservative or Republican party. Among them are people who own stock in corporations, hold high managerial positions, own their businesses, possess large farms, enjoy regular salaries as white-collar workers, or belong to the more "respectable" Protestant churches (for example, Episcopal, Congregational, or Presbyterian).

An examination of the party divisions in Congress over the decades will show that these broad cleavages in voter support are reflected in how senators and representatives vote. After all, that is what they promised to do, in exchange for voter support. Republicans (usually in alliance with *Southern* Democrats) are somewhat more likely to vote for tax benefits for large corporations, the interests of larger property owners, weaker controls over the safety or health standards in industry, or income tax loopholes for owners of stocks and bonds; they are *less* likely to vote for increased aid to unmarried mothers, governmental ownership of utilities, tighter controls over timber cutting in publicly owned forests, or higher minimum wages. The voting differences between parties are not large, but they appear

regularly when we examine either a series of bills in Congress over time, or the less visible political manipulations within the various congressional committees that give preliminary hearings to proposed bills.[14]

In Europe other cleavages play a large role, though the class divisions remain fundamental. Given a wider range of choices, those cleavages are clearer—for example, some tiny parties may support the restoration of a monarchy toppled long ago or denounce a revolution that happened a century ago. (Even in this country there have been Vegetarian and Prohibition parties.) As in the United States, left or liberal voting is associated with insecurity of income, unsatisfying work, low prestige rankings, the isolation of workers who nevertheless communicate with one another (lumbermen, miners, fishermen), and a low expectation of social mobility.

In addition, special religious allegiances are important; some of these have their roots in conflicts hundreds of years in the past. In most European countries *practicing* Catholics are more likely to be conservative in their party preferences. (Note the contrast with countries settled by the British, such as the United States, Canada, and Australia, where Catholics came mostly as lower-class immigrants and are now more likely to vote for a Labour or Democratic type of party; while members of the Anglican or Episcopal church, of a somewhat higher class position, are more likely to vote Conservative or Republican.) In general, the more regular the church attendance in Europe, the more likely a person is to vote for one of the religious parties.[15]

[14]Warren E. Miller and Donald Stokes, "Constituency Influence in Congress," chap. 16 in Angus Campbell et al., *Elections and the Political Order,* New York: Wiley, 1966.

[15]For a good discussion of religious factors in voting, see Lipset, *The First New Nation,* pp. 433ff.; Philip Converse, "Religion and Politics: The 1960 Election," in Campbell et al., op. cit., pp. 96–124. See also Robert Wuthnow, "Religious Commitment and Conservatism:

Although people are likely to view themselves as independently choosing among candidates, several interesting regularities in party preference cast some doubt on that view. One of those is the overriding weight of people's past preferences. As against those regularities, current data suggest there is a steady increase in the percentage of "independent" or "uncommitted" voters, who feel free to switch parties on the basis of emerging political issues, even when they still call themselves Democrats or Republicans. Let us consider the regularities as well as this new trend.

Perhaps the most striking regularity is the extent to which voters continue to follow the party preference they have shown in past elections and the preference of their own parents.[16] Most voters whose parents have regularly voted for only one party are likely to vote for that party, too.

A second pattern is that people who might be considered uncommitted voters, who have not yet decided on a set of candidates and thus seem to be carefully weighing their options, are *least* likely to be informed about politics in general or any particular election. In fact, voters who are more committed to one party are also more likely to have more knowledge about all candidates who are running for office (although they pay far more attention to their own choices).

Those who are most undecided are also the most *apathetic* about the election. Among those who are more undecided are those who feel they are under strong social

cross-pressures—being Democratic in a Republican neighborhood or a conservative church, being married to someone whose party preference is different, or being Republican but belonging to an automobile workers' union. People under cross-pressures are not only more apathetic; they are also more likely not to vote at all. People are sometimes genuinely apathetic about both sets of candidates simply because neither seems to be adequate, and these people are also likely to vote late or not at all. If they do finally make a decision, however, they are likely to vote for the party they have supported in the past.

PROTEST MOVEMENTS

Data from many countries show that people in democratic countries feel they have more control over the larger decisions that affect their fate, are given more respect as individuals, and trust their governments more than do people in less democratic nations.[17] However, governments of democratic nations, too, may fail to confront the important problems of the day, may handle them badly, and may not express the wishes and needs of the people they supposedly represent (because the upper social strata enjoy far more political influence than do the lower strata).

In the short time since World War II, in a period that has witnessed the downfall of more governments than any comparable generation, the democracies of the world have been relatively stable compared to other nations. Yet they too have experienced a widespread set of protest movements that have simultaneously evoked much sympathy from some segments of the society and outrage from others. One conse-

---

In Search of an Elusive Relationship," in Charles Y. Glock, ed., *Religion in Social Perspective,* Belmont, Calif.: Wadsworth, 1973, pp. 117–132; and Gerhard Lenski, *The Religious Factor,* rev. ed., Garden City, N.Y.: Doubleday, 1961.

[16]For a discussion of the influence of one generation on another in voting, see Herbert H. Hyman, *Political Socialization,* Glencoe, Ill.: Free Press, 1959. A classic analysis of the regularities is found in Paul F. Lazarsfeld, B. Berelson, and H. Gaudet, *The People's Choice,* New York: Columbia, 1948.

[17]For a variety of data on these points, see Gabriel A. Almond and Sidney Verba, *The Civic Culture,* Princeton, N.J.: Princeton, 1963; and Alex Inkeles, *Becoming Modern,* Cambridge, Mass.: Harvard, 1974.

quence is a growing distrust of the government and considerable dissent within the society. These processes are as evident in Japan or Belgium as in Germany or the United States.

Estrangement from Government

In the United States a growing distrust of the government began long before Watergate, and very likely even before the revolts of students, blacks, and women in the 1960s. Figure 13-4 makes this evident. It shows how the amount of support for the government has fallen, or the amount of estrangement from the government has risen, over time. Almost certainly, the curve would be at an even lower point in the mid-1970s. The Index of Estrangement is based on the following five questions, asked of a random sample of American people:

1   Do you trust the government in Washington to do what is right?

2   Is the government in Washington pretty much run by a few big interests looking out for themselves, or for the benefit of all the people?
3   Do you think the government wastes the money we pay in taxes?
4   Do you think the people running the government are smart people who usually know what they are doing?
5   Do you think the people running the government are a little crooked?

In general at any given time the people in somewhat higher socioeconomic ranks are less distrustful than others; it is they who typically benefit more from governmental policies. Nevertheless, *all* groups have become less trusting in recent years.

As can be seen, the confidence of blacks in the government has dropped sharply (other data suggest that of Northern blacks has dropped more than that of Southern blacks). However, better-educated blacks and those who have been upwardly mobile have increased their distrust or cynicism more than others over this period. It is they who see the greatest discrepancy between governmental promise and fulfillment (as an example, in the 1970s the greatest discrepancy between the incomes of blacks and whites was at the college graduate level).

In the mid-1970s people became more fearful and pessimistic about the economy than in two decades. Over half of all workers (both blue- and white-collar) felt "they were getting less pay than they deserved."[18] About 70 percent of black workers felt that way, but older blue-collar workers (black and white) were not far behind. A right-wing populist, Governor George Wallace, claiming to speak for "the little man," continued to arouse much enthusiasm among those who believe that "in spite of what

Figure 13-4   Election study results, 1958–1972, showing estrangement by race. (*IRS Newsletter*)

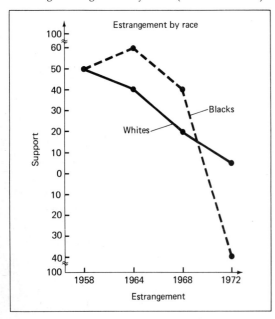

[18]See "Pay Inequities Bother Large Number of Workers," *Newsletter*, Institute of Social Research, University of Michigan, 2 (Summer 1974), p. 2.

some say, the condition of the average man is getting worse, not better."[19] At the same time, people who are considered "important" by *others*—in higher managerial posts and in the professions—increasingly felt that they no longer had much influence on "The System,"[20] and many people believed "The System" was at fault for everything from our involvement in Vietnam to the Watergate scandal.

Finally, although the percentage of Republicans had dropped in 1976 to 22 percent, the lowest figure in decades, that did not create much optimism for Democrats (46 percent), since the percentage who called themselves Independents had risen to a high point of 32 percent.[21] All this would imply that the party system is changing, or that it is being weakened by a failure to respond to a widespread discontent.

The College Generation

Evidence of discontent with the current political system is disputed, however, by evidence that the organized protest movements of the 1960s can no longer arouse much enthusiasm or even sympathy. The rebels' bright hopes of rapid social change, or even revolution, have apparently all been stifled. The dissidents of the 1960s learned that

[19]The question was a good predictor of a political preference for Wallace in 1968: See Philip E. Converse et al., "Continuity and Change in American Politics: Parties and Issues in the 1968 Election," *American Political Science Review,* 63 (December 1969), pp. 1098–1099. He appeals, however, to such people in the 1970s as well. On that appeal see Gary Wills, "The Man the Democrats Need," *New York Review of Books,* 21 (January 1975), pp. 14–16.

[20]One factor in this sense of possessing less influence, even among people whose advantages are many, is the growing power of all *corporate* agencies, such as unions, governmental agencies, and corporations. On this point see James S. Coleman, *Power and the Structure of Society,* New York: Norton, 1974, especially chap. 2. See also the chapter on formal organizations in this book.

[21]Gallup Poll, reported in The Gallup Opinion Index, 1976.

they could not persuade the United States populace or defeat the government. News stories report they are now quietly pushing baby carriages or worrying about a steady job. Young people who announced a revolution against both United States liberal politics and the crass accumulation of material possessions are now managers of Long Island branch banks. We have, it is alleged, entered a more conservative period. Men are digging in their heels to prevent women from getting the best jobs, whites are rioting to preserve segregation, and college students have abandoned the barricades for the library. Even fraternities and sororities have taken a new lease on life.

This portrait of conservatism is what one might expect after an unsuccessful revolution—or indeed even after a successful one. It is characteristic of revolts or revolutions, if they are not crushed immediately, that radical extremists take them over and try to move the country to build an entirely new society. However, *after* the revolution, even if successful, a conservative reaction takes place. The populace wants order and continuity, not a perpetual call to arms. Many of the older customs, scorned when the spirit of revolt was high, once more seem worthwhile. For example, after the Russian Revolution the Communist leaders decided that a modified form of free enterprise or capitalism would be useful in the early 1920s—until the people were ready for genuine communism. After the French Revolution of 1789, efforts toward abolishing the stigma of illegitimacy and giving more rights to women were similarly dropped or postponed. Is the United States now experiencing the same type of conservative reaction after the spurt of liberal and radical militancy in the 1960s?

This is a unique moment in history, and no science can predict the unique. We can only guess the future on the basis of the data we now have. However, to consider the problem at all helps us better to understand the relationships between the social and the political processes.

Two important facts can help our thinking about this problem. The first is a simple descriptive fact: For all the talk of *backlash*—that is, of people becoming *more* prejudiced after seeing how far women, blacks, and the lower classes want to go toward equality—there is little evidence of it. Every poll shows a steady increase in the approval of giving equal rights to these disadvantaged (and overlapping) segments of the population. On political or economic issues the United States population has not been moving backward, toward the values, norms, and ideologies of decades ago.

The second fact has a more general application, and is also helpful in understanding the peculiar place of college people in modern industrial society. The protest movements of the 1960s, except for possibly the "nonviolent" demonstrations against race discrimination in the South, aroused widespread disapproval and anger in the United States. A majority of the population perceived the riots, sit-ins, marches, speeches, bombings, and thefts of government documents as immoral and un-American. A majority disapproved of *legal* protest meetings, demonstrations, and marches.

Nevertheless, those protests, both legal and illegal, violent and nonviolent, did speed up reforms in many areas of political, social, and economic life, from giving up control over undergraduates' sex life to reducing United States military involvement in Vietnam; from forcing universities to reduce or stop secret military research, to attacks on the government's spying on its own citizens. Some of those protests were violent. Others were nonviolent but forceful, as when protesters passively occupied an office, peacefully barred an entrance, or merely sat in a restaurant where blacks had been refused service. And still others were more peaceful actions, for example, people simply not using segregated buses or carrying placards outside a corporation that discriminated against women.

Yet all were *perceived* by most of the United States population as a challenge to the system, and as disorderly and disrespectful. The protests were viewed as a threat of revolution, a threat of force. Those who disapproved often argued for the use of strong counterforce, and indeed some protest actions (both peaceful ones and threatening ones) were put down with violence. Nevertheless, as a whole the United States leadership has *acted* by initiating a wide range of reforms in order to reduce the militancy of that protest. In short, force, the threat of force, and the *perceived* threat of force from the protest movement have moved United States leaders to accept more reform than they wanted at the time. In effect, those threats have changed their minds about the relative costs of different courses of action: To avoid still more threat, they accepted some reforms.

Earlier, we analyzed some of the relationships between force and force-threat, legitimacy and authority, and the values and norms of the society. We noted that people support their government and their society because they believe in it, and yet the threat of force plays a role even in a peaceful democratic society. Public protests, especially those in which some violence *happens* (whether or not the protesters start it), have several effects that relate to those underlying patterns discussed earlier.

First, a protest action announces to leaders as well as the populace that *some* citizens deny the authority of the government or the legitimacy of a particular policy—be it the pricing of bread or going to war. A public protest is always taken more seriously than even valid knowledge that people do not approve of a current policy. It is taken more seriously because most people believe the protesters must be *intense* in their disapproval. They would not run the risk of counterdisapproval, anger, beatings, arrest, and jail sentences if their commitment were not strong.

This is not a modern interpretation of protest. For hundreds of years rulers have supposed riots and rebellions told them that some part of the populace (or all of it) intensely disapproved of a policy.[22] Rulers have typically answered such outbreaks with counterviolence, sometimes imaginative in its sadism, but also typically with some effort at reducing the grievance, at improving the policy.

Of equal importance is a structural element in this process: Higher-level administrators need to maintain peace, just to keep their jobs. Higher-level officials—sub-chieftains, managers, Chinese provincial governors, and mayors—have long understood that however excellent they believed their policies were, or however wise their execution, *their* superiors—heads of bureaus, chiefs, emperors, presidents of corporations or nations—would hold them responsible for such protests and demonstrations, especially if violence and counterviolence broke out. People in charge are supposed to maintain order, by arousing fear or respect or both. Protests that escalate into riots, no matter who is responsible, let the secret out that the officials are not doing their job. When, as in many protests of the past decade, the heads that were bloodied belonged to the sons and daughters of respectable or important parents, the suspicion of official incompetence may become widespread.[23]

In the historical past, in every nation, landowners, merchants, and the aristocracy have generally felt threatened by protests, riots, and rebellions, and quite rightly, for they were at least the immediate targets.

They have called for a swift, ruthless end to that threat. However, when the event occurred five hundred miles away, on another baron's lands or in another city, the news came late and was too distant to be immediately threatening. Recently, however, television may have intensified the fear of people who were not sympathetic with the protesters. Television makes the viewer feel that the threat is already *here*, aside from the possibility that some local viewers will be stirred into imitation. In addition, television reporters and camera people focus on the most dramatic event, that is, violence, and so exaggerate its intensity as well as the numbers of people taking part.

People who are unsympathetic, now or in the past, demand that officials put down such protests, but the more general message that officials hear is, *Do* something! Since the cost of using force to put it down must be weighed against alternatives, they may also decide to reduce the grievances if they can.

For these reasons the protest movements of the recent or distant past have frequently moved rulers (even in authoritarian or monarchical systems) to soften or improve their policies. Thus, in spite of the antagonism the Black Muslims aroused among whites, they improved the lot of United States blacks by changing the calculations that whites made about the possible costs of maintaining strict discrimination policies. The protest movements of ethnic groups in other parts of the world are having similar effects.

However, protests in the most advanced countries have recently been spearheaded by the college generation, which might superficially appear to be the most unlikely source of political organization, for young people are, in all countries for which we have data, the least likely to vote or to be seriously interested in politics. In addition, people in college come from the more affluent, successful families, and might be expected to

[22]For an excellent sociological analysis of historical violence and its various "messages," see Charles Tilly, "Collective Violence in European Perspective," in Hugh Graham and Ted Gurr, *The History of Violence in America*, New York: Praeger, 1969, pp. 4–45.

[23]For some theoretical propositions that illuminate these facts, see Goode, op. cit., pp. 516–517.

believe that a system that so favors them cannot be very wrong. Moreover, they will eventually enjoy a higher-than-average socioeconomic rank in adult life, and usually such people feel more committed to the social system that promises such rewards. True, college students were in the *age group* that could be drafted for the Vietnam war, but in that too they were privileged. For most of that period few were drafted who kept up their grades. It was the lower classes and blacks who experienced most of the combat deaths.

We should note, however, that college education itself was not associated with antiwar sentiment in the 1960s. A higher percentage of people with grade school education were against the war than of people with a high school or college education.[24] Thus, the relationship between protest and the college generation is complex and deserves further analysis.

First, let us note that although younger people are in general less political than older ones and are less committed to any party, they are typically more liberal as well. Even when they are not—remember that both the Nazis and Mussolini's Fascists appealed to the young—they are less attached to the past and instead support the new political movements of their generation. In the United States they have contributed to the slow leftward trend of political policies over the decades. College students engaged in less spectacular public politics in the 1950s than during the Depression of the 1930s, but their opinions were not more conservative.

Thus, the place of college students and the college-educated in the politics of industrial countries is made up of several contradictory factors. We do not believe it is possible as yet to predict the outcome of the next few years. One set of such tensions or strains can be seen in the fact that the larg-

er society is far more tolerant of radical politics among college students than among adults, and especially adults in steady jobs. College has become a kind of enclosed community, permitting many deviant life-styles. Nevertheless, the creation of such islands of nonconformity or radicalism does not occur on most college campuses. That is not typical, contrary to much public opinion. It is more likely to occur at great universities where more of the social elements of a *community* can be found: leadership from graduate students and professors who enjoy local prestige; students who live in the area of the university, and so interact with one another frequently; a large enough *number* of students and faculty to make up a community that is not overwhelmed by the surrounding city, large enough that even a *small percentage* of dissidents can create a crowd; access to means of communication (Xerox and mimeographing machines, walkie-talkie radios, bullhorns, newspapers, radio, television), at which these people are more competent than most; a range of common concerns, from housing and food to improving the world; and enough leisure time to engage in political talk.

Illustrative of this generally left-leaning attitude are the poll data in the table on the next page.

A second set of elements in tension is the extent to which a radical social or political style is the creation of a small number of people. Even within such tolerant university communities the percentage of students who are radical, or who were in the 1960s, has remained very small. About one in ten is very alienated and very dissident. Only 3 percent express revolutionary views. Nevertheless, in the 1960s a majority of those campuses followed their lead in picketing, signing petitions, demonstrating, and marching. Even in the 1970s they show no sign of turning to a conservative leadership.

A third set of contending factors focuses on political *opinion* as contrasted with action. Even in strong monarchies, where the

[24]For an extended analysis of these sentiments, see Milton J. Rosenberg, Sidney Verba, and Philip E. Converse, *Vietnam and the Silent Majority,* New York: Harper & Row, 1970, especially pp. 55–73.

TABLE 13-1 ATTITUDES OF COLLEGE STUDENTS

Poll Question or Statement	% Answering "Yes"
The American way of life is superior to life in other countries.	12%
We are a sick society.	35
Business is too concerned with profits and not with public responsibility.	94
Our foreign policy is based on our own narrow economic and power interests.	88
People's privacy is being destroyed.	86
Basically we are a racist nation.	79
Groups discriminated against by U.S. society:	
American Indians	82
Homosexuals	82
Long-hairs	68
Poor people	71
Mexican-Americans	73
High school dropouts	59
Blacks	71
College students	26

SOURCE: Daniel Yankelovich, *The New Morality: A Profile of American Youth in the 70's,* New York: McGraw-Hill, 1974.

outspoken sometimes lose their heads, kings have permitted intellectuals more freedom in speech than in action. Modern industrial democracies give some respect to the academic community because it is a major source of new science and it helps to preserve knowledge and scholarship. They also give college students and professors much tolerance for their ideas, as long as their hands do not touch any of the important levers of political action.[25] When people graduate and leave that community to take positions of influence, their peers and bosses are more critical of radical political comments, and are still less tolerant of *overt* political protests. Thus, even when people do not become much more conservative in their political *views* after college, their actions are much more conservative. They do not enjoy any encouragement for such activities, as they once did as students, and they are now too busy with their jobs and families. A higher percentage of the college-educated do vote than of the the rest of the population, but they do not continue the protests of their student days.

A possible view of the future is, therefore, that for many people the college experience will be only a short phase of intense, very liberal political talk and action, followed by a lifetime of action that is more conservative than the person's opinions. That pattern seems to be observable in Japan, where student activism has been much more extreme than in the United States; the college-educated adults are sympathetic to socialist movements, but those same adults are relatively docile both in public politics and as employees of the government or of large corporations.[26]

An additional set of tensions was implied

[25]For an analysis of the intellectual as political critic, see Seymour M. Lipset and Asoke Basu, "Intellectual Types and Political Roles," in Lewis Coser, ed., *The Idea of Social Structure,* New York: Harcourt, Brace, 1975, pp. 433-470.

[26]See the extended analysis of political movements among Japanese students by Don Wheeler, "The Japanese Student Movement: Value, Politics, Student Politics and the Tokyo University," Ph.D. dissertation, Columbia University, 1974. See also Lipset and Schneider, op. cit., pp. 477-481.

Figure 13-5 People who participated in demonstrations as students usually become bystanders after leaving college. (Bill Anderson, Monkmeyer.)

in the previous analysis, one between the political and social opinions of students and those of blue-collar workers. Although many members of the academic community express sympathy with workers as exploited victims of the capitalist system, they have been unable to create an effective political coalition with them, to elicit a feeling of brotherhood or sisterhood from them, or even to engage in a continuing political dialogue with them. Moreover, during the 1960s the antagonism of workers toward dissenting college students was strong. This is not the first time in history that a small intellectual vanguard has offered itself as the advocate for the "inarticulate masses," without being accepted by them—although successful revolutions *have* typically been led by that group. However, the present situation occurs in most democracies and deserves a further step in the analysis.[27]

College and Noncollege Populations

In the 1960s the population in college had moved toward social and political opinions that were very different from those of the noncollege population of roughly the same age (sixteen to twenty-five). Differences between the people in college and the adult noncollege people were even stronger. One might have speculated that this split would become a continuing set of tensions in United States political life, those in college making a set of radical attacks on the fundamental institutions of the society, while people with less education held to traditional values.

However, that divergence has narrowed considerably. Although college students have continued to express opinions that would have been considered radical fifteen years ago, they have become somewhat more "conservative" only with reference to such traditional notions as opposition to the use of violence to gain worthwhile objectives, the value of working hard, the acceptance of law and order, and the value of education.[28] At the same time, noncollege youth have moved substantially toward the opinions of students with reference to many aspects of social life, life-style, and politics. The gap is now much narrower.

[27]For a good analysis of why the New Left political leaders were unable to persuade workers and others to follow them, see Hamilton, op. cit., pp. 547–555.

[28]See the detailed data in Daniel Yankelovich, *The New Morality*, New York: McGraw-Hill, 1974.

Since news reports frequently discuss the "new conservatism" of college students, it must be repeated that opinions on almost every topic have *not* become conservative. For example, there has been a continued rise in the percentage of students who believe that big business needs fundamental reforms; over 90 percent believe that business is too concerned with profits and not with public responsibility; and patriotism as a personal value has declined. College students express much less willingness to engage in political battles and more concern about jobs; that is, they are somewhat more "quiescent," but they have not become conservative.

Moreover, with reference to life-style or social values, the trend toward more liberal attitudes has continued: More students welcome the new sexual freedom and reject "patriotism, religion, and the traditional view of a 'clean moral life'" as important personal values. They are more tolerant of homosexuality, premarital sexual relations, or abortion, and stress privacy as a value.[29] These attitudes do not suggest a trend toward greater traditionalism or conservatism.

Of more importance, however, is the apparent movement of noncollege youth in the direction of college student attitudes. This has especially occurred in the areas of social life or life-style. Here are some examples where the gap between the two groups has narrowed: approval of abortion, homosexuality, and casual premarital sexual relations; a slightly lesser emphasis on law and order, or respect for authority; a lowered acceptance of "containing communism" as an excuse for going to war; a greater acceptance of marijuana; and the opinion that political parties need reform or elimination. Gaps remain, but the trend is unmistakable. The attitudes of college students now have more noncollege support than in the past, even if the two groups do not engage in much social interaction together.

29Ibid., p. 57ff.

Noncollege *women* remain very conservative in comparison with college women students in just one major area: the feminist movement. However, it is highly unlikely that women students and noncollege women will continue to diverge so much in the future; without question, among college and noncollege women and men the trend is clearly toward more approval of greater equality for women.

SUMMARY AND CONCLUSION

For generations both sociologists and political scientists have analyzed the political process in this and other countries. Political scientists have focused far more on the detailed machinery of governments, while sociologists have emphasized political allegiances and shifts of influence. The overlap has been substantial, and it has yielded much knowledge about political systems.

Whether we begin by imagining people in isolation who decide to band together, or by observing actual daily behavior, we can see that people must agree to a body of rules for dealing with their inevitable conflicts, for creating new rules when that is desired, for cooperating on large enterprises like war or highway construction, and for deciding how the privileges and rewards of the society shall be divided. Many different systems, or sets of rules, have been created over the past several thousands of years, but no large, diverse society can exist without some kind of charter or constitution, whether or not it is set down in writing. How the rules work, and who decides on the rules, is a central object of analysis in political research.

The ultimate resource of all political systems is force and thus the threat of force. Governments possess more firepower and can enforce their will. On the other hand, both sociological theory and ordinary observation argue that using arms on the citizenry is an inefficient way of eliciting loyalty. Governments are more secure when the citizens of the country are given a voice in decisions and believe that the traditional political rules are being followed. When people believe their government is legitimate, they will support its decisions with force or force-threat. Thus, we note the seeming paradox that political systems with the least need to use force are themselves supported by the greatest amount of potential force in the form of a loyal body of citizens.

The modern era has been marked by high political instability, and especially by the rapid turnover of revolutionary governments that achieved independence from foreign or local despotic rule, without being able to gain the allegiance of their own citizens. They have typically failed to achieve political authority, for their people eventually refused to concede their *right to command.* Here we have considered several difficulties such regimes have faced. Among them are (1) the need for the support of rich and powerful families, versus the need for programs those families will oppose; (2) the need to promise much in order to gain power, versus the inevitable disappointments of only minor success; and (3) the necessity of attacking older traditions in order to gain control, versus the need for some traditional authority and loyalty for a *new* regime.

In general, the changes in social, economic, and political life that new governments create in their efforts to modernize appear to be correlated with civil strife, turmoil, and rebellion. However, the reader should analyze the possibility that leaders who aim at a genuinely socialist society may well arouse less citizen revolt by very *rapid* social changes that aim at quickly giving to the masses whatever benefits the new regime can muster.

It seems obvious that people in somewhat higher class positions would generally support the political system as it exists, for clearly it gives them handsome rewards. Consequently, they are more likely to vote for the more conservative Republican party.

Similarly, people who get fewer rewards from the system, and thus have a lesser stake in it, are more likely to vote for a liberal or left party (in the United States, the Democrats). Happily, that reasonable speculation is borne out by the facts. However, in an effort to illuminate the relationships among authority, tradition, political competence, and party choice, we have considered the case of lower-class voters for the Conservative party in Great Britain. Although they are less likely to vote Conservative than are middle-class voters, they have made a major contribution to the success of the Conservative party over a period of almost a century.

Because of the increasing influence of governmental actions on all aspects of social and economic life, people and organizations try to shape those actions. They do so through legislators who are already in office and through commissions and agencies whose administrative decisions and rulings determine the price of oil, health conditions in factories and mines, where dams and highways are built, how much taxes we pay, and a host of other aspects of our lives. Nevertheless, who wins the elections will also affect the actions of governments. Thus, the drama of the electoral process is not hollow; all of us have a stake in the outcome.

Political analysts have studied party preferences in great detail, and have often described the process of choice as a market competition in which parties can win only by changing their programs to fit the wishes of the voters. On the other hand, we must also note the many factors that limit how far the candidates and their parties will shape their political principles to the desires of the electorate.

Whether or not the political system contains a fully fledged party system and free elections, in all countries there will be some political action outside traditional channels: riots, rebellions, demonstrations, petitions, boycotts, and sit-ins. Violent or nonviolent, such events set in motion a number of political processes, such as repressive counteractions by the government, changes in political opinions, government attempts to improve conditions, and even successful revolutions. Consequently, although such protests are typically viewed as "outside" the political system, in fact they occur in all countries from time to time, and have always affected how political leaders calculate the costs or benefits of their political programs.

The decade of the 1960s was marked by many such demonstrations, in which college students played a large role. While many observers report that these students have moved toward "conservatism" in this decade, we have presented contrary data and have examined the present situation. We have done so, not to "predict" the future, but to lay bare some of the factors that influence contemporary political processes—for example, the relatively low political participation of youth; the liberal, left, or uncommitted political preferences of younger people; the tiny percentage of college youth who held (or hold) radical opinions; and the shifts of social and political opinions among college and noncollege populations over the past decade. Many people have moved toward some acceptance of the new "life-style freedom" that was preached by political radicals in the 1960s, without much acceptance of their political opinions. On the other hand, there is little evidence that political opinions in the United States have become more conservative. Moreover, if the past is any guide to the future, political opinion will continue to move toward support of programs that will help people who suffer disadvantages under the present system.

READINGS

Michael Aiken and Paul E. Mott, *The Structure of Community Power,* New York: Random House, 1970.

Gabriel A. Almond and Sidney Verba, *The Civic Culture,* Boston: Little, Brown, 1965.

Crane Brinton, *The Anatomy of Revolution,* New York: Vantage, 1957.

Robert Dahl, *Modern Political Analysis,* Englewood Cliffs, N.J.: Prentice-Hall, 1963.

Amitai Etzioni, *The Active Society,* New York: Free Press, 1968.

William A. Gamson, *Power and Discontent,* Homewood, Ill.: Dorsey, 1968.

Richard F. Hamilton, *Class and Politics in the United States,* New York: Wiley, 1972.

Samuel P. Huntington, *Political Order in Changing Societies,* New Haven, Conn.: Yale, 1968.

Herbert H. Hyman, *Political Socialization,* Glencoe, Ill.: Free Press, 1959.

V. O. Key, *The Responsible Electorate,* Cambridge, Mass.: Harvard, 1966.

Paul F. Lazarsfeld, B. Berelson, and H. Gaudet, *The People's Choice,* New York: Columbia, 1948.

Seymour M. Lipset, *Revolution and Counterrevolution,* New York: Basic Books, 1968.

——— and Philip G. Altbach, *Students in Revolt,* Boston: Beacon Press, 1970.

——— and William Schneider, "Political Sociology," in Neil J. Smelser, *Sociology,* 2d ed., New York: Wiley, 1973, pp. 399–491.

C. Wright Mills, *The Power Elite,* New York: Oxford, 1956.

Alexis de Tocqueville, *Democracy in America*, 2 vols, 1835, 1840, trans. by Henry Reeve, Francis Bowen, and Phillips Bradley, New York: Vintage, 1954.

CHAPTER FOURTEEN

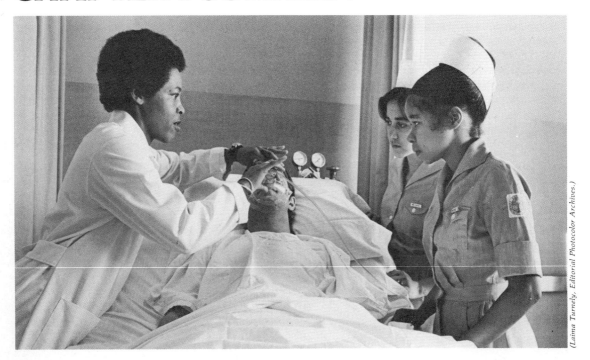

(Laima Turnely, Editorial Photocolor Archives.)

OCCUPATIONS AND PROFESSIONS

Why is work so important sociologically? In this as in other societies the work that we do affects much of our existence. It takes up a large part of our time and energy budget, even for those who live on that legendary tropical isle where delicious fruits conveniently drop into one's lap. The economic rewards for our work determine the level of physical comforts we can command, and indeed affect how long we shall live to enjoy them. Within all the contemporary nations, people's jobs—and how well they do them—determine their class position and even whom they will marry.

Stereotypes about different kinds of jobs often appear in fiction—the lawyer who suspects everyone's motives, the jovial innkeeper, the reckless young lieutenant, the skulking spy, or the uncultured business person. That is, it is thought that by spending years in a particular occupational world,

people take on its special perspective, and both see and weigh the rest of life from its point of view. Mark Twain once argued that to be a United States senator or a Mississippi River steamboat pilot marked one's character forever afterward, because both of these jobs gave their occupants such unlimited authority and surrounded them with a circle of admirers who catered to their every whim.

Since much of our social life is affected by our relations with our jobs and with our fellow workers on the job, a sociological analysis of work should help us to understand better an important part of our social experience. In Chapter 7, "Formal Organizations," we analyzed the kinds of jobs that are found in large bureaucracies. Here we focus on more general aspects of work, whether or not it occurs in a bureaucracy.

THE SOCIAL MEANING OF WORK

Two general themes are to be found in both literary and philosophic commentaries on the place of work in people's lives. The first is that work was not viewed as a central part of a man's existence (women did not enter such analyses) until the Protestant revolution in the sixteenth century. It was a necessity for most, a curse for many, and, ideally, it was to be avoided if at all possible. Religion, philosophy, war, politics, and even play were much more important. The second theme is that at some unspecified time in the past (the Middle Ages are a favorite, if vague, choice), the artisan or worker made the whole product from start to finish, using whatever creativity he possessed, and took pleasure from a job well done.

It is alleged that all this has changed. People now work compulsively, driven by an inner feeling that leisure is almost sinful. People must sell their labor as a commodity on the market, like wheat or iron ore, and their work self is alienated from their true self. Occupied at trivial tasks, they serve a soulless machine or corporation, but not their fellow human beings, nor the society, nor God. As a consequence, their identity is lost, and their lives are dull, gray, and meaningless.[1] Writers and sociologists who have had direct experience with what some consider the most extreme version of modern industrial work, the automobile assembly line, assert all that is true for such occupations.[2]

To Work or Not to Work

Doubtless, the meaning of work *has* differed from society to society, and certainly the human *dedication* to labor and production has varied a great deal. At one extreme, the eighteenth-century sailors who first encountered the Polynesians on various Pacific islands reported that they were happy, friendly, and far more attentive to the delights of food, sex, and festivals than to the grim duty of hard work. At the other extreme, in some Melanesian and West African societies, adults seemed to be constantly concerned with hard work and productivity.

In contrast to both extremes, the Athenian Greeks asserted that one should not waste one's time in the grubby, unrewarding business of making money, and especially not in manual labor. The only worthy life was one dedicated to discussing philosophy, art, architecture, and poetry, or perhaps creating them. The Hebrews learned from the Old Testament that work was a punishment, meted out by God because Adam and Eve violated his command when they were in the Garden of Eden.

Medieval Christianity certainly approved of work, but not because working in itself was a higher good. Rather, labor was a necessity, and it kept people out of mischief. However, the higher duty of human beings was to focus their hearts and minds on spiritual matters and the life hereafter. By the late Renaissance or the early Protestant Reformation, this had been changed somewhat to the notion that labor was a way of serving God. Hard work was an expression of one's piety. To be successful at work was a sign that one was spiritually excellent.[3]

[1]These views have been discussed with special eloquence by Sebastian de Grazia, *Of Time, Work and Leisure,* New York: Twentieth Century Fund, 1962, chap. 1; see also Harold L. Wilensky, "Varieties of Work Experience," in Henry Borow, ed., *Man in a World at Work,* Boston: Houghton Mifflin, 1964, especially the section beginning p. 126, "From Curse to Craft"; and Theodore Caplow, *The Sociology of Work,* New York: McGraw-Hill, 1954, chap. 1.

[2]See Eli Chinoy, *Automobile Workers and the American Dream,* New York: Doubleday, 1955; and Harvey Swados, *On the Line,* Boston: Little, Brown, 1957.

[3]This transformation in belief was analyzed at great length in Max Weber's monumental study on the sociology of religion, which tried to show that in many great societies of the world, most of the preconditions for the development of modern capitalism existed at one time or another, but they were not energized or transformed appropriately by an ideology or religion comparable to ascetic Protestantism. Against this, Kurt Samuelsson, *Religion and Economic Action,* New York:

More recently, by contrast, Western capitalists who tried to establish plantations or factories in less developed societies complained steadily that native workers would not work as hard or conscientiously as European or United States workers. They ceased working when not driven to it, and generally felt lackadaisical, if not downright frivolous, about their jobs. There are no known cases in which capitalists tried the daring experiment of paying high wages to elicit a more disciplined productivity, but their reports cannot be completely discounted.

The upper class in Latin America expressed a philosophy closer to that of Athenian Greeks, and often complained about the crass business orientation of the Yankees they encountered. They viewed manual labor and even engineering with distaste. They held that men (again, women were irrelevant) should be evaluated as persons, as unique human beings, as intellectuals or leaders, but not on the basis of their financial success or their contribution to the economy.

The Need to Work

Although these differences in the meaning of work cannot be dismissed, we should be probing, if not skeptical, as with all descriptions of the values and norms of past societies. First, we should remember that such statements largely came from aristocrats, philosophers, and literary people. They express essentially the *ideal* viewpoint of people in the top social strata, not the attitudes of ordinary persons, and very likely not even the actual attitudes of people at such higher social levels. Such comments are likely to be reports about how persons of

higher rank in those societies would have *liked* to believe or feel.

Leaving aside such privileged members of past societies, there is no reason to suppose that people in the middle and lower social strata took great joy in hard labor once upon a time, or that they viewed it as an opportunity for self-expression and creativity. When intellectuals now compare modern work with the supposedly harmonious integration of self and labor in the past, they are indulging in rhetoric; they are not reporting historical data. Hoeing and plowing the fields in the past were not guided by the creative impulse, but by local tradition and economic necessity. Artisans once produced traditional objects for traditional markets. They were not "free spirits" whose skilled labor expressed their true inner selves; or to be more cautious, if they were, we have no evidence that they were.

What we can assert with more security is that in past societies, as in the present, *people had to produce in order to survive.* Whatever productive labor they did was a central source of their personal and social identity. With few exceptions, people who did not take part in work did not take part in society at all, and at the present time that relationship still holds. That is, when work ties are severed, people participate in the community far less and feel more isolated from their fellow human beings.[4]

It is unlikely that an obligation so universal and so generally accepted in the past would have not been supported by a set of justifications, rationalizations, and even theological doctrines to give it a certain amount of dignity. Workers at all levels give more respect to those who work competently and hard. Even dukes and barons were always partly evaluated by how well they carried out their appropriate duties—even if they did not call them work. In short, although the *ideal* meaning of work has certainly varied from one society to another, and the

Basic Books, 1961, argues that the dedication to work, diligence, thrift, and asceticism was preached long before the Reformation. Weber's most famous essay on this topic is *The Protestant Ethic and the Spirit of Capitalism,* trans. by Talcott Parsons, New York: Scribner, 1930.

[4]Wilensky, op. cit., pp. 131–134.

dedication of human beings to work has varied in intensity, for most people in most societies, to be adult at all is to take part in the productive process. Loafing has never been viewed as an ideal way to live in any society. Even when aristocrats were able to loaf because they were supported by their peasantry, they invented a wide range of honored activities that would give some dignity to their lives, at least within their own value system.

Human beings who perform more menial jobs have never been deluded into believing that work was an unmitigated pleasure—had they been convinced, philosophers would not have written so many arguments to persuade them that work was an excellent thing. Nevertheless, in all societies people have given respect to adults who worked, that is, who administered, labored competently in their gardens, produced objects or services other people wanted, or delivered goods safely to their destination. People may have secretly envied those few who could idle their days away; they did not respect them for it. To earn esteem among ordinary people in perhaps all societies, men and women had to take part in the productive labor that maintained their community. To work was to take part in the society; to reject work would have meant rejecting the members of one's own society as well as one's kinfolk.

When work itself is not viewed as a direct pleasure, human beings have tried, and mainly with success, to take some pleasure from social interaction on the job, whether it is the gossip and chitchat of a modern office or the sea chanties and dancing of sixteenth-century English sailors who were engaged in exploring the North Sea routes through the ice fields.

Though work occupies a central place in people's lives in harsh as well as kindly environments, the impact of work is different in different kinds of occupations. The division of labor places people in very different social positions and thus affects what they experience or perceive. Let us now consider this fundamental aspect of work.

THE DIVISION OF LABOR

In some societies technology is little developed, and labor is divided only by sex and age. For example, children and women may gather roots and vegetables and occasionally catch small animals, while men do all these things and also hunt larger animals. However, in larger societies the division of labor goes much further so that there may be ironsmiths and arrow makers, priests and warriors, weavers and hut makers. In the United States there are at least 25,000 different kinds of jobs.

With each step toward a greater division of labor, several other social developments occur. First, those who specialize can usually produce more of their product in a given hour than can those who attempt many tasks. If they can produce more, then it becomes profitable to trade with others who specialize in a different type of product. Consequently, as the labor of a society becomes more finely divided, there is an increase in total trade, and eventually a spread of markets where people go to exchange their surplus products.

However, that development is not automatic; there is no iron law of progress that pushes every society to move indefinitely toward a more complex division of labor. The reason is simple: Specialization does *not* always yield many extra products for the market. For example, where fish are plentiful and everyone fishes, an individual who proposes to specialize may not be much better at it than others, and they have no reason to buy what that person catches. Second, a person might offer a specialty service or product that others simply do not want. For example, seventeenth-century New England Puritan villages would not have been willing to support a specialist in dancing or in Catholic theology.

Only if *others* can *also* create a surplus by *their* specializing can they have something to exchange with each other. Indeed, at low levels of productive efficiency, as in many peasant villages of the past, increased specialization would not have been a useful step to take toward prosperity. The wrong specializations might have been chosen, specialists would not have produced enough to trade with one another, and some necessary things might not have been done.

Thus, it cannot be assumed that all societies move automatically toward a great division of labor over time or that division of labor is always efficient. Such a steady progression has been rare in world history, and its most extreme example has occurred in the modern era of industrialization. To take that step, a society required (1) a large economic surplus that could support specialists in one narrow service or product, and (2) new techniques that were more productive, so as to create that surplus for the market. In eighteenth-century England much of that surplus was furnished by more efficient agriculture. In late-nineteenth-century Japan, when the Meiji regime attempted to industrialize, the surplus was obtained by paying low wages to factory workers and low prices to farmers.

By contrast, some societies developed a minute division of labor that was essentially unproductive. For example, in India even a decade ago some people did no more than sweep a few yards of a hotel floor, sell a few packs of gum a day, or wait around for an occasional task as messenger. Until a generation ago dozens of rajahs' courts contained from a handful to hundreds of hangers-on, all specialists who enjoyed some small title but who contributed nothing to the economy.

Results of Division of Labor

As productivity and the division of labor increase, however, the following large-scale changes also take place in the society:

Figure 14-1 Although medieval warriors used arrows in battle, the specialized occupation of fletching—putting feathers on the ends of arrows—continues to the present day, as these workers in South Carolina demonstrate. (United Press International Photo.)

1   There is growth in the size of work units or factories. It becomes profitable to bring together larger numbers of specialists, whether they are to make pins or to weave cloth.
2   New cities are built and older ones expand to offer more opportunities for people to exchange goods and services.
3   The job of manager or supervisor becomes more important; someone must see to it that all cooperate in the total process.
4   Because productivity increases, new markets must be found, and a flow of raw materials must be assured.
5   Larger enterprises need more capital, and as a consequence, all the variegated tasks of banking and credit become more specialized as well.

Because losses can be greater when enterprises are bigger, and because specialization is more productive only if it is based on better knowledge and skills, such a society moves away from traditional practices and begins to apply rationality, science, and engineering in deciding how to do things.

Ultimately, then, the occupational structure of a society is radically transformed by division of labor. The transformation may also be seen in a dramatic contrast: In the past almost every able-bodied male was a hunter in a hunting and gathering society, and about 85 to 95 percent of the population in a peasant society were poor farmers; but in the modern United States, whose agricultural production is one of the highest in the world, less than 5 percent of the population make a living from farming, and over 65 percent are white-collar workers.

It seems unlikely that productivity could ever be great enough to support the extreme division of labor in modern industrial societies without the widespread use of machines. Since these have a profound effect on occupations and on the social structure generally, it is to these we now turn.

Machines and Automation

The spread of machine technology has been accompanied both by gloomy predictions that machines would replace all workers and by optimistic prophecies that some day no one would *have* to work, because all our labor would be done by mechanical servants. Both readings of the future were incorrect. In fact, more people have jobs than ever before, thus disproving the first prediction. Modern automation also increases productivity but does not reduce the total number of jobs in the society. As to the second prediction, machine technology requires a good deal of care and will not operate at all unless a vast army of occupations work together to design, build, and repair the machines; to produce the skilled people who will operate them; to distribute what they will make; and to repair the social and psychological damage they generate in a society dominated by them. It does not seem very likely, then, that in the future we shall go

from cradle to grave, nursed and cared for by wise, agreeable machines. On the contrary, as we make that long trek, we are more likely to serve as nursemaids to machines.

As Marx pointed out, a machine is not just any labor-saving device, for example, an axe, a lever, a bucket; all of these save labor, but they are not machines. Nor is a machine "something run by motors"; for it may be moved by water, a horse, or even a human being. What sets a machine apart is that it *duplicates some operation previously done by the human hand,* and thus makes that human hand unnecessary: twisting cotton to make thread, turning off a flow of water when it reaches a certain level, or making chemical tests of oil as it flows through a refinery.

When the operation of the human hand is replicated, several possibilities emerge for transforming production. First, some kind of driving force other than the human body can be harnessed: Water power, then steam, and later electricity. Second, the machine does not tire, so that it can work long hours, and at almost any speed. Third, although the machine is not so subtle and clever as the hand, it is possible to break down almost all complex tasks into simple steps, each of which even the stupid machine can do.

The next development in machine technology is *automation* and a self-regulating, or feedback, mechanism known as a *cybernetic control.* Cybernetic controls are not at all new: Mechanical devices that direct the machine operation to *adjust itself* were found in the earliest machines. One of the first, a "governor," was a set of spinning knobs on a steam engine; if they spun too rapidly, they closed a valve and thus slowed down the engine; if too slowly, they opened up the valve and thus speeded up the engine.

The Effects of Machine Technology

The change from human to machine technology has transformed work in the industrial era in several respects.

The first major change was the imposition of a *steady pace* or rhythm for work. In traditional societies work may have been rhythmical at times, and even accompanied by singing, but people typically controlled their own pace. Having worked hard for a while, they could rest, change the pace, or turn to a different task. The machine eliminated all that; and indeed the most widespread complaint of modern industrial workers is precisely that they cannot control their own pattern of work, for how much work they do in a given day is determined by the machine. This is not simply a matter of speed, although the machine does force people to work faster. It is rather that the machine does not adjust itself to the varying tempo of human wishes.

A second major change in work resulting from the introduction of the machine has been the *discipline* imposed on workers. Everything must be organized, and everything must be in its place. Whether it is a tiny shop or a giant factory, there must be high control over the flow of material in and out of the work unit. A machine cannot adjust itself to the infinite variety of human beings; they must adjust to it. Since all parts of the machine process are integrated with one another, workers must be organized around the machine's schedule.

Third, both workers and work become increasingly *time-oriented* as a result of the machine's discipline; workers have to arrive and have to work at set times. People cannot simply drift in and out of their workplace whenever they please; they cannot decide to ignore work for a while. The increased emphasis upon time has affected other areas of our lives as well—and time has become more widely recognized as a major resource. Although the variables of time and space affect social relations in all cultures, as we noted in Chapter 8, "Geography and Social Life," a microscopic attention to time schedules is found only in modern industrial society.

The emphasis on time is not the result of mere whim, perversity, or compulsiveness.

When those who work together are not in close enough contact to permit coordinated messages to go back and forth, they must agree to be available for work at a particular time. So, similarly, every stage in the productive process requires an exact coordination of time. A widespread set of social consequences flows from this continued calculation of how much time is worth. One can argue, indeed, that for many people in modern society time has become almost as precious as money. For example, industrial society has increasingly become a "throwaway economy"; products are no longer meant to last or to be repaired, but are expected to be thrown away when they stop working. The cost of repair is high, but more importantly, people do not have enough free time to take them to be repaired or to do without the convenience they offer. They simply buy a new one. And because people feel time-driven, they wish to make a peak experience out of each moment of their leisure time. Consequently, they invest large sums of money in their recreational equipment and vacations. When the economy yields an ever-expanding, vast array of products, we feel pressed and deprived if we do not have enough time in which to enjoy all of them. It is indeed this aspect of modern social life that creates the paradox of the supposedly shorter workweek (which may not be in process anyway) while we increasingly feel we "have no time."[5]

The fourth major impact of the machine on occupational life stems from the heavy *investment of capital* that machines require. While machines increase profits, the capitalist must put together a great deal of money or credit to purchase them. Consequently, there must be high control over every phase

[5]For a thoughtful analysis of time as a resource, see Staffan Linder, *The Harried Leisure Class*, New York: Columbia, 1970. By now, the formal economic analysis of time as an allocatable resource has been considerably elaborated, largely following the explorations of Gary S. Becker. See, for example, his article "A Theory of the Allocation of Time," *Economic Journal* (September 1965), pp. 493–517.

of production to guarantee profits, to protect the capital, and to thus maintain the investors' enterprise. As banking and credit systems expand, people invent many systems for gaining command over the necessary capital. In fact, the modern corporation was designed to bring together large sums of money for investments. The focus of the class system and of society in general has turned away from land and to investments and jobs in corporate enterprises. Moreover, because the monetary investment in machinery must be ensured, a vast array of new occupations arise to drive the bureaucracy, which must organize the flow of materials, labor, and products that are part of the whole machine process.

A fifth important development of machine technology was first observed by Marx: the *reduced need for individual dexterity* and skill. But Marx incorrectly predicted that it would be a continuing wave of the future. Because the machine dispenses with the human hand, high skill is no longer needed *at that task*. Long years of training are required to weave good cloth, but a spinning or weaving machine can be tended by almost anyone after a short period of instruction. Consequently, both women and children could enter the factory and supervise a machine as well as a trained man could. Since factory owners thus had a much larger source of labor, they could reduce wages to an extremely low level. Those who did not would simply go bankrupt in competition with others who did.

In the early stages of industrialization, as a consequence, both children and women were widely utilized. Lower-class families found that *everyone had to work as wages were reduced*. Only by *combining* their wages could they survive at all. However, this trend did not continue indefinitely, and the case illustrates the important principle that the machine alone does not determine social life. People can and do decide how to use machines. In fact, it was political action that changed the direction of factory work that Marx observed in the middle of the nineteenth century. Since that time numerous regulations, the political threats of workers, and union pressures forbade the use of children and increased the wages of all workers—both male and female.

The Limitations of Machines

Our attention has so often been directed to the dramatic impact of machine technology on modern life that we forget how *narrow* is the scope of problems that machines solve. This limitation appears in several ways.

First is the ironic finding that machines do not typically "save" labor; instead, they *increase productivity*. That is, they do not increase the amount of leisure we enjoy, but merely push us to produce more in a given time period. Modern homemakers do not spend less time at their whole range of domestic duties than they did seventy years ago (although the physical labor then was greater). The mechanical appliances of the home simply permit more work to be turned out. A careful analysis of time budgets not long ago came to the conclusion that "the greatly touted gains in free time since the 1850s, then, are largely myth."[6] Any extra hours that have come from shortening the workday all seem to have been gobbled up completely by additional time in commuting to work, traveling for shopping and recreation, do-it-yourself tasks, and moonlighting.

Second, machines do a few things, and do them well, on a large scale; but they need human attention. They cannot repair themselves, design themselves, furnish raw materials to themselves, or maintain the elaborate paper work that is necessary to keep the entire operation going. In a modern chemical plant or oil refinery, the machinery seems to be taking care of itself, and few human beings are to be seen. But a large

[6]De Grazia, op. cit., p. 86.

Figure 14-2 In a highly mechanized oil refinery, specialized workers are needed to watch the machines that watch the flow of processes. (Deutsche, Texaco.)

army of jobs must exist in order to maintain the flow of those processes. And many more of these people must be experts, because a breakdown anywhere is very expensive. Problems must be solved immediately.

A third limitation of machines, and perhaps the most important for the future, is that machines are best in situations that yield *economies of scale*, that is, for tasks that can be done more efficiently in large batches. By contrast, some tasks are so small and so special in character that machines cannot do them cheaply or even well. Thus, if we need a million yards of the same cloth, the machine can weave that very well; but if we want only one yard of a special cloth, a handloom may be more efficient. Similarly, a machine cannot pick up diapers or straighten up the living room, nor can it prepare and deliver a hot meal to a neighbor who is ill. The machine is least useful for *most problems of human and social relations,* for they require a unique and flexi-

ble approach that does not yield economies of scale.

Thus, we observe the seeming paradox that in this most industrialized of all societies the percentage of workers who attend machines has not increased by much. Further, it is much less than the percentage of workers who are engaged in the wide array of tasks whose aim is to *help people* in one way or another.

One important implication of this change should be noted. National productivity can continue to increase only where economies of scale can be created. However, a larger and ever-expanding sector of our economy is devoted to human relations tasks in which economies of scale are impossible. Machines cannot take over the tasks of satisfying human needs because human beings have needs that machines cannot satisfy; machine products cover too narrow a range of human life. Thus, if a larger part of the society is devoted to occupations in which there is no way of "processing a batch" of human needs in larger and larger quantities, inevitably the expansion of the Gross National Product must slow down over the long run.

Some of these changes are revealed in Table 14–1, which shows relatively minor growth in machine workers in contrast to the major growth in the occupations that process human needs. The reader may encounter a few surprises in Table 14–1. First, it indicates that over the past seventy-five years of high industrialization, the percentage of "operatives"—semiskilled workers, factory workers on assembly lines, people who tend machines—has *not* risen by much. A second surprise is that although many commentators lament the passing of the skilled worker, that segment of the work force has actually shown a slight increase.

As Table 14–1 shows, private household workers (servants, domestics) have dropped substantially, and so have the farming cate-gories. A large increase has occurred, as we noted before, in "Professional and technical workers," many of whom deal with the tasks of helping people; here the increase is about 350 percent. Similarly, "Clerical workers" has expanded even more. As the industrial system depends on monitoring a flow of papers and documents, this category has expanded by over 600 percent since 1900.

Thus, the job opportunities within a modern society change over time. Not only are people competing for jobs; but jobs themselves are expanding and contracting and thus competing with one another. In the following sections we will consider these changes in the structure of jobs.

OCCUPATIONAL MONOPOLY: TOWARD INDEPENDENCE OR SELF-CONTROL

A sociological view of occupations cannot confine itself to the relations between the

TABLE 14–1   CHANGES IN THE OCCUPATIONAL DISTRIBUTION OF U.S. WORKERS (1900–1975)

Occupational Group	1900	1920	1940	1950	1960	1970	1975
Professional and technical workers	4.3%	5.4%	7.5%	8.6%	11.4%	14.2%	15.1%
Managers and administrators	5.8	6.6	7.3	8.7	10.7	10.5	10.6
Salesworkers	4.5	4.9	6.7	7.0	6.4	6.2	6.4
Clerical workers	3.0	8.0	9.6	12.3	14.8	17.4	18.5
Artisan	10.5	13.0	12.0	14.2	13.0	12.9	12.8
Operatives	12.8	15.6	18.4	20.4	18.2	17.7	15.4
Nonfarm laborers	12.5	11.6	9.4	6.6	5.4	4.7	4.5
Private household workers	5.4	3.3	4.7	2.6	3.0	2.0	1.4
Service workers except private household	3.6	4.5	7.1	7.9	9.2	10.4	12.4
Farmers and farm managers	19.9	15.3	10.4	7.4	4.2	2.2	1.8
Farm laborers	17.7	11.7	7.0	4.4	3.6	1.7	1.3

NOTE: Figures for 1900–1950 are based on the Economically Active Population, and this includes unemployed workers; the figures for 1960–1975 include only the employed.
SOURCES: 1900 to 1950: from U.S. Bureau of the Census, *Historical Statistics of the United States*, 1960, p. 74; 1960 and 1970: from *Statistical Abstract of the United States*, 1974, pp. 350–351; 1975: from U.S. Department of Labor, *Employment and Earnings*, vol. 21, no. 8 (February 1975), p. 41.

worker and the job or to relations among coworkers. It must also view occupations themselves as "social actors" and thus extend to the relationships among occupations. This more extended view brings into focus some important processes that help us to understand the place of jobs in any large society.

At some phase in the history of certain occupations, mainly the skilled trades and professions, their members make an effort to gain control over their work. Specifically, they attempt to control who may enter the occupation, the training of recruits, standards for certification and competence, salary scales and fees, the quality of work performance, standards for deciding about misconduct and expulsion, and the nature of the tasks included within their area of expertise. In short, they try to get a charter, a mandate, or a license; they seek a monopoly.

The people in all occupations would prefer to take such a step, since any such control yields many advantages. In all work settings workers would prefer to have greater control over what they do, when they do it, and how they do it. In a fundamental sense, all occupations are in competition with each other to some extent, and each is trying to carve out an area in which to enjoy a partial monopoly. Over the short run, the total amount of services bought is limited, so that if one occupation succeeds in its monopolistic efforts, it can derive economic benefit from that control.

However, it is not possible for every occupation to be autonomous; if some are to be freer to make their own decisions, others will have to integrate their efforts with them. Consequently, occupations must compete for control, and only a few succeed. Typically, the skilled crafts (electricians, plumbers, diemakers, printers) and the professions do.

As might be expected, competition is greatest between occupations whose areas of expertise overlap to some extent. Thus, physicians are not likely to be in much conflict with plumbers with respect to the problems of control, but they may well be in conflict with clinical psychologists (who take patients that would otherwise go to psychiatrists), with nurses, and with hospital administrators. Similarly, pharmacists, apothecaries, bonesetters, chiropractors, podiatrists, bleeders, barbers, and witches have all competed with physicians at times, and some still do. Similarly, a blacksmith commands a set of skills that other skilled workers do not, but most metalworkers (tinsmiths, coppersmiths, farriers) can do *some* of the blacksmith's tasks.

In addition, those who are only partially trained may compete with skilled workers. In the rural United States and on the frontiers of the past there were many jack-of-all-trades whose wide range of skills overlapped with those of their fully trained colleagues. Apprentices who never advanced to journeyman in the skilled trades could usually do most of the tasks of that craft. Thus, many people and many occupations have always challenged the monopoly of a particular occupation.

Resistance against Occupational Monopoly

We can observe two regularities in the resistance against occupations' gaining a full charter or greater control over their work: (1) Occupations with similar or overlapping areas of expertise are likely to oppose that effort. (2) When a skill is widespread in the population, it is unlikely that only one craft can successfully claim it as theirs. This rule applies to fence builders, field laborers, and fruit harvesters in rural areas, and to clerks and typists in modern urban life. Many of these tasks can be done by many people who do not work full time at that job, or by people who simply carry out the tasks for themselves. Even in a highly specialized society like the United States, people make dresses for themselves, cook their own meals, plant their gardens, paint their homes, repair their cars, type their own letters, balance their own financial records, write their own computer programs, and diagnose and treat their own illnesses.

Whether people do these tasks only for themselves or their friends, or for customers who pay for them, all these activities do offer some competition to regular members of those occupations and do frustrate their attempt to gain full control over the area they claim as their own.

There is a third regularity in the resistance to complete control within an occupation: The occupations that succeed in gaining control over their members and work are not only distinctive in their command of skills that most people do not have. In addition, the skills they have are typically those which a potential recruit cannot usually acquire alone. These skills must be learned under the supervision of a practitioner in the trade or by working with the practitioner along with some supplementary training in a vocational school. Thus, even the high-level job of management is not viewed as a monopoly, because people do not believe that the skills can actually be learned by an apprenticeship with those who are successful. Even though many administrators are trained in graduate schools of business, successful corporation presidents do not believe that the skills and talents they possess can be simply passed on to junior managers or recruits in training programs.

A fourth limitation on control within an occupation is due to the fact that many high and low positions in modern countries are obtained through election. Again, people do not believe that a person can become an effective mayor, governor, or county clerk by serving an apprenticeship with the incumbents of those positions. In any event, those incumbents do not command a monopoly, since they are under constant threat of being removed in the next election.

A fifth source of opposition to a job monopoly is the state itself. Although the state has some interest in limiting who may practice any occupation so that it can control their practice in some fashion, the state's interest does not always extend any control over skill and competence and thus does not give control to one occupational group. For example, waiters, waitresses, and restaurant owners may be controlled only with respect to health needs, and licensing or inspection focuses on that area almost entirely. Control over liquor licenses is nearly universal, but it has little to do with competence. Rather, its aims are to ensure the collection of taxes and to prevent infiltration by organized crime. Prizefighters, performers in New York City nightclubs, and owners of gambling resorts in Nevada are similarly subjected to some control, because of the state's wish to bar people who have some connection with crime.

When controls are imposed by the state, the occupation itself does not have as much influence or authority. The state itself denies control to the occupation. The state allows almost anyone to be licensed, and state control therefore does not limit by much the number of people who are permitted to compete. Second, even when the numbers are limited, the occupation does not typically choose who is allowed to enter, does not organize the training or the examinations, and does not set the standards of performance that the practitioner must meet. Only a few occupations or professions gain that control.

We have been noting several sources of resistances against the efforts of those within an occupation to obtain a charter or mandate within their area of expertise, and thus to control it: the amateurs or the partially trained; the practitioners of similar occupations; and the state itself, which has the final authority in these matters. Only a few occupations—mainly the skilled trades and the traditional professions—can escape much of this control. These are typically licensed, put their representatives on the examination and licensing boards of the state, and also control the standards for entrance, performance, and working conditions.

Factors That Support Occupational Monopoly

Occupations that successfully secure autonomy, as noted earlier, typically command *rare skills*. What are other characteristics that set them apart and give them advantages in the competition among other types of occupations? A minor one is that their skills are in *demand* anywhere in the society. By contrast, many jobs are so narrowly specialized that the worker can be employed only in a particular type of plant or industry, for example, the automobile assembly line, meatpacking plants, oil and chemicals, or electronics.

When an occupation requires rare skills, occupants also have more influence in the social and political processes through which control could be obtained over their type of work. More importantly, they claim, with some justification, that it is *dangerous or unwise* to let in just any practitioner who can get customers. That is, it is not merely that the skills are *rare*; their expertise *solves problems* or difficulties that may become serious if a poorly trained amateur or self-appointed practitioner tries to solve them. The risk is so dangerous that consumers should not be *permitted* to hire anyone they choose outside the occupation, for laypeople cannot judge the quality of the professional's skills. For example, medical quacks have never lacked for clients. Unskilled plumbing can cause pollution that leads to illnesses within the household or neighborhood, without anyone ever knowing why. A poorly installed electric circuit may cause fires. Following amateur legal advice may lead to bankruptcy or jail.

Those unfortunate outcomes are less likely where the employer is an expert, or has access to expert opinion, and can thus judge the work being done. One example of this is engineering, one of the most technically advanced occupations, which is not organized as a single group but is split into dozens of specialized associations. As a "community" its members do not exercise much control over each other or over the occupation as a whole.

A usual characteristic of the professions and skilled occupations with great autonomy is that members can practice without much capital or equipment and thus can work independently. The only large exception is medicine, but physicians do not have to *buy* a hospital in order to practice. After all, their own colleagues are in charge of it, and they can use it without owning it.

Perhaps of equal importance in maintaining their independence and bargaining power is that in such occupations there seem to be *no* great economies of scale; that is, putting *many* electricians, steamfitters, or diesinkers together does not yield much more output *per person*. By contrast, in most of modern industry the organization of many specialists, together with their machines, has typically led to large gains in productivity per person.[7]

The building trades especially have succeeded in gaining considerable control through effective *union* activities over many generations of struggle. They cannot control the economic cycle of boom and depression; but even when times are poor, these unions have largely maintained discipline, especially in the cities. How has this been done?

Ordinances require a certain level of performance if building inspections are to be passed. In turn, building contracts specify that payment will not be made until those official inspections have been passed. Consequently, numerous ordinances must be

---

[7]Bureaucratic organization as a support staff does create economies of scale in some occupations; for example, consider hospitals and libraries.

observed—but these ordinances were drawn up in collaboration with the craft unions. More importantly, when union control has been challenged, members have been able to impose severe penalties on rebel workers and employers. Aside from physical force, they have exploited the peculiar vulnerability of the construction job itself. A tiny vial of acid can be broken in a bathtub that has already been installed, electric wires can easily be cut, and fine paneling scratched. Political pressure can be brought to bear on building inspectors, who then find that the work violates the building ordinances. Contractors, employers, or corporations have often found the experience costly when they have hired nonunion labor. Coal mining is especially vulnerable, too.

In fact, both the highly organized crafts and the professions have succeeded in making an implicit "exchange" or bargain with the society. They have agreed to furnish services of an adequate standard and to police their own members—a task they claim laypeople are not competent to do since only experts know when the job is well done. In exchange, they obtain an effective monopoly over the sale of their service.

However, as in all social relations, such agreements are constantly being renegotiated. More and more organized groups are asserting their right to check on the quality of medical service provided by doctors. They charge that organized medicine is more interested in its income than in the patient. That challenge could not be mounted if it were not supported by many young physicians who believe their accusations are correct and are willing to give data to prove them.

The professions and crafts have also been charged with discriminating against talented women and minorities. Those charges are largely correct. Both medical and law schools have made some effort in recent years to permit more blacks and women to enter. But the building trade unions have been almost adamant in their refusal, and almost no change is as yet visible in their discriminatory practices. In the highly con-

Figure 14-3 Some trade unions have systematically discriminated against minorities, as is reflected by the members attending this union meeting. (Burk Uzzle, Magnum Photos.)

trolled crafts, blacks make up less than 5 percent of the total. It is especially in the building trades that the practice has grown of allowing mainly kinfolk or family friends to become apprentices. Although the monopoly itself has not been challenged in any of these occupations and professions, their discriminatory practices have been under attack by both private and governmental organizations, whose efforts have mainly focused on opening up opportunities to people who had been previously barred from them.

HOW MANY OCCUPATIONS CAN BECOME PROFESSIONAL?

As part of the general competition among occupations, we can observe that some are seeking to rise in income, influence, and prestige by trying to become "professions." Over the past seventy years the category of "Professional and technical workers" has increased faster than any other category in the labor force—except clerical workers—about 350 percent since 1900. Occupations at these higher prestige levels gain great advantages from being thought of as professions. They earn more money and enjoy more autonomy in their daily work. Consequently, many occupations organize propaganda campaigns in which they lay claims to professional rank. Since existing trends fit in with the aspirations of high-ranking occupations, the question may be asked, *Are there limits to the process of professionalization?*

Very few of the aspiring occupations and semiprofessions will in fact become professions; they will never reach the levels of knowledge and the dedication to service the society considers necessary for that rank. Aspiring occupations include schoolteaching, nursing, librarianship, pharmacy, stockbroking, advertising, business management,

and others.[8] Moreover, most occupations that do rise will continue to be viewed as collectively different from the four great "person professions"—law, medicine, the ministry, and university teaching.

These aspiring occupations will continue to be less able to exhibit professional *traits* such as cohesion, commitment to the norms of service, the percentage of members remaining in the profession through their lifetime, homogeneity of membership, or control over professional violation. In this narrow sense, the occupational structure of industrial society is *not* becoming *generally* more professionalized, even though a higher percentage of the labor force is in occupations that enjoy high prestige rankings and incomes and that *call* themselves professions.

Some occupations manage to strike an implicit "bargain" with the society, by which they guarantee a standard of service and in turn are granted some kind of monopoly over selling that service. Such transactions may take decades, generations, or even centuries to accomplish, and it is unlikely that any occupation can so delude the public that they can conspire to exploit it without giving anything in return. What is the basis for the claims made by the high-ranking professions?

Traits of Established Professions

The two essential characteristics that generate most of the well-known traits of the established professions are (1) a basic body of abstract knowledge, and (2) the ideal of service. Both qualities contain many dimensions or subtraits, which we will examine below.

[8]For a more extended analysis of these processes, see William J. Goode, "The Theoretical Limits of Professionalization," in *Explorations in Social Theory*, New York: Oxford, 1973, pp. 341–382; as well as Amitai Etzioni, ed, *The Semi-Professions and Their Organization*, New York: Free Press, 1969.

With respect to *knowledge,* the traditional professions claim a command over a body of abstract knowledge that is thought to be applicable to the concrete problems of living. Thus, the knowledge is different from philosophical speculation or abstract theories of art. Moreover, it is necessary that the members of society believe that knowledge can actually help to solve their problems and that it is appropriate for people in trouble to seek professional help for those problems. The profession has command over that knowledge, usually through the organization of schools or research institutes. Finally, since the individual profession is in control of that knowledge, it is believed that in any disputes about how good a technical solution is, the profession itself must be the final judge.

With respect the *ideal of service,* the traditional profession asserts that the *practitioner* must decide what the client's needs really are and must make this judgment without regard to self-enrichment. The patient may come to the physician with his or her own diagnosis, just as the client may come to the lawyer with his or her own legal solution, but the professional must decide what the client really ought to do. It is a violation of professional ethics to offer a solution whose main goal is a larger fee for the practitioner: The goal is supposed to be to help the client, not the professional.

In addition, the traditional professions demand some real *sacrifice from practitioners,* both as ideal and in fact. For example, the student professional must be willing to study for years to acquire skills, thus deferring material comforts and the privileges of adulthood for several years. In addition, there are some situations in each profession where the practitioners are exposed to threats or dangers if they live up to the highest ideal of the profession: For example, the military officer must be willing to die in battle, the scientist should persist in expounding the truth against the opposition of laymen or influential colleagues, and the

lawyer should defend the unpopular murderer. The profession should allocate some of its own resources and talent to the development of new knowledge, even though that may make obsolete some of the knowledge of people already in practice.

Perhaps of most importance, the profession must attempt to work out some system of *rewards and punishments* that yields greater honor and even income to those who live by the ideals of the profession. As with most such social arrangements, those who are honored most may well not earn the highest possible incomes, though typically they do earn far more than the average.

Let us consider for a moment the interlocking and reinforcing character of some of the social traits of the professions. Their *incomes* are higher than those of other occupations because their services are needed and there are no satisfactory alternatives: They have a monopoly over a valuable product. Their product is also valuable on the *prestige market* because of their dedication to the service ideal, because their education is high, and because their performances are above those of average people. They enjoy a monopoly because the society believes no one else can do the job, and it is dangerous to try other kinds of practitioners. They are given more autonomy (a charter) because they claim, more than others, to be concerned about the client's interest. For the same reasons the shape of legislation, the manning of control and examination boards, and standards for licensing and expulsions are more likely to be in the hands of professionals.

Because all professions have some kind of ethical code that is somewhat different from that of the larger society (for example, lawyers and medical professionals should not advertise[9] and should not guarantee results, and military officers should be willing to risk

[9]In 1975–1976 legal attacks as well as professional opposition to the rule against advertising may well lead to its abolition.

their lives), some period of adult socialization is more necessary than in other occupations: People have to be *trained* to believe in such norms. Finally, because the rewards are high and adult socialization is more intense, members are more *committed* to the profession, are less willing to leave it, and are more likely to claim they would choose the same work if they were to begin their careers once more.

Thus, in order to move far toward being accepted as one of the established professions, it is not enough merely to achieve a high income, make speeches, or even write a code of ethics. Professionals must command a body of abstract knowledge and show they are motivated by the ideal of service.

Social Determinants of Professionalism

If social reality, not the claims of aspiring occupations, determines professionalism, we can make some predictions about what occupations will or will not become accepted as professions. It seems likely that these occupations have actually become professions in the last generations: dentistry, certified public accountancy, clinical psychology, and some high levels of the scientific and engineering fields (electronic engineering, cryogenics). It is likely that these semiprofessions will achieve professionalism over the next generation: social work,[10] marital counseling, and perhaps city planning.

These occupations will not become professional, although all of them have such aspirations and have made such claims: managerial jobs for nonprofit organizations (executives for philanthropic organizations, supervising principals), schoolteachers, librarians, and the higher levels of business management and advertising.

---

[10]It should be emphasized that here we refer to the social worker who has undergone professional training that culminates in the M.S.W. or the doctorate in social work; we are not referring to the welfare worker or caseworker in urban departments of welfare.

The contrasted cases of librarianship and dentistry illustrate the importance of the knowledge base. It is only within the past generation that dentistry in the United States began to build adequate scientific foundations for general practice as well as specialties. Correlative with that change has occurred a rise in income as well as prestige. In the past, dental problems were not viewed as important enough to require so much investment in the necessary research for this new development. Indeed, precisely because it was not viewed as important, it was never incorporated into the general medical industry, by contrast with midwifery, surgery, and bloodletting.

On the other hand, though librarians as a class are doubtless more learned than members of most other occupations, and are as committed to service as they are dedicated to knowledge, the public is not convinced there is a basic *science* of librarianship. The skill is thought to be only clerical or administrative. There are university curricula whose content is devoted to the organization and codification of library materials, and even to the development of principles about information retrieval. But the most relevant occupational group, university professors, have not been convinced that this knowledge base deserves the respect given to the traditional professions.

At a deeper level, these continuing decisions are essentially based on whether the society believes it suffers great costs because the members of an occupation do not command a body of codified knowledge. Doubtless, work of almost any type—nursing, chauffeuring, or waiting on tables—would be done better if much research were devoted to those specialties, but social decisions have consistently denied that that investment is worthwhile.

On the other hand, knowledge may not be thought to be the key to high performance anyway. For example, there *is* a considerable body of scientific knowledge about the principles of corporate management,

FOCUS

HOW WORK SHAPES THE PERSON

The weightiest social relationship of the teacher is his relationship to his students; it is this relationship which is teaching. It is around this relationship that the teacher's personality tends to be organized, and it is in adaptation to the needs of this relationship that the qualities of character which mark the teacher are produced. The teacher-pupil relationship is a special form of dominance and subordination, a very unstable relationship and in quivering equilibrium, not much supported by sanction and the strong arm of authority, but depending largely upon purely personal ascendency. Every teacher is a taskmaster and every taskmaster is a hard man; if he is naturally kindly, he is hard from duty, but if he is naturally unkind, he is hard because he loves it. It is an unfortunate rôle, that of Simon Legree, and has corrupted the best of men. Conflict is in the rôle, for the wishes of the teacher and the student are necessarily divergent, and more conflict because the teacher must protect himself from the possible destruction of his authority that might arise from this divergence of motives. Subordination is possible only because the subordinated one is a subordinate with a mere fragment of his personality, while the dominant one participates completely. The subject is a subject only part of the time and with a part of himself, but the king is all king. In schools, too, subordinated ones attempt to protect themselves by withdrawing from the relationship, to suck the juice from the orange of conformity before rendering it to the teacher. But the teacher is doomed to strive against the mechanization of his rule and of obedience to it. It is the part of the teacher to enforce a real obedience. The teacher must be aggressive in his domination, and this is very unfortunate, because domination is tolerable only when it stays within set bounds. From this necessary and indispensable aggressiveness of the teacher arises an answering hostility on the part of the student which imperils the very existence of any intercourse between them. The teacher takes upon himself most of the burden of the far-reaching psychic adjustments which make the continuance of the relationship possible.

That inflexibility or unbendingness of personality which we have mentioned as characterizing the school teacher flows naturally out of his relations with his students. The teacher must maintain a consistent pose in the presence of students. He must not adapt to the demands of the childish group in which he lives, but must force the group to adapt to him, wherefore the teacher often feels that he must take leave of graciousness and charm and the art of being a good fellow at the classroom door. The teacher must not accept the definitions of situations which students work out, but must impose his own definition upon students. His position as an agent of social control, as the paid representative of the adult group among the group of children, requires that when he has found a pose he must hold it; to compromise upon matters where adult morality runs would be thought treason to the group that pays his salary.

SOURCE: Willard W. Waller, *The Sociology of Teaching*, New York: Wiley, 1932, pp. 383–384.

and many millions of dollars have been devoted to research on these problems. Nevertheless, the society at large and even managers themselves continue to believe that success or failure does not depend upon mastering those principles. Instead, most people believe that a good manager can be an intuitive master without knowing them at all. Moreover, managers do not seek wise solutions except in their own interests, not for those of the society.

A crucial structural element in the claim to independence or autonomy is whether the profession *has to be trusted if it is to do its work at all.* Members of any occupation prefer independence if they can achieve it, and typically claim that they should be trusted. The deciding variable, however, is whether the professional *can* do harm if the work is not done properly, and cannot do the work at all if she or he is *not* in a position to *do* harm.[11]

This means, typically, that the stakes are higher in professional work. That is, to do a professional job at all will at times require that the client be *vulnerable.* The physician must be allowed to explore the patient's body in ways that outsiders are not permitted; the lawyer must be free to obtain answers to questions that others are not allowed to pose; the military officer must be able to know the weaknesses of the country's defenses.

In such a position the client cannot measure adequate performance correctly. Such professions, which have less *technical* control over outcomes—law, psychiatry, medicine, the military, the university, and the

clergy—can more easily protect their inept colleagues, because laypeople may never learn that incompetence caused the failure. For example, the lawyer whose client goes to jail can always assert that the term of imprisonment would have been much longer if another lawyer had handled the case.

Because of these mutually reinforcing factors, which allow for laxity or incompetence, the *internal* controls on the professional must be stronger, and *colleague* controls must be imposed when those internal controls weaken. Thus, ethical problems loom larger and are more frequent in the types of professions that deal less with technical solutions and more with "person-problems." Far more personal gossip is focused on those professions, more fiction is devoted to those problems, the temptations to violate trust are more frequent, and the control systems themselves doubtless fail more frequently.

If we look at the occupations that have much *greater* technical control over their problems—which include some specialties in medicine (radiology, pathology), architecture, and the engineering specialties—we see that the client-professional relationship is much more likely to be simply a contractual one. That is, price and definite results are part of the agreement. Clients are more likely to demand proofs of competence and are less likely to demand proof of some devotion to their own interest. The personal authority of the professional plays a far lesser role, simply because the proof of competence can be found in the measurable results. In addition, far fewer problems of unethical behavior are likely either to occur or to be suspected—after all, the opportunities are much more limited there.

JOB SATISFACTION

Over the past generation hundreds of studies have attempted to find out what makes

---

[11]Everett C. Hughes points out that many occupations cannot be carried out "without guilty knowledge." For example, the priest must know of heresies and sins; the lawyer, the newspaper reporter, and the private secretary must all acquire and keep some embarrassing information. Moreover, members of such occupations must be permitted to talk in shocking ways, that is, plainly and objectively, about such matters, at least when only colleagues are present. See his "License and Mandate," in *Men and Their Work,* Glencoe, Ill.: Free Press, 1958, pp. 78–82.

workers satisfied, presumably in the belief that contented workers will produce more, or at least that discontented ones will produce less. The volume of this research suggests, at a minimum, that corporate leaders suspect work is not in itself very entertaining. If people streamed to their jobs each morning full of joyful anticipation, it would not be necessary to ask these questions.

The central (and perhaps surprising) finding of these inquiries is that only about 20 percent of all workers are clearly dissatisfied; about two-thirds claim their work is interesting and they are satisfied.[12] We need to understand why this response is so widespread, when artists, fiction writers, commentators, social philosophers, and union representatives assert the contrary; and we should also examine the social conditions that create more or less satisfaction with the job.

The reasons why workers say they like their job are partly to be found in our earlier comments on the meaning of work.[13] If holding a job is part of being a person in our society, if social interaction at work is part of a person's identity, and if wages are necessary to survive, then people do gain certain kinds of satisfaction from work. People may not be enthusiastic about the *tasks* they perform on the job, but the entire package of the job yields, on balance, some satisfaction. For most workers such inquiries pose "a choice between no work connection (usually with severe attendant economic penalties and a conspicuous lack of meaningful alternative activites), and a work connection burdened with negative qualities (routine, compulsory scheduling, dependen-

cy, etc.)."[14] Thus, the worker will say she or he chooses to work, if those are the alternatives.

Questions about job satisfaction may be almost meaningless for that part of the labor force that is frequently unemployed, marginal, and working irregularly under substandard conditions. They do not have a steady relationship with *any* particular job, and certainly no strong hold on one.[15] For them job changes are frequent, unpredictable, and uncontrollable; such workers do not really have a job of their own. To the worker in that situation, "the central fact of his work experience is job chaos—the lack of any stable work milieu, organizational context, or career to which he could respond in a cheerful or alienated way."[16]

By contrast, workers with *steady* jobs can say they are "satisfied" with the job. That is, people may not find much joy in their work, as they are alleged to have done in the rosy, mythical past, but some of their needs are satisfied by working.

What Yields Satisfaction?

Differences in job satisfaction do support the arguments of the intellectuals and artists who have proclaimed the soullessness of modern work life, that is, of those who have correctly stated what kind of work is most satisfying: It is, in fact, their own kind of work. A higher percentage of people are satisfied in jobs that permit more independence, control over the pace of work, and self-expression; that earn more esteem from other people; and that pay more. Indeed, the curve of job satisfaction corresponds rather well to the prestige ranking of occu-

[12]See *Work in America*, Task Force, Department of Health, Education, and Welfare, Cambridge; Mass.: M.I.T., 1973, pp. 13ff.; and Harold L. Wilensky, op. cit., pp. 135ff.

[13]We leave aside the methodological point, that queries like "Do you like your marriage? Are things OK?" stimulate people to give socially approved responses. Just how much bias these answers contain is not known.

[14]Robert L. Kahn, "The Meaning of Work: Interpretations and Proposals for Measurement," in Angus Campbell and Philip E. Converse, eds., *The Human Meaning of Social Change*, New York: Russell Sage, 1972, p. 179.

[15]Wilensky, op. cit., p. 131.

[16]Ibid.

Figure 14-4 Job satisfaction is generally higher among managerial than among lower-level occupations. (Merrin, Monkmeyer.)

pations. Job satisfaction is therefore least in lower-level manual or assembly line occupations; it is highest in the professional and managerial occupations. The data even contain an irony: Urban university professors are almost at the top in all prestige rankings, and highest in job satisfaction, and it is they who mainly carry out studies of job satisfaction. These relationships hold in other industrialized countries as well.

When work is done under close supervision, the pace of work is determined by others, and the tasks lack variety or meaning, then job satisfaction is *lower*. Assembly line occupations fit that description, but only about 2 to 5 percent of the work force in the United States in such classically alienating occupations, and 60 percent of workers even in automobile factories report that their jobs are satisfactory just the same. However, a second type of question yields an important and deeper truth: Most would *prefer* to *change* their jobs. Moreover, in answer to the fantasy question about whether they would keep on working if they inherited enough to live on comfortably, most workers do say "Yes"—but only about 9 percent claim they would keep on working because they enjoy that kind of work (the other an-

swers focus on keeping busy, avoiding trouble, not feeling lost, and so on). As Wilensky remarks, "What the vast majority seem to be saying is that they want to remain among the living."[17]

Similarly, the fantasy question about what the worker would do with the extra two hours, if the day were twenty-six hours long rather than twenty-four, elicits similar responses. That is, the people in repetitive, mechanically paced, closely supervised work—those at the "bottom" of a large corporation ladder—are not very likely to respond that they would use that extra time in work-related activities or in working at their jobs. In contrast, most professors would, as might be guessed from Table 14–2. This table, which shows the percentage of people who would enter the same kind of work if they could start over again, indicates a strong relationship between job satisfaction and the job level.

We can see that the jobs likely to be cho-

[17]Harold L. Wilensky, "Work as a Social Problem," in Howard S. Becker, ed., *Social Problems*, New York: Wiley, 1966, p. 136. The data are from a study by N. E. Morse and R. S. Weiss, "The Function and Meaning of Work and the Job," *American Sociological Review, 20* (April 1955), pp. 191–198.

TABLE 14–2 PERCENTAGES IN OCCUPATIONAL GROUPS WHO WOULD CHOOSE SIMILAR WORK AGAIN

Professional and Lower White-Collar Occupations	Percent	Working-Class Occupations	Percent
Urban university professors	93	Skilled printers	52
Mathematicians	91	Paper workers	42
Physicists	89	Skilled autoworkers	41
Biologists	89	Skilled steelworkers	41
Chemists	86	Textile workers	31
Firm lawyers	85	*Blue-collar workers, cross section*	24
Lawyers	83	Unskilled steelworkers	21
Journalists (Washington correspondents)	82	Unskilled autoworkers	16
Church university professors	77		
Solo lawyers	75		
White-collar workers, cross section	43		

SOURCE: *Work in America*, Task Force, Department of Health, Education, and Welfare, Cambridge, Mass.: M.I.T., 1973, p. 16.

sen "if people could do it over again" are those with greater freedom, higher incomes, higher prestige, more control over work pace and more choice over the task to be done. That relationship holds generally, but it is not perfect. For example, at almost *any* occupational level there are *some* dissatisfied workers. Some people feel their work is useless (much of advertising and the public promotion of corporations). Some know their labor is simply featherbedding, or make-work (extra printing required by union rules, extra workmen in railroading), and thus do not enjoy their work as much. Well-educated people in low-paying, routine, specialized white-collar jobs are unlikely to gain much satisfaction from work, and annual turnover rates in these categories run about 30 percent a year. The most dissatisfied segment of United States workers are young black people in white-collar jobs. Since the educated young black workers are more militant politically, they are also more sensitive to the racial experiences they suffer while on the job—and white-collar blacks report more discrimination than blue-collar blacks.[18]

Toward Greater Satisfaction

Job satisfaction may be of some importance because it increases productivity. One can also argue that making work more pleasurable is surely as worthwhile a goal as turning out more cigarettes, TV sets, or Crunchy Boxtop sugar-coated breakfast cereal. It may also have some effect on health. Diet, exercise, medical care, and genetic inheritance account for only about 25 percent of the risk factors in coronary heart disease; and some researchers believe that work role and work conditions account for part of the rest, that is, such factors as job dissatisfaction, low self-esteem, occupational stress, or rapid employment changes.[19] Such factors also af-

[18]Ibid., pp. 52ff.
[19]Caplan, "Organizational Stress and Individual Strain," in A. J. Marrow, *The Failure of Success*; New York:

fect the mental health of workers negatively.[20]

Much industrial research has aimed at developing better machines and a more efficient work flow to reduce the burden on workers (as well as to lessen the dependence of the corporation on the worker). Other analysts have instead suggested that the *job be redesigned* to fit the needs of human beings. In some factories the assembly line is discarded, and a team builds a product from start to finish. A more modest change is to permit each worker to do several different kinds of job each day, a form of "job rotation."

Still more far-reaching plans have been put into effect. These contain several key elements. The most central is that the *workers themselves* decide on such matters as methods of production, who is to do which tasks, the hours of work, who is to be in charge of the work unit, and even how new workers are to be hired. These have always been the rights of management, but workers are like managers: They work better if they can decide the matters that concern them most. Ordinarily, such plans call for some kind of profit-sharing, so that efficiency pays off immediately. In this, again, the workers receive some of the benefits that higher-level *managers* typically get now— that is, bonuses, fringe benefits, extra rewards for higher output[21]—and that presumably increase the dedication of managers to their work. It seems reasonable to suppose they would have the same desirable effect on workers.

Such plans have been widely criticized, and often both management and workers are initially somewhat skeptical about their possible success. However, when a thoroughgoing redesign of jobs has taken place in any plant, higher productivity results as well as a greater feeling of satisfaction on the part of workers and managers. Since they run counter to work traditions and they reduce the managers' authority somewhat, it is not likely that these improvements will be immediately accepted. Nevertheless, if the quality of life becomes more important in work, a larger number of companies will adopt some version of this program.

MISTAKES AT WORK

Coworkers and managers view mistakes as a problem, something to be *stopped* if possible or at least to be reduced. However, mistakes are sociologically interesting in their own right: When mistakes cause some slowdown in the work process, how does a group mobilize itself to handle the problem? Or how do different groups in an organization evaluate different kinds of mistakes (*my excusable* error may be *your* catastrophe)? Some tasks are inherently risky (for example, fighting a battle); how do practitioners deal with that risk? Let us consider the apparently simple matter of mistakes at work.[22]

All workers make errors, whether trivial or serious. And some errors are costly. The cost may fall primarily on the consumer, as when a jeweler fails to adjust a watch properly; but if errors are frequent, they may be costly to the jeweler, too. Other errors affect an employer, as when a worker loses or breaks a valuable tool. And some errors can harm an entire community, as when a biologist fails to detect a disease-bearing organism in the water supply.

Since we all bear the cost of these errors,

American Management Association, 1972; as well as John R. P. French and Robert D. Caplan, "Psychosocial Factros in Coronary Heart Disease," *Industrial Medicine and Surgery*, 39 (September 1970), pp. 383ff.

[20]Arthur Kornhauser, "Toward an Assessment of the Mental Health of Factory Workers," *Human Organization*, 21 (Spring 1962), pp. 43ff.

[21]The Appendix to *Work in America*, pp. 188–201, gives a list of companies that have adopted some version of this plan.

[22]A perceptive analysis of this difference is found in Everett C. Hughes, "Mistakes at Work," op. cit, pp. 88–101.

everyone at some time attempts to prove that someone made an error or to locate the person who committed it. But people who make errors do not usually show much enthusiasm about confessing them and do not reward the diligence of those who uncover them.

Mistakes are important not only to their victims and to the people who committed the blunder; they are also important to some lower-level occupations that can assert their importance in the scheme of things, and the dignity of their members, by claiming that they save others from the consequences of their mistakes. The pharmacist and the nurse both say this about the doctor. Clerks of various kinds, and especially administrative secretaries, claim that they save their bosses from making blunders by reminding them of the facts. Accountants correct errors in addition that the chief engineer has made, and so on. On the other hand, higher-level occupations can sometimes hire others to carry out some lower-level tasks in order to avoid making the mistake themselves. In turn, however, because lower-level persons may not have the same motivation to be error-free, the number of errors may increase.

Who Did What to Whom?

Practitioners and customers would both prefer to avoid errors, but when they inevitably occur, the various involved parties have different stakes in the outcome. The employer would like to punish an *employee* but to prevent the *customer* from knowing that a real error was committed. If the practitioner is self-employed (physician, cab driver, plumber), he or she would like to claim there was no error at all. These very different stakes in the outcome create several sets of processes in the social menaing of mistakes at work.

The first important difference in perspec-

tive between the customer or client and the practitioner is that for the customer the initial problem is an emergency, but it is a routine experience for the practitioner. One consequence of this difference in perspective is that the customer has a large emotional investment in an effective solution, while the practitioner feels less strongly about it. Essentially, the customer views the problem as a unique experience: It is *his* tooth that aches, or *her* TV that has blacked out. By contrast, the practitioner can view the problem as *statistical*, as one in a series of similar problems. Correspondingly, the practitioner may know that a particular solution works, say, 95 percent of the time, and is calm when it fails. But the customer experiences the recurrence or continuation of the difficulty after it was supposedly solved and is likely to be angry about it.

This type of conflict is to be found in all occupations in which practitioners confront customers. How much social conflict results is partly a function of how costly the mistake is and whether the customer understood the chances of success or failure beforehand. People accept with resignation or only mild annoyance the common blunders that everyday life imposes on them—for example, the bookshelf that is not quite level, the spot that was not entirely removed by the dry cleaners, the carburetor that still does not start quickly in cold weather—because the cost is not very high. On the other hand, when the cost is high, people are less likely to respond serenely. In addition, if they know or believe that the problem was not difficult, and the chance of error was low, most people will be less tolerant about it.

Since these processes are often encountered in the relations between customers and practitioners, and between boss and employee, it is typical that practitioners can draw upon a standard set of rationalizations, evasions, explanations, and excuses in order to cool down the other person's annoyance. In more general terms, where conflict is common, there are likely to be social patterns for reducing it. What are some of these?

Resolving the Conflict

How well polished a set of techniques exists for handling the conflict is determined by whether the members of the occupation form a "community", that is, whether they share many work values and norms in common, know each other, and feel solidary with one another.[23] Physicians make up such a group, and very likely protect one another from wrathful ex-clients more than the members of any occupation except that of police officers. However, the practitioners of other trades have occupational communities as as well—for example, printers, plumbers, diesinkers, coal miners, overland truck drivers.

The crux of the conflict is whether an error has been committed, and who is competent to decide that issue. Many patients die, and until about 1912 physicians probably harmed as many patients as they helped. Yet the physicians were not usually blamed for their ignorance or error. As one historian phrased the situation, "The medical therapy itself was never listed as the cause of death."[24] It is not only medical practitioners and funeral directors, however, who can bury their mistakes. Members of most occupations that run the risk of cus-

tomer indignation attempt to do the same thing. When the client protests, the practitioner is typically able to assert that a proper understanding of the situation would show that (1) there was no error, or (2) it was not the practitioner's fault.

In those claims the members of an occupational community are likely to be supported by their fellows: The lawyer lost the case, but it was a difficult one; the carburetor was repaired correctly, but the automatic choke failed later on, after the car was driven away; the passenger did not speak clearly in giving the address to the cabdriver. Practitioners support one another in these matters because they have experienced similar conflicts, feel that customers are not likely to be right, and suppose that their fellows honestly tried to do well.

Note that a special type of problem arises in those occupations where some part of the task is carried out by students (interns in a hospital, apprentices in the skilled trades). To acquire the necessary skills, the trainee must be permitted some independence; but since the trainee is not yet skilled, errors are likely to be made. Thus, very often the customer or client is not permitted to know that the student is "practicing," or how much autonomy the trainee is given, while the mature practitioner-teacher has the ethical responsibility of adequate supervision. Indeed, the supervising practitioner has conflicting ethical obligations to *both* the trainee and the customer.

One protection in such situations is to carry out the task according to *accepted procedures*. That is, if the practitioner can claim that the traditional ways of doing things were followed, then the error cannot easily be laid at his or her door.[25] If a wise surgeon discovers early in the operation that the patient will die soon anyway, to avoid later accusations he or she will be especially

[23]William J. Goode, "Community within a Community: The Professions," *American Sociological Review*, 22 (1957), pp. 194–200, applies this notion primarily to the professions, but clearly the question can be asked about any occupation.

[24]Richard H. Shryock, *Medicine and Society in America,* New York: New York University Press, 1960, p. 111, as quoted in Eliot Friedson, "Dilemmas in the Doctor-Patient Relationship," in Arnold M. Rose, ed., *Human Behavior and Social Processes,* Boston: Houghton Mifflin, 1962, p. 210.

[25]Ibid., pp. 96–97.

careful to follow approved procedures when sewing up the patient as well as in emergency room care afterwards. This avoids the risk of failure and also reduces criticism.

Among themselves practitioners have a more complex view of mistakes at work than do their employers or customers. True, they share each other's complaints about unreasonable customers, their unfairness in blaming the practitioner, and their failure to understand that no one is perfect. However, practitioners also share judgments about which practitioners are more or less competent or which ones follow high standards of professional conduct. They assert the excellence of most workers in their craft, but they also differentiate among them, ranking some as dishonest or bunglers and others as admirable. In this they act as do members of other kinds of communities; that is, they protect one another against "outsiders." But within the group they are willing to condemn or criticize those who fail to live up to the group norms or values.

OLD AGE AND RETIREMENT

Sociologists often note that in traditional agrarian or hunting societies the elders were repositories of useful knowledge and skills, were heads of their kinship units, and were closer to the spirits of the dead. Consequently, they were given far more honor in such societies. It should not be forgotten, however, that in agrarian societies they were also owners of the land (however ownership was defined) and thus could maintain considerable economic and social influence. Moreover, except in a few harsh environments (the polar regions, the Kalahari Desert of South Africa) the elders were no great economic burden. As a consequence, in perhaps every society of the past, it was assumed that elders would continue to produce as best they could, as long as they were able to work. Industrial societies have changed that social definition by excluding older people from the work force. In the United States, this usually occurs at age sixty-five.

One consequence is that as people move into their sixties, there is a drop in their job satisfaction as well as their participation in social organizations. People who are squeezed out of the labor market, whether they are simply unemployed or are retired, are the most socially isolated segment of our society. The importance of work in modern life is revealed with great clarity as workers move into the older years. Their time schedules, income, plans for the future, and network of social relations are all likely to change. Gently or firmly, they are "disen-

Figure 14-5 Rigid retirement-age rules are widespread; the style of implementing them varies, though the overall effects on the person forced to retire are the same. (Lorenz, *The New Yorker.*)

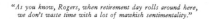

"As you know, Rogers, when retirement day rolls around here, we don't waste time with a lot of mawkish sentimentality."

gaged" from their connection with social activities.

Retirement at sixty-five is an arbitrary social definition, for people were not forced out of productive activities in societies of the past if they were able to continue work. The arbitrariness is also shown if we compare most jobs with the handful of occupations in which people are permitted to work as long as they are able: Musicians, lawyers, actors, physicians, the self-employed, and politicians, among others, may well continue working into their seventies or even eighties. Although all these occupations have a middle to high prestige and income ranking, the key variable is not that ranking, but whether their income is decided by free negotiations with clients or customers, rather than by holding a job in a bureaucracy. After all, presidents of large corporations have a high income and prestige ranking, but they, too, are retired arbitrarily at age sixty-five or earlier.

As many analysts have noted, setting an iron rule for retirement permits the employer to avoid gracefully the embarrassing problem of how to let go the less-competent older employee. No one has to decide whether that person is still competent or not; the older person in turn does not lose much dignity, since the rule is nearly universal and is widely understood to have no connection with ability. Moreover, retirement opens jobs for younger people who are ambitious. Finally, many blue-collar workers do not experience much pleasure from the job itself, and indeed, lower-level workers are more willing to retire early than are upper-level workers, if given the chance. For these reasons, rigid rules for retirement are widespread in all industrial countries.

As the structural position of older people has changed, so has the social definition of what is appropriate to that age group. When older people did not yield up their authority at an arbitrary age, stayed within the community, and continued to pass on their

knowledge about how to plant, harvest, or hunt, the aged enjoyed a specific position in the society and took on the social roles expected of older people. For the most part they were expected to be grave or at least serious, to take part in collective decisions, and to represent and to support ancient traditions. In Western countries, it was expected that old people would not embarrass others by exhibiting much interest in sexual activity, and this rule was especially severe for older women. Older people were also expected to make some effort, if they could, to maintain or to continue building an estate or property for the younger adult generation who would be their heirs.

Today older people have much greater freedom and flexibility; they can dress and act as they wish and no longer feel constrained to be retiring grandparents. Many have moved to Florida and California, where they can be free of any censure by their adult children and lead active social lives. Many older people are enjoying this wider range of acceptable behavior. Those who wish to sit on the front porch in their rocking chairs, dressed in black, may still do so, but there are no great rewards for that.

Older people do not feel as much concern as they once did for the *continuity* of an estate through succeeding generations, whether landed property or negotiable securities. Since marital stability is lower, they do not wish to invest in the marriages of the younger generation through dowries. They feel less responsibility about controlling the behavior of their adult children. A larger percentage of the old seem to feel that they themselves should enjoy any money they may have accumulated.

As to residence, they do not wish to live with their adult children, and their children do not want them to join their household. Thus, not only is there now a higher *percentage* of the population in the age bracket sixty-five or over than in the past; in addition, a far higher percentage of them are *living apart from their own children*, are living in independent households, and often (since one spouse may have died by that time) are living alone.

Disengaged from their kin network and work relations, many older people have moved to villages of the retired, where facilities are organized around common recreational interests and many of the small chores of cooking, house repairing, and cleaning are managed by a small bureaucracy, paid for by those in the village. In moving to such communities, older people do not lose as much as they might have one hundred years ago, when leaving their own village or even their city neighborhood would have meant leaving all the accumulated friendships, available services, and kinfolk who might have helped them from time to time in crises. In many such retirement villages, people support one another in their willingness to try new tasks, games, and activities—in short, to take on new identities, unhampered by a lifetime accumulation of social pressures from neighbors, kinfolk, and their own children. They are in a sense freer than they had been before, even though they are somewhat limited in their social experiences: Almost everyone else is within a fairly narrow age range, death and disease rates are high, and the possibility of really new, large-scale enterprises is much lower than it would be in a major city.

On the other hand, we should keep in mind that this "solution" to the problem of old age yields no such pleasures to most of the old. In many retirement villages the old live dreary, uninspired, and unchallenging lives.[26] A large portion of the poor in the United States are the old, most of whom have not managed to build up an estate for their own retirement, do not own houses, do not receive additional income, and are eking out a scanty and precarious existence on social security checks plus some form of Medicaid or Medicare, supplemented when that is possible by food stamps or welfare.

It is possible to argue that the development of old-age pensions has to a great extent been spurred by the unwillingness or inability of the adult younger generation to care for their own parents.[27] People are able to assuage their guilt feelings about the old by supposing that their needs are few and that they are getting along fairly well. The fact is, however, that social security does not furnish an adequate income for people in the United States at present.

Moreover, almost no private pension fund has worked well: The overwhelming majority of workers who have contributed part of their salary to their own pension fund while working for a corporation do not receive any benefits at all when they retire. Some work for companies that have no pension plan. Under the rules of most corporation pension plans, the majority of workers do not serve long enough to obtain any "rights" to the money they have actually paid in to the fund. Most change jobs from time to time; and as a consequence they enter retirement with nothing but their social security to live on, though in fact they have been paying into a private pension fund for decades. New congressional laws have attempted to deal with this problem in part, but in the main the situation remains as it has been for the past ten years: Corporation pension systems come perilously close to being a fraud. Thus, social security is *typically* not supplemented by a private pension that derives from one's work over a lifetime.

In spite of the fact that the elderly do not have much political power, and they have little economic influence because their wealth is minute, many people have offered various suggestions for "solving" the problem of old age. One has been the develop-

---

[26]See the grim account in Jerry Jacobs, *Fun City*, New York: Holt, 1974. The lives of the old in commercial old-age homes is much worse.

[27]See the excellent study of Harold L. Wilensky, *The Welfare State and Equality*, Berkeley: University of California Press, 1975.

ment of retirement villages, noted already. Another plan is to increase pension funds. However, the larger the pension funds, the greater is the burden that old age puts on younger people, and that burden grows every decade.

Another solution that has been offered is to change the rules of retirement, so that people can continue to work after age sixty-five. The suggestion has been made, for example, that people in their older years might be permitted to work at a reduced pace, during a smaller number of hours, or for a shorter workweek, so that they could continue to earn some income and at the same time would enjoy the social and psychological well-being that comes from being needed. Coupled with this suggestion has been the idea that large organizations of all kinds should hire some percentage of the elderly as a form of "tax," taking for granted a somewhat lower productivity, which would be viewed as a contribution to the collective quality of living in the contemporary United States.

In any event, though the percentage of the elderly will not continue to increase indefinitely, it will increase somewhat. The United States gives less support to its elderly than most societies do, but it seems likely that a sociologically wise solution cannot be merely monetary. To be successful, it must embody some plan for actually utilizing the potential contributions of the elderly to the productivity of the nation. It must contribute at the same time to the dignity as well as the economic independence of older persons. So far, no such plan has been proposed, and it is not likely that the position of the elderly in this society will improve by much over the next decade.

SUMMARY

In this chapter we have examined some of the social processes of work. We began with the social meaning of work in various societies, and argued that in contrast to the philosophies expounded by writers and aristocrats, most ordinary people found much of their dignity in discharging adequately the work tasks imposed on them by their society. Societies do vary in how intensely they believe people should labor, but none has given much respect to those who prefer to idle their time away.

Work has changed greatly in the modern era of capitalism. It has been increasingly marked by a minute division of labor. Workers can turn out more production, since they can become more adept at it. However, the division of labor itself is not the prime source of higher productivity; tasks can be divided very finely with no gain at all. In many civilizations of the past and present, people have been specialized at unproductive tasks that yielded no surplus. This has especially occurred at royal courts (for example, the King's Cup-Bearer), but any visitor to an underdeveloped country can see people whose tasks are minute but yield little surplus for the market.

For specialization or the division of labor to be worthwhile, surplus capital must be invested in new techniques; exchange of products must be facilitated; urban markets must be created; the flow of materials, labor, and finished goods must be accelerated; and production must be based on rational knowledge. In the modern epoch this has especially taken the form of investment in machine technology.

The machine has a different relationship with human beings than does the tool, not only because workers do not own machines but can own tools. More importantly, a machine can replace the human hand and can be made more efficient than the hand. Then it can be driven by any kind of power, at a steady speed, much longer than any human being can work. It enlarges the pool of labor and thus drives down wages—unless workers can use political pressure to impose rules that prevent that type of exploitation.

The life of ease that machines, and especially automated machines, were supposed to usher in is not likely to occur. The number of people needed to watch them does not rise; but the number of people needed to design and build them, repair them, ensure a flow of materials to them, handle the records for all these processes, or send the products on their way later has expanded. Machines are good at very narrow tasks, those which yield economies of scale; but they are poor at "person-problems," at solutions that fit individual or unique needs or that demand great flexibility. For these reasons managerial and professional jobs continue to expand, but machine-operative jobs do not.

It is not only people who compete with one another: Occupations do, too. The members of occupations seek a monopoly over their chosen type of task and a higher control over their work situation. Most do not succeed at obtaining this type of charter from the society, because amateurs, workers who can perform some of the tasks, other occupations, corporate employers, and the state all resist such a grant of autonomy.

The higher-level occupations called professions seek a charter as well, and against resistance from many sources. They must prove that they are masters of an abstract body of knowledge applicable to important problems and that they will police themselves in the interest of the client. Some professions (the "person-professions") must also assert that they must be trusted to have confidential information about their clients, to "get inside the client," as in psychotherapy or the confessional, military intelligence, or surgery. That is, their clients *must be* vulnerable if their problems are to be solved.

We considered the conditions under which work is more satisfying because the problem is of practical and human importance and because it throws some light on the social meaning of work. Hundreds of studies show that the majority of workers are "satisfied," but that may mean no more than that they see no delightful alternatives available. Clearly, however, some jobs are more fun than others. These are occupations in which people have more freedom to set their own pace, to choose how they will solve a problem, to arrange their own hours—in short, jobs that yield greater respect and pay, but above all are not under the close supervision of others with authority. To counter the dullness and mechanical pace of machines, some programs have been developed under which workers not only build a complete product as a team, but actually decide how that will be done, during which hours, and who will be team members. Generally, such programs have been successful, though they require giving up the comfortable, if boring, habits of traditional work.

We have also examined mistakes at work sociologically, by asking how they are defined by customer, employer, or worker and what each does about them. Practitioners view both their customers' crises and their own mistakes statistically, as part of the ongoing flow of work. They are also likely to develop various rationalizations and socially accepted defenses against the efforts of employers or customers to pin the blame on them. At the same time that they defend one another by various techniques, they make occupational judgments within their own group about the competence of fellow workers.

The social definition of work is seen with special clarity if we consider the position of the retired in modern industrial societies. Most people have to retire, but many do not, and we noted what distinguishes such occupations (for example, composers, politicians, lawyers) from others. They are permitted what all the elderly once could take for granted: the right to contribute as long as they are able. Modern societies have created various pension plans, most of which do not work adequately, to take care of the increased number of the retired, who wish to live independently. Those plans do not work well, and the opportunities of the eld-erly to live out a meaningful life have been steadily dwindling. At present, no solutions for this complex problem are being devel-oped.

READINGS

Howard S. Becker, *Outsiders,* New York: Free Press, 1963.

———, ed., *The Other Side,* New York: Free Press, 1964.

Eli Chinoy, *Automobile Workers and the Ameri-can Dream,* New York: Doubleday, 1955.

Sebastian de Grazia, *Of Time, Work and Leisure,* New York: Twentieth Century Fund, 1961.

Fred H. Goldner, "Demotion in Industrial Man-agement," in Frank Baker et al., eds., *Industri-al Organizations and Health,* vol. I.: Selected Readings, London: Tavistock, 1969, pp. 390–410.

William J. Goode, "The Theoretical Limits of Professionalization," in *Explorations in Social Theory,* New York: Oxford, 1973, pp. 341–381.

Richard H. Hall, *Occupations and the Social Structure,* Englewood Cliffs, N.J.: Prentice-Hall, 1969.

Everett C. Hughes, *Men and Their Work,* Glen-coe, Ill.: Free Press, 1958.

John Irwin, *The Felon,* Englewood Cliffs, N.J.: Prentice-Hall, 1970.

Jerry Jacobs, *Fun City,* New York: Holt, 1974.

Morris Janowitz, *The Professional Soldier: A So-cial and Political Portrait,* New York: Free Press, 1960.

Robert L. Kahn, "The Meaning of Work: Inter-pretations and Proposals for Measurement," in Angus Campbell and Philip E. Converse, eds., *The Human Meaning of Social Change,* New York: Russell Sage, 1972, pp. 159–203.

Sar A. Levitan and William B. Johnston, *Work Is Here to Stay, Alas,* Salt Lake City, Utah: Olympus, 1973.

Staffan Linder, *The Harried Leisure Class,* New York: Columbia, 1970.

Gavin McKenzie, *The Aristocracy of Labor,* Lon-don: Cambridge, 1973.

Max Weber, *The Protestant Ethic and the Spirit of Capitalism,* trans. by Talcott Parsons, New York: Scribner, 1930.

Harold L. Wilensky, "Varieties of Work Experi-ence," in Henry Borow, ed., *Man in a World at Work,* Boston: Houghton Mifflin, 1964.

W. M. Williams, eds., *Occupational Choice,* Lon-don: G. Allen, 1974.

Work in America, Task Force, Department of Health, Education, and Welfare, Cambridge, Mass.: M.I.T., 1973.

PART SIX

SOCIAL CHANGE

CHAPTER FIFTEEN

THEORY AND METHODS IN THE ANALYSIS OF SOCIAL CHANGE

SOCIOLOGY AND SOCIAL CHANGE

Almost all great social philosophers and scientists of the past devoted much thought to social change. The dramatic fall of both people and nations over the centuries has given rise to much speculation about what creates such processes. From the middle of the nineteenth century until World War I, social change as *progress,* or evolution, was a dominant theme in sociology. Thereafter, sociologists turned mainly to the development of more rigorous research techniques. To gain precision, it seemed necessary to move from the library or office to actual work in the field. Since the only observations one can make oneself are *contemporary,* most research over the half-century between World War I and the 1960s focused on twentieth-century life, especially in the cities.

Renewed Interest in Social Change

Over the past decade—perhaps indicative of greater confidence in research techniques and perhaps partly to answer criticism from younger sociologists—a larger number of studies have given more attention to the problems of social change. Although this current impulse may grow in part from a clear notion that these inquiries may yield some scientific value, perhaps the greater impulse comes from a *growing awareness* of social change and how pervasive and consequential it is.

That renewed impulse also derives from a greater awareness that social structures are not simply stable, tightly integrated, or harmonious. Rather, they are unstable, loosely put together, and torn by dissension. Consequently, a sociology that is true to the facts must give a more central place to the analysis of social change.

Doubtless, too, social scientists feel as do ordinary citizens in our time: That is, at an *emotional level* perhaps most people welcome any progress and improvement in their lives, but the general rapidity of change in our generation makes many people uneasy. Many alterations seem to bring losses, not gains. The security that people enjoy from adjustments already made is lost when any day may render obsolescent some old habits, attitudes, or knowledge. Thus, more people turn their attention to the threatening newness of the world.

A *political impulse* may also be evident in the increased attention to social change. To view all parts of the social world as being created and still in the process of being made suggests that the world as it exists is not good enough. The concern with social change is likely to be especially strong among those who feel the world should be altered because it is not adequate.

Other people may be moved in part by a *pragmatic concern* about social change. It is evident that things are changing already, but if they are to be altered in the direction we desire, they must be controlled now. Perhaps most of the research that has been done on social change—and by far most governmental research—has focused on the problems of charting the future, in hopes of guiding it in some fashion.

These many concerns that create a renewed interest in social change do not specify which kinds of problems are most important, which *theories* might be useful in interpreting social change, or which research strategies are worth using if we want to study social change. Certainly, without that knowledge we shall fail to understand or create the future as we want it to be.

Types of Social Change Problems

Let us attempt to classify the many types of problems that are called *social change,*

meaning any alterations in the social behavior of any group or society. Then we can see more clearly why some of these are more difficult than others to carry out. We can also understand better why it is unlikely that sociology will very soon make great progress at some of these tasks.

We must begin with a basic methodological distinction, the difference between (1) analyses of particular events, sometimes called *historical,* or *idiographic, inquiries,* and (2) the *search for social laws,* or *nomothetic* inquiries. Neither of these can be called more scientific than the other, for both attempt to find out *why* changes occur as they do.

The difference between the two is that the events of the first type are *unique.* The French Revolution occurred only once. It was a concrete event, and no other revolution has been quite like it. Innumerable conditions or causes shaped its particular characteristics. Everything inside and outside France at that time affected it, from climate to the unique individuals who took part in it. In analyzing that specific phenomenon, we use any social laws we think will help us in understanding it, such as these: (1) A shortage of goods or the free printing of money will increase inflation. (2) In a period of social turmoil many traditional customs begin to weaken.

Similarly, the evolution of human societies occurred only once in the history of the world. Commentaries and analyses of that great drama are therefore focused on one particular event. On a much smaller scale, we might analyze the causes for a unique trend within a special time span, such as the gradual drop in the United States birthrate during the nineteenth century, the increase in voting rights in England during the same period, or the expansion and decline of railroad travel in the United States. All these are unique, special to their time and place, and are affected by a wide variety of causes.

In contrast to the analyses of such singular events are studies that attempt to search out patterns, abstract models, types, or laws. Thus, we might consider the French Revolution, not in its particularity, but as an example of a more general kind of process or occurrence, the *radical revolution.* Then we lose some of the uniqueness of that special revolution, but we can locate more cases, for example, the Russian, Chinese, and Cuban revolutions. We might then try to discover the major factors that maximize the chances of this *kind* of social-political change.

A much simpler example would be the hypothesis that if newly married couples are expected to be economically independent, they will marry relatively later, probably in their late twenties. But if economic opportunities expand to permit people to become independent at an earlier age (as when the factory system began), then the age at marriage will drop. This is a hypothesis about social change, but it is essentially a *timeless proposition.* That is, these relations should be observable under a wide variety of conditions in almost any historical epoch. Knowing such general relationships also permits us to understand better any unique time period we examine, for we can use those general hypotheses to explain a part of what happened. For example, when the potato was introduced into Ireland in the late eighteenth century, couples could then marry earlier because they could settle on poorer, cheaper land. They did not have to acquire as much money before marrying.

Beyond such "timeless" propositions are much more difficult social change problems that we have only begun to attack. The two main types are (1) the *evolution of human societies,* viewed not as a unique event but as a general pattern of development, and (2) particular *patterned sequences of evolution* that are phrased in this fashion: Phase Z is unlikely to occur until phase Y has occurred, and phase Y is unlikely to occur before phase X.

The clearest examples would be found in the development of technology. For example, we can safely assert that the wheel and axle had to be developed before the fancy carriage with springs, that the successful *heavy* self-propelled vehicle (the steamboat or train) would be created before the lighter automobile, and neither automobile roads nor a self-starting mechanism for cars would have been developed before a relatively light self-propelled vehicle. A simple example that combines both technological and social variables would be this sequence: Printing must arise before typewriting, writing before printing, speech before either of these, and various scratched or shaped symbols before writing. Social scientists have for some years been attempting to discover such sequences in linguistics, kinship systems, economic systems, and types of social structures.[1]

If we combine all the types that we have noted up to this point, we arrive at the following list of social change problems:

1   The analysis of *particular events* (idiographic)
  a   Trends
    (1)   The grand evolution of humanity
    (2)   Particular epochs or time spans
  b   Causal interpretations of particular events (for example, French Revolution)
2   The search for *laws* or *general patterns* of social change (nomothetic)
  a   Timeless propositions
  b   Patterned sequences in time
    (1)   General evolution
    (2)   Limited evolution

Analysis of Social Change Problems

Let us now comment briefly on each of these social change problems. Thereby we shall better understand the various processes involved as well as the greater or lesser difficulty of analyzing social change.

[1]For a theoretical analysis of the development of different types of social structures, see Talcott Parsons, *Societies,* Englewood Cliffs, N.J.: Prentice-Hall, 1966.

The rise of humanity The great thinkers of the past who mused on the economic meaning of humanity's rise from the primordial slime did not bother to grapple with the difficulty of obtaining data about it. The earliest philosophers and social commentators were moralists, and they were preoccupied as well with the mythical or religious question of the *origins* of humankind. Most such analyses were not empirical descriptions of humanity's great drama, but were attempts at moral persuasion. To most moralists each generation seems to be falling constantly away from a virtue that lies in the past (for example, Adam and Eve driven from the Garden of Eden). Indeed, it was not until the eighteenth century that some philosophers, contemplating changes in society over many generations, came to believe in progress and to assert that the present was better than the past, while the future would be better still.

Causal analyses A trend within a particular time span may not be a law even if it continues for a long time. It is more likely to be a particular historical process. Thus, the divorce rate in the United States has continued to rise since the Civil War, but this rise is a unique historical event. It did not happen everywhere else at the same time, and we do not know precisely what will happen in the future. As is often the case, we do not know precisely why the gradual change took place.

In the United States since 1900, the following trends can be observed: a higher percentage of women in the labor force, higher average education, a higher per capita income, heavier taxation, increased power and responsibility given to the federal government, and a higher average life expectancy. The reader can consider for a moment some causal influences that have created this array of trends. Since all of them are unique events, it may be difficult to develop general hypotheses that would explain any one of them adequately. Some thought will suggest at least a few factors that have played a major role in each one of them, though no explanation would account for all those trends together.

An example of such an explanation was Karl Marx's attempt to explain the trend

Figure 15-1 Since 1900 there has been a trend toward a higher percentage of women in the labor force. In recent years, women have been moving increasingly into executive positions. (Mini Forsyth, Monkmeyer.)

toward family disintegration under the newly emerging factory system of the early nineteenth century. He drew his trend data from a mass of field reports, many drawn up by British government commissions. He showed that as wages dropped and almost everyone in the family was required to work in order to survive, these changes were observable: the neglect of children, the lack of time to engage in family activities, the failure of women to sew or cook, the decline of domestic skills, the loss of family unity, and the increasing participation of married women in the labor force.[2]

From the earliest Greek historians to the present, social analysts have also attempted to make causal analyses of particular events. This type of explanation does not aim at achieving generalizations of wide validity or at testing a scientific hypothesis. It rather attempts to use social laws or generalizations in order to understand a *particular* historical event, such as women's suffrage, the Reformation, or industrialization in Japan. The explanations range from social factors peculiar to the society at that time to generalizations that might be expected to apply to almost any kind of social situation. Some of these generalizations are no more than comments of a commonsense nature: for example, that cousin marriage used to be more common in the rural United States because families wanted to retain the land within the kin network; or that in any period of rapid social change, parents and children will engage in an increased amount of social conflict, since the child rapidly adjusts to the newly emerging culture while the parents do not.

The explanations can be more elaborate. Some generalizations that might be brought in to help explain the unique case of Japanese industrialization in the latter part of the nineteenth century include these:

1 To transform a feudal society peacefully into an industrial one, it is necessary to gain the cooperation of the aristocracy (since typically they have some independent basis of military power).

2 It is easier to do this if the aristocracy has been trained to believe they should sacrifice themselves to the common good (that is, in this case, to industrialize so as to defend Japan against the imperial Western countries).

3 All social strata will cooperate more if each is given important opportunities in the new system, or if they are paid (as were the great princes of Japan) for giving up old privileges.

4 A nation that is already disciplined to work hard, that builds on a moderate base of literacy toward a much higher one, and that collectively decides to invest heavily in technological growth can industrialize more easily than one whose citizens are relaxed and leisurely in work, are mainly illiterate, and spend their surplus (as did the sixteenth- and seventeenth-century Spanish with their New World gold) on ostentation and luxury.

5 Lacking valuable resources (gold, silver) for trade, an industrializing country will have to obtain investment capital from its existing economy. Given the typical class system in large nations, this will usually be obtained from heavily taxing the lower social strata or by paying them low incomes.

These general statements are not meant to be a full explanation of Japanese industrialization. They are rather meant to illustrate the process of looking for broad patterns or social regularities, applicable to many societies, in order to explain a particular major historical process or event.

Timeless propositions Timeless propositions or general regularities are useful in

[2]Karl Marx, *Capital*, New York: Modern Library, 1936, especially pp. 429ff.

explaining social change, but it should be emphasized that in any scientific field most research is devoted to such general relationships, *without regard to change*. In every major field the phenomena of great changes over time are least studied, partly because of the difficulty in finding out the distant past. For example, in physics the motion of the planetary bodies was explained with a high degree of elegance in the seventeenth century. That formulation did not explain changes, but rather explained an equilibristic system. That is, a small set of factors was used to explain why the system would continue as it does, generation after generation. As against those precise predictions, based on highly general laws, speculations about the origins and changes in the universe, or even the origins of the earth, remained the hobby of imaginative amateurs and of a tiny minority of astronomers and physicists until well into the twentieth century.

Social Change and Theory

It is evident that no grand theory of evolutionary processes, and no hypotheses about limited sequences of evolution nor about great changes in social structures, can be discovered until we have accumulated a *vast amount* of timeless propositions, hypotheses, and regularities. That is, there can be no theory without laws that seem to be applicable to a wide range of societies. Mere speculation about what might happen or could have happened in the past is not enough, and in any event, cannot be tested without such general hypotheses.

As in other fields, these regularities can be used to weigh the validity of speculations or hypotheses about the past. Whether we wish to peer into the future or simply to understand the changes that are taking place in contemporary social structures, we can test our explanations only by confronting them with a firm, precise set of observations and generalizations that are much more modest in scope.

Nevertheless, social analysts have attempted to work out a set of evolutionary laws *without* that firm base. From the late eighteenth century to World War I, evolutionary theory dominated most studies of social change. In this view the scientific problem was a search for universal evolutionary "laws" of social development. Its underlying assumption was that if there had been many lines of evolution, or if the grand process has occurred many times, they would all have followed a similar form. Thus, the ancient philosophical or religious problem—the significance of the human destiny—was transformed from a unique case (humankind arose only once, really) into an empirical analysis of a hypothetical *type*, to be stated in *general* laws of evolution.

As the nineteenth century drew to a close, actual field observations of many societies became common, gradually replacing the often curious and sometimes incredible stories of missionaries or hunters. A flood of empirical research about past and contemporary societies stimulated numerous theories as to exactly which stages human societies had gone through, and what caused those great changes. Unfortunately for the larger theory, the data did not always fit a simple evolutionary scheme. In most of anthropology and sociology such schemes were discarded just after World War I, and analysts focused far more on how any particular society actually works now, rather than on attempting to fit it into some evolutionary sequence.

Though that evolutionary framework has been judged a failure, it should not be forgotten that writers such as Louis Henry Morgan, Robert Briffault, Edward B. Tyler, and Herbert Spencer addressed themselves daringly to the problems of social evolution. They attempted a grand synthesis of the then-known facts of social behavior. In doing so, they made four great assumptions that we do not now accept. Yet these assumptions undoubtedly are a first step toward solving the difficult problem of measuring social change over great time spans:

1 That the social behavior and cultural patterns of a society with a low level of technology are closer to, say, Paleolithic (that is, early Stone Age) human beings than to modern people. Consequently, we can reconstruct the time stages in between by observing contemporary societies and arranging them by their level of technology, such as hunting and gathering, nomadic and herding, simple agriculture, and so on.

2 That we can view a "cultural survival"—such as ritual wife-capture, the handshake, or a religious ceremony—as the equivalent of a social "fossil" and thus reconstruct the past just as we do when we dig up the bones of an extinct animal.

3 That the social patterns we can observe or learn about evolved because once they contributed more to the survival of the society than did the patterns that were discarded in the past.

4 That (as in biological evolution) a standard set of sequences could be found through which all social systems would pass eventually.

Modern social change theory does *not* accept these assumptions. On the other hand, modern theorizing about social change has not developed a more adequate substitute body of either theoretical or measurement assumptions. Nineteenth-century theorists of evolution felt free to speculate about a past they could not know. They had a special difficulty, however, in *proving* that some specific causes created the various sequences they described. That problem still remains, but renewed attempts have been made in the past two decades to develop an intellectually defensible set of sequences. It is likely that this interest will continue in the future.

Limited sequences As our list of social change problems suggests, some theorists of evolution have attempted to work within a smaller compass, trying to locate *limited sequences of social change*. That is, instead of working out a large-scale set of phases for all of human history, they have tried to work out a few more specifically defined sequences over a *shorter* time span. It then might be possible to reconstruct an immediately past set of successions, and thus to discover some determinate sequences with reference to language changes, industrialization, or changes in family patterns.

In one such reconstruction the authors assert that a change in the sexual division of labor (which tasks are done by men or by women) should take place *before* an alteration in the rules governing where a couple should live after marriage (with the wife's family, the husband's family, or independently). These residence rules, in turn, should change *before* rules about land tenure, descent (whether ancestry is mainly traced through the female or the male line), and kinship terminology (the various names people give to relatives). And *all those changes should occur in that order*, that is, just as they have been listed in the previous sentences. Here, then, we have a set of hypotheses that state a set of changes has to occur in a certain order: That is, change will take place in the first set of variables before occurring in the second set, and so on.

It should be emphasized, however, that even the attempt to establish limited but determinate sequences of social change pushes us much further back in time than our observations can go. We can dig up the tools, and we can infer the technology of societies that died out thousands of years ago, but we do not really know about their social patterns. Those sequences lie far beyond recorded history, written or unwritten. Nevertheless, the search for such sequences and for better modes of testing them will continue, for these inquiries are one way of attempting to ascertain how human society developed over time.

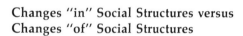

Figure 15-2 A sagging economy producing increased numbers in the unemployment line is a change *in* the social structure; the introduction of slavery was a change *of* the structure. (Left: United Press International Photo; right: Culver Pictures, Inc.)

Changes "in" Social Structures versus Changes "of" Social Structures

When sociologists charge that the field has developed no adequate theory of social change, they refer mainly to general laws of evolutionary change, either the great evolution of human societies over the past several hundred thousand years or a more limited set of evolutionary sequences or phases. More specifically, however, this type of inquiry refers to changes *of* the social system or social structure, rather than to changes *in* such a system. Although this distinction is widely used, there is no general agreement on how the observer can tell when a change *of* the system itself has occurred, that is, when the social *structure itself* has changed.

In somewhat technical terms, changes *in* the system occur all the time: For example,

the homicide rate, the percentage of unemployed, or factory output rises or falls over a period of years. By contrast, we speak of changes *of* the social structure when a change occurs in the social factors that actually *cause* those many alterations in rates.

Let us consider an example of such broader changes and then examine the distinction again. A clear example might be drawn from the work patterns in a small factory over time. If we are referring only to changes within the system, then we note that both output and quality may vary. However, if either of them rises very far, then it is likely that the workers will begin to resent the difficult standards they are meeting and will relax their efforts. If output or quality drops very much, management is likely to take steps to increase discipline by either firings or a new incentive system.

So far, we observe no changes *of* the system itself because the *same* social structure exists. That is, all personnel are doing the same jobs, authority is still in the hands of management, and the factory must continue to compete in the same way with other factories. That will be true even if many workers are replaced or even if the management is replaced.

However, a change *of* that small social structure can also occur. For example, the owner might give the factory to the workers, who must then assume responsibility for the operation of the whole system. They now have more authority, they can allocate jobs differently, and they will enjoy any profits or suffer any losses.

We see, then, several possible indexes or criteria by which we would decide that the *system itself* or the social structure has actually changed. The simplest, but most difficult to apply, is that we are referring to *large changes,* as when there is a revolution and the entire aristocracy is driven out. However, it is difficult to come to much agreement as to when a change is to be considered large. For example, in spite of the considerable new legislation passed during the Depression period under the leadership of Franklin D. Roosevelt, it is generally agreed by most social analysts that no *structural changes* were made in the American economy or society. On the other hand, many members of the Republican party thought that nothing short of a revolution was taking place. In short, there is much disagreement about how large a change must take place before we must call it a structural change.

A second type of change that seems to betoken a structural alteration is the emergence of new statuses or positions, new groups, or new organizations that now make up the system. For example, the introduction of slavery is a change of the system itself, and it alters the structural position of other people in the society. Similarly, the disappearance of major positions or organizations in the system is an index of a significant alteration in the social structure, as when the nobility is eliminated. On the other hand, some new positions can be introduced in a large organization or society without a significant change in the social structure, as when the new position of calculating-machine operator or librarian is created. This index of a structural change is useful, but not very precise.

Third, in some cases we are referring to the growth of some *part* of the social system to a point where the sheer size of it affects the working of the organization or community. For example, when the middle classes began to form a large and prosperous part of the English population in the seventeenth century, or the percentage of unionized United States workers became large in the late 1940s, the political and economic structure seemed to operate in a somewhat different way.

Fourth, when we have to use *different social factors* to *explain* the relationships or social behavior we observe, we are likely to say that is a change of the social structure. An example has occurred in the past generation, when the profits of many major corporations are determined more by their political success in manipulating government contracts, loans, or tariffs than by their cost-output effectiveness in manufacturing and in specific market competition with other corporations.

Though these various definitions or indexes convey an intuitive sense of what a structural or even an evolutionary change is, none is very precise. Unbiased social scientists will still disagree about whether a given example of change is *basic* or *structural*, and about whether it represents a new evolutionary phase in the history of society or of a smaller social system. It is, in any event, such far-reaching changes that represent the more difficult challenge, both theoretically and methodologically, to the social scientist concerned with the problems of social change.

FOCUS

SOCIAL CHANGE: CAUSAL ANALYSIS
OF THE FRENCH REVOLUTION

The point, however, on which I would lay stress is that exactly the same feudal rights were in force in every European land and that in most other countries of the continent they pressed far more heavily on the population than in France. Take, for example, the lord's right to forced labor, the *corvée*. It was rarely exercised and little oppressive in France, whereas in Germany it was stringent and everywhere enforced.

Moreover, when we turn to the feudal rights which so much outraged our fathers and which they regarded as opposed not merely to all ideas of justice but to the spirit of civilization itself (I am thinking of the tithe, irredeemable ground rents, perpetual charges, *lods et ventes*, and so forth, all that in the somewhat grandiloquent language of the eighteenth century was styled "the servitude of the land"), we find that all these practices obtained to some extent in England and, indeed, are still found there today. Yet they do not prevent English husbandry from being the best organized and most productive in the modern world; and, what is perhaps still more remarkable, the English nation seems hardly aware of their existence.

Why then did these selfsame feudal rights arouse such bitter hatred in the heart of the French people that it has persisted even after its object has long since ceased to exist? One of the reasons is that the French peasant had become a landowner, and another that he had been completely emancipated from the control of his lord. (No doubt there were other reasons, but these, I think, were the chief ones.)

If the peasant had not owned his land he would hardly have noticed many of the changes which the feudal system imposed on all real estate. What could the tithe matter to a man who had no land of his own? He could simply deduct it from the rent. And even restrictions hampering agriculture mean nothing to an agriculturist who is simply cultivating land for the benefit of someone else.

Moreover, if the French peasant had still been under his lord's control, the feudal rights would have seemed much less obnoxious, because he would have regarded them as basic to the constitution of his country.

When the nobles had real power as well as privileges, when they governed and administered, their rights could be at once greater and less open to attack. In fact, the nobility was regarded in the age of feudalism much as the government is regarded by everyone today; its exactions were tolerated in view of the protection and security it provided. True, the nobles enjoyed invidious privileges and rights that weighed heavily on the commoner, but in return for this they kept order, administered justice, saw to the execution of the laws, came to the rescue of the oppressed, and watched over the interests of all. The more these functions passed out of the hands of the nobility, the more uncalled-for did their privileges appear—until at last their mere existence seemed a meaningless anachronism.

I would ask you to picture to yourself the French peasant as he was in the eighteenth century—or, rather, the peasant you know today, for he has not changed at all. His status is different, but not his personality. See how he appears in the records from which I have been quoting: a man so passionately devoted to the soil that he spends all his earnings on buying land, no matter what it costs. To acquire it he must begin by paying certain dues, not to the government but to other landowners of the neighborhood, who are as far removed as he from the central administration and almost as powerless as he. When at long last he has gained possession of this land which means so much to him, it is hardly an exaggeration to say that he sinks his heart in it along with the grain he sows. The possession of this little plot of earth, a tiny part, his very own, of the wide world, fills him with pride and a sense of independence. But now the neighbors aforesaid put in an appearance, drag him away from his cherished fields, and bid him work elsewhere without payment. When he tries to protect his seedlings from the animals they hunt, they tell him to take down his fences, and they lie in wait for him at river crossings to exact a toll. At the market there they are again, to make him pay for the right of selling the produce of his land, and when on his return home he wants to use the wheat he has put aside for his daily needs, he has to take it to their mill to have it ground, and then to have his bread baked in the lord's oven. Thus part of the income from his small domain goes to supporting these men in the form of charges which are imprescriptible and irredeemable. Whatever he sets out to do, he finds these tiresome neighbors barring his path, interfering in his simple pleasures and his work, and consuming the produce of his toil. And when he has done with them, other fine gentlemen dressed in black step in and take the greater part of his harvest. When we remember the special temperament of the French peasant proprietor in the eighteenth century, his ruling interests and passions, and the treatment accorded him, we can well understand the rankling grievances that burst into a flame in the French Revolution.

SOURCE: Alexis de Tocqueville, *The Old Regime and the French Revolution,* trans. by Stuart Gilbert, Garden City, N.Y.: Doubleday, Anchor, 1955, pp. 29–31.

SOME THEORIES OF SOCIAL CHANGE

Although we shall go on to discuss some of the factors that cause social change, that examination will be more fruitful if we first consider briefly some common theories of the past.

Monistic Theories

Most past theories were *monistic,* or *unifactorial.* That is, they asserted that major social changes were caused by a single factor. The most frequent candidates have been race, the survival of the fittest, climate and/

or geography (discussed in Chapter 8), technological innovation, or the economic relations of production (discussed in the section on the Marxist theory of stratification in Chapter 9).

These monistic theories all suffer from a major difficulty in both theory and measurement. Their central theoretical difficulty is that they claim that all social change is caused by factor X. If the critic suggests that other factors (values, temperament, technical skill, literacy) might also contribute, the author responds by claiming that factor X includes *those* factors as well. Thus, for example, if the critic argues that the values of a culture make a difference, then the firm believer in the overriding influence of economic relations argues that values, too, are determined by economic relations! If the critic of a racial theory claims that cultural level and education make a difference in social change, the race theorist proclaims that race determines *these,* too. In short, factor X causes all the stages in human relations, all the different kinds of social structure, because X *is* everything, and surely everything does cause everything.

The problem of measurement is equally obvious. If the single great factor is everything, or affects everything, how can one *empirically* separate it out in order to ascertain how much weight it has? Moreover, since the factor cannot be measured easily (because it is mixed with everything), it is not possible to formulate precise hypotheses of the type "More or less of factor X causes a rise or fall in some social pattern Y." Or, more generally, a *constant* type of factor cannot be used to explain all the *variability* in social behavior.

Race   The heyday of racial theories (about 1870 to World War I) is past, but it should be remembered that for many generations dedicated social scientists believed that races were real divisions of the human family, that each race developed a particular kind of culture, and that the evolution of human

society seemed to suggest that the "more backward" races could not develop the higher type of civilization that Western societies represented. Awkward difficulties such as the high achievements of some African kingdoms in the past or the creativity of the Central American Mayans were either ignored or brushed aside. Long generations or centuries of stagnation in Western countries (that is, the white race) were interpreted as a temporary degeneration of racial stocks, caused by intermixture with other races. There were temporary epochs in which the "oriental races" threatened the rule of the white races, but the inevitable success of white people seemed assured.

Survival of the fittest   After the publication of Darwin's *Origin of Species* in 1859, the notion of the survival of the fittest was applied to human societies as a way of explaining social change. It seemed clear that nations and societies competed with one another. In that competition the "fittest" would survive better. Thus, over time this competition would create many changes in social structures, as a tribe or nation sought better solutions for the problem of competition. Again, the great achievements of China or India in the past could be passed over or ignored, because they represented only a temporary stage in the slow but sure triumph of Western societies.

Social theorists of this persuasion also ignored the fact that the "fittest" simply meant the ability to succeed in war. Had they followed out that logic more rigorously, they would have agreed that the Huns were superior to Rome, and the Mongols superior to China. Almost certainly, the competition among nations does cause important changes in their social structures, but we would no longer agree that winning a war is an adequate index of being superior.

Geographical factors and climate   As we noted in Chapter 8, the belief that geographical factors, including climate, determine the various types of human societies is very ancient, appearing with the early Greeks. It also appears in a somewhat more sophisticated form more recently, in Arnold J. Toynbee's great work, *A Study of History,* in which the author asserts that high civilizations are created only when societies face a moderate degree of environmental challenge (rather than a very easy life or a severe continuing threat). Such theories are attractive, for they accord in part with our observation. Thus, when we travel to a different geographic region of the world, people *are* different. In almost every country it is thought that the Southerners are "different."

Here again, as with the previous factor (the survival of the fittest), it must be conceded that geographical variables do constitute part of the environment to which a society must adjust. In adjusting, necessarily the social structure is altered. In that alteration, how members of society view the geographical reality to be adjusted will also change, and so will their new adjustment. Unfortunately, even the most thoroughgoing geographical determinist has not been able to demonstrate that any *specific* sequence or set of changes in the social structure can even mainly be attributed to geographical factors.

Marxist Theory

In the manifesto of the Communist party, Karl Marx and Friedrich Engels asserted, "All history is the history of class struggle." According to the Marxist view, a class is determined by its relationship to the factors of production. In the feudal past the most important relationship was the ownership of land, but in the modern period of industrialization it became the ownership of capital, that is, money to control factories and businesses. It is the struggle for that control that causes all the great changes in social structures over time. Under capitalism political control passes to capitalists. They deter-

mine how the legal system works, and they create new laws where needed to protect their property and to amass still more political control. They also determine the philosophy and more generally the values by which people decide what is right or wrong. Universities thus become, in the Marxist view, merely devices by which educated people are indoctrinated to believe in and to serve the interest of the ruling stratum, the upper class.

However, according to the Marxist theory, the very success of the capitalists is their undoing. In order to compete, they continue to exploit the workers and to drive smaller capitalists into the working class, so that eventually the society is polarized, the rich against the poor. The revolution that occurs then will usher in a new type of society in which all property is communally owned and the large political apparatus of the state decreases in size, since its main activity was protecting the rich and that is no longer necessary.

Determinism

The previous theories are *deterministic;* that is, the successive changes of the social structure are not caused by conscious human planning. The Marxist theory does not entirely ignore human decisions, since Marx conceded that the wheels of history must be pushed by the deliberate acts of people. Nevertheless, what people decide is rational or wise to do is also determined by economic necessity.

Although very likely a larger number of people believe in the Marxist theory than in any other, social change itself has not dealt kindly with it: Its specific predictions about the future turned out to be simply wrong. The major radical revolutions have not taken place in capitalist nations but in agrarian ones (Russia, China, Yugoslavia, Cuba). In the capitalist nations workers have not become increasingly poor and downtrodden, and the middle classes have not been pushed down into the laboring class. Nor, for that matter, is there any evidence that after the revolution the communist state is withering; indeed, the opposite occurs.

On the other hand, this theory correctly alerts the sociologist to the conflicts among classes as they struggle for political influence or economic gains and thus change the social structure over time. It also reminds us that even if people are guided somewhat by their values, these are shaped in part by their social position, and by people's judgments as to what is in their best individual or class interest to do.

Diffusionism

As can be seen by now, many theories of social change draw our attention to one important source of change while ignoring others. Another such theory is *diffusionism*,

Figure 15-3 McDonald's in Tokyo: a modern instance of cultural diffusion. (Fred Ward, Black Star.)

which flourished in the 1920s. Its hypothesis is that few inventions or discoveries are ever made; most of what we see in any culture is simply borrowed from another. That is, social change occurs by *diffusion* from one society to one or more other societies. Thus, the coins, printing, books, felt hats, beds, bread, fruits, clothing, dishes, and a wide array of other items in United States culture came from other societies in all parts of the world. In extreme forms of this theory, almost all sociocultural patterns were traced to a few major sources, or even to one (usually Egypt).

The more careful work of diffusionism discarded the socioevolutionism of the nineteenth century as being insufficiently precise and not in accord with the data. Diffusionism attempted instead to trace carefully the exact path a given art form or agricultural technique took as it spread from one center to one or many other societies. In doing so, these social scientists developed hypotheses about which kinds of social or cultural patterns were diffused most easily, which social traits of the receiving society made them more willing to borrow, and the best ways of ascertaining that diffusion had taken place.

The contribution of this mainly German school of thought to our knowledge is to be found in our contemporary awareness of how much of our sociocultural heritage we owe to other societies, and in our better understanding of the conditions that facilitated that borrowing. Modern programs of foreign aid have had to understand these processes much better, in order to persuade people in underdeveloped societies to adopt new techniques, such as more productive seeds or agricultural techniques, improved health practices, or modes of house construction.[3]

[3]For a thoughtful analysis of many such problems and processes, see George M. Foster, *Traditional Societies and Technological Change*, 2d ed., New York: Harper & Row, 1973.

Immanent Change

A final theory to be noted emphasizes the theme with which we began this chapter, that everything is changing all the time. Pitirim A. Sorokin's Theory of Immanent Change argues that the forces and factors that operate in any social or cultural system are never static.[4] Each part is different at every successive time point, because all the other causes that affect it are also changing. These changes are called *immanent* because they emerge from the interplay of forces within the society itself.

These forces are intensified by all the external challenges of the social and natural environment the society faces. Within the social system even small changes have continuing consequences, because these affect still other factors, which have consequences for still others; in short, nothing remains the same, even if the people within a society attempt to keep it so. All the stresses and strains within any social or cultural system set various adjustments in motion, which in turn cause still other changes. On the other hand, Sorokin also postulates a Principle of Limits, the rule that whatever the pressures toward a given change, it cannot continue in one direction indefinitely. Population, homicide, and divorce rates may rise, but they drop eventually; both the prosperity and the poverty of a society are limited; only in a smaller time range do the curves of change seem to continue without limit.

One important conclusion from this theory is the somewhat troubling thought that over many centuries, for most sociocultural phenomena, we observe neither progress nor decay, but "trendless fluctuation," that is, ups and downs which may seem to show a definite trend for a while, but which in

fact are kept from continuing indefinitely by the principle of limits. This thought is a somewhat sobering reminder that whether we indulge in a gloomy pessimism about the future or a rosy optimism, we are likely to be correct only if we confine our predictions within a modest time frame.

SOURCES OF SOCIAL CHANGE

Our analyses up to this point have singled out numerous possible sources of change. In this section we shall attempt to state these in a more systematic fashion, without at all denying the importance of those previously mentioned.

Strains within Society

The most important principle in any discussion of factors that cause change is that *no special factors* cause stability, and no special factors uniquely cause social change. Almost any factor that we can think of might cause either, under some circumstances. Punishing dissidents may stifle a small outbreak of rebellion at one time, but at another, may trigger a full-scale revolt. The creation of a large standing army to stabilize the defenses of a country may eventually change the social structure by giving the military a much larger role in the nation's political decisions.

If, then, we focus on the kinds of forces that are likely to cause change, we must also recognize that there are situations in which those factors may instead help to restore the system, or at least to keep it operating in a relatively adequate fashion. This is even true for our first factor, the *existence of strains within the society*. At any given time, different parts of a social system are pulling and hauling against each other, and indeed one can argue that the strains hold it together or keep it operating in about the

[4]His more elaborate statement is to be found in his four-volume work, *Social and Cultural Dynamics*, New York: American Book, 1937–1940. See a more succinct sketch in Pitirim A. Sorokin, *Society, Culture and Personality*, New York: Harper, 1947, pp. 696ff.

same way.[5] For example, the strains that are created by the expanding power of the presidency, a sudden increase in the crime rate, or the poor performance of generals at the beginning of a war may lead to counteractions that keep these trends from going very far. Indeed, this is the set of dynamics that underlines Sorokin's Principle of Limits.

On the other hand, as Marx emphasized, these inner strains and contradictions may continue to grow, and thus alter the social structure in important ways. Moreover, as Wilbert E. Moore points out, the consequences of any attempt to bring things back to normal also create tensions, and may alter people's behavior in still further unpredictable ways.[6] This is especially likely, since no social structure is rigid; all are flexible to some extent, and thus the effort to change part of them will succeed in changing still other parts. This is so on both the societal as well as the individual level, for everyone can and does change his or her actions when the surrounding situation changes in some degree, but almost no one returns to exactly the same pattern as before.

The Conflict between Ideal and Real

Part of the strains and tensions within any system may be observed in our second factor, a problem that all groups and individuals constantly face: the *conflict between the ideal and the real,* or the conflict between the high standards that are set up for people or organizations to meet and what are considered adequate or barely adequate levels of conformity. It is said, with more cynicism than accuracy, that we merely pay lip service to ideals. In fact, it is safe to say that every reader of this book has experienced some troubling moments when this type of conflict has occurred: We want to live by an ideal, and we fail. Almost everyone, as we have noted in our discussion of norms and values, does attempt to live by the standards she or he has accepted. But everyone also fails frequently. Organizations attempt to accomplish great goals, but typically fail. On the other hand, if those ideals, standards, or goals were simply empty of meaning, people would not strain to try to reach them. Moreover, they would not feel either embarrassed or upset if other people pointed out that they were failing, or even were falling below an adequate level of performance.

In a radical revolutionary period it is typical that the population sets for itself nearly impossible goals and pours great energy into those new tasks. Often the new revolutionary system continues for some time to make high demands on its citizens. People find that tiring, and the constant challenge of reaching for the nearly impossible becomes somewhat less satisfying over the long run. Thus, there is a falling away from such high aspirations. At the other end of the scale, however, when an organization becomes lax and inefficient, or a government becomes rife with corruption, typically there is a concerted attempt to restore some balance by insisting once more that people attempt to come closer to the ideals. It is unlikely that they will ever come back to exactly the same types of social patterns that once were observed. Sometimes the new reforms are far-reaching. And organizations do perish because of their failure to work hard enough toward the ideals they are supposed to represent. In any event, the strains and tensions occasioned by the attempt to balance the difficulties of living by

---

[5]On this theoretical point see William J. Goode, "A Theory of Role Strain," in *Explorations in Social Theory,* New York: Oxford, 1973, p. 119: ". . . The total balances and imbalances of role strains create whatever stability the social structure possesses."

[6]Wilbert E. Moore, *Social Change,* 2d ed., Englewood Cliffs, N.J.: Prentice-Hall, 1963, p. 11; as well as Wilbert E. Moore and Arnold S. Feldman, "Society as a Tension-Management System," in George Baker and Leonard S. Cottrell, eds., *Behavioral Science and Civil Defense,* Study no. 16, Washington, D.C.: National Research Council, 1962, pp. 93–105.

group ideals (with its attendant great costs), and the temptation to live comfortably or corruptly (while violating the group's ideals), may be a source of either large- or small-scale change over time.

Changes in Personnel

Although we are focusing on the structure of societies or organizations, we should not overlook the importance of a third factor, *changes in personnel,* as a factor in the gradual shifts in social patterns over time. These changes may be extremely gradual, measured only by periodic censuses, as when the percentage of the population sixty-five years of age and over increases, or the percentage of people with different ethnic backgrounds shifts. Such changes may also be occasioned by the appearance of a major political leader or a religious prophet.

Sociological analysis has generally rejected the "great man" theory of history, according to which major social changes have been the creation of a strong magnetic figure such as Napoleon or Henry VIII. Sociology has rather held to the thesis that most of these changes, like inventions or scientific discoveries, would have occurred even if their particular originators had not lived.[7]

However true that may be in general (and it is very difficult to prove), it seems unwise to suppose that people are infinitely substitutable, that if a major leader with the ability to command great loyalty (called a *charismatic* figure) had died early, another just like him would have arisen, or that the policies of one historic leader would have been exactly the same if a different person had been in the same position. A society is not a blind, automatic system. Whatever a society does is decided upon and executed by individuals whose particular needs, ideas, and capacities shape whatever social system can be observed. This is likely to be true for social change.

Environmental Challenges

A fourth source of change is environmental challenges of all kinds, including catastrophes. These comprise such slow alterations as the encroachment of an Ice Age, driving people farther south or forcing them to change their hunting and gathering techniques; or the altering climates experienced by the people who crossed from Asia to Alaska twenty to thirty thousand years ago and then moved south to warmer climates. They also include sudden catastrophes such as tidal waves, storms, atomic bombs, or volcanic explosions.

Such challenges, however, can also be social, as when a nation becomes powerful and begins to engage in military conquest, for example, the Manchu conquest of China, the expansion of the Bantu-speaking tribes in Africa, or the growth of the Inca empire in South America. As the modern European nations gradually took form, they created for one another a different kind of environmental challenge, for increasingly they competed in war, trade, manufacturing, and even science.[8] However, on a smaller scale that was also true of preliterate societies, who almost never lived in isolation, and thus who faced an ever-changing social challenge from their neighbors.

Not all of this contact can be called environmental challenge, in the sense that a given society was actually threatened. Much of it has been relatively peaceful, and that contact often facilitates such change through diffusion, or borrowing. Neighboring societies trade toys and types of clothing; tech-

---

[7]With reference to significant discoveries or inventions, the thesis seems unquestionably valid. On this point see Robert K. Merton, "Singletons and Multiples in Science," in *The Sociology of Science,* ed. by Norman W. Storer, Chicago: University of Chicago Press, 1973, pp. 343–370.

[8]For a major analysis of this process, see Immanuel A. Wallerstein, *The Modern World-System,* New York: Academic, 1974.

niques for riding horses; ideas about spirits, gods, and magic; or songs (but not often family patterns). We have discussed this process at some length in Chapter 2, and here we need only remind the reader that that process has occurred whenever societies interact with one another.

Planning and Design

Just as societies can learn from one another, whether through outright challenge or simply a peaceful competitiveness, so can they invent and discover and thereby change their society by *direct planning or design.* Modern societies engage in more of this than any previous ones, but no society ever lived for centuries utterly unchanged by this process. As Moore notes, one should not suppose that a group of elders once sat around a campfire and voted "to establish a prize and exclusive patent privilege for the

person who would invent the wheel."[9] Not only does most planning not take this form, but people do not typically applaud the innovator. Nevertheless, people at even low technological levels do make plans to change some aspects of their environment, techniques, and social structure.

Just how much social change is caused by invention is not easy to ascertain. We discussed this problem in earlier analyses of culture and the diffusion process. The "invention" of agriculture certainly changed social life a great deal, and very likely this great invention was hit upon in many parts of the world at different times, though it was also transmitted by cultural diffusion. Even if agriculture was invented by people already living in communities and was further developed by townspeople who continued for thousands of years to farm outside

[9]Moore, op. cit., p. 22.

Figure 15-4 We are living in a "society by direct planning," a graphic example of which is Levittown, Pa. (Monkmeyer.)

the cities,[10] it did eventually permit the growth of very large cities, as farmers produced enough to feed urban people who did not engage in agriculture.

However, few inventions are so momentous as agriculture. Most are as trivial as looking in a new area for edible roots or making a new ornament on a shield. This is true for social inventions as well, which we often overlook when we speak of discoveries. No one follows exactly the customs of his or her parents or the society. Everyone makes small changes in them over a lifetime. Most of these changes are minute, though they may accumulate over time to become or cause larger social changes. For example, an individual may extend a canoe trip to visit another tribe and trade with some of its members. This contact is then repeated over time to increase greatly the interaction between the two groups, or even to become a regular market system. The minor social invention of spontaneous, friendly help given to neighbors at harvest-time may over generations come to be guided by complex rules that are enforced by the community. At the beginning, such changes may not even be seen as real inventions. But whether small or large, quickly enacted or slowly growing, social inventions may come to have substantial effects on the social structure.

Linked closely with inventions, both technical and social, are changes that arise from *planning*. These range from decisions to move to a new village site where mosquitoes are less abundant to the planning that goes into a revolution. In all these, we observe that at times people do foresee the possibility of improvement and deliberately set

[10]The argument that Jane Jacobs presents in favor of cities having developed first, and agriculture later, seems very plausible. See *The Economy of Cities,* New York: Vintage, 1970, chap. 1: "Cities First—Rural Development Later."

about achieving it. Planning may be based on a new invention, or on borrowing, or simply on the utilization of existing knowledge.

As we noted before, modern societies doubtless engage in far more planning than did previous ones. That is so for many reasons. First, we possess much more *knowledge*, and thus can make a better assessment as to whether a given plan might yield some improvement. That is, our added knowledge makes planning less costly and more profitable.

Second, the cost of *not* planning is much greater. The consequences of simply barging ahead without much further thought may be far-reaching when every part of the society becomes so dependent on every other, as in a modern nation. For example, building a new town requires advance calculation for transportation, size of markets, schools, roads, fire-fighting equipment, sewage and garbage disposal, libraries, and entertainment facilities. All these parts must be calculated *together,* with respect to time, place, and cost. This necessity is so widely accepted that social planning has become a recognized profession. Moreover, aside from the group called city planners, almost every large organization now contains a special planning section.

A third reason for the importance of planning in contemporary society is a change in evaluating change. As we noted before, by the eighteenth century many social philosophers had come to believe that human beings were achieving *progress,* that the present was better than the past, and that the future would be better yet. This *idea of progress* has been widely accepted since that time. However, it has taken a new form in the twentieth century: The *idea* of progress has become the *norm* of progress.

This is a norm in the strict sense. People believe the nation, organization, club, or group *should* move ahead, become larger or more successful, or generally improve in some ways. Merely to maintain is to fail, to be deficient. Since people do believe in this standard, they expend some energy and capital in order to live up to its demands. Other people criticize them if they do not. The head of a large organization or the president of a nation who admitted he or she had no intention of even trying to make any progress would be viewed as unworthy of the office.

Since in the modern era very little planning is aimed at trying to keep things as they are—two notable exceptions are the rearguard activities of conservationists; and town councils in upper-class and upper-middle-class communities—this strong emphasis contributes to social change. After all, planning does make it more likely that a particular goal will be reached, and here the goal *is* change.

RECEPTIVITY TO SOCIAL CHANGE

That almost any major factor can, under some circumstances, lead to social change or to stability reminds us that many possible sources of social change have little effect, because one or more contrary forces resist them. Let us, then, consider the main factors that increase or decrease receptivity to change.

Many of these were discussed in Chapter 2, where we analyzed the factors that lead to alterations in cultural patterns. The two sets of factors must be similar, because whether a cultural pattern is accepted or rejected is mainly determined by the *social relations* between the borrowing and the receiving cultures. And the compatibility between the two cultures is likely, in turn, to affect their social relations. Earlier, we emphasized diffusion or borrowing, and here we broaden our perspective to include changes from *within* the society as well as those alterations that come from other societies.

The Extent and Speed of Change

One of the most general factors that affect a society's ability or willingness to change is simply how big a change, within a limited time period, is contemplated. This factor can be observed in many situations. A simple illustration is the brief attempt in the nineteenth century by the United States government to transform some Plains Indians on reservations from hunters of buffalo (which had almost disappeared) into cattle herders. To these governmental innovators the change appeared easy. All the Indians had to do was to change their taste in eating meat. In fact, however, it required the Indians to stay in one area rather than move around as nomads; to give up hunting (actually, they shot the cattle anyway); to abandon their system of giving high esteem to greater hunters, expert horse thieves, and courageous warriors; and to earn a living by making profits from cattle raising in a market economy. In short, they were being asked to transform completely their social patterns. Thus, the costs were high, and the rewards seemed slim.

Adding to the old   By contrast, merely *adding* a new social pattern to the old is more likely to be viewed as less costly. Then, even if the advantages are small, the change is more likely to be accepted. For this reason there is nothing mysterious about the spread of the practice of chewing gum or drinking Coca-Cola in distant lands. In these instances, only very small social changes need be made. In many societies, sociability permits a wide variety of drinks, alcoholic and nonalcoholic. A new one competes with others to some degree but does not require changing many of those social patterns. Chewing gum may get in the way of chewing tobacco, coca leaf, or betel nut, but in many regions chewing gum will not require any great social change.

Replacing the old   Still further illustrations may be seen in two areas where one might suppose large changes are required: medicine and religion. Both may eventually require large changes, but much of both can be introduced without actually supplanting the old social patterns. It is commonplace for both modern public health measures (sewage disposal systems, a clean water supply, insect control) and the individual cure of pathologies to be accepted while people *continue* for decades to visit with doctors, herb sellers and—in modern societies—a wide array of quacks, faith healers, and sellers of worthless drugs. In both Latin America and Africa missionaries have typically had to ignore their converts' continued allegiance to traditional worship. Their converts simply added Christian rituals to their social activities.

Vested Interests

Linked with the extent and speed of social change is the resistance of what are called *vested interests*—groups which derive much benefit from the existing social arrangements and which have considerable political influence. As ordinarily used, the term has a negative tone, since it suggests these people selfishly resist progress or improvement. People who benefit from high tariffs oppose free trade; professors oppose changes in the university structure that would give much influence to students; and men in all societies resist giving equal opportunity to women. Indeed, it is sometimes asserted that in the modern United States city it is difficult to introduce any important change, because the number of such vested interests is so great and their combined influence is so large that almost any change will arouse them to effective opposition.

Individual Leaders

Sometimes charismatic people can persuade others to accept their policies, and so can leaders with much prestige or political influence who are somewhat less charismatic or

Figure 15-5 The charismatic leader Gandhi had enormous influence in the movement for independence in India. (United Press International Photo.)

magnetic. In all group decisions the traits of the person who proposes the change will affect the group's willingness to assume the burden of learning new ways. This can be seen in small changes as well, which sometimes cumulatively affect the social structure to a substantial degree. Some small changes that were first accepted by people with higher prestige, and only later were widely diffused, are contraceptives, radio, television, a lower birthrate, and automobiles.

A much more extreme example is the influence of dictators with a broad program for radically changing the society, for example, Hitler, Mussolini, Kemal Ataturk in Turkey, or Stalin. Whether left-wing or right-wing in politics, and whether or not they are viewed as the outcome of a popular movement that would have found a substitute leader if they had not appeared, it must be conceded that such men wielded tremendous influence and thus could engineer greater changes than other people could have.

Stability of the Society

A factor that is more difficult to weigh—in part because it is determined to a considerable extent by the foregoing factors—is the *relative stability of the society,* its flexibility, or the willingness of its members to look for new solutions. This factor is not entirely dependent upon the previous forces, however. First of all, it is partly a function of its current resources, of the amount of surplus energy or capital it commands that can be invested in social innovations. In general, very poor societies that have remained so for a long time are less open to large changes, for any new possibilities require that they give up some of the little they have, while the chances of any substantial gain may not be high.

However, the relative stability of a society is also a function of the current crises it faces. For example, analysts of revolution have noted that governments which continue to mismanage their finances or which have been defeated in a major war are more prone to radical or revolutionary changes. Major crises or widespread disorder are both more likely to persuade people that their traditional social patterns deserve less support. Their allegiance dwindles in those circumstances, and social changes that are proposed come to seem more attractive.

CONCLUSION

Over the past decade sociology has begun to give more attention to the problems of social change than it did in the period between World War I and the 1950s. Prior to World War I change was a dominant theme in all social science, and before that had been a major interest of social philosophers from the beginnings of social analysis.

The reasons for this renewed interest are many. They include a greater awareness that social structures are not tightly integrated or harmonious, and in fact are constantly changing. In addition, social changes in the modern world, as we document with more attention in the succeeding chapter, have created considerable unease among many people. Many alterations seem to bring losses, not gains, and such threats arouse a wish to understand them.

There is also a political impulse in the increased attention to social change, because more people are concerned about the possibility of changing the world and, it is to be hoped, improving it as well. Finally, there is a pragmatic concern about social change, since without considerable practical knowledge we cannot possibly alter the society in ways that we deem desirable.

In this chapter we devoted considerable attention to the various types of social change problems, specifically noting both the theoretical and methodological differences among (1) social changes that occur only once in world history, such as the rise of human societies or the European Middle Ages, and (2) underlying processes or recurring events from which social scientists might be able to discover laws and regularities. It is important to distinguish among these various types, because they require somewhat different research techniques and strategies, and some problems are much more difficult than others. For example, the attempt to develop a satisfactory theory of large-scale changes over time, that is, laws of evolution, is not likely to be successful until we have achieved many small-scale regularities or laws. Moreover, it is characteristic of all fields of science that large-scale evolutionary changes lag far behind the development of what are called here timeless propositions.

Throughout this section we gave many examples of the different types of causal explanations, for example, charting of trends, interpretations of historic events, limited or large-scale evolutionary laws, and timeless propositions. In order to illuminate further the methodological and theoretical differences among different kinds of social change problems, we attempted to explain a distinction that is of some importance in modern theories about social change, that is, changes *in* social structures as contrasted with changes *of* social structures. The latter generally refer to the larger social factors that *cause* the day-to-day changes that we constantly observe, such as alterations in the homicide rate, the divorce rate, or the percentage unemployed. We noted, however, that this distinction is somewhat difficult to maintain, and analysts may argue among themselves about whether a particular change is fundamental, altering the structure itself, or is merely one more small-scale change within the structure.

In general, changes *of* the social structure refer to larger changes; the emergence of new statuses, positions, or organizations; the growth of some part of the social system until its sheer size affects the working of the organization or the community; or changes in the operation of an organization or a nation that can no longer be explained by factors that once were of great importance, so that we have to bring in new ones (an example might be the introduction of the mass, draft army in modern warfare).

We also presented a wide array of hypotheses that social analysts of the past have put forward in order to explain social change. Most of these, as we noted, were monistic theories. That is, they claimed that major social changes were caused by a single factor such as race, the survival of the fittest, climate, or technological innovation. However, we went on to present the basic hypotheses of diffusionism and Sorokin's theory of immanent change as well as his principle of limits. Though each of these may have some measure of truth in it, we have pointed out both methodological and theoretical criticisms that have been directed against these hypotheses.

We analyzed still other sources of

change—specifically, the existence of strains within the society, the conflict between the ideal and the real, changes in personnel (including the rise of a "great man"), environmental challenges of all kinds, and direct planning and invention. The last of these has become especially important in the modern world, both because there is more knowledge available and because change without some planning has become much more dangerous in a society where almost every sector can be affected by actions taken in any other part of the society.

Finally, we analyzed some of the factors that affect the *receptivity* of a social structure to changes of various kinds. Some of this discussion paralleled our earlier presentation of the social factors that affect the acceptance of new cultural patterns. Some of the variables that affect the willingness of a group or a society to change its social structure are whether the change is large and rapid, or small and slow; whether the new social pattern is merely being *added,* or instead is suggested as a *substitute* for an older pattern; the resistance of vested interests; the persuasion and force used by leaders; the energy or capital a society has available for risking an investment in social innovation; and how desperate are the current crises the society confronts.

We have, then, considered a wide array of theoretical and methodological problems in the analysis of social change. We have also offered a few generalizations that have been drawn from many studies of social change. In the following two chapters we shall consider several of the massive changes now occurring throughout the world. In the final chapter we shall also examine the possibility that since all of the world is becoming increasingly interlinked, and faces very similar challenges and problems from these massive forces, perhaps a world order or community might emerge.

READINGS

Bernard Barber and Alex Inkeles, eds., *Stability and Social Change,* Boston: Little, Brown, 1971.

Daniel Bell, ed., *Toward the Year 2000,* New York: Houghton Mifflin, 1969.

Warren G. Bennis, Kenneth D. Benne, and Robert Chin, *The Planning of Change,* New York: Holt, 1969.

Kenneth Boulding, *The Meaning of the Twentieth Century: The Great Transition,* New York: Harper & Row, 1964.

James S. Coleman, *Resources for Social Change: Race in the United States,* New York: Wiley, 1971.

Amitai Etzioni, *The Active Society,* New York: Free Press, 1968.

George M. Foster, *Traditional Societies and Technological Change,* 2d ed., New York: Harper & Row, 1973.

Alex Inkeles, *Becoming Modern: Individual Change in Six Developing Countries,* Cambridge, Mass.: Harvard, 1974.

Peter Laslett, *The World We Have Lost,* 2d ed., New York: Scribner, 1971.

Marion J. Levy, *Modernization and the Structure of Society*, 2 vols., Princeton, N.J.: Princeton, 1966.

Wilbert E. Moore, *Social Change,* 2d ed., Englewood Cliffs, N.J.: Prentice-Hall, 1963.

Robert A. Nisbet, *The Twilight of Authority,* New York: Oxford, 1975.

Eleanor Sheldon and Wilbert E. Moore, eds., *Indicators of Social Change: Concepts and Measurements,* New York: Russell Sage, 1968.

Pitirim A. Sorokin, *Social and Cultural Dynamics,* 4 vols., New York: American Book, 1937–1940.

Alvin Toffler, *Future Shock,* New York: Random House, 1970.

Immanuel A. Wallerstein, *The Modern World-System,* New York: Academic, 1974.

Max Weber, *The Protestant Ethic and the Spirit of Capitalism,* trans. by Talcott Parsons, London: G. Allen, 1930.

CHAPTER SIXTEEN

MAJOR WORLD CHANGES: URBANIZATION, POPULATION GROWTH, AND INDUSTRIALIZATON

Social analysts generally agree with the commonsense observation that major social changes are taking place more rapidly now than at any earlier period of history. In the previous chapter we stated some of the ways we can distinguish important or structural changes from the innumerable small, day-to-day alterations in our individual lives or social groups. We also considered some of the important theoretical and methodological issues in social change analysis.

Let us now consider some of the massive social changes that are taking place in the modern world. Perhaps the reader would suggest additions or substitutions in our list, but most of those noted below should be in any such inventory. Certainly, they have created and are creating massive shifts in social structures all over the world, and they have been noted at various points throughout this book. They are, then, *world* chang-es. In this chapter we shall discuss only the first three of these, reserving the remainder for a brief analysis in our final chapter.

1 Urbanization
2 Population growth
3 Industrialization
4 The disappearance of kings and the spread of dictators
   a The increasing power of national governments
   b The decline of communal networks relative to the influence of national patterns
   c The loss of privacy
   d The loss of authority and deference
5 The social effect of the atomic bomb
6 Pollution and the exhaustion of natural resources
7 The growth of science

As can be seen, most of these are not

causes for rejoicing. Rather, they are challenges, or even threats to life itself. Their consequences are far-reaching, and their ultimate effects cannot be foreseen as yet. On each of these topics literally hundreds of books have been written, because many analysts have perceived their importance. We shall discuss each of them briefly, hoping thereby to call the attention of the reader to some of the great forces that shape the life of everyone now living, and very likely the life of everyone who will be born during the next several generations.

THE ORIGINS OF CITIES

Of all the changes that human beings have made in the physical appearance of the world, perhaps none is more striking than the construction of cities. At the tip of what was once a large, wooded island at the mouth of the Hudson River one can now see only stone, asphalt, and concrete surfaces and dozens of buildings towering hundreds of feet into the air. The fertile valley of the Thames River a few miles inland from the sea is now covered by the urban agglomeration whose center is London. In some industrial regions one can fly for dozens of miles without ever losing sight of one city after another.

The city differs from the countryside in physical appearance, and the two differ in their social reality as well. The city is one of the important human inventions of the past. As with so many other fundamental social inventions (the family, bureaucracy), the people who first began this one probably did not know they were doing so. Almost certainly, it was independently invented in the Americas, China, and the Near East, and possibly elsewhere, but we do not know just what the social conditions were under which it first thrived.[1]

However, we do know approximately where and when the first cities arose—in the Near East, in what is now Iraq and Turkey, about nine or ten thousand years ago.[2] Before those little towns began, there were many hamlets or relatively permanent settlements in what is now Europe, the Near East, and India; these date back to perhaps fifteen thousand years ago. Since human beings may have appeared more than two million years ago, and the modern species of human beings over fifty thousand years ago, cities are—on this broad time scale—relatively recent.

It is generally asserted that cities could not develop until human beings invented agriculture, that is, the deliberate cultivation and planting of the soil in order to gather its fruits, and especially the seeds of certain grasses (wheat, rice, barley, maize). This was supposedly necessary because some people had to produce the food if city people were to eat. This guess seems unlikely, but we do not as yet know the correct answer.

It is just as plausible to suppose instead that hamlets and permanent settlements began first, and then human beings gradually invented agriculture to fill the needs of the settlement. First, we know already that numerous small settlements (not yet cities) did continue for generations in areas where an adequate supply of fish and shellfish was found. That is, a permanent hamlet can be fed before agriculture is invented. In any event, the earliest cities may have had no more than 150 inhabitants at their beginnings, and such a small number could have

---

[1]For a somewhat technical article on the difficulties of pinning down what these conditions were, the se-

quence of development of cities, the relations of central cities to smaller ones, and so on, see Robert McC. Adams, "Patterns of Urbanization in Early Southern Mesopotamia," in Peter J. Ucko, R. Tringham, and G. W. Dimbleby, *Man, Settlement, and Urbanism*, Cambridge, Mass.: Schenkman, 1972, pp. 735–749.

[2]The reader must keep in mind that even radiocarbon dates contain a large margin of error, and that over the past generation of research the dates for the "earliest" stages of almost any aspect of human history have been steadily pushed back to earlier and earlier periods.

easily supported themselves by various combinations of hunting, collecting plant food and shellfish, fishing, or even part-time agriculture. Even late in European history, a high percentage of townspeople were not supported by farmers; they were also farmers, growing part of their food outside the town walls. Moreover, trade—much more important as the basis for urban life—certainly began while human beings were hunters and gatherers.[3]

Whichever came first, agriculture or cities, the two seem to have evolved closely together. As cities grew larger, specialization became more widespread. By about 3000 B.C. cities as large as twenty thousand inhabitants had arisen; and in such a city far more people would have devoted themselves to tasks other than farming, while trade would have attracted agricultural and other products from greater distances.

However, because of the anticity bias that pervades United States thought, we must be careful not to impose our own preconceptions on that somewhat unknown past. It is tempting to suppose that peasants sweated in the fields to support a large number of city people. It is easy to make that assumption, since less than 5 percent of the United States labor force feeds the entire population and sends a large surplus to other parts of the world. However, peasants in the ancient world did not produce that much. One estimate is that it probably took fifty to ninety farmers to support one city dweller at this early stage of history; and even now the farmers in the less developed countries produce no more than enough to feed 1.3 city dwellers.[4] Indeed, we should keep in mind

that most city dwellers were simply workers and producers themselves. They produced both food and other kinds of goods (arrows, spears, wheels, bricks) that farmers and other urban citizens needed. Since by 3000 B.C. militaristic kings ruled the cities we know, we can take for granted that they oppressed their peasant subjects much as they oppressed their urban ones. However, we cannot assume that city dwellers were able to erect an urban civilization by doing little more than taking a large food surplus from farmers.

Thus, at some time between five thousand and nine thousand years ago (approximately) there were settlements that we would consider "real" cities, and not simply permanent hamlets. What is the difference between a genuine city and an overgrown hamlet? Even today, nations differ as to whether they consider a town of 2,500 to 5,000 inhabitants urban, or not. However, for that time period, most agree that some or all of these traits would be considered urban:[5]

Permanent, dense settlements

Specialists other than farmers

Taxation

Public buildings

Writing

Trade

City citizenship as a basis for community membership (that is, not merely kinship)

It is not necessary to add the production of art, since all nonurban societies do that as well. Taxation implies the development of a state or political system. It seems unnecessary to add (as some do) the growth of a

[3]Jane Jacobs, in *The Economy of Cities*, using archaeological data, suggests a hypothetical development of a small city on the basis of trade (New York: Vintage, 1970, pp. 18ff.).

[4]For these estimates see Kingsley Davis, "The Origin and Growth of Urbanization in the World," *American Journal of Sociology*, 60 (March 1955), p. 430; and Kingsley Davis, *World Urbanization 1950–1970*, vol. II: *Analysis of Trends, Relationships, and Developments*, Population Monograph, ser. no. 9, Berkeley: University of California Press, 1972, p. 46.

[5]See Noel P. Gist and Sylvia F. Fava, *Urban Society*, 5th ed., New York: Crowell, 1966, pp. 10ff.; and J. John Palen, *The Urban World*, New York: McGraw-Hill, 1975, pp. 15–17. These traits were enunciated by V. Gordon Childe, "The Urban Revolution," in *Town Planning Review*, 21 (April 1950), pp. 3–17.

class or stratification system to this list. Certainly, it is not one of the foundations of city life, and is found in many nonurban societies. In any event, what was emerging was a new way of life.

THE INFLUENCE OF CITIES

From the time the first cities arose, they have had a major influence on how people interact with one another and on the larger society as well. With rare exceptions, kings have ruled from urban residences, not from rural ones. Cities have been the center of economic transactions—as we noted in the chapter on geographic factors, it is more convenient to trade or communicate if people are closer. Cities have been the source of most new ideas and inventions, including those in agriculture. Conquered by nomadic warriors, they have transformed their conquerors into city people. The history of great civilizations is largely the history of what was accomplished in cities. The "fall" or decline of great empires is marked by the temporary failure of their cities.

The reasons for this dominance seem clear enough, and can be drawn from analyses that are found throughout this book. Cities are organized and concentrated groups of people, while peasants are scattered. Thus, peasants are unable to communicate or organize with one another in large units (an observation that Karl Marx once made, as one explanation for the failure of peasants to mount revolutions). Thus, peasants have not often been able to resist the military forces of the city. In turn, they have typically been compelled to pay heavy taxes and rents, which supported the urban military units.

Larger numbers of people in one place make specialization profitable; experts in a single task such as making wine or shipping goods can find a large market. People learn from and are stimulated by one another, so

that new ideas arise. There are enough people to support the development of various arts. Political and economic records can be kept. Thus, whether literacy is high or low in the nation as a whole, it will be concentrated in the city. Since the city is the center of economic life, productivity is higher there, and wealth accumulates. (It is for this reason that many believe a complex class system is first developed there.) In short, the processes that are set in motion by the emergence of cities will assure their dominance over many aspects of national life.

THE CHARACTERISTICS OF URBAN SOCIAL INTERACTION

Social philosophers and analysts have written at length about these processes. In one of the classic statements, the sociologist Louis Wirth defined a city as a "relatively large, dense, and permanent settlement of socially heterogeneous individuals."[6] He then argued that these factors generated the social patterns that have become accepted as the common experience in city living: (1) There is much social contact among different kinds of individuals, which breaks down traditional customs and creates social disorganization. (2) Social interaction is segmental; that is, we do not know the other person, except in a particular and special context, such as buying milk or working (sometimes we say that the interaction is *impersonal*). (3) Neighbors are not friends, but remain strangers, and do not help one another in crises. (4) There is much *seg-*

---

[6]Louis Wirth, "Urbanism as a Way of Life," *American Journal of Sociology*, 44 (July 1938), pp. 1–24. For criticism of Wirth's reasoning and facts, see Herbert J. Gans, "Urbanism and Suburbanism as Ways of Life: A Reevaluation of Definitions," in Robert Gutman and David Popenoe, eds., *Neighborhood, City, and Metropolis*, New York: Random House, 1970, pp. 54–69; as well as Herbert J. Gans, *The Urban Villagers: Group and Class in the Life of Italian-Americans*, New York: Free Press, 1962.

regation; that is, people of a given class or ethnic group live closely together. (5) Life is anonymous, for most people we see do not know us. (6) This means there is an emphasis on maintaining one's privacy, but most people do not even want to interact much with most people they meet.

That description suggests a purely *Gesellschaft* type of society, but we pointed out in our chapter on primary groups that such a society is never encountered. Always there are other kinds of social relationships within it. Yet most people do act as strangers to most people, since no one has time enough to stop and chat with the hundreds of people encountered each day. Urban dwellers learn to sidestep unpleasant events, to pass them by, or to be tolerant of differences.

On the other hand, much of any large city is made up of somewhat *stable* residential neighborhoods or blocks. In cities of the Far East in the past, as in modern cities, many such neighborhoods have been made up of subgroups or ethnic communities. Far from being anonymous or rootless, most people have frequent interactions with friends, and in fact the frequency of interaction with relatives is probably greater than in villages of the past.

Thus, much of any large city is made up of many different parts (that is, it is heterogeneous, as a whole); but it also contains many relatively *homogeneous* neighborhoods.[7] Large cities can be thought of as collections of small towns. Even areas of low income may not be slums, in the sense of being disorganized, crime-ridden places. If residents remain for years, so that they have a stake in the neighborhood, both the richness of daily social life and safety in the streets are likely to be high.[8]

When so many people and groups with

Figure 16-1 San Francisco's Chinatown is a striking example of an ethnically homogeneous neighborhood. (Bloom, Monkmeyer.)

very different goals and values live together, they must develop some tolerance for one another, and traditional customs will inevitably erode. However, it is incorrect to infer that as a consequence the city is therefore disorganized. After all, some cities are more than a thousand years old, and by now they would have ceased to function if only disorganization took place there. Though traditional *rural* patterns break down, and most traditions are under threat in the city, new customs and values emerge as well. This is but another way of noting that the city is where innovation takes place, in techniques and the arts as well as in social customs.

WORLD URBANIZATION

While intellectuals deplore the city[9] as they have in the past, and political leaders wring

---

[7]On these and related points see Jane Jacobs, *The Death and Life of Great American Cities,* New York: Vintage, 1961, Part I: "The Peculiar Nature of Cities."

[8]See ibid., chap. 15, "Slumming and Unslumming."

[9]For antiurbanism among intellectuals, see Gist and Fava, op. cit., pp. 534ff.

their hands in the face of insoluble urban problems, a flood of people all over the world is streaming to the cities, at a faster rate than at any previous time in history. Let us consider this massive process, which is both an indicator of social change and a cause of it.

In 1975 the world's population was about 4 billion, and about 40 percent of this total lived in an urban place. "Urban place" is defined somewhat differently from one nation to another, with the bottom limit usually in the range of 2,500 to 5,000 people. However, the fraction in urban places would not change by more than 5 percent even if the bottom limit were 10,000.[10] We are accustomed to thinking of the United States as urban, and so it is: About three-fourths of the population lives in urban places, and slightly more than half in cities of 100,000 or more inhabitants. Still more urbanized are Great Britain and Australia, with about four-fifths in urban places.

That contrast between highly urbanized countries and the rest of the world should be emphasized. For the world as a whole, about 60 percent is *rural*. Of those classified as urban, about 40 percent live in towns of *less* than 100,000 inhabitants. Thus, the population *not* living in cities above that limit constitutes about three-fourths of the world's population. If we make the cutting point smaller still, say 12,500, then almost two-thirds of the world's population would be found in towns or villages that small or smaller, or simply in rural areas.[11]

On the other hand, keep in mind that if we focus *only* on people living in an urban place, *most* of them live in relatively large cities. This follows from the elimination of rural populations from our calculation, and

the greater weight of giant metropolises in the equations.[12] Moreover, as we have noted many times, the political and economic influence of those larger units is much higher.

To emphasize the contrast between highly urbanized countries and the rest of the world helps us keep some perspective on the urbanization process. That is, it has some distance to go. However, it is moving at a rapid rate. Let us view it in time perspective. As recently as 1850 no *country* in the world was as urbanized (about 40 percent) as the *world* as a whole is now. Shortly after that time Great Britain reached that level, and the United States followed in about 1900. Other countries have begun to follow. In the world as a whole, the rate of urbanization has been fastest since 1950. Between 1950 and 1970, the urban population in cities of 100,000 or more actually *doubled*, and the percentage or *fraction* of the world's population in cities of that size increased over 20 percent in each of these two decades.

This is a fast rate of change, and indeed is the fastest on record, but the process has been going on for many decades. A high rate has been *usual* for a century. This can be seen in the accompanying table.

We can see, for example, that a rate of increase *per decade* of about one-fifth (19 to 24 percent) in the fraction of the world's population in cities of one hundred thousand inhabitants or more has been typical for a century.

The absolute *numbers* involved in this process get steadily larger, since the world population itself has been growing, and at a faster rate than ever. This population growth actually affects the urbanization process, since the *rural* population has been growing at an unprecedented rate, too. Ob-

[10]Davis, *World Urbanization, 1950–1970,* vol. II, p. 31. The data in the succeeding pages are mainly from this volume. The most adequate compilation and analysis of world urbanization data are in these two volumes.

[11]Ibid., p. 41.

[12]The hypothetical mean urban dweller lived, by this calculation, in a city of 1,575,000 in 1970; and the median urban citizen, in a city of 250,000. The large difference arises from the great weight of large cities in the calculation of the mean.

TABLE 16-1 THE RATE OF CHANGE IN URBANIZATION IN THE WORLD AS A
WHOLE: 1800–1970

	Percentage Change in World's Population per Decade			
Years	In All Urban Places	In Places 20,000+	In Cities 100,000+	Combined Index*
1800–1850	16.4	12.4	6.3	12.9
1850–1900	16.3	16.4	19.1	16.8
1900–1950	15.7	19.7	24.1	18.8
1950–1970	16.9	19.3	21.1	19.1

*Ibid., Table 13 (modified), p. 51.

viously, the *fraction* that is urban will not increase as fast if the rural population grows at a high rate. In the decades 1950–1970, the world rural population grew by 434 million people; if all that increase had been added to the world's urban population, the growth rate in the urban population would have been *twice* as fast.

The percentage of the world's population that lives in cities of one million or more is also rising fast; this proportion doubled in the decade 1950–1970, while the proportion in urban places of less than one million rose by only one-fourth. That is, a larger fraction of the world's population is moving toward the giant cities. From this, some conclude that the larger the city, the faster it grows. However, the data are somewhat more complex. First, the larger cities actually appear to have slower growth rates. They contain a larger *fraction* of the total population, because more and more cities enter that class of one million or more in size, but the individual city does not increase that fast in size.

Is there an optimum size to cities, so that as they grow bigger they slow down in growth? One might conclude this from, say, the example of New York City, which changes little in size, and seems to face complex problems of finance and social control. Some social philosophers have in fact argued for one or another optimum size,

reasoning on the analogy of an organism (there are in fact structural limitations on the possible size of a land-dwelling animal). Plato believed there was a proper size to his ideal republic (which was a city), and the idea has appealed to many urban planners. However, no one has yet observed any special effects of size that might slow down the expansion of large cities, and what anyone considers "optimum" is likely to be determined by personal preferences.

In any event, careful examination of the relationship between size of city and rate of growth suggests that none can be proved at all. Very likely, the apparent slowdown is caused by (1) the difficulty of taking an adequate count as the city expands geographically, and (2) the fact that most of the very large cities are in countries that are already highly urbanized (and thus the rate of change cannot be very high).[13]

Note what is implied by the explanation above: Modern cities grow by (1) *geographical expansion*, in addition to (2) the emigrants they receive, and (3) their own excess of births over deaths. Since they grow by spreading outward, we encounter the paradox that as cities grow, the overall *density* of cities (the number of inhabitants per acre) is actually being reduced.

[13]Davis puts both these explanations to the test (ibid., pp. 101ff.).

In the less developed regions of the world, *both* the urban and the rural populations are growing faster than in the industrialized countries. As a consequence, about forty cities one million or more in size can be found even in countries that are predominantly agricultural and tropical. Since almost every traveler reports squalor, hunger, and poverty in the shantytowns of these large cities, and the economic development of cities has not been fast enough to absorb all these people, why does the migration continue?

First, in such countries the poorer rural population itself is growing fast, so that these migrants would have faced a growing competition if they had stayed in their rural region. Second, even the poorest in Latin America or Indian cities feel they are better off than in the country. The average income in the city is higher, and they at least perceive that some opportunity for mobility exists. Social services and welfare are more easily available. They can enjoy at least part of the network of community facilities such as public transportation, water supply, or even the entertainment of radio or television. National leaders in many countries have tried to restrain this flow, but to no avail.

Keeping in mind that in the United States no more than 5 percent of the work force *could* leave agriculture for the city, let us note a final contrast. The highly urbanized, industrialized, and wealthy countries have a lower *rural* density (number of people per square mile) than the poorer, less urbanized countries. Since the rural population in poor countries is expanding fast, but the land is not, the people who stay on the land are likely to be worse off over time. By contrast, in the industrializing countries outside Europe, agricultural land is still expanding somewhat, but the agricultural population declines or does not grow by much. Consequently, the countries at the higher income levels show a *drop* in the number of males in agriculture per square mile of farming soil, and the reverse is true in the poorer, less urbanized and industrialized countries.[14]

Davis argues that the recent trend in world urbanization "cannot have existed very long in the past and certainly will not endure long in the future." It began somewhat slowly "in the 16th and 17th centuries, with the entire world probably between one and two percent urban . . . The pace picked up some in the 18th century, but really got under way rapidly in the 19th, continuing and perhaps accelerating a bit around the middle of the 20th century. Within another century—certainly by the year 2100—the entire process of world urbanization should be finished."[15]

PROBLEMS OF THE CENTRAL CITY

Perhaps human beings have always had an uneasy relationship with the city. Rural people have felt awkward, ignorant, and fearful when they visited it. They have known—especially in the Near and Far East—that new taxes and oppressive laws came from the city. Urban people, and especially philosophers, have argued that city life is unnatural, artificial, and dangerous to both physical and spiritual well-being. More recently, because of changes inside the city, many analysts have wondered whether the problems of the city can be solved at all.

In the United States that question has taken a particular form:

1 Although the average wealth of urban dwellers is higher than that of rural people, most of the nation's poor are concentrated in the cities. They include most of the mother-headed families (black and white) as well as the aged.
2 Middle-class and stable working-class

[14]Ibid., pp. 300–307.

[15]Ibid., pp. 48, 52–53.

families have been moving from the city to the suburbs, which means that a major source of social and political leadership is lost to the city. Even when these people continue to work in the city, they have much less stake in it, and invest less of their time and energy in solving its problems.

3 Although about half of black families are now middle-class, and housing restrictions make it difficult for them to move to the suburbs, an increasing number surmount that barrier just the same, thus abandoning civic decisions to white political leaders left in the city.

4 Much or most of the revenue of city government comes from property taxes, which have become so heavy that many individuals and businesses cannot afford to stay.

5 Since welfare and child aid payments are higher in cities, whatever migration of the poor occurs is toward the city, thus increasing its financial difficulties. Federal taxes come mainly from cities, but federal help to the cities does not fill this gap entirely.

These difficulties are made still more intense by the attitudes of both federal and state legislatures. Although the United States population is urban, a majority of legislators came from small-town or rural backgrounds, are white, and well-to-do. Since three-fifths of all blacks live in the central city of major metropolitan areas (versus 28 percent of the white population), and blacks make up from 40 percent to a majority of thirteen United States major cities,[16] many white legislators do not have a keen interest in making an organized attack on urban problems and do not believe they know what to do about them.

Within the central city area, crime rates are many times higher than elsewhere, un-

employment rates are higher, overall rates of poverty are higher—and on all these measures the rates for blacks are higher than for whites. Many political leaders view the central city areas as hopeless regions of urban decay.

All these problems have been intensified in the past decade by the growing recognition at the national level that many antipoverty programs have not worked well, and by the gradual failure of city government to cope with the elementary difficulties of ordinary civic housekeeping. Special-interest pension systems, borrowing money for short-term expenses, incompetent record keeping and mounting welfare rolls (a smaller percentage of the total population is below the poverty line than a decade ago, but a higher percentage of those who *are* poor get some welfare) have brought many large cities close to bankruptcy. Politically, many city governments have given political influence to many special groups (sanitation workers, clerical unions, ethnic groups, teachers, or particular political clubs and organizations that deliver small blocs of votes) who have little power to accomplish anything, but great power to stop or stall almost any program. Thus, no concerted, overall program for civic betterment seems to have much chance of being put into action.

As noted already, one consequence is that a very large percentage of urban people not only would live in the suburbs if they could, but many are actually moving there, especially when their children are young. In the last two decades many suburbs as well as small towns distant from metropolitan regions have begun to show some of the same disturbing phenomena that were once thought to be characteristic only of slums: vandalism, juvenile crime, senseless violence and general lack of safety, youthful drug addiction, and even traffic jams.

The modern "crisis of the cities" is, then, following people to the suburbs. Neverthe-

[16]Palen, op. cit., pp. 211ff.

Figure 16-2 Governments as well as people are having increasing difficulty

less, the decline of the central city has proceeded much further than anything yet to be observed in the suburbs. Whether the quality of life can be improved in the major slum areas of the United States remains to be seen. The efforts at urban renewal have been studied sufficiently to make it clear that very likely a majority of them have been been failures, and very expensive. At the present time it is difficult to think of any obvious ways in which major cities have been successful in meeting their problems, with the possible exception of attempting to cleanse somewhat the air that city people breathe. Moreover, no prospect of any substantial improvement in the near future seems credible.

POPULATION DYNAMICS

Both urbanization and population growth are examples of massive changes that have a profound effect on people's lives, but are not the result of decisions made by political leaders. They are the result of billions of small-scale decisions made by individuals, for their own goals, all over the world, often against the wishes of those leaders. Few people decide to move to the city, or to have more or fewer children, because they believe their country should be more or less urbanized, or should have a larger or a smaller population.

The consequences of modern population growth are far-reaching, and in some countries, sure to be catastrophic. The present rate of world population growth is 2 percent a year, which means that the world's population doubles every thirty-five years. At the end of 1975 the world's population was about 4 billion people, so that by the year 2000, it will be between 6 and 7 billion. This rate cannot continue indefinitely; there is not enough space on the earth to hold so great a number as would be eventually reached at this rate. It will either slow down because people decide to have fewer children, or death rates from war, starvation and disease will rise.

Such a gloomy forecast is not like the prophecy of a moralist who peers into the future and tells us the social fabric will tear apart at some date. In population dynamics many of the factors that will determine the near future are already at work. For example, 90 percent of the people who will be alive in 1985 have already been born. We already know how many people will be in the childbearing ages in 1995, since almost all of them are alive now to be counted. We can also "predict" backward in time, and assert flatly that *deaths closely balanced births through most of human existence.* Simple arithmetic will show us that even a tiny rate of increase would have covered the earth with human beings in the short time between the Neolithic period (eight to ten thousand years ago) and the rise of the Greek and Roman civilizations.

Let us now consider the process of population growth, for their outcome affects all the major world changes that are taking place, and they have consequences for the daily decisions that individuals make: pollution, who may be available for marriage, how many sons are likely to survive to adulthood, the exhaustion of natural resources, war, employment opportunities, the economic development.

Basic Population Variables

Demography, or the analysis of population, focuses mainly on three great variables, that is, births, deaths, and migration. Each of these is affected by many factors, and it is typical that the demographer cannot explain *why* the death rate has risen or fallen in a given century, or the birthrate among United States mothers with two children has dropped sharply. Instead, the analyst attempts to find out how such changes affect the numbers of people of a given age and sex, the expectation of life, or the number of children in completed families. That is, the

demographer does attempt to find *correlations* between such factors as industrialization and birthrates or death rates, or between birth and death rates and the resulting age and sex distribution of the population, but he or she generally believes that the precise causal factors are so very complex that they cannot often be pinned down with great precision.

Fecundity and Fertility

Population dynamics is a set of biological processes that are highly structured by social variables. Let us begin with a distinction that demography makes between *fecundity,* the biological ability to bear children, and *fertility,* the actual number of children born. The latter is usually expressed as some kind of *birthrate,* for example, the number of children born each year per thousand population.[17]

The reader can immediately think of various factors that might affect the biological ability to reproduce. For example, some people are born with physical defects that prevent conception or make childbearing unlikely.[18] Some genetic defects cause a high fetal mortality, that is, a high death rate of the fetus before it can be born. Any biological factors that increase the general health of individuals will increase their fecundity. This includes diet as well, for the lack of food in general or of specific minerals or vitamins will reduce the ability to conceive or bear infants. Some analysts once believed the opposite, because they observed that people with inadequate diets had high birthrates. They failed to see that they were

---

[17]For most technical computations, the demographer is much more likely to focus on the number of children born each year per 1,000 females in specific ages, usually the childbearing years.

[18]A good summary of the factors involved in fecundity can be found in William Petersen, *Population,* 3d ed., New York: Macmillan, 1975, pp. 190–200.

merely observing a difference in birth control practices between the well-to-do and the poor.

Since fecundity is a biological variable, age affects it. The very young are not fertile, but become increasingly so through adolescence. As middle age approaches, the ability to conceive drops, more slowly in males and rather swiftly in females.

All such statements about age summarize large *individual* differences. Some boys produce adequate sperm cells at age eleven, and some women continue to produce fertilizable eggs well into their fifties. Moreover, these ages vary with the health of individuals, while the ages at which young people can first conceive change over time, and differ from one country to another. For example, the age at first menstruation has been dropping in this and other well-fed countries for many decades, and is lower by several years than in poor countries (twelve to thirteen years of age versus fifteen to sixteen years). The period between first menstruation and full physical maturity varies in length, and during that growth phase the female is less likely to conceive or bear normal children. Whether a mother breast-feeds her infant will also affect fecundity: females who are giving milk are less likely to produce an egg.

Fertility

It is already evident that this biological factor of fecundity may be affected by social behavior. For example, in a society in which breast feeding is approved, it is likely that the intervals between births will be two or three years. However, let us view the processes of fertility more broadly, by considering the wide range of factors that affect whether the birthrate is high or low.[19]

The first point to be made is that in *no* society is the social structure so organized as to maximize fertility. All societies socialize their children to become parents, and give some disesteem to adults who do not become parents, but always there are some social rules that reduce the actual fertility well below the biological maximum.

Second, depending on their values and the techniques at their disposal, societies can choose *where,* in the total process from sexual intercourse to the acceptance of a child as a family member, to affect the fertility outcome. Whether or not they consciously make a choice, their behavior varies a good deal in this emphasis.

Third, in general the societies in which death rates are very high are more likely to emphasize techniques that affect the *later* phases of the birth cycle, such as abortion or infanticide. Then, after a major epidemic or mass starvation, the existing social patterns that support a high rate of conception will rapidly replace the population if the latter techniques are not used.

All societies impose some control over the first phase, in any event, by limiting sexual intercourse in various ways. There are celibate groups (for example, priests) in some societies, and many societies have imposed some form of guarding nubile girls from adolescent or mature males. Many have customs that forbid sexual intercourse between wife and husband at certain ritual periods (which may not be the least fertile ones). In the countries of Western Europe the age of marriage has been in the mid-twenties for females and late twenties for males over many centuries, thus eliminating almost a decade of possible childbearing for most individuals. All such customs have *aims* other than reducing the total fertility of the society, but they have that *result* just the same.

---

[19] A systematic statement of the many points of the birth process where social factors may affect fertility can be found in Kingsley Davis and Judith Blake, "Social Structure and Fertility: An Analytical Framework,"

Economic Development and Cultural Change, 4 (1956), pp. 211–235. See also Petersen, op. cit., pp. 204ff.

At the second major point in the phases of reproduction, that is, conception or the fertilization of the egg, for thousands of years people have tried to introduce various barriers and obstacles. Perhaps most of these forms of contraception have been imaginative rather than effective, and have been based more on magic than on a sound knowledge of either anatomy or physiology. Even as late as the eighteenth century, a man as keenly observant in these matters as Casanova could not distinguish between effective and ineffective techniques. It was only in the nineteenth century, when it became possible to make serviceable articles of rubber, that a reliable contraceptive device (the condom) was invented.

Nevertheless, even techniques that are less than perfect will have an important effect on the fertility of a whole population. Better techniques will yield better control, but if a population wishes to limit the number of children per family, they are likely to find some crudely useful ways to accomplish that goal. Until recently, the commonest form of contraceptive in most of the world was *coitus interruptus,* that is, withdrawing from the female at the point of ejaculation. This mode has been used especially in sexual intercourse *within* marriage, or wherever the male had to take responsibility for contraception because he would have to bear the costs of rearing the child (as in European courtship among peasants).

This technique is open to many accidents, but when used by large populations it does reduce the birthrate. Fertility in France began to drop in the last quarter of the 1700s, long before modern contraceptives were available. Within that long-term decline over the ensuing one hundred fifty years, it rose with prosperity and fell with hard times. Thus, we know that the French masses were controlling the number of children they had. Similarly, the United States birthrate began to drop in the early part of the nineteenth century, when it was still

scandalous even to mention publicly the idea of birth control.

With reference to the phases of both conception and pregnancy, or gestation, folk knowledge has, in all societies, contained a mixture of shrewd guess and wild speculation or magic. That sexual intercourse was connected with pregnancy seemed clear enough, but no systematic observations or experiments were made to discover the complex processes that make up the development of a healthy infant. In fact, research over the past ten years has revealed that process to be much more complex than biologists had known.

Folk belief was much more handicapped, because people did not report to one another about this very private area of action. However, people would have easily learned that most acts of sexual intercourse, even without contraception, did not result in pregnancy. Some couples never conceive, although they try. A large percentage of first pregnancies result in natural, or spontaneous, abortions, and many infants are born dead. Some couples conceive, although they use supposedly reliable contraceptives. Most amateur attempts at abortion in past centuries—strong laxatives, drugs to induce heavy vomiting, deliberately falling downstairs, poking objects into the female body—were not successful. Considering this array of contrary observations, it is not surprising that physicians and laypeople have generally held some odd beliefs.

Modern abortion is both safe and effective. Throughout most of human history it was neither, but it was used just the same. On the other hand, it did not have to be very effective in order to reduce the fertility of a large population. It was a traditional method of family limitation in peasant Japan, for example, where it was called "thinning" (a comparison with pulling out rice plants, to let the remaining ones grow better). It was denounced by the Church over many centuries of European history, but it continued anyway. Since World War II it has been given governmental approval in several countries at different times (Japan, Hungary, the United States), and it invariably reduces the birthrate sharply.

Infanticide as Population Control

Infanticide is the technique that is used at the last phase of the birth process. It permits a choice when the couple has the most knowledge about their ability to care for the child. At this time they (or the society) can also inspect the child to ascertain its acceptability. In the Greek city of Sparta defective children were exposed and left to die. In some societies twins were killed. In all societies where infanticide was practiced, female infants were more likely than males to be killed, or to be neglected so that they would be more likely to die. The poor have used this technique more because they were less able to care for their children.

Since at least the ninth century A.D. church and political leaders have denounced the shocking practice of killing infants or leaving them to die. More recently, historians have used both these repeated expressions of outrage and the continued practice as proof that parents (and especially mothers) once felt callous and indifferent towards their children.[20]

If such data can be viewed as proof, then parents all over the world have cared little for their children, since all major societies for which we have evidence engaged in infanticide. The practice proves little about parental attitudes, but much about the demographic situation in which most peasants and urban masses have lived in the past. That is, most have lived under constant threat from starvation or death by disease, knowing that most of their infants would not live as long as five years, facing a grind-

ing and hopeless poverty in which one more mouth to feed might well reduce the whole family to the danger point. Some infanticides were cases where young mothers thought to hide their shame from a harsh society. As a method of population control, infanticide is wasteful and inhumane, but in times past it was an answer to an inhumane demographic and social situation.

Mortality

In any given cohort of 1,000 infants, the likelihood of death is high at birth, and drops to a low point at about ten to fourteen years of age. It remains fairly low until the maturity of these survivors, and then begins to rise more rapidly. From middle age onward, the curve of mortality rises still more steeply, toward that inevitable point where all have died. In societies where infectious diseases are common and sanitation is primitive, some 20 to 40 percent of all newly born children may not survive the first year. In most societies before the twentieth century, most families did not include three generations living in the same household (as was often the ideal) because only a modest number of people survived to become grandparents in a large household.

The universality of death has many social consequences, and is itself affected by many social factors. First, it requires all societies to devise orderly procedures for handing over social roles as well as property from one generation to another. Second, because death itself appears arbitrary or unfair to both the unlucky individual and those who care for him or her, human beings have created religions and philosophies (as we noted in our discussion of culture and symbol systems) that view such events as part of a cosmic plan that may even be based on justice. Third, since death awaits us all, at unexpected moments, people must prepare for it in some way. For example, parents may have more children, knowing that only

[20]One such example is Edwin C. Shorter, *The Making of the Modern Family*, New York: Basic Books, 1975.

a few of them will survive long enough to become an economic support when the parents are old. Or, when a high percentage of people live to old age, as in industrial countries, some forms of old-age benefits are created, which the whole society must pay for.

A fourth consequence is the large number of commercial or governmental programs that are based, not on the whimsical and arbitrary character of death, but on its opposite. Though death is not easily anticipated as an individual event, as a mass event it can be predicted with considerable accuracy. Insurance companies have relied on this fact for several hundred years. Demographers compute what is called—with no intentional irony—*life tables.* They are summarized from the sex-specific chances of death at any given age, and are called *life* tables because in each succeeding column the number of *survivors* from the previous age group is shown. In effect, they carry a cohort of 100,000 individuals from birth until death. If the death rate of, say, men aged forty to forty-nine years rises, then the number surviving to age fifty and beyond will be lower, and the table must be revised. From it, one can calculate whether an annuity that is bought by women aged sixty-five will on the average have to be paid in ten, twelve, or more years.

Over the past century the rise in expectation of life in industrial countries has been caused mainly by a reduction in infant mortality. That is, the large rise since the nineteenth century (about forty years in the United States) to about sixty-eight years for white males and seventy-six years for white females occurred only partly because modern medicine keeps older people alive much longer. When infant mortality rates drop to, say, 40 to 50 per 1,000, the increase occurs because most babies live out their life-span. As a specific example, if we compare a life table from the mid-nineteenth century in England and Wales with one for 1970, we

see that about 150 infants would have failed to survive the first year in 1840, while that number had dropped to only 18 in 1970.[21]

All countries that introduce modern sanitation, insect control, vaccination, and other public health measures show quick drops in mortality, and correspondingly rapid increases in life expectation—again, because infant mortality drops quickly. However, *historical* changes in mortality, unless they were catastrophes such as the Black Death, the great epidemic of fourteenth-century Europe and Great Britain, are not so easy to demonstrate. For example, the British population increased from 1760 to 1840, that is, in the first stages of the industrial revolution; but historical demographers continue to argue about whether this was caused by a drop in mortality, a rise in fertility, or both.[22]

Differences in mortality are related, then, to many biological and socioeconomic factors. Let us note several of these:

Long-lived parents are more likely to have long-lived children—but note that they may share both a similar biological make-up and more healthful habits.

Groups or societies (for example, South Sea islanders, South American Indians) that had not been exposed to European diseases (smallpox, measles, syphilis) were unable to resist them, and thus exhibited high mortality rates at first contact with the whites.

Because of small genetic differences, some ethnic groups and races are especially susceptible to some diseases that are rare in the general population.

The poor have higher death rates than the well-to-do, United States blacks have higher death rates than whites, and Unit-

[21]Petersen, op. cit., pp. 579, 582.

[22]For a summary of the data and arguments on this point, see ibid., pp. 435–455.

ed States Indians have higher rates than either. These differences are growing smaller.[23]

From the beginning at conception in the womb, males show a higher mortality than females. In societies where childbirth deaths were or are high, the male death rate may drop below that of the female

[23]For a brief discussion of especially the first point, see David M. Heer, *Society and Population,* 2d ed., Englewood Cliffs, N.J.: Prentice-Hall, 1975, chap. 4. The first of these points is contested by some analysts, in part because of a confusion between death rates and disease rates, and in part because the differences themselves are growing smaller.

Figure 16-3 Mass starvation, one catastrophe aggravated by enormous growth in the population, is already being felt in a number of countries, including India. (Michael Putnam, Peter Arnold.)

during the childbearing years, but otherwise this female advantage exists throughout life. Doubtless, some part of the difference arises from the greater physical risks that males run, even in childhood, but it is also a *biological* difference. As life expectancies rise in modern societies, the gap between males and females grows larger.

Death rates from specific diseases (for example, certain types of cancer) may be rare in the general population, but extremely common in certain occupational groups, such as people who work with asbestos, coal, hardrock, phosphorus, or various plastics. Diseases caused by substances which industrial society finds useful but against which the human body has no defenses will doubtless continue to increase in the future.

The Modern Surge in World Population

Earlier in this chapter we noted that the modern rise in world population is more rapid than it has ever been, and that it will eventually come to a halt. The earth is geographically limited in its area as well as its resources. Either higher death rates or lower birthrates will stop that growth. Given the human capacity for blundering into catastrophe, it is unlikely that birthrates will drop in time to prevent large-scale disasters over the next few generations. Let us consider the dynamics of this massive process of population growth.

Prior to the British census of 1801, social analysts argued among themselves about whether the population was growing or declining, and most analysts of that time agreed that a growing population was good for the nation, both economically and militarily. In 1798 Thomas R. Malthus made a major contribution to that debate with his *Essay on Population,* and revised it many times over the ensuing decades to take account of criticisms. Even today, demographers continue to analyze the issues he raised.

In his first formulations Malthus argued that the human population will double every generation unless it is checked. That is, population grows *geometrically*: 2, 4, 8, 16, ... However, food from agriculture increases only arithmetically: 2, 4, 6, 8, 10, ... Later he amended this notion, but continued to assert that the tendency of human populations is to outstrip their food supply. Positive checks (misery, war, diseases, hard labor) may keep that tendency under control, and so may preventive checks (birth control devices, moral constraint, vice). His choice was moral constraint, for example, marrying late or not at all, or controlling one's sexual appetite in order to keep the number of children under control.

Malthus thought he had discovered that human populations differ from the things that are grown to feed them, for they grow at a different rate. In fact, what he was reporting and did not see clearly is that human beings are *like all* other growing things: *All* produce far more progeny than can survive to adulthood. That is, weeds, birds, wheat, cows, and human beings are all limited by nature. If far more are produced than the environment can sustain, then the mortality rate will increase. In a temporarily benign situation populations will expand fast, and soon they will be too large for that previously encouraging environment. Then stronger population checks will appear: For example, foxes expand fast, eat up the surplus rabbits, and then die off when the surplus is gone. Malthus argued that high wages will permit people to marry early and to produce more babies; but then the surplus labor will be paid less, and many will starve. He also argued that it does no good to give charity to the poor, for that only encourages the poor to have more babies, and wages will then drop still more.

As a set of specific predictions, Malthus's ideas were simply wrong. Populations in all countries since his time have expanded, but people's lives have not worsened as a result. In fact, more food is available in most countries, and more production of goods for people's comfort.

On the other hand, as a statement of dynamics, or as a general relationship, his basic idea is true by definition. *If productivity does not increase as fast as population, certainly the amount available per person must decrease.* If that gap widens by much, as it has in recent times in very poor areas such as Ethiopia, Bangladesh, and the strip of land (the *sahel*) running across Africa just south of the Sahara Desert, hundreds of thousands or even millions of people will die of starvation or of diseases and malnutrition. If, on the other hand, productivity continues to increase faster than population, again by *definition* the amount per person will also increase.

It is equally self-evident that at some as yet undefinable point it is extremely unlikely that the resources of the earth are sufficient to permit a continued *increase* in the amount of productivity per person—for all increases in productivity must be bought by using some part of the earth's resources. The scientific and humanitarian question remains, whether it is possible to create the socioeconomic conditions under which a maximum rise in productivity will also be accompanied by a drop in the birthrate, so that we shall not reach that point at which disaster becomes inevitable.[24] Scientific advances will increase the food supply over the next generation, but productivity cannot increase indefinitely. Water, minerals, and fertilizers will eventually be insufficient. Without question, the earth can support a population of

[24]For an especially gloomy statement of the near future, see Donella H. Meadows et al., *The Limits of Growth*, New York: Universe Books, 1972. Its predictions have been widely criticized, but the optimists have not offered a credible solution for the problems posed in this and similar books.

20 or even 30 billion, but with equal certainty we know that the quality of life will drop as a result.

The dynamics of the immediate situation have been described many times, and can be briefly summarized here. In the Western nations that became industrialized in the course of the nineteenth century, the birthrate dropped gradually in the countries that entered industrialization earlier, and somewhat faster in other Western countries, but in all of them this transition was gradual enough to permit some balance between birth and death rates while productivity increased. That is, although death rates dropped, so did birthrates. Births did not drop as fast as deaths, but the natural increase did not outstrip *production* increases.

Before that time, that is, throughout most of human history, we know that the world's human population grew very slowly, and in many areas may have grown little or none over hundreds of years. That is, populations exhibited a high fertility (perhaps forty to fifty births per thousand population annually) and an equally high mortality. In prosperous times the population rose, and in times of pestilence, war, or starvation it dropped.

In almost all societies a high value is placed on fertility, and a good part of childhood socialization is focused on training to become parents. Perhaps societies emphasize reproduction because it is *not* self-evident that being very fertile is advantageous for the *individual;* it is simply useful for the *society.* That emphasis on fertility is useful to the society as long as death rates remain high, for it permits the society to recoup its losses whenever a catastrophe occurs.

However, modern science has created a totally new situation in the less developed nations, that is, a swift drop in death rates, while people's attitudes about fertility have changed very little. Tens of millions of dollars have been spent over the past two dec-

ades in birth control experiments in various parts of the underdeveloped world, and most of these have been failures. Although many participants will take part in such experiments, they do not usually change their basic patterns of behavior. Individuals may claim that they would like to know about birth control methods, and even express some wish to limit the number of children, but the number of children they would like to have will be large enough to double the country's population in one generation just the same.

Note the nature of the social processes that social scientists and political leaders are attempting to set in motion. Public health measures can generally be introduced with little change in the individual habits of a population. Sanitation measures can be introduced, clean water can be supplied, insects can be sprayed, and mass innoculations or vaccinations can control many diseases. In addition, no great changes in attitudes are required to persuade people to utilize at least some modern medical techniques. After all, most people do want to continue to live. *Contraception .*

By contrast, the advantages of <u>contraception</u> are not always clear to the individual. Without question, if a couple uses <u>contraception,</u> they will be just as poor a <u>month</u> from now. No change in their socioeconomic condition will result. Moreover, using contraceptives of any kind requires discipline and a new set of habits. Most contraceptive devices require that some specific action be taken almost every time that sexual intercourse takes place. Parents continue to believe, especially in agricultural areas, that their future welfare depends at least in part on rearing sons to adulthood who can care for them in their old age.

It is not surprising, then, that in spite of some temporary success, there are very few large-scale and continued drops in fertility in most of the underdeveloped nations of the world. It should be added that the United States population, too, continues to grow, and that there has been no large-scale change in ideal family size in this country.[25]

Between the gloomy forecasts of some demographers and the optimistic assurances of people who believe that science will somehow find a solution is the possibility that some of the socioeconomic changes now taking place within less developed countries will reduce fertility substantially, though they cannot reduce fertility fast enough to prevent a doubling of the population over the next thirty-five or forty years. Urbanization, for example, typically reduces birthrates somewhat. The entrace of women into the industrial labor force (as contrasted with being a part of the agricultural labor force) also reduces birthrates somewhat. When parents learn that under the new patterns of infant survival it is almost certain that many of their children will grow to maturity, it is at least plausible that many will begin to control their fertility. Where abortion has been approved by the government, birthrates also drop.

On the other hand, in almost no countries has a full-scale effort been made to reduce birthrates to a level that would actually balance death rates. Consequently, we can expect a continued rise in world population in the generations to come.

INDUSTRIALIZATION AS A FACTOR IN WORLD CHANGE

Since the impact of industrialization has been noted in almost every chapter of this book, we shall comment on it only briefly at

[25]For data on this last point, see Judith Blake, "Ideal Family Size among White Americans: A Quarter Century's Evidence," *Demography,* 1 (1966), pp. 154–173; and "Can We Believe Recent Data on Birth Expectations in the United States?" *Demography,* 11 (1974), pp. 25–44. On the acceptance by Catholics of contraceptives, see Charles F. Westoff and Larry Bumpass, "The Revolution in Birth Control Practices of U.S. Roman Catholics," *Science,* 179 (1973), pp. 41–44.

this point, with special reference to it as a *world* process.

Clearly, populations that move to the city must increasingly rely on industrialization, simply because modern technology is needed for the transportation of food and individuals, for water supply and sanitation, medicines, chemical fertilizers for the farms that feed the cities, and factories for other production. Industrialization at a rapid rate is also necessary for higher productivity if the growing populations of the world are to be saved from disaster. Thus, the three great factors discussed in this chapter are closely interlinked.

Our continuing concern with industrialization has highlighted its importance as a *transforming* factor. Countries that industrialize also change their social structure. In order to gain the benefits of a single machine, people may not have to change their social patterns; but to develop a whole productive system based upon machines, much of the social structure will change, whether or not people desire that result.

However, we must consider more closely what is meant when social analysts assert that a wide variety of consequences flow from industrialization or urbanization. Both factors are sometimes thought to be the cause of most of what is viewed as bad or good in the modern epoch. Generally, social analysts are simply recognizing that almost everyone is absorbed or enmeshed somehow in these large-scale processes, but it is somewhat difficult to pinpoint exactly how these processes create those supposed results: for example, high crime rates, high divorce rates, intellectual creativity, high illegitimacy rates, the rise in relief rolls, unemployment and depression, war, or social change generally. In fact, it is difficult to *prove* just how much *either* of these great processes contributes to *any* of those outcomes.

The reason for this difficulty is that urbanization and industrialization constitute a *total* social pattern that includes almost any single factor we can think of. We cannot test whether either is a single but large social factor, or instead simply constitutes the whole fabric of modern society. Specifically, we cannot find a society that is just like the United States *except* for industrialization or urbanization, so that we then can compare exactly what either great factor does. Instead, we are tempted to compare small, preliterate, traditional societies with the United States, and then to suppose that some unitary process called industrialization or urbanization caused all those differences.

Yet a broader historical view informs us that industrialization itself once had to be *caused* by factors operating in societies that were not yet industrialized. Perhaps it is the spread of such underlying factors that caused both urbanization *and* the peculiar characteristics of modern societies. As that development proceeded, Western societies changed in many ways, but industrialization includes so wide a set of subprocesses that we cannot set it apart as a single factor whose direct effect can be easily tested. This is also the case for urbanization.[26]

Nevertheless, we can discern the central technical factor that defines the degree of industrialization that any nation exhibits, and we can observe some of the social patterns that are characteristic of a general process of industrialization.

As we noted in our extended discussion of work and occupations, a technological system can be defined as more or less industrialized to the extent that it uses more or less inanimate power and harnesses that power to drive machines.[27] Inanimate power in-

cludes wind and water flow, but the amount utilized in most societies is fairly small before the development of dams for hydroelectric power. The use of inanimate power rises high only when steam engines are built, and spurts to still higher levels with the development of electrical energy. As we noted earlier, a machine is a tool that can substitute for some skill formerly done by hand, such as twisting cotton to make thread or weaving cloth. Harnessing the two together, as Marx pointed out, generates a vast number of social and economic changes—or at least does so when they interact with other social factors. Some of these have been noted in various chapters and need not be discussed at length. Here, however, let us simply summarize a few of them:

The first important result is that machines can substitute for human beings. Thereby all skills become downgraded because a machine can execute them, but new skills are required (repairing machines, furnishing raw materials, designing new machines, supervision) so that though some segments of the work force lose temporarily, there is a *general* upgrading of labor skills in the total work force over time. This has now continued for generations in Western countries.

Because industrialization in this narrow sense requires a heavy capital investment (that is, paying for the machines and the power), it becomes necessary to obtain more control over the entire production and selling process in order to ensure less waste and more profit, whether this occurs in a capitalist or a communist nation.

Thus, evaluation of individuals is increasingly made by reference to their *job effi-*

---

[26]For an extended commentary on the fact that family patterns can change without much industrialization, but industrialization does not cause a breakdown in all family patterns, and that preindustrial family patterns may well have eased the development of industrialization in the West, see William J. Goode, *World Revolution and Family Patterns* (1963) New York: Free Press, 1970, especially pp. ix–xxx, chap. 1, and "Conclusion."

[27]This is close to Marion J. Levy's definition of "mod-

ernization." See his *Modernization and the Structure of Societies*, Princeton, N.J.: Princeton, 1966, vol. 1, p. 11.

ciency and the level of skills they command, and far less by reference to the prestige rank of their families.

Because machines are best at repetitive tasks linked together in complex ways, both factory production and business increasingly support the development of bureaucratic organizations and especially corporations (this process was discussed in greater detail in Chapter 7, "Formal Organizations"). Thus, much of modern life is enmeshed in bureaucratic processes.

Because even small improvements in machine or bureaucratic techniques may yield great advantages (for their output may number in the millions of units), much energy and talent can be wisely invested in both *innovation* and *planning*. Thus, prestige and economic rewards are given to people who carry out those tasks well.

As industrialization develops in this manner, thousands of new, specialized jobs are created.

Land ownership decreases in importance, and the control over capital becomes a more significant base for both political influence and social rank.

Aristocracy of birth becomes less influential politically; the lower social strata lose whatever allegiance they once felt to their lords; and workers can threaten strikes or disorder to gain economic and political advantage.

Since education or training becomes the most important basis for getting a job, and people are less dependent on their family elders for jobs or promotions, young people need not obey the wishes of their parents in decisions about mate choice or other matters.

Whether or not the links we suggest above are easily proved, it is at least clear that whenever industrialization begins to spread in a society, these and many other changes also appear.

Figure 16-4   The miniskirt and the kimono together illustrate the acceptance of both old and new in modern Japan. (Barry J. Shlachter, Nancy Palmer Photo Agency.)

These changes are supported by an *ideology* of industrialization, which gains converts before any factories are built. This ideology is frequently supported by a politically revolutionary ideology, typically Marxist, that presents a vision of a future society in which prosperity for all will come from industrialization. Before many factories have been built or the society has been transformed by industrialization, some people come to believe that individuals *should* be hired on the basis of merit, not family connection, and that industrialization is a necessary step toward improvement (though in many countries more efficient agriculture will increase the national income faster). They also come to believe that education and training programs should be geared to industrial needs, and that traditional ways should be discarded because they impede industrialization.

For these reasons the ideology of industrialization has a large political impact. Since only the upper classes in most underdeveloped countries have the capital with which to exploit the new opportunities, at the first stages of attempted industrialization they are likely to become still richer. On the other hand, the steps toward industrialization may well create a considerable amount of dissension among members of the upper social strata, because former leaders would prefer to follow traditional ways, to use the new opportunities for enriching family members, and to keep people from the lower social strata from obtaining political influence or new economic opportunities; other members of the same strata may view themselves as the vanguard of the future. At some phase, political attacks on the upper strata may become widespread. In the modern world any major steps toward industrialization are accompanied by considerable economic and political turmoil.

Almost all the political leaders of the less developed new nations—now comprising most of the world's population—argue (with considerable merit) that their economies have been held back by the exploitation of the Western capitalist nations. All have embarked on a program of industrialization. Thus, political freedom as a political cause is closely linked with industrialization as an ideology. Consequently, almost all these countries are attempting to alter their socioeconomic structures. Because few of these "revolutions" have removed from power all the formerly privileged groups, bitter fighting about these plans and programs continues to break out.

Moreover, as we pointed out in our chapter on political processes, industrialization is much more difficult to achieve than was once believed. By now, hundreds of millions of dollars have been spent in various countries in order to implement an industrialization program, but only a few countries can claim general success. Economists, sociologists, and anthropologists from both capitalist and communist nations have worked on both the theoretical and the practical problems of such programs, and there is little agreement about the best solutions.

There is general agreement on one important point, that the model of development followed by Western nations is not likely to occur in other nations. Each of the new nations begins from a very different base, for example, a lower level of literacy, higher birth and death rates, a lower level of both wealth and productivity, a greater need to move fast, stronger controls for the government. Even Japan, the only case of a feudal nation that moved independently into industrialization, did not follow the Western model.

As a consequence, neither Western advisers nor the leaders of less developed nations can solve their problems by simply finding out how the industrial revolution unfolded in Europe and the United States during the nineteenth century.

The difficulty of industrialization increases the political instability of the less developed countries. Modern industrialization requires a national mobilization of effort as well as capital, political trust as well as technical competence, a politically and socially legitimate government as well as engineers. Almost no new government enjoys all these advantages, as we pointed out earlier in this volume. New governments can get those advantages primarily by producing the desired results quickly. Since they are not likely to achieve those goals swiftly, these governments are likely to be soon under threat, just as the *former* governments were.

All these prophecies are widely observable in the modern world. It seems likely that in the near future we shall continue to see these political and social effects of the global press toward industrialization.

SUMMARY

In this chapter we have analyzed the dynamics of three massive world processes that are affecting everyone's life. They are all extremely complex in their causes and widespread in their effects. They are also closely intertwined with each other, while none of them can simply be thought of as completely caused by the others.

The first two, urbanization and population growth, are the result of countless decisions made by individuals, for their own purposes and often against the wishes of their political leaders. The third, industrialization, is a process in which leaders of less developed nations as well as industrial ones have invested much money and talent, often with little success.

Debates continue about what were the conditions that first caused genuine cities to arise and flourish at some point about nine to ten thousand years ago in what is now Iraq and Turkey. We reported some guesses about that process; and we pointed out that whether agriculture or cities arose first, two did accompany one another. And even if the first cities were very small, they did engage in trade and taxation, erect public buildings, use writing, and have a central government (and very likely, warlike kings); and they probably counted as community members all who were legally citizens, rather than using kinship as the basis for being part of the community.

Even those few differences suggest a new set of social forces in human life. As we noted in our earlier discussion of *Gemeinschaft* and *Gesellschaft,* social analysts have continued to speak of these differences for well over two thousand years. One result of the differences (including the accumulation of wealth, the control of taxation and laws, innovation and the arts, control over trade) is the dominance of the city in almost all aspects of national life, whether the country is urban or rural.

We also pointed out that many social analysts have described urban life as cold, impersonal, rootless, and disorganized. However, human beings have always had a somewhat uneasy relationship with the city; and the city is partly a victim of stereotypes, which usually emphasize its less attractive qualities. These only partly fit the reality. In modern cities people visit their kin very likely as much as people did in rural regions a century ago, take part in neighborhood social interaction, are known to many others, protect each other's safety in most neighborhoods, and are much less anonymous than one would suppose from journalistic accounts of the city.

We documented at some length the increase in world urbanization, that is, the greater *number* of urban people and the greater *fraction* of the world that is urban. Both are increasing more rapidly than in the past, although for about a century the rate of increase has not changed much. The present changes are more spectacular than in the past, because the sheer numbers of people involved are much greater: For example, about 1.6 billion people live in an urban place, and there are about forty cities in agricultural and tropical countries with over one million inhabitants.

We pointed out both some basic data and some seeming paradoxes within these world processes. For example, more people in mainly rural countries than in industrial ones are streaming toward cities; but the increase in the *fraction* or percentage that is urban grows at a more rapid rate in industrial countries, because in the rural countries the rural population itself is growing at the fastest rate ever in history.

In addition, although major cities are growing fast, they are becoming less *dense,* because they grow outward (taking in more territory) rather than upward. Also, rural populations in the more developed countries outside Europe are dropping or only growing slowly, while little agricultural land is being added. Therefore, the number of agricultural workers per square mile of arable land is *decreasing* in the *well-off* nations, but increasing in the poorer nations. This is one more factor in the push of people toward cities. In the poorer countries they are fleeing a lack of rural opportunities, rather than being attracted by large urban ones.

Though world leaders have deplored the squalor of life in the shantytowns huddled within great cities of the less developed countries, the United States has been confronting urban decay in the central districts of its metropolises as well. We have analyzed this process, noting the many factors that create that result. The financial mismanagement in large cities is accompanied by a flight to the suburbs of middle-class citizens, both black and white, and by the failure of the federal and state legislatures to make any organized plan to improve urban life.

The world population of 4 billion people is now doubling every thirty-five years. Its rate of growth is 2 percent a year, and in some tropical countries the rate is 3 percent. By the year 2000 the world population is likely to be 6 to 7 billion people. This rate cannot continue indefinitely. There is not that much space on the earth. Long before we run out of space, we shall run out of food or other natural resources. However, in many less developed countries the amount of income per capita is already dropping as population rises faster than productivity. Local disasters caused by the combination of food shortages, diseases, and malnutrition have already occurred here and there. They are likely to occur on a larger scale in the future if the rate of natural increase (births minus deaths) does not slow down drastically.

As we noted, such forecasts of a dismal future are based on more than guess. For example, we already know how many people will move into the childbearing ages by 1995. We cannot predict exactly when and where the next substantial shortages and epidemics will occur, but they are most likely to happen where the natural increase is fast outrunning productivity. In our analysis of this world process, we considered the factors of fecundity (the biological ability to reproduce), fertility (the actual birthrate), and mortality. For the purposes of our analysis, we did not consider the other important demographic variable, migration, for on a global scale this cannot increase population at all.

We noted that social factors affect fertility and mortality at many points, just as the rates of births and deaths affect social structures eventually. For most of world history, human populations showed a very high rate of births and deaths, roughly in balance over literally hundreds of years. The world's population increased extremely slowly throughout all its history, until about the eighteenth century. In general, human societies have attempted to control fertility at various phases in the reproductive cycle, and we noted some of the consequences of controlling at the earliest points (sexual contacts between fecund males and females) or when the child is actually born (the possibility of infanticide). The modern world has witnessed a fundamental change in the balance between births and deaths that was typical throughout almost all of human history. Modern science has permitted the drastic reduction of death rates, especially infant mortality rates, in many countries, without being able to make corresponding changes in birthrates.

One reason for this is the fact that all societies attempt to socialize their children to want to become parents, and also teach them that parenthood is one of the few sources of economic support in old age. By contrast with the contemporary scene, in the early stages of the industrial revolution, births began to drop, and so did death rates. Although the rate of natural increase was fairly large, productivity continued to rise faster than population, and over time both births and deaths continued in some fair balance. In the Western world, then, the change to a lower death rate was not sudden, and people had literally generations in which to adjust to the new demographic pattern, that is, the high likelihood that almost all of one's children would in fact survive to adulthood.

Optimists continue to believe that the forces that apparently reduce population growth in Western countries (urbanization, industrialization, the entrance of women into the labor force, the survival of most children to adulthood, abortion) will also succeed in bringing a balance between births and deaths in less developed countries. On the other hand, the populations of Western nations (including that of the United States) continue to increase, though all of them already face some serious shortages of natural resources. In our discussion of Malthus's theories of population, we noted that his specific predictions were incorrect, but that some of the dynamics he presented are correct by definition. At a minimum, it is clear that there are varying limits to population growth, depending on when different kinds of shortages may develop, how willing we are to tolerate a substantial drop in the quality of life, and the unforeseeable outbreak of various kinds of epidemics or local shortages of food.

Industrialization is the third great world process we analyzed briefly in this chapter, drawing on comments and discussions that have been presented throughout this volume. The close dependence of all populations on industrialization is a new phenomenon in world history. If modern technology were to cease tomorrow, people would rapidly be unable to survive at the high population densities the world now contains, and cities would cease to function almost immediately.

Industrialization is dependent on the use of inanimate power harnessed to machines.

However, it permits a great number of options in economic and social relations that do not exist when the tool is directed only by the human hand and power only comes from horses or from other people. The industrial revolution began with machines that could outperform any human being in existence, and the technology on which machines are based permitted a continuing development of efficiency. Consequently, machines could gradually supplant human beings in a wide array of skills and activities. We noted some of the far-reaching social consequences of these changes.

The ideology of industrialization affects many of the political events that take place in less developed countries as well as industrial ones. All over the world, both world leaders and illiterate farmers are likely to believe that it is necessary for the poorer countries to industrialize as quickly as possible, and that industrialization will yield opportunities for people who suffer disadvantages under their present system. Frequently, the press toward industrialization is intensified by a vision of a future society in which there will be prosperity for all, and in which the entrenched privileges of upper-class families will be reduced or abolished.

The importance of industrialization as a political issue on a global scale is underscored by recurrent political instability in the new nations of the world, a process which we have analyzed in this chapter and which we shall take note of in the following chapter as well. Here we have emphasized the technical difficulty of industrialization, a large theoretical and practical problem that has engaged the talents and investments of both capitalist and communist countries. Modern governments in less developed nations are under great pressure to get results quickly, but the task is now seen as more difficult than analysts once believed. It is at least clear that the less developed nations cannot simply follow the historical model of Europe, Great Britain, and the United

States. At the present time there are few cases of general success in the steps toward industrialization. Japan's success is striking; but it did not follow the model of the West, and it is unlikely that other nations could follow its footsteps, for they began from very different bases.

Whatever the difficulties and however unknown the steps toward industrialization, it is at least clear that at the present time no other road toward solving these world problems is likely to be taken seriously by most of the world's population.

READINGS

David E. Apter, *The Profits of Modernization,* Chicago: Univeristy of Chicago Press, 1965.

Norman Birnbaum, *The Crisis of Industrial Society,* New York: Oxford, 1969.

C. E. Black, *The Dynamics of Modernization: A Study in Comparative History,* New York: Harper & Row, 1966.

Kingsley Davis, *World Urbanization 1950–1970, vol. I: Basic Data for Cities, Countries, and Regions,* Population Monograph ser. no. 4, Berkeley: University of California Press, 1969; and vol. II: *Analysis of Trends, Relationships, and Developments,* Population Monograph, ser. no. 9, Berkeley: University of California Press, 1972.

Thomas R. Ford and Gordon F. DeJong, eds., *Social Demography,* Englewood Cliffs, N.J.: Prentice-Hall, 1970.

George M. Foster, *Traditional Societies and Technological Change,* New York: Harper & Row, 1973.

Francine R. Frankel, *India's Green Revolution: Economic Gains and Political Costs,* Princeton, N.J.: Princeton, 1971.

Herbert J. Gans, *The Urban Villagers: Group and Class in the Life of Italian-Americans,* New York: Free Press, 1962.

David V. Glass and D. E. C. Eversley, eds., *Population in History,* Chicago: Aldine, 1965.

David M. Heer, *Society and Population,* 2d ed., Englewood Cliffs, N.J.: Prentice-Hall, 1975.

Jane Jacobs, *The Death and Life of Great American Cities,* New York: Vintage, 1961.

———, *The Economy of Cities,* New York: Vintage, 1970.

Robert E. Kennedy, *The Irish: Immigration, Marriage and Fertility,* Berkeley: University of California Press, 1973.

Marion J. Levy, *Modernization: Late-Comers and Survivors,* New York: Basic Books, 1972.

Thomas R. Malthus, *An Essay on the Principle of Population,* Totowa, N.J.: Rowman & Littlefield, 1973.

Carl Meadows and Ephraim H. Mizruchi, eds., *Urbanism, Urbanization, and Change: Comparative Perspectives,* Reading, Mass.: Addison-Wesley, 1969.

Donella H. Meadows et al., *The Limits of Growth,* New York: Universe Books, 1972.

William Mengin, ed., *Peasants in Cities: Readings in the Anthropology of Urbanization,* Boston: Houghton Mifflin, 1970.

Wilbert E. Moore, *The Impact of Industry,* Englewood Cliffs, N.J.: Prentice Hall, 1965.

Lewis Mumford, *The Culture of Cities* (1938), New York: Harcourt Brace Jovanovich, 1970.

J. John Palen, *The Urban World,* New York: McGraw-Hill, 1975.

William Petersen, *Population,* 3d ed., New York: Macmillan, 1975.

Stephen Thernstrom and Richard Sennett, eds., *Nineteenth Century Cities: Essays in the New Urban History,* New Haven, Conn.: Yale, 1969.

Charles F. Westoff and Larry Bumpass, "The Revolution in Birth Control Practices of U.S. Roman Catholics," *Science,* 179 (1973), pp. 444.

CHAPTER SEVENTEEN

(United Nations, T. Chen.)

EPILOGUE: AN EMERGING WORLD SYSTEM?

SOCIOPOLITICAL CHANGES

In this and the previous chapter we speak of *world* changes because (1) they are happening over much or all of the world; and (2) what happens anywhere will affect the rest of the world, since no part of it is insulated from any other part. In the previous chapter we considered three massive, complex sets of forces—urbanization, population growth, and industrialization—which have been extending their impact on social structures for the past two centuries, and at a somewhat increasing speed for the last fifty years.

In this final chapter we consider briefly some additional changes. They are:

1 The move from kings to dictators
   a The increasing power of national governments
   b The decline of communal networks
       relative to the influence of national patterns
   c The loss of privacy
   d The loss of authority and deference
2 The social effect of the atomic bomb
3 Pollution and the exhaustion of natural resources
4 The growth of science

Because these changes have such far-reaching consequences, they have all appeared at various points in this volume. However, we bring all of them together here because we wish to look at them all with reference to their effect on the world, on the social structures of individual nations, and on the relations among nations as part of the world community.

Moreover, all of our long list of changes can be considered together, even though each has an independent effect, because all of them are interlinked to some extent. For example, the atomic bomb and pollution are an outgrowth of scientific and industrial developments; science gives new modes of control to dictators; the loss of authority has helped to remove kings and colonial rulers; the ideology of industrialization has helped to put new dictators in power; population growth feeds urbanization and increases the impact of pollution. Though these changes are interlinked, they do not grow from one great cause, and each deserves an independent analysis.

The first set of changes may be viewed as sociopolitical, and in fact we discussed some of them in our chapter on political processes. The atomic bomb, pollution, and the exhaustion of natural resources are all caused by industrialization and the growth of science, but here we shall take note of them only with respect to their importance for world social changes. Similarly, we shall consider the growth of science only with reference to its importance for solving some of these world social problems. That is, in our brief comments on these changes we are mostly concerned with the ways that industrial and scientific developments affect the nation and the social order of the world, and whether the science that led to these problems may help to solve them.

Finally, we shall consider a major question that confronts the entire world: Since nations are changing in similar ways because of these geographical, biological, technological, and social factors, and thus are becoming interlinked in so many ways, is it likely that a new world community will emerge?

From Kings to Dictators

Let us consider the set of political changes that we have put under the general heading of the decline of kings and the rise of dictators.

Just before the outbreak of World War I,

most of the earth's population was ruled by monarchs. Some dynasties had been in power for hundreds of years, while others were much more recent. At the end of that war, which marks a major watershed in world history, many of those empires and kingdoms began to dissolve. Shortly after World War II almost no countries were ruled by emperors or kings, and most of the remaining monarchs were simply figureheads, as in Norway and England. Even after World War II some countries still had colonies under their control. Now there are almost none.

However, this destruction of a traditional authoritarianism did not lead to an increase in democratic governments. Instead, a bewildering succession of dictators arose, to hold power briefly or for decades (as in Portugal and Spain). They were kept in power by military force and secret police and by their ability to persuade their subjects that they would lead the nation to glory, freedom, and economic success.

There is little reason to lament the disappearance of monarchies, with their expensive, colorful aristocracy; and we need not suppose, with American ethnocentrism, that all these nations really had the choice of setting up constitutional governments that would guarantee civic liberties but also raise per capita income. True enough, most of these dictatorships fail in maintaining order, achieving legitimacy (discussed at some length in the chapter on political processes), and creating an adequate economy. The problems they face were and are difficult; and even after the fact, one cannot be sure what wiser courses should have been pursued.

We are not concerned, then, with criticizing this change but with noting that it has had great effects on social structures the world over. One can ask the question, "Are there any differences at all?" After all, one might say that once there were kings who repressed freedom and exploited their subjects, and now there are dictators who do the same thing.

However, modern dictatorships are different from both monarchies of the past and old-style Latin American rulers in the past and present, in ways that affect the social order. Or, to reemphasize the sociological orientation that looks for still deeper factors, we may instead say that the massive forces that shape the modern world make monarchies intolerable, but permit dictatorships to flourish. In any case, we can note some of the sociostructural differences between the two.

Kings once faced different problems than modern dictators do, and thus their solutions were different. To rule in a stable manner, even a "good king" had only to persuade his subjects that he was trying to protect them from invasion and from daily injustices *within* the nation: for example, the cruelty of a baron, or overly high prices for bread. He did not have to promise that he would alter the system so as to achieve new freedoms and economic development. He could count at least on his subjects' passive acceptance of his right to rule. That is, unless really serious difficulties arose, he was considered legitimate.[1]

By contrast, as we noted in the chapter on political processes, the modern dictator *typically* faces the problem of establishing legitimacy, or authority to rule. To gain office the dictator had to overthrow another one and to persuade followers that older traditions

Figure 17-1 Spanish dictator General Francisco Franco arranged that after his death he would be succeeded by Prince Juan Carlos de Bourbon, whose family had ruled in Spain before Franco held power. (Wide World Photos.)

should not be followed. However, since people do not obey on the basis of traditional authority, the dictator must act quickly and effectively to achieve the results that were promised. Success is unlikely. National achievements, economic development, or civic freedoms are goals that may require generations to establish. However, if success is not quick, still other groups will threaten to take over the government. In the modern world the life of dictators is dramatic, and it offers many temporary rewards of adulation and material pleasures, but not stability.

Even temporary dictators may have a substantial effect on the social structure, because (at least briefly) they can muster some national support for change. They have, after all, gained their position by committing themselves to great changes. To carry out those promises, they must use all their force and persuasion to alter many parts of the society. To do this, they must try to *mobilize* their people, that is, arouse their interest, involve them in new programs,

[1] The general loss of authority by people in power, that is, their unquestioned right to command or their *legitimacy*, has been noted by many commentators for decades. For an insightful discussion of deference see Edward A. Shils, "Deference," in Edward O. Laumann et al., *The Logic of Social Hierarchies*, Chicago: Markham, 1970, pp. 420–428. See also the data in Robert MacKenzie and Allan Silver, *Angels in Marble: Working Class Conservatives in Urban England*, Chicago: University of Chicago Press, 1968, which suggest that authority and deference have been of importance in the maintenance of conservative political parties in Great Britain over nearly a century. This topic was discussed in our chapter on political processes.

loosen their allegiance to traditional ways by force or by new opportunities, and increase their willingness to sacrifice for collective goals.

To make such changes, dictators seek to establish a direct relationship between each subject and themselves, or at least between each subject and the national government. In traditional societies of the past, although the king's authority was officially absolute or nearly so, his legitimacy was partly based on the support of many smaller social units to which the individual citizen also owed allegiance: an aristocracy, a landed gentry, groups or councils of village elders, local peace officers, guilds, or kindred. On a day-to-day basis, the individual was controlled by those *communal* ties, and these support-ed the king as long as he ruled in traditional ways.[2] Such communal units served local interests, commanded group loyalties, and thus were never entirely subservient to the king's will except as he followed custom.

By contrast, modern dictators must weak-en those community relations precisely be-cause they have some independence and they do support older traditions. They must persuade their subjects to give their loyalty to the dictator personally.

Modern technology can be harnessed to these ends. Command of radio, television, and the newspapers permits the dictator to appeal directly to subjects, and especially to prevent any groups or organizations that are not simply the dictator's agents from using the media. Techniques for spying are more effective than in the past: Independent radio broadcasts can be tracked down, letters can be opened and sealed again without leaving a trace, and hidden microphones listen in on conversations.

Thus, the ordinary citizen feels, and is

vulnerable to, a direct supervision of his or her life by the national government and thus by the dictator. In addition, because no one can be sure who might be listening, and people who are listening may feel loyalty to the dictator, people have far less trust in even their friends. The result of that distrust is that even the links of friendship are less likely to grow into cells of opposition to the dictator.

Though the privacy of both individuals and independent groups is undermined, it should be remembered that in traditional monarchies also people had little privacy. After all, villagers have always kept a close watch on each other's actions, and so have aristocrats at court. Little is hidden for long. The differences now are that (1) the de-struction of that privacy is in the service of the dictator and the national government, not the local group and its autonomy; (2) technology makes it easier to know what many people are doing and to keep records about them; and (3) the consequences of being found out are likely to be imprison-ment and torture, rather than the disapprov-al of one's neighbors.

Thus, we observe the seeming paradox that modern dictatorships create powerful national governments, but they are also more fragile and less stable than govern-ments of the past. They are much more *active* than monarchies of the past in seek-ing change, but they also fail at accomplish-ing the greater goals they have set for themselves. They offer freedom, but attack people who try to get it. As a consequence of these complex forces, the social structures of most societies are undergoing great changes. There is little evidence that dicta-torships will be any less prevalent in the generations to come than at present.

The Social Effect of the Atomic Bomb

The existence of various kinds of atomic bombs and missiles capable of delivering

[2]A recent work that laments the decline in the authori-ty of communal relationships such as the family, the church, or other community organizations, in *Twilight of Authority,* by Robert A. Nisbet, New York: Oxford, 1975.

them to particular targets constitutes literally a threat to the entire human population, and thus the bomb inaugurates a new phase in history. However, it is not clear how much, or through what processes, all this affects social structure. Doubtless, for many people this threat is as abstract a potential catastrophe as a large-scale earthquake in San Francisco. That is, everyone knows it may take place; but since people do not know when and they feel there is little they can do about it, they give it little thought. As a result, they do not change any of their social behavior. That now it is possible for almost any nation to manufacture a bomb does not change by much their attitude or how they interact with one another.

The bomb and mass war generally have nevertheless changed the United States sociopolitical structure and its economic patterns as well, in ways that are well known. They have had similar consequences in other industrial nations. Let us simply note them here:

1 The great destructiveness of such a war has convinced even high government leaders in both Russia and the United States that neither country should develop war machines as fully as possible, since either can kill much of the citizenry of the other country, and both countries feel these costs are too high. It is pointless to increase this killing capacity. After all, under perfect conditions both have enough bombs to kill everyone on the other side many times over, and surely even once is enough.

2 Since an atomic war is too destructive, small wars or military operations are used instead to exert political pressures on other nations. As a consequence, for the first time in its history, the United States has continued to maintain a large standing army at great cost to its economy.

3 The size and complexity of defense and attack systems have enmeshed much of the political and economic structure in these activities; a high percentage of the population now has a political and economic stake in maintaining or developing military systems.

4 Because the nation itself cannot use all the war systems it manufactures, but needs the industries themselves in case of an emergency, the United States has become the largest source of war material in the world: It now sells arms to other countries at an annual rate of over $9 billion a year. However, other industrial nations do compete in this trade, and thus we must view this as a change that affects the world.

Pollution and the Exhaustion of Natural Resources

These two changes arise mainly from technological developments, and they threaten the quality of life everywhere. In the United States critical changes in technology after World War II shifted production from natural organic materials (cotton, wool, wood) to various kinds of synthetics, and to a wide array of new chemicals (growth hormones for livestock, pesticides, propellant gases for spray cans) whose side effects have turned out to be lethal. In addition, we have learned that many older substances (asbestos, preservatives, smoke) also increase death rates. As we noted in our chapter on geographic processes, this humanly created geography effects a new environment that is dangerous to humanity.

We also pointed out in that chapter that the currently known supply of many raw materials essential to industrialization (oil, copper) will not last for more than a few more decades at current consumption levels. Still more important is the fact that not enough of them exist to permit underdeveloped nations to rise to the industrial levels

Figure 17-2   Pollution has become so bad that this river near Cleveland caught fire. (Kendzierski, *Plain Dealer.*)

of any of the rich countries. For example, the known reserves of copper are not sufficient to allow India to industrialize at the level of the Netherlands. Thus, the aspiration toward full industrial development in one part of the world is barred by consumption rates or shortages in another. The ultimate sociopolitical consequences of this cannot be foreseen at present.

The Growth of Science as a Solution?

Most engineering and manufacturing knowledge in the Western countries developed independently of science until well into the nineteenth century. However, by the end of that century almost all the new technologies were made possible by scientific discoveries. The modern world is the first ever to base much of its productivity and even many of its social decisions on scientific research.

Science has also become one of the major social institutions of industrial nations. From being a part-time activity of scholars and amateurs in the seventeenth century, it has come to absorb the attention and energies of millions of workers, as well as billions of dollars in research budgets. New nations rapidly attempt to set up research laboratories, for they are a mark of progress. The general ethic and ideology of science is taught to school children: for example, that the scientist should be skeptical toward traditional knowledge; that the scientist should discard his or her own ideas if research proves them wrong; that esteem should be given to those who make new discoveries, not simply to one's cronies; that research results must be publicly communicated; and that the scientist-hero is one who resolutely puts forward daring discoveries, even though he or she might be punished for doing so.

In short, science as an institution contains large organizations and vast numbers of personnel, a set of community ideals, heroes of the past and present, and numerous political relations with the communities and governments that support it.

Many citizens wisely view science with a mixture of high respect and slight suspicion; respect for its great achievements and anxiety about what dangerous discoveries it may make this or next year. However, it has also been viewed as the potential savior of mankind. Some have supposed that science will somehow replace all the natural resources that the industrialized countries have been consuming; will alleviate the pollution that threatens our lives; and will sove the problems of unemployment, the flow of money, taxation, racism, and perhaps mental disease.

We should not be overly optimistic about that likelihood. It is true that since about 1750 the number of scientific journals in the world has increased by a factor of ten every half-century, expanding from about ten such journals to about a hundred thousand.[3] The same factor of growth can be found for the number of scientific papers published, and in newly emerging fields the rate of increase is even faster.

From this vast growth, and from the obvious fact that science does solve *some* problems, we cannot infer, however, that the major world problems we are discussing can be solved even mainly by science. First, there are limits to the growth and development of science itself. It is true enough that the number of people in science continues to grow at a rate much faster than that of the population, but obviously that rate cannot continue indefinitely upward. After all, there cannot be more scientists than there are people. Over the next few generations it is likely that the rate of scientific development will slow down. The number of papers that scientists publish in their lifetime is very small (one to three per author), and there is no evidence that the quality of those papers is rising. Since, however, the number and

magnitude of problems we have been noting does increase, it seems likely that their solution cannot depend upon breakthroughs in science on all fronts.

On a much more fundamental level, however, as social scientists we must become aware that many of the most important human problems are *not* solved by science. They are essentially problems of values, ideologies, disagreements as to priorities and allocations; in short, fundamental differences in evaluations of what is worthwhile.[4]

Social scientists have made this point for some decades. It is as correct for world problems as it is for much more localized ones. For example, many people object to prostitution; but they tolerate it just the same, because in fact their attitudes and interests are somewhat in conflict. Businessmen make money from it, and so do prostitutes. It is supported by the same set of supply-and-demand forces that maintains any other industrial enterprise. Aside from economic stakes, many people do *not* disapprove of prostitution. So, similarly, white people will not give up racism, while the various ethnic groups in the United States continue to feel prejudice toward each other and to express that prejudice in acts of discrimination.

That is, people have a stake in their evaluations, for those evaluations essentially state what they prefer. People are willing to pay some costs in time, money, and energy to support what they want. With reference to most of the programs that governments attempt to implement, some part of the citizenry approves them, but many of those same citizens also disapprove of various aspects of them. Consequently, the attempt to

[3]For these and related findings, see Derek J. de Solla Price, "Diseases of Science," in Wilbert E. Moore and Robert M. Cooks, eds., *Readings on Social Change,* Englewood Cliffs, N.J.: Prentice-Hall, 1967, pp. 49–68. For contributions to the study of science as a social institution, see Robert K. Merton, *The Sociology of Science,* ed. by Norman W. Storer, Chicago: University of Chicago Press, 1973.

[4]For a wise discussion of the difference between problems that call for political solutions and those which require merely factual knowledge, see Daniel P. Moynihan, *Coping,* New York: Vintage, 1973, especially chaps. 13 and 14.

solve social problems at the local level is a slow and sometimes futile task.

However, the solution to such problems lies in political and evaluative mobilization, rather than simply more knowledge. That is, although more facts would be useful in working out any program for human betterment, most such programs do not founder and fail because of simple ignorance or lack of scientific research. They fail because the community does not truly support them.

So it is on the global scale that we have been discussing here. Whether we examine population growth or pollution, the threat of the atomic bomb or the spread of dictatorships, we are confronting precisely the kind of problem that science is least equipped to solve. Science and engineering can best solve a problem when there is a clear goal in mind, for example, the production of a satellite system to be used for communication or watching one's enemy. It is least equipped to solve a problem when people disagree fundamentally about what the problem is, or even about whether anyone should attempt to solve it at all. All too commonly, people nod sagely in their agreement that a particular problem exists. For example, people deplore pollution of waterways in the United States, but few are willing to give up their own polluting practices, for that would be a cost to them. More generally, people are often willing to admit there is a problem, but will not accept any conceivable solution.

In all these cases, in short, the crux of the problem is not the lack of technical knowledge; it is the lack of a moral consensus. It is the lack of a shared, fundamental evaluation of the problem, or of the goal people and governments should seek. Sociologists can contribute to that analysis, for they can at least ascertain what people's values, attitudes, and political ideologies are, how they conflict with one another, and even which ones might be more easily changed than others because people do not hold them so

firmly. Though that knowledge is useful, it cannot be a substitute for the development of community agreements about which social goals are more worthwhile.

WILL A WORLD SYSTEM EMERGE?

It is evident that the major processes of change treated in the previous sections not only affect every society in the world; many of them also have the effect of *linking* every nation to every other one, for good or evil, and thus perhaps creating a grad society of nations. Nations use and pollute each other's sea and air, consume and use up each other's raw materials, impinge upon each other's space through their expanding population, and share in each other's fate to an increasing degree.

Cheaper transportation and communication decrease the cost of both trade and other kinds of social interaction, while the need of all nations for both of these increases. Even if we are pessimistic about the ultimate benefits of these exchanges, we are nevertheless becoming citizens of the same world community. Whatever index we use—world trade, number of students who go abroad to study, tourist travel, number of international or supernational agencies—the interlinkages become ever more numerous.

Several regularities are observable in these processes (discussed earlier, in the chapter on geographical factors). One is that the contacts or exchanges between two countries depend on the *specific* need of one country for specific things the other can supply, and a corresponding, reciprocal need in the other country (this was called complementarity in that chapter). Exchanges are also dependent on how easy it is to transport something (knowledge, a telephone message, a ton of coal) to another country relative to the advantages the exchange brings to both countries. It can also be observed that large and rich countries exchange more in total *quantity* than do poorer and smaller ones, but they exchange a smaller percentage of their own total trade, output, mail, students, or skilled personnel. They constitute a more nearly complete world than do smaller and poorer countries. In addition, the richer countries also have more contacts with each other than they do with poorer ones.

However, that countries interact more with each other than they did once should not lead us to suppose that they can or will come to form a *social unity.* In many ways, as we have been noting, they are also becoming more alike—industrialization, a greater dependence on science, bureaucratization, planning for social change, and even "modern" attitudes about how the world operates and an awareness of what is going on in the world—but this does not mean a willingness to unify with other countries. The various international and supernational agencies, including the United Nations, have facilitated a considerable exchange of information and technical help and even the codification of some agreements about the rights of human beings under international law. However, none of this has lessened in any degree the determination of every country to give up none of its nationalism or its rule over its subjects, or to avoid sharing political authority with any other nation. This is as clear for the communist countries as it is for capitalist ones.

The amount of exchange or contact between countries need not increase by much the willingness of nations to share their rule with one another and need not even cause much change in their attitudes toward one another.[5] Moreover, the sheer fact that such exchanges or interactions form so small a part of each individual's life makes them relatively insignificant, as compared with the amount of interaction those people have

Figure 17-3 Astronaut Thomas P. Stafford and Cosmonaut Aleksey A. Leonov meet during the docking of American and Soviet spacecraft, a new step in international sharing and cooperation. (NASA.)

with one another within their own country. Few citizens of any country, whatever their participation in international travel, exchanges, or supernational agencies, come to feel that a supergovernment or supersociety is desirable to unite their country with others.

A genuine world system requires the building of a real *community*—that is, sharing common goals, values, and norms with reference to most aspects of social life, such as religion, family, civic liberties, or even friendships; an agreement to subordinate private or national interests to the same collective, political system; and a deep belief that the citizens of other countries are "sis-

[5]On these and related points, see Amitai Etzioni, *The Active Society: A Theory of Societal and Political Procedures,* New York: Free Press, 1968, pp. 554ff.

ters" and "brothers." Such a process very likely has not even begun as yet in the world.

On the other hand, at least one precondition for this step is gradually being achieved:

a slowly growing recognition that ultimately we do share a similar fate in many ways. To make that destiny, because it must be shared, a desirable one, the present and future citizens of this earth will have to unite.

READINGS

Barry Commoner, *The Closing Circle: Nature, Man & Technology,* New York: Alfred Knopf, 1971.

Amitai Etzioni, *The Active Society: A Theory of Societal and Political Processes,* New York: Free Press, 1968.

R. Buckminister Fuller, *Operating Manual for Spaceship Earth,* Carbondale: Southern Illinois University Press, 1969.

John McPhee, *Encounters with the Archdruid,* New York: Farrar, Straus & Giroux, 1971.

Henry Menard, *Science: Growth and Change,* Cambridge, Mass.: Harvard, 1972.

Derek J. de Sola Price, *Little Science, Big Science,* New York: Columbia, 1963.

Barbara Ward and Rene Dubos, *Only One Earth: The Care and Maintenance of a Small Planet,* Middlesex, Eng.: Penguin, 1972.

GLOSSARY

Acculturation The process by which individuals or groups acquire the culture of a different group or society.

Achieved role or status A role or status that is attained through one's own performances or decisions (whether or not one wanted to achieve it).

Age-specific mortality or fertility rate The number of persons who die per 1,000 persons in a specific age group; the number of infants born per 1,000 women in a specific age group.

Alienation Feeling that one does not share the goals or norms of one's group; feeling that one is no longer part of one's group; loss of interest in one's daily activities; feeling of social isolation or lack of social influence.

Anomie A condition in which the society or a group no longer accepts a set of norms or values as social standards; a condition in which people do not feel integrated in a group.

Anthropomorphism Assuming that animals, spirits, or things have the same feelings, motives, and thought processes as those of human beings.

Anticipatory socialization The process by which people are led by others to learn the norms or behavior patterns of a role or status before they have entered that role or status.

Ascribed role or status A role or status that is assigned to the individual without regard to personal achievements and on the basis of traits that the individual cannot control, such as age, sex, caste, and nationality.

Assimilation The process of cultural diffusion, by which a subordinate group is absorbed into a dominant group; the process through which two or more groups come to share the same social and cultural patterns.

Authority The right to give certain orders or commands that are defined as legitimate by the group.

Birthrate Usually refers to *crude* birthrate, i.e., the number of births per 1,000 population in a given area in one year.

Bureaucracy A system of administration, within government, business, or voluntary associations, that is characterized by specialized functions, explicit rules, and a hierarchy of authority.

Caste System The organization of a society into social strata, marked by different degrees of ritual purity or pollution, socially defined as unchanging in prestige ranking, into which the individual is born and from which he or she may not rise (although it is possible to be cast out for some violation of caste rules).

Charismatic leader A leader whom people follow in part because they feel or believe he or she has special qualities, magnetic appeal, or extraordinary wisdom.

Class A social stratum within a class system; one of several categories of people with roughly similar rankings in prestige, economic position, and political influence; people who share a roughly similar relationship to the means of production in their society.

Class consciousness The degree to which members of a class believe or understand they share a common economic fate, and are willing to support each other in a political struggle.

Community Sometimes used as an English translation of *Gemeinschaft;* a group or society characterized by primary relations, shared values and norms, and a feeling among members of concern for the group as a whole; a folk society.

Conjugal family A social unit made up of a married couple and their children, socially linked with relatives through marriage or kinship.

Correlation A measure of the relationship between two variables or characteristics (e.g., income and prestige); the degree to which one variable rises or falls when the other changes.

Crude birthrate The number of births per year per 1,000 members of a population.

Crude death rate The number of deaths per year per 1,000 persons in a population.

Cultural relativism A value or an ideological position that asserts that we should evaluate others' behavior by reference to their own norms and standards or that the culture, values, attitudes, customs, or norms of other societies should all be respected.

Culture The total array of customs, beliefs, attitudes, philosophies, social patterns, and modes of economic production that characterize a given society; in a more restricted sense, the complex of beliefs, norms, values, philosophies, and knowledge of a society (thus, omitting social be-

havior); all the social and cultural patterns that are learned by members of a society and are transmitted to the next generation.

Deviance, deviation Violation by an individual or a group of the norms or values of their own group; violation by an individual or a group of the norms or values of the larger society.

Diffusion The transfer or spread of cultural or social patterns from one group or society to another.

Discrimination Denying social, economic, or civic rights to members of a group *because* they are members of that group, more loosely, denying opportunities or rewards to individuals because they belong to a particular race, religion, sex, or ethnic group.

Dyad Any two people in social interaction; any two people whose interaction continues for more than a brief encounter.

Endogamy A marriage rule that requires individuals to find mates within their own group (but not their own family).

Ethnic group Any segment of the population that is socially viewed as having a shared national history (e.g., Poles, Irish), whether or not they actually form a group now or have maintained much of that culture.

Ethnocentrism Considering one's own group to be superior; measuring other groups by the values or norms of one's own group.

Ethnomethodology The study of the social rules or regularities by which people construct the social reality they interact with and inhabit.

Extended family A group of related persons, larger than the married couple with their children, forming and contributing to a single household; sometimes also used to include the network of relatives, not in the same household, with which the conjugal family members are in close interaction.

Fecundity The biological ability of an individual or group to bear children (distinguished from *fertility,* which means the actual birthrate).

Fertility rate The number of children born per year per 1,000 potentially fertile females in a population.

Folk society *Gemeinschaft;* community; usually a small, relatively isolated community whose members feel much solidarity with one another, follow traditional rules, and control each other by informal means rather than by courts and policemen.

Formal organization Bureaucracy; any organization whose day-to-day administration is based on explicit rules, procedures, regulations for both rewards and punishments, and a specification of the obligations members owe to one another; social patterns typical of a *Gesellschaft.*

Formal organization Bureaucracy; any organization whose day-to-day administration is based on explicit rules, procedures, regulations for both rewards and punishments, and a specification of the obligations members owe to one another; social patterns typical of a *Gesellschaft.*

Function A consequence; any effect that one institution or social behavior has on any other part of the society.

Gemeinschaft A folk society; a society in which social relations are mainly primary, social controls are informal, and members identify with one another.

Generalized other The individual's general conception or view of the values, norms, and customs of the group, which the individual has made a part of his or her own inner self; the moral order, which the individual makes his or her own.

Gesellschaft A secular society; a society based on explicit, formally stated rules and obligations; a society based on contractual agreements rather than traditional and informal ones.

Ghetto Traditionally, a section of a European city in which Jews were required to live; now applied primarily to Negro districts in large cities, and less often to economically depressed urban districts.

Group Any set of individuals numbering two or more, engaged in any social interaction; a set of individuals who maintain a pattern of continuing social interaction; a set of individuals who share a common body of norms and customs and who feel solidarity with one another.

In-group Any group of which one feels a member, and which one also views as being superior in some ways to outsiders or others.

Institution A set of social processes and activities, including the norms or values they express

or embody, focused on some major societal goal (e.g., law, family, war).

Labeling process The social patterns by which members of a group define someone as deviant (or, less often, as vituous), whether or not that person's acts are out of the ordinary.

Legitimacy The extent to which an act or behavior is approved socially; lawfulness; the extent to which political acts, systems, or persons are backed by authority or are viewed as having the right to command.

Looking-glass self Selfhood that grows from the individual's perceiving how others react to her or him, and thus coming to view herself or himself in a similar way.

Marginal man Any person who grows up in one culture and then participates in another, so that he or she does not feel completely at home in either.

Mass society Modern industrialized societies that are viewed as having lost their community characteristics and having become instead aggregations of anonymous, atomized individuals whose relationships are mostly dominated by contract and utilitarian calculation.

Minority group Any segment of the population, usually in fact a statistical minority and usually an ethnic group, that is given a lower social ranking than the dominant group, and suffers various disadvantages in economic and social competition.

Mores (singular: mos) Patterns of behavior that are traditional and are strongly backed by community rewards or punishments.

Norm Any standard or criterion by which behavior is defined as appropriate, right, good, or aesthetically pleasing; social expectation, backed by some punishment or reward meted out by the group.

Nuclear family A social unit consisting of a married couple and their children.

Out-group Any group other than one's own in-group, and usually viewed as inferior to one's own.

Peer group Any grouping or aggregation of individuals of about the same age and social position who interact with one another and shape each other's behavior; any group of equals.

Power The ability to gain one's ends, even against the resistance of other persons; the ability to gain one's ends through force or force-threat.

Prejudice A preexisting, usually negative, attitude an individual or group holds toward another group; responding to a group or an individual by reference to the supposed negative traits of that group, without ascertaining whether the individual or group actually possesses that trait; responding on the basis of social stereotypes.

Primary group or relationship A relationship or a small group in which people interact with one another personally and as unique individuals; a relationship that is viewed as an end in itself, and not merely as a means to some goal; contrasted with contractual, secondary, impersonal, or formal relationships.

Primitive society A human society that is at a relatively low technological level, and mostly preliterate; does not refer to "early man."

Reference group Any group whose social standards, norms, or values an individual uses as a basis for deciding on her or his actions or making evaluations.

Relative deprivation Feeling deprived or disadvantaged relative to members of some group; feeling more (or less) deprived, not so much because of the absolute amount one gets (low or high), but because of the amount that others get, with whom one compares oneself—usually, one's reference group.

Role Any social behavior; a social expectation; a regular, recurring way of acting and feeling that is viewed as appropriate to a social position; a standard mode of behavior, backed by group rewards and punishments.

Secondary group or relationship A relationship in which interaction is viewed as appropriately impersonal, contractual, and guided by one's own end or goals; contrasted with a primary, or a *Gemeinschaft*, relationship.

Sect Any religious group, typically small, with intense commitment to its particular religious doctrines, and marked by high control over any possible deviations.

Self-fulfilling prophecy A prediction that initiates changes in people's behavior such that their actions make the prediction come true (e.g., people spreading the rumor that a bank does not possess enough money to cover its deposits).

Sex roles Patterns of behavior that are socially viewed as appropriate for one sex but not for the other; approved patterns of interaction between the two sexes.

Social distance The extent to which members of a group or individuals are willing to interact with varying degrees of intimacy (being neighbors, inviting to dinner, sitting side by side) with members of another group.

Social mobility The extent of movement upward or downward from one class or social stratum to another.

Socialization The process by which a person comes to believe in the norms, values, attitudes, and customs of his or her group; the development of the self; the process by which an individual comes to act in conformity with the rules of his or her group.

Status A position in a social system; the set of rights and obligations that are viewed as part of a social position; a post, position, or rank that is socially recognized (e.g., chief, mother, witch-doctor); a prestige ranking.

Stereotype A fixed belief, resistant to evidence, that a given group or occupation possesses certain social traits, usually negative ones.

Subculture The social behavior and cultural pattern of a subgroup of the society, which are distinct from those of the dominant society but nevertheless closely akin to them.

Symbol Any gesture, object, thing, or behavior that is used by a group to stand for or to represent something else.

Value Any general criterion or standard by which actions, beliefs, or indeed any social objects whatever are evaluated; a criterion that a group imposes as a measure of goodness, rightness, virtue, ritual purity, or aesthetic excellence; distinguished from a norm mainly by greater generality and thus a greater difficulty in applying it to specific behavior.

Voluntary association Any formal organization; more commonly applied to organizations or clubs that one joins because one approves their explicit goals, as distinct from economic relationships or organizations (corporations, governmental bureaucracies) that one joins because one must earn a living.

INDEX